There Is a River

There Is a River

by Vincent Harding

Vintage Books
A Division of Random House
New York

First Vintage Books Edition, January 1983

Library of Congress Cataloging in Publication Data
Harding, Vincent.
There is a river.
Originally published: New York:
Harcourt Brace Jovanovich, 1981.
Bibliography: p.
Includes index.
1. Afro-Americans—Civil rights.
2. United States—Race relations.
3. Afro-Americans—History.
I. Title.
E185.H29 1983   323.1′196073   82-4901
ISBN 0-394-71148-3   AACR2

Manufactured in the United States of America
Cover illustration by Bob Ziering

To the memory of Howard Thurman,
Father in the faith,
Companion in the way,
[...] peaceable warrior

W ho loved [...]

For those and all the old ones of our struggle
now dancing among the ancestors.

For Sue Bailey Thurman
For Ella Harris Freeney
For Mabel Broome Harding,
Still proudly walking among us,
Whose continuing love and strength
Have opened a way of life and hope
For all the generations of your children,
Seen and unseen, known and unknown,
Now and always.

Contents

Illustrations

Introduction

This work is an experiment...
of a continuing attempt to discover and develop the source...
tension among my responsibilities as a historian, my commitment to
human liberation, and my urgent determination to keep faith with that
magnificent company of witnesses—my mothers and fathers—whose lives
form the wellsprings of the black struggle for freedom in America.
Ultimately, what I have written is also meant as an offering to the
children, all our children, who shall live and prevail. These pages are
my encouragement to them, the expression of my hope that they may
join their lives with all life in love and courage, daring to create and
become much more than we ever dreamed was possible on these shores
of darkness and light.

Affirming objectivity and subjectivity as equally necessary to any
compassionate rendering of our flawed and splendid human strivings, I
have tried honestly to tell the story and to provide a rigorous analysis of
the long black movement toward justice, equity, and truth. At the same
time, identifying fully with the subjects of my study and the substance
of their hope, I have freely allowed myself to celebrate. For I could
not possibly remain silent and unmoved in the presence of the mysterious,
transformative dance of life that has produced the men and women,
the ideas and institutions, the visions, betrayals, and heroic dreams renewed in blood that are at once the anguish-and the glory of the river of
our struggle in this land.

Yet if I understand the essence of what I have done, then beyond
celebration and analysis, beyond narrative and documentation, there is
still more. Somewhere near the heart of the work is a search for meaning,

an attempt to apprehend and share with others my own tentative grasp of the harrowing and terrifying beauty of my people's pilgrimage in this strangely promised land. Why did it happen? Why were we chosen to be chosen, if we were? How in the midst of such death and suffering could we find so much strength to love, so much determination to live, fight on, and be free? In permanent and grueling exile, how could a people dance and create songs and art, fashion institutions of hope, bear so many children of beauty? In the land of our captivity, subject to a host of attempts at dehumanization and humiliation, how and why did we become the nation's foremost champions of human freedom and social justice, creators of many of its most native rhythms of life? And what now is our future, and this nation's destiny, if those costly, creative black visions of hope, long nurtured in the fires of persecution, should be broken and bastardized—or meanly forgotten—in a ruthless and unprincipled process of Americanization?

Such a quest for meaning in history, such attempts to lift our eyes from the past toward the future, at times to venture beyond both past and future, are not often fashionable in the realms of academe (which is one reason why I have spent so much of my time on the blurred and questionable edges of its domain). Nevertheless, this kind of search is neither new nor unexpected in our human adventure, especially among the children of a captive people who have known what it is to live "far from [our] native clime/Under the white man's menace, out of time," and who may once again sense some furtive but urgent call to rendezvous with the life-giving forces of the morning.

Indeed, in my view, such persistent probes toward meaning are absolutely necessary, not primarily as a source of psychic comfort or as diversionary, apolitical spiritualizing, but because there is no truly human history without them. For just as each of us at one time or another is fiercely driven to seek coherence and purpose in the deciphering of our own personal stories, so it is in this collective venture toward wholeness. A sense of meaning—which we surely create out of our particular responses to the "facts" of experience—is crucial if we are to join ourselves to the past and the future, to commune with the ancestors as well as the coming children. Without it we lose touch with ourselves, our fellow humans, and other creatures, with the earth our mother, and with the cosmos itself. Without the search for meaning, the quest for vision, there can be no authentic movement toward liberation, no true identity or radical integration for an individual or a people. Above all, where there is no vision we lose the sense of our great power to transcend history and create a new future for ourselves with others, and we perish utterly in hopelessness, mutual terror, and despair. Therefore the quest is not a luxury; life itself demands it of us.

I do not know when this concern for the meaning of our history in the United States as black and white and red (and all our neighboring, contributing varieties) began fully to grasp me. Having been raised in a tightly knit, Bible-centered black church community in Harlem, I was surely open to such a search from the outset. Moreover, it is likely that ~~~~~~~~~~~ own unorthodox pilgrimage helped to fortify ~~~~~~~~~~~~~~~~~~~~~~~~~~~~~~~~~~ and I first moved

The very songs of the struggle, buried in my grave," proclaimed the sources of their historical being. And in the early 1960s, when the young band of freedom-loving believers first spoke of offering their own lives to create "the beloved community" in America, more than naive rhetoric was at work. For they had broken loose from much of the *Angst* and constriction of the Cold War mentality and the Silent Generation of the 1950s, to dare to dream a society where this nation's men, women, and children would no longer live under racial hatred, oppression, and fear. In doing so, they were not only following and joining Mahatma Gandhi and Martin Luther King, Jr., and the participants in anticolonial struggles across the globe, but also revisiting their own black ancestors in America and Africa; indeed, they were resurrecting the most ardent hopes of all humankind. Willing to live and die in hope for what they believed, working with a steadily increasing company of white allies, they planned, they marched, they sang, they laughed, they stood up under the blows of their enemies and kept moving.

As they moved, as we moved, we encountered much that would eventually contribute to the shaping of this written history. Most important were the people we met. In such beautiful and dangerous places as Americus, Leesburg, and Albany, Georgia; Nashville and Memphis, Tennessee; Montgomery and Birmingham, Alabama; Greenwood, Cleveland, and Ruleville, Mississippi; and scores of equally compelling places in between, the men and women we encountered were a revelation. In every place touched by those early Movement actions we discovered—and were discovered by—witnesses who had been standing their sometimes solitary ground in harsh and threatening circumstances for a long time; people who refused to lose hope, black people (occasionally linked by faith and adversity to a few beleaguered white friends) who had contributed their lives and their deaths to prepare the way for the great outpouring of the freedom movement. Their names were legion, some well known but most anonymous, often invisible to the written documents, unknown to the rest of the world. Among them were Moma Dolly, Hartman Turnbow, Rev. E. D. White, Septima Clark, Oliver Holmes, Amzie Moore, Herbert Lee, Fred Shuttlesworth, Slater King, L. D. Reddick, Mrs. A. W. West, Rev. J. A. DeLaine, and Harry Briggs. These were some of the human bridges between the past and the future, the stubbornly continuing elements in the river of our struggle. It was they—in their lives, in their quiet courage, in their songs and silences—who first told us that there was a significant history behind what we called "The Movement," a long time of surging toward freedom. It was they who called us to see a movement older and deeper than any one life, any one generation. It is with them that I must keep faith, for it was among them, in the 1960s, that the informal, largely unconscious research for this work began. Their churches and homes, the marching lines, the confrontations with sheriffs and deputies in front of the county courthouses, the cars on the treacherous back-country roads, the jails and cemeteries—these were my first archives, my first living sources for the story of our river.

It was a heady time. It was a time of hope, a time of great expectations, a moment in history when it seemed as if ordinary men and women led by a band of hard-working and sometimes confused young dreamers might well come in touch with all the extraordinary, transformative powers within their own beings and stretch out to remake the realities of their world. In a fundamental sense, this was the gestation period for my work.

By the time I began consciously to formulate the concepts and carry out the initial research for the book, however, we were all living in another time. By the summer of 1967, the Southern-based freedom movement had already passed its apogee and the cities of the North and West were on fire. Malcolm X, the "shining black prince" of the Northern movement, was two years gone, but by then it was apparent that his assassination—combined with the posthumous publication of his *Autobiography*—had opened the way for his life to touch us more deeply than ever before. The love he bore to his people, the overwhelming power of his black consciousness, and the force and integrity of his spirit offered a powerful testimony to the possibilities of human transformation. Meanwhile his words and ideas were still sweeping through the nation's black communities, especially the explosive urban centers, connecting with

Introduction xv

many forms of black nationalism, helping to roil the deep waters of
disaffection, anger, rebellion, and pride.

The old Movement dreams seemed to have exploded into nightmares.
Tanks and troops of the U.S. Army and the National Guard were in the
streets. Helicopters sent their powerful lights and intimations of death
down into the fiery nights. The call for Black Power, the cry of "Burn,
baby, burn!" and the image of young Black Panthers with guns in their
hands could be heard and seen across the land. Now countless men and

black liberation

King pressed

Through a variety of experimental actions, he searched for a way to
with the new times he had helped to create. Though he and his organization were often ill prepared to deal with them, King tried to work more
actively on the economic and political problems of the urban North. At
the same time he continued to raise his voice against the nation's destructive misadventure in Vietnam. For Martin King felt the anguish of
the Vietnamese people and readily identified it as part of the same pain he
met daily in the broken black cities of America. At great cost to his
standing with the black and white liberal establishment, he eventually
insisted on joining his voice with that minority of activists who linked
the war in Indochina to this country's refusal to deal adequately with its
own racism and gross economic inequalities. Indeed, by the summer of
1967 the urgency of the situation at home and in Vietnam had evoked
from King a hesitant public call for a national, nonviolent revolutionary
force to carry out massive acts of civil disobedience in the cause of racial
freedom, economic justice, and a vaguely defined transformation of the
nation's political structures. Meanwhile the leadership of the federal
government responded to such signs and callings with more bombs and
troops in Vietnam, more covert subversion of the movements for freedom,
peace, and justice in America, and just enough money for antipoverty
programs to reveal the stark difference between its will to make war and
its commitment to heal the wounds of its own people. As a result, both
black and white activists were talking about revolution.

In those days, I was teaching history at Spelman College, one of the schools in the predominantly black Atlanta University complex, where the evidence of our people's evolving and expanding freedom struggle was all around us, burrowing deep within our own lives. Some students and faculty on these campuses recognized and welcomed the impressive national flowering of black consciousness and cultural renewal that had re-emerged from the surging mass movements. Often we were especially impressed by the itinerant band of radicalized poets, playwrights, historians, and musicians who joined the political organizers and moved among us, detonating their announcements of the coming black new day wherever we gathered to organize, confer, and celebrate.

Living in the spirit of that time, my students and I—like our counterparts on scores of other campuses—were encouraging one another to explore the complex riches of the black cultural heritage. We reached out to gain a sense of the grandeur and responsibilities of our unique and dangerous vocation as children of Africa in a universal quest for freedom, independence, and justice, especially as that explosive search rose up from the Third World. (In some of our circles, the writings and examples of men like Frantz Fanon, Amilcar Cabral, Chairman Mao, Che Guevera, and Ho Chi Minh had become the focus of study groups and extended rap sessions.) Compelled by the mounting demands for black solidarity and our own need for revolutionary transformation, we looked urgently for new means by which our education might become a bridge rather than a barrier to our people and their aspirations.

Naturally, these explorations into the future and the past, into the world of revolutionary theory and practice, led us to question and challenge the leadership, purpose, and direction of the traditional Negro colleges and universities—as well as their white models and counterparts. So we participated deeply in the national call for the creation of politically conscious and culturally sensitive black universities, black studies programs, and general educational strategies for renewal and reformation. In fact, a group of us in Atlanta had already begun to meet regularly to share our visions and plans for a politically committed Black Studies Institute that might be related to the Atlanta University complex.

By then, of course, the black struggle of the early 1960s had at once inspired and been significantly challenged by the meteoric rise of the new white Left, whose antiwar and antiestablishment movements burst forth from hundreds of college campuses. Often these assaults on the American status quo were led by white students who had received their own baptism of fire and their awakening to the harsh realities of their native land as allies in the Southern-based Afro-American freedom movement. Thus their campuses and their lives were filled with the sounds of our struggles.

It was in the midst of this exciting new time that I received an invitation from Professor Alfred Young of Northern Illinois University, asking me to contribute an essay to an anthology he was editing on the history of American radicalism. Most of the other participants represented the progressive and radical historiographical approaches that had been developing among white scholars over that decade, spearheaded by persons like Staughton Lynd and Howard Zinn, whom I had first met in ～～～～ ～ollege teachers and coworkers in the Southern black move-

～～～～～～～～ ～ ～ ～ ～ ～ ～ ～ for Staughton and

Martin King went ～～ ～～～～ ～
of the city's striking garbage collectors. I did not see ～～ ～ ～ ～ ～ ～ ～ the long surreal night when I stood vigil over his body as it lay in state in the Spelman College chapel, available to that steady stream of ordinary black men and women who came in from the darkness of the early morning to bid their last farewell to the dreamer. A few weeks later Coretta Scott King, his widow, asked me to be the first director of what would become the Martin Luther King, Jr., Memorial Center in Atlanta. Even though I was still flooded with outrage over the murder of King and over what many of us thought the likely complicity of some of this nation's official institutions, my love for Martin and for the people he represented left me no choice. But first I had to complete the interrupted essay on black radicalism.

As often occurs with my writing, the finished article turned out to be more than twice as long as it was supposed to be, so only the section on the post-1954 period was used in the anthology. However, several persons, including C. L. R. James, the black Marxist revolutionary scholar; Julius Lester, then a photographer, resident philosopher, and musician with the Student Non-Violent Coordinating Committee; and Al Young of Northern Illinois encouraged me to develop the longer manuscript into a book on black radicalism in America. But by then, I was deeply engaged with others in creating the first element of the King Center, a library-documentation project that we envisioned as a major archive for the modern black freedom movement.

As I look back now on the meandering development of this manuscript, and consider the several periods of as long as a year when no

ostensible work was done, it would be easy to view the demanding task
of creating the King Center as only the first of a long series of interrup-
tions in the path that led from the original article to the completion of
this volume. But the library-documentation project proved to be far
more than a distraction. Rather, it provided a crucial opportunity for me
to rethink the concept of a history of black radicalism in the United States.
Most important, as we gathered the Movement documentation from across
the South and elsewhere, as we dealt with the people out of whose lives
it came, I was taken back in person and in memories to some of those
places where Rosemarie and I had first worked in 1961–64. Revisiting
and revisioning the settings and the people, we were able to understand
in a new way the continuity and ubiquity of the river, the depths and
the power of its movement, the need to keep faith with its unique sources,
its people, and their vision.

While the responsibilities of the King Memorial Center took me again
toward such reflections on the meaning of our earlier Movement experiences, they provided almost no time for sustained work on the book.
For in addition to the library-documentation project, some of us were
also creating the Institute of the Black World, a center for research,
organizing, and advocacy. The fruit of our earlier Atlanta discussions,
it evolved into the second element of the King Memorial Center. Here
again, this interruption provided another positive and crucial development in the creation of the work. Beginning in 1968–69, IBW brought
together in Atlanta a group of black scholars, artists, and organizers who
engaged in constant dialogue and work on the meaning and the future
of our struggle for freedom in the United States. Persons like William
Strickland, Gerald McWorter, Stephen Henderson, Lerone Bennett, Joyce
Ladner, Councill Taylor, A. B. Spellman, Larry Rushing, and Chester
Davis became the nucleus for an expanding network of sisters, brothers,
and colleagues. In the midst of such collective work and reflection, constantly involved in a variety of personal and political re-evaluations, I
was encouraged to test, develop, and reshape my own perspectives on this
work.

Perhaps of most importance to the ultimate content of the book was
the decision that rose up like a powerful mandate from the experiences
of the Southern black struggle. It was now clear to me that a history
of black radicalism in the United States was too narrow, too abstract, too
European a means of developing my subject, far too constricted a way to
keep the faith. Instead, I knew that what I wanted and needed to write
about was something that had never been developed in one work: a
narrative, analytical, and celebrative history of the freedom struggle of
black people in this country, beginning before there was a country. I was

especially concerned to try to convey its long, continuous movement, flowing like a river, sometimes powerful, tumultuous, and roiling with life; at other times meandering and turgid, covered with the ice and snow of seemingly endless winters, all too often streaked and running with blood.

At first, as the river metaphor took life within me, I was unduly concerned about its apparent inexactness and ambiguity. Now, with the .... of time and the deepening of our vision, it is possible to recognize .... time that the river is more

....

States has always taken ...
of its movement have continually gathered others to itself, ...
filled other men and women with the force of its vision, its indomitable hope. And at its best the river of our struggle has moved consistently toward the ocean of humankind's most courageous hopes for freedom and integrity, forever seeking what black people in South Carolina said they sought in 1865: "the right to develop our whole *being.*"

Beyond my concern about the metaphor of the river, I was also uncertain for a long while about how my own deep immersion in its flow and my clear identification with its movement toward a transformed future would be received by those who considered "scholarly objectivity" the measure of all things. For I knew that my first commitment was not to the ambiguous abstractions of "objectivity" or "scholarship," but to the lively hope and faith of a people in struggle for a new chance to be whole. Gradually, through the process of the work, in conversations with others, in the course of dreams and inner struggles, and especially with the constant encouragement of my wife, the force of this concern was broken, and the worry about such things as my use of "we" and "us" as well as the conventional "they" and "them" in the manuscript became unimportant. Somehow I believed that my vow to keep faith with the creators and the children of the river would also lead me to be faithful to the truth of their experience as I saw it, read it, felt it. I knew that I must not be afraid to let that commitment speak for itself, to let my own baptized voice be heard.

So, too, I began to understand that it was only in the context of the ongoing movement of black struggle, changing and yet continuing, that we could speak adequately of black radicalism. Now I understood it as that element of the movement that at any given moment in our history develops the most fundamental challenge to the social, economic, political, spiritual, or intellectual domination of white people and their power over black lives. Increasingly, too, I defined it as that movement, those ideas, that way of organizing and living that produced the most profound prospects for transformation and hope, beginning with black people and burgeoning to the entire society. In all of this I recognized, of course, that many words, ideas, and actions that are radical at one time may not be so at a different time or place. Even more important, though, I came to understand that it was only in the context of the overall, continuing flow of the river that it was possible to keep faith with all those blacks who struggled for transformation, whatever their setting, their time, their limitations.

Although I am trying in my work to express a holistic vision of the continuous black movement toward freedom in this country, I have chosen not to try to make this book another general survey history of black people in the United States. In their various, distinctive ways many of my elders and teachers in the historian's art have done that work, and I owe them a tremendous debt. Here I think especially of George Washington Williams, Carter G. Woodson, W. E. B. DuBois, Benjamin Quarles, John Hope Franklin, and Lerone Bennett. (Indeed, each of the last three has added a very special benison to my efforts, encouraging and instructing me at many points along the way, in spite of differences in perspective and approach.) Building on their foundations, moving through the larger story that they have so skillfully told, I am attempting to focus on what seems to me the central theme of black history in the United States, a theme that Earl Thorpe and others identified before I did: the active black struggle for freedom and justice. So wherever it is faithful to its own best intentions, my work should complement the survey histories of my friends and mentors.

Just as this is not a history of black radicalism or a general survey history of black people in the United States—though I attempt to come to grips with both these perspectives—so, too, it is not a history of "black protest" in this country. The modern writing that has been done on protest and resistance within the black community by persons like Herbert Aptheker, Mary Berry, Lerone Bennett, Robert Brisbane, John Bracey, James Forman, Eugene Genovese, August Meier, Jane and William H. Pease, Robert Starobin, Sterling Stuckey, and others has, of course, been essential to the development of my own work and of great value to us all. However, in *There Is a River*, I have tried to set what I call the Great Tradition of Black Protest and other forms of reaction to white oppression in the context of the river's larger movement. I have also attempted to emphasize the development of the many creative black initiatives in the quest for freedom. Beyond protest, I have focused on the need to understand what our people were fighting, dying, and hoping for, suggesting some of the ways in which those goals and purposes were developed or repeated over time. In other words, I have operated on the assumption that the attempt to keep faith with a people's best hopes demands that we ... to search out the positive vision of truth and justice that caused them

... forces all around them. Beyond

For better and ...

comprehensive and organic historical survey of the black ... ward freedom, of our search and struggle for justice, equality, and self-determination in the United States. Important studies have been developed on particular periods of the struggle, or on such subjects as rebellion and resistance during slavery, the quest for a new society during Reconstruction, the movements for equality and self-determination at the turn of the twentieth century, the Garvey Movement, the rise of organizations like the National Association for the Advancement of Colored People, and the Congress of Racial Equality, as well as on the massive new dynamic of the freedom movement in the post–World War II period. Significant work has also been done on a relatively few individual leaders like Paul Cuffee, Nat Turner, Frederick Douglass, Martin Delany, Ida B. Wells-Barnett, Paul Robeson, DuBois, Garvey, Malcolm X, King, and others. But up to now these movements, experiences, and individuals have not been gathered up and placed in the larger context of our historical development in the United States, or studied extensively for their relationships and debts to each other.

Obviously, it required a certain amount of foolhardiness to take on such a task, and if I had foreseen its magnitude I might well have backed away to engage myself in some far more limited responsibility. Besides, I am now not only open to the slings and arrows of outraged (or bemused) specialists in any given period or subject matter, but also heir to the problems arising from the relative lack of specialists on any aspect of the black struggle for freedom in this country. Obviously, then, this work is only a beginning, bearing all the hopes and limitations of beginnings. The first of two volumes, this opens with the slave-ship rebellions off the coast of Africa, and carries the story on to the destruction of the legal institution of slavery in the United States in 1865. Even when the full work is complete and has brought the account into our own generation, it will make no claim to be a definitive survey of the subject. Too much basic research still needs to be done in scores of local communities and archives on thousands of participants in this centuries-long movement toward freedom. So here, as in the forthcoming volume, I have primarily attempted to provide an overview of that movement, to introduce or reexamine certain major and lesser-known participants and creators, to suggest some of the critical issues, themes, ideologies, and questions. In every period I have tried to indicate the internal contradictions and external opposition to the surging of the river, always seeking to comprehend the sources of hope that drew people forward in spite of the terrors of the night.

As might be expected in such a broadly ranging effort, my work in this volume has been based largely on monographic studies, published collections of documents, oral histories, journals and periodicals, and some work in the primary sources, as well as many hundreds of secondary works. I have tried to make my major sources clear and accessible through the Notes, and for those wishing to explore any aspect of the study in a more serious way I have included a select bibliography of books and journals. However, if I understand it correctly, much of the strength of my work rests not on newly discovered archival materials, but on the attempt to clarify and interpret the black movement toward freedom, to suggest its meaning for all of us who live in the nation that may prove to be the perilous heartland of this grand and terrifying century.

Though others must ultimately be the best judges of my contributions, I consider myself essentially a harbinger of things to come. So in my Notes I have often called attention to some of the work yet to be done if we are to have a truly helpful picture of the creators, the varieties, and the depths of this river of struggle. I trust that those who are younger, more skilled, or more adequately endowed with time and resources will take up some of these concerns—as well as others of their own choosing—and carry them on. In other words, I am part of a cloud of working witnesses, no more, no less, a member in fairly good standing of an ongoing company of investigators, participants, critics, and testifiers. Following the lead of men and women like DuBois in *Black Reconstruction*, C. L. R. James in *Black Jacobins*, Lerone Bennett in *Confrontation: Black and White*, Lorraine Hansberry in *The Movement*, Langston Hughes in *Fight for Freedom*, and Robert Brisbane in *Black Vanguard* and *Black Activism*, I am simply carrying on a tradition, trying to write and to live the story of our struggle, creating a history that has already created me, seeking to keep the faith.

Of course the only way I can do that with any integrity is to be faithful to my own deepest impulses, visions, and concerns. I must raise the questions and suggest the insights that come out of my encounters with the documents of the past, the personal and social upheavals of the last quarter century of radical movement, and the constant groundings with my brothers and sisters in the river. Largely as a result of such grapplings with history, self, and community, I have felt a renewed urgency to em- [illegible] for this ailment of the spirit, but I am now more [illegible] it has been at work throughout the history of our black and white—and red—encounters in this land, and that there will be no hope for a truly just society on these shores until we address the issue of the human spirit and its role in our struggles for political transformation. (When Martin King first came among us speaking of the need to carry on a struggle for justice and truth that would "redeem the soul of America," many of us tended to smile patronizingly or to turn away in annoyed disbelief at such naiveté. It appears to me now that we rather than he may well have been the innocents.)

Understandably, then, I have tried especially to be faithful to the soul of the river, of its people, the living and the dead, the many thousands gone. It seemed essential that I try to convey the spirit of struggle and hope, of laughter and despair, of fear, determination, and sacrifice, to capture the apprehension of waiting for sunrise through all the terror-filled hours of darkness. To keep faith with a people meant being in touch with them and their feelings, recognizing how many were my feelings, and somehow reflecting these in the pages of the book. With the songs and poetry of the black experience (including my own), with the words of the participants and their antagonists, I have tried to convey the aliveness, the deep feelings, the spirit of a community in hard and costly movement toward freedom. At the same time I have had to nurture my own spirit, to recognize the significant transformations taking place within me over the years since I first entered the cauldron of the Southern freedom movement. Thus the work is also an attempt to keep faith with the man who lived then, the one who lives now, and the continuing passage toward the development of my own "whole being." The creative tension inherent in that task will be apparent to all who have followed my writing.

Recognizing the dangers of this tension, I have persisted in my sense that the black struggle for freedom is at its heart a profoundly human quest for transformation, a constantly evolving movement toward personal integrity and toward new social structures filled with justice, equity, and compassion. Though it has often seemed to be a restricted political, economic, or racial struggle, it has always tried to help men and women discover their tremendous capacities as individuals and as members of an empowering community. Thus at its deepest levels the river moves toward a freedom that liberates the whole person and humanizes the entire society, pressing us beyond the boundaries of race, class, and nationality that serve temporarily, necessarily, as our organizing, stabilizing bases. From my perspective, this is the magnificent opening toward which the river has been moving, the great ocean of humanity's best hope that it has always held and nurtured at the center of its own bursting life.

This was the source of the opportunity we presented to the young white nation in the eighteenth century, when we challenged it to free all slaves and begin to fulfill its own most important promises. This black vision of a new American community beyond slavery and white superiority was the main impetus behind the "right hand of fellowship" that we offered to the former slavemasters after the Civil War. This was the dream nurtured in the hearts of those workers for "the beloved community" who helped create the cascading river of the 1960s.

Because it is my river, both by ancestral heritage and by personal choice, I care deeply about both its past and its ultimate destination. Though the title comes from one of the Psalms of my childhood, the metaphor was revived sharply a decade ago when I read the words of a Jamaican Rastafarian poet, Bongo Jerry, singing, lilting, and strong:

> Sooner or later.
> But mus'.
> The dam going to bus' and every man will break out
> and who will stop them?
> The force?
> What force can stop this river of man
> who already know their course.

Now, pausing at the end of this first volume, considering the precarious terrain of our current lives, I am concerned about the one force that may surely stop the river: the self-destructiveness and despair that overwhelm us when we no longer know our course, no longer remember our origins.

So I write in hope that some men and women will read the words and recognize that they/we are the essential force, are the river, are the vision. I write, trusting that some parents and grandparents and teachers will read aloud and share this with the children, will become new sources of memory, will remind one another that our destination has always been a new, transformed humanity, a new humanized society (not "equal opportunity" in a dehumanized one), will remember that we have come this far at great cost.

. . . . of hope. The only history I

American society, . . .

our courage and hope the barriers of all the political, . . .

social institutions that now hold us in bondage to our worst selves.

Indeed, as a result of the history I have explored, I am foolish enough to identify the decade of the 1980s as a time of hope. In the face of all the predictions and signs of breakdown and great danger that I see and hear all around me, I hear and see more as well. (Has this not always been one of the great strengths of our people, to face the storm without flinching, but then to see hope at its center: "Nobody knows the trouble I seen . . . Glory, Hallelujah!") I sense a time of tremendous opportunity, not an easy time, but a period of great possibilities. I think it is especially significant that when this decade ends we will have come to another Bicentennial, this time the anniversary of the nation's Constitution. From the perspective of the black river, considering the struggles of women, Native Americans, Hispanics, and many others, we can now understand that the first constitutional creation of the American nation was more like a poorly attended dress rehearsal, with most of the rightful and necessary performers and creators barred from the stage. Women were locked in homes, black people held in thrall in both South and North, Native Americans harassed, destroyed, and driven from their land, and poor people of every hue taught to let their propertied "betters" make the crucial public decisions for them. Now, nearly two hundred years later, all the hidden, driven, enslaved improvisers are thronging toward the stage, walking on it, creating the drama, reshaping the sets, reflecting the realities of the modern world. Of course many of the old-line actors think that the show is still theirs, that they are at least in charge of saying which of the "newcomers" will be allowed to participate and how; they believe that their access to the levers of destruction gives them ultimate power to deny new creation. But I am certain that they are wrong. The making of the United States—like the making of the modern world—is beginning again:

> O, let America be America again—
> The land that never has been yet—
> And yet must be—

And the central question of our history is the question of our future: what kind of a nation do we want?

We know, of course, that there are no prefabricated answers to that question. Rather they are most often the product of much study, experimentation, hard struggle, failure, and hope, beginning with the innermost levels of our lives. That is the center of the drama, the heart of the enveloping river. Now, as we dare to take responsibility for our own future as individuals and peoples, as we give up the fantasy that presidents or the best charismatic leaders can solve the most basic problems of our society, the moment of great possibility opens before us. Now, some of us who were here for thousands of years, as well as some of us who came from Europe and from Asia, from Mexico and India, from Puerto Rico and the wide ranges of Latin America, may join with those children of Africa in the United States who remember their course. Together we may stand in the river, transformed and transforming, listening to its laughter and burning with its tears, recognizing in that ancient flow the indelible marks of human blood, yet grounded and buoyed by hope, courage, and unfathomable, amazing grace. Keeping the faith, creating new faith, we may enter the terrible and magnificent struggle for the re-creation of America. For all who seek that way, for all who join the compassionate seekers of the past and the future, I share this work of history as an act of solidarity and a testament of hope.

Pendle Hill
Winter, 1981

There Is a River

1

From the Shores of Africa

The Forerunners

. . . us
and wounded many . . . and many
and drowned themselves in the ocean with much resolution . . .

John Barbot
Slave Ship Captain, 1701

It began at the edge of our homeland, where the verdant forests and tropical bush gave way gradually to the sandy stretches of the Guinea coast. It began at the mouths of the rivers, from that northern point where the Senegal and the Gambia pour their troubled streams into the waters around Cape Verde, down the thousands of miles of coastline to the place where the mighty river Congo breaks out into the ocean. On these shores near the mouths of these rivers, we first saw the ships.

There was no way to know it then, but their crews of men and boys came from many ports and many pasts to find the shores of Africa. They sailed from Amsterdam and Lisbon, from Nantes and La Rochelle, from Bristol and London, from Newport and Boston on ships with strange names. They came to us on *Brotherhood* and *John the Baptist*, on *Justice* and *Integrity*, on *Gift of God* and *Liberty*; they came on the good ship *Jesus*. But by the time our weary lines of chained and mourning travelers saw the vessels riding on the coastal waves, there could be but one name, one meaning: captivity. Thus it was on the edges of our continent—where some of us gulped down handfuls of sand in a last effort to hold the reality of the land—that the long struggle for black freedom began.[1]

Struggle was inevitable for the captives, and preparations began early. There were many times when the forced marches from the interior or the long rides in the river canoes brought our people to their terrible rendezvous with slavery long before the *Morning Star* and *Mary* had arrived to receive them. Often, even when the ships were anchored in the bay, the involuntary black pilgrims were kept waiting weeks at a time until a slaver's full human cargo had been collected. Then, guarded by other Africans who had made a tragic choice, huddled together in rows of wooden shacks known as "baracoons" and "factories," forced into dungeonlike castles and forts which the Europeans had built on the coasts, or simply settled in open clearings by the riversides, a troubled and bewildered people had time to consider the past and the future, time to ponder this new captivity which dominated the present, time to grapple with the need to break free.[2]

As is so often the case with human struggles for liberation, the first stages of the baracoon-based movements toward black freedom required internal action, exertions of the will. In many places it was probably necessary to break through all the real and fancied barriers of each particular geographic, tribal, and national history represented in these first confused and unlikely pan-African assemblies. For within the flexible matrix of our continental oneness, over the long millennia of the ages, Africa has produced great diversity. Even in the relatively limited setting of the western portions of the continent, which supplied most of the men, women, and children who filled these prison spaces, there was a fascinating, compelling variety of human experience. Wherever they were gathered, in the slave castles at York, or at Cape Coast on Bena Island, or at Atim, or in scores of other places, the African captives were themselves a testimony to this multiformity. They had come from the ocean-tempered coastal area as well as inland forests, from the villages in the mountain shadows and from riverside towns. Some were the products of peoples and nations with long traditions of strong kings, elaborate courts, and well-defined civil services. Most of the others had heard of such things only through the stories of their traders; the sole kingdom they knew was that which encompassed their family, clan, and small tribe. As they identified themselves to one another and spoke their names in those dark prison places, the sounds of their tribes and nations must have tumbled like a waterfall out of the river of the past: Bambara, Malinka, Fon, Dinka, Ewe, Bakongo, Ibo, Yoruba, and hundreds more.

In the same way, the African people who waited against their will for the coming of the European ships were also living testimonies to the breadth and variety of the work and skills of their continent. Imprisoned now in the heart of the earth they had known so well were miners familiar with the long African traditions of iron, gold, and diamond mining. Blacksmiths, their companion artisans, were also captives. Weavers and potters; workers in bronze, copper, and gold; traders whose wide-ranging movements had long ago put Africa in touch with Asia, Asia Minor, and Europe—all of them were now among the prisoners in these cramped and fetid waiting rooms of history. Here were herders, perhaps captured while pursuing their lonely, roaming occupation, and fishermen and fisherwomen. But surely no group was more fully represented in the baracoons than the vast body of farmers. And none was more essential to the life of the people than the priests and musicians who illuminated, intensified, and celebrated the ritual integument and vital religious center

in these terrible temporary settlements

stories of the captive people who had followed a certain Moses. By the time the ships arrived, there could no longer be any doubt that we had been captured in our homeland to prepare us for a greater, uncharted, wholly terrifying captivity across the endless waters "far from [our] native clime / Under the white man's menace, out of time."[4]

From the European side, the way to this place of struggle had been ploughed by powerful movements of peoples and institutions. That relatively small continent was bursting with new cultural, political, and economic forces. Religious, civil, and commercial revolutions were creating new men and women, new institutions, new hungers for the riches of other people's lands which could only lead to harsh conflicts. In the fifteenth and sixteenth centuries the recently established monarchies and national states, burgeoning commercial classes, trading companies, and adventurers were all drawn together. The common magnet was the search for gold and other precious goods, for the wealth and power these created, and the new trading routes to the Orient which led to them. At the same time, while their newly redefined religion and philosophy taught these men that human freedom had few limits for the strong, their advances in weaponry convinced them that there was no strength to match their own. Other technological developments, often borrowed by the way of North Africa and Asia Minor, gave them greater confidence on the ocean, new capacities to navigate its reckless wastes, stronger ships to carry them into the sun. Most often the kings, queens, and trading companies, as well as the new public treasuries, provided the capital for the bold explorations. Popes, bishops, and professors provided the blessing and the rationale for their incursions into the lives and histories of other civilizations. Their developing nation states and national consciousness promised glory and recognition to the most successful conquerors and exploiters. Men and boys newly uprooted from the countryside and towns provided the crews and cannon fodder for fierce mutual warfare and for the larger European assault on the peoples of Africa and the Western Hemisphere.

With the merchant marine of Portugal and Spain taking the lead, the men and the ships who carried the banner of this new Europe blundered into the Americas while seeking the way to China. At the same time, still looking for alternative routes to the Orient, searching out trading posts on the way around "the Dark Continent," they discovered Africa's gold and its people. So Christopher Columbus and Vasco de Gama, Bartholomeu Diaz and John Cabot went out in search of wealth, adventure, and a place in history, and they barged into the future on a rising tide of blood. As a result, by the end of the sixteenth century many Europeans realized that across the Atlantic they had found a sparsely populated hemisphere to conquer, exploit, and settle. South of their so often cold and crowded lives, they had also come upon a great, warm black continent to provide the slave workers who would create much of the wealth of the New World. That brutal connection between the vast, potentially profitable lands of the Western Hemisphere, and the apparently inexhaustible sources of captive labor in Africa, became the critical nexus in the minds of Europe's ruling and commercial classes, as they anticipated the wealth and power these human and physical resources would bring to them. Out of that combination of vision, enterprise, and avarice, the African slave trade was born.[5]

Of course long before the ships of Europe arrived, there was a form of human bondage in Africa, just as there was on most of the world's continents. But there is no evidence that the kind of chattel slavery which Europe was to perfect in the New World had taken root in West Africa. The slavery in existence was—as slavery goes—far more humane, since often it was only for prescribed periods of time, and involved no laws aimed at dehumanization. This slavery was not established by the Africans primarily for profit; it did not impose on the victims a mark of essential, intrinsic inferiority; and it was not necessarily passed on to the children of the bondsmen. When the ships came, they brought with them the European passion for profits, the European disease of racism, and the European fondness for power of arms. When these forces encountered all the weaknesses—all the tendencies to fear, deception, and greed—that Africans share with the rest of humankind, the earlier, more flexible patterns of African bondage degenerated into the African slave trade—

financed, fueled, and directed by the peoples of Europe, and all too often aided and abetted by African allies.[6]

Attempts had already been made in various places to use the indigenous peoples of the Western Hemisphere, as well as poor white prisoners and indentured servants from England and the continent, as slave workers in the Americas, but none of these experiments had proven successful. In the case of the Indians, escape was too easy on their own native ground.
_____ ____ were limited, and few had any preparation for the
_____ _____ ____ _____an exploitation

America was the fur trade _____
latter would endanger. For these and other reasons, the _____
developed beyond relatively isolated instances.[7]

On the other hand, even those whites brought out of the prisons of England and elsewhere to work as slaves or indentured servants often still had some link to the home countries. Consequently, knowledge of their permanent servitude could produce serious political problems at home for the colonizers of the royal territories, as well as stop the flow of other white servants to the colonies. Besides, the common color and culture that these white servant-slaves shared with other whites in the colonies created thorny social, religious, and psychological problems, and also rendered re-capture more difficult when they escaped. Perhaps even more important was the fact that, as in the case of the Indians, there were simply not enough of them, and they had not developed the natural immunities necessary to become the massive, intensive, often semi-tropical labor force required to satisfy the desire of the companies and monarchs for the largest profits in the shortest time.[8]

As a result, by the end of the seventeenth century, as England and other white-settler countries shifted their attention north from the Caribbean, established claims along the North American coast, and explored the wilderness, Africans became the chosen people for American slavery. Here they were far from home with no natural allies around them, and with no regular means for word of their fate to get back to any political centers which would affect the sources of supply. In most cases they had the needed agricultural experience and natural tropical immunities, and the supply seemed inexhaustible. Then, too—surely of the greatest importance—they were an alien, non-Christian, nonwhite people, easily providing a negative source of identity and a negative rallying point for the New World's white society. And so they were chosen. We were chosen.

By this time England had established its hegemony over "the Trade," as its participants and others euphemistically referred to this commerce in human bondage. With the Royal African Company and scores of independent "adventurers" leading the way, the vessels called *Morning Star* and *Charity*, *Young Saint Paul* and *Good Intent* were making their laden way from the Guinea coast to Barbados and Jamaica, to Charleston and Norfolk, carrying the peoples of Africa into captivity. There were often impressive profits to be made now in the Trade itself, and especially in that great flowering of agriculture, shipping, and commerce which accompanied the colonizing of the New World, a world that the captive Africans built. Individual owners, trading companies, churches, monarchs —all shared in the wealth. Of course these financial gains were based on working hundreds of thousands and eventually millions of men, women, and children for their lifetime without pay. And so, beginning with their first experimental presence on the tobacco plantations of the Caribbean, Africans gave their involuntary labor to the creation of the new settlement. They blazed the trails, cleared the forests, built the dwellings, tilled the land, planted the seed, harvested the crops, dug the ore, kept the livestock, nursed the children, created and maintained the wealth of the New World—without pay. As a result, there were great profits in Barbados and Hispaniola, in Carolina and Virginia. Indeed, before the American War for Independence, one contemporary English economist would say, "The daily bread of the most-considerable part of our British manufacturers, are owing primarily to the labor of Negroes." That, essentially, is what Eric Williams, C. L. R. James, and Walter Rodney have told us since: Europe's Industrial Revolution, that engine of revolutionary change which released the social, economic, and political energies of the modern world, was built on the black and bloody foundations of our African forebears. That is why the ships continued to come to the coast of Guinea and to wait at the mouths of the rivers.[9]

As the "Black Gold" began pouring into the English colonies of the New World, new patterns of captivity, betrayal, and confusion were established on the continent. African nations like the Fulas, the Mande, the Susu, and the peoples of Dahomey devoted themselves to capturing and keeping other Africans for the slave trade. Ancient political balances and structures of power and alliances were shattered through the introduction of Europe's firearms into the hands of one side or another. Often the arms were used as bribes to encourage leaders to capture men, women, and children from adjoining nations and tribes. Wars were declared for no other reason than to obtain prisoners. Villages were razed; hunting parties never returned home. Families and tribes, and centuries of traditions, were broken. And eventually the trails of the West African lands were beaten smooth by the bare feet of millions of our ancestors, as they made their way down to the rivers and the sea. For a long time the Europeans, sustained by their guns and Bible, and by arrogance and cruelty, were convinced that all things white and Christian were possible.

... of internal weaknesses among the non-

tribes, nations, and empires—who had known ... of their fathers, no other rule but the rule of their African peoples—must have developed within themselves a powerful will to break free from this captivity. Even the Africans who had been prisoners, the disgraced, the twice-captured, must have recognized the desperation of their plight. Too much human life, too much human creativity, too much human hope was compressed in those castles and dungeons for the struggle to be denied.

And so, by the time the ships arrived out of the glaring mirror of sun-swept waters, or moved like a visitation of giant fireflies against the darkness of the sea—by the time *Integrity* and *Liberty* and *Black Boy* arrived at Whydah and Malemba—the issues and nature of those early stages of black struggle were starkly defined. At that moment in our history, as the ominous shadows hovered near the coasts, we fought to remain in our homeland, to continue in the experience and tradition our peoples had created, to build and protect the societies we had fashioned under the guidance of the spirits. Our struggle was to resist the breaking of our nations, our families, and the chain of our existence. Our struggle was to free ourselves from the already obviously brutal captivity which was spreading over the people like some cloud of foreboding and death, to free ourselves for the life that our forebears had willed to us and our children. Our struggle was to resist both the European captors and their African helpers, to challenge and seek to break their power to take us away from our homeland. In doing this, we denied the European right to hold us, to rule our lives, to control our destiny. We affirmed our own freedom, our own being.

Struggle was inevitable, and captains of the slave ships knew that they must be prepared for our attempts to break free, especially while their vessels were still near the African coasts. On board an English ship in 1693 (was it *Brotherhood* or *Constant Mary*?—we no longer know) the captain wrote: "When our slaves are aboard we shackle the men two and two, while we lie in port, and in sight of their own country, for 'tis then they attempt to make their escape and mutiny; to prevent which we always keep centinels upon the hatchways, and have a chest full of small arms, ready loaden and primed, constantly lying at hand upon the quarter-deck, together with some granada shells; and two of our quarter-deck guns, pointing on the deck thence, and two more out of the steerage."[11]

If chains and guns were necessary when Africans were stuffed down in the brutal darkness between the decks, then even greater force and threat of force were often deemed necessary when we came up on deck to eat. The captain continues: "They are fed twice a day, at 10 in the morning, and 4 in the evening, which is the time they are aptest to mutiny, being all upon deck; therefore all that time, what of our men are not employ'd in distributing their victuals to them, and settling them, stand to their arms; and some with lighted matches at the great guns that yaun upon them, loaden with partridge, 'til they have done and gone down to their kennels between decks." Such testimony from the men who manned the ships of black captivity was repeated hundreds of times throughout the centuries of the Trade. In spite of their names, many of the vessels were indeed meant to be "kennels" where human beings were forced to exist for weeks and months in condition not fit for animals. That is why so many hundreds of thousands of our ancestors were ravaged by disease, lying for days in their own excrement, dying in these cattle ships.[12]

Yet the ships were also prisons for humans. That was the meaning of the chains, the guns, and the fearful white men standing with lighted matches at the cannon. For ultimately they knew that we were more than animals, that the secret conversations of the baracoons and lower decks could turn into rebellion at any moment. So as in all prisons, an inordinate amount of the captors' time was spent in simply watching and guarding against any black movement toward freedom. And the life of the sailor guards, locked in a captivity parallel with our own, was often filled with sheer wretchedness.[13]

In the course of the struggles, it developed that the ships were even more than prisons. Ultimately they provided black people with an introduction to the Euro-American state, for they were mini-states with their own polity, their own laws and government; the common sailors were the ships' own indigenous oppressed class. When the Africans were brought on board, much of the machinery of these floating miniatures of England and France, of Virginia and Massachusetts, could be geared toward our captivity, but the internal contradictions did not disappear. At the core of the mini-states, prisons, and kennels it was always possible to discover the social, economic, and political scourges rising out of Europe: racism, capitalism, and the deep human fears they engender. The tie of the ships to European capitalism was evident in the decision to call _____ their relationship to the slave "factories," and to _____ that they brought

an African who had killed a ___
Snelgrave had the black man hoisted as high as possible abo___
and shot to death in the presence of his fellow Africans. Then, he said, "I ordered the Linguist to acquaint the men-Negroes, 'That now they might judge, no one that killed a white Man should be spared.'" Snelgrave probably did not know it then, but even if he had hoisted the insurrectionary up into the clouds, the struggle would not have ended. Though few of their words survive, the actions of our fathers and mothers in those ships along the coasts declared that many of them were determined to carry on a relentless struggle for freedom. They wanted freedom from the status of animals, the role of prisoners, the domination of white Europeans. They wanted to continue in their people's long stream of history.[14]

In the early struggles on the ships in the coastal waters, the African captives used every available tool to strike for freedom. Sometimes they even broke their chains and transformed them into weapons. Near the end of the seventeenth century, off the shores of the Gulf of Guinea where the castle of Elmina stood, a Dutch captain underestimated the power of the will of his black captives. He fished up an anchor left behind by another ship, and put it down in the hold where the male Africans were being held. The anchor became a signal and a forge. A Dutch writer and a participant in the slave trade, William Bosman, wrote:

[the men,] unknown to any of the ship's crew, possessed themselves of a hammer; with which, in a short time, they broke all their fetters in pieces upon the anchor; after this they came above deck and fell upon our men; some of whom they grievously wounded, and would certainly have mastered the ship, if a French and English ship had not fortunately happened to ly by us and immediately came to our assistance with chalops and men, and drove the slaves under deck: Notwithstanding which before all was appeased about twenty of them were killed.

The lessons then being written in the reddened coastal waters soon entered into the long history of the struggle: blacks have never lacked ingenuity, wisdom, courage, and a deep longing for freedom. But in captivity these were not sufficient: it was not enough to break the chains; it was necessary to master the ship.[15]

Along the African coasts, it was possible to hope for such mastery. So in spite of constant and costly defeats, the struggles for freedom went on. Often women took a crucial part, making full use of the special status and greater freedom of movement accorded them. While the men, except for prescribed times, were kept chained in the communal hole between the decks, the women were allowed to move around the upper decks by day, and not infrequently after the day had ended. Why? Partly because they were judged less dangerous than the men. Partly too because the captains, who considered themselves humane and Christian, often thought it necessary for the children to be on deck, and wanted the women to be able to care for them. But also, on many vessels, so that white men from the captain to the cook's helper could unleash their lust against them.[16]

Fortunately for the black struggle, many black women refused to submit to or be corrupted by this most personal of white invasions; instead, they turned the situation to the purposes of their people's fight for freedom. Samuel Waldo, the owner of the slaving ship *Africa*, which operated out of Boston, wrote to his captain in 1734: "For your own safety as well as mine, You'll have the needfull Guard over your Slaves, and putt not too much confidence in the Women nor Children lest they happen to be Instrumental to your being surprised which might be fatall."[17]

By the time of his letter there was much evidence to support such a warning, for black women were regular participants in the struggle for freedom. Their role was exemplified in the events on board the English ship *Robert* as it stood off the coast of Sierra Leone in 1721. Among the thirty captives on board was a man who called himself Captain Tomba, one of the earliest identifiable leaders of the struggle. He and several other African men and an unnamed woman had developed a plan to attack the crew, overcome them, and make their way back to the shore. The woman, because she had greater freedom of movement, was chosen to inform the men of the best time for the attack.[18]

One night as she roamed the deck, she noted that the number of sailors in the night watch was small enough to make a surprise move feasible. After she managed to inform Tomba, he prepared to act immediately; but only one of the African men who had promised earlier to assist him was now ready to join Tomba and the woman. Nevertheless, these three moved to strike for their freedom. The smallness of their force and an accidental sounding of an alarm worked against them, so that after killing two of the crew they were overwhelmed by others, beaten to the deck, and placed in chains. The ship's doctor who preserved this story of black

over her privileged bondage among white men: we are told

woman he hoisted up by the Thumbs, whipp'd and slashed her with Knives, before the other Slaves till she died." And so, not far from the shores of the homeland, the swaying, bleeding body of a sister in struggle bore terrifying witness to the cost of the decision for freedom. Yet perhaps she would have considered this lonely vigil above the sea a better use of her body than any that the crew members had had in mind.[20]

It is only by accident that we learn a name such as that of Captain Tomba, or even catch the disturbingly grand outlines of the woman from Sierra Leone. Most of those Africans who carried on the earliest phases of the movement toward justice are now nameless. This is unfortunate, yet not wholly so, for their very anonymity is a reminder of the broad basis of the struggle, an encouragement to see the relentless surge toward freedom as a movement from the outset belonging to the people.

Even without the faces or the names, what begins to be clear is the stunning, perhaps frightening power resident in those early struggles. For instance, we know only that in 1730 the captive Africans of the Massachusetts schooner *William* conspired together and killed almost all the crew, then made their way back to the nearby shores. On another Massachusetts ship of the same period, "the Negroes got to the powder and Arms, and about 3 o'clock in the morning, rose upon the whites; and after wounding all of them very much, except two who hid themselves; [the blacks] ran the Vessel ashore a little to the Southward of Cape Lopez and made their escape." So too, near the end of 1732, a contemporary account reported that a group of captives from Guinea on board a Bristol slaving ship "rose up and destroyed the whole crew, cutting off the Captain's Head, Legs and Arms."[21]

The sheer ferocity of such confrontations makes it clear that some of the men and women who battled in the coastal waters anticipated the violent future ominously as when, in 1735, the captives on the English ship *Dolphin* "overpowered the crew, broke into the powder room, and finally in the course of their effort for freedom blew up both themselves and the crew." In February 1759, in the Gambia River, a battle on board a New England ship produced a similar outcome. When the vessel had taken on its captives, it was attacked by other Africans from the shore. According to a contemporary white account, the crew "made a good defence; but the Captain finding himself desperately wounded, and likely to be overcome, rather than fall into the Hands of such merciless Wretches, when about 80 Negroes had boarded his Vessel, discharged a Pistol into his magazine, and blew her up; himself and every living soul on Board perished."[22]

In spite of the constant danger of such suicidal white defense, black men and women continued to resist. Still, there were always captains and other white men who claimed to be surprised at such persistent struggle. On another occasion a group of Africans fresh from the Gold Coast attempted an uprising while the ship of the familiar Captain Snelgrave was still near the shore. The fifty white men in the slaver's crew were healthy and well armed; black resistance had not been expected. When the revolt had been crushed, Snelgrave had his translators ask what had induced them to mutiny. According to his own account, the Africans told him that he was "a great Rogue to buy them, in order to carry them away from their own Country, and that they were resolved to regain their Liberty if possible."[23]

It is likely that the version of either the translators or the captain was much milder than the original sentiment; nevertheless, both the words and the deeds of the rebellious Africans were significant, and their meaning was not lost. The captives were challenging the justice, authority, and legitimacy of their captors. Their words, which surely represented the speeches—and the screams—of many other men and women on those voyages, were among the earliest forms of what we shall call the Great Tradition of Black Protest. As such, the speakers and others like them were the first bold face-to-face petitioners against slavery. But they were more besides, for if those European ships indeed represented the rising white racist nation-state and its developing systems of economic and cultural exploitation, then the black voices of the Gold Coast were also part of a beginning tradition of radical challenge to such a state. Albeit unwittingly, they called into question the very roots of the mechanisms of white power and control. Essentially, they declared that for them this system had absolutely no legitimacy; they persistently acted accordingly and often took the consequences. This was black radicalism at the outset.[24]

Everywhere, though, the joint tradition of protest and radicalism raised problems which needed to be solved—harsh questions involving both the goals of the struggle and the nature of the men and forces which opposed black freedom. How could black struggle best break the power of men who were at once driven and imprisoned by the glittering promises of

. . . . blinded by the racism and fear which burrowed

introduction to the civilization of the European

pulses, and its conception of our place. Near the coast our challenge was clear, fundamental, and radical in its essential nature: our total struggle on each ship was a total challenge to the control of the white captors, a movement to smash their power, to repossess our history and our future. We wanted their little ships only long enough to return us to our vast continent. Indeed, sometimes we spared their crews if they did not hinder our homeward flight. So for the most part, black struggle and black radicalism were at the beginning a single stream encompassing both words and action.

But what happened on those ships, those thousands of ships which took us out into the ocean, away from the sights and smells of our land, beyond even the far-ranging flight of our birds? What did black struggle for freedom mean out in the vast and seemingly endless arena of that ocean? Was any struggle possible? In such situations African men and women must surely have asked, why challenge the captains and crews, why risk the certainty of death for the uncertainty of the land beyond the ocean, why fly in the face of the eternal east wind?

Already it was evident that from place to place, time to time, and setting to setting, the nature of our struggle was to be transformed and the questions reshaped. So it was on the ocean, as we moved further from the black shores into the agonies of the middle passage. Under those new, unprecedented circumstances the only possible struggle for most captives was to stay alive—an arduous task on many ships, usually demanding all our energies. On too many vessels the focus of this struggle for survival was the food, stingily apportioned by the captains or the owners, while Africans and their children slowly starved. Sometimes our attention was focused on filth and on the disease it engendered, as well as on the strange new diseases brought from the wharfs of Bristol or London—and from the captains' bedrooms—and insinuated into our bodies just as arrogantly as the boats moved into the rivers of our land. Often the focus was on the extended suffering of countless hours in chains, lying on our backs and sides in spaces made for narrow, rigid corpses. But it is likely that for most of us the heart of the new darkness was imprisonment itself. Most of us had not experienced it before—neither the physical imprisonment of kennels, chains, and guns, nor those mental dungeons that white fear and disdain now created around us. In many instances, the shock they induced proved fatal.[25]

It was a long journey to the Western Hemisphere—usually from one to three months, depending on tides and storms, and on the points of departure and landing. Under these circumstances, when even the birds of the homeland could no longer be seen, survival was an understandable obsession, and it was not always possible to perceive the meaning or purpose of any other struggle. In the midst of the journey, on many ships they made us sing and dance. But like so much of our singing and dancing at white command ever since, the activity was not primarily for our benefit or entertainment, but for white profits, ordered because dancing was considered therapeutic, was supposed to ensure us against the "melancholy" that drove countless thousands of Africans to suicide in the course of the middle passage. It was also supposed to help prevent scurvy, though as some observers noted, dancing "was a useless torture for men with swollen limbs." Nevertheless, "while sailors paraded the deck, each with a cat-o'-nine-tails in his right hand, the men slaves 'jumped in their irons' until their ankles were bleeding flesh." The men and women often danced separately, their music supplied by a fellow captive who beat on a broken drum or played on the upturned kettle which was, and would continue to be, so ubiquitous in our cultures.[26]

And what were the songs that we sang? One doctor who served on the English ship *Young Hero* probably spoke with great accuracy when he said, "They sing, but not for their amusement. The captain ordered them to sing, and they sang songs of sorrow. Their sickness, fear of being beaten, their hunger, and the memory of their country . . . are the usual subjects." Then late at night, after the songs were over, from the darkness of the lower decks of the *Young Hero* and a thousand other ships, the sailors often could hear "an howling melancholy noise, expressive of extreme anguish." On one such occasion, the ship's doctor said that he asked his black female interpreter to go inquire the cause·

of the wailing noise. According to the doctor, "she discovered it to be owing to their having dreamt that they were in their own country, and finding themselves when awake, in the hold of a slave ship." At every period of our history, in every place of our captivity, men and women have dreamed that long collective dream of home and then awakened to the brutal reality of the endless night.[27]

On many ships in the Atlantic, out of sight of the shores, there were other awakenings as well. Even in such desolate places, where all cause ... seemed destroyed, many Africans awoke and insisted on the

Ship's Company, distant from Land. ...
but these Europeans did not think we would struggle against them simply because we knew that we did not belong to them, simply because many African men and women considered any fate better than the continued subjugation they had already experienced briefly among Europeans. Therefore the whites said they could not understand those apparently reckless last stands which often ended with death in the ocean.[28]

One of many such desperate battles took place near the beginning of the eighteenth century on the English ship *Don Carlos*, which had sailed up the Congo River and down again, and was now out to sea. Several crew members had died on the river and others were sick. Nevertheless, in an act of careless overconfidence, the crew had given knives to many of the black men. In addition, the captain later wrote:

others had pieces of iron they had torn off our forecastle door, as having premeditated a revolt, and seeing all the ship's company, at best but weak and many quite sick, they had also broken off the shackles from several of their companions feet, which served them, as well as . . . all other things they could lay their hands on, which they imagined might be of use for their enterprize. Thus armed, they fell in crouds and parcels on our men, upon the deck unawares, and stabb'd one of the stoutest of us all, who received fourteen or fifteen wounds of their knives, and so expir'd. Next they assaulted our boatswain, and cut one of his legs so round the bone, that he could not move . . . others cut our cook's throat to the pipe, and others wounded three of the sailors, and threw one of them overboard in that condition.[29]

Before long, however, the ship's company rallied behind the ever-present firearms. As the captain later reported, "We stood in arms, firing on the revolted slaves of whom we kill'd some, and wounded many: which so terrified the rest, that they gave way, dispersing themselves . . . between decks, and under forecastle; and many of the most mutinous, leapt over board, and drowned themselves in the ocean *with much resolution, showing no manner of concern for life*."[30]

What was the basic goal of such desperate struggle, and what manner of men and women were these who threw themselves into the ocean "with much resolution," rather than submit to slavery a long way from home? Obviously, the captain's answer is not that of the black people. The captors and the captives never have the same answers to the basic questions of struggle; most often, not even the same questions. Those who threw themselves resolutely into the ocean in fact had great "concern for life." That was why they fought so relentlessly in a seemingly hopeless situation, driven by a vivid urgency that only those who face bondage can know. They were incited by a wild and terrible hope which winds its way through all the history of our struggle against white domination. They lost the battle to live and be rid of their captors, but they won the struggle to die and be free.[31]

The question then arises: after the struggle to break the oppressors' hold upon our lives is stymied, is suicide another form of battle against that domination? Thousands upon thousands of Africans—we cannot know the number—took that path. For many, of course, it was the traditional pathway back to the homeland, for they believed that death would deliver them to the unseen but well-remembered shores. Sometimes, after the firearms had overwhelmed them, black men and women moved resolutely back into the hold and methodically, unwaveringly—in spite of knives ripping them and hot coals placed at their mouths—starved themselves to death. Others, countless others, took some new occasion to leap over the side of the vessels. This response was so common that the watch was constantly on guard, and special nettings were rigged up to baffle such attempts. Still, this black action was so often successful that schools of sharks followed the vessels.[32]

Consistently, even the reluctant white witnesses spoke of the active resoluteness of the suicides, and at times perceived suggestions of ecstasy in their daring acts. On the French ship *Le Rodeur*, which had left Bonny Town on the Guinea Coast and was several days at sea, there was a sudden commotion. The Africans began charging across the decks in every direction. Eluding the flailing arms of the crew, avoiding the nettings, they hurled themselves into the ocean. An eyewitness later wrote: "The Negroes . . . who had got off, continued dancing about the waves, yelling with all their might, what seemed to me a song of triumph and they were soon joined by several of their companions still on deck. Our ship speedily left the ignorant creatures behind; their voices came fainter and fainter upon the wind; the black head, first of one, then another, disappeared, and then the sea was without a spot; and the air without a sound." On another ship the captain declared—typically—that he would fight the epidemic of suicides among the Ibos on board by public beheadings of all who attempted it. At one of these white rituals several Africans tried _____ overboard, and one succeeded. A crew

be forever blotted from the pages of the world ___

own time more recent versions of conventional wisdom would relegate such black action to the category of unfortunate, ineffectual escapism, or of limited passive resistance at best. Contrary to such opinions, both the songs and the singers remain embedded in the black freedom movement in America. No struggle against oppression is ignorant, and to label it escapist is in itself an evasion, an escape from the meanings of the long battle. These forerunners who fought and sang, who starved themselves to death in the darkness of the ships' holds, have forced their way into the ever-flowing river of black struggle. To call such acts "passive resistance" is to deny the existence of vast realms of the spirit, to count resistance only by its outward physical modes. Anyone who has seriously contemplated suicide or attempted fasting surely understands what tremendous action of the will was performed by those men and women who leaped voluntarily into the waters, or who refused food until they died. There was nothing "passive" in such decisions and deeds.

Their form of resistance again challenged and denied the ultimate authority of the white traders over their lives and their spirits. Their actions were unmistakable attacks on the system of slavery and the slave trade, for they refused the system some of its profits, some of its parts— perhaps even threatened some of its self-righteousness of spirit. Whatever else they did, these men and women made a radical break with the situation of their captivity, denying that their lives could belong to any man, especially to the representatives of Europe. Doing so, they took charge of their future, joining it with their own past. Out on the Atlantic, such an action was often the highest form available to many persons who found themselves far from the sands of Africa's shores, far from the birds of the mainland, under the white man's menace, but determined to be free.

Suicide was a last resort. Before its final word was spoken, all the other possible avenues of struggle were often attempted; just as they had been attempted near the shores. The movement never abated, and we are told by a major authority on the subject that from the third decade of the eighteenth century to the end of the slave trade, "tales of mutinies abound in the literature of the slave trade. . . . There is little question but that they became more common as the trade fell into the hands of independent traders, who probably were more careless in their supervision of the negroes, and who carried smaller crews in comparison with the size of their cargoes than had the company vessels." This was a strange but telling testimony, not only to the determined resistance of the forefathers, but to the way in which the very racism and greed for profits which fueled the trade created openings for new struggle and revolt. For this carelessness was a form of disdain for the Africans' love of freedom, a disbelief in their willingness to strike when the opportunity arose. And the smallness of the crews was a way of saving on the initial investments, so that the profit might be even higher. Out on the ocean the captives took advantage of both of these circumstances wherever possible.[34]

In 1727 the English ship *Ferrers* was ten days out from the Guinea Coast. Its captain, surely considering himself liberal and humane, regularly sat among the African captives while they ate their main meal on deck. One day, we are told, the Africans "laid on him, and beat out his Brains with the little Tubs, out of which they eat their boiled Rice." Nor was this an unplanned, impetuous act.

This mutiny having been plotted amongst all the grown Negroes on board, they run to the forepart of the Ship in a body, and endeavored to force the Barricadeo on the Quarter-Deck, not regarding the Musquets of Half Pikes, that were presented to their Breasts by the white Men, through the Loop-Holes. So that at last the chief Mate was obliged to order one of the Quarter-deck Guns laden with Partridge-Shot, to be fired amongst them; which occasioned a terrible destruction: For there were near eighty Negroes killed and drowned, many jumping overboard when the Gun was fired. This indeed put an end to the Mutiny, but most of the Slaves that remained alive grew so sullen, that several of them were starved to death, obstinately refusing to take any Sustenance.[35]

Eventually, after another attempted uprising, the *Ferrers* was lost in a hurricane off the coast of Jamaica.

Meanwhile the struggles of the forerunners continued on the Atlantic, out beyond the birds of the coasts. In the spring of 1730 the Rhode Island vessel *Little George,* with ninety-six Africans on board, had left the Guinea Coast almost a week behind. Somehow the African men slipped out of their chains and overpowered the crew. Throwing some crew members overboard, the captives gained control of the ship. The remaining crew took refuge in a cabin, holing themselves up there with _____ _____ firearms and gunpowder as they were able to gather. If _____ _____ eventually become

continent from ports ___ __ the rivers, befouling the shores, to carry black people as ___ rising patriots of Virginia, the Carolinas, and Maryland. Our fathers and mothers made no distinctions between those slave ships whose owners were fighting for "freedom," "liberty," and "independence" at home, and the ones who were not; there was no cessation in their struggles when they were herded aboard the North American vessels in the time of freedom's ferment. In 1765 a ship from Providence, Rhode Island, had filled its lower decks with captives and was on its way to the high seas. According to one account, soon after they left the coastal area extensive sickness among the crew forced the captain "to permit some of the Slaves to come upon the Deck and assist the People." An invidious distinction between "Slaves" and "People" had obviously been impressed upon the minds of the Americans, but not the Africans. Indeed, we are told that "these slaves contrived to release the others, and the whole rose upon the People, and endeavored to get Possession of the Vessel; but was happily prevented by the Captain and his Men, who killed, wounded and forced overboard Eighty of them, which obliged the rest to submit."[37]

Meanwhile, the ironies and contradictions built up. So, in the spring of 1776 Thomas Jefferson, representing the cause of American freedom, wrote into his draft of the Declaration of Independence a sharp attack on the English crown for supposedly forcing the colonists to participate in the African slave trade in order to fill the mother country's coffers. At the same time, these Americans seemed to be unreluctant slave traders and slave owners and were actively engaged in suppressing shipboard rebellions carried out in the cause of black freedom. For instance, that fall of Independence, there was word of another African uprising, this time on the Rhode Island–based vessel *Hope*. The ship's doctor told the story:

We had the misfortune to lose 36 of the best slaves we had by an Insurrection; this unlucky affair happened . . . when there was only the Boatswaine, Carpenter, 3 White people and myself on board. . . . We had 160 Slaves on board and were that day let out of the Deck Chains in order to wash, about 2 O'Clock. . . . They began by seizing upon the Boatswain . . . but he soon got disengaged . . . after receiving a wound on his breast and one under his Chin. . . . They continued to threw [sic] Staves, billets of wood, etc., and in endeavoring to get down the Baricado, or over it for upwards of 40 minutes, when finding they could not effect it all the Fantee and most of the Accra Men Slaves jumped over board.[38]

At the end of his narrative, this doctor found it difficult to account for the struggle: "The only reason we can give for their attempting any thing of the kind, is, their being wearied at staying so long on board the ship." But these captives knew why they struggled, and it had nothing to do with the boredom of the ship. Like the independence struggles of the American colonists—indeed, *more than* the white battles in America—the issue was simply freedom.[39]

Sometimes, of course, other related matters were involved. On June 6, 1796, the captain of the *Mary* out of Providence, Rhode Island, wrote in his log: "This morning found our women slave apartments had been attempted to have been opened by some of the Ship's crew, the locks being Spoiled and Sundered." Four days later the African men attempted an uprising. They failed, but they knew why they rose.[40]

Struggle was inevitable.

We do not know how many battles were actually won in those days of the forerunners, or how often the Africans were able to take over the ships and return to the homeland. Similarly, we do not know how many repossessed their own lives by means of suicide. But we do know that the struggle continued relentlessly, from the river Gambia to Charleston's bay, filling the waters and lining the ocean floor with the bones of those first many thousands gone. Of course we also know that the large majority of uprisings failed, because of the overwhelming fire power of the captors. Nevertheless, even in their failure these battles often led the most honest among the white men to marvel at the unyielding determination of the Africans. In 1790, such testimony emerged from the simple reportage of the English sailor, William Richardson, whose crew had gone to the aid of a French vessel where the Africans were rebelling: "I could not but admire the courage of a fine young black who, though his partner in irons lay dead at his feet, would not surrender but fought with his billet of wood until a pistol ball finished his existence. The others fought as well as they could but what could they do against fire-arms?"[41]

What the learned medical doctor had not been able to see, an ordinary sailor saw clearly. And the question and the issue remain with us through all our history. As the sailor rightly sensed, the issue was never—nor is it now—a matter of superior white cultures, more satisfying ways of life, democracy, free worlds, or higher civilizations. Always, beneath these _____ lurked the demonic forces of white racism and _____ and protected

historical realities of our _____ amazing endurance, can we properly understand the river of _____ and help to guide its continuing movement toward freedom.

2

American Bondage, American Freedom

Shaping the Struggle

Reason and Revelation join to declare that we are the creatures of that God, who made of one Blood, and kindred, all the nations of the Earth; we perceive by our own Reflection, that we are endowed with the same Faculties with our masters, and there is nothing that leads us to a Belief, or Suspicion, that we are any more obliged to serve them, than they us, and the more we Consider of this matter, the more we are Convinced of our Right . . . to be free . . . and can never be convinced that we were made to be Slaves.

Prime and Prince, "in behalf of themselves
and the other Petitioners," 1779

And the black seed of Africa was ruthlessly cast into the winds, into the hungry soil, into the mines, into the furrows, into the forests, into the rivers and the sands, into the eyes and minds and white nightmares of North and South America. And the harvest has not yet fully come.

Just as we had been cruelly gathered from many places along the coasts of the homeland, so by the end of the seventeenth century the prison ships were making their stops at many ports in the New World, from Brazil and Barbados to New England, bringing us to coasts we had never dreamed of, moving us into rivers far from home.

Though the coasts and rivers of North America were unfamiliar, the racism and economic greed of Europe had arrived there before us. They had already begun to prepare a way, driving the natives of this continent relentlessly from the grounds of their ancestors, from the mounds of their spirits. That was the meaning behind the words of Peter Stuyvesant, the Dutch governor of New York, when in 1660 he wrote: "It is evident that in order to possess this country in peace and revenge affronts and murders we shall be forced into a lawful offensive war against [the Indians]."[1]

That was the meaning behind the traditional Indian version of the earlier New Amsterdam massacre in 1643, as told by Chief Flying Hawk:

The Indians had befriended the helpless adventurers when they came among them, and for their kindness the settlers attacked them one night and killed more than a hundred and twenty men, women and children while they were

̇ ̇ ̇ the first massacre. But it was a white-

coming of the Africans.

Europeans had declared themselves owners and governors of the lands of others—nonwhite, heathen others. Then, when these others finally and inevitably resisted, Europeans were regularly "forced into a lawful offensive war" against them to "revenge affronts and murders." Since the Europeans had brought the laws of their churches and states with them, they could decimate the others legally and morally, in apparent quietness and righteousness of conscience. The Euro-American search for "peace" by means of legal genocide had begun, and the drive to possess this country was on. For better and for worse, it developed concurrently with the campaign to possess the bodies and spirits of the children of Africa—and neither the search nor the campaign has yet ended. So the way had been prepared when *Brotherhood* and *John the Baptist,* when *Justice* and *Integrity,* when *Gift of God* and *Liberty* and *Jesus* arrived in the New World, carrying the burden of our people's captivity.

Meanwhile, the shipboard struggles which had begun in the rivers and on the coasts of Africa continued right to the shores of the Americas. Rebellions, suicides, and in a few cases capture of the vessel, occurred in sight of the new land. But the overwhelming majority of those who neared the strange coasts had no such alternatives. By the tens, then the hundreds, then the thousands, we walked onto the new shores and wept by the new rivers, forced by the men and the systems of Europe into a new history, a history to be shared in relentless struggle with them, a history we never wanted. At first, many entered the new North American settlements by way of the West Indies, often experiencing a period of "season-ing" in a place like Barbados. Later the connections were direct, un-mediated, and stark.[3]

It was a new time and place, yet it was not. The middle passage had ended, yet it had not. We were no longer on the slave ships, yet we were. We were plunged into a new era, yet we were heirs of untold thousands of years of our past. In the midst of such contradictions, what was the nature and meaning of our struggle in the New World? Now that we could no longer fiercely possess the ships on the ocean, no longer turn them back to our shores, now that the African birds were gone, and all the familiar scents of our rivers were captured only in our dreams, now—in America—what was black struggle, that one river which we could not leave behind?

The answers to these questions did not come easily, but were worked out in all the actual situations where we found ourselves, were developed in harsh dialectic with the varying circumstances of this new bondage. Well into the midst of the seventeenth century, the situation we discovered was fluid and uncertain, for colonists like the early Virginians seemed at first unclear about the status of the black people they were purchasing from the traders and pirates. Although the landing of the first group of captive Africans in Jamestown, Virginia, in 1619 is traditionally consid-ered the beginning of the institution of black slavery in the North Ameri-can colonies of England, the fact is that the category of "slave" was not yet clearly defined at that time. Nor were the Africans who arrived in the early period limited to or by that status. For several decades, indeed, blacks in Virginia and elsewhere had a status within the laboring classes that varied from indentured apprentice and servant to free man and free woman; the nature of the quest for justice, the definition of the struggle for freedom, was also fluid. But within less than a generation the circumstances had changed, the options were narrowed, and the early mold of oppression was formed.[4]

In this change the Southern colonies—especially Virginia and later South Carolina—played a crucial role. As the number of Africans in-creased, as they indicated their firm desire for the privileges of other men and women, they became more visible, more of a troublesome pres-ence. At the same time the European demand for Southern crops such as tobacco, indigo, and rice was sharply rising, opening up to white men and women new visions of the vast profits to be made from slave labor. Then, as blacks began to be chosen for that role, all the recently imported, constantly developing legal system of Anglo-America was brought to bear, forcing a clearer, sharper definition of the black (and therefore the white) status, building slavery into the heart of the new society, confirming the chosen people in their anguished calling.

So in the course of the seventeenth century, the freedom-loving English colonies developed a series of laws and judicial rulings to define the black situation. Beginning in Virginia at the end of the 1630s, laws establishing lifelong African slavery were instituted. They were followed by laws prohibiting black-white intermarriage, laws against the ownership of property by Africans, laws denying blacks all basic political rights ... the time). In addition, there were

... the use of the drums. In many places they also banned ...
Thus they attempted to shut black people out from both cultures, to make them wholly dependent neuters.[6]

Finally, because the religious and legal systems were so closely intertwined, everywhere in the colonies a crucial legislative decision declared that the Africans' conversion to Christianity did not affect their enslavement. Some whites had expressed scruples on this matter, others fear. For while they wanted to introduce their slaves to the blessings of the Gospel, they were concerned lest such Good News disturb the sensitive workings of the new black-white society as a whole, and the marked advantages of their own role as slaveholders. Again, Virginia led the way: in 1667 its Assembly passed an act declaring that "the conferring of baptism doth not alter the condition of the person as to his bondage or freedome." Such laws freed many whites to do their Christian duty of evangelization and to reap the profit and the social standing of slave ownership at the same time. Blacks could be at once Christians and slaves—a status unique for that age.[7]

It was all very convenient and very ironic. The great collections of colonial law—landmarks of early American liberty—shut the door in the face of black freedom. Whether it was the highly lauded Massachusetts Body of Liberties or the Fundamental Constitutions of Carolina, presumably wrought by John Locke, or Virginia's colonial statutes, the intentions of the propertied white rulers were unvarying: a formal denial of black rights, an affirmation of African slavery, all providing a clanging antiphony to their own gathering struggles for self-determination, posting a guard against their own very real internal class conflicts.[8]

This last element was of great importance, for as the laws sought to provide legal sanction to the economic, political, and cultural domination and definition of the black captives from Africa by the whites from Europe, many of those laws at the same time, as part of the same objective, aimed at building a new, fundamentally false solidarity between the upper and lower classes of the white population—a solidarity based on race and racism. For the laws which placed the onus of perpetual bondage and subordination on black shoulders were also meant to help many whites forget that they had only recently been victims of the Anglo-Saxon law themselves, had barely escaped from debtors' prisons, poorhouses, indentured service, and the cold underside of English society. By defining the black workers as permanent slaves held out of the mainstream of human development; by defining Christian whiteness as automatically privileged; by developing a situation in which the economic welfare of every white seemed to rest on enslaved black labor—by all these means and more, the dominant classes of the colonies consciously worked to create a white laboring force isolated from and antagonistic to black concerns. Such a white group, it was rightly assumed, would be more prepared to serve as an armed force for social control against the expanding African population.

Thus the planters and commercial leadership, especially in the South, were free to bring in ever larger numbers of Africans, to increase their own profits and status, and to share some minor part of these benefits with their white laboring group, knowing that the dangers of black-white solidarity at the bottom of society were decreased as poorer whites were legally and socially defined in a distinctly favorable status relative to Africans, and as Africans were forced to become the slaves and the subalterns of the entire society. By such means the leadership of a colony like Virginia was able to defuse and redirect some of the dangerous class tensions building up in the last quarter of the seventeenth century. At the same time, there and in South Carolina especially, the colonial leaders were creating a white armed guard against the possibility of insurrection by these ever more numerous and very profitable African slaves.[9]

From the outset, then, European laws for African people meant black subjugation and repression, arbitrary advantages for whites, and racist distinctions among laboring forces. Always behind the laws were the whips, the scaffolds, and the guns, buttressed in turn by the ever deepening layers of fear and mistrust. In this way, many of the essential experiences of the slave ships were transferred to the shores of American slavery, to the fields of Virginia and South Carolina, to the crooked streets

of Boston and New York. There, in the heart of the prison states, the
experience was elaborated and expanded. Gradually, the black awakening
from the dreams of the middle passage became an unrelenting reality in
the New World.

Before long, through laws and social practice, our forebears in America
were being pressed into three basic categories, just as they had been
packed into the kennels of the ships. Roughly, the categories were political, economic, and cultural; but there was constant interpenetration, lack
of . . . . First, Africans were defined as

only the power to hold them as prisoner-laborers for . . . . .
of their children's children: even more profoundly, it was the power to
define them in North American terms according to Euro-American social,
political, and economic needs. Whites in this way attempted to deny
millennia of African history, pressing the tragic ironies of European
names, faiths, and categories upon the black present, seeking in that and
other ways to guarantee black co-operation and submission far into any
future created by white racism and greed.

But many African men and women were no more ready to accept the
imprisonment of white categories and laws in Virginia, South Carolina,
and New York than they had been prepared to submit peacefully to the
life of the kennels on the ships. Indeed, in the face of such concerted
legalized attempts at political, economic, and spiritual enslavement, it is
not surprising that the movement of black struggle quickly leaped from
the slave ships to the North American prison-states. Nor is it strange that
its shapes and forms often corresponded to the categories of white oppression and invoked memories of the shipboard experiences. Soon the struggle for black freedom in the colonies began to resemble a small river
gathering its early force, moving against the domination of white power,
against the debilitating definitions of white society, against the control
of black lives by Euro-America and its systems of slavery and racism.
Within that young river, the black radical streams were those which posed
the most basic challenges, offered the most fundamental and wide-ranging
resistance, raised the most profound questions about the nature of white
society and the legitimacy of its power to control and define black people.

By the middle of the seventeenth century, as the laws of slavery fell into place like ponderous nets of words and deeds, and the laden slave ships poured their cargo onto the shores, the freedom struggles of the black forerunners often followed the patterns of rebellion established earlier. Steadily the number of fugitives increased, as African men and women denied the power and legitimacy of white laws and white enforcers. Some engaged in individual acts of outward rebellion before breaking free; most simply ran to the wilderness, to the rivers, to the docks. At times the runaways attempted to consolidate their strength and their gains by developing what were essentially small guerrilla bands, maintaining a constant opposition to the surrounding white society and its laws. (Occasionally these bands contained white and black members alike.) Elsewhere in the Western Hemisphere, where they usually operated in large numbers, these bands were called "maroons." In North America they were most often called "outlyers," and the colonial laws of slavery and bondage were filled with persistent concern for runaways and insurrectionists, an early "troublesome presence."[10]

Thus in Virginia, as early as the 1650s, there were reports of fugitive Africans attempting "to form small armed groups in various sections of the colony and to harass neighboring plantations, at the same time creating bases to which others might flee." Every year the reports were repeated in all parts of the colony, becoming even more threatening when, as in Glouster County in 1663, blacks and whites were discovered together in a conspiracy to overpower their masters and make a break for freedom. Joint action of this sort was not exceptional, and helped explain why the wedge had to be driven between blacks and poor whites. Indeed, the urgency for such racial separation became clearer in 1676, when scores of blacks joined a motley group of white indentured servants, unemployed workers, and other lower-class and not-so-lower-class whites in Bacon's Rebellion, Virginia's closest approximation to a large-scale, class-based insurrection. Although the motives of Bacon and many of his white comrades now appear ambiguous, and there was unmistakable anti-Indian racism and much greed for plunder mixed in, the available evidence nevertheless indicates that blacks in the rebellion believed themselves to be fighting for their freedom. The black participants in this seven-month antigovernment and sometimes anti-upper-class revolt seem to have been among its stanchest supporters. In the fall of 1676, even after its leader was dead and its potentially revolutionary course corrupted, armed black members of the rebellion held out until, heeding false promises of freedom, they were betrayed, captured, and re-enslaved.[11]

However, as the laws and the mores isolated the African captives more effectively from white laborers, the essential black thrust had to become

increasingly independent and self-reliant, taking many forms. In 1687 a
plot was uncovered in which blacks in one part of the colony planned to
use the occasion of their funerals to stage an insurrection. A few years
after that, an African named Mingoe and his guerrilla band of fugitives
were stirring many fears among the whites in Virginia's Middlesex County,
especially since the black men were stealing not only livestock and clothing
but guns.[12]

In 1694 Sir Edmund Andros, the English governor of the colony,
control laws in Virginia, "in conse-

find peace only by keeping black people under
unallied with lower-class whites.[13]

A similar testimony developed out of South Carolina, where the English
planter-colonists from Barbados had established a new colony, with its
inevitable backbone of captive black laborers. Steadily, as a part of their
struggle to break the white power and be free, these workers ran away,
stole their own labor, deprived the colonists of invaluable lifelong investments, and in many cases made their way to Saint Augustine, the center
of Spanish influence in Florida. As Carolina's rice and indigo plantations
spread, as a largely absentee ownership gave over the semitropical areas
to their African laborers, running away became an even greater option
than in Virginia, and the environs of Saint Augustine soon began to
build up with Carolina's fugitive blacks. By 1710 South Carolina's whites
were expressing fears about more than runaways. For blacks had so begun
to outnumber whites throughout the colony that the threat of insurrection
was a constant source of conversation and, as in Virginia, a motivation
for policy.[14]

But it was not in Virginia and South Carolina alone, not only among
white Southern society, that the fear of a black quest for freedom existed;
the same attitude permeated much of Northern colonial life. In the Northern colonies blacks had already given evidence of their struggle for freedom. As early as 1657 Africans and Indians in Hartford "joined in an
uprising and destroyed some buildings" in the settlement. Such incidents
were regularly repeated. In 1706 Lord Cornbury, the English governor of
New York, put forth an edict "requiring and commanding [all officers]

to take all proper methods for the seizing and apprehending of all such Negroes as shall be found to be assembled—and if any of them refuse to submit, then fire upon them, kill or destroy them, if they cannot otherwise be taken. I am informed that several Negroes in Kings County [Brooklyn] have assembled themselves in a riotous manner, which if not prevented may prove of ill consequence." The English governors provided a critical insight for any proper understanding of black struggle and black radicalism in America: they appeared to believe that in a racist society built on white domination, black submission, and black invisibility, the unsupervised black presence itself, especially in the aggregate, was a threat, a challenge, an element of the struggle for control. Later their white Revolutionary opponents and successors would agree totally—which suggests, of course, that more than white revolution is necessary to break the power of white racism.[15]

The official statements of colonial governors were not simply ravings of racist minds; they knew whereof they spoke. The record of black rebellion and resistance, of arson and flight, was already written in the private papers and public journals of the land. In New York early in 1712—a few years after the warning from Lord Cornbury—"some Negro slaves of the Cormantine and Pawpaw nations, together with a few Indians, resolved to revenge themselves for 'some hard dosage they apprehended to have received from their masters' and to obtain their freedom," and so on March 25 formed a plot "to destroy all the whites in the town."[16] On April 6, when the plans were put into motion, centuries of African tradition could not be broken, especially in such a crisis of struggle: the rebellious Africans swore themselves to secrecy by sucking the blood of one another's hands, and "a free Negro who pretended sorcery gave them a powder to rub on their clothes to make them invulnerable." Then they set fire to an outhouse and waited for the white inhabitants of the area to respond to the alarm, being "prepared to slay each person who came to put out the blaze." Their resolve, their weapons, and the element of surprise made it possible for the conspirators to kill nine persons and wound seven others before soldiers were ordered out. Then the insurrectionists retreated and scattered into the night. The next day the colonial troops were joined by the local militia. In the course of the ensuing battles, some black rebels committed suicide rather than submit to capture, one of them a husband who first killed his wife. Among those Africans who remained alive to face the consequences, several were burned alive and one was broken on the wheel.[17]

Men and women who joined such allies, risked so much and fought so hard, were surely seeking more than revenge, and it is likely that the keepers of white power knew that. Even when there was no open, costly confrontation, white men and women understood that black struggle was a radical challenge and might take many forms. A decade later in Boston, Lieutenant Governor William Dummer thought he saw black hands behind a rash of fires which had just swept the city, and claimed that they were "designedly and industriously kindled by some villainous and desperate Negroes."[18]

Still, the major struggles by these "villainous Negroes" were based in the South, especially in South Carolina, where by 1720 they outnumbered the white settlers two to one, and in Virginia, where the demand for

to attack planters, "to rob and plunder us," to capture (or rescue) enslaved blacks.[19]

As noted earlier, the threat of black struggle was used as a means to solidify white people, to array lower-class whites into a colony-wide police force against the black quest for freedom. In South Carolina in the 1720s, the local slave patrols were merged with the colony's militia, reflecting a shift from concern with an outer enemy to increased surveillance of the enslaved, resisting blacks. Similarly, in Virginia in 1727 a special slave patrol was established to deal with "the great dangers that may happen by the insurrection of negroes." Thus in the life of the Southern colonies the military system became at once a testimony to, and defense against, the reality of the black struggle for freedom.[20]

Even when there were no open confrontations, white men and women dreamed of them, expected them, feared them, sometimes expanded actual events to epic proportions. Thus an African named Samba, who had already attempted insurrection struggle in the coastal baracoons, was credited in 1730 with trying to organize a conspiracy from Virginia to Louisiana. Could this have been true? No one can now be certain, but what seemed most important, distorting all reality, was the black presence itself, unnerving and troubling: a subterranean, self-fulfilling part of the struggle which raged through the minds of white people wherever Africans were in bondage. So in the same year it was reported from Charleston that "the Negroes . . . had conspired to Rise and destroy us, and had almost bro't it to pass." And in South Carolina several years later, the threat of black and white solidarity had still not passed, for the white authorities complained that "several white persons and Blacks, have committed many Outrages and robbery and lye in the swamp at the Head of Wando River, where they bid defiance to the chief Justices warrant."[21]

In Virginia such fears were sharp. In 1736 Colonel William Byrd expressed his apprehensions: "We have already at least 10,000 men of these descendents of Ham fit to bear Arms, and their Numbers increase every day as well by birth as Importation. And in case there should arise a Man of desperate courage amongst us, exasperated by a desperate fortune, he might with more advantage than Cataline kindle a Servile War. Such a man might be dreadfully mischievous before any opposition could be formed against him, and tinge our Rivers as wide as they are with blood." Thus while Africans dreamed of the black and beckoning waters of the homeland, guilt-seared Americans lay down in darkness and were overwhelmed by rivers of blood. In the movement of black struggle, in the development of our convulsively joined black and white history, the two dreams were destined to merge more than once.[22]

Three years after the colonel had written his letter, in a place far (yet not so far) to the south of his native Virginia, the dreams merged in a minor stream, a tentative, suggestive streaking of blood. The place was Saint Paul's Parish, near the western branch of the Stono River, some twenty miles from Charleston. Blacks in this area and elsewhere had already run so often for freedom that their "desertion" had been anxiously broached in the colonial legislature. But here at Stono, early on a Sunday morning in September 1739, there was more than running, and no question of hiding, as an enslaved African named Jemmy led some twenty of his fellow captive workers in an uprising against their white masters. Having first successfully raided a store for arms and ammunition and executed the two storekeepers, they elected a captain and set out boldly in search of freedom. Moving "at a slow pace," they marched toward the southwest, heading for the relative safety of Saint Augustine. "With colors flying and two drums beating," the black men advanced "like a disciplined company," and it is said that on their way "they called out liberty." Also they killed every white person who came within their reach, burned and sacked houses and barns, and eventually built up a company of some seventy to eighty marching Africans.[23]

In the annals of our struggle for freedom in America, this tradition of black men marching flamboyantly in military formation is persistently repeated. On the surface, such a formal though deadly parade may have been mere imitation of the military forces of oppression; but at Stono and elsewhere it was more likely a radical statement of identity, a message of self-possession, for what was ultimately at work was a movement toward self-transformation. A group of black people whom the white world had identified as slaves chose to organize and see themselves as soldiers of liberty, crusaders for freedom. Sounding the forbidden drums, they were warriors again. Living under the white man's menace, but no longer in his time, they had declared their own small but significant revolutionary war.[24]

Of course all the marchers could not open themselves equally to such a new direction for their lives. Late that Sunday afternoon, when the militia _____ _____ _____ prematurely, there were varied re-

lost their lives.[25]

Just as it had been on the ships, so it was on the land: death could not stem the flow of the young black river. Later that fall, even while some of the Stono marchers were still being hunted, and the severed heads of Jemmy's defeated army looked down from mile posts on Pons Pons Road, new threats and rumors of black insurrection broke out in the areas surrounding Charleston. Then in June 1740 a group of from one hundred and fifty to two hundred Africans in the Goose Creek area "got together in defiance" of their white overlords. Like the Stono forces, they had no arms and were reportedly planning to break into a Charleston arsenal and then take over the city. As it happened, their plan was betrayed, an ambush was set, and fifty blacks were seized. All these were hanged, at the rate of ten per day, the aim being, as a white official said, "to intimidate the other negroes." Still the struggle continued, and some contemporary observers called the series of risings in South Carolina the "Gullah War," identifying elements of an armed conspiracy in Saint Paul's, Saint John's, and Charleston parishes.

Nor was such movement confined to the larger colonies. In 1740 in Maryland, the courts received depositions from several black persons in Prince George's County "relating to a most wicked and dangerous Conspiracy having been formed by them to destroy his Majesty's Subjects within the Province, and to possess themselves of the whole Country." Again, the white-kept record was vague but instructive. On the sea they had rightly understood black people to be fighting to possess the ships. On land, at least in this instance, the fight was for black possession of "the whole Country."[26] Although the words of the African participants themselves did not survive, their situation and their dilemma were obvious. The slave ships had once been the kennels, the prisons, the ministates. Now, in eighteenth-century America, those institutions had been transferred to the plantations, the counties, and the colonies themselves. A struggle for freedom in a sprawling land where slavery prevailed throughout was a far more complex matter. Where was the river headed? Was it indeed possible that black men and women were forced to struggle to possess—or transform—"the whole Country," before any of the children of Africa could really be free?

These were not trifling questions for the forerunners in America— just as they are not trifling now. Slavery was cruel in all its forms; in some, it was savage. Nowhere did the savagery of the keepers emerge more clearly than in the face of African movements toward freedom. So black people could not afford to play with struggle in a land claimed by white men and women whose very lives seemed increasingly to depend upon the maintenance and justification of black slavery. By and large, in the middle of the eighteenth century, these realities of the cost of struggle were the same in the North and the South. In the late winter and early spring of 1741, while the British empire was carrying on a costly and unpopular war with Spain, New York City was struck by a rash of fires and robberies, including the burning of the governor's residence. Immediately a large proportion of the two thousand enslaved Africans and the far smaller number of Indians came under suspicion—especially a group of blacks recently captured among the crew of a Spanish vessel. White citizens remembered the insurrection of 1712; some said that they recalled overhearing black threats to "set the houses on fire, and kill the white people . . . in order to be free."[27]

Although no white deaths were recorded in the wave of arson, the disputed evidence seemed to indicate a deep black involvement. Indeed, Mary Barton, a white indentured servant, claimed that she had heard three Africans planning with a white man to burn the town down, kill all the other whites, and establish a monarchy with the white conspirator as king and one of the blacks as governor. As a result of such testimony, coming in the midst of an extremely tense and fearful situation, thirteen Africans were burned at the stake, sixteen others hanged, and more than seventy banished to places as distant as Newfoundland, Surinam, and Spain. (The list of the dead and banished men carries a fascinating, already Europeanized, but still pan-African resonance, including such names as Antonio, Cuba, Cuffee, Africa, Diego, London, Sussex, Jamaica, Quamino, and Othello.) Meanwhile that same spring, just across the river in Hackensack, New Jersey, the militia stood duty day and night as three black persons were burned at the stake for burning seven barns.[28]

While such explosive, turbulent events periodically broke through to the surface, always there was a more quiet, less dramatic, but never-ceasing movement of black struggle against the rising walls of slavery, carrying its own high hopes and harsh penalties. By the middle of the eighteenth century, wherever the system of bondage had established itself in the North American colonies, the African captives were still running away, becoming fugitives from the repressive law, breaking to-

New Brunswick in New Jersey; they left Annapolis and Baltimore in Maryland; Culpepper and Stafford Courthouse in Virginia. Like solitary tributaries feeding into the river of struggle, these men, women, and children moved toward freedom. Leaving plantations, estates, private residences, farms, and factories, they headed toward the Virginia swamps, toward the caves by the Cooper River, toward the relative safety of Florida, to cities like New York and Boston, to relatives and "paramours" wherever they were—some as far away as London. Indeed, there were African people who were evidently "persuaded that they could find the way back to their native country," if only they walked far enough. By every possible means, with many levels of hope, they broke loose from bondage and moved toward a new life.[30]

Often these fugitives carried strange bundles and burdens. Some expropriated large sums of money from their masters' coffers; others took guns and powder. A few even ventured to ride off on horses, and a good many black musicians took their violins—forerunners of the generations who would walk the roads with guitars strapped to their backs. Many times they stole as much clothing as possible, like the man named Sam who in 1755 left Prince George's County in Maryland with "one Cotton Coat lined with blue, one red waistcoat and Breeches, one blue Silk coat, one light Cloth Coat, some five shirts, and one or two good Hats." (If clothes indeed make the man, this man clearly meant to be free.) Some women took men's clothing as a disguise.[31]

Just as often, of course, the fugitives left with nothing but their own coarse apparel on their backs. Under the clothing, deep in their flesh,

many also carried scars and unhealed wounds from whips and sticks and branding irons, and some even had to bear certain irons, like Hercules who had "Irons on his feet," and Bill who had "a chain and pad lock on his Neck" when they left South Carolina's bondage. Fortunately, they all took more than that. In their minds and bodies they carried a variety of skills, some surely brought over from Africa and passed on, some acquired in the New World. Among the runaways were blacksmiths, carpenters, barrelmakers, shoemakers, musicians, and a number who had a reputation "as a doctor among people of his color."[32]

Interestingly enough, in spite of the efforts to separate them, during the first half of the eighteenth century a number of black runaways left their bondage in the company of white indentured servants, again testing an alliance which had a painful future. In the spring of 1754, for example, a black man from Annapolis joined with two white "convict servants" to rescue another black and a white, murder a sea captain, and abscond toward freedom in the captain's small boat.[33]

For those who remained in bondage on the plantations and farms or in the towns, the range of resistance was significant. Arson was always a weapon, either by itself or in connection with larger plans. In addition, the colonial records bear consistent testimony of poisoning. In 1756 a well-known Charleston physician named Alexander Garden declared, "I greatly and do suspect that the Negroes bring their knowledge of the poisonous plants . . . from their own country." So five blacks were sentenced to death in one parish for the "horrid practice of poisoning their masters." Still, five years later, the word went out: "The negroes have again begun the hellish practice of poisoning." Meanwhile, on less obvious, less dangerous levels, many Africans were resisting by simply refusing to learn how to use a tool without breaking it, how to work without setting up deep currents of quiet, persistent, noncooperation. Others, with great but silent determination, were learning how to re-create their religious experience, in order to possess their soul in the midst of a destructive and soulless situation.[34]

At the same time the sharper, more pointed confrontations regularly ripped their way to the surface, forever facing black people with the brutal necessities and cruel costs of open rebellion. Near Christmastime in 1769, a group of blacks on a plantation in Hanover County, Virginia, decided to turn on their new steward and a neighboring overseer. They tied up the two men and, perhaps remembering their own experiences under the lash, whipped their white bosses "till they were raw from the neck to the waistband." Some forty to fifty persons were involved in this action, and when armed whites called upon them to surrender they refused, until their leader and several other rebels were killed.[35]

Not long after, in Louisiana, several men and a woman, including at least one who was African-born, killed their master and attempted to organize a larger insurrection. They failed, and the penalties were brutal. Two of the leaders were "condemned . . . to death by hanging . . . dragged to the gallows from the tail of a pack-horse with an . . . halter tied to the neck, feet and hand." By some strange coincidence the black leader of this movement was called Temba, evoking memories of Captain _____ ____ Sierra Leone. It was decreed that Temba was "to remain on _____ _____ nailed on the public roads.

blow up her master's ___ __ powder. She succeeded, and one can only conclude that __ the cost of the serious injury she sustained. Consistently, blacks in struggle confirmed the judgment of the colonial official who had called them "a people whom no example can reclaim, no punishment deter, or leniative appease."[37]

Rather than faltering, some major currents of black resistance were only beginning to come into focus. By then it was obvious, for instance, that the continuing attempts at insurrection made by small groups like the one led by Temba and Mariana were essential to the struggle. In addition, there were the armed bands of outlyers. In 1772 a grand jury document from Georgia provided a glimpse of one such group when it complained "that a Number of fugitive slaves have Assembled . . . on or near the borders of the River Savannah and are frequently committing depredations . . . with impunity." Only after the Georgia authorities set up a strong system of patrols were they finally able to drive many of the runaways deeper into Florida.[38]

The outlyers in fact had a significant role in the struggle everywhere. Throughout the history of slavery, their existence and widespread activities demonstrated the willingness of relatively large numbers of black men and women to live outside the nets of white law and order, especially when that system mandated their degradation. In essence, their very existence was an act of radical disobedience. But of even greater importance than their radical witness as individuals was the fact that these runaways organized as groups. Hidden in swamps, caves, and forests, they often created tentative new communities outside the domination of the masters, summoning up memories of Africa and adapting them to the hard realities of the new land. So their rebellion was not only an act of negative will, and their organizing not only a source of strength to their active resistance: their action moved forward into the creation of alternatives. Admittedly, these alternatives were often temporary, rugged, and dangerous, but they clearly challenged the existing order of slave society with another, self-determining black way.

This may have been their greatest significance. For as more than one white official noted, the countercommunities of fugitives became bases to which others might flee. Even beyond that, they became a living message for the enslaved people of the plantations, farms, and homes. The organized existence of the runaways meant that those black men, women, and children who lived within the apparently total institution of slavery could not view its power as all-encompassing so long as they knew of the black outlaws. And there was no doubt that they knew. Their own relatives and close friends were often among the outlaws. At night many of the fugitives found physical and spiritual sustenance in the cabins of the farms and plantations. Thus the outlyers represented a hidden, submerged black power that the masters could not break. They were a radical presence, challenging blacks and whites alike.[39]

However, in those days—as in all other times—most participants in the movement toward freedom were not really organized. Rather, the mainstream of the river was filled with innumerable individual acts of protest and rebellion. Today there is a tendency to place such individual action outside the compass of black struggle, but that is wrong. From the earliest times in America the quest for a new and self-determining life has been measured not only by the organization of black hope and black rage, but also by individual, private lives whose number was legion and whose only link was the river of struggle itself.

There were men like Caesar, a New England slave who had somehow lost both legs, but who in 1769 still managed to join the relentless company of runaways. In 1772 a black captive named George was giving much trouble to a slave dealer in Reading, Pennsylvania. The dealer wrote to the Philadelphia slave-trading firm that had sent George to him:

I took your Negro George some time ago home, thinking I might be the better able to Sell him: who after being with me a night behaved himself in such an insolent manner I immediately remanded him back to the Gaol. About a week since I put him up at Public Sale . . . where there was a number of Persons who inclined to Purchase him. But he protested publickly that he would not be sold, and if Any one should purchase him he wou'd be the Death of him and Words to the like purpose which deter'd the people from biding. I then sent him back with Directions to the Gouler to keep him at Hard Labor which he refuses to do & goes on in such An Insolent Manner that's impossible to get a Master for him there.[40]

Understandably, the dealer's letter asked for instructions on what to do with George, who at that point was "almost Naked and if not furnished soon with some Cloathes I fear he'll perish. . . . He's now Chain'd & Hand cuff'd on Account of his Threats."[41]

George's fate is not known, but his words and actions helped to il-

his rebelliousness from

The year of George's imprisonment, 1772, was a year in which the white colonists intensified their own talk of freedom from tyranny— a year in which they organized the Committees of Correspondence for serious discussion of their common means of defense against the oppressive acts of the British Parliament, while the name of another George grew increasingly unpopular among them. For any Africans who could see and hear the discussions of white men, the colonies were clearly in crisis. From the time of sickness and death among the white crews on slaving ships to the burgeoning experiences of enslaved and colonized men throughout the New World, the black struggle for freedom had never failed to benefit from white crises. So in those pre-Revolutionary days of the 1770s, many black men and women carefully appraised the rising struggle and searched for opportunities, advantages, cracks in the wall. As the patriot slave traders and the patriot slaveholders moved to break their colonial bonds to the English Crown, the captive Africans also moved—not in massive insurrections, as some later observers think they should have done, but in growing daily defections from the system. It is not clear at this point how many black captives used this time of white struggle to break for freedom, but we know that thousands escaped to Florida, Canada, and the Indian lands, or to service in the merchant marine, and that many finally boarded departing British ships. Later Thomas Jefferson estimated that by these means Virginia lost some thirty thousand in one year alone.[42]

There were, of course, thousands of black men who considered service in the Revolutionary armies as a possible path to their own freedom and, eventually, to the freedom of their people. But it was not until the British colonial governors—especially Virginia's royal governor, Lord Dunmore —began appealing for black support, that George Washington and other American leaders saw fit to permit blacks officially to enlist. Even then, there were fewer blacks fighting for white American Independence than were engaged in the large, unorganized, fugitive army in flight toward their own independence.[43]

However, while the confusion, crisis, and chaos of the Revolutionary period opened an escapeway for many thousands of black fugitives, and at the same time drew some five thousand black men into the American army, it is likely that other results were even more significant for the long-range development of black struggle: specifically, the ideology of the white American Revolution and the uses that blacks made of it. As democratic dogma and revolutionary rhetoric filled the colonial legislatures and reverberated through the Continental Congress, and were proclaimed in local communities seeking justification for armed rebellion for the sake of Independence, many black people took careful notice. Was it so hard to grasp that the ideas of no taxation without representation, the equality of all men under God, and the divine right of humankind to freedom and self-government had some direct reference to their own lives? Indeed, in the fall of 1774 word spread among them that the Continental Congress had formally approved a resolution pledging the colonies to forsake the African slave trade altogether. Before long the radical rhetoric, promises, and ideas were firmly grasped by Africa's children in America and transformed for the purposes of their own freedom struggle.[44]

Especially in the North, on many occasions during the War for Independence—in petitions to legislatures, freedom cases in the courts, and speeches—black people resolutely turned the professed revolutionary faith of their captors into outright challenges to the system of American slavery. The deism of the white Enlightenment, the Natural Rights doctrines of the white philosophers, the pietistic religion of the white churchmen—all were marshaled in verbal and legal attacks against the bases of black bondage. In many instances this assault continued the tradition of oral protest established on board the slave ships. Eventually this sort of protest, based on American democratic principles and too often on naive faith, became the broadest single element—the mainstream—in the river of black struggle in America. In the short run such protest, especially when backed up by actual flight, seems to have helped break the power of Northern slavery.[45]

Needless to say, during the war there was something about such ideol-

ogy in the hands of black captives and their partially free comrades which
was clearly radical and revolutionary in potential. The direction was
often suggested in the black petitions and suits for freedom which appeared throughout the period. In May 1774, just as armed hostilities
were mounting, a "Grate Number of Blacks" in Massachusetts petitioned
that patriotic legislature, saying, "We have in common with all other
men a natural right to our freedom without Being depriv'd of them by
. . . we are a freeborn Pepel and have never forfeited this
. . . ."[46]

who made . . .
by our own Reflection, that we are endowed . . . .
masters, and there is nothing that leads us to a Belief, or Suspicion, that we
are any more obliged to serve them, than they us, and the more we Consider
of this matter, the more we are Convinced of our Right . . . to be free . . .
and can never be convinced that we were made to be Slaves.

In seeking legal emancipation, they said, "we do ask for nothing, but
what we are fully persuaded is ours to claim." The petition itself was an
act of challenge, but beneath it was an essential black radical consciousness which denied their definition as "slaves," which refused to allow
their captors to think for them. From that point on, petitions for freedom
based on reason, revelation, and reflection became recurrent features in
the history of black struggle, and black people remained unconvinced of
their inherent fitness for slavery.[47]

When the Connecticut petitioners referred to "Revelation" as an
element of their position on black freedom, they were pointing specifically
to the teaching of the Bible and the theoretical doctrines of the white
churches. Black people knew, of course, that the contradictions between
theory and practice were often as intense in this sensitive area as in any
other, and they chose to struggle within the churches with such contradictions in mind. With certain notable exceptions, the white church, like
every other institution in the North American colonies, had been used to
defend white supremacy and justify black slavery. In many cases blacks
had been brought into its precincts as part of the continuing assault on
African history and traditions, as part of the attempt to root out all
living connections with the homeland, as a program of pacification.

Consequently, there were also contradictions within the black community, especially in its adherence to the white-controlled churches. For in spite of the many crushing experiences of the slave ships and seasoning grounds, in spite of the attempts of America to deny them access to their own being, Africans continued to hold the religious experience at the center of their lives. Therefore the struggle in the churches was critical. So when black people moved beyond petitions to seize the time and break the white control over their lives in these religious institutions, they were obviously engaged in radical action on behalf of self-definition and self-determination. At its best, their struggle in the churches was to repossess their souls.

This movement in the churches took various forms. In the course of the War for Independence, there was a noticeable expansion in the number of independent black Baptist churches in the South, especially in Savannah, Georgia, and in Petersburg and other communities in Virginia, as black people moved out from under white ecclesiastical control. In essence, this was a sign of the larger attempt to break free, and it was not ignored. During the wartime confusion such black action was tolerated, but when the struggle for Independence had ended, white officials struck out against these attempts at African self-determination. In at least one church in Georgia the whites imprisoned a black preacher, Andrew Bryan, and whipped several of his members. However, with some crucial assistance from a leading white citizen, Bryan and his congregation persevered, and went on to become the organizational center for the black Baptists of Georgia.[48]

In the North the critical struggle in the churches came in Philadelphia. By 1787 Richard Allen, Absolem Jones, and their friends had discovered that the white institution in which they worshiped, Saint George's Methodist Episcopal Church, was really another slave ship, christened with another deceitful name. Within the place of worship blacks were being pressed to accept white definitions of their place—definitions which had nothing to do with the spirit of a living and just God. So one Sunday morning when Allen, Jones, and others were yanked from their knees and denied their right to unsegregated prayer, they had already formulated their response: the creation of a new institution under black direction.[49]

It was no easy choice for Allen and his friends. They were making a sharp and costly break with a church which meant much to them. Allen, who had been born in slavery in Philadelphia and sold into Delaware, had been converted to Methodism while still an adolescent. Soon after purchasing his freedom, the ardent black Christian became a preacher and moved about in the itinerant Methodist manner, earning a living with his hands, preaching the Gospel wherever he found an audience. This double mission had brought him back to Philadelphia in 1786. There Allen soon discovered that the white Methodist officials were quite prepared to have him evangelize black people into their structures, but not at all prepared to let him form a black Methodist church with significant black control. So in the spring of 1787 Allen and his friends formed the Free African Society as a temporary substitute for their desired church,

_____ _____ already conscious of their potential powers and dangers when

_____ ____ _____ __ ____ [50]

and women in ____ _

had made their final break with white ecclesiastical ___ __

on their own paths. Eventually these paths led to the creation of the powerful forces of African Methodism in America, Denmark Vesey being only the most obvious and immediate inheritor of their work.[51]

Meanwhile, in 1787 Philadelphia's black people were given additional evidence that white American political leaders were no different from the religious leaders when it came to black freedom. For it was not hard to see that the Constitutional Convention then meeting in the city did not intend to take the rhetoric of their American Revolution into the threatening realms of black slavery, just as most white Christians did not intend to take the love of Jesus out to the auction block. Thirteen years earlier, in 1774, when some of these same white leaders had met in Philadelphia for the First Continental Congress, in their revolutionary fervor they had proclaimed: "We will neither import nor purchase any slave imported after the first day of December next, after which time we will wholly discontinue the slave trade and will neither be concerned in it ourselves nor will we hire our vessels nor sell our commodities or manufactures to those who are concerned in it."[52]

This had been a logical statement for patriot-philosophers preparing to affirm the equality of all human beings as part of their Declaration of Independence. But neither logic nor revolutionary fervor was finally able to overcome white racism, fear, and greed—not even in the Declaration itself. (There, Jefferson's disingenuous claim about the slave trade's having been forced upon the colonies had been deleted from the final draft, not because his colleagues hated lies, but because they—and Jefferson—

loved the gains of the Trade and feared the freedom of blacks.) Therefore it was not surprising that once the war was over and these momentary fervors had died away, and the Constitutional Convention met in 1787, America wrote both the institution and the benefits of slavery into its Constitution. This basic set of national laws shielded the slave trade against any legislative prohibition for a minimum of twenty years; at the same time it made provision for the federal government to levy import fees on each new African who survived the middle passage. In the document the black population was included in the determination of Congressional representation, based on a formula which allowed enslaved people to be counted as three-fifths of a person. The Constitution also guaranteed the right of slaveowners to track down black fugitives across state lines and have them delivered back into captivity. It promised the use of federal armed forces in any struggle against insurrections. In fact, so firmly etched was the guarantee of black bondage that only a grim and bloody war would begin to expunge it from the laws. Thus the revolution for white liberty ended with black slavery carefully protected in the basic document of the new, "free" nation.[53]

The power of the king had been destroyed, but the slave trade which he had supposedly forced on the colonists had not ended. Indeed, since the Revolution it had markedly increased. So much so that in 1796 the British governor of Sierra Leone would write to a white American abolitionist: "You will be sorry to learn that during the last year, the number of American slave traders on the coast has increased to an unprecedented degree. Were it not for their pertinacious adherence to that abominable traffic, it would in consequence of the war, have been almost wholly abolished in our neighborhood."[54]

The Revolution had set the white Americans free to press on with their part in the breaking of African society and the raping of her children, just as white laborers in the Southern colonies had earlier been granted greater freedom in exchange for their aid in repressing black struggles to achieve the same liberty. Therefore, in spite of the onset of a gradual movement toward the freeing of the African slaves in the Northern states, and in spite of continued black uses of the Revolution's rhetoric and ideology, many blacks realized that they would have to look elsewhere for true revolutionary inspiration. The white American Revolution was not ours.[55]

Before the eighteenth century was over, the inspiration had come. Very near to them, in the immediate environs of the New World, in the French colony of San Domingo, all the shibboleths of freedom had exploded in bloody confrontation in a black revolution for freedom. There, beginning in 1794, Toussaint L'Ouverture, a trusted black plantation steward, with a reputation for unshakable rectitude and courage, had moved to the leadership of a revolution which had begun a few years earlier. It was a revolution whose clear direction was to fulfill the Biblical promise of the last becoming first, for the slaves had arisen and seemed determined to break the power of their European masters. The black river on the mainland was in ferment. Along the grapevine that had already begun to connect the African community in North America, the words were passed: Toussaint . . . San Domingo . . . Liberty or Death. Freedom and

. . . . . . they heard the words

While the . . . . . . similar ideas, words, and revolution among the Africans of their . . . while they passed laws and wrote letters and published hundreds of thousands of words against the epidemic of this black revolutionary fervor, Africans in America listened, pondered, and passed on the word. In more places than can be known, they worked toward the day when it might be said of them, as it would be said of Toussaint, "he decided that the old life was over and a new one had begun." Of course black people in North America knew that they were not in San Domingo. They did not make up the vast majority of the population here. They were not separated by an ocean from the vital civil center and the military forces of the system of white oppression. So while San Domingo could provide continuing inspiration, it was not a final model. By and large, black people knew that the struggle here would have to grind out its own difficult and costly channels toward freedom.[56]

In many cases, the evidence of these post-Revolutionary black movements toward freedom was quickly covered over by white censorship and fear. Only brief, fleeting accounts of African-American rebellious actions during the period of the San Domingo uprising leaked out of Louisiana in 1791, 1792, and again in 1795. Similarly, reports seeped through about Africans in the area of Norfolk, Virginia, who had broken with slavery and were organized into bands to attack whites nearby. But little more was known. Even where documents endured, it was hard to assess their meaning in such an atmosphere of fear and repression. There is, for instance, a letter reportedly picked up on the street in Yorktown, Virginia, in August 1793, apparently sent from a black rebel

leader in Richmond to his coworker in Norfolk; it is signed, "Secret
Keeper Richmond to Secret Keeper Norfolk," but nothing more is known
of them.[57]

By now a fresh stream of black fugitives from slavery had begun their
movement toward the North, where the post-Revolutionary period had
brought a series of state laws gradually abolishing slavery. Already the
future of the black runaways had become a source of controversy between
the Northern and Southern states, and within each section as well. The
first federal Fugitive Slave Law, passed in 1793, was both a result and
cause of this controversy. It grew naturally out of the language and intent
of the fugitive slave clause of the Constitution ("[Any] Person held to
Service or Labour in one State, under the Laws thereof, escaping into
another . . . shall be delivered up on Claim of the Party to whom such
Service or Labour may be due."). It was a federal attempt to find some
more effective way to deal with the self-liberating action of black men
and women.[58]

Meanwhile many fugitives in the South continued to refuse to leave the
section, joining the outlyer ranks instead. While their camps were often
secret, their confrontations with white society were not. Indeed, one band
of black outlaws, operating near the mouth of the Savannah River, appeared to be continuing their own version of the War for Independence.
The group had served with the British during the siege of Savannah and
now, years later, still called themselves "the King of England's Soldiers,"
while carrying on guerrilla activities in the Georgia and South Carolina
countrysides, often with Indian allies. Toward the close of the century,
many Atlantic coast outlyers were drawn to the vicinity of Wilmington,
North Carolina. With the ocean on one side and swamps on another,
Wilmington had become the scene for much significant black resistance
activity. In the late spring and early summer of 1795, the white community of the area complained of being harassed by "a number of runaway Negroes, who in the daytime secrete themselves in the swamps and
woods . . . at night committed various depredations on the neighboring
plantations." The leader of the outlyers was known as the "General of the
Swamps," and a price was placed on his head. Then, in the heat of that
summer, special hunting parties were sent out to find the fugitives, and
the General was caught and killed.[59]

But outlying would not die. It was a continual reminder to the masses
of African captives in America that their freedom still lay outside white
law and order. It offered a constant opportunity to both free and enslaved
blacks to participate in the struggle, as they provided the fugitives with
travel documents, food, shelter, and moral support. From prison ships
to prison states, those black men and women who sought freedom were

compelled to move against the law, to defy the order of America, to
organize independently in search of justice, challenging many of their
brothers and sisters to help them. In their own ways, with the assistance
of their silent black partners, the outlyers made signal contributions to the
heritage of black radicalism and black struggle. As a result, though the
white posses in a place like Wilmington did not know it, there were other
fugitives and other generals to come before the issue of black freedom
was settled, and it is not unlikely that the General of the Swamps had
            ͏   ͏   black boys growing up in Wilmington—

and Elizabeth in New Jersey, and in Savannah and ͏
ubiquitous flames streaked the skies of the young nation, there was intense excitement concerning their mysterious origins. Almost without
exception they were ascribed to the Africans in those cities. Although
the accusations were never fully proven, it was not hard to agree with the
suspicion, especially when men recalled events in San Domingo. Referring to the burning of the plantations there, C. L. R. James, the pioneer
modern historian of that revolution, comments: "The slaves destroyed
tirelessly. Like the peasants in the Jacquerie or the Luddite wreckers, they
were seeking their salvation in the most obvious way, the destruction of
what they knew was the cause of their sufferings; and if they destroyed
much it was because they had suffered much." In many times and places,
fire was struggle. In America too, black fire was black struggle.[60]

By the end of the eighteenth century, America clearly invited black
fire, demanded black struggle, required the continuing development of
black radicalism, if the children of Africa were ever to be free. For by
then America had fully committed itself, revealed itself. The slave ships
were no aberration. The massacred Indians were no accident of history.
Faced with the clear choice, both the patriot slave traders and the patriot
slave owners had opted for slavery as an American institution. Experienced at the uses of names, they had decided to leave the "peculiar
institution" unnamed in their Constitution. They had decided that Africans should be noncitizens, lesser beings, that the vast majority of black
people should continue to be prisoners in a free land. By the end of the
century the white Founding Fathers, led by Alexander Hamilton, had

also committed the federal government to the encouragement and protection of private business, including the burgeoning business of African slavery and the Indian-killing business of Western land speculation. In other words, America had committed itself to the practice of racism and to the eventual related development of capitalism.[61]

In the midst of such developments, what were the priorities of the black freedom struggle as the century ended? Especially in the South, for our ancestors the institution of slavery was the clear, present, and primary danger. As they faced the "new" America, as they became part and yet not part of the nation, that nation's injustice was most fully manifested in the institution of black bondage. Because that institution so often appeared to promote the destruction and dehumanization of the Afro-American community, the mainstream of the struggle was often given over to the simple fight for survival. The maintenance of black life and spirit was crucial, and struggle was geared to that end, just as on the slave ships. Remaining alive; maintaining sanity, strength, and inner dignity regardless of outer poses; carrying children toward the future—these were major thrusts.

Out of that context, black radicalism continually developed. Though it is sometimes difficult to conceive of radicalism among the enslaved, the difficulty is more a testimony to the captivity of the observer's imagination. In a setting where slavery was considered both a natural and a legal right, where it had clearly become part of the social, economic, and political structure of the nation, the fight of enslaved Africans for freedom was a critical and essential aspect of black radical struggle in America. Each person who broke with the system contributed to a rudimentary level of radical challenge. Such persons denied its legal and political power, chipped away at those parts of the economic system based on their own submissive bodies. They continued to run away, carrying clothing, instruments, scars, memories, and children, determined to meet the new century with new life.

Moreover, in the case of black men and women who encouraged, organized, and participated with others in the struggles for freedom, there was another level of radicalism at work. Here more fundamental threats were created, simply because they broadened the level of participation, expanded the questioning of white legitimacy. Wherever black struggle against slavery implied consciousness of a larger battle against the system itself, a larger and deeper radicalism was at work.

Finally, in some cases those who fought to break away from white domination were also creating new orders of the spirit and the mind within themselves and others. Therefore their goal was not simply the absence of chains but the presence of a new society, if only within their own lives, if only within the narrow confines of their outlyer community. Paradoxically, for some of Africa's children this newness involved returning to the older dreams of the slave ship holds, and discussions began among them in the North and South concerning the wisdom and means of return to the homeland. Still others recognized that they were forging a dream not yet dreamed in America, the dream of a truly new nation in which justice and not whiteness would prevail.[62]

By the beginning of the new white century, then, many basic currents

arsonists, the poisoners and the creators of new hope moved at various depths. Through their own lives the forerunners had established each current as part of the river. A new stage of movement was about to begin.

3

Rebels, Resistants, and Outlyers

Building the River's Power

I have nothing more to offer than what George Washington would have had to offer had he been taken by the British and put to trial by them. I have adventured my life in endeavoring to obtain the liberty of my countrymen, and am a willing sacrifice to their cause.

> Courtroom Testimony,
> Anonymous Black Insurrectionist, 1804

It was a new century and we were a long way from home.

In America we were still largely people of the coasts and the rivers, people of the verdant fields, forests, and mountainsides, but this was not the land, these were not the waters, not the hills which had been the dwelling places of our fathers and mothers from the beginning of human time. Instead we were here as unwilling accomplices in the intrusion upon the spirits of other men's forebears, prisoner companions to the desecration of the mounds of the natives of these lands, worker captives in a place which was itself being taken captive.

We were a long way from home. Yet all of America had become our home. In the cities and settlements of the Atlantic coast, from Boston to Savannah, we were the dark and dangerous presence. In New York and Norfolk, in Philadelphia and Charleston we were on the wharves unloading the ships, watching—with what mixed feelings in our hearts?—the new bewildered children of Africa arrive. We were the carpenters and the cooks, the ironworkers and the porters, the chimney sweeps and the coopers, the butchers, sailors, and blacksmiths.

Back in the limitless rural area where the vast majority of Americans lived, we also lived and worked. In the darkness of the mornings we

walked out from our cabins into the vast expanse of cotton, fields of to-
bacco, rows of corn; waded in the paddies where the endless acres of rice
plants awaited our coming. Often the crops and the earth reminded us of
our homeland, but we were a long way from home.

We were by the rivers again, but not the Gambia and the Sierra Leone,
not the Congo and the Niger. Instead we worked the crops and built the
houses and guided the boats along rivers whose very names evoked the
unquiet spirits of the land: Roanoke and Potomac, Chattahooche and Alle-
gheny, Mississippi and Tennessee. And we followed the rivers and the
paths, and helped slash new roads into the countless acres of land being
wrested from the natives of this place.

We moved with the nation across the Appalachians and found new
homes in places like Cincinnati and Pittsburgh, and out in the Indiana
Territory and down in the flatlands of the Mississippi Territory. (Soon
after, when the victorious revolution of Africa's children in San Domingo
helped to convince Napoleon to sell the Indian land the French had
claimed as their own, we moved there with the white slaveholding settlers
and found children of Africa already in the territory called Louisiana.)
We were everywhere, but in some places there were only lonely scatterings
of blackness, for our locus was the South, and the South had now ex-
tended westward beyond the Mississippi River.[1]

We were far from home, yet some of us were not sure if we were near
or far. For some had been in North America, living and enduring here
with the people from England and Ireland and Scotland and Europe, for
five and six generations. At the same time, with every movement of a
slave ship into the Eastern harbors, new African captives arrived, bearing
word and proof of a homeland, lending credence to the stories passed on
through the generations, affirming the songs sung in the brush arbors of
the night. Where was our home?

The new century cast into painful relief all the strange complexities
and profound dilemmas which time and the increasingly long exile had
brought to our situation and our struggle. By 1800 there were somewhat
more than one million children of Africa living in the new nation, comprising approximately twenty percent of the population. Most of us—
some 900,000—were held in legal slavery. The rest occupied that limbo
assigned to men and women who live as "free" in a society committed to
their slavery.[2]

The situation was crowded with hard choices, with brutal tensions
that bore directly on the nature and status of black struggle. As a people
they had been in America for generations, but there seemed no end to
slavery. Indeed, the cotton mills of England had now found new life in
the use of steam, and the cotton fields of America promised fantastic new

yields with the coming of the cotton gin. Neither of these developments carried any hope of relief for Africa's children at the outset of the new century. Neither seemed to clarify the direction black struggle should take. Meanwhile the voluminous laws which supported black bondage were constantly being reproduced, reshaped, and redefined. The purchase of Louisiana in 1803 soon provided new lands for slavery, new impetus for the slave trade, new justifications for the nation's commitment to our bondage.[3]

Indeed, in these turn-of-the-century years tens of thousands of new Africans were poured into the cauldron of American slavery. Even in the North, where some sixty percent of the small black minority lived as "free" people, and where slavery was on its way to legal death, the dilemmas were similarly harsh. For in 1800 there was no state in which black people could educate their children, earn a living, find proper housing, exercise voting rights—in short, exist in dignity—without constant, often brutal struggle against the white majority and its laws and customs. And when the beleaguered Northern blacks tried to raise their voices on behalf of their kinsmen in the South, they encountered even more evidence of the depths of white racism.[4]

Thus in 1800 the outspoken black community of Philadelphia, under the leadership of Absolem Jones, sent a petition to Congress calling for legislative action against the African slave trade as well as for laws which would gradually abolish slavery. It was put forward in a respectful tone, a quiet call for justice. In Congress the usual treatment for all antislavery petitions from white constituents was to refer them to a committee and kill them. However, in response to this black petition Harrison Gray Otis, a Massachusetts congressman, opposed even that negative form of recognition. To acknowledge this word from black people, he said, "would have an irritating tendency, and must be mischievous to America very soon. It would teach them the art of assembling together, debating and the like, and would soon . . . extend from one end of the Union to the other."[5] After a two-day debate, devoted largely to the promulgation of views like those of Otis, the House voted 85–1 to offer "no encouragement or countenance" to such messages from the children of Africa in America.

As the new century began, it often appeared as if the future lay wholly, securely, with white men like these, deniers of black rights, opponents to the development of black humanity. On the surface, the new age seemed only to have reinforced the old bondage now spreading across the land. But white surfaces concealed many things, especially the insistent black river, steadily moving, beating against and beneath the walls of slavery. In 1800, rising from under the surface, black people made it clear again that men and women born into slavery were not necessarily born to be slaves. That was the testimony from Henrico County, Virginia, where a group of Africans had been born into bondage but had grown to love freedom. The three brothers had been given names which perhaps revealed the quiet, radical hope of their family: Solomon, Martin, and Gabriel—Biblical monarch, religious leader, angel of God. According to the law of Virginia and America, they were slaves, property of a tavern keeper named Thomas Prosser. Still, by the time they reached their twenties, these tall, sturdy young men knew they were meant to be free, and they were prepared to wage hard and decisive struggle for that costly freedom, not only for themselves but for others as well.[6]

In the spring of 1800, as the sharp, sometimes fiercely divisive sounds of the white Federalist and Republican debates echoed through the states, the Virginia brothers and their comrades began to organize among their people, and the leadership passed finally into Gabriel's hands. At twenty-four he was the youngest—and the tallest, standing well over six feet. With his dark complexion, prominent scars, and Ethiopian features, he was a striking figure. Later he was described by the Virginia authorities as possessing "courage and intellect above his rank in life." White authorities did not know Gabriel's rank in life, but his fellow Africans evidently did, for by the summer he and his two brothers had gathered an impressive cadre of comrades for the proposed struggle. Under the cover of funerals and other black religious gatherings, and in the hours after sundown when the exiled African community reaffirmed its integrity through singing and praying and loving and planning and escaping—in those times and hours, Gabriel presented his plan. It was strategically simple and seemed sound. Several hundred men would make a surprise midnight attack on Richmond to capture arms, burn warehouses, and perhaps take the governor as hostage, thereby inspiring a general uprising among thousands of Africans.[7]

In addition to their own fierce determination to be free, Gabriel and his two brothers had been spurred on by two rather different models, and they systematically shared this inspiration with all potential recruits. Wherever they gathered, the three young men spoke of the brilliant example of the Africans of San Domingo, and of God's assistance to the children of Israel. Martin was a preacher, and he backed up Gabriel's love of Toussaint with his own encouragement from the Scriptures. When doubts were raised, it was Martin who told the people that "their cause was similar to [the] Israelites," and he read the Bible to them: "God says, if we worship him . . . five of you shall conquer an hundred and a hundred a thousand of your enemies." For his own personal statement, Martin simply said, "I can no longer bear what I have borne."[8]

The men they recruited realized that they were being called to make a fundamental break with their own past, to offer a radical challenge to white society, and therefore to risk their lives and the lives of their families. In the course of organizing, one of the group's lieutenants (who later testified against the others) told a potential recruit named King, "The negroes are about to rise, and fight the white people for our freedom." King's response was chilling and direct: "I was never so glad to hear anything in my life. . . . I could slay white people like sheep." At the same time some sensed the need for their struggle to maintain an essential continuity with the African past. So a key recruiter named George proposed that the conspirators make full use of the peculiar gifts of those native-born Africans who had remained close to the cultic practices of the homeland, suggesting that "he hire his own time, travel down country to what he called the 'pipeing tree,' and enlist the 'Outlandish people,' for they were supposed to deal with Witches and Wizards and this would be useful in Armies to tell when any calamity was about to befall them."[9]

The fate of this proposal is not known, but there is evidence that Gabriel did not take the traditions of Africa as seriously as did others in his group. Indeed, in black lore there is a suggestion that such a move as George proposed would have saved the plot from its untoward ending. But Gabriel had his mind set: they would move at midnight on August 30, 1800, carrying a flag with the motto "Death or Liberty"—the battle cry of San Domingo. Although it was later said that Gabriel had planned "to subdue the whole of the country where slavery was permitted, but no further," we are not certain how well the bold leader understood the nature of the forces which could ultimately be brought to bear against his insurrection, including the troops of the national government.[10]

By the end of August widespread organizing had evidently gone on among the black community of Henrico County and the surrounding areas. Many of the rebels held regular transport jobs as boatmen and as carriage and wagon drivers, and so enjoyed a mobility that was of great importance to their organizing work. When the time for the attack came, accounts of what finally happened vary, but certain matters are sure: at noontime on the appointed day it began to rain, and soon the worst storm in living memory broke over the area. The invasion of the city was called off by Gabriel when it was clear that several rivers and creeks on the way to Richmond would not be fordable, and that the planned operations would be impossible in the storm.

No one knows how many men and women were gathering when the word of delay was given; estimates range from dozens to more than a thousand. However, before the rain had stopped, the mission was betrayed by informers, and white search parties were soon scouring the countryside. Although his two brothers were captured early in the search, Gabriel managed to escape for a time. Finally, near the end of September, he was apprehended at Norfolk, while hiding on board a coastal schooner, the *Mary*. By this time most of his fellow leaders had been captured and executed, along with many persons whose involvement was at best peripheral. Nevertheless, Gabriel refused to confess or to discuss the planned insurrection, even when confronted by Gov. James Monroe. One morning in October, he went to his death without flinching.

Even in his failure, the Virginian had deeply stirred the black river of struggle. His name was on the lips of his people in many parts of the state and elsewhere. That was why Monroe could write from Richmond, "It was distinctly seen that [the plot] embraced most of the slaves in this city and neighborhood," and that "there was good cause to believe that the knowledge of such a project pervaded other parts, if not the whole state."[11]

Did it reach Southhampton County, not far away, where a child named Nat was born on Benjamin Turner's plantation? And what of Charleston? Did Denmark Vesey, just purchasing his freedom, hear of Gabriel and the price he had paid?

Although the fear of widespread black rebellion was akin to an occupational disease among Southern white officials, Monroe did not speak from idle anxiety. Not only did he recognize seething radical power and possibilities when he faced a man like Gabriel, but he must have known of other disquieting events. In the weeks following the trials there was word of "a series of small, insurrectionary actions" throughout Virginia. For example, it was reported that in Hanover County black people had been "very riotous and ungovernable" following the discovery of Gabriel's conspiracy. Some black men had gone so far as to break into a jail "and set free two insurrectionists who were handcuffed and chained to the floor." After they had been set free, the prisoners themselves attacked the guard, knocked him down, stamped on him, then escaped. It was against such a background that Monroe concluded his letter: "Unhappily, while this clas of people exists among us we can never count with certainty on its tranquil submission." His opinion was widely shared throughout Virginia, while as far away as the territory of Mississippi, Gov. Winthrop Sergeant informed his fellow slaveholders of Gabriel's attempt, "warning them to be watchful of a similar uprising in the vicinity."[12]

Actions like those attempted by Gabriel caught most attention and fired the imaginations of blacks and whites alike, but always, behind and beneath those larger, organized attempts were the subterranean acts of individual defiance, resistance, creative rebellion, sabotage, and flight.

This anonymous, pulsating movement persisted wherever there was slavery in America. It rose out of the broad base of all the men, women, and children who offered their personal, rudimentary challenges to the system. One time it was manifested in the decision of a solitary person to kill his master on a dark road as they traveled home at night. Another time it came when a group of black men determined that white patrolmen had broken up their social gatherings once too often and chose to resist to the death.[13]

Most often the efforts at resistance were on a small scale; only by accident did they leap into wider significance. Such an incident occurred in York, Pennsylvania, where in the spring of 1803 a black woman was convicted of attempting to poison two white persons. But after her conviction, other blacks in the town made several attempts to burn major sections of York to the ground; within three weeks eleven buildings were destroyed. Only after the militia and special patrols were called out, and a curfew was enforced against the black population, did the black fire cease in York.[14]

In the minds of the keepers of America's law and order, all such fires had to be watched carefully. This was no time to take lightly rebellious black action anywhere, for the revolution in San Domingo was still erupting, and everywhere in white America it was a source of conversation and fear. The African revolutionaries on the island were successfully resisting all Napoleon's efforts to break their will. Indeed, by the spring of 1803 their implacable resistance had utterly destroyed some of France's finest—and most cruel—military forces, and driven them from San Domingo. This totally unexpected turn of events helped convince the French ruler that his vision of an American empire must be abandoned. (As a result, he was willing to sell the entire Louisiana Territory to the United States, doubling the nation's area in one stroke.) But few whites anywhere seemed able to hear the indomitable General Dessalines when he and his comrades in leadership on San Domingo declared in 1803: "Towards those men who do us justice, we will act as brothers." Neither the white Americans, who had no special desire for African brothers, nor the French, who still hoped desperately to find a way to reassert their domination over these black revolutionaries, were able to absorb such words. Instead, most whites could only tremble when on January 1, 1804, the revolutionaries declared the creation of Haiti, a new independent African nation, and Dessalines put forth its motto: "Independence or Death! Let these sacred words serve to rally us . . . let them be signals of battle and of our reunion."[15]

Then, after a year of military, diplomatic, and political threats and maneuvers, extending beyond San Domingo to the rivalries of the

European and North American worlds, after several attempts by Napoleon to use the local French settlers to help undermine the revolution—after all that and more, the time for threats and maneuvers was up. Now, the overwhelming thirst for revenge against French treachery and brutality which had been building up within some of the Haitian revolutionaries finally won the day. Before March 1805 was over Dessalines "the liberator" became Dessalines "the avenger." His order for the death of all French settlers who had refused the hand of brotherhood was mercilessly carried out by Haitian soldiers and civilians. The terrible burdens of a land already engorged with blood were multiplied, and the cries of thousands of white men, women, and children became a bitter counterpoint to the agonizing, echoing calls of the tens of thousands of the island's people who for years had fallen under the fire, guns, and swords of the armies of the motherland.[16]

There was no way to contain these cries of anguish, rage, and victory, and when news of the latest developments in Haiti reached America, new tremors of excitement ran deep within the black community there. For years afterward, memories of this time when neighboring Africans seized their own freedom, created a nation, and repelled elements of Europe's greatest military force would live and grow in black tradition. As for American whites, they were understandably stunned and fearful. Although they held an overwhelming numerical advantage in the nation, there were many localities in Virginia and South Carolina, for instance, where slaveholders and their white neighbors were far outnumbered. And in spite of their denials, whites had every reason to believe that the Africans around them also loved liberty and craved independence. So the developments in Haiti stimulated a renewed campaign in America to erect every possible legal barrier against that revolutionary incubus.[17]

But some men were not content with laws and regulations. In 1804, shortly after Dessalines's cry of "Death to the whites" resounded throughout Europe and its colonies, William Claiborne, the new governor of the Louisiana Territory, reported on the special precautions he had taken: "All vessels with slaves on board are stopped at Plaquemine, and are not permitted to pass without my consent. This is done to prevent the bringing of Slaves that have been concerned in the insurrections of St. Domingo; but while any importations are admitted, many bad characters will be introduced." It was, of course, too late: the "bad characters" had been coming by ship for decades and so were already there, waiting for the day. Indeed, such characters were everywhere. In the year of Governor Claiborne's searches, a black insurrectionist in Virginia declared in the course of his trial: "I have nothing more to offer than what George Washington would have had to offer had he been taken by the British and put to trial by them. I have adventured my life in endeavoring to obtain the liberty of my countrymen, and am a willing sacrifice to their cause." This was indeed bad: black men were comparing themselves to the heroes of the white "revolution," claiming a legitimacy which was dangerous in slaves.[18]

Meanwhile, after several years of intermittent debates in Congress, the white heirs of the American revolutionary tradition were finally developing a new version of their own response to black slavery—one which avoided the central issues and affirmed the deepest contradictions. In the late winter of 1806–07, when they finally kept a promise of their Revolution and legislated an official end to American participation in the African slave trade, the bill was intentionally so weak that its provisions proved easy to circumvent. More ironic yet, the law proposed that any Africans found on interdicted slaving ships, instead of being hastened toward freedom, should be sold into bondage in the South. The law was to go into effect in January 1808. Not long before that, two boatloads of Africans brought to Charleston for sale had offered their own response to the slave trade: while awaiting sale in the slave pens, a number of them starved themselves to death.[19]

In the North, the options for struggle were usually not so harshly limited, especially for those free blacks who had been in the country for some time, learned its language, and studied its contradictions. Though their resistance was generally less stark and less costly than that in Charleston's slave pens, their continuing uses of white American political and religious assumptions contributed an important element to the developing protest traditions of black struggle. In 1808, a member of Boston's African Society spoke to that organization on the topic, "The Sons of Africa: An Essay on Freedom." In the course of his lecture he put forward words which held significant portent, saying, "Men have exercised authority over our nation as if we were their property, by depriving us of our freedom as though they had a command from heaven thus to do. But, we ask, if freedom is the right of one nation; why not the right of all nations of the earth?"[20]

Quietly, forcefully, certain questions were being raised by the blacks in America. Didn't black people have the same right and responsibility to fight for their liberty as white America had to fight for its independence? And were Africans in America not a nation? In the decades ahead these basic, radical questions would moil the river, thrusting black struggle onward with their force.

The seemingly confident surface of America's Natural Rights philosophy was not the only white theory and practice under constant attack from the underground black struggle. The religion of white America, which in most situations was meant to assure the tranquil submission of its captives, was insistently, continually wrested from the white mediators by black hands and minds, and transformed into an instrument of struggle. The Scriptures, the theology, the doctrine, the very places of worship were repeatedly transmuted in the alchemy of the black movement. This was seen in Gabriel's use of the preaching meetings, and explains the laws against independent black gatherings for worship, and the anger of Richard Byrd of Virginia in 1810, who "felt that slave preachers used their religious meetings as veils for revolutionary schemes." He was right—not only about one General Peter, a religious revolutionary operating from Virginia's Isle of Wight, but about others as well, such as those who in that same year sent messages of rebellion from nearby North Carolina, saying, "Freedom we want and will have, for we have served this cruel land enuff." Such men, like their ancestors on the slave ships, would hammer any object, any doctrine, into a weapon for the struggle toward freedom. Indeed, to love freedom so fully in the midst of slavery *was* religion, *was* radical.[21]

Nor were such radicals difficult to find, even after slave ships had been searched to weed them out, and laws passed to guarantee their death. They appeared in the Pointe Coupée section of Louisiana in January 1811, even though some twenty-five men and women had been executed less than two decades earlier in the same area for the same kind of thrust toward freedom. This time several hundred black men organized, secured some guns, flags, and drums, and on the night of January 8 began "marching from plantation to plantation, slaves everywhere joining them." It was a familiar scene, though in their march the group managed to kill only one white person (or so the records say). Nevertheless, their marching presence was so threatening that wagons and cartloads of white refugees were soon pouring into New Orleans seeking safety. However, before long a group of well-armed planters, assisted by militiamen of the territory and almost three hundred troops of the U.S. Army, met the poorly armed black forces, broke the uprising, and killed scores of other black persons in the days that followed. Thus the forces of the American government moved again to guarantee black bondage, presenting a harsh challenge to the radical black movement toward freedom.[22]

By then it had become strikingly apparent that the military power of the democratic American state would be used insistently to tighten the chains of slavery. Nevertheless, the movements of the river went forward, often buoyed by the desperate hope that some countervailing, supporting forces might be brought to bear on their behalf against the overwhelming weight of white America's national power. That hope was sometimes based in magic powers brought from the homeland, sometimes in the mysterious arrival of African forces from Santo Domingo or elsewhere. Often, hope was focused on America's white national enemies, chief among whom was still Great Britain.

Thus during the War of 1812 thousands of fugitives broke loose from slavery, and in some places tried to organize insurrections, expecting help from the English. In 1813, along the South Carolina coast there was much excited talk of a British invasion, and an insurrection was planned to coincide with it. In the course of the almost nightly planning meetings, black people on one of the Sea Islands apparently developed a song expressing their commitment to the struggle, a song lacking any of the ambiguity that usually attached to black songs of struggle and faith. At the beginning and close of each meeting, they are said to have sung:

> Hail! all hail! ye Afric clan
> Hail! ye oppressed, ye Afric band,
> Who toil and sweat in Slavery bound;
> And when your health & strength are gone
> Are left to hunger & to mourn,
> Let *Independence* be your aim,
> Ever mindful what 'tis worth.
> Pledge your bodies for the prize
> Pile them even to the skies!
>
> Firm, united let us be,
> Resolved on death or liberty
> As a band of Patriots joined
> Peace and Plenty we shall find.

After stanzas of similar sentiments, the song ended with these lines:

> Arise! Arise! Shake off your chains
> Your cause is just so heaven ordains
> To you shall Freedom be proclaimed
> Raise your arms & bare your breasts,
> Almighty God will do the rest.
> Blow the clarion! a warlike blast!
> Call every Negro from his task!
> Wrest the scourge from Buckra's hand,
> And drive each tyrant from the land.[23]

Current knowledge of the origins of this song is third-hand. If it was indeed created by the children of Africa out of the river of their struggle, it testified to a deep wrestling with the white American world. It called for independence for black people. It saw the liberating possibilities of the religion of Jesus and the Israelites. It demanded that all who loved tyranny be driven from the land—a demand which could be made only by those who now believed that they had some firm right to the land themselves. At every level, this was a radical statement for black bonds-people, and the call to arms was only the most obvious level of its radical thrust.

Africans in America were a long way from home, separated in some cases by several generations, and yet, if such things as presence, work, and blood counted, there were few places in the young nation which black people could not rightfully call home. But the claims of black work and blood, and the undeniable, troubling reality of black presence, were insistently denied by whites; and among black people themselves, America was often considered only a second home. Therefore Africa's children had only begun to make those just claims which flow out of a people's right to the territory they have helped develop and create. In its talk of driving tyrants from the land, the Sea Island battle hymn implied a contrast between prison ships and prison states, recognizing that while the ocean-going ships might be taken over only to be abandoned on Africa's coasts, this new land might have to be taken over to be transformed into a new home.

Of course, at profound and difficult levels, the claim to the American land as a home was complicated by the relationship of black struggle to the dark natives of North America, and to the fight they were waging in various parts of the continent. In fact, throughout the American sojourn Africans found themselves in a special and often cruelly difficult relationship to those beleaguered people who had invested their spirits in this land for thousands of years. That relationship between Africans and Native Americans affected the black struggle, from the earliest days of flight right down to the Seminole wars.[24]

For the black people of the Southern states, Florida was a focal point for this intertwined struggle. For three hundred years—from the initial Spanish settlements through the brief period of British domination, to the time when the United States forced its rights to the area—the territory had been a crucial sanctuary for black outlyers and other runaways, who made it a base for their attacks in various Southern states and a beacon of freedom for other captives. In doing this, they were often assisted by the Native Americans who shared the area with them. Then, during the War of 1812, hundreds of militant Creek Indians fled to Florida following their defeat by the white Americans in the Creek War of 1813–14, while thousands of additional black fugitives made their way into the area as well. During the war the British sought to recruit these disaffected groups, both of whom responded; by the end of 1814 at least four hundred black fugitives had enlisted, and were armed and uniformed as part of the British forces. In exchange for this service, the black men were promised their hard-earned freedom, as well as land in either Florida or the British West Indies.[25]

At the war's end, when the British finally withdrew and Spain resumed nominal control, both blacks and Indians were once more on their own in the grueling struggle for freedom against the American forces. Although some black people departed on the British transports, most remained to carry on the fight. They were aided in this when, just before they pulled out in the spring of 1815, British officers turned over to a group of the black soldiers and their families, plus a few of their Indian allies, one of their newest and best forts on the southwest coast of Florida. The fort at Prospect Bluff on the Apalachicola River was renamed "the Negro Fort" and occupied by more than three hundred men, women, and children, mostly black, commanded by a fugitive slave named Garson and a Choctaw chief. In addition, approximately a thousand men, women, and children lived in settlements along the river under the fort's protection. Immediately the group began both to symbolize and to demonstrate possibilities of such a sanctuary in the heart of the South, by using the fort as a base for marauding expeditions against slaveholders and as a haven for other fugitives. Men, women, and children came there from Georgia, the Mississippi Territory, and as far away as Tennessee. Thus not only were black people defying white law and order and creating new visions of their own possibilities, but valuable white property was roaming free, and even more of it was being daily endangered—all with the co-operation of those perennial "bad characters," the Indians.[26]

Obviously, this situation presented fundamental dangers to the keepers of the society. On June 26, 1816, the *Savannah Journal* said of the black fort: "It was not to have been expected, that an establishment so pernicious to the Southern States, holding out to a part of their population temptations to insubordination, would have been suffered to exist after the close of the war. . . . How long shall this evil requiring immediate remedy be permitted to exist?" Within a month the question had been answered, not simply by "the Southern States," but once again by the military forces of the federal government. Gen. Andrew Jackson—whose fame had recently been made, with a certain black assistance, in the battle of New Orleans—was the commander of the Southwestern Military District of the United States. In July 1816 he sent a unit of federal troops, backed by naval gunboats, to destroy the fort "and restore the stolen negroes and property to their rightful owners."[27]

After an initial encounter in which the waiting blacks and Indians captured a small vessel on reconnaissance and killed several crew members, the United States forces sent a delegation to call for the fort's surrender. Garson and his Choctaw comrade refused the demand, and the delegation reported that the black fugitive leader had "heaped much abuse on the Americans." Indeed, it was said that Garson declared he would "sink any American vessels that should attempt to pass" the fort. Learning of this defiant spirit, one of the American officers commented: "We were pleased with their spirited opposition . . . though they were Indians, negroes, and our enemies. Many circumstances convinced us that most of them were determined never to be taken alive."[28]

Most of them were not. Early in the morning of July 27, 1816, after four days of negotiations, skirmishes, and waiting, the American gunboats moved into position near the fort. The inexperienced gunners of the fortress fired first and missed. The first shot fired in return found its way into a powder magazine which had been left open. The terrifying explosion which followed was so powerful that it was reportedly heard and felt in Pensacola, some sixty miles away. Fewer than fifty of the fort's inhabitants survived the disaster, many of them so burned and mutilated that there was little hope for their survival.[29]

In a sense, the battle at the Negro Fort was a prelude to the First Seminole War, and announced the crucial role of black people in it. But for the long run the blinding explosion signaled something even more important: the fact that black men and women who broke away toward freedom had always to estimate the range of the cannon of the American government. In essence, then, the chilling sounds of the guns at Apalachicola were meant to deny the captive children of Africa—and the native peoples of America—any sanctuary from white domination, exploitation, and destruction, any right to claim the land as their own. Apalachicola meant that all such claims were guaranteed to drive endless streams of blood into the river of struggle; and the harrowing cries of the dying were harsh reminders of the realities which surrounded every black fortress in the midst of a hostile white society.

Faced with these bitter truths, some Africans were again exploring return to the homeland as a path toward that new life which seemed so hard to find on the bloody American ground. Indeed, under the leadership of stalwart men like Paul Cuffee, some Afro-Americans had already returned home: surely there was something tempting in letters they sent to friends here. One said: "Be not fearful to come to Africa, which is your country by right. . . . Though you are free, that is not your country. Africa, not America, is your country and your home." The letter was obviously addressed to the black "free" minority. Did it have any meaning for those who had to defend their "illegal" freedom in the forts of Florida, the swamps of North Carolina, the bayous of Louisiana?[30]

Some answers came slowly. But Denmark Vesey, one of the "free" minority in Charleston, South Carolina, had clearly answered the question of African repatriation for himself. In 1800 Vesey, then in his thirties, had bought his freedom from the ship's captain who held legal possession of him, and with whom he had already spent many years on voyages. In the course of those trips Vesey had traveled through the Caribbean, where in his adolescence he spent three months in San Domingo. He had apparently spent some time in Africa also. Since the beginning of the century, Vesey had lived in the ambiguous world of a free black in Charleston, working as a skilled and much-respected carpenter, while serving as a leader in the powerful African church there. His tall, spare figure was well known on the streets of the city and in the country districts surrounding it. By 1817 he had amassed savings of several thousand dollars, probably making him one of the wealthiest black men in the city. On at least one occasion he had been offered a chance to return to Africa as a free man. For it was a time when white, usually Southern-dominated organizations like the American Colonization Society were developing programs and raising funds to encourage the voluntary emigration of free blacks—those thorns in the side of slavery—from the United States to West Africa and other locations. But Vesey clearly shared the sentiments of the free black persons in Philadelphia who responded directly to the Colonization Society in 1817 by declaring: "We will never separate ourselves voluntarily from the slave population of this country; they are our brethren by the ties of consanguinity, of suffering and of wrong; and we feel that there is more virtue in suffering privations with them, than fancied advantages for a season."[31]

By that time Denmark Vesey was intimately familiar with many aspects of "the ties of consanguinity, of suffering and of wrong." At least one of his wives and some of his children were in slavery. He had seen the oppression and injustice meted out by the white community all around him, and he stood firm as a symbol of defiant resistance in the black community. However, it was not mere sentiment or ties of blood and oppression which kept him in Charleston when he could have begun a new life elsewhere. By 1817 Vesey had evidently decided that the only new life he desired was a struggle for the freedom of his people. One of his companions said that Vesey often rebuked any of his friends who offered the customary black gesture of bowing to a white person on the street. Vesey claimed that "all men were born equal, and that he was surprised that anyone would degrade himself by such conduct; that he would never- cringe to whites, nor ought any who had the feelings of a man." Such feelings were not uncommon in the black community, and were often expressed within its confines. It was not common, however, to act on them publicly or urge others to do the same. Denmark Vesey did both, and plunged forthrightly into the stream of black radicalism.

He acted because he believed that, both in Charleston and outside of it, history was evolving in ways which could be bent for the purposes of black freedom. Within the port city those historical developments were focused in the church, the heartland of institutional black concern. By the end of the War of 1812 the black Methodists in Charleston—the single largest black denomination—outnumbered the white membership ten to one. They had developed a quarterly conference of their own, and had custody of their own collections and control over the church trials of their own members. This independence was intolerable for the supervising white Methodists (and probably their non-Methodist friends as well). In 1815 they had acted against this black freedom, taking away privileges that they claimed were theirs to give, asserting that the African people had abused their freedom.

This was the decisive signal for a secession movement which had been stirring within the African churches. In 1816 Father Morris Brown and other black Charleston church leaders had gone to Philadelphia to confer with Richard Allen and other founders of the newly formed African Methodist Episcopal Church. Later in that year Brown and another elder were ordained for pastorates in Charleston. By 1817 an independent African Association was organized in the city. Then in 1818, on the occasion of a dispute over a burial ground, more than three-fourths of the six thousand black Methodists of Charleston withdrew from the white-dominated churches. Morris Brown was appointed bishop, and the independent African Church of Charleston was established.[32]

The Charleston movement for religious independence was a crucial form of mass black struggle which would be revived in and through the black churches more than a century later. Following the Philadelphia example, it challenged white domination, white control, white definitions of religious life and church polity. It participated in the growing movement among African people in America to establish relatively autonomous religious institutions where black life could be shaped and affirmed under black control. In the context of American slavery, the secession was a budding radicalism, and if the religious authorities of Charleston did not recognize it, the white secular authorities certainly did. (In many cases, of course, they were the same.) That was why the city consistently harassed and broke up the meetings of the newly established independent black congregations. That was why there were periodic arrests—sometimes of the leaders alone, and sometimes of large numbers of members—and why some were kept in jail, some banished, and others publicly whipped and otherwise punished. Finally, in 1821, the city of Charleston closed the Hamstead church, which had provided key leadership in the movement.[33]

The spirit of resistance and struggle had been lodged deeply in the black community's religious life, and the white authorities were not the only ones who recognized its larger potential. Denmark Vesey and certain special companions of his had known it long before; indeed they had helped to nurture it. But the closing of the church was the stimulus for organizing black discontent and resistance into something more effective than anger. Vesey had been a member of the Hamstead church, as had his friends Rolla Bennett, "Gullah Jack" Pritchard, Monday Gell, and Ned and Peter Poyas. They began meeting with some of the discontented members of the black community, often in Vesey's own house, sometimes in the areas for religious gatherings on plantations, at other times in the brush arbors outside the rural cabins. Vesey and his comrades believed that the suppression of the church had provided the issue around which they could rally the Charleston-area black community in a full-scale rebellion against white power. Within Charleston itself history had moved, and Vesey interpreted its movement to the black community. As one participant remembered it, the black leader said again and again that "we were deprived of our rights and privileges by the white people and that our Church was shut up so that we could not use it, and that it was high time for us to seek for our rights, and that we were fully able to conquer the whites if we were only unanimous and courageous, as the Santo Domingo people were."[34]

The San Domingo revolution was the second movement in history to which Vesey turned the minds of the people. He had been to the island as a boy. There is evidence as well that one of Vesey's comrades, the brilliant Monday Gell, had corresponded with the president of the troubled black republic. So as an insurrection was organized, Africa's children in and around Charleston were told that "Santo Domingo and Africa will assist us to get our liberty, if we will only make the motion first." That recurring pan-African element of black struggle, which had originated in the slave castles and on the ships, was now revived again in a fierce hope of help from elsewhere in the African diaspora. Of course, in Gullah Jack the Charleston conspirators already had Africa and its spirits with them in a peculiar way: he was a conjurer from among the Gullah people who lived on the coasts of the homeland, and his comrades in the conspiracy believed that he would call upon the fathers in their behalf, and would develop potions and powders to protect them.[35]

But neither Haiti nor Africa was the center of their hope. Rather it was another movement in history, another diaspora, which was used more effectively in rallying the insurrectionary forces. At almost every meeting, it was said, Vesey or one of his comrades "read to us from the Bible, how the children of Israel were delivered out of Egypt from bondage." That theme was struck insistently: the deliverance from Egypt, the movement of God among his captive people. (No wonder, then, that in some black traditions it is said that Vesey or his fellows were the inspiration for the ageless black song of faith and struggle, "Go Down, Moses." Was it out there in the fields, late in the Carolina nighttime, that a voice first lifted the slow and halting melody?)[36]

But Vesey went further. He did not merely speak of the mysterious action of God in plagues upon an Egyptian people, for that might have been misunderstood as a call to wait passively for divine intervention. Indeed, he constantly read to the people: "Behold the day of the Lord cometh, and thy spoil shall be divided in the midst of thee. For I shall gather all nations against Jerusalem to battle; and the city shall be taken. . . . And they utterly destroyed all that was in the city, both man and woman, young and old, and ox and sheep, and ass, with the edge of the sword." That message was unambiguous. And assurance for the faint of heart was there, too: "Then shall the Lord go forth, and fight against those nations, as when he fought in the day of battle." Even one of the noncanonical books of the Old Testament Apocrapha, *Tobit*, was brought to bear, to strengthen, to urge the children of Africa into battle for justice, for freedom.[37]

They needed every available encouragement, for even though blacks outnumbered whites in the city of Charleston, and held nearly a ten-to-one advantage in the surrounding areas, they lacked arms. The plans, similar to those of Gabriel, were to sweep into the city from seven different points, capture arms from the arsenal, set fire to the whole area, kill all whites who came into their path, and if necessary make good an escape to the Caribbean or Africa.[38]

As with many of the attempted insurrections in this phase of black struggle—as is the case, indeed, with insurrections everywhere—there was considerable vagueness concerning ultimate objectives. Part of that ambiguity lay in the dilemma of their basic situation: assuming immediate victory, how would thousands of black people make their way in safety to Haiti or Africa, as the armed forces of the white American national government bore down upon them? Could there really be any mass abandonment of the Southern prison-state at this stage of history? And if it could not be abandoned, how could it be held and sustained as a free territory in the midst of a white-dominated country?

The existing records do not provide any real sense of how Vesey and his comrades answered such questions. However, there is a possibility

that the resolute leader believed history to be moving so decisively in
favor of black freedom that such desperate flight or beleaguered military
action might not be necessary after their victory in Charleston. He had
read accounts of the recent bitter debates in Congress over the Missouri
Compromise, and there is some evidence that Vesey had either himself
come to believe, or at least had convinced others, that the federal government was abandoning its protection of slavery. If that were true, it might
not be necessary to face any forces other than those of South Carolina.[39]

Whatever their ultimate objective, Vesey and his companions apparently did an outstanding job of organizing. This was evident from the
first comrades in arms whom the black leader had chosen. One white official wrote:

In the selection of his leaders Vesey showed great penetration and sound
judgement. Rolla was plausible and possessed uncommon self-determination;
bold and ardent, he was not to be deterred from his purpose by danger. Ned's
appearance indicated that he was a man of firm nerves, and desperate courage.
Peter was intrepid and resolute, true to his engagements, and cautious in
observing secrecy where it was necessary; he was not to be daunted nor impeded by difficulties. . . . Gullah Jack was regarded as a sorcerer, and as such
feared by the natives of Africa, who believe in witchcraft. He was not only
considered invulnerable, but that he could make others so by his charms. . . .
His influence among the Africans was inconceivable. Monday was firm, resolute, discreet, and intelligent.[40]

Such were Vesey's lieutenants. Together they prepared for a deadline
in the second week of July 1822. Blacksmiths were making bayonets and
spikes. Others were to obtain daggers, swords, fuses, and powder. Dis-
guises, wigs, and false mustaches were to be contrived. The draymen,
carters, and butchers were to supply the horses. Plantation people were
recruited from the surrounding areas, some from as far away as eighty
miles outside of the city. They were to bring whatever weapons they
could obtain. However, most of the active participants were from the
urban black artisan population, both enslaved and free. Within the limitations of the time, Denmark Vesey and his comrades had built an all-
class black movement.[41]

Of course, a rebellion which meant to capture an important city needed
quantity as well as quality and breadth, and the leaders seemed to have
made hundreds of contacts over the months of patient organizing. But
that success carried within it the elements of defeat; for as knowledge
of at least the general plans spread among an ever-widening circle of
black people, so did the likelihood of betrayal become more an imminent
danger. At the end of May 1822, the possibility became a reality when a
slave who had been contacted as a likely recruit reported the contact to

African captives, caught in the net of the Europeans' slave trade,
on their way from the interior to the ships.

Africans on the slave ships rebel
and are thrown overboard
by crew members.

An enslaved African
convicted of participation
in a wave of arson and robberies
in New York City
in 1741 is burned at the stake.

Andrew Bryan,
founder of one of the
first independent
black churches in the United States,
in Savannah, Georgia.

Richard Allen,
a key founder and first bishop of the
African Methodist Episcopal Church.

The building that housed
the first Baptist Church
of Savannah.

Toussaint L'Ouverture,
leader of the successful
revolution carried out by the
enslaved Africans of San Domingo.

A scene from the San Domingo revolution, which led to
the establishment of the Republic of Haiti in 1804.

Negro Abraham,
an interpreter and comrade of the Seminole Indians
in their fight for self-determination
against U.S. military forces.

Captive Africans brought ashore in Florida for their introduction
into the slave system of the United States in the early nineteenth century.

Massacre of whites by blacks and Indians in Florida, in December 1835.

Slaves working with cotton, the basis of the South's economy.

RAFFLE

Mr. Joseph Jennings respectfully informs his friends and the public that, at the request of many acquaintances, he has been induced to purchase from Mr. Osborne, of Missouri, the celebrated

DARK BAY HORSE, "STAR,"

Aged five years, square trotter and warranted sound; with a new light Trotting Buggy and Harness; also, the dark, stout

MULATTO GIRL, "SARAH,"

Aged about twenty years, general house servant, valued at *nine hundred dollars*, and guaranteed, and

Will be Raffled for

At 4 o'clock P. M., February first, at the selection hotel of the subscribers. The above is as represented, and those persons who may wish to engage in the usual practice of raffling, will, I assure them, be perfectly satisfied with their destiny in this affair.

The whole is valued at its just worth, fifteen hundred dollars; fifteen hundred

CHANCES AT ONE DOLLAR EACH.

The Raffle will be conducted by gentlemen selected by the interested subscribers present. Five nights will be allowed to complete the Raffle. BOTH OF THE ABOVE DESCRIBED CAN BE SEEN AT MY STORE, No. 78 Common St., second door from Camp, at from 9 o'clock A. M. to 2 P. M. Highest throw to take the first choice; the lowest throw the remaining prize, and the fortunate winners will pay twenty dollars each for the refreshments furnished on the occasion.

N. B. No chances recognized unless paid for previous to the commencement.

JOSEPH JENNINGS.

Black men and women advertised
in the same category as material possessions.

Samuel Cornish,
editor of *Freedom's Journal*,
the first black newspaper
in the United States.

John Russworm,
the first black college graduate
in the United States,
later co-editor of
Freedom's Journal.

David Ruggles,
leader of New York City's
Vigilance Committee.

Frederick Douglass fighting a white mob
in Indiana in the 1840s.

For many, running away to freedom was the only appropriate response to slavery.
Polemical art like this emphasized the great danger involved.

his master. From that point on, the carefully constructed plan began to break down as the white authorities initiated a series of probing arrests, questionings, and releases, followed by new arrests. Though their initial information was fragmentary and did not immediately include Vesey's role, they were clearly on the trail.

Near the beginning of June, before the whites had worked their way through to the heart of the insurrectionary plans, Vesey attempted to recoup the situation by moving up the time of the attack to June 16. But by then not only was it impossible to reestablish contact with his far-flung network of recruits in time, but the authorities were sufficiently alerted to stymie the move before it could take on any real life. By June 22, Vesey and the rest of his comrades had been rounded up for a long, involved trial that was held under a law enacted "for the better ordering and governing of Negroes and other slaves in this state."[42] Even during the trial it was not easy to order and govern the African people of the Charleston area. They knew what the planned insurrection might have meant to them, and attempted to get close enough to the courtroom to receive news of its action. But black people were not allowed within several hundred yards of the building; indeed, federal troops "guarded the prison and court day and night to prevent blacks from freeing prisoners and continuing the conspiracy."

Within the courthouse, most of the leaders of the insurrection remained faithful to their commitments and refused to identify their comrades. Then, before the trial was over, the deepest meaning of black radical struggle was set in relief by the words of the oppressors. When Denmark Vesey was being sentenced, the presiding magistrate said to him: "It is difficult to imagine what *infatuation* could have prompted you to attempt an enterprise so wild and visionary. You were a free man; were comparatively wealthy; and enjoyed every comfort, compatible with your situation. You had therefore, much to risk and little to gain. From your age and experience you *ought* to have known, that success was impracticable."[43]

If one forgot the slavery of Vesey's own children and wives for the moment, then it was possible to say that he was especially fortunate—an unusual and even well-to-do Negro, since assets of eight thousand dollars would have been impressive for any Charleston white man at the time. But Denmark Vesey had chosen to identify himself as an integral part of the black river, of Tomba's river, of Gabriel's river, of Temba's river, of the river that was created by the countless thousands before him. Neither his freedman's status, his wealth, his age, nor his relative security could cut him off from the oppression and injustice his people suffered. He had rejected the precarious security of his "class" to join the struggle to overcome the entire system of white supremacy and slavery, and to smash all the false distinctions it had created, even among the children of Africa. At the age of fifty-five, Denmark Vesey had chosen to die.

The white rulers could not, or would not, understand such things. The magistrate concluded: "Your professed design was to trample on all laws, human and divine; to riot in blood, outrage, rapine, and conflagration, and to introduce anarchy and confusion in their most horrid forms. Your life has become, therefore, a just and necessary sacrifice, at the shrine of indignant justice." According to the record, Denmark Vesey and his men "mutually supported each other, and died obedient to the stern and emphatic injunction of their comrade, Peter Poyas: 'Do not open your lips! Die silent, as you shall see me do.' "[44] In Peter's trunk a letter was found with these words: "Fear not, the Lord God that delivered Daniel is able to deliver us." Perhaps he believed it.[45]

> Didn't my Lord
> Deliver Daniel,
> Then why not ev'ry man?

Nor was Peter the only one. There is evidence that on July 2, 1822, the day of their execution, another attempt at insurrection was made by the persistent, committed black people who had joined the struggle in Charleston. State militia held back the demonstration, but "so determined, however, were they to strike a blow for liberty that it was found necessary for the federal government to send soldiers to maintain order." The basic testimony of the slave ships remained: almost any serious black movement toward liberty confronted white law, white firearms, and the quest for white order.[46]

While major plots like Vesey's presented the most obvious challenges, they were constantly sustained by thousands of nameless black people like those in Charleston who attended the execution of their leaders, who were arrested and beaten for wearing black to mourn the death of Vesey and Poyas, of Gullah Jack and Ned, and more than thirty others. At the same time the poisoning, the arson, the flight from slavery still fed the subterranean streams.[47]

Throughout this period the fugitive outlyers who stayed in the South continued to be a persistent judgment and challenge. In the spring following Vesey's death, the profound effect that a company of outlyers might have on the workings of slavery was seen in the southern portion of Virginia's Norfolk County. In May 1823 it was reported that the white residents of the area "have for some time been kept in a state of mind peculiarly harassing and painful, from the too apparent fact that their lives are at the mercy of a band of lurking assassins, against whose fell designs neither the power of the law, or vigilance, or personal strength and intrepidity, can avail."[48]

This group of what Governor Claiborne of Louisiana would have called "bad characters" were in fact former slaves of the area. "These desperadoes are runaway negroes (commonly called outlyers). . . . Their first object is to obtain a gun and ammunition, as well as to procure game for subsistence as to defend themselves from attack, or accomplish objects of vengeance." In the course of their struggle to remain free, and as part of their warfare on slaveowners and patrollers, the self-determining black band had killed several white men. One slaveholder in the area received a note from the group, "suggesting it would be healthier for him to remain indoors at night." He took the suggestion.[49]

Finally the state militia was dispatched. In June they captured the reputed leader, Bob Ferebee, a black who had lived independently as a free man and fugitive for six years. In July 1823—just one year after the execution of Denmark Vesey and his comrades—Bob Ferebee met the logical results of white justice, became another strange fruit, witnessing in the wind of Virginia.[50]

As usual, the executions were not deterrents. Ferebee and his band had already offered their contribution to the struggle, and their existence had made a point to both blacks and whites. They were "bad niggers" —"desperadoes" elevated to an organizational level. They had inspired deep, open fear in the white community, and for a time had been the hunters rather than the hunted. Their leader had remained free for six years; others had most likely been outlyers for even longer, for the Dismal Swamp offered protection for many children of Africa for long periods of time. (Some persons were said to have been born and died in such refuges.) This band and others like it provided an essential and unambiguous challenge to the system of slavery and its law and order.

A manifestation of black radicalism which rises out of swamps does not fit into easy categories, but black struggle is not easy to wage. Unquestionably these self-determining African men and women were part of the irrepressible struggle which was destined to meet its counterparts in the streets of the Northern cities a century later. But even in Virginia in 1823, their ultimate destiny might have been suggested through a glimpse at the life of one of the state's enslaved black men, Nat Turner. For it was during this period that Turner ran away for thirty days. Other fugitives from Southhampton had gone to the Dismal Swamp. Did he go, too, perhaps following the footsteps of his fugitive father? Was the inspiration of such men as Ferebee's outlyers part of the sound which eventually burst like a trumpet in his soul?[51]

The time may yet come for such questions to be answered. All that is certain now is that the early nineteenth-century black community in slavery—the community that knew names like Gabriel, Vesey, and Fere-bee—lived close to the active, radical depths of the river of black strug-gle. Occasionally they were swept in by its force; most often, they oper-ated at less costly levels, but knew of the radical movements. Engaged in day-to-day survival to maintain integrity, identity, and life, the vast majority who formed the mainstream were constantly in touch with the runaways, outlyers, and arsonists, and with those men and women who sneaked back into their cabins before dawn after attending secret plan-ning meetings. In addition, the fugitive, exciting word from white politi-cal sources, telling of arguments and debates over the operation of the institution of slavery, continued to seep into the life of the Southern black community, hinting, suggesting, revealing the basic tensions which lurked deep in the larger white society. Always, too, there was word from farther away (and nearer), from San Domingo and other parts of the African diaspora in the Caribbean—word of struggle and victory, even of emancipation. Then, beyond and above all these, was the word from the Lord, word from the Word, word of delivering Daniel, word that "Jesus do most anything/Oh, no man can hinder me." There were words not only to hear, but to eat and drink, words to ponder, words to surrender to.

The river of black struggle held all these speaking, acting, and enliv-ening words, all these bold, challenging heroic lives, and it was always moving, rising in the midst of the slave community. Therefore this was not a community caught in the flatness of despair. It was not a commu-nity without hope. It lived with brutality, but did not become brutish. Often it was treated inhumanely, but it clung to its humanity. There was too much in the river which suggested other possibilities, announced new comings, and hurled restless movements against the dam of white oppression. Always, under the surface of slavery, the river of black strug-gle flowed with, and was created by, a black community that moved actively in search of freedom, integrity, and home—a community that could not be dehumanized.

4

Symptoms of Liberty and Blackhead Signposts

David Walker and Nat Turner

I speak Americans for your good. We must and shall be free . . . in spite of you. You may do your best to keep us in wretchedness and misery, to enrich you and your children, but God will deliver us from under you. And wo, wo, will be to you if we have to obtain our freedom by fighting.

David Walker, 1829

I heard a loud voice in the heavens, and the Spirit instantly appeared to me and said . . . I should arise and prepare myself, and slay my enemies with their own weapons . . . for the time was fast approaching when the first should be last and the last should be first.

Nat Turner, 1831

There was much about America in the 1820s that made it possible for white men and women, especially in the North, to live as if no river of struggle were slowly, steadily developing its black power beneath the rough surfaces of the new nation. Indeed, the newness itself, the busyness, the almost frenetic sense of movement and building which seized America, were all part of the comfortable cloud of unknowing that helped preserve a white sense of unreality. Nor was the incessant movement of the majority simply imagined. Every day hundreds of families were actually uprooting themselves from the more settled areas of the East and seeking their fortunes beyond the Appalachians, even beyond the Mississippi River. Other whites from Europe and the British Isles were landing regularly at the Eastern ports, making their way into the seaboard cities and across the country to the new West, providing an intimation of the waves of immigrants soon to come. Thus the sense of movement in America was based on a concrete, physical reality.[1]

Naturally, much attention and energy were invested in the political, economic, and social institutions being developed and refined to serve the new American society. The national government was defining its own sense of purpose and power. Courts, banks, corporations, systems of transportation, and religion—all were being molded, reshaped, and re-examined, set in motion to serve a nation of settlers intent on dominating a continent. Because of that goal, the natives of the land were receiving their share of attention, too—much to their regret. Relentlessly, the collective white behemoth pushed them from river to river, back into the wilderness, smashing the cultures of centuries as if the Anglo-Americans and their cousins were agents of some divine judgment in the land.[2]

As a matter of fact, major segments of white America were possessed by just such visions of divine action in their midst, saw America as a Promised Land, as a staging ground for the earthly manifestations of the coming (white) Kingdom of God. Such godly visions, built strangely on the deaths of significant portions of the nonwhite children of this Father, contributed their own peculiar busyness to the blurring of American vision. For from the stately church buildings of New England (many built on profits from the Trade), to the roughhewn meeting houses of the Northwest and the sprawling campgrounds of the South, men who considered themselves agents of God proclaimed the need of the people to prepare the way for His Coming. Whatever the differences in their theology or lack of it, from Unitarians to Hard-Shell Baptists, they were united in their sense that the God of Israel was among them in a special way, and busily announced the various implications of that presence among the (mostly white) people. Partly as a result of such holy activism and fervent conviction, various sections of the nation were periodically swept by paroxysms of religious ardor, and the enthusiastic style of evangelical Protestant revivalism set its mark on large sectors of American life.

It was a time for building, whether canals or corporations or Kingdoms of the Saints, a hectic time of new buildings when busy men and overworked women might understandably ignore certain dark and troubling movements among them. It was a time that some called the "Era of Good Feelings," when party strife among whites seemed less pronounced than during the earlier founding periods. But the harsh and bitter debate which was then being carried on in Congress and across the country over the expansion of slavery's territory spoke to a different reality, one which often seemed about to break out and threaten all the white kingdoms.[3]

Meanwhile, down in the kingdom that cotton was building, there was just as much movement, building, and expansion, but of a somewhat different quality. Louisiana had become a state in 1812. Alabama entered the Union in 1817, and Mississippi two years later. Within the decade from 1810 to 1820, the population of the Alabama-Mississippi area alone had increased from 40,000 to 200,000 persons, including more than 70,000 enslaved Africans. Since the official closing of the Atlantic slave trade to America, the internal traffic in human bondage had burgeoned; Virginia served as its capital, while the nearby slave markets of Washington, D.C., provided an appropriate commentary on the state of American democracy. With the rise of this domestic trade, which eventually took hundreds of thousands of black people from the seaboard breeding and trading grounds into the interior of the developing South, new sectional bonds were established across that entire area, helping to create a self-conscious South which was tied together in many ways by the chain of black lives.[4]

The nation had committed itself to slavery, and the South was the keeper. In the 1820s the Southern black population grew from 1.6 million to more than 2 million persons, comprising some 40 percent of the section's total population, and ranging as high as 70 to 90 percent in some plantation counties and parishes. In this kingdom that cotton was building, enslaved black people were everywhere, and it was at once harder and easier for white men and women to deceive themselves. But there was no escape from the realities represented by the radical black presence in America. Thus private and public writings from the South continually referred to deep levels of fear—fear of insurrection, fear of death at black hands, fear of black life, fear of blackness, fear of repressed and frightening white desires. Usually it came out in references to "an internal foe," or "the dangerous internal population," or "the enemy in our very bosom," perhaps revealing more than the writers ever knew.[5]

Yet even in the South, even there where all the busyness of America could not shield white men and women from the stark black reality, it was still possible not to see where the objective enemy really was. In the 1820s, in Virginia's Southhampton County, who would have chosen Nat Turner for the role?

On the surface, Nat Turner appeared to represent much of that development which allowed men who called themselves masters to rest in the rightness of their ways. The ascetic Turner seemed to have imbibed deeply all the best elements of evangelical Southern white religion, all the proper anesthesia against the knowledge of who he had been, what he had lost, and what there was to regain. He did not use tobacco or liquor, he seemed to live a perfectly disciplined life among men as well as women (though not all owners would think well of *that* fruit of the Spirit); by and large, he caused no real trouble for the keepers of the status quo. Indeed, around 1821 the young black man had vividly demonstrated to whites the exemplary advantage of his high standing among the other Africans by returning voluntarily to Samuel Turner after having run away for about thirty days. Such a faithful black exhorter and singer of spiritual songs was of great value in the eyes of the white world. Of course the eyes of the white world did not see into the deepest level of Nat's real relationship to the black community, or into his real relationship to his God. Therefore whites could never have predicted that Nat, once harshened and honed in the burning river, would be possessed by a driving messianic mission to become God's avenging scourge against the slaveholders and their world.[6]

After his birth in 1800, the first community Nat Turner knew was that of his mother, father, and grandmother, a family not far removed from Africa but held in slavery by one Samuel Turner. Had they considered themselves or young Nat simply to be "slaves," he would never have become a Messenger. Rather, from the outset they taught him that he was meant for some special purpose (and therefore so were they), and they led him in that path. For instance, the immediate family and the surrounding black community were evidently convinced—as was Nat—that he had learned to read without instruction. Soon they were fascinated by his experiments in the ancient crafts of Africa and Asia: pottery, papermaking, and the making of gunpowder. Perhaps this was seen as another manifestation of the esoteric knowledge the community was convinced that he possessed—knowledge that included events and times before his own birth. Meanwhile his grandmother Bridget, a "very religious" woman, instructed him in what she knew from the Scriptures and other sources, nurtured him in the songs of nighttime and sleep.[7]

We are not sure of all that Nat learned from his immediate family, but his father taught him at least one thing: slavery was not to be endured. While Nat was still a child his father had joined the ranks of the fugitives. (Who can imagine the conversation in that family before his father ran away into the shadows of history? How much of their substance did Nat carry to his own grave?) From the rest of the community of captives Nat learned the same lesson, which was often taught in the captives' own flight from slavery, in spite of the high costs involved. He knew of the injustices suffered by his community. He learned its ritual songs and prayers, and the stories of heroes like Gabriel. But Nat claimed that his most profound lessons came in his own lonely, personal struggles with the spirit, whom he identified as "the Spirit that spoke to the prophets."[8]

By the time he was twenty-five, Nat had wrestled many times in the night with the Spirit of his God, the God of his Fathers. He had been pressed especially hard by the words: "Seek ye first the Kingdom of God and all things shall be added unto you." As he attempted to plumb the meaning and mystery of that promise, he had been driven into his own month-long experience of the wilderness, but then had returned to the Turner farm. Steadily he became more convinced that the Kingdom he sought was not the one preached by most of the white men he had heard. Instead, he saw the promised Kingdom of righteousness as one which would somehow be realized on the very farms and fields of Virginia, a Kingdom in which the power of the slavemasters would be broken. What made the vision chilling and exhilarating was his vivid awareness of being a chosen instrument for the bringing in of this Kingdom.[9]

Still, the way forward was not yet really clear, and Nat Turner went about his life and work, waiting. By this time Turner was a familiar figure in Southhampton County and the surrounding areas. Of about average height, muscular in build, coffee-tan in complexion, with a wide nose and large eyes, he walked with a brisk and active movement among his people, marked within himself and among them as a special man. On Sundays and at midweek meetings he exhorted and sang in black Baptist gatherings. At one point, word spread that Nat Turner had cured a white man of some serious disease, and then had baptized the white believer and himself in a river. Such a story only added to his renown.[10]

None of these developments, none of this high regard, moved Turner from his central purpose and passionate search. He waited and worked and married, but knew that all these things were only a prelude. Then in 1825 a clearer vision came: "I saw white spirits and black spirits engaged in battle, and the sun was darkened—the thunder rolled in the Heavens, and blood flowed in streams—and I heard a voice saying, 'Such is your luck, such you are called to see, and let it come rough or smooth, you must surely bear it.' " Again, one day as he worked in the fields Nat claimed to have "discovered drops of blood on the corn as though it were dew from heaven." On the leaves of the trees he said he found "hieroglyphic characters, and numbers, with the forms of men . . . portrayed in blood." Through this African imagery the white and black fighters had appeared again, but this time the meaning was even clearer in his mind. What it signified to Nat was that "the blood of Christ had been shed on this earth . . . and was now returning to earth." Therefore, he said, "it was plain to me that the Saviour was about to lay down the yoke he had borne for the sins of men, and the great day of judgement was at hand."[11]

On one level, Turner was obviously living within the popular nineteenth-century Euro-American millenarian religious tradition, marked by a belief in the imminent return of Christ to rule his earth. Often, for persons thus convinced, a terrible and sometimes beautiful urgency caught fire and burned within them, annealing and transforming their being.[12]

But the burning within Nat Turner came from an at once similar and very different fire. That became evident in the spring of 1828, when the fullest description of the Kingdom he sought, and of his own role in its coming, were spoken to Nat's third ear. With very rare exceptions, white American evangelical religion could not contain such a Word, had no ear for it. On May 12, 1828, Nat said, "I heard a loud voice in the heavens, and the Spirit instantly appeared to me and said the Serpent was loosened, and Christ had laid down the yoke he had borne for the sins of men, and that I should take it and fight against the serpent, for the time was fast approaching when the first should be last and the last should be first." As if to clear away any lingering doubt he might have had, Nat heard the spirit's clear instructions, that at the appearance of the proper sign "I should arise and prepare myself, and slay my enemies with their own weapons." After that he waited, he bided his time.[13]

> Oh praised my honer, harshener
> till a sleep came over me,
> a sleep heavy as death. And when
> I awoke at last free
>
> And purified, I rose and prayed
> and returned after a time
> to the blazing fields, to the humbleness.
> And bided my time.[14]

For twenty-eight years Nat Turner had been nurtured by the black community, instructed by signs on the leaves and in the skies. Now he was clear about who the enemy of righteousness was, and who were the servants of the devil; he had only to wait for the sign. But it may have been difficult to wait: about this time, it seems, Turner was whipped by Thomas Moore, his present owner, "for saying that the blacks ought to be free, and that they would be free one day or another."[15]

A bustling, growing, building white nation could miss the sign that such a man carried in his own flesh, but for persons who were willing to see, more obvious signs were available. These were the years of black insurrections in Martinique, Cuba, Antigua, Tortola, Jamaica, and elsewhere in the Western Hemisphere, and black people in the States were not oblivious of them or of their promise. This was demonstrated in the fall of 1826, when twenty-nine black people were being taken by sea from Maryland to Georgia on the *Decatur*, a vessel owned by one of the nation's largest slave traders. The black captives rebelled, killed two members of the crew, then ordered another crew member "to take them to

Haiti" because they knew of the black struggle there. The boat was captured before they could reach their destination, but when the *Decatur* was taken to New York City, all but one of the captives escaped.[16]

Two years later a group of four black slave artisans were on a similar journey by ship from Charleston to New Orleans. Before leaving South Carolina, they vowed that they would never be slaves in New Orleans. By the time the boat docked, they all had committed suicide. At about the same time, fragmentary reports of rebellions and death on island plantations seeped out of other parts of Louisiana.[17]

There was no surcease. While Nat Turner saw visions and waited for signs, others continued to fight. In Mobile County, Alabama, a black man named Hal had led a group of outlyers for several years. By the spring of 1827 the fugitives were organized to the point where they were building a fort in the swamps. One day while the construction was still going on, they were surprised, attacked, and defeated by a large group of whites. Later one of the white men reported: "This much I can say that old Hal . . . and his men fought like spartans, not one gave an inch of ground, but stood, was shot dead or wounded fell on the spot."[18]

While Nat Turner waited for the sign, and black people fought on ships, in forests, and on plantations, there were still other options and other signs, especially for those who could no longer bide their time. David Walker was one such man. He had been born legally free in 1785 in Wilmington, North Carolina, the child of a free mother, but he knew that he was not free, that his status ultimately depended upon the good will of white men. By the 1820s, while Nat waited for signs and saw visions, Walker had traveled across the South and into the trans-Appalachian West, had seen what America was doing to black people in slavery, and had become concerned about what slavery might yet do to him. Later, two scenes from those journeys stood out especially in his mind. He claimed to have watched the degradation of two black men: a son who was forced to strip his mother naked and whip her until she died; and a black husband forced to lash his pregnant wife until she aborted her child. Walker knew that, if faced with such savage choices, he would kill white men—and most likely be killed. "If I remain in this bloody land," he told himself, "I will not live long." By 1826, led by his own signs and visions, David Walker had moved to Boston.[19]

By then he was forty-one years old. A tall, slender, handsome man of dark complexion, Walker was a bachelor when he arrived. Perhaps he had thought it unwise to give too many hostages to white fortune while living and traveling in the South and West. Perhaps he wanted to be untrammeled in his passionate work on behalf of black freedom, a task he took up in very concrete ways soon after arriving in Boston. Almost immediately, the North Carolinian's house became a refuge for all black people in need of aid, especially the fugitives from slavery who came regularly into Boston. Walker was also an organizer and lecturer for the General Colored Association of Massachusetts, a black abolitionist organization, and when *Freedom's Journal*, the first black newspaper in America, began publication in 1827, Walker became an agent for the paper in Boston.[20]

The meeting of David Walker and *Freedom's Journal* in the Northern phase of the struggle raised a question of great moment: what is the role of the word—the spoken word, the preached word, the whispered-in-the-nighttime word, the written word, the published word—in the fight for black freedom?

In the slave castles and by the riversides of Africa, where our ancestors had gathered for the long journey into American captivity, the spoken word had many functions. It provided a bridge between and among them, to draw them together for the unity those first efforts demanded. On the ships the word was used to strengthen men and women and urge them toward the dangers of participation. It was often on the ships that the word, for the first sustained length of time, was directed toward the white captors. Early, in such a setting, the word was used in protest, in statements of black rights and white wrongs, of black people's determination to be men and women in spite of European attempts to dehumanize them. There, too, the word publicly spoken to white men often served as a rallying point for the Africans. For in many cases the word was openly uttered in spite of the rules and laws of the whites, spoken in the face of threats and punishment and even death. Such courageous speakers of the word understandably evoked strength and courage and hope in other captives.

Similar situations often prevailed when the black-white struggle moved from the prison ships into the fields and forests of the New World prison state. In the South, the word was used as an organizing tool for the flight into the outlyers' camps or toward the North. In many such situations it spoke the truth about white oppression, black suffering, and the potential power of organized black will. Such a word strengthened and encouraged friends to continue the struggle to survive, to bide their time toward the struggle to overcome. And on many occasions, the prison states exacted the same cruel penalties as the prison ships for the honest, defiant, encouraging black word. For such words were radical acts.[21]

No less dangerous to white power in the South were the words spoken honestly from the Bible, the Word, telling men and women of a humanity no one could deny them, reminding a people that God opposed injustice and the oppression of the weak, encouraging believers to seek for messianic signs in the heavens, for blood on the leaves. On the tongues of black people—and in their hands—the Word might indeed become a sword.

On the other hand, in the antebellum North the role of the word developed somewhat differently, progressing less starkly but in the same essential direction. There, in situations where black men and women brought that word to bear against their oppressors, they usually addressed two intersecting realities: the bondage forced upon their brothers and sisters in the South, and the racist discrimination practiced against their own immediate community in the North. When they spoke or wrote against slavery, the fate of their word often depended upon where it was spoken and to what audience it was directed. Put forth among black people or white sympathizers, words from black speakers and writers denouncing slavery and its defenders usually did not present the same outright, abrasive challenge as in the South. However, such words could never be confined to those circles. They carried their own resonance and therefore their own dangers. No black critics, whatever their audiences, were suffered gladly, and it was not unusual—especially as the nation's argument over slavery grew more heated—for white mobs to break in on abolitionist meetings and especially attack the black men and women who dared stand as public judges of white law and order.[22]

As the debate over slavery intensified, the black word from the North became more provocative, more slashing in its condemnation, more daring in its encouragement to resistance. Then, when attempts were made to publish and distribute those words among the Afro-American captives of the South, radical words and deeds were clearly joined, and the challenge was explosive. In the same way, as black men and women pressed their fierce arguments against the conditions of Northern racism, they found increasing hostility in that section, too. For the word often called upon their brothers and sisters to struggle for changes in their status there, to resist, to fight back. Ultimately, the words against slavery in the South and discrimination in the North were joined, for the black community of the North was finally called upon to resist the laws which endangered the fugitive slaves who came among them. From pulpit, platform, and press the black word would urge them to take up the struggle of the enslaved on free ground, thereby proclaiming all American soil to be contaminated, unfree, and in need of the rushing, cleansing movement of the river.

So the word had many roles and many places in the Northern struggle. In 1827 the almost simultaneous appearance of David Walker and *Freedom's Journal* represented one of the earliest institutional manifestations of what we have called the Great Tradition of Black Protest. As such, it was in the mainstream of the river, closer to the surface than the churning depths. In its first issue this pioneer black periodical announced: "The civil rights of a people being of the greatest value, it shall ever be our duty to vindicate our brethren when oppressed, and to lay the cure before the publick. We also urge upon our brethren (who are qualified by the laws of the different states) the expediency of using their elective franchise; and of making an independent use of the same. We wish them not to become the tools of party." For the *Journal*, the word meant quiet, sound advocacy of the black cause, an encouragement to acceptable black social and political development, and a source of information and advice for any whites who might be concerned about black needs. In 1827 the word of the Great Tradition was less strident than it had been on the slave ships, but it was the same tradition, and the time for its renewed stridency would come.[23]

By the following year, David Walker began his brief career as a goad to moderate voices like that of *Freedom's Journal*. For even as he moved within the Great Tradition, Walker's history, temperament, and commitments urged him toward deeper and more radical levels of struggle. In the fall of 1828 he delivered an address before the General Colored Association of his adopted state, calling on blacks to organize and act on their own behalf. In the address Walker first spoke of the need for political and social organization within the black community, identifying such structured, inner cohesion as a prerequisite to any effective struggle for freedom. "Ought we not to form ourselves into a general body to protect, aid, and assist each other to the utmost of our power?" Proceeding beyond this, he also said that "it is indispensably our duty to try every scheme we think will have a tendency to facilitate our salvation, and leave the final result to . . . God."

This last sentiment was not escapist. Rather, it suggested a certain affinity between Walker and the waiting Nat Turner. For David Walker was a staunch and faithful member of a black Methodist church in Boston, and he firmly believed that people—especially oppressed people— were called upon to act as well as pray, always placing their ultimate confidence in God. It was that context of active faith which illuminated the final words of Walker's speech to the Colored Association: "I verily believe that God has something in reserve for us, which when he shall have poured it out upon us, will repay us for all our suffering and misery."[24]

In February 1829, two months after the publication of Walker's December speech, a document which seemed to express certain elements of his thought more explicitly appeared in print. One Robert Young, a black New Yorker, published a pamphlet called *The Ethiopian Manifesto*, evidently intending to put forward a longer version later. It appears now that the larger statement never came, but the *Manifesto* picked up the themes from Walker's work and carried them forward. For Young, as for many Biblically oriented blacks of the time, the word Ethiopian was synonymous with African: where Walker had spoken generally of the need for political and social organization, Young seemed to advocate the establishment of a theocracy of Ethiopian people in America. Calling for the "convocation of ourselves into a body politic," Young said that "for the promotion of welfare of our order," it was necessary "to establish to ourselves a people framed into the likeness of that order, which from our mind's eye we do evidently discern governs the universal creation. Beholding but one sole power, supremacy, or head, we do of that head . . . look forward for succor in the accomplishment of the great design which he hath, in his wisdom, promoted us to its undertaking."[25]

Equally important, perhaps more so, was the *Manifesto*'s announcement to the black people of America and elsewhere that "the time is at hand, when, with but the power of words, and the divine will of our God, the vile shackles of slavery shall be broken asunder from you, and no man known shall dare to own or proclaim you as his bondsmen." This was a deliverance rather different from the kind Nat Turner pondered in Virginia, or that David Walker would soon propose. It depended solely on "the power of words" and the will of God. But according to Young, it would be manifested through a mulatto Messiah chosen by God from "Grenada's Island" in the West Indies. This Messiah would be the means whereby God would "call together the black people as a nation in themselves." Thus Young could say to white people: "Of the degraded of this earth, shall be exalted, one who shall draw from thee as though gifted of power divine, all attachment and regard of thy slave towards thee."[26]

Here was true messianic promise: divine intervention on behalf of the Ethiopian nation in America, to provide a savior to draw black people together as a nation, and somehow miraculously break the shackles of slavery. Its pan-Africanism, its sense of nationhood, its radical hope all marked this rather mysterious announcement as part of the stream of radical ideas in the struggle. But by then both David Walker and Nat Turner had heard other voices.

Not long after his arrival in Boston, David Walker had set up a new and used clothing shop on Brattle Street. That provided his living: but the freedom struggle of black people in America was his life. Not only did he regularly attend the abolitionist meetings and assist all the fugitives he could, but those who knew him noted that Walker was devoting very long, hard hours to reading and study. Driven by an urgency that he attributed to the spirit of God, his special role was taking shape, only faintly suggested by the speech near the end of 1828.

Sometime during this period Walker took time to get married, but there was no release of the internal pressure, no relaxation in the harsh schedule of reading and writing which he had set himself. Finally, having developed a series of notes and drafts, in September 1829 Walker supervised the printing of his explosive seventy-six-page pamphlet, *Walker's Appeal . . . to the Colored Citizens of the World But in Particular and very Expressly to those of the United States of America.* It read as if all the passion and commitment of his life had been poured into the document. In its pages, filled with exclamations and pleas, with warnings and exhortations, one could almost hear the seething, roaring sounds of the black river, from the wailings of the African baracoons to the thundering declarations of Dessalines, and the quiet signals of the outlyers in Wilmington's swamps.[27]

Near the beginning of the work, Walker proclaimed it one of his major purposes "to awaken in the breasts of my afflicted, degraded and slumbering brethren, a spirit of inquiry and investigation respecting our miseries and wretchednesses in this REPUBLICAN LAND OF LIBERTY!!!!!" Essentially, he was demonstrating several of the major functions of radical teaching among dominated African peoples: to raise questions about the reasons for their oppression, to speak the truth concerning both oppressed and oppressor, to clarify as fully as possible the contradictions inherent in both communities, and to indicate the possible uses of these contradictions in the struggle for freedom. Actually, he accomplished even more than he set out to: for over a century, Walker's *Appeal* remained a touchstone for one crucial genre of black radical analysis and agitation. As such, its primary strength lay in the breadth and honesty of its analysis, in the all-consuming passion of its commitment to black liberation, and in the radical hope which lifted it beyond the familiar temptations to bitter despair. Understandably, then, David Walker's heirs, both conscious and unconscious, have been legion.[28]

In the pamphlet, which quickly went through three editions (with new material added to the later ones), ten major themes were addressed:

1. The profound degradation of African peoples, especially those in the United States, as a result of the racism and avarice which supported and shaped the system of slavery. (Walker was perhaps the first writer to combine an attack on white racism and white economic exploitation in a deliberate and critical way.)

2. The unavoidable judgment which a just God would bring upon the white American nation, unless it repented and gave up its evil ways of injustice and oppression.

3. The imperative for black people to face their own complicity in their oppression, and the need for them to end that complicity

through resistance in every possible way, including the path of armed struggle.

4. The need for black people to develop a far greater sense of solidarity, especially between the "free" and captive populations within the United States, and between the children of Africa here and Africans in the rest of the world. (This was the first clear, widely publicized call for pan-African solidarity.)

5. The need to resist the attempts of the American Colonization Society to rid the country of its free black population.

6. The need to gain as much education as possible as a weapon in the struggle.

7. The possibility that a new society of peace and justice could come into being if white America were able to give up its malevolent ways, especially its racism and avarice.

8. The need for an essentially Protestant Christian religious undergirding for the black struggle for justice.

9. The likelihood that he, Walker, would be imprisoned or assassinated as a result of the *Appeal*.

10. The repeated statement of his own essential sense of solidarity with his brothers and sisters in slavery.

Actually, this last-mentioned sense of solidarity was the deepest source of Walker's radicalism. He was impelled not by a hatred of white America, but by a profound love and compassion for his people. It was this commitment to black people, and his unshakable belief in a God of justice, which led inevitably to an urgent statement of black radicalism, a call for uprooting and overturning of the system of life and death that was America.

Because of the nature and preoccupations of American society, the *Appeal*, in spite of its other urgent concerns, gained its greatest notoriety through advocacy of black messianic armed resistance to white oppression and slavery. Of course it was this advocacy which posed the most obvious, if not the most profound, threat to the American social order. Combining social, political, and economic religious messianism with the secular natural rights doctrine then current, Walker urged black people:

Let your enemies go with their butcheries, and at once fill up their cup. Never make an attempt to gain our freedom or *natural right*, from under our cruel oppressors and murderers, until you see your way clear—when that hour arrives and you move, be not afraid or dismayed; for be you assured that Jesus Christ the king of heaven and of earth who is the God of justice and of armies, will surely go before you. And those enemies who have for hundreds of years stolen our *rights*, and kept us ignorant of him and his divine worship, he will remove.[29]

A black man had again taken products of white civilization and transmuted them for purposes of black freedom. In the *Appeal*, the two major
systems of belief in early nineteenth-century America—Protestant evangelical Christianity and natural rights philosophy—were lifted up and
bound in blood as a weapon in the struggle of black people toward justice. For Walker, the cause of freedom was the cause of God, and the
cause of black justice was the cause of Jesus Christ; he readily promised
the divine presence to all black people who would stand up and fight in
that "glorious and heavenly cause" of black liberation.

Obviously such conclusions had never been dreamed of on the campgrounds of the South, in the churches of the North, or in the town halls,
universities, and legislatures of the white nation. But whatever those white
assumptions, Walker knew his own purposes, and his urging of a divinely
justified armed struggle against oppression was relentless. Calling upon
black people to fight openly against all who sought to maintain them in
slavery, he wrote: "If you commence, make sure work—do not trifle, for
they will not trifle with you—they want us for their slaves, and think
nothing of murdering us in order to subject us to that wretched condition—therefore, if there is an *attempt* made by us, kill or be killed." He
also added: "It is no more harm for you to kill a man who is trying to kill
you, than it is for you to take a drink of water when thirsty; in fact the
man who will stand still and let another man murder him is worse than an
infidel."[30]

As he saw it, the fight for black freedom was in reality a holy crusade.
Black resistance to slavery was sacred obedience to God; continued submission was sinful and risked God's judgment. Nor was Walker reticent
about his own views on the need for such judgment: "The man who would
not fight under our Lord and Master Jesus Christ, in the glorious and
heavenly cause of freedom and of God . . . ought to be kept with all of
his children or family, in slavery, or in chains, to be butchered by his
cruel enemies."[31]

(Had Walker read the words of Dessalines? A quarter of a century
before, calling for the blood of the white oppressors, the Avenger had
asked: "Where is that Haytian so vile, Haytian so unworthy of his regeneration, who thinks he has not fulfilled the decrees of the Eternal by
exterminating these blood-thirsty tyggers? If there be one, let him fly;
indignant nature discards him from our bosom . . . the air we breathe
is not suited to his gross organs; it is the air of liberty, pure, august, and
triumphant.")[32]

For those who needed a different kind of encouragement, Walker
offered the promised Messiah, a figure first raised up by Robert Young
and now militarized by Walker. Thus the passionate Boston radical prom-

ised the black nation that "the Lord our God . . . will send you a Hanni-bal," and urged black people to fight valiantly under his leadership, since "God will indeed deliver you through him from your deplorable and wretched condition under the Christians of America." There was no doubt about the warlike intentions of *this* Messiah, for under him, Walker said, "my colour will root some of the whites out of the very face of the earth." Indeed, David Walker was so certain of his God's judgment upon the evil of white American society that he foresaw the possibility of another route of judgment in case black people and their Hannibal-Messiah did not prove adequate. Here, his prediction was eventually and vividly confirmed: "Although the destruction of the oppressors God may not effect by the oppressed, yet the Lord our God will surely bring other destructions upon them—for not infrequently will he cause them to rise up against one another, to be split and divided, and to oppress each other, and sometimes to open hostilities with sword in hand."[33]

Did David Walker see signs and visions, as the waiting Nat Turner had seen them? Did such revelations explain the accuracy of his prophe-cies regarding the nation? Although he did not claim this sort of inspira-tion as explicitly as Nat Turner, Walker did reply to some of his critics by saying: "Do they believe that I would be so foolish as to put out a book of this kind without strict—ah! very strict commandments of the Lord? . . . He will soon show you and the world, in due time, whether this book is for his glory." So perhaps there really were visions; but there was something less esoteric as well. For it was obvious that Walker was driven to many of his conclusions not by kaleidoscopic images and voices whirring in the wind, but by a profound, unshakable belief in the justice of God, an element of faith which remained consistently present in the radical streams of black struggle. Confidence in that divine justice led to an assurance of divine retribution against America, which in turn en-couraged black struggle in the cause of that justice and retribution. At one point in the *Appeal*, Walker asked: "Can the Americans escape God Almighty? If they do, can he be to us a God of justice?" To Walker the central answer was unmistakably clear: "God is just, and I know it—for he has convinced me to my satisfaction—I cannot doubt him."[34]

But even more than this lay behind Walker's fiercely accurate conclu-sions. Not for nothing had he spent years of travel, reading, and research examining white oppression in America, seeking to clarify his people's situation. For instance, his observations across the land led him to refer again and again to the economic motives behind white oppression. Early in the *Appeal* he said that, after years of observation and reading, "I have come to the immovable conclusion that [the Americans] have, and do continue to punish us for nothing else, but for enriching them and their country." This he called "avarice." Pursuing the theme of white avarice and greed, Walker moved to conclusions which would appear repeatedly in radical black analysis. Thus he continually referred to whites as "our *natural enemies*." He conceded that "from the beginning [of international contacts between blacks and whites], I do not think that we were natural enemies to each other." But he quickly added that since the opening of the slave trade, the whites by their avarice and cruel treatment had made themselves the natural enemies of blacks. It was therefore logical for him not only to call for relentless struggle, but also to explore the possibility of emigration: he suggested Canada or Haiti.[35]

The use of such a term as "natural enemies" raised questions which continued to arise: precisely who were the enemies of black freedom, of black humanity, natural or otherwise? Were they all white Americans, thereby positing a struggle of white against black? Were some white Americans not the enemy? What was the role of the federal government in this conflict? Was it also the enemy? These were crucial questions, profoundly affecting the ways in which black people looked at whites as well as themselves, and the ways in which they organized themselves for struggle toward freedom.

In the *Appeal* it was not always clear where Walker was focusing his attack, and who was included among the "natural enemies." At times he mentioned "slave-holders and their advocates," but he also included Northern white racists, perhaps classifying them also as "advocates." On one occasion he pressed the issue to the critical point, saying, "Is this not the most tyrannical, unmerciful and cruel government under Heaven?" Generally, the primary enemies that he identified—with sometimes more, sometimes less clarity—were these: the system of slavery and its advocates in North and South alike; the American government, which supported that system and other aspects of white supremacy; and the white citizens of the country at large who co-operated in any way in the degradation of black people. To identify the government, the system of slavery, and most of the people of white America as the enemies of black freedom, was to put forward a radical analysis in keeping with the slave-ship experience.[36]

His sound and basic analysis of the American situation and of the human condition led Walker also to explore further the matter of black self-government which he had originally raised in 1828, and which Robert Young had put forward in a more spiritualized form in February 1829. Now, in the fall of 1829, Walker found no inconsistency in advocating implacable struggle on these shores, and at the same time preparing for self-government here or elsewhere. In the course of the *Appeal*'s powerful attack on the racism of Thomas Jefferson's *Notes on Virginia*, Walker wrote: "Our sufferings will come to an *end*, in spite of all the Americans this side of *eternity*. Then we will want all the learning and talents among ourselves, and perhaps more, to govern ourselves."[37]

Whatever the future of black people in America, by 1829 Walker had also developed a mature and fascinating sense of pan-African identity, tying together past, present, and future. He not only identified black people with the past greatness of Egypt and the rest of Africa, but went on to identify the bonds of future struggle. He spoke to all black people in America, especially those who "have the hardihood to say that you are free and happy." For him there was no true freedom or happiness apart from his brothers and sisters in slavery; moreover, he insisted to black people that it was "an unshakable and forever immovable *fact* that your full glory and happiness, as well as that of all other coloured people under Heaven, shall never be fully consummated [without] the entire emancipation of your enslaved brethren all over the world. . . . I believe it is the will of the Lord that our greatest happiness shall consist in working for the salvation of our whole body." For those who doubted and said such pan-African liberation could never be accomplished, Walker spoke out of his profound faith in the God of our ancestors: "I assure you that God will accomplish it—if nothing else will answer he will hurl tyrants and devils into *atoms* [!] and make way for his people. But O my brethren! I say unto you again, you must go to work and prepare the way of the Lord."[38]

Everything in Walker's mind led back to "the way of the Lord," the way of justice for the Lord's oppressed African peoples. This way demanded harsh judgment upon white America. Or did it? In spite of Walker's passionate commitment to black freedom and God's justice, the *Appeal* shows a certain ambivalence toward white America and its future, as in this ambiguous warning: "I tell you Americans! that unless you speedily alter your course, *you* and your *Country are gone*!!!! For God Almighty will tear up the very face of the earth!!!!" In his mind, then, there seemed to be some alternative: America might "speedily alter" its course. But was it really possible? He doubted it: "I hope that the Americans may hear, but I am afraid that they have done us so much injury, and are so firm in the belief that our Creator made us to be an inheritance to them for ever, that their hearts will be hardened, so that their destruction may be sure." Nevertheless, in a tradition soon to be firmly set, Walker continued to speak to the hopeless white "Americans," continued to call them to new possibilities. Perhaps there was no other choice, since black people jointly occupied with the "Americans" the territory which was to be torn up by God's judgment. Who could be eager for a judgment on America, when its land was filled with Africa's children?

Thus he spoke as a kind of angry black pastor to white America: "I speak Americans for your good. We must and shall be free . . . in spite of you. You may do your best to keep us in wretchedness and misery, to enrich you and your children, but God will deliver us from under you. And wo, wo, will be to you if we have to obtain our freedom by fighting." And what if the miracle occurred, and America decided that it wanted to change its ways, to seek justice and love misery, to let the oppressed go free? What would repentance require where black men and women (to say nothing of the natives of the land) were concerned?[40]

Here, as in the case of many of his later heirs, Walker was vague: "Treat us like men, and . . . we will live in peace and happiness together." What did that mean? What did justice and manhood require? Ending slavery was, of course, one obvious requirement, and Walker cited it. But beyond that, his answer was less clear: "The Americans . . . have to raise us from the condition of brutes to that of respectable men, and to make a national acknowledgment to us for the wrongs they have inflicted upon us." Perhaps that statement implied compensation to the African captives for the generations of unpaid labor. Perhaps it meant reparations in other forms. Perhaps it suggested some special role of honor in the society for those who had been so long humiliated by its racism and greed.[41]

At this point, we cannot be certain what David Walker saw as the proper acts of white repentance and restitution. Whatever he meant, his "Americans" did not care. As the three editions of the *Appeal* came rushing off the presses between October 1829 and June 1830, white men were in no way drawn to Walker's pastoral/prophetic calls to penance for the oppression of black people. What they reacted to in the *Appeal* were the sanguinary calls to black men, the ringing summonses to armed struggle against the white keepers of the status quo. For the "Americans," *that* was Walker's *Appeal*, and it constituted sedition.

Of course it was precisely because they were not interested in Walker's invitations to repentance that white people were forced to be frantically concerned with his summonses to divinely ordained rebellion. They were right to be concerned. In the months following publication there is some evidence that David Walker, in addition to distributing it among Northern blacks, made distinct attempts to see that his *Appeal* reached black captives of the South, sometimes sewing copies into the inner linings of coats he traded to Southern-bound black seamen, sometimes using other clandestine methods—including at least one white courier—to circulate it. Word came back from Georgia and Louisiana, from the Carolinas and Virginia (did it reach Southhampton County?) that the message was breaking through.[42]

Meanwhile white condemnation erupted from many sources. The governor of North Carolina, most likely mindful of the swamps around Walker's native Wilmington, denounced (and praised) the *Appeal*. He called it "an open appeal to [the black's] natural love of liberty . . . and . . . totally subversive of all subordination in our slaves." He was, of course, totally correct. More unusual was the response from Benjamin Lundy, the best-known white antislavery publicist of the time: "A more bold, daring, inflammatory publication, perhaps, never issued from the press of any country. . . . I can do no less than set the broadest seal of condemnation on it." Thus conservatives who placed the preservation of their way of life before black freedom, and liberals who placed the validity of their own solutions before black-defined struggle, were equally dismayed.[43]

Some of Walker's "Americans" were more than dismayed. Shortly after whites in the South first gained access to the *Appeal*, it is said that "a company of Georgia men" not only vowed that they would kill David Walker, but offered a thousand-dollar reward for his death. When Walker's wife and friends heard of this, they frantically urged him to go to Canada at least for a time. It was useless advice to David Walker. He replied: "I will stand my ground. *Somebody must die in this cause.* I may be doomed to the stake and the fire, or to the scaffold tree, but it is not in me to falter if I can promote the work of emancipation."[44]

Nor was he alone in this determination. Walker's message electrified the black community of the North and provided new sources of courage for those among them who saw no ultimate solution apart from the sword of the Lord. Even more important, perhaps, scores of now anonymous black people throughout the South risked their lives to distribute the *Appeal*. In Savannah an unidentified "negro preacher" distributed it after it had reached the city by boat. In February 1830 four black men were arrested in New Orleans on charges of circulating the *Appeal*. That same winter, thirty copies of it were found on a free black man in Richmond, Virginia. Meanwhile black seamen carried it along the coast at similar peril.[45]

If he was able to follow the progress of the *Appeal* into the South, it is possible that David Walker may have been most moved by its appearance in his home town of Wilmington, North Carolina. As a result of it, much "unrest and plotting" were noted in the black community. But there was also a great cost to pay. Early in 1830, a report from Wilmington announced that "there has been much shooting of negroes in Wilmington recently, in consequence of symptoms of liberty having been discovered among them."[46]

Walker had said it: "I will stand my ground. *Somebody must die in this cause.*" On the morning of June 28, 1830, in Boston's fair precincts of liberty, David Walker became suddenly and mysteriously afflicted, and fell dead in a doorway near his shop. Almost all of black Boston was convinced that the dauntless crusader had been poisoned.[47]

And what of Nat Turner? Did Walker's *Appeal* ever reach him as he waited for the proper sign in Southhampton County? No record exists of that contact, if it ever occurred. But the contact was not necessary, for Nat Turner had long been convinced that the God of Walker's *Appeal* had always been in Southhampton.

By the time of Walker's death, Turner had moved to a new home in the country, on the farm of Joseph Travis near Barrow Road. Legally, as such madness went, Nat was now owned by Putnam Moore, an infant. The child's father, Thomas Moore, Nat's last owner of record, had recently died, and in 1830 Moore's widow—Putnam's mother—married Joseph Travis. At that point she and the child moved with Nat to the Travis home and land. But wherever he was, working for whichever white person currently claimed to be his owner, Nat Turner knew that he had only one Master, who spoke in thunder and lightning and through the swaying, leafy trees. This was the Master who possessed his life, who had honed and harshened him in the wilderness, in the midst of the black community, in the movement of black struggle. This was the leader of the black angels who would scourge the white oppressors and pour judgment like a red bloodtide over the land. So Nat did his temporary work and bided his time, watching for the sign.[48]

> *Green trees a bending*
> *Poor sinner stands a tremblin'*
> *The trumpet sounds within-a my soul*
> *I ain't got long to stay here.*

The sign came in February 1831, with an eclipse of the sun. White men seeking a sign may have thought it marked an end to their bleak season of economic suffering in Virginia and North Carolina, but Nat found a different message: the movement of the last into their proper place had begun. And so, soon after the eclipse, he told his closest comrades that the time of battle and blood was approaching. With him in the initial leadership cadre were four men: Henry Porter, Hark Travis, Nelson Williams, and Samuel Francis. Evidently there was a group of some twenty-five who would form the core of the fighting force at first, convinced that others would be recruited as the struggle was openly joined.[49]

The Fourth of July, that prime symbol of white American contradictions, was chosen as the date for the uprising. But as the time approached, Nat became ill (were there fears or premonitions?) and the date was abandoned. Another sign had to be sought. On August 13, 1831, there was "a day-long atmospheric phenomenon, during which the sun appeared bluish green," and Nat knew that he had found the way again. One week later he met with Hark and Henry to agree on a final plan. The next night they met again, this time with several others; they agreed on their work, and ate a final meal together. In the dark hours of the morning of August 22, Nat Turner's God pressed him forward at the head of his band of black avenging angels, drove him in search of what seemed the ultimate justice: that "the first should be last and the last should be first." According to a black tradition, Nat's final words to his followers were: "Remember, we do not go forth for the sake of blood and carnage; but it is necessary that, in the commencement of this revolution, all the whites we meet should die, until we have an army strong enough to carry out the war on a Christian basis. Remember that ours is not a war for robbery, nor to satisfy our passions; it is a *struggle for freedom*." Whatever the words, this was the goal, and the river now was churning.[50]

They began at the Travis household with hatchets and axes, and no life was spared. At that point, with very few exceptions, all whites were the enemy. It was not a matter of "good" and "bad" masters; all were involved in slavery. And the children—even Putnam Moore—were the heirs. Temporarily filled with such resolve, organized into rudimentary cavalry and infantry sections, Nat's men continued down the Barrow Road, storming house after house, destroying family after family: Francis, Reese, Turner, Peeples, Whitehead, each in its turn experienced the terrible slaughter, not alien to the children of Africa.

At the height of the advance, there were apparently some sixty men in Nat Turner's company, including several described as "free." Together, in a breathlessly brief period of solidarity, they were marching to Jerusalem, Virginia, and their leader was now "General Nat." Once again a captive black prophet, wresting the religion of white America out of its hands, had transformed it and had in turn been utterly changed. Now, as an insurrectionary commander carrying out the sanguinary vengeance of a just God, Nat Turner took up the spirit of David Walker's *Appeal* and burned its message into the dark and bloody ground of Virginia, streaking the black river with blood.[51]

Apparently, he had hoped to move so quickly and kill so thoroughly that no alarm would be given before his marchers reached Jerusalem, and had captured the cache of arms stored there. As in the case of Gabriel and Vesey, the steps beyond that action were not certain. Perhaps they would seek out a new word from Nat Turner's heavenly Master. Perhaps they planned to head toward the swamps. There were even rumors that they expected somehow to find their way to Africa. But in the brutal light of August, it was still Virginia, U.S.A. The skies had not broken open, the earth had not erupted in divine power and judgment—and they were not fully angels of light. Indeed, as time wore on that Monday there was a growing sense of confusion, disarray, and sometimes drunkenness among some of Nat's men. Often the prophet himself seemed distracted, and rode at the rear of his troops rather than at the front. Added to these internal problems was the tragic fact that General Nat's men "had few arms among them—and scarcely one, if one, that was fit for use." So it was still Virginia. They had not moved as rapidly, mobilized as effectively, transformed themselves as fully; nor destroyed as efficiently as Nat had expected. Before they reached the road to Jerusalem, the alarm had been spread, leaping like fire from one blanched and trembling set of lips to another, echoing in the clashing sound of church bells across the countryside. The alarm struck fear in the heart of some of Turner's band and they deserted. Others, still on plantations, decided that the struggle was now hopeless, and decided to remain with their masters, biding their time.[52]

Nevertheless, Nat had already challenged Virginia, the government of the United States, and all the fierce and chilling fears which raged within the depths of the white community everywhere. So vigilante groups, militia companies, and the ever-present military arm of the federal government were soon on their way to the battleground. By noon on Monday, in the blazing heat of a cornfield, Turner's insurrectionaries had their first encounter with the white militia and the volunteer companies which had rushed to organize. The blacks were heavily outgunned and, after suffering significant casualties among some of their best men, were forced to retreat. Still, with less than a third of his army remaining, General Nat maintained his resolve to reach Jerusalem. But the path was blocked each way he moved, fear was rising among his decimated command, and night was now upon them. So they hid and prayed and hoped, while isolated members of their company were being trapped, captured, and sometimes murdered in the woods.

By the next day, Tuesday, August 23, it was hard to see how hopes or prayers would prevail. The countryside was swarming with hundreds of armed white men from surrounding counties, cities, and military bases in Virginia and North Carolina, and Turner had fewer than twenty rebels remaining. Even in the face of these odds, Nat and his men were determined to fight on, if only they could draw more blacks to their side. Before daybreak they moved to attack a large plantation near their encampment, daring to hope they would attract fresh recruits out of the slave quarters there. Instead, Turner's fighters were repulsed by a defending force made up of the owners and their enslaved blacks. At least one of the rebels was killed there and several were severely wounded, including Nat's close friend, Hark. That may have been the decisive experience of defeat. Soon after, in one last skirmish with the militia, three more of Nat's little band were killed; others were wounded and captured, becoming offerings to a fearful spirit of vengeance which raged through the white community. Only Prophet Nat and four followers managed to escape. Finally, before Tuesday was over, as the beleaguered black remnant force separated in desperate search for other possibly surviving companions, all save Nat were killed or captured.

The march to Jerusalem was over. The band of black avenging angels was crushed. Still, Nat Turner was not captured and was not defeated. That night he hid and hoped. As hundreds of men and animals searched him out he dug a hole in the ground and lay there, daring to nurture the dream that he might yet regroup his forces, refusing to believe that the promised time of judgment for Virginia's slaveholders had not come (or had arrived in some form unrecognizable to him).[53]

In spite of Turner's desperate hope, there was no regrouping for his troops. Rather, while the residue of the black men hid or were rounded up, the outraged, terrified white forces struck back in overwhelming fury. Estimates range from scores to hundreds of black people slaughtered, most of whom evidently had no intimate connection with the uprising. Meanwhile, the prophet-turned-general was alone in the woods again, hiding, biding his time, most likely wondering if there would ever be another sign. He remained in hiding, avoiding capture for six weeks after the attempted revolution. But the signs were not propitious. His wife was found and lashed until she gave up those papers of his in her possession, papers "filled with hieroglyphical characters," characters which "appear to have been traced with blood."[54]

"The blood of Christ . . . was now returning to earth."

His friends were being captured and killed. Perhaps, though, there may have been some comfort afforded him if Turner learned that many of them manifested an amazing spirit of courage and commitment, even in the face of death. Of some it was said that "in the aggonies of Death [they] declared that they was going happy for that God had a hand in what they had been doing."[55]

While Nat was still hiding, another black preacher—this time one named David—attempted to enter the radical stream. In Duplin County,

in southeastern North Carolina, far from Nat's place in the woods,
David planned rebellion. With other enslaved Africans he plotted an
insurrection for October 4, 1831, to culminate in a march on Wilmington. Were these some of David Walker's heirs, readers of the *Appeal*,
marching on his native city in his honor? Or were they, as the authorities
feared, part of Nat Turner's band of avengers? No one was certain, and
the insurrection was blocked before it could demonstrate the direction of
its flow. So even in Duplin County signs were not good, though the river
was clearly in ferment.[56]

Out of that ferment, while Nat was still hiding, a fiery letter reached
the town of Jerusalem, sounding almost as if the most stunning visions of
Turner, Walker, and every other black insurrectionary leader had been
put on paper and thrust into the Southern furnaces. Arriving from Boston, signed simply by "Nero," the missive proudly and provocatively
announced to the white authorities that a paramilitary organization of
black men was forming which would eventually lead hundreds of thousands of black people to take up arms in revenge for all the oppression
of their people. According to Nero, their leader was even then traveling
throughout the South, visiting "almost every Negro hut and quarters
there." Key cadre members were training in Haiti, learning from the
surviving leaders of that celebrated revolution. Everywhere in America
they were recruiting, telling blacks "that if they are killed in this crusade
that heaven will be their reward, and that every person they kill, who
countenances slavery, shall procure for them an additional jewel in their
heavenly crown." Had David Walker finally arrived in Southhampton
County, vindicating the hidden Turner and his scores of dead companions? Or was this simply another of those radical, bloody visions which
must soar wildly out of the river of a people's freedom struggle, expressing all the yearnings buried in the spirits of the mute sufferers?[57]

The silence which followed the letter offered no answers for the future
and no concrete hope in the present, least of all for the fugitive insurrectionary. Then on October 30, 1831, Nat Turner was captured. His
sign had not come; Nero's army had not appeared. Charged with "con-
spiring to rebel and making insurrection," he told his counsel that he
wished to plead not guilty, because he "did not feel" that he was a guilty
person. Guilt was not a relevant category for an instrument of divine
judgment—even if the last sign had not come.[58]

Perhaps he was sign in himself. Thomas Gray, a local slaveholding
attorney who produced his own widely read version of Turner's confession, described Nat in prison as "clothed with rags and covered with
chains, yet, daring to raise his manacled hand to heaven, with a spirit
soaring above the attributes of man." Then Gray added, "I looked on him

and my blood curdled in my veins." Turner's presence provoked similar terror and awe in other white observers, as well as deep levels of rage. Clearly some of that rage—and terror—had been spent in the postrebellion bloodletting, but lynching was still a possibility, so during the trial the court ordered the normal detachment of guards increased "to repel any attempt that may be made to remove Nat alias Nat Turner from the custody of the Sheriff." Nevertheless, when whites faced the reality of Nat Turner, other feelings and emotions seemed to overwhelm their rage. Indeed, there was something approaching fascination in the words of one contemporary: "During the examination, he evinced great intelligence and much shrewdness of intellect, answering every question clearly and distinctly, and without confusion or prevarication." Nat had no reason to be confused or to lie. Indeed, he did not hesitate to say that if he had another chance he would take the same bloody path to God again.[59]

It was on November 11, 1831, that Nat Turner went to the gallows, refusing to speak any final word to the crowd gathered to see him die, knowing that it was his living which had been his last, best testimony. Then, in its quiet, secret ways, the black community of Virginia and of the nation took his life into its own bosom and pondered it, just as some had done at the outset of his life. They continued to see signs, beginning with the day of his execution, for on that day, according to black tradition, "the sun was hidden behind angry clouds, the thunder rolled, the lightning flashed, and the most terrific storm visited that county ever known."[60]

> My Lord He calls me, He calls me by the thunder
> The trumpet sounds within-a my soul
> I ain't got long to stay here.

Perhaps, though, in keeping with all the irony of the history of our struggle, it was the terrified and ruthlessly driven white community which provided the ultimate sign of meaning for Nat Turner's movement. In the course of the massacre of blacks following the insurrection, the severed head of a black man had been impaled on a stake just where the Barrow Road, Nat's way of judgment, intersected the road to Jerusalem. The juncture became known as Blackhead Signpost and was meant, as usual, to be a warning against all future hope of black freedom.[61]

In spite of the white world's intentions, that macabre roadmark, with its recollections of similar slave-ship rituals and other bloody American roads, may have been the awaited black sign, fraught with many meanings: the suffering and death continually interwoven with the black march toward the freedom of Jerusalem; the white force of arms forever placed in the way of the life-affirming black movement. But even that terrible sign may have been transmuted to mean much more, just as Nat Turner meant more. Perhaps above all else it was a statement of the way in which all black people were a collective Blackhead Signpost for America. By the time of Nat Turner, that possibility was clearer than ever before. For white America's response to the black struggle for freedom might well determine the ultimate destination of its own people, moving them toward greater, truer human freedom, or eventually closing all pathways into a dead end of tragic, brutish varieties of death. So black struggle and black radicalism had no choice but to continue as an active, moving, relentless sign, forcing the issue of the nation's future, never allowing any of our God-driven, freedom-seeking, Jerusalem-marching fathers to have died in vain, pointing the way.

5

Many Thousands
Crossing Over

Two Decades of Struggle in the South (1830-1850)

It always appeared to me that I wanted to be free, and could be free. No person ever taught me so—it came naturally into my mind. Finally I saw that my case was pretty bad if I had to live all my lifetime subject to be driven about at the will of another. When I thought of it I felt wrathy at the white men. At length I said—this will not do—if I stay here I shall kill somebody—I'd better go.

> Henry Brant,
> Fugitive from slavery, c. 1850

David Walker and Nat Turner: the word of black radicalism had been made flesh. The life of the black community, the oppression of the white society, and the relentless, pursuing power of their God, had driven these two men deep into the river of struggle. Their entrances were made from strange but fitting places. From the streets of the city built by the slave-trading patriots of Boston, from the roads of the countryside claimed by the slaveholding patriots of Virginia, they had come to the river. They streaked it with their own blood, with the blood of those who stood with them and followed their heavenly voices, with the blood of the oppressors. Of course such thin red lines were as nothing in comparison to the over-whelming floods of Africa's blood shed in the slave trade and slavery, but it was more than enough for white America.

Actually, in the case of both these men, more than blood was involved, and America knew it. Walker and Turner had come speaking words of judgment, proclaiming news received from the living God, messages which white America found unbearable. Both men presented profound chal-lenges to American definitions of their white-owned God, questioned the white commitment to the nation's espoused religion, flatly declared that the American people did not know the ways of their own Lord. This was a black radicalism which delved into matters of great sensitivity to the divinely chosen Euro-Americans. It attacked the roots of their being. Indeed, it suggested that whites were chosen only for destruction, unless black people were set free.

Such words were bad enough on paper, quietly yet boldly insinuating their way into the hands and minds of black people, and a man like Walker might well be poisoned in white attempts to deflect the words. But Turner had transformed the Word and the words into a roaring passion, into hatchets and axes, into muskets and swords, into courage, into the blood of many free white people—and Turner was a preacher.

Predictably, then, one major white reaction was to attempt to intercept and oppose all such black messengers from God, who brought the Word to the captive African people of America. Shortly after the Turner insurrection, the Richmond *Enquirer* raised the alarm: "The case of Nat Turner warns us. No black man ought to be permitted to turn a preacher through the country. The law must be enforced—or the tragedy of Southhampton appeals to us in vain." From Washington, D.C., an unidentified, but not atypical, correspondent wrote to express a widespread white fear of the power of such independent black religion: "It is much to be regretted that many insurrectionary plots are instigated by fierce, ignorant fanatics, assuming to be preachers. . . . I foresee that this land must one day or another, become a field of blood."[1]

Out of such fear, a congeries of new laws swept across the South. There were laws prohibiting the captives from being taught how to read and write, and forbidding them to preach; laws insisting on increased white vigilance; laws interfering with black meetings—all of them testifying to the fact that similar earlier laws simply had not worked. Yet the strenuous legal effort went on. Just as on the slave ships it was necessary for white men to pour out great expenditures of time, energy, and money to keep the hidden black forces from springing into sight, so the white South remained constantly on its guard lest the rebellious black presence break out like fire, like flood, onto the decks of the society. So in Mississippi, shortly after Turner's insurrection, this statute was enacted: "It is unlawful for any slave, free Negro, or mulatto to preach the gospel upon pain of receiving thirty-nine lashes upon the naked back of the . . . preacher."[2]

But since when had lashes, even to the death, impeded the movement of the river? Before long, black people responded to the laws inspired by Nat Turner with an answer whites could hear without really understanding. Like so many black answers, it was disguised in a song:

> You might be Carroll from Carrollton
> Arrive here night afo' Lawd make creation
> But you can't keep the World from movering round
> And not turn her back from the gaining ground.[3]

Only when that last ambiguous line was repeated again and again might it become clear that "not turn her" was old Prophet Nat in disguise, alive on the lips of his people, still on the gaining ground.

So the prophet-general—like the fleshly word, like the river itself—was often hidden but always alive in the black community, especially in the South. Even where there were no actual uprisings, no battles in the road, no burning of barns and houses, it was yet possible to sense the profound disequilibrium building in the society, to feel the underlying, restless, eruptive movement of the river, gaining ground. Those who had the proper ears could hear and feel, in spite of laws and patrols and lashes. Young people seemed especially attuned. Martin Delany said he heard about Nat Turner in Pittsburgh, and it helped to shape the direction of his future. Harriet Tubman said she heard in Maryland, and pondered his meaning deep within her. Frederick Douglass said that he heard, too, and the knowledge almost cost him his life.[4]

This happened in 1833, when Douglass was still Frederick Augustus Washington Bailey, living in slavery on the eastern shore of Maryland. At sixteen years of age he was a tall, muscular, long-striding youth. Frederick had surely heard about Nat Turner earlier, when word of Turner's deeds ran like a flood through the black communities, but it was two years later that the knowledge became a threat to his life. Young Frederick had been attempting to organize a local Sunday-school class among the other black youths of the area, and freedom was already on his mind. A group of white men suspected as much, and they stormed the house of a freedman where the class was being held. They chased the other young people away and then, according to Frederick's own account, "They told me that I wanted to be another Nat Turner, and if I did not look out, I should get as many balls into me as Nat did into him." Although the whites were mistaken about the mode of Turner's execution, they were not wholly wrong about Douglass's relationship to Turner. Frederick was bursting into manhood, and was tied to Nat Turner by their common and insatiable hunger for freedom. But unlike Turner, Frederick did not see hosts of angels; his visions were simpler and more direct.[5]

In the year that he lost his Sunday-school class, Frederick had been sent to the farm of a professional slave breaker named Edward Covey. It was this man's task to see that the impudence and stubbornness becoming noticeable in young Frederick did not build up into a vital inner strength and courage that might challenge the system of slavery and its keepers. There on Covey's land Frederick often looked out at Chesapeake Bay and saw his own visions and thought his own thoughts of the way to freedom: "It cannot be that I shall live and die a slave. I will take to the water. This very bay shall yet bear me into freedom." Meanwhile Covey was doing his job. Representing the system of bondage, he was physically punishing Frederick in order to exorcise the spirit of freedom.[6]

After several months the white man had almost succeeded, but something drove Frederick beyond his own best resources to the point of open personal resistance. He was never sure what it was. Because of his later tendency to a respectable rationalism, he could not admit that his resistance might be related to the root and the dust from Africa that a conjurer had given him, promising they "would render it impossible for Mr. Covey or any other white man to whip me." Or perhaps he was simply remembering Nat Turner again. Whatever it was, the radical break came the day after he received the conjurer's gift. On that occasion, Covey came at him in a barn. In Douglass's words: "At this moment—from whence came the spirit I don't know—I resolved to fight; and . . . I seized Covey hard by the throat; and as I did so, I rose. . . . He asked me if I meant to persist in my resistance. I told him I did, come what might; that he had used me like a brute for six months, and that I was determined to be used so no longer. . . . We were at it for nearly two hours. Covey at length let me go." Later, when Douglass understood more completely the meaning of that wrestling in the barn, he said, "This battle with Mr. Covey was the turning point of my career as a slave." According to Douglass, the fight "rekindled the few expiring embers of freedom, and revived within me a sense of my own manhood." With that, he entered the river.[7]

It is important to note the path of Douglass's movement into the active struggle for black freedom. His first break with the system of slavery, an internal experience, had occurred earlier, when he dared to believe he could be free. That step was absolutely necessary, and cannot be underestimated as the essential preparation for any external struggle. In the barn, in the fight with Covey, the determined young man had taken the second step by offering a personal, open, individual challenge to white slaveholding society. And at least for the time being, Douglass had prevailed.

Though the precise details may have differed from individual to individual, Douglass's movement toward the struggle for freedom was typical of many rudimentary, defiant, individual eruptions which constantly shook the black community of the South. Not long after Douglass's battle with Covey, another young black man in nearby Frederick County, Virginia—one destined to less renown—wrestled with his own fear of the consequences and then courageously broke with the system of slavery. Later, Henry Brant said of his action: "It always appeared to me that I wanted to be free, and could be free. No person ever taught me so—it came naturally into my mind. Finally I saw that my case was pretty bad if I had to live all my lifetime subject to be driven about at the will of another. When I thought of it I felt wrathy at the white men. At length I said—this will not do—if I stay here I shall kill somebody—I'd better go." Expressing the same desperate sentiments as David Walker when he left the South, Brant made his own bid, and refused to stop until he had reached the relative safety of Canada.[8]

Such men, and the women who made similar decisions, were part of the activist mainstream of Southern black struggle. They made a personal break, offered a personal challenge. Although most of them did not follow David Walker, Nat Turner, or the countless bands of outlyers into more radical acts of challenge and resistance, the steps they took and the escapes they made were of great significance as acts of civil disobedience, as persistent, living challenges to white power. Indeed, like an unrelenting river breaking against the dams, they were central to the unmaking of the structure of white control.

While it has certain weaknesses, historian Kenneth Stampp's earlier description of that white system—of what was put forth as the ideal methodology for the making of slaves—is still useful here. Only in the context of such a methodology can the decisions of men like Frederick Douglass, Henry Brant, and their innumerable comrades be adequately appreciated and understood. For it was this slave-making system that they challenged most directly. According to Stampp, the slaveholders' methods for creating slaves out of free men and women, for developing slave mentalities from childhood, could be broken down into six related elements:[9]

1. The establishment of strict discipline over the captive African community in America; the development of "unconditional submission."
2. The development within black people of a sense of personal inferiority, especially in relation to their African ancestry.
3. The development of raw fear, "to awe them with a sense of their master's enormous power." (Of course, behind the power of the master stood the power of the local and national governments.)
4. The establishment within the enslaved person of a sense that the master's welfare was really synonymous with his own.
5. The creation of a willingness within the Afro-American captives to accept the slaveholders' standards of conduct as their own.

6. The development within the captive people of "a habit of perfect dependence" upon those who claimed to be their masters.

Inevitably, every black man and woman who began to think about freedom—every decision to protest, to resist, to break the chains of fear and doubt; every final tearful parting; every passage into the darkness of the future—presented a challenge to the system which sought to create slaves. Black fugitive literature suggests that the movement toward freedom was often like an act of self-conversion for its participants, like the coming of a new birth. Few persons expressed that sense more vividly than William Parker, who escaped from Maryland in the 1830s and later said: "While a slave I was, as it were, groping in the dark, no ray of light penetrating the intense gloom surrounding me. My scanty garments felt too tight for me, my very respiration seemed to be restrained by some supernatural power. Now, free as I supposed, I felt like a bird on a pleasant May morning. Instead of the darkness of slavery, my eyes were almost blinded by the light of freedom."[10]

Meanwhile, there in Maryland, Frederick Augustus Bailey continued his own movement toward this path. As was the case with many others, Frederick's initial decision to break with the system of white domination needed to be further nurtured. His spirit needed to be tested—perhaps like Prophet Nat's—if he was to go any farther. Still, he was moving, and by 1835 the determined young rebel had begun to meet with other captives to plan a group escape. Douglass's later reports on those meetings in Maryland provide great insight into the significance of the act of escape, and the tremendous psychic costs it exacted. These human costs must be added to any estimate of the significance of running away as an act of struggle and resistance.

Describing the inner conflict of his own small group of conspirators, Douglass said that they "met often, and consulted frequently, and told our hopes and fears, recounted the difficulties, real and imagined, which we should be called on to meet." Again, this was no isolated struggle: Douglass articulated the experiences of many thousands who had gone before him, of tens of thousands who would follow. Douglass said of his group: "At times we were almost disposed to give up, and try to content ourselves with our wretched lot. . . . Upon either side we saw grim death, assuming the most horrid shapes. Now it was starvation, causing us to eat our own flesh;—now we were contending with the waves and were drowned;—now we were overtaken, and torn to pieces by the fangs of the terrible bloodhound [or] after swimming rivers, encountering wild beasts, sleeping in woods, suffering hunger and nakedness,—we were overtaken by our pursuers, and, in our resistance, were shot dead upon the spot!" These were very different visions from Nat Turner's. Douglass said that they "sometimes appalled us, and made us 'rather bear those ills we had,/Than fly to others, that we knew not of.' "[11]

In the light of such inner struggles—which almost always precede premeditated, radical breaks with oppressive institutions and systems—Douglass said unequivocally: "In coming to a fixed determination to run away, we did more than Patrick Henry, when he resolved upon liberty or death. With us it was a doubtful liberty at most, and almost certain death if we failed." He was right. That is why the hundreds of thousands who eventually challenged the masters and defied the system, who tried to make the break to freedom through individual and group action, must be seen as crucial elements of black struggle in the South.[12]

Within that movement of the river there was significant variety, but the break with the system and the challenge to white domination were persistent themes. Men and women who poisoned their masters and mistresses had obviously made a decisive internal move, breaking with fear, refusing to identify the owners' welfare with their own. On many occasions those blacks who turned to the uses of fire, either as a diversionary action to cover the flight, or as a self-contained, purposeful act of destruction, were making similar breaks, similar decisions. The continuous testimonies concerning those enslaved persons who fought overseers, patrol members, and occasionally masters—fought them with their hands, their hoes, their wits, and their spirits—confirmed the constant breaching of the system, the refusal "to stand in awe." Meanwhile, suicide periodically re-emerged as a terrible final act of independence.[13]

By the mid-1830s, of course, each concrete situation of slavery, each locale of white control, evoked its own particular expression of black struggle. For example, in the same year that Douglass's group dreamed fearful dreams of freedom's cost, the very different situation of New Orleans caused some black struggle there to take more openly defiant though perhaps less effective forms. One historian, Joseph Tregle, wrote of the city's life in that year: "The whole behaviour of the Negro toward whites . . . was singularly free of that deference and circumspection which might have been expected in a slave community. It was not unusual for slaves to gather on street corners at night, for example, where they challenged whites to attempt to pass, hurled taunts at white women, and kept whole neighborhoods disturbed by shouts and curses. Nor was it safe to accost them, as many went armed with knives and pistols in flagrant defiance of all the precautions of the black code." Influenced by its independent-minded free black population, New Orleans was obviously experiencing a significant manifestation of the "bad nigger" phenomenon. It was a development which always held dangerous potential for the system of slavery, but in 1835 there was also the danger that this black challenge would do no more than win a louder voice, and more elbow room and privileges, within the system of oppression.[14]

On the other hand, in Texas that year the stakes of struggle were higher. Slavery had carried thousands of blacks out into that vast area which was then still a part of Mexico, but the center of intense political battles. The white settlers were challenging the legal control of Mexico, seeking ultimately to provoke war and have the area annexed by the United States. In the summer of 1835 there was great tension and confusion over the status of the land, and as usual the enslaved black people tried to take advantage of the situation, making attempts at armed insurrection along the borderline Brazos River. If the extant contemporary records can be taken seriously, the rebels sought far more than escape to Mexico and freedom—nothing less than control of the area. In the course of their planning, according to one informant, "the Negroes . . . had devided [sic] all the cotton farms . . . and they intended to ship the cotton to New Orleans and make the white men serve them in turn."[15]

Whatever the details of the plan, it did not succeed, and more than a hundred black persons were arrested, some beaten, and others hanged. Nevertheless, the conspirators had raised a critical issue, for they were not only challenging the right of whites to control their lives, but also claiming power over the produce which black hands extracted from the land. It appears that these black men and women were demanding the right to be free without having to leave the soil which they had nurtured and developed, without fleeing to Mexico, Canada, or even Africa. In the expanding kingdom of cotton the rights of blacks to the land, and to the control of their own produce, were issues which would not die.

By 1835, from the waters of Chesapeake Bay to the shores of the Brazos, certain patterns of the Southern struggle had been established, often as variable in their specific movements as the waters themselves, and just as unmistakably present. Flight and hidden resistance, arson and insurrection, outlyers and preachers of freedom, suits in court for emancipation, struggles for the land and its products—all these and more were part of the movement, building ineluctably, undermining the foundations of slavery. Then, late in that same critical year, in another disputed section of the American land, one of the most complex aspects of the struggle came to the surface again.

In Florida the strangely mixed waters of black and Indian liberation still flowed together. During the First Seminole War (1816–18) the efforts of the renowned Indian fighter and slaveowner, Gen. Andrew Jackson, had failed to break the dark alliance. Now, in 1835, Jackson was President of the United States. With the passing of time he had not lost his predilection for driving Native Americans away from their land, and had

so increased his holdings of black men and women that he could be
called "one of the biggest slaveholders in Tennessee." Meanwhile, not
only was Congress developing every possible means to shut off the divisive
and dangerous debate on slavery, but the old Indian fighter had carried
his preferences and policies with him into the White House, and had had
them approved by the national legislature in the Indian Removal Bill
(1830). Once again it was declared legal and constitutional to dispossess
the natives from their land, and to claim that land for the expansion of
slavery and its products.[16]

But the Seminoles of Florida would not co-operate. In 1835 several
thousand of them were still there, many driven from Georgia and the
Carolinas, and their black allies were with them. At that point, three
groups of blacks were in the Florida Territory: a small group of legally
free black people, concentrated especially in the Saint Augustine area;
slaves—the largest group—on the white-owned plantations, especially in
the Saint John's valley; and also—the most explosive group by far—the
several hundred Africans who lived among the Seminoles. Technically,
some of this last group were in slavery, having been purchased by Indians from Spanish, English, or American settlers. Most often such
purchases had been arranged to rescue the black people from the Europeans, and none of the slaves was held as mere chattel. But most of the
Africans with the Seminoles were self-liberated refugees from white
slavery, fugitives and the descendants of fugitives. According to a well-
informed observer, all the black people with the Seminoles were "thoroughly identified in customs and interests with the Indians, at worst their
favored dependents, at best advisers to the chief men of the tribe."[17]

The white people of Florida, South Carolina, Georgia, Tennessee, and
elsewhere were well aware of the continuing relationship between the Indians and the Africans. This was one of the major reasons they became
increasingly adamant in their insistence that the Seminoles be removed
across the Mississippi, by the use of whatever federal force was necessary.
Determined to rid themselves of the threat from this black and brown
alliance, the whites were no less resolved to claim for their own property
as many of the African people as possible when the Seminoles left. For
their part, the blacks and Seminoles realized these white intentions, and
had determined to stand their ground. First they presented armed resistance to any attempt at forcible removal; later they insisted on a guaranteed right to Western territory which would not be subject to white land
theft again, as well as an assurance of the safe passage out of the South
for the black people among them. The American government and its
white constituents responded to these demands with military attacks on
the one hand, and deceptive subterfuge and false promises on the other.

As a result, by December 1835 the Second Seminole War was officially launched in Florida.

In the struggle against the national government and the militia of Florida, Georgia, and Tennessee, the black allies of the Seminoles played a crucial role, for many of Florida's so-called Indian guerrilla bands were made up largely of blacks. This was the case with Chief Osceola's warrior group, for instance. These black men had already existed apart from the power of white oppression, sometimes for more than a generation, and were determined to maintain their freedom. Therefore, during the seven years over which the Second Seminole War extended, black guerrillas served and fought with impressive and fierce tenacity, as a contemporary white historian begrudgingly conceded: "The negroes, from the commencement of the Florida war, have, for their numbers, been the most formidable foe, more bloodthirsty, active, and revengeful than the Indians."[18]

During the war one of the most important roles of the black allies of the Seminoles was to establish contact, recruit, and gain information among their brothers and sisters enslaved on the white plantations. Two key men in this operation were John Caesar, who was second in command to Chief Emathla, better known as King Philip; and a man we know only as "Abraham," adviser to Chief Micanopy. These efforts were noted; in the summer of 1836 Maj. Benjamin A. Putnam reported to the Secretary of War that "many slaves have escaped to and joined the Indians, and furnished them with much important information, and if strong measures are not taken to restrain our slaves, there is but little doubt that we should soon be assailed with a servile as well as Indian war." Indeed, late in the same year Gen. Thomas S. Jessup wrote, "This . . . is a negro, not an Indian war," and added: "If it be not speedily put down, the South will feel the effects of it on their slave population before the end of the next season."[19]

The black and brown guerrilla movement in Florida was not "speedily" put down; it survived even slave-tracking bloodhounds imported from Cuba and it lasted several years. However, the struggle was isolated in areas of Florida, and was ended in 1842 without spreading through the South. By that time most of the Seminoles and many of their black comrades had decided that a move across the Mississippi was better than the ceaseless warfare of the Everglades. Of far greater importance, however, was the struggle itself, and the role of its black participants. Former captives who decided to break for freedom had once more joined with the oppressed natives of the land to offer a direct challenge to the military and political power of the American government and its states. They had fought long and were not finally destroyed. In the course of their struggle they made a clear and radical contribution to the river.[20]

In the struggle on the land, as in the early struggles on the sea, no voice was wholly lost, no contribution finally wasted. While the guerrillas fought in Florida, quiet, anxious voices could be heard in the woods in Maryland where black people had gathered. When those voices sang, "O Canaan, sweet Canaan/I am bound for the land of Canaan," another voice pierced the darkness: "I ain't got long to stay here." Then, having given the signal, having gathered for the last prayers and broken their fears, one more group moved northward in the darkness, entering the struggle in their own best way. Others did not leave, but waited in the South with unnerving patience after singing their portentous song:

> Gwine to write to Massa Jesus,
> To send some Valiant soldier
> To turn back Pharaoh's army, Hallelu![21]

Each situation of slavery required its own response. While the black guerrillas challenged the army, and the singing voices broke the chains of their internal or external slavery, in a place like New Orleans other blacks gathered regularly in "a makeshift church" and were arrested there, accused of having developed "the habit of repairing to this place for the joining in singing hymns and cantiques which was followed by sermons the subject of which was of the most inflammatory character." Fire was struggle, even when it burned only in words.[22]

Of course most black churches in the South were not, and could not be, such obvious keepers of the fire. Nevertheless, by the end of the 1830s black people had overcome the worst of the post–Nat Turner white reaction, and were now establishing and re-establishing their once proscribed churches throughout the South. For these institutions, and the African schools and benevolent societies which they spawned, were all elements of the struggle for self-definition, for identity, ultimately for a certain degree of autonomy. So even where there was no fire apparent, many of these institutions played their role, sometimes openly, sometimes in clandestine arrangements, helping a people to name, re-create, and re-possess themselves.

At the same time, there were many moments in that period of the struggle when institutions could not serve as a focus, when the turbulent river concentrated its being in a single solitary life. So it was in Tennessee in 1840, with a teen-aged youth named Jacob. He had been playing when his master, Robert Bradford, thought he ought to be working. Bradford threatened to whip Jacob and sell him, and was amazed to hear the boy say that "he was as tired of the master as the master of him." When Bradford tried to whip him, "Jacob snatched the whip . . . broke it up and ran off." He came back in a day or two, but still refused to be whipped. Then Bradford recruited two of Jacob's brothers to help break his spirit, to hold him while the master asserted his mastery. When Jacob heard this, he found a large butcher knife, carefully sharpened and concealed it, and waited.[23]

It was later said that "Jacob was not in the habit of carrying deadly weapons of any description," but obviously he had been pressed to the limits. When the two brothers seized Jacob and wrestled him to the ground, the young man pulled the knife out of his shirt, leaped up, and stabbed the white owner. As he struck, he shouted, "Damn it, clear the way!" In the terror and confusion the boy escaped, and Robert Bradford died soon after. Then, at the end of a search of several months, the black youth was finally captured in another state and returned to Tennessee for trial. When the defense claimed that Bradford's action had provoked Jacob's act, the court ruled as a court of the slaveholders must: "The Law cannot recognize the violence of the master as a legitimate cause of provocation." Therefore Jacob went to the scaffold.[24]

Neither the court's ruling nor Jacob's action was unique. Many lives had known that same final, bursting moment when injustice could no longer be endured; there were many echoes to his desperate cry, "Clear the way!" Jacob simply leaped out into history, representing all the rest, standing for the thousands who were forced to sharpen knives, wrestle with men and with fears, and strike for freedom at whatever cost.

> *Rassal Jacob, rassal*
> *   as you did in the days of old,*
> *Gonna rassal all night*
> *   till broad day light*
> *And ask God to bless my soul.*[25]

Beyond the countless individual acts of resistance and rebellion, black struggle in the South continued in all its other recurrent, often radical forms. In the same year that Jacob struck toward a clear way, word filtered through from Louisiana concerning a considerable number of black people who had been involved in large-scale conspiracies against slavery. Like Jacob, their immediate actions failed, and they were lynched or legally executed, but all such deeds fed the mounting pressures of the river.[26]

Nor were the slave ships forgotten in those times. Indeed, as long as there were slave ships, the battles to take them over continued. Among the best known of those battles in which America's black captives were involved took place in the fall of 1841. On October 25 of that year, 135 blacks sailed from Hampton Roads, Virginia (with all of its memories of

Gabriel, Turner, Ferebee, and more). The group was imprisoned on the slaving brig *Creole*, headed for New Orleans. Somewhere in the journey, perhaps even before it had begun, at least nineteen of them decided that they would seize this opportunity for freedom. Their leaders included Madison Washington and Ben Blacksmith.

On the night of Sunday, November 7, as they drew near one of the Bahamas, the insurrectionists attacked the crew, killing one man and wounding the captain, but sparing the lives of the rest. Remembering that the struggle was also one for self-definition, they seized all the arms on board, and with great coolness and presence of mind, took possession of all documents related to their slavery. Then they threatened to throw the officers and crew overboard, if they were not taken to an English colony in that area. On November 9 they arrived at Nassau. With the assistance of their fellow Africans on the island, who came out in small boats to surround the *Creole*, and in spite of many official American protests, the temporary black masters of the brig escaped being returned to slavery.[27]

But such relatively large-scale radical challenges to the power of American oppression were available to comparatively few of the Africans in bondage. Usually the struggle had to be manifested in more clandestine forms in the fugitive bands in the Everglades of Florida, the nighttime signals in Maryland, conspiracies in Mississippi and Louisiana, or individual acts of resistance in Tennessee. A plantation home burned, a plantation manager "shockingly murdered," a new insurrectionary plot uncovered, a black man shouting to an overseer who had hit him, "If you will give me a white man's chance, I will whip you like damnation!" Everywhere the familiar struggle persisted, developed, deepened. And as the Southerners, with aid from the North, built and refined the prison called slavery, everywhere the outlyers were always present: in the early 1840s they practiced theft and arson north of Mobile in Alabama, gathered in the swamps near New Orleans, haunted the areas near Wilmington in North Carolina. They were part of the unconventional radicalism of the struggle, part of the force which would help tear the building down.[28]

On the other hand, some black men refused to be hidden. They insisted that their challenge to white oppression be open, that their break with the system be clear. How else can we explain the group which, in 1845 in Maryland, appeared apparition-like on a road leading to the free state of Pennsylvania? They were there for all who dared to see: "a group of slaves numbering about seventy-five men . . . in marching order headed for the free state of Pennsylvania. One of the slaves had a gun, another a pistol, and the rest carried scythe blades, swords and clubs. They went

six abreast headed by a powerful negro fellow, sword in hand." Like the
men of Stono, South Carolina, like the silent avengers on Barrow Road
in Southampton, Virginia, these black men were marching to freedom.
The radicalism of their journey could be sensed in their decision to go six
abreast—not in stealth, but in triumph. *"Jordan's stream is wide and
deep, halleluja!"* Clearly the first battle—against the inner chains of
slavery—had already been won. Then—fifty miles short of the Pennsylvania line, near Rockville, Maryland—the second battle was joined, and
the power of white guns finally overcame them. Some evidently escaped,
others were killed, and thirty-one were recaptured. But none of them
could be hidden.[29]

Considering the realities of the post–Nat Turner period, it is most
unlikely that any such companies of renewed black men were able to
march openly from the South into the ambiguous freedom of the North.
Nonetheless, many did run and hide and run again to break the hold of
slavery's chain. In companies as large as twenty and thirty, in smaller
groups and families, and temporarily as lone individuals, they defied
white power and seized their freedom. As in the past, they carried clothes
and money, used stolen horses and canoes, and took the tools of their
trade. The flight of one woman from Tuscaloosa, Alabama, surprised her
owner, who said the fugitive was "very pious" and "prays a great deal,
and was, as supposed, contented and happy." But Fanny ran, and in
doing so remained true to her own best self, since she "carried away with
her . . . a Bible with a red cover," and was probably praying all the way
to freedom land. Were such seemingly unheroic actions any less a part of
the struggle? Prudence and calculated wisdom had always been more
truly African ways than flamboyant heroism. These people knew that
freedom seized quietly—Bible in hand—was freedom nonetheless.[30]

In the harsh, exciting years between the death of Nat Turner and the
1850s, these self-liberating blacks moved out of slavery by the thousands.
In Washington, D.C., a group of seventy-seven men, women, and children
sought to escape together one night by boat. In Richmond, Virginia,
Henry Brown "called out . . . a prayer to Almighty God, then had himself packed in a wooden crate for delivery to Philadelphia." In their
creative, desperate, relentless movement, the fugitives continued to shape
the mainstream of the Southern struggle. Many went no further than the
surrounding forests and swamps, creating microcosmic new societies that
remembered the ways of Africa. Others attempted to blend into the growing anonymity of cities like Mobile and Charleston, Richmond and New
Orleans, remaining within traveling distance of family and community,
receiving assistance from the members of that community in food, in
clothing, in love.

However, it appears that a large proportion left the South and made their way to the North and West. This self-liberating defiance of slavery involved tremendous additional risks and often exacted great costs. Most who made the trip north had no idea of the terrible pilgrimage to which they were committing themselves. (Sometimes, of course, relatives did come back to accompany them, bearing word of both the difficulties and the promise.) They knew that, if caught, they might be sold into an even crueler slavery than the one they had left. Recapture could mean severe, sometimes crippling beatings for themselves and their loved ones. It could mean maiming by the specially trained "Negro dogs." It could mean death.

The choice of running away meant leaving the ambiguous security of their slavery to venture into the stark unknown of the wilderness. It meant a painful hardening of their lives in order to consolidate the radical break they had already made within them. It meant being possessed by all the dreadful visions of Frederick Douglass and his band. It meant moving through the hills of Kentucky or Tennessee in the dead of winter, wearing the scant clothing of Mississippi's slavery. It meant never erasing from one's mind the terrible baying of the bloodhounds on a summer's night. It meant frozen feet and lost toes, tracing a path of sorrows which sometimes extended a thousand miles or more (reminiscent of a path which once led out of the forests to the African shores). It meant buckshot wounds and broken limbs. It meant the terror of all the worst visions come true, nearly drowning in the Ohio River, or wandering through the woods for weeks. It meant children—many children—buried in shallow graves by the wayside. It meant all this and more, yet the black flow out of slavery was never stanched.

Nothing in the melodramatic stories told by white and black abolitionists can convey the profound drama and courage, the overwhelming determination and hope, in the lives of these many thousands gone. They were the measure of the mainstream of black struggle during the pre–Civil War generation. Most often they were not conscious of their role in the larger struggle, but that does not diminish it. Their lives were concrete challenges to the system of slavery. They defied its power. They robbed its profits. They encouraged and inspired its opponents. In the widening disputes over their escape, recapture, and return, they drove the black wedge of their bodies between the two sections of the nation. Thus in their quiet courage these nameless masses not only seized their own freedom, but released a radical power and a turmoil in the river which would not be quieted until legal slavery was smashed in the holocaust of war.

Nor did they move alone. All along the way toward the freedom places they had fashioned in their hopes and dreams, there were points of refuge, conveyances of hope managed by other blacks and their white allies. Sometimes these points of refuge were no more than a clearing in the woods where food and clothing could be found. At times they were the upper levels of a barn, the fastness of a trunk, the false bottom of a wagon, the hold of a ship that now had black crewmen and was headed out of slavery. All the black people who offered their food and clothing, their homes and wagons, and at times their lives—all these, with white allies, were engaged in serious civil disobedience against the laws of the United States. Often this informal system of disobedience was called the Underground Railroad; in its deepest reality it was the underground river of black struggle.

In years following David Walker's death it would become clear that these varied points at which the black people of the North joined their own struggle most actively with that of the urgently flowing movement from the South were precisely the points where the most profound challenges to the white system of oppression would be mounted. For the two struggles were ultimately one, and could find their best strength only at the points of confluence, where the movement of the South met the movement of the North in the river.

> *Runs falls rises stumbles on from darkness into darkness*
> *and the darkness thicketed with shapes of terror*
> *and the hunters pursuing and the hounds pursuing*
> *and the night cold and the night long and the river*
> *to cross and the jack-muh-lanterns beckoning beckoning*
> *and blackness ahead and when shall I reach that somewhere*
> *morning and keep on going and never turn back and keep on going*
> >   *Runagate*
> > >   *Runagate*
> > > >   *Runagate*
>
> *Many thousands rise and go*
> *many thousands crossing over.*[31]

6

Strange River in Canaan

The Paradoxical Search for Freedom in the North

O Canaan, sweet Canaan
I am bound for the land of Canaan

Canaan was a strange place. The land created in songs and dreams of black hope in the South bore little resemblance to the cold and disappointing realities developing in the states of the North. Considering the usual relation of dream to reality, that was not surprising; indeed, in the light of the specific, equivocal history of this particular Canaan, the conflict was unavoidable.

By 1830, when official slavery had finally ended in the North, some 150,000 persons of African descent were living there. But what replaced chattel slavery was not freedom, justice, and equality for black people. Rather, the demise of legal slavery in the North had actually ripped the mask from the enduring blights on the land: self-righteous white racism, rapacious economic greed, and deep-seated, irrational fear of blackness. Although slavery no longer served its purposes, a society so fully committed to those terrible scourges needed to find some substitute arrangements for keeping blacks in their proper place. Some substitutes were necessary if Africa's children were to be allowed to share Canaan land at all, even in the barest physical sense of the word. With the end of slavery in the North, some whites were questioning the reason for a continuing black presence there. In that context, new legal and extralegal barriers to black equality and freedom had to be built, and new discouragements devised against the development of white conscience and humanity. By the time the most recent dark pilgrims from the South had arrived, the truly strange career of Jim Crow had already begun.[1]

It emerged in the antebellum North, not in the post-Reconstruction South. It began there at that time because the North was the first settled area of the country to find itself without a total social, economic, and political system for the legal control and exploitation of black people. As a substitute for slavery a varied, uneven, widespread system of discrimination, segregation, and often cruel repression developed, which was eventually called Jim Crow, the term apparently growing out of a black-face minstrel show of the late antebellum period. In the many places where black men and women touched Northern soil in their flight from the South, the details of the system were different, but the essence was the same: Canaan was by no means sweet.

Legally, Afro-Americans were quasi-free people, their precise status often depending upon the whims and prejudices of federal, state, and local officials. They had no secure rights which the masses of white people were bound by law to respect. Under the various land-grant bills, they were denied access to public land and therefore to important economic opportunities. They were pressed into the most menial jobs, and often pushed out again in times of economic panic, depression, or increased white immigration. White artisans and laborers usually guarded their realms of work against black applicants with a grim fury. In most communities, there were no provisions for black children to attend the publicly supported schools, but their parents were taxed nevertheless. In the vast majority of Northern states, especially with the rise of Jacksonian democracy, black people were systematically denied the right to vote. Perhaps Philadelphia provided the most vivid symbol of the over-all Northern situation: for many years, when black people sought to join the July Fourth celebrants at historic Independence Square, they were driven away by the whites.[2]

Beyond symbols, many black men and women were also literally hounded away from even their most limited freedom, for slave catchers and kidnappers continually used deception, and the co-operation of America's laws, to snatch blacks back into slavery, and even capture some who had never been slaves at all. But the agents of slavery were not alone in their attacks on black life and liberty; in a number of communities, Afro-American lives were broken under the cold and raging anger of white mobs who attacked the huddled neighborhoods and drove the inhabitants into new exile or death. All the while vicious, slanderous attacks on black character, morals, health, and intelligence were broadcast across the land from pulpits, through the press, and in the legislatures. When a minority of black folk, in spite of these terrible obstacles, continued to push their way forward economically, educationally, and professionally, they were persistently discouraged. Indeed, some white friends in the American

Colonization Society and elsewhere continued their attempts to rid the
country of its "problem" by developing their own plans and their own
terms for the return of free blacks to Africa.[3]

It appeared as if the slaveholder's formulae for making good slaves
were at work again, only on a different level. In the North, the method for
keeping Africans in submission was more systemic than personal. The
attempt to instill a sense of inferiority was carried on through the denial
of schools and jobs and land, through the vituperative verbal attacks,
and the constant, overwhelming presence of a normative white culture.
The mobs, the local Black Codes, and the federal fugitive slave laws
were reminders of white power. At the same time there were efforts to
imbue black people with a certain level of patriotism, and with the
middle-class white community's sense of moral uprightness. In subtle
ways, an unmistakable dependency was also encouraged, both by liberal
white abolitionists on the one hand, and by unscrupulous private employers and public officials on the other. Thus while slavery had ended
in the North, its undergirding forces of white supremacy, economic exploitation, and fear were firmly in place, offering troubling intimations of
the future of an American society in which all legal slavery would eventually be destroyed.

Canaan was a strange land. In many crucial ways, it had been easier
to understand black struggle in the South. At the most personal levels, the
objective there was to break with slavery and move to a land where the
institution was no longer legal, defying the dominance of the slaveholders
over black lives. In the Southern setting all white people often seemed
to be the institution's defenders; therefore, in the ultimate sense, all
could be considered the enemy. That was the meaning of Nat Turner, of
Vesey, of the depredations of many of the outlyers. Below the Mason-
Dixon line, then, the nature of the white system appeared in sharper
relief. The individual plantation or farm, the local community patrols,
the courts and prisons, the churches, the state militia, sometimes the
federal troops—all were a part. The opponents of black freedom were
out in the open, or so it seemed.

Matters appeared more complex in the North. Black people were free,
yet not free. They were their own men and women, and yet they were not.
They were protected by laws, yet many statutes left the black community
open to its enemies. And who precisely were the enemies? David Walker
had pointed to the slaveholders, their advocates and supporters. But
advocacy took many forms. Andrew Jackson was an advocate. There were
advocates in the halls of Congress, and silent, consenting supporters in
every Northern community. The advocate enemies were also the many
persons and institutions, including the federal government, who were

creating and condoning the complex system of Jim Crow, with all its debilitating effects. This network would seem to include most white people. Scattered as blacks were, comprising not more than a small minority in the population of almost any Northern state, how should they struggle against such complex, elusive, pervasive enemies? What were the goals? What did "freedom" mean in the free North? What did any freedom mean there, when the vast majority of the black community was enslaved elsewhere?

Undeniably, it was a perplexing, often exasperating set of questions, through which the total pattern of struggle was not easy to discern. Nevertheless, for those black persons in the North who determined to take up the fight for freedom and justice in whatever forms it came, there were certain rather unambiguous tasks immediately available. Then, as they directly confronted these more obvious responsibilities, they discovered that they were inevitably drawn into other struggles at once more difficult and more radical.

In the two decades following David Walker's death (1830–50), at least five clear responsibilities confronted participants in the freedom struggle of the North. First, the black community had to face the stark, immediate needs of their kinsmen who were repeatedly coming under physical attack from white mobs in the Northern cities, and who needed food, shelter, clothing, and public advocacy, as well as comrades in defensive warfare. Second, the black North had to protest and struggle against the less physical but equally destructive and more widespread systems of segregation and discrimination arrayed against them in every area of Northern life. Third, it was absolutely necessary to build black institutions wherever they could in the North, partly as a base for the ongoing fights against white injustice, but largely as repositories for the visions and hopes of the future. Fourth, black voices in the North had to be raised incessantly against the institution of American slavery, on behalf of their fellow Africans in Southern chains. Like David Walker, they recognized that their situation was indivisible from that of the enslaved community. Fifth and last, they must also identify, protect, and otherwise actively assist the black fugitives who daily found their way to the North.

As black people in the free states addressed themselves to each of these less ambiguous elements of their struggle, they found certain concrete answers to the puzzling issues of their larger situation, discovered new levels of struggle which often bore their own set of questions. Indeed, as they attempted to grapple with each of the obvious, specific tasks, they were often unwittingly building the basis for their own new community of struggle, defining its shape, scope, and directions. Thus when, in 1829 and 1830, savage white mob action forced more than a thousand blacks to leave Cincinnati—most of whom headed for Canada in desperation and great need—the determination of their Northern brothers and sisters to develop organized assistance for the exiles led to the creation of the National Black Convention movement of the 1830s. In turn, the conventions provided a crucial platform for the development of new leadership in the Northern freedom struggle, and made available a sounding board for much of the mainstream black protest of the time. Similarly, broad black participation and leadership in the organized national anti-slavery movement provided many of the same opportunities for growth and development, and also taught Northern black leaders some hard and necessary lessons about the inadequacies of certain white allies. However, it was the determination of a broad spectrum of black people to help their fugitive brothers and sisters from the South—even to the point of civil disobedience—which finally drove the Northern black community as a whole to its deepest level of radical struggle in the three decades before the Civil War.[4]

As long as there had been runaway slaves in the North and the South, there had been black civil disobedience on their behalf. By the 1830s, as the fugitive movement out of slavery grew in significance, so too did the black response. Every Northern city participated, but Detroit, standing as it did on the edge of Canada's relative freedom, was especially noted for such action. There, for instance, in the summer of 1833, the black populace's determination to rescue a fugitive was so powerful and organized that members of the apprehensive white community took up arms against them. Indeed, the situation was so volatile that the mayor eventually requested federal troops to assist the whites in putting down the defiant black action.[5]

Then, in the National Black Convention of 1835, one of the first and most important organizational statements of this civil disobedience was put forth. Meeting in Philadelphia, a city with one of the strongest black communities in the North, the delegates resolved: "That our duty to God, and to the principles of human rights, so far exceeds our allegiance to those laws that return the slave again to his master . . . that we recommend our people to peaceably bear the punishment those [laws] inflict, rather than aid in returning their brethren again to slavery." The language was not abrasive or militant, but appropriate to the uncompromising resolve. Quietly, black folk were moving toward radical action.[6]

As a matter of fact, the official resolution was a testimony to inner resolves which had already been made, to actions well begun before the meeting. Throughout the cities and towns of the North, black men and women had formed vigilance committees to organize their assistance to the fugitives from the South. These committees provided initial hiding places and often armed protection against the federally approved slave catchers. They made food and lodging available for the hungry and weary travelers, and provided comfort and understanding to those overcome with distrust and fear. For the ones who would not stop until they were off the soil of this bloody Canaan, they provided means of transportation to Canada, and sought jobs for the majority who decided to stay. All this assistance came out of a seriously embattled and widely persecuted Northern black community. All this placed that community in direct opposition to many of the statutes of the federal and state governments.[7]

At times, the black-dominated vigilance committees took defiant action which exacerbated the contradictions within the American slave system. Often when fugitives—or free blacks who had been falsely pursued—were captured by agents of the masters and brought before magistrates, the vigilance committees organized rescue parties. Such action involved a broad spectrum of the black community, and was sometimes quite humorous. For instance, late in 1836 a black vigilance committee in Boston organized such a rescue and precipitated what became known as the "Abolition Riot." Under the provisions of the Fugitive Slave Law of 1793, two young black women had been claimed as the property of a Baltimore man, whose attorney brought the women into a Boston court to secure the right to return them to his client. Just as the lawyer was addressing the official, "someone in the spectators' section shouted 'Go, go,' whereupon some colored people rushed to the bench and bore the prisoners down the courthouse steps and shoved them into a waiting carriage." One of the participants was described as "a black woman of great size who scrubbed floors for a living"; she threw her arms around the neck of one officer, so that he could not join in the pursuit. The two young women were never recaptured, and their black rescuers were never prosecuted, including the woman "of great size."[8]

The existence of the vigilance committees obviously encouraged many enslaved black Southerners to flee northward, and at the same time sharpened the disputes between the whites of North and South over the protection of Southern property and the prosecution of Northern blacks and their white allies for their actions. The struggle over fugitives, heightened over the decades by the relentless civil disobedience of individuals and committees, played a central role in forcing the system of slavery to its breaking point. Just as important, this organized resistance movement helped develop many black leaders: Charles S. Ray, Henry H. Garnet, Jermain W. Loguen, William Wells Brown, Lewis Hayden, John Mercer Langston, and others. All these men, many of them former slaves, moved from leadership in the vigilance committees to broader activities in the Northern-based freedom struggles, helping to shake the society's foundations.[9]

Among these vigilance leaders, one especially represented the critical importance of this work, and its costly contribution to the cause of black freedom. His name was David Ruggles. Born in 1810, Ruggles had made his way to New York City when he was seventeen. Although he drifted into many modes of earning a living, from selling butter to selling books, he resembled David Walker in making the struggle for liberty the center of his life. By 1835 the young and vigorous advocate had become the leading force in a biracial New York vigilance committee. In that year he paid a double price for his role: his bookstore was burned and he was almost kidnaped by slave catchers.[10]

None of this deterred Ruggles. There seemed to be a basic purity of heart, a singleness of mind about his devotion to the hundreds of fugitives who came under his care. His commitment was a radical one, both in its persistent civil disobedience and in the level of its sacrifice. He had no patience with those blacks who counseled prudence or expediency, considering these attributes to be "the offspring of obedience and cowardice." At times some of his more moderate colleagues were put off by the younger man's aggressive, outspoken ways, but Ruggles was determined not to be a slave mentally or otherwise. With dogged perseverance, he continued his work on behalf of the fugitives. Not only did he provide food, lodging, and friends for those blacks who made it to New York, but when slave agents apprehended them, Ruggles trailed them from magistrate to magistrate, refusing to leave the black captives at the mercies of a racist law. Also, taking another tack, he knocked without hesitation on the doors of many white families, demanding information on black servants suspected of being held there against their will.

Over a period of some five years, displaying an evangelistic tenacity which led to his being jailed several times before he was thirty, and which finally broke his health and took away most of his sight, David Ruggles helped more than a thousand fugitives to escape. So it was not surprising that in 1838, when Frederick Augustus Bailey—using an assumed name and borrowed identification—finally broke loose from Maryland and, lonely and afraid, ventured into New York City, it was Ruggles who took him in. It was Ruggles again who brought to his home his brilliant friend, the black clergyman J. W. C. Pennington, secretly to marry Bailey and Anna Muray, the woman whom Frederick later called "the wife of my youth." Finally, Ruggles quietly sent the couple off to New Bedford, Massachusetts, where the young fugitive could practice his trade of caulker in the shipyards. Later Frederick Douglass would say of this patron, "He was a whole-souled man, fully imbued with a love of his afflicted and haunted people." It was an appropriate and familiar testimony, a reminder that Ruggles was another of the black radicals who had been drawn to the depths of the river—and to the sacrifices those depths demanded—by the love of his people, rather than coerced into such streams by a slavish, vengeful reaction against the whites and their ways.[11]

When he met Ruggles, Douglass was on his way to add his own talents and his own complex soul to the Northern-based struggle. In a sense the two lives provided the necessary confluence of the Southern and Northern branches of the river. Once more, through the integrity of the Northern black response to the flight of the Southern fugitives, the two movements had been joined. Moreover, in Douglass's case, as with so many others, out of that encounter a new black man had been created, set free to enter the larger struggle. Indeed, within a decade this giant of a man would become the best known of a striking company of black abolitionists, bearing within himself a personal force that was immeasurable, contradictory, and often controversial, emerging as a powerful witnessing voice for a great and unheard assembly of his people.[12]

By the time Douglass arrived in New York, abolitionism was a crucial part of the black struggle in the North, perhaps its mainstream movement. By that time, too, white abolitionist organizations, springing from different roots, had established themselves as significant dissident elements in the life of America. Most often these white antislavery groups built on the base that the independent black struggle for freedom had prepared, for blacks had provided the first abolitionists, the first martyrs in the long battle, starting in the slave castles, on the ships of the middle passage, continuing on the soil of the new land. At the beginning of the 1830s there were some fifty local and national predominantly white abolitionist groups, and these often depended upon black churches for meeting places. In Afro-Americans like Charles Remond and his sister, Sarah Remond, of Boston, J. W. C. Pennington of New York, Robert Purvis of Philadelphia, Sojourner Truth of everywhere, and soon Douglass himself, the organized antislavery movement found many of its most effective speakers, organizers, and exemplars. Thus by the 1830s black people had provided much of the base and the heart for the abolitionist movement.[13]

Nevertheless, by the time Douglass arrived in the North, there were many troubling questions among black leaders concerning their proper relationship to the white abolitionists. The problems stemmed from harsh organizational and personal realities alike. For instance, although three black men were on the board of the all-important American Anti-Slavery Society when it was organized in 1833, this was a white Protestant middle-class organization with its essential internal machinery in white hands. From the outset men like Theodore Dwight Weld, Arthur and Lewis

Tappan, Elizur Wright, and James G. Birney molded and directed the organization and, through it, the organized abolitionist movement. Chief spokesman, curmudgeon, and embattled leader among them all was William Lloyd Garrison, the prophet, publicist, and courageous moral reformer. It was this combative practitioner of nonresistance whose weekly, Boston-based *Liberator* newspaper and whose presidency of the AASS set the tone and established the agenda of struggle—both internal and external—for much of American abolitionism in the three decades prior to the Civil War.[14]

No one could deny the personal courage and self-sacrifice of such men as these, and the women who worked by their side. Relentlessly, often at the cost of fortunes, families, and friends, they crisscrossed the nation lecturing, preaching, and agitating in the antislavery cause, facing white mobs that were sometimes murderous. But by the same token, no one among them would have doubted that their movement and its national and state organizations were meant to be white, under essential white control, and for the healing of a white-defined nation. In theory their dual purpose was "the entire abolition of slavery in the United States" and the "elevation" of black people to "share an equity with the whites, of civil and religious privileges." In practice, the second part often proved very difficult for the white abolitionists, which created a thorny set of problems in their dealings with black coworkers.[15]

On certain levels, of course, agreement among black and white abolitionists could and did exist. Many members of the two groups were inspired by the same Protestant revivalist religion and democratic rhetoric of the age. They could agree that slavery was an evil system which went counter to the justice and goodness of God, and contradicted the best insights of natural law. They also agreed on the cruelty and exploitation inherent in the system, and gave unrelenting broadside publicity to the many available examples of this ruthlessness. Together, black and white, they were at least rhetorically opposed to any talk of gradualism, urging slavery's immediate overthrow. To be sure, as time went on they found it increasingly difficult to agree on whether or not the American Constitution actually condoned and protected slavery, but that was not simply a black-white disagreement, and both groups were fully in accord that no constitution of a democratic republic *ought* to give such aid and comfort. But then, sometimes subtly, at precisely this point emphases tended to shift, and differences were more starkly revealed.

To a large degree, most white abolitionists saw slavery as a dishonor to their vision of the real America—the democratic, divinely led, essentially just America. For almost all of them, slavery was a sin against God, an obstacle in the way of His Kingdom's establishment in an otherwise generally fair land. (Of course some of the strongly evangelical Protestant abolitionists did indicate that slavery was only one of the many sins to be fought, in order to clear the way for the coming Kingdom. Among other evils, for instance, were intemperance, Sabbath-breaking, profanity, prostitution, and Roman Catholicism—especially that variety of Catholicism which accompanied the rising tide of non-Anglo-Saxon immigrants from Europe.)[16]

From this white vantage point, the fight against slavery was, on the one hand, a negative battle against an evil which was undeniably immense, but in most cases not very close to them; and on the other hand, a positive struggle for the honor of America, in which they felt great personal involvement, not only to right the wrongs of the present, but also to vindicate their divinely inspired forefathers—sometimes Puritans and Pilgrims, sometimes the Revolutionary leaders, often all of them. Among white abolitionists, then, the positive aspects of the fight against slavery emerged primarily out of their commitment to a special vision of America, its righteous origins, and its no less righteous destiny.[17]

The struggle in which the black abolitionists were involved was at once more personal and more profound. They were fighting against slavery but also, and more importantly, *for* the enslaved people. These were not simply "the slaves"; they were fathers and mothers, sisters and brothers, uncles and cousins immediate or several times removed. They were "our people," toward whom objectivity was neither possible nor desirable. Firm in the minds of black abolitionists was the conviction that the end of slavery would be the beginning of freedom for their people. Often they were far more sanguine in this conviction than they might have been, but the conviction was fully evident and operative. Black abolitionists fought for the chance to join unshackled hands with their kinsmen in the South. At their best, like David Walker, they wanted the body of black people to be one in freedom and self-determination. Even on the most selfish levels of the struggle, they knew that their own ultimate freedom depended upon freeing the black people in the South.

Although black abolitionists often used the rhetoric of the times, for tactical purposes as much as any other, the vindication of America was at best a secondary cause on their agenda. Instead the freedom, dignity, and self-determination of black people were central to the struggle. Even when they were most confident about the coming of a society of justice and brotherhood in America, these black abolitionists knew that it would be neither a return to America's bloody Eden nor an extrapolation from the white-interpreted Promised Land. Rather, the transformed society would have to be hewn out of the American experience as a new creation, extending in depth and meaning beyond anything that white men and women—or blacks—had ever known before.

The significance of the differences between the black and white antislavery workers became most apparent when members of the two groups faced each other in common tasks in the North. Many of the black abolitionists had been captives in the South, had made the courageous inner break with the system of white domination, and now presented something other than the popular image of the humble, grateful slave. Because many of the white abolitionists usually had no desire to know—in the best sense of the word—a truly free black man or woman, tensions and conflicts inevitably developed between them. Since many white abolitionists assumed that they were to be the saviors of the American society and its black underclass, they often treated their black coworkers with patronizing disdain at worst (or was awestruck idolatry the worst?), or at best as almost equal but clearly subservient allies of their white-defined cause.[18]

Martin Delany, an occasional black participant in the early biracial abolitionist partnership, was one of its most perceptive critics. He not only saw the dangers of black dependence on whites for freedom work which only blacks could do, but also, in those areas where whites could make legitimate contributions in the North, found whites a source of constant disappointment. As he reviewed his own involvement in this black-white movement, Delany pointed especially to two shattered hopes: that of equality with whites in the abolitionist organizations that these whites controlled; and that of equitable treatment and hiring in the businesses owned and managed by many of these same white allies. In both situations, said Delany, "we find ourselves occupying the very same position in relation to our Anti-Slavery friends, as we do in relation to the pro-slavery part of the community—a mere secondary, underling position, in all our relations to them, and anything more than this, is not a matter of course affair—it comes not by established anti-slavery custom or right, but . . . by mere suffrance."[19]

This was typical of the black experience with the Northern white abolitionist forces. It was a reminder not only of the complex ideological roots of a Martin Delany, but of white abolitionism's inability to deal with many black problems in the North. An abolitionism that was unclear about its own relationship to electoral politics found it hard to fight against the black disfranchisement which was sweeping the North at the time. An abolitionism deeply entrenched in the burgeoning capitalism of white America did not force the issue of economic exploitation and discrimination against blacks in the North. A middle-class, largely professional and mercantile white movement had little access to the white working class, and almost no leverage against its antiblack attitudes and actions. Men and women who were not prepared to examine closely the nature of their own deep fears and conflicts concerning black people could not easily deal with the irrational elements which surfaced in the responses of their fellow whites. A movement affirming the white-dominated origins and destiny of America was not easily stirred to consider the meaning of full black participation in the present. Moreover, those who believed in white-defined Canaans and white-controlled Kingdoms of God often backed away from the implications of an independent, self-affirming black presence in either. So the making of slaves went on in the most unexpected places in the North.

Of course, even with the best intentions and attitudes—and white antislavery leaders like William Lloyd Garrison, Theodore Dwight Weld, and James G. Birney often possessed both—no one in the late 1830s could forget two central realities in the struggle: not only were the white abolitionists developing deep divisions among themselves, but within white society they constituted a small and routinely despised minority. Unlike their black coworkers, they were not a part of the mainstream aspirations of their own community. On many levels, then, these white allies could be considered a burden, adding to the problems of black people in the North; even in their most helpful manifestations, they were themselves a beleaguered justice-seeking minority whose real influence is still questionable. In a sense, their most important role was as a signal of the problems black struggle would continue to face when it was allied with white men and women whose first, overarching commitment was not to black freedom, but to the past and future of white America. By the end of the 1830s, black men and women in the abolitionist movement felt these vibrations deeply even as they preached, lectured, organized, wrote, and engaged in civil disobedience at the side of their white allies. By the end of the 1830s, it was obvious that the visions and dreams which moved the brothers and sisters of David Walker and Nat Turner were most often not those which motivated the middle-class leaders of white abolitionism.[20]

By the time Frederick Douglass moved north, black participants in the antislavery struggle understood many of these issues, but were not always certain how to master them. Thus they continued to work with the whites, while recognizing the dilemmas that such co-operation presented. At the same time black crusaders like Sojourner Truth, David Ruggles, John Vashon, and Charles Reason carried on their day-by-day tasks of personal and group protests, the writing and circulation of petitions, the raising of one continual *cri de coeur* from hundreds of outposts across the North, constantly facing danger and death at the hands of hostile white mobs.

But beyond the mainstream activities, beyond the debate over the role of white allies, there were other black forces rising, some of which would challenge the white power of allies and enemies alike. One such force was the call for new and independent black organization; another, the black summons to emigration. Martin Delany personified both.[21]

In Pittsburgh, as the 1830s ended, Delany was still a young man, working in various ways to realize his hope of becoming a doctor, while wrestling at deeper levels with his truest sense of vocation. Delany had been born of a free mother in Charles Town, in what is now West Virginia, on May 6, 1812. His parents and maternal grandmother, deeply conscious of their noble African heritage, passed on this sense of pride to the boy. Then, when he was ten years old, the family moved north to Chambersburg, Pennsylvania. Nine years later, in 1831, the young man went to Pittsburgh, where in the following year he was one of the first students in a school established there by the city's newly organized African Educational Society. Lewis Woodson, a brilliant young minister of the African Methodist Episcopal (A.M.E.) Church, was the teacher.[22]

The summer in which Martin Delany crossed the Appalachian Mountains in search of his future was the summer of Nat Turner's march to Jerusalem. When Delany reached Pittsburgh, all the snatches of news he had heard on the road finally coalesced into the explosive reality of the black uprising in Virginia; from that time on, the meaning and power of Nat Turner's sacrifice bore deeply into his own life. It signified several things to him: a new commitment to the struggle to free Nat's enslaved brethren, to free Delany's own people of Charles Town; the steady rise of a spirit of fierce defiance to the white world; an even deeper sense of pride in his own burning black, almost ebony-hued complexion, and in his African forebears. But in the months and years which followed this crucial meeting with the reality of Nat Turner, what weighed most with Delany was his developing conviction that the fight against slavery must necessarily be joined to the positive struggle for truly independent black people and black minds. So while he continued to aspire to a medical career, becoming one of Pittsburgh's experts in "cupping and leeching," and occasionally practicing the primitive dentistry of the time, Delany could not rid his mind of these larger concerns.[23]

In its essential direction, Delany's thought represented a thrust beyond the black abolitionist mainstream. It appears that he became aware of this divergence while still in his twenties. He and his teacher Woodson, only seven years apart in age, had become personal and intellectual companions. There is evidence that Delany's struggles were really a part of a mutual search by the two young men for a sense of direction for themselves and their people. In 1836, when Delany wrote down some of his thoughts concerning "a plan . . . for the elevation of the colored race," it was probably the product of much discussion between himself and the articulate black preacher.[24]

The need for a national black "Confidential Council" was central to this early version of the plan. In Delany's words, such a body was necessary so that the claims of black people might be "presented in a national capacity." The Council would not simply serve as a revival of the Black Convention movement, but would be "a great representative gathering of the colored people of the United States." Actually, what he proposed was a national black assembly invested with certain planning and legislative functions on behalf of the entire black community. Such a call carried the seed of radical challenge, for it raised implicit and explicit questions concerning the legitimacy of the conventional white national institutions for the governing of black people. Indeed, moving to a most explicit level, in his early draft Delany also proposed that one of the first actions of the Council might be to establish a board of commissioners to investigate suitable locations for black emigration from the United States. For him, his calls for independent black organizing, and his explorations into black-directed emigration, were part of the movement toward a positive freedom which was the core of his larger vocation.[25]

Considered abstractly, there seemed to be no way in which Delany's proposals could be tied together in the movement of black struggle. The call for independent black organizing on a national, representative scale in the United States, combined with a call to explore sites for black emigration, appeared contradictory and illogical. But if one left the level of rigid abstraction and entered the ongoing experience of African people in antebellum America, it was not at all difficult to see the connection between inner organization and outward-bound emigration, as well as the relationship of both to the continuing fight for freedom. Historically, independent black organizing had long been established as a necessary element of all our struggle. In rudimentary forms it had taken place earlier on the slave ships. It was taking place at that very moment in brush arbors, isolated churches, and darkened cabins across the South. It was part of the black challenge to white control. On the ships as on the land, independent organizing was tied to the defiant black movement beyond the white structures of slavery. On the ships, men and women organized to take them over, to return to the homeland. When the black paths led from prison ships to prison states, they continued to organize, to plan for their break with slavery's power, for their movement into the swamps, into the cities, up toward the North, sometimes toward Africa. Indeed, organization was a testing, a proof of black capacities for "self-improvement," a denial of white rights to create the black world.

Thus organized struggle always carried the seed of hope for new beginnings. Whether toward Canaan or Africa or a temporarily unelaborated
"freedom," the best movement was always toward a renewed people and
a renewed, self-authenticated community. There were always black men
and women who considered freedom as the opportunity to conquer the
past of slavery and all its debilitating effects: people like Delany, who
recognized the brokenness of the black community and searched urgently for the setting in which healing might take place. Concretely, then,
Delany's call was a reminder that independent black organizing was in
itself an intimation of the future's wholeness, a suggestion that black
people might one day repossess their lives. Therefore it was not anachro-
nistic for that call to have as its ultimate goal the search for a new black
national ground of healing, renewal, and repossession.[26]

Although there was an intense and crucial logic to the joining of his
two major concerns, Martin Delany found the 1830s a less than propitious
time for their full development. Not only was he still young and relatively
unknown, but the Northern black community also had other options to
test, other lessons to learn. (For instance, because of firm Southern white
control within the American Colonization Society, black people North and
South tended to distrust any talk of emigration that sounded too much
like the ACS's plans for ridding the nation of its black population.) Almost two decades would pass before plans for the independent organizing
of blacks would develop beyond the lives of men like Delany and his
friend Woodson. In the intervening years, the black community was
honed and driven toward Delany's logic by its constant disappointments
with many of the white abolitionist leaders, and by the harsh movements
of American history.[27]

Meanwhile the self-confident, aggressive young man seized certain elements of that history in his own hands. By the fall of 1839, without benefit of a black Confidential Council (other than himself and perhaps a few
friends like Woodson), Martin Delany became his own Board of Commissioners in the search for the new place. Temporarily putting aside his
medical practice, he set out alone to see if he could identify those
sparsely settled sections of the North American continent most suitable
for emigration and for the creation of a renewed black nation. He headed
southwest and went at least as far as Arkansas, Louisiana, and Texas, as
well as to parts of the Indian Territory. There is also some evidence that
the intrepid traveler passed through several other Southern states on his
return—a courageous pilgrimage for a solitary black man still in his
twenties. He was potentially valuable property, and even though he had
a copy of his "free papers" with him, at any one of a hundred places
along the way he could have been captured and enslaved. Apparently

such considerations could not deter Delany, for he was in search of a new land, a place of new hope. But he did not find it. Instead, everywhere Delany went he met the ubiquitous white presence, with its passion for control and exploitation of nonwhite peoples, with its deeply impressed fears. By the time he returned to Pittsburgh in the early fall of 1840, Delany was convinced that his search must lead elsewhere.[28]

Ever increasing numbers of black people were looking beyond the boundaries of the white American nation for opportunities to be free men and women. They had tasted Canaan in all its white bitterness, they were experiencing all the hardships of the nationwide economic depression following the Panic of 1837, and now they looked toward Africa, toward the Caribbean, toward Canada. But those leaders who represented the mainstream struggle of that time were not committed to such searches. Instead, they continued to hope that America would somehow change, that slavery would end, that the status of black people in the North would be radically altered for the better.[29]

While Delany was still on his journey, such thinking was being put forward in New York City by Charles Ray, the editor of the *Colored American*, an heir of the moderate tradition of *Freedom's Journal*. In April 1840, Ray wrote: "While we know that God lives, and governs, and always will, that he is just and has declared that righteousness shall prevail, we believe, despite all corruption and caste, we shall yet be elevated with the American people here." Following this statement of faith— faith in the midst of contradictory evidence—Ray indicated the path he believed black people ought to take: "We believe . . . that it is our duty and privilege to claim an equal place among the *American people*, to identify ourselves with American interests, and to exert all the power and influence we have, to break down the disabilities under which we labor, and look to become a happy people in this extended country."[30]

By the 1840s, that was the essential quality of the developing Great Tradition of Black Protest, the mainstream line. It began with the same evidence that Delany was gathering in his travels. It presumed the existence of the same God of justice that David Walker had known. But it ended with a non sequitur, a statement of faith in the peaceful working out of the American situation, rather than in the announcement of divine retribution, the clashing of opposing forces, or a call for blacks to emigrate. At its most dangerous level, such an approach encouraged black identification with the goals and interests of an oppressive white society, an identification which had long contributed to the making of American slaves.[31]

Still, in spite of its pitfalls, the black protest-abolitionist position was in many ways attractive and powerful. It was the position that Frederick

Douglass was approaching in his steady movement toward the abolitionist camp. It was the ground already occupied by many black persons in that group, including the brilliant young ministerial student, Henry Highland Garnet. He too had been born into slavery in Maryland, but his escape had come sooner than Douglass's: in 1824, when Garnet was only nine years old, his family had managed to make its way into New York. Since that time his life had been filled with the excitement, terror, and high promise so familiar to black people in the North who asked more of freedom than a mere release from slavery.[32]

Garnet spent several years at one of the African Free Schools in New York as a classmate of Samuel Ringgold Ward, Alexander Crummell, James McCune Smith, and other men who would play significant roles in the struggle. As a young teen-ager he worked for a time as cabin boy on ships sailing to Cuba. Once, on his return, he learned with horror that in his absence his family had been terrified and dispersed by an unsuccessful slave-catching kidnap attempt, whereupon he stalked the streets in search of the would-be abductors. By 1835 Garnet had decided on a career in the Christian ministry; along with Crummell and another friend, though constantly suffering from a diseased right leg, he began a course of study at Noyes Academy in Canaan, New Hampshire. The presence of the three young black men was too much for that particular Canaan; shortly after their arrival the Academy was burned to the ground. When the arsonists seemed intent on attacking the house where the young men were huddled together, Garnet fired a shotgun blast which drove the marauders away. Nevertheless, it was necessary for the crippled youth and his friends to leave the area, and Garnet continued his schooling at Oneida Institute, a center for radical white abolitionists in western New York State. In the spring of 1840, just before his graduation from Oneida, he made his first major abolitionist speech at the seventh-anniversary meeting of the American Anti-Slavery Society in New York City.[33]

The Society was, of course, only the best-known among an extensive informal network of voluntary reformist groups spawned by America's white Protestants in their crusade to prepare the land for the coming Kingdom of God. However, by the time Garnet was chosen to speak at the meeting, the organization's unity was being rapidly eroded by the zeal of its most famous participant, William Lloyd Garrison, and by the unreadiness of many of his less single-minded associates to move in the radical directions which he deemed necessary. Indeed, the meeting of May 1840 produced a permanent split in the organized abolitionist ranks. Prior to that development, Garnet was called upon to speak in favor of a resolution which declared: "That all the rights and immunities of American citizens are justly due to the people of color, who have ever been, and still are, willing to contribute their full share to enrich and defend our common country." Garnet's speech was important for several reasons: it gave him an opportunity for significant national exposure within the abolitionist movement, and to exhibit all the eloquence, power, and slashing humor for which he was to become known. Also, the statement provided a background for his more famous performance (that word is used advisedly) of 1843. Most important, however, was the fact that Garnet's well-received oration revealed some of the most profound dilemmas of the black abolitionist position—cruel predicaments not yet resolved even today in the Great Tradition of Black Protest.[34]

The setting itself was indicative of the contradictions: tall, black, broad-nosed Henry Garnet, limping on his bad leg, pacing the platform in his peripatetic style, before a vast sea of mostly white faces, almost all of whom claimed to endorse immediate abolition of slavery. Yet many parts of his speech, filled with harsh, sarcastic, biting condemnations of slavery and its supporters, sounded as if addressed to a congress of slaveholders. At the same time the young black preacher voiced unstinting praise of the Puritans and the Pilgrim Fathers, referring to them as "our" forefathers, identifying them as "men who had no communion with tyranny and oppression." (No one had invited a New England Native American to speak of these righteous "forefathers," and the echoes from the holds of the Massachusetts slave ships appeared to have died away.) In the same generous spirit, but with somewhat more reserve, Garnet de-clared: "We would not question the sincerity of purpose, and devotion to freedom which seemed to wield the swords of most of the fathers of the revolution." According to Garnet, they too were "our fathers," but he felt compelled to "complain . . . of the base conduct of their degenerate sons." Did he include blacks there, too?

While standing on such precarious scaffolding, Garnet presented his vision of the black claim to liberty in America: "In consideration of the toils of our fathers [this time he was speaking of the black ones] we claim the right of American citizenship. Our ancestors fought and bled for it, but I will leave it with this assembly to decide, whether they fought and bled as wise men or as fools." It was a strange set of judges he had chosen, these contentious men who had found it difficult to decide even if their own contemporary white coworkers were "wise men" or "fools." It was a strange ground on which to stand, identifying with the purportedly "great" and blameless founders of the white nation, schizophrenically claiming as "fathers" both them *and* the black men they oppressed and destroyed. Still, Garnet pressed on to the inevitable peroration, putting forth the core of the black abolitionist demand: "With every fibre of our hearts entwined around our country, and with an indefeasible determination to obtain the possession of the natural and inalienable rights of American citizens, we demand redress for the wrongs we have suffered, and ask for the restoration of our birth-right privileges."

The tensions and implications inherent in Garnet's speech were part of the life of many black abolitionists. They affirmed the mainstream position of the struggle, identified with America and its traditions of liberty, and sought to turn these traditions to the black cause. Yet they also knew that the founding whites had not really intended their words, deeds, and institutions for such black causes. They identified with the white fathers of freedom, but knew that these had also traded in their black fathers and mothers, had been the owners of their captive African ancestors. The black abolitionists offered wartime service by their people as evidence of a deserving status, yet knew that black men should not have to prove their right to freedom by their capacity to kill in white men's wars. And yet, what alternatives did they have? It was the hard search for alternatives to the black abolitionist mainstream that drove black men and women into the more radical depths of the river.

By the time the meeting of the Anti-Slavery Society had ended in May 1840, the division in the antislavery ranks had achieved organizational reality as Garrison's opponents went on to create the American and Foreign Anti-Slavery Society. As with all such splits, the issues were both personal and ideological. The former largely stemmed from Garrison's radical positions and his merciless tongue and pen. The ideological issues were not all clearly defined, but the uses of political action and electoral politics, the role of women in the movement, and the relationship of antislavery to other social and religious issues were among the central questions dividing the two organized groups at the time. (Other divisible issues appeared over the next several years.)[35]

Whatever the issues, it may be that the most important result of the split in the white-controlled antislavery forces was the impetus it provided for black people in the movement to search for new alternatives. Along with a significant number of white members of the American and Foreign Anti-Slavery Society, some blacks began to investigate the possibility that the recently formed, abolitionist-oriented Liberty Party might offer the basis for a new alignment with white allies. But they found that a party committed to the death of slavery "within the limits of the national jurisdiction" was not necessarily committed to destroying white racism in America and working for true equality, beginning in its own ranks. The Liberty Party had been formed in April 1840, but by the fall of the year there was a conspicuous absence of black candidates on its state and national tickets. A black critic observed: "The professed object of this party is to secure the rights of *colored men* in THIS country; [but]

they have given no opportunity to the poor colored man to speak for himself, by placing him in the legislature where he *ought* to be heard with themselves. . . . In view of this state of things, what better is this third abolition *party* for us than either of the other parties?"[36]

This critic, Thomas Van Rensselaer, happened to be one of the black men who had remained with the American Anti-Slavery Society, and it would be possible to identify his views as nothing more than the opposition to electoral politics associated with Garrison and others of that Society. To do so would be to deny the presence of an independent radical black analysis of the black-white situation in antebellum America. Of even more importance were some of the long-range implications of Van Rensselaer's question. For he was asking his people whether they ought to depend on any white-dominated political parties (especially those not yet clearly committed to black equality) for fundamental solutions to white-created problems in America. Nor was that the only criticism Van Rensselaer brought against the black protest mainstream. For he also attacked it on one of its greatest articles of pride: the willingness of black people to fight for America. Late in 1840 there were hints of war with England over Canadian border disputes and other matters. To those prepared to dispatch black soldiers to fight for the American cause yet again, Van Rensselaer said: "The colored people have always been among the foremost to take up in defence of this country, and what is our REWARD? oppression! from one end of the country to the other." Therefore he asked, "Is it the duty of colored men, in case of war, to take up arms against the English?" His answer was adamant and clear: "Never! while we are denied almost all the privileges of the institutions of this country; and while [the] British government offers the only asylum for our enslaved countrymen."[37]

By its very nature, a position like Van Rensselaer's disturbed the ongoing movement of black protest, challenged its affirmations and assumptions, invited men and women to more radical levels of struggle. Thus it provoked response. Again, Charles Ray of the *Colored American* took up the cudgels for the mainstream abolitionist position. In response to Van Rensselaer's call to refuse military service, Ray wrote that he "was not disposed" to take up arms against anybody, but "if we were compelled to do so, we should stand in defence of our country, because it is our country, and because we expect, as people, to have our rights in it, and to share the destinies of it." Ray somewhat lamely added that such defense did not necessarily mean defense of slaveholding or "colorphobia." On this matter the Mexican War would soon prove the editor wrong, but meanwhile Van Rensselaer had hurled back his own proposed black policy: "Let it be distinctly understood from one end of the country to the other, that we will *never again* take up arms in defence of the institutions of this country, unless *all* these institutions are thrown open to us on equal terms."[38]

For those who believed that black freedom ultimately depended upon the ability of black people to win the approval of the white keepers of American society, Van Rensselaer's position was, and still is, a most dangerous one. But for those who were convinced that the children of Africa could not afford the new slavery of patriotic obedience to an oppressive society, there was no other honest path in struggle but this dangerously radical one. Van Rensselaer was saying that black people needed to make the country truly "ours" before it could be honorably defended as a black possession. That meant making America responsive to black needs for freedom, to black visions of a new humanity, to black aspirations for a transformed and just society—one that would include the original inhabitants of the land. To make such demands probably meant a long period of radical disobedience to white America's martial calls.

One of Van Rensselaer's colleagues in the American Anti-Slavery Society was Charles Remond, the handsome, spellbinding pioneer among full-time black abolitionist lecturers. At the time of the debate in the *Colored American*, Remond was touring the British Isles on behalf of the American Anti-Slavery Society. In the course of that trip he often put forth ideas which contributed another element to the search for black alternatives. Remond's ideas were also identified with Garrison, but they had a strong black tradition behind them. It was a largely mistaken tradition, but in those days of searching, all positions were possible openings into the radical stream and needed to be explored. One of Remond's standard speeches during that 1840–41 tour called for the dissolution of the union of North and South—a position which on the surface carried much strength and logic. Remond usually brought it forward in response to those who feared that radical abolitionism would press the South to secession. He said he would favor this, for "the moment when the American Union is dissolved, that instant the power of the slaveholders is prostrated in the dust. Hopeless, helpless, friendless, they become an isolated class of beings, having nothing to depend upon but their own strength, and that is weakness indeed. Then will rouse the crushed worm, turning on its torturer, and, in the fierce indignation of outraged men, the slaves will demand the right of measuring arms with their masters."[39]

As with so much of Remond's work, there was something compelling and exciting about this vision. It seemed an excellent example of a radical solution to the problem of slavery: to dissolve the union with slaveholders, free the black captives from the fear of federal intervention, and release them to turn on their captors. But as Remond would see clearly in 1861, it was not in keeping with reality, and thereby failed as an adequate black analysis. His solution seemed to assume, as did so many black and white abolitionists all too facilely, that the American Union consisted of a nonslave (or even antislavery) society in the North, constitutionally linked to a slave society in the South, and that such a bond could therefore be broken by secession or separation. What it did not face was that all America was a slave society, that between the white North and the white South the ties of sentiment, consanguinity, and capital were deep, that they would not be broken by anything less than profound and bloody trauma, if even then. The doctrine of "no union with slaveholders" refused to face the stark reality that white racism, white economic exploitation, and white fear all lurked together beneath the system of slavery and the system of Northern prejudice, and that this infrastructure would not be destroyed by a break with the slaveholding states. Remond did not take seriously enough the fact that the slaveholders were white, the government was white, the army and navy were white—that in the mind of its white majority, America was a white man's country. Therefore, even after disunion, it was naive to expect that in any armed struggle of black against white in the South, the slaveholders would be "hopeless," "helpless," or "friendless." In such a contest, the rest of white America would be their hope, their help, their comrades in arms.[40]

Remond's talk of "friendless" white Southerners could not deal adequately with such harsh realities as those faced just then by the beleaguered black population in the Northern city of Cincinnati, which white mobs had again attacked in 1841. Once more it was the black people who were friendless, and forced to rely upon their own courage, guns, and ammunition to repel the surging mob. In the end, they fell before the forces of white violence when the mob obtained a cannon and fired it into the ranks of black defenders. If this continuing, relentless, defensive struggle was what peaceful blacks in the North had to deal with, how would they fare at the hands of white Northerners in the event of a massive slave insurrection?[41]

While Remond's position could not handle the Northern realities, other lines of black thought did. When the white abolitionist organizations split, the call for independent black organizing activity was renewed in the North. It was time, many blacks believed, to revive and expand national and local Black Conventions, under black control. Even though the new appeals for black solidarity did not yet approach the radical vision Delany had espoused, this discussion of independent black organizations caused some people to balk. They considered it a form of self-segregation, claimed it would hamper the anti–Jim Crow campaigns, and warned against offending their white friends and allies. In the influential East, much of this thinking was focused among the black middle classes of Philadelphia and Boston, while its antithesis was centered in New York City, where blacks had recently formed the New York Association for the Political Elevation and Improvement of People of Color. Out of this latter setting, in response to the ironic black fears of all-black institutions, a writer in the *Colored American* declared in 1841:

As long as we attend the Conventions called by our white friends we will be looked upon as playing second fiddle to them. They will always form the majority of such Conventions, and the sentiments and opinions thus promulgated will go forth as the sentiments and opinions of white men, but when *we act* then they will see that the worm is turning. . . . We should enter upon the work with the honest conviction that we are doing what no others can do for us, and what cannot be effected under any other circumstances.[42]

The words and stance were those of the young veteran of the vigilance committees, David Ruggles. With his usual tenacity, he insisted on the need for organized, independent black action: "We have no right to hope to be emancipated from thralldom until we honestly resolve to be free." In his statement, Ruggles included a brief but crucial analysis of the black situation in the North: "We must remember that while our fellow countrymen of the south are slaves to individuals, *we of the north are slaves to the community*, and ever will be so, until we arise, and by the help of Him who governs the destiny of nations, go forward, and, like the reformed inebriates, ourselves strike for reform—individual, general and radical reform, in every ramification of society." With far less emphasis on divine intervention, but with no less sense of urgency, Ruggles stood in the tradition of David Walker. For him, black self-determination and black action were crucial. Out of that sense of urgency he called to his brothers in struggle: "Strike for freedom, or die slaves! . . . In our cause, mere words are nothing—action is everything. Buckle on your armour, and appear at the Black Convention, remember that our cause demands of us union and agitation—agitation and action." This was the Great Tradition of Black Protest at its best.[43]

Beyond the North Star

Testing the Great Tradition
of Black Protest

We solemnly dedicate the *North Star* to the cause of our long oppressed and plundered fellow countrymen. . . . It shall fearlessly assert your rights, faithfully proclaim your wrongs and earnestly demand for you instant and even-handed justice. Giving no quarter to slavery at the South, it will hold no truce with oppressors at the North. . . . Every effort to injure or degrade you or your cause . . . shall find in it a constant, unswerving and inflexible foe.

> Frederick Douglass
> *North Star*, 1847

In spite of reservations on the part of some black leaders, the struggle-conscious sectors of the Northern community generally heeded admonitions like those of David Ruggles, and black-dominated conventions were held again on local and national levels in the 1840s. Generally they focused on the hard issues of black life in America, attempting to participate effectively in the antislavery vanguard, opposing racism and discrimination in the North while constantly searching for alternatives to both systems of black oppression. A minority of whites regularly attended the black-led conventions, but it is clear that the work of the sessions moved in far more radical directions than was possible under white leadership. For instance, in March 1842 the black people of Troy, New York, came together to discuss the action required of them in the face of a recent Supreme Court decision which appeared to nullify the "personal liberty" laws of states like New York, thereby exposing black people even more fully to fugitive-slave hunters. With Henry Highland Garnet as chairman of the Resolutions Committee, the group announced that they were in total agreement "with the statement of Patrick Henry,

and solemnly declare that we will have liberty, or we will have death."
Although they quoted the white Virginian, the Troy assemblage had
certainly been touched by the spirit of David Walker—an influence that
Garnet would soon make more evident.[1]

The 1843 convention was held in August in Buffalo, and Garnet was
the main speaker. Western New York—Garnet's home territory at the
time—was a section of the nation which had generally developed a more
radical brand of abolitionism, both black and white. By the time of the
meeting there was a sense in many parts of the society—and certainly
among black people—that the power of American slavery was on the
increase; throughout the North the words of David Ruggles seemed to
ring within the black ranks: "We . . . are slaves to the community." As
a result, black men and women everywhere were being pressed to reexamine the precarious situation, to test their own commitment, and seek
out the next steps. A new generation of leaders was disturbing and challenging the movement of the river; Garnet, recently ordained as a Presbyterian pastor in Troy, was important among them.

Perhaps this sense of the deepening crisis and the desperate search
weighed on the young man's mind as he prepared his message. Besides,
in an angry, aggressive opening address, the president pro tem of the
convention had called for independent black action on behalf of their
freedom, "with the use of every means in our power." This prepared the
way for the main speaker. When Garnet began to speak, it appeared that
he had moved well away from the mainline protest position he had taken
in 1840. As he held his audience in thrall with another matchless performance, the black leader now seemed far more in touch with the radical
levels that Walker had plumbed. The very title and subject he had chosen
suggested it: *An Address to the Slaves of the United States.* For Garnet
had decided to address the brothers and sisters in slavery, and not the
blacks and their white allies in Buffalo.[2]

The religious ground that he took resembled Walker's, yet it was not
the same. In his *Address to the Slaves* Garnet told the Southern bondsmen
that they must resist slavery because the white-controlled system of bondage made it impossible for them to obey the Biblical commands "to keep
the Sabbath day holy . . . to search the Scriptures . . . and bring up
your children with respect for God's laws, and to worship no other God
but him." Therefore his central, motivating call was a strange one, placing an almost bizarre burden upon the black children of bondage: they
must seek freedom from slavery, because only as free men and women
could they keep God's laws and reap their heavenly reward. Garnet
warned the enslaved masses, "You are not certain of heaven, because you
suffer yourselves to remain in a state of slavery, where you cannot obey

the commandments of the Sovereign of the universe." It was within the context of this rigid evangelical Protestantism, with its clearly implied threat of divine damnation, that Garnet urged the enslaved black people to break their bondage. He said, "IT IS YOUR SOLEMN AND IMPERATIVE DUTY TO USE EVERY MEANS, BOTH MORAL, INTELLECTUAL, AND PHYSICAL, THAT PROMISES SUCCESS." The words were Walker's, but the spirit and the vision were far short of his soaring scope.[3]

Not only was Garnet placing the major burden for their slavery upon the bondsmen, but his call for rebellion had rather limited ends. Essentially, it appeared to include only a physical freedom from slavery and the ability to work for wages—and to keep the Sabbath day holy. For instance, while urging the enslaved forces to reason with their owners, he proposed a systematic campaign of noncooperation, a general strike. Promoting this idea, Garnet told the brethren to "promise the slaveowners renewed diligence in the cultivation of the soil, if they will render to you an equivalent for your services." There was no question of black land ownership, of black participation in governing the society they had done so much to create. Indeed, the best model that Garnet could supply was the halfway house between slavery and freedom which the British West Indies had recently provided in their system of apprenticeship. He advised black people to "point the slaveholders to the increase of happiness and prosperity in the British West Indies since the Act of Emancipation. . . . Inform them that all you desire is FREEDOM."[4]

Even so limited a definition of freedom was, of course, a wild radicalism in America in 1843. For the enslaved children of Africa to hear and follow it—even in the realm of organized noncooperation—would mean extensive bloodshed, which Garnet considered inevitable: "However much you and all of us may desire it, there is not much hope of redemption without the shedding of blood." Garnet in fact went on to call for armed insurrection, but only if systematic noncooperation through a general strike failed. This insurrectionary call was the context for his best-known and most incendiary counsel: "Brethren, arise, arise! Strike for your lives and liberties. Now is the day and the hour. Let every slave throughout the land do this, and the days of slavery are numbered. You cannot be more oppressed than you have been. . . . RATHER DIE FREEMEN THAN LIVE TO BE SLAVES. REMEMBER THAT YOU ARE FOUR MILLION! . . . Let your motto be resistance! *resistance*! RESISTANCE! No oppressed people have ever secured their liberty without resistance."[5]

In many ways it was a spectacular performance. Sometimes overly theatrical, sometimes immaturely militant, the speech nevertheless was a significant one, an indelible contribution to expanding radical thought in the North. Because of his eloquence, and his sensitivity to the state of the black community and its needs, Garnet, according to a contemporary source, "had his audience laughing or crying, almost at will." Still, after the laughing and crying were over, after all the overwhelming emotions had begun to drain away, a sober responsibility rested with the convention. Garnet had not called for action from the black people gathered there in the Mohawk Valley of New York. Rather, his words had been explicitly addressed to those brothers and sisters down in all the lonesome valleys of slavery. The *Address* was an invitation to the shedding of *their* blood and the risking of *their* lives. It was ultimately a call for *them* to challenge all the military power of the American government—without plans, supplies, or significant allies.[6]

Inevitably, the debate on Garnet's address extended over four of the five days of the meeting, breaking through other discussions irresistibly, forcing the delegates to prolong the convention by a day. For after the tumult and the shouting, they had to decide whether they would officially recommend such a course of action to their people in the South. They had to ask what it meant to be responsible in the struggle, to stand in the tradition of Walker. Understandably, there was sharp disagreement. Frederick Douglass was present, and complained with others that there was "too much physical force" involved in the content and manner of Garnet's address; besides, Douglass said, he was personally unprepared to instigate black insurrection in the South. After voting, appointing a revision committee, and then voting twice again, the convention finally decided not to send forth Garnet's *Address* as its own document. On one occasion, however, only a single vote divided the opposing sides. The pressures of slavery and white supremacy were building.[7]

Part of Garnet's appeal lay in the fact that everywhere black people turned, they saw an expansion of forces arrayed against their freedom. In the decade ending in 1845, three new states—Arkansas, Michigan, and Florida—had been admitted to the Union, either with slavery permitted or with severe restrictions against black exercise of the franchise; and by the end of that year Texas and its millions of acres had been added to the slave states, for the exploitation of black labor. Beyond Texas, Manifest Destiny coveted the wealth of Mexico and the great Indian plains of the Southwest, conjuring up images of a limitless white American domination which might extend even down into the Caribbean and South America.

All this was threatening to black interests, for everywhere the nation expanded it took along its racism, exploitation, and fear. Almost everyone it welcomed to its shores from Europe—and each year now they were coming by the hundreds of thousands—seemed to imbibe its racism as part of the rites of passage into this land of free whites. Hence the resolution passed by the German settlers of Mercer County, Ohio, near the end of 1846: "*Resolved* That the blacks of this county be, and they are hereby respectfully requested to leave the country [*sic*] on or before the first day of March, 1847; and in the case of their neglect or refusal to comply with this request, we pledge ourselves to *remove them, peacefully if we can, forcibly if we must.*" As an example of the peaceful means envisaged at the outset, they passed another resolution: "That we who are here assembled, pledge ourselves not to employ or trade with any black or mulatto person, in any manner whatever, or permit them to have any grinding done at our mills, after the first day of January next." Beyond threatening words, beyond economic strangulation, the final pledge made the immigrants' position brutally clear: "We will resist the settlement of blacks and Mulattoes in this country to the full extent of our means, the bayonet not excepted." Ohio's German settlers had discovered a typical white freedom in America and fully exercised it.[8]

These Northern signs were obvious enough for de Tocqueville to have written as early as the 1830s that "the prejudice of race appears to be stronger in the states that have abolished slavery than in those where it still exists; and nowhere is it so intolerant as in those states where servitude has never been known." Of course, if such signs were clear to a perceptive European visitor, they were like a searing white ball of light to the alien black natives of the land, and there was no hiding place. So each day black people faced more fully the need to break down the gates, to smash the dams, to defeat the slave power in the Northern white community, to rise toward freedom. But the way was unclear.[9]

According to a black tradition, this highly charged time of uncertainty led to the formation of an underground force of black guerrilla fighters. In 1846 twelve young black men were said to have gathered in Saint Louis to form a group called the Knights of Tabor. Following their own Biblical interpretations, members of the black community later identified them as men "who like the Twelve Apostles, commenced the great work of Liberty," undertaking to organize a full-scale liberation army to be called the Knights of Liberty. They allowed themselves a decade for preparation and then, if necessary, would strike for black freedom sometime after 1856. To date, however, only the oral traditions trace their history; for the time, they disappeared from the surface of events.[10]

Whatever their potential, such an obscure incipient force could not have dispelled the brutal reality then facing the black community. The situation was still cruel and cloudy, and no one exemplified the complexities and confusions of the Northern mainstream more poignantly than Frederick Douglass. It had proven impossible for him to work many years at his caulking trade in the shipyards, for he had seen Ruggles and Pennington, had heard Remond and Garrison, so that before long his true vocation had grasped him. Having joined the organized antislavery movement in the early 1840s, Douglass first became its prime traveling exhibit of the powerful potential for freedom existing among enslaved black people. Then, increasingly, he stretched out to become his own man, to possess his own fullest identity. Soon his powerful, towering frame and his thundering, eloquent voice were known across the North, as he toured the lecture circuit of the American Anti-Slavery Society, participated in the activities of other elements of the white-dominated reformist network, and attended the Black Conventions.[11]

But like so many of his lesser-known fellow fugitives from slavery, Douglass had discovered that freedom was elusive, that the struggle led through many deceptive ways. It was one thing to overcome the fears of escape, to wrestle with a Covey, to plan and fail and then finally succeed in the physical break with bondage. Those battles were clear and well defined. It was another matter to move beyond the state of the fugitive in the South to that of a quasi-free black man in the North, and even more difficult to ponder and understand how all the bondsmen, fugitives, and semifree black people would one day enter the full freedom of the children of God.

Douglass's life vividly illustrated this predicament. In his antislavery travels he quickly discovered that Northern segregation presented very real and harrowing challenges which at times had to be fought with the same energy that combating a Covey had demanded. On railroad cars, in carriages, on steamships and canal boats he was constantly, literally fighting for his right to sit, to ride, to stand, to occupy the same area as his white companions. On various occasions he was physically thrown off public conveyances, sometimes showered with rocks or rotten eggs at speaking engagements, and periodically threatened with murder. All this was part of the struggle for freedom in the North, and Douglass remained in the heart of it.

Then in 1846 the popular black abolitionist made his first voyage on what had become a regular antislavery itinerary to the British Isles, and became enmeshed in a far more complicated aspect of the dilemma of freedom. England's ambiguous act of emancipation and its full array of Protestant reformist groups made it appear a natural ally to the American abolitionist cause. (The ritual journey, regularly filled with admiring corteges of white English female supporters, was often deceiving and distracting—to say the least—for black male abolitionists.) Like others before him, Frederick Douglass went there as a representative of the

American Anti-Slavery Society, but even more as a striking human symbol of the great cause of black freedom. Consequently, many persons
on both sides of the Atlantic were troubled and deeply disappointed when
Douglass, still legally a fugitive, yielded to his understandable fears of
re-enslavement and agreed to allow some of his English supporters to raise
the necessary funds to pay the Maryland slaveowner, Thomas Auld, for
the freedom of Frederick Augustus Washington Bailey.

It was a questionable move—one which some abolitionists claimed actually justified and gave legitimacy to slavery; when reported in America,
it exposed the proud black spokesman to withering attacks. In the course
of a rather weak defense, Douglass said that under American law Auld
still had the right to seize him at the dock if he did not have legal
emancipation papers, in which case the white slaveowner would most
likely be "aided by the American government to bind the fetter and drag
me from my family." So while Douglass justified his need for legal purchase papers, he also declared that such federal complicity in any attempt
to capture him would simply offer clear "proof of the plundering character of the American government . . . stamping the nation in whose name
the deed was done, as a great aggregation of hypocrites, thieves, and
liars." From that he drew a logical, profound, and radical conclusion:
"The contest which I have to wage is against the government of the
United States."[12]

Here again, as with Van Rensselaer and Remond, one could identify
such a radical position simply as a part of Douglass's "Garrisonian
phase," but this would fail to convey the progress—the spurting, suddenly
clarifying leaps—of black radical analysis. Here, in 1846, Douglass had
seen through to the critical core of the issue, but it was apparent that he
could not remain there, could not follow the logical thrust of an insight
which identified the government of the United States as possibly the
central enemy of freedom-bound black people.

Instead, by the time he returned to the country and appeared at the
1847 National Convention of Colored People in Troy, New York, the
legally free man was again identifying with the mainstream position that
left the enemy unnamed and ambiguous. At the convention Douglass
sponsored a resolution which said:

Resolved, that our only hope for peaceful emancipation in this land is based
on a firm, devoted and unceasing assertion of our rights and a full, free and
determined exposure of our multiplied wrongs.

Resolved, that in the language of inspired wisdom, there shall be no peace
to the wicked, and that this guilty nation shall have no peace, and that we will
do all we can to agitate! *Agitate*!! AGITATE!!! till our rights are restored and
our brethren are redeemed from their cruel chains.

Struggle waged against a "guilty nation" might tend to be less precise, more oratorical in nature, than one against "the government of the United States." It might also be safer.[13]

Still, it was impossible to deny the inspirational appeal of this black agitational approach. Later in the year, when Douglass published the first issue of his newspaper the *North Star*, the Great Tradition of Black Protest was put forth in what would become a classic and exciting format. The new editor declared:

We solemnly dedicate the *North Star* to the cause of our long oppressed and plundered fellow countrymen. . . . It shall fearlessly assert your rights, faithfully proclaim your wrongs and earnestly demand for you instant and even-handed justice. Giving no quarter to slavery at the South, it will hold no truce with oppressors at the North. While it shall boldly advocate emancipation for our enslaved brethren, it will omit no opportunity to gain for the nominally free complete enfranchisement. Every effort to injure or degrade you or your cause . . . shall find in it a constant, unswerving and inflexible foe.

We shall energetically assail the ramparts of Slavery and Prejudice, be they composed of church or state, and seek the destruction of every refuge of lies, under which tyranny may aim to conceal and protect itself.[14]

In the thirtieth year of his life, and in the ninth year of his physical freedom, Frederick Douglass had surged forward against the advice of his closest white advisers to establish in print an authentic black voice. In doing so, he immediately set forth most of the major elements of the Great Tradition of Black Protest—a tradition which he had inherited, one which he would strengthen and embellish, and one which would move far beyond his own long day to inform the struggle for more than a century. In their sheer energy, the ideas leaped from the newsprint: the proclamation and exposure of wrongs, the assertion of rights, the demands for justice *now*, the boldness of advocacy, the constancy of defense, the fearless assaults, the commitment to the destruction of all refuges of lies, and everywhere—unceasingly—the promise to agitate. The only thing missing was the pledge to defend America, come what may.

It was *Freedom's Journal* revived and moved forward, but it was far more as well: pure Douglass. A basic, vital force constantly surged forth —a language, a rhetoric of action and warfare. But the action, the militancy, and the warfare were essentially confined to the word and focused in Douglass, the spokesman for the people; they were not expressed in a call for ubiquitous movement *by* the people, for self-liberating deeds emerging out of the radical presence of the total community. To call for and organize widespread resistance and disobedience would have taken Douglass and his *North Star* into the depths of black radicalism. But the time had not yet come, the time had not returned. Nevertheless, it must be clear that when such *North Stars* appear in situations where men have agreed to be silent in their dark deeds, where honest protest and advocacy of rights and justice come at great personal and communal cost, and where the word itself challenges white domination, then the Great Tradition carries important radical weight. Often Douglass's words carried that weight. Often his life took the weight, as he transformed his own words of protest into deeds, facing mobs, braving harassment and attacks and threats of death.[15]

Douglass struggled, yet his radical insight of 1846 was not carried forward, was not immediately focused. Why not? Partly because he was not prepared for the outcome of the logic of 1846, not ready to meet the federal government as enemy. Perhaps, though, his *Narrative* suggests something about the nature of those times, that man, and the elements of black struggle. In the *Narrative* Douglass refers often to his belief in a "divine Providence," a "kind Providence" which, he said, "has ever . . . attended me and marked my life with so many favors." He credited this Providence, this mysterious divine opening of the blank walls of history, with many developments which eventually led him out of slavery: "From my earliest recollection, I date the entertainment of a deep conviction that slavery would not always be able to hold me within its foul embrace; and in the darkest hours of my career in slavery, this living word of faith and spirit of hope departed not from me, but remained like ministering angels to cheer me through the gloom. This good spirit was from God."[16]

These were not idle words, nor written simply to appeal to his evangelical Protestant readers. Douglass was not deeply involved in organized religion, neither while in slavery nor as a free man, but he did imbibe intensely of the nineteenth-century understanding of Providence, of the rational, loving, guiding hand of the Divine. This religious conviction was of great importance, for it brought to his thought and life what might be called a radical hope, a strange and mysterious faith which was a two-edged sword. On the one hand, it had a profoundly strengthening effect, allowing Douglass to maintain himself in the midst of discouraging realities. But it also held the possibility of blinding him to the ultimate harshness of those realties, decreasing the sense of need to face them and organize against them with more than hope and faith, without losing either. Everywhere the Great Tradition carried in itself much of this religiously inspired hope, sometimes desperately, sometimes with great quietness of spirit. And everywhere, as with Douglass, it was both strength and weakness, for it often caused black men and women to avoid the deepest levels of the river, allowing them to draw back from the harshening that a Nat Turner or a Black Jacob knew, encouraging them to believe that emancipation in a corrupt land could come without the shedding of blood, without direct confrontation with "a great aggregation of hypocrites, thieves and liars" and their government.

Perhaps Douglass was admitting the presence of a softer, more uncertain side to his nature when, in 1847, he chose a partner to help him edit, promote, and sell the *North Star*. For in those days Martin Delany was a counterpoint—in some ways, a corrective—to Douglass. Not only was he a few years older, more widely traveled in America, and more convinced of white intransigence and the need for independent black action than was Douglass, but also, since 1843 in Pittsburgh, he had operated his own highly regarded, outspoken newspaper, the *Mystery*. He was giving up the paper to join Douglass, but not before he had suggested the quality of his own inner development by dropping a Biblical quotation from the banner of the journal, and replacing it with the declaration: "Hereditary Bondsmen! Know Ye Not Who Would Be Free, Themselves Must Strike the Blow?" (In contrast, Douglass had chosen as a motto for the *North Star*: "Right Is Of No Sex—Truth Is Of No Color—God Is The Father Of Us All, And We Are All Brethren.")[17]

Partly because of his own sad loss of contact with his black family in slavery, Douglass was also far less conscious of his African roots than Delany, far less assertive concerning his black identity. As Douglass himself once noted, he was satisfied to "thank God for making me a man simply; but Delany always thanks him for making him a *black man*." Nor did Delany intend that the consciousness of heritage which he had received from his parents should end with his own life; for he married in 1843, and his first son, born three years later, was named Toussaint L'Ouverture, beginning a family trend in which the names of black heroes and heroines were given to the children, the last of whom was a daughter named Ethiopia.[18]

Of course, as the chaotic 1850s approached, Douglass and Delany agreed on many issues regarding black freedom. For instance, while the nation engaged in an expansionist war against Mexico (1846–48), both Douglass and Delany condemned it, especially for the ways in which it would strengthen the slaveholding South. For a time both editors regularly raised the cry of "No union with slaveholders," and Delany boldly faced its consequences. Accused of treason by some of his opponents, he replied, "In what manner may I be treasonous to a country which I am not allowed to call mine?"[19]

Like so many of their black crusader comrades, both men had encountered the white mobs of the free North with their threats of tar and feathers, and their cries of "Burn them alive!" and "Kill the niggers!" It is likely, then, that Delany had such painful experiences in mind when he appeared before the National Convention of Colored Freemen in Cleveland in the summer of 1848, and proposed this resolution: "Whereas we find ourselves far behind the military tactics of the civilized world, Resolved that this Convention recommend to the colored Freemen of North America to use every means in their power to obtain that science, so as to enable them to measure arms with assailants without and invaders within." With Douglass in the chair, the convention voted down Delany's resolution, but the ferment could not be denied. Black men and women were seeking ways of struggle to resolve their urgent needs. A deepening sense of crisis was upon them. The positions which had seemed tenable when the decade began were not always sufficient as it ended. Slavery was on the march, apparently prepared to establish its hegemony as far west as the Pacific, while many supporters of the "peculiar institution" talked even more boldly of rounding out its domain as far south as Cuba and Central America. All over the North, moderate white men sought for ways to compromise, to limit slavery's expansion, not to destroy it. Coming from another direction, the abolitionist persuasion still seemed weak in influence and ineffective in its political alliances. Black people were changing their minds.[20]

Henry Garnet was certainly changing his. Back in 1843, in the midst of his spectacular *Address to the Slaves*, he had included a little-noticed and very wise warning to those who pondered the possibility of mass black emigration from America: "It is impossible, like the children of Israel, to make a grand exodus from the land of bondage. The Pharaohs are on both sides of the blood-red waters." By this, he said he meant that no mass movement was possible to Canada, for it would have to pass through the white ugliness of the American North; nor could he anticipate an escape through Mexico, for even then, three years before the Mexican War, Garnet had clearly seen that "the propagators of American slavery are spending their blood and treasure, that they may plant the black flag of [tyranny] in the heart of Mexico and riot in the halls of the Montezumas." But by 1848 Garnet was looking at the red waters again. The end of the Mexican War had added new impetus to the call for slavery's expansion. Moreover, in November of that year Gen. Zachary Taylor, a career soldier who was both a Mexican War hero and a Louisiana slaveholder, was elected President of the United States, while Henry Highland Garnet—black, crippled, and resisting—was still being ousted from segregated trains and coaches. Late in that year he announced, "I hesitate not to say that my mind of late has greatly changed in regard to the American Colonization scheme. . . . I would rather see a man free in

Liberia than a slave in the United States." A year later he said he thought that any country offering freedom and enfranchisement would do.[21]

Garnet was not alone. Thousands of black people who had not done so before were also looking anew at the waters. In Ohio John Mercer Langston, an eloquent young student at Oberlin who had been born into slavery (the son of his master), spoke the thoughts and convictions of many when he said "he loved his freedom more than his country, and would be happy to see the emigration of Negroes and the establishment of a Negro nation."[22]

In those days of increasing desperation, emigration was not the only alternative to the Great Tradition which was being considered by black men and women. Some found it more helpful to remember the Henry Garnet of 1843 and to ponder even earlier proposals. In 1848, Garnet's five-year-old Buffalo *Address* was finally published and distributed widely as a pamphlet. It was said that an enigmatic white man named John Brown, a dealer in wholesale wool in Springfield, Massachusetts, had paid for its publication. Whoever paid, the historical context of Garnet's speech, and the exigencies of the late 1840s, were well understood, for the *Address* was placed under the same cover with David Walker's *Appeal*.[23]

By now, more blacks were prepared to ponder such words, to consider their meaning and their cost. At times—true to the black style—the foreboding appeals were mixed with humor and insight. In June 1849, partly in response to an extensive American lecture tour by Louis Kossuth, the Hungarian revolutionary leader, the state legislature of Louisiana had passed resolutions of sympathy with the revolutionary forces of Hungary, urging them to continue in their struggle against Austrian rule. The governor of the state also added a word of encouragement. That summer, in his short-lived, outspoken black newspaper, the *Ram's Horn*, Thomas Van Rensselaer seized upon the Louisiana action to put forward his own call, reminiscent of Garnet and Walker: "Slaves of the South, Now Is Your Time! Strike for your freedom *now*, at the suggestion of your enslavers. Governor Johnson, one of the largest slaveholders in Louisiana, encourages you to strike at once. You may be sure of his sympathy for liberty."[24]

Then, in a more serious vein, the *Ram's Horn* picked up the Garnet proposal of radical noncooperation: "We do not tell you to murder the slaveholders; but we do advise you to refuse longer to work without pay. Make up your minds to die, rather than bequeath a state of slavery to your posterity."[25]

Resistance was in the air, taking many forms. Blacks in the North continued to practice civil disobedience, but in constantly new and cre-

ative forms. In the spring of 1848 a group of slave catchers appeared in
a small Michigan town looking for a fugitive family, and drew out a
black Paul Revere. According to Martin Delany, when the slave agents
accosted the family, "An old gentleman mounted his horse, rode through
the streets ringing a bell, crying 'kidnappers—the Crosswait family.' "
Soon the whole town was aroused and a group of blacks quickly escorted
the entire family out of town. That same summer, a company of black
women in Cincinnati, armed with "shovels, tongs, washboards and rolling
pins," took on a posse of slave agents and prevented the recapture of a
group of fugitives who had just crossed the Ohio River.[26]

Every form of resistance was necessary, for the national situation
appeared to be worsening. Congress was seriously debating the proposal
that the lands lately wrested from Mexico be completely thrown open to
slavery. Northern states like New York, Wisconsin, and Pennsylvania
were actively refusing black political enfranchisement, and in some cases
were still calling for the expulsion of their black citizens. In the South,
legislatures and local officials were dangerously narrowing the options for
free blacks, hoping to drive them out or force them back into slavery.
After banning importations for almost twenty years, the border state of
Maryland officially reopened itself to the slave trade. Black people were
being pressed against the white wall of America; sanguine hopes were
being stripped away. Late in the winter of 1849, traveling across the
Pennsylvania mountains on the route he had followed in the days of Nat
Turner, Martin Delany wrote: "The thunders of God's mighty wrath must
sooner or later break forth, with all of the terrible consequences, and
scourge this guilty nation for the endless outrages and cruelty committed
upon an innocent and unoffending people. I invoke the aid of Jehovah, in
this mighty work of chastisement."[27]

When spring came, Delany's colleague Douglass was in Boston, also
dealing with thoughts of judgment and justice, perhaps raising new, private questions concerning the ways of Providence. In June 1849 the
masterful black orator spoke to his customary packed audience in Faneuil Hall. His speech had nothing to do with slave insurrection, but near
the end of it he suddenly roared out his response to the brothers and
sisters in bondage, touching again the radical depths: "There are three
millions of slaves in this land, held by the United States Government,
under the sanction of the American Constitution." But Douglass did not
call for disunion. Instead, he threw his Garrison-oriented audience into
an uproar as he proclaimed that "he would welcome the news that the
slaves had risen and that the sable arms which have been engaged in
beautifying and adorning the South were engaged in spreading death and
devastation there."[28]

The calls to radical levels of commitment and struggle were coming from the subterranean levels of black history. The old voices in the Atlantic's waves were again inviting, compelling responses from their kindred on the ship. Douglass and Delany, Langston and Garnet—these were only symbols of the agitated movement in the North. Then in the South, before the decade closed, the struggle narrowed again into one critical life: one black woman on Maryland's eastern shore who had heard of Nat Turner, who had seen her own visions and dreamed her own dreams of God. Once her name had been Araminta Ross, now it was Harriet Tubman. Like many others of her brothers and sisters in bondage, she bore the marks of slavery—large, testifying scars on her head and back and neck; but her dreams and visions were of freedom. Unlike Nat, she had been told by her voices to continue her stubborn resistance to slavery by stealing away from its power.

In 1849 she broke free. Running with two of her brothers, hiding in caves and graveyards, eluding wild men and wild dogs, wading through the waters, she made her way to Philadelphia. But her destiny was to return. She said: "There are three million of my people on the plantations of the South. I must go down, like Moses into Egypt to lead them out." Working as a domestic servant to obtain the necessary funds, she began her sorties back into the South on rescue missions.[29]

As Harriet Tubman joined the Northern and Southern movements in her own scarred body, the God of the river appeared to have many voices —perhaps one for each eager listener—and many tasks in the struggle to free a people from their bondage. But the way was still cloudy. For even as Harriet entered the City of Brotherly Love, blacks there were being forced into radical action. In October 1849, under attack from white mobs for a night and a day, Philadelphia's blacks picked up guns, tore up paving stones, seized bricks, and defended themselves vigorously against the onslaught. Resistance was in the air.[30]

8

A Ferment of Fugitives

The Confluence of Northern and Southern Struggle

We do not wish to offer violence to any person unless driven to the extreme, in which case we are determined to defend ourselves at all hazards, even should it be to the shedding of human blood, and in doing thus, will appeal to the Supreme Judge of the Social World to support us in the justness of our cause. . . . We who have tasted of *freedom* are ready to exclaim . . . "Give us Liberty or give us death."

Convention of Chicago Black People
Protesting Fugitive Slave Law, 1850

Late in November of 1849, still doing battle with the bitter realities of Canaan, Frederick Douglass wrote in the *North Star*:

We deem it a settled point that the destiny of the colored man is bound up with that of the white people of this country. . . . It is idle—worse than idle to think of our expatriation, or removal. . . . *We are here*, and here we are likely to be. To imagine that we shall ever be eradicated is absurd and ridiculous. We can be remodified, changed, and assimilated, but never extinguished. We repeat . . . that we *are here*; and that this is *our* country; and the question for the philosophers and statesmen of the land ought to be, what principles should dictate the policy of the action toward us? We shall neither die out, nor be driven out; but shall go with this people, either as a testimony against them, or as an evidence in their favor throughout their generations. We are clearly on their hands and must remain there forever.[1]

In a way, these words reflected the young leader's continuing battle against the rising tide of emigrationist thought within the black community. But beneath that level, his statement and his life also raised other profound and lasting issues concerning the ultimate struggle between white and black in America, among white and black for America.

Regarding certain matters, Douglass's words were undebatable. Black people were surely in America. They had multiplied more rapidly than almost any other group of Africans in the New World. By the time of his *North Star* statement, the radical, explosive black presence amounted to almost four million persons, more than fifteen percent of the total American population. They were scattered in every part of the land, with more than 400,000 of them living in the free states. But was it really their country? Did all the unrequited labor, all the valiant battles, the quiet blood, the broken bodies, and the midnight screaming in the wind make it theirs? Could America be theirs when black people could not vote, could not serve on school boards, could not sit in any legislatures, on any courts, were not in any official positions of authority to give direction to the nation? Even Douglass faltered here, for he spoke of his people only as a waiting presence, as the all-too-passive recipients of white action, as objects of the policies of white "philosophers and statesmen." He identified the children of Africa solely as dependents, as problems for the nation and candidates for assimilation. These were not descriptions of a people who shared possession of a land—and the responsibility for it.

Douglass was not alone in his uncertainty concerning the meaning of the black presence in America. As in all previous periods, many blacks were now in deep anguish over the question of possession, and like Douglass many still hoped—with that strange hope of the embattled Great Tradition—that Africa's sons and daughters would indeed finally become a testimony in favor of America, rather than a judgment against it. But by the middle of the century, such hope was being slashed to red and ragged shreds in the vituperative disputes over the expansion of slavery into the new states and territories. In 1849–50 the specific matter at hand was the future of the millions of acres recently annexed from Mexico: the land west from the Louisiana Purchase all the way to the Pacific Ocean, the land of white Manifest Destiny. Would slavery be allowed in this territory? In which parts? How far north and west? Who was to decide?[2]

The debate raged on in Congress and across the nation, but nowhere in the white political community was the issue of black rights seriously broached. (Even those few whites who cared about such things were well aware that, if the issue were voiced publicly, the racism and fear of their kinsmen would distort it viciously and use it to inflame the debate.) In the commons and the churches, in the cities and on the lovely hills, on the prairies and in the halls of Congress, there were no doubts in most white minds about whose country this was. Though Barnburners and States-Righters and Whigs and Free-Soilers battled fiercely among themselves, nothing in their struggles concerned the right of black people to claim and deeply share America. Rather, the basic argument was over which white vision of America would prevail. When they took up Douglass's question in Washington and across the country, when they asked what principles should dictate policy toward black people, these white leaders continued to see blacks essentially as objects. Their principles were the principles of white supremacy. At best, their policy was one of compromise over the future of slavery, the future of the South, the future of black men, the future of the nation. And in their minds, almost all the sacrifices on the altar of compromise were to be made by blacks.

Slaveowners and other advocates and beneficiaries of the system pressed for total license to carry the "peculiar institution" wherever new territories were opened and states established. Their opponents were essentially seeking to avoid competition with slave labor, to give free white labor the upper hand in the new areas; they were determined to check that increase in Congressional membership which the expansion of slavery would provide to the slaveholding section under the Constitution's three-fifths arrangement for counting the enslaved black population in apportioning representation to the lower House. By and large, it was the same battle which had been waged at various levels of the nation's life since the days of the Constitutional Convention. Now the three major white positions in the bitter debate were often grouped under the rubrics of Free Soil, Popular Sovereignty, and Proslavery. Generally, the Free-Soilers were most adamant in the call for federal legislation against the expansion of slavery into the new areas, but most of them were just as adamantly opposed to a free black presence in the West. The advocates of Popular Sovereignty demanded that the voting population in each territory be allowed to decide the issues for themselves through their legislatures. (Here again, blacks would be excluded from the decision-making process, since in most places they had not been granted the right to vote.) The Proslavery group demanded that federal protection of slaveholding be extended into the new areas, and the strong fugitive-slave legislation be developed to guarantee their property. Even before 1850 the struggle had become so intense that white men and women in both North and South were freely debating secession and disunion as real alternatives. At the heart of it all, beneath the level of the John Calhouns, the Daniel Websters, the Henry Clays, and the Stephen Douglases, lurked the unadmitted but unavoidable issue of the black presence.[3]

Then, early in January 1850, as the opposing forces mounted their ferocious arguments, and the fabric of the white union seemed dangerously threatened, a compromise proposal was worked out by the Congressional leaders, the chief architect being Henry Clay. As part of the Compromise of 1850, Free-Soilers were given California as a free state; Popular

Sovereignty supporters (and hopeful Southerners), the organization of New Mexico and Utah as territories in which the free white people would decide for or against the introduction of slavery; and Southerners, what turned out to be the most controversial and explosive piece of the legislative package: a new fugitive slave act.

Under the Fugitive Slave Law of 1850, it appeared that no black people would be safe. Federal power, in the person of marshals and commissioners, would provide new force to the thrust of white domination. Only a sworn affidavit would be necessary to claim a black man, woman, or child as someone's escaped slave, to seize them from streets and houses and hiding places, and haul them before a federal commissioner. The apprehended individual had no right to a trial by jury, nor could his or her testimony be admitted in any legal proceedings which challenged the capture. The commissioners were to receive ten dollars for each case in which a black person was sent into slavery, and five dollars for each release. Moreover, federal marshals were empowered to summon any citizen to aid in the capture of a fugitive, and the penalties for interference with this legal kidnapping process were to be maximum fines of a thousand dollars and imprisonment for up to six months. Southern spokesmen, skeptical about the proposed compromise in general, said that they would judge its value largely by the effectiveness of this law in the North. So in 1850, when the white "philosophers and statesmen" considered the black people whom Frederick Douglass had desperately put "on their hands . . . forever," they gave black people the back of those hands, the teeth of their laws, the threat of even more efficient action against black freedom. At least, that was the thrust of the legislative package presented to Congress late in January 1850.[4]

Fortunately for the movement of black struggle, there were many people, including Douglass himself in his more realistic moments, who were not satisfied to be on—or behind—the hands of the white rulers, simply waiting for their decisions and actions. As the acrimonious debates on the Compromise ran on in Congress and the country through spring and into summer, black people in the North met together in every community where their numbers and status made it possible, and tried to decide what their own hands might need to do. More than any other single issue, they were deeply concerned about the proposed new Fugitive Slave Law, and the severe threat it posed to the life and liberty of hundreds of thousands of their people. The desperation of the hour was sharply stated in the angry, booming voice of Samuel Ringgold Ward, the abolitionist lecturer, who spoke that spring in Boston's Faneuil Hall; a fugitive himself, he said: "Such crises as these leave us to the right of Revolution, and if need be, that right we will, at whatever cost, most sacredly maintain."[5]

Before turning fully to such fearful possibilities, some black persons followed the time-honored practices of the abolitionist tradition by asking white friends and supporters what they thought should be done. One such adviser, William Jay, wrote to a New York group: "You ask me how you shall secure yourselves from the kidnapper. God only knows." What Jay knew, he said, was that black people should not turn to violence, but should leave "the pistol and the bowie knife to 'Southern ruffians and their Northern mercenaries [meaning the U.S. Army?].' " When another black group asked Thaddeus Stevens, the abolitionist Congressman from Pennsylvania, for his advice, he said that the brutal new act would no doubt be enforced in federal courts. Therefore, he told them, he could "advise nothing better than the subjects of it put themselves beyond its reach."[6]

But no white advice was sufficient. By the time President Millard Fillmore signed the Fugitive Slave Law in September 1850, tens of thousands of black people across the North had recognized more fully than ever before how intimately and inextricably their struggle for freedom was joined with that of their brothers and sisters in slavery. The net cast by the law could obviously entrap legally free black people, as well as authentic fugitives in the North. Thus Canaan's dark minority was being pressed, driven to move toward the masses of the South in joint actions of defense, defiance, and resistance; the radical streams of thought and action were gaining in power.

If their often overflowing meetings and tumultuous speeches were any indication, by the fall of 1850 a large number of black people had prepared themselves to stand fast in the face of federal power, to defend their own beleaguered liberties and the freedom of their fellow Africans who came streaming north. In all the crowded meeting places of that anxious season, the thrust of the shouted pledges and hard decisions was undeniably toward a more widespread and defiant level of civil disobedience than Northern blacks had ever practiced before. In New York City, at a tightly packed meeting called to discuss the new law, an excited crowd heard the first speaker call out: "You are told to submit peacefully to the laws; will you do so?" They shouted and screamed, "No, No!" Again he called out: "You are told to kiss the manacles that bind you; will you do so?" In deafening tones they again replied, "No, No, No!" For many, this familiar question-and-response pattern was much more than ritual, more than words; they promised to stand immediately against the laws. Up in Elmira, New York, in that radical western district of the state, the black people who gathered in one of the meetings "vowed they would defy the Fugitive Slave Law at the sacrifice of their lives." In Philadelphia, the usually irenic Robert Purvis was defiant; speaking before an audience where many whites were present, with his own pale complexion now flushed in anger, Purvis cried out: "Should any wretch enter my dwelling, any pale-faced spectre among ye, to execute this law on me or mine, I'll seek his life, I'll shed his blood."[7]

White advice was not sufficient. In Alleghany, Pennsylvania, shortly after the Fugitive Slave Law was signed, a mass meeting was held in the market house. The mayor, the local Congressman, and prominent white local citizens all urged black people and others to obey the law and petition for its repeal. Then came Martin Delany, providing the sober, radical assessment black people needed. He said that petitioning was futile, for the law was necessary to maintain the Compromise, the national compact between the white people of the North and South. So when he pledged his own active resistance, he was also stating his fundamental opposition, his radical challenge, to the Compromise and to the governments which upheld it. Turning his coal-black face toward the mayor, he said:

If any man approaches [my] house in search of a slave—I care not who he may be, whether constable, or sheriff, magistrate or even judge of the Supreme Court—nay let it be President Millard Fillmore surrounded by his cabinet and his bodyguard, with the Declaration of Independence waving above his head as his banner, and the constitution of his country upon his breast as his shield —if he crosses the threshold of my door, and I do not lay him a lifeless corpse at my feet, I hope the grave may refuse my body a resting place, and righteous heaven my spirit a home. O, no! He cannot enter that house and we both live.[8]

Wherever he went in that period, although the precise words and vows varied slightly, Delany offered essentially the same promises, undergoing that peculiar process of honing which the radical movement of the river provided for those who pressed themselves into the depths.

In a sense, of course, it was not surprising to hear such words from Delany. But what of Frederick Douglass, now that the white philosophers and statesmen had flung their response in his face? The two men had given up their joint editorial venture in the previous year. The official reason had been lack of funds to support both, but underneath ran the mounting ideological tensions between them. Although Douglass was now listed as the sole official editor of the paper, he was relying heavily on the editorial, business, and political skills of Julia Griffiths, his white English confidante. In a controversial action, she had recently moved into the Douglass household. Against this background, it is fair to speculate on the possibility that Griffiths' presence may have adversely affected Delany's relationships with his comrades in arms.[9]

Still, for a time, the relentless evil of the society and the surging pace of the black movement brought the two men together, moved them to common ground. In Boston, one of his favorite lecture sites, Douglass was heard voicing the same threatening, defiant sentiments as Delany, joining his hands with those black persons in the city who had recently pledged "to resist unto death any attempt on their liberties." Douglass declared, "We must be prepared . . . to see the streets of Boston running with blood . . . should this law be put into operation."[10]

Douglass's reference to a resistance group was more than likely directed to the League of Freedom, which blacks in Boston had formed that summer "to resist the law" and "receive and protect the slave at every hazard." The organization's existence was a reminder that the struggle over fugitive slaves was not only binding the Northern and Southern blacks, but also at least temporarily breaking down class barriers among the Northern black community. For the organizers of the League proudly affirmed its lower-class base, declaring that it was "composed of Actors and not speakers merely," that the members were "men of overalls, men of the wharf, who could do heavy work in the hour of difficulty." Nor was it confined to men; the women in the organization who did washing and cleaning in various hotels and boarding houses, were instructed to be "on the constant lookout for the Southern slavecatcher and be prepared for any emergency." It was such a group, extending well beyond the predominantly middle-class makeup of the Black Conventions, which said of the slave catcher, "when he rushes upon our buckler—kill him."[11]

As the decade developed, the resistance groups in the North repeatedly exhibited the same tendencies to cut across the incipient class lines of the black community, and to strike out toward bold action. Among the famous and the unknown, among the countless thousands in the struggle, the response was overwhelmingly toward radical disobedience, toward resistance and new levels of black unity. In New York City a recent fugitive from South Carolina, John Jacobs, spoke on behalf of many of his nameless brothers and sisters. His message was in the language of the New Testament, and the tradition of Turner and Walker: "My colored brethren, if you have not swords, I say to you, sell your garments and buy one. . . . They said that they cannot take us back to the South; but I say, under the present law they can; and now I say unto you; let them only take your dead bodies [Tremendous cheers]. . . . I would, my friends, advise you to show a front to our tyrants and arm yourselves . . . and I would advise the women to have their knives too."[12]

In Chicago, the words of Patrick Henry were again echoed, but as usual the spirit and the meaning were indigenous to the black struggle. There, that momentous autumn, some three hundred persons—more than half the black population of the city—gathered in the A.M.E.'s Quinn

Chapel to pass a grim resolution. "We do not wish to offer violence to any person unless driven to the extreme, in which case we are determined to defend ourselves at all hazards, even should it be to the shedding of human blood, and in doing thus, will appeal to the Supreme Judge of the Social World to support us in the justness of our cause. . . . We who have tasted of *freedom* are ready to exclaim, in the language of the brave Patrick Henry, 'Give us Liberty or give us death.' "[13]

Words were not sufficient. The black assemblage in Chicago went on to set up a Liberty Association with teams of men assigned "to patrol the city, spying for possible slave-hunters." In cities across the country, black people met in the churches (those ambiguous but precious bases of operation through all the long struggle), in homes, in the lodge halls and the streets. First they spoke the necessary, angry, determined words, then they organized to act in civil disobedience against federal power on behalf of black freedom. In Cleveland and Cincinnati, black paramilitary companies had already been formed, and other cities now followed suit, reviving and responding to Delany's call for military preparedness. Before the year was over, many unofficial but very real black vigilance groups had sprung up in places where they had not existed before, while organizations already active renewed their commitment to armed resistance. One already existing group was in the rural area of Christiana, Pennsylvania. Led by a long-time fugitive named William Parker, they resolved to prevent any of their brethren being taken into slavery, at the risk of their own lives.[14]

The North, that bitter Canaan, was the battleground. Some fought to stay, to survive, to prevail; others, to leave, to survive, to prevail. Many left for Canada, often in the spirit of the two hundred who set out from Delany's Pittsburgh in October 1850, just days after the Fugitive Slave Law was signed. Like many fugitives who were coming directly from the South, the Pittsburgh group—most of them waiters in the city's hotels—carried guns, vowing that "they would die before being taken back into slavery." In Syracuse, New York, one of the leading black abolitionists, Jermain W. Loguen, recalled his own escape from Tennessee as a teenager, and now decided to flee again across the border. But he soon returned, declaring, "I don't respect the law—I won't fear it—I won't obey!" Then, true to his word, he eventually shepherded some fifteen hundred black pilgrims through Syracuse and on to Canada. Many thousands were soon gone, often leaving behind their families, homes, and property, and the flotsam of shattered hopes. In the harsh years between the signing of the Fugitive Slave Law and the Civil War, fifteen to twenty thousand men, women, and children—four to five percent of the black population of the North—made the cruel journey in search of free-

dom and reconstructed hope. Canaan was a bitter land, a place of aliens
and exiles, of black men and women pressed insistently into the radical
streams of the river.[15]

More than ever before, the Fugitive Slave Law made the North a
battleground, but at the same time it revived strange memories of past
struggles. In the West, for instance, the law transformed the future of
several hundred black people who had originally emerged with the Seminole Indians from the long struggles against the federal government in
Florida. These freedom-loving black nomads had gone from Florida to
the Indian Territory (later Oklahoma), but in 1850 the Fugitive Slave
Law convinced them that they were no longer safe—if they ever had been
—on any American territory, whereas a tradition of friendliness to black
freedom had been clearly established in Mexico. So, routing a body of
Creek Indians sent to oppose them, the group made its last move in the
American struggle and fled to Mexico.[16]

Soon after this dash toward freedom, other reports came of "a large
number of negroes" from the Galveston area who were reported also to
have "succeeded in escaping to Mexico." In this case, the reports were
accompanied by the enigmatic news that "the late extensive plot was only
partly frustrated." The break with slavery—and with America—was still
part of the struggle toward freedom, but not all fugitives in the Southwest made the same choice. In the year of the Compromise it was also
reported that some fifteen hundred former black slaves were fighting in
Texas alongside the Comanche Indians, resisting the encroachments of
the white settlers and armies upon their lands and liberties. As always,
the struggle had many elements, and the red and black alliance in defense
of land and rights was not the least of them.[17]

However, the vast majority of black people were still in the Deep South,
and the major fight for freedom continued there, often expressed in
rhythms and methods characteristic of the black South's own special history. For instance, although it is hard to grasp in a secular age, large
numbers of black people believed that their best contribution to the struggle was through unremitting prayer. Like some widespread, unorganized,
unrecognized corps of spiritual resistants, these black men, women, and
children were everywhere disciplining their wills, turning themselves to
the work of praying for freedom. At least a few such persons existed
within each attempt at organized insurrection, but most of them remained quietly in the background, sending forth their agonized petitions
like the first bittersweet offerings from the African baracoons. Wherever
they were, these black men and women considered their prayer a serious
thing, inextricably bound to the living of their lives, transforming those

lives, directing them toward antislavery purposes over which the white members of the community could have no control.[18]

Remembering slavery in Dawson, Georgia, one black man later said: "I have heard slaves morning and night pray for deliverance. Some of 'em would stand up in de fields or bend over cotton and corn and pray out loud for God to help 'em and in time . . . He did." In Tennessee a young man who heard the older people praying thought at the time that it was "foolishness," but later recalled that "the old time folks always felt they was to be free." Down in Florida it was said that "there was a praying ground where 'the grass never had a chancet ter grow fer the troubled knees that kept it crushed down.' " Because certain whites recognized the troubling, unfathomable power of spiritual resistance, not a few blacks were lashed unmercifully for such prayers, but the victims kept on, always feeling "they was to be free."[19]

Black people continually attempted other unorthodox forms of resistance, and were rewarded with even more unorthodox punishment. As noted earlier, there is every indication that, in spite of the laws, significant numbers of enslaved black people were trying to learn how to read and write. In some Southern cities schools sponsored by churches and private individuals were tolerated. In other urban areas they had to operate secretly. Usually such activity was considerably more difficult and dangerous in the plantation areas; according to black tradition, it was not unusual for rural blacks to have fingers or hands cut off, if they were caught in this defiant act. But nothing stopped the attempts, not even in some of the most repressive areas of the South. There were many places like Greene County, Georgia, where it was said that "dere was some Niggers dat wanted larnin' so bad dey would slip out at night and meet in a deep gulley whar dey would study by de light of . . . torches." Unorthodox though it may have been, this was an unmistakable form of resistance: at its simplest level, a challenge to white laws and white men; at its best, a forceful, personal movement toward self-determination and independence of the mind. Collectively, this secret learning represented a people's thrust toward new self-definitions, toward the creative transformation of a culture.[20]

Of course one of the most persistent forms of Southern black resistance took place out in the fields in the unending battles against white overseers (and sometimes black drivers). These men—often despised, or at least patronized by the planters and owners—were the wardens and guards of slavery's prison. They had replaced the poorly paid and abused seamen of the slave ships. Since for black people who worked on plantations they were often the major continuing contact with the larger system, by the 1850s the tradition of resistance to them was well established. Repeatedly, black men and women struck out against these whites, often using their hoes as weapons, smashing at faces and heads, offering this limited but real evidence of their determination to be free, authentic persons, even while engaged in slave labor. One woman who grew up in slavery in Hillsboro, Tennessee, transmitted a typical story when she recounted how one day in the 1850s an overseer approached her father while he was chopping cotton and said to him, "Bob, I'm gonna whip you this morning." When her father replied that he had done nothing to deserve the familiar, bloody punishment, the overseer responded, "I know it, I'm gonna whip you to keep you from doing nothing," and came down on her father with the cowhide whip. Immediately her father had countered with a quick, slashing stroke of his hoe to the white man's head, killing him on the spot. His penalty was to be sold away into Mississippi—away from his family, but not from his daughter's memories.[21]

Some prayed, some read by torchlight, some fought and killed. Others ran, fighting cold and fears and sickness, like two black fugitives from North Carolina who, in those anguished days of the early 1850s, traveled for 101 days, refusing to stop anywhere for more than a night until they reached Canada. Meanwhile, all around the plantations and the cities, the outlyers continued to build their own insistent challenge, their counterculture. In Louisiana one contemporary observer reported black runaway colonies in the swamps of Saint James Parish and elsewhere: "The swamps were never free of Negroes. They constituted a species of asylum, and that fact had its effect upon the working of the system. As a general thing, the negro became more self-reliant, and the master more wary." It was an important observation, for the rise of black self-reliance meant the certain death of slavery.[22]

Elsewhere, especially where there were no swamps, an even more unusual form of self-reliance was created among the runaway groups. In parts of Georgia and Alabama, black men and women who broke with slavery often dug holes in the ground to live and hide in. Sometimes they stayed in such dwellings for years, emerging only at night for supplies and visits, and sometimes for attacks. On occasion, children were born in those strange underground homes, some of whom never knew daylight until emancipation. It was a high price for freedom; but it was paid, sometimes compounded in the blindness of a child.[23]

Children were constantly and often centrally involved, especially where runaways and outlyers were concerned. Often, because they would rarely be suspected, children from the plantations and houses were used to take food and messages to the fugitives who lived in the woods. Obviously, these children caught some sense of the danger and the challenge of that life.

In some places, for boys who sought to assert their manhood, the defiant act of running away for short or long periods became part of the rites of passage. One young man who grew up in Christian County, Tennessee, later recalled, "I would let [the master] see the bottom of my heels all day. . . . I commenced doing just like the men were doing."[24]

All the while, the movement of these fugitives still provided the main link with the Northern river. Indeed there were times when crucial events tied the Southern situations directly to the rising, radical movement in the North. For instance, a letter might arrive by devious means from a black woman in Philadelphia, saying, "Tell my brothers to be always watching unto prayer, and when the good old ship of Zion comes along, to be ready to step aboard." Harriet Tubman was on her way down from Philadelphia, still joining North and South in her person and her work. Then, in the brush arbors, a song might go up: "Get on board, little children/There's room for many a more."

In other places, anticipating the arrival of such strengthening and encouraging help (many besides Harriet came back from the North on rescue missions), the large iron pots were again turned face down on the ground in the cabins and the woods, and the secret meetings prepared men and women for their own part in the never-ending struggle to break with slavery. On one of these meeting grounds, it would not have been strange to hear a voice caressing the night:

> Swing low, sweet chariot
> Coming for to carry me home,
> Swing low, sweet chariot
> Coming for to carry me home.

In the morning both chariot and singer might be gone, with nothing remaining but a testimony like that of young Henry Gross of New Orleans after he had made his way to Canada in 1851: "After my wife was gone I felt very uneasy. At length, I picked up spunk, and said I would start. All the time, I dreamed on nights that I was getting clear. This put the notion in my head to start—a dream that I had reached free soil and was perfectly safe. . . . I had many doubts. I said to myself . . . I can't die but once; if they catch me, they can but kill me; I'll defend myself as far as I can. I armed myself with an old razor, and made a start alone."[25] So modest a desire as a place to be "perfectly safe" drove men and women to dream dreams, to break laws, to get clear. Some got clear by sharpening knives, some by carrying old razors, some by following Harriet Tubman.

In this troubled decade, never had it been more obvious that the places where the rushing movement of the Northern and Southern streams met

were the critical points for the development of black radicalism. As the
runaways broke out of the South, defying the Fugitive Slave Law, the
pledges which had been made in scores of meetings across the black
North were kept. In countless covert and open places of contact, determined civil disobedience on behalf of the fugitives deepened and broadened. Men, women, and children risked their own security on behalf of
the runaways. Black people again were posing fundamental challenges to
the national government and its laws because of their commitment to
their kinsmen.

In Boston, in February 1851, a man popularly known as Shadrach was
seized by slave catchers and brought into court. During the hearing some
fifty black persons "pressed into the courtroom, lifted Shadrach in the
air, and bore him to the street. His clothes half torn off, Shadrach was
placed in a carriage and soon the rescued and the rescuers were moving
away 'like a black squall.' " (Or was it a river?) Three days after the
rescue, President Fillmore issued a special proclamation calling for legal
proceedings against the "aiders and abettors in this flagitious offense."
Lewis Hayden, the acknowledged leader of the rescue squad, was one of
the eight blacks and whites indicted—but not convicted—for obstructing
the Fugitive Slave Law. (Such a role and its consequences were not new
to Hayden, who had himself escaped earlier from Kentucky; soon he was
one of the most consistent leaders of such civil disobedience.) Later that
year, a similar rescue of a fugitive whose alias was "Jerry" took place in
Syracuse, New York. There the black man was taken right out of the
police station. Once more, eighteen persons were placed under federal
indictment; but here, as in Boston, the jury would not convict them. Obviously, the failure to obtain convictions reflected the deeply divided state
of the nation.[26]

Still, in the light of such challenges to the federal government from the
black community, and in the light of the attempted federal legal attacks
in response, there was something logically unreal—if tactically sound at
the moment—about the position that Frederick Douglass took in the
spring of 1851. By that time he had come to the conclusion that the Constitution was not meant to protect slavery. He wrote in the *North Star*:
"We hold [slavery] to be a system of lawless violence; that it *never was
lawful and never can be made so*; and that it is the first duty of every
American citizen, whose conscience permits so to do to use his *political*
as well as his *moral* power for its overthrow." While this statement has
been most often interpreted in the context of Douglass's break with William Lloyd Garrison, it is possible that something more was at work.
Douglass, who tended at times to back away from the grim political realities, seemed to suggest that black men and women could oppose slavery

and the Fugitive Slave Law without really challenging the federal government and the power of the American state.[27]

Tactically, Douglass may have seen this as a way to encourage even greater participation in the mounting resistance movement in the North, or to justify significant actions already being taken, but the position entailed profound strategic pitfalls. His views flew in the face of the reality represented by the Compromise of 1850, by the determined federal prosecution of the vigilance groups, and the Constitution-makers themselves. Douglass tended dangerously to dissociate the institution of slavery from its roots in the racist, exploitative American society. Such a point of view could well leave him unprepared for the time when the institution might be destroyed without the roots having been seriously affected.

There was another, younger Douglas in those days who was not so sanguine, who for a time saw America and its Constitution far more clearly and therefore made a more significant contribution to black radical thought at that point in history. Too little is yet known of the tall, lithe, light-skinned Afro-American named H. Ford Douglas. Born in Virginia—very likely in 1831, the year of Nat Turner's rebellion—as a teen-ager he escaped from slavery during the late 1840s and, after a sojourn in Louisiana, settled for a time in Cleveland, Ohio, where he earned his living as a barber. Though not yet twenty years old, by 1850 Douglas was a highly regarded orator in black abolitionist circles in Ohio. In 1851 the forceful young speaker attracted even more attention when he attended the Ohio Convention of Colored Men, where he was soon locked in debate with William Howard Day and Charles H. Langston, two black abolitionists who were his superiors in years and reputation, though not in intellect or lucidity of thought.[28]

The convention reflected all the excitement and anxieties of the period. Day and Langston had taken a position similar to that of Frederick Douglass, endorsing the integrity of "the founding fathers" and calling upon blacks to participate in the political process under the Constitution. Reading both the Constitution and the black experience in America with searing honesty, H. Ford Douglas attacked their arguments: "I hold . . . that the Constitution of the United States is pro-slavery, considered to be so by those who framed it, and construed to that end ever since its adoption. . . . Now, I hold, in view of this fact, no colored man can consistently vote under the United States Constitution."[29]

Although there would be continued debate over the specific (and most often hypothetical) matter of whether blacks should or should not vote, the younger Douglas's analysis of the relationship of the national government and its Constitution to black people was in the vanguard of Afro-

American thought at the time. Indeed, black people were already acting on some of its implications. From the Canadian side Henry Bibb, one of the best-known black exiles and leaders of the period, was organizing his people to respond to the Fugitive Slave Law. Since his own initial flight from Kentucky in 1837—and his many recaptures and escapes in an attempt to rescue his wife—the light-skinned popular orator and organizer had explored many aspects of the struggle. He had been a leading figure in the mainline abolitionist movement, traveling, lecturing, and singing across the North. For a time he had also participated actively in the campaigns of the Liberty Party, searching for a political solution to slavery. During most of this period he repeatedly proclaimed that emigration was wrong for black people. But in 1850 the Fugitive Slave Law drove him across the Canadian border, where he began immediately to organize blacks and whites to aid the rising flood of fugitives, and to encourage massive black colonization in that country. In those efforts, Bibb's major propaganda vehicle was the newspaper he edited from Canada West (now Ontario), the *Voice of the Fugitive*.[30]

In September 1851 the self-educated black leader brought together a North American Convention of Colored Men in Toronto. The very decision to hold such a meeting in Canada was meant to be a radical move—a formal, organized announcement of the break with America and its laws, a break that many had decided to make. When the convention opened, a message from James T. Holly, a leading black emigrationist, challenged the delegates to move beyond the symbols of their separation and begin to create concrete, new, self-reliant reality. Living in Vermont at the time, the twenty-one-year-old Holly did not attend the meeting in person, but the Vermont delegates brought the message, which was clearly inspired and probably written by him. Raising the issue of parallel institutions as a part of the struggle, the message said at the outset: "We regard your assembly as the sovereign representatives of the colored people of the United States and the Canadian provinces. You have the supreme right to legislate for their interest, and adopt measures for their advancement. . . . And if other associations have been formed with the same or similar objects, it is to be hoped if they are sincere in the cause, that they will immediately rank under the banners that you will unfurl at Toronto."[31]

Holly, a close friend and colleague of Delany, was putting forth a proposal related to Delany's proposed black Secret Council and the establishment of formal links among African peoples in the New World. Concretely, the Vermont letter called for the Toronto convention to set up a Canadian-based "North American Union" of black people, and a legislative assembly representing the citizens of the proposed Union. Thus it was one of the first statements in the history of the American freedom struggle which specifically proposed a black government-in-exile. In essence, it was a call for a black peoplehood, along with a black assembly to represent a people who were steadily being driven to declare their independence from a racist, persecuting American government. In the debates over Holly's proposal, Delany—for some reason not now evident —opposed the plan, and it was not adopted. Perhaps Delany thought his own ideas about linkages among African peoples in the United States, South America, and the Caribbean a more likely alternative for those black men and women who sought secure places for nation-building. Nevertheless, Holly's idea was not permanently lost.

At conferences like the one in Toronto, it was always possible for black people to become caught up in the net of their own words, to equate struggle with talk. Of course such debates, such searches for analytical clarity were an essential part of the struggle, but more was required, as events in the United States soon made clear. In September 1851 Edward Gorsuch, a slaveowner from Baltimore County, Maryland, came to Pennsylvania to find four black men who had escaped from his legal possession some two years before. Having recently heard that the black men were in the vicinity of Christiana, Gorsuch—accompanied by his son, two relatives, and two neighbors—went to Philadelphia to obtain the proper federal warrants and the assistance of a deputy U.S. marshal. Having received such federal power and with a marshal accompanying them, Gorsuch's group set out for the place where an informer had indicated the fugitives could be found.[32]

Active in Christiana, however, was a group of black resistants who had organized several years earlier under William Parker, vowing to protect their fugitive kin with their lives. On several occasions they had already engaged in significant rescue operations, and during the uproar of 1850 had renewed their vows of solidarity. Moreover, in Philadelphia William Still's vigilance committee had a spy at work near the federal office where Gorsuch had got his warrants, so that a messenger was quickly dispatched to warn Parker's force. When news of the Gorsuch party reached Christiana, some of the black people there counseled immediate flight for the hunted men, as well as others who might be endangered. But Parker insisted that they all stand their ground at his house, keep their word, and resist to the death. Still in his twenties, but highly respected in the community, he prevailed.[33]

When Gorsuch and his company arrived at the house, the armed black group waited in a barricade on the second floor. The Maryland slaveowner entered the dwelling with the deputy marshal and said, "I want my property." Parker responded from the second floor: "Go in the room down there, and see if there is anything belonging to you. There are beds and a bureau, chairs and other things. Then go out to the barn; there you will find a cow and some hogs. See if any of them are yours." At that point the marshal began to talk of burning the house down. Hearing the suggestion, Parker's wife sounded a horn from the second-floor window, braving gunfire to do it. Gorsuch and the marshal then left the house, and continued to argue outside. Soon other black people appeared, surrounded the house, while at the same time whites also gathered, largely as spectators. When the black folk learned that Gorsuch was a Methodist class leader with a reputation for being a "good master," they responded with a song:

> Leader, what do you say
> About the judgment day?
> I will die on the field of battle,
> Die on the field of battle,
> With glory in my soul.

It was no song of happy escapism, but a challenge and a warning. Still, Gorsuch insisted on having his property.[34]

By then, from twenty-five to fifty black people had gathered at close range, armed with guns, corn cutters, staves, clubs, and stones. In a sudden explosion of weapons and bodies, they attacked the Gorsuch party. Guns were fired on both sides. The younger Gorsuch was critically wounded and driven back from the melee, while his father, who had been shot, was beaten to the ground by one of the men he had come to reclaim. Then, as Edward Gorsuch lay dying in that circle of blackness, the women burst upon him. They came leaping out of the rivers of Africa, urged up from the depths of the Atlantic, lithely moving from off the decks (and down from the masts) of the slave ships, forcing their way out of the mourning grounds of the South. These black women, we are told, "rushed from the house with corn cutters and scythe blades [and] hacked the bleeding and lifeless body."[35]

Meanwhile, although the marshal had managed to escape by beating a quick retreat, forty-five U.S. Marines from Philadelphia arrived. Recognizing the radical nature of the direct challenge, the federal government not only sent its military forces, but eventually charged thirty-six black persons and five whites with treason. But the charges could not hold, partly because Parker, the obvious leader, and several of his closest comrades had made good their own escape north, being sheltered by Frederick Douglass at his house in Rochester before going on to Toronto.[36]

The fight at Christiana provided further proof that the freedom struggle and its future could not be decided in conventions, but in personal, physical struggles to be free. Across the North—as far west as San Francisco—black people affirmed this truth and "treason" as their own; in scores of rallies they spoke of "the victorious heroes of the battle of Christiana," and sent hundreds of dollars for the legal defense of those indicted. Eventually, all the accused were acquitted in court. Meanwhile, in angry, flaming newspaper editorials, all the proslavery forces of the North and South called this resistance treason. In the North, the white men and women who loved white union more than they cared for black freedom condemned the act. But the loudest and deepest cries came from the South, charging that the action of 1851 and the acquittal which followed it were a sure sign that the Compromise of 1850 could not work, that the South must go its own way even at the cost of its blood. No doubt many white Southerners were serious, and their very seriousness confirmed the fact that black flight from slavery and black resistance to the Fugitive Slave Law played a critical role among the forces driving the nation toward its hard and bloody day of reckoning.[37]

9

Called to Go Forward

Protest, Emigration, and Radical Destiny

. . . no people can be free who themselves do not constitute an essential part of the *ruling element* of the country in which they live.

. . . the white races are but one-third of the population of the globe—or one of them to two of us—and it cannot much longer continue that two thirds will passively submit to the universal domination of this one third.

The time has now fully arrived when the colored race is called upon by all the ties of common humanity, and all the claims of consummate justice, to go forward and take their position, and do battle in the struggle now being made for the redemption of the world.

Martin Delany, 1852

It was another of the ironic contradictions which constantly marked the black-white struggle in America. Without question, the Fugitive Slave Law, the keystone of the Compromise which was meant to keep the whites of North and South together, was actually serving another—a blacker—cause. It was not only exacerbating white disputes, but also relentlessly drawing together the streams of struggle in the black South and North, urging men and women to conventions like the one at Toronto, to struggles like the one at Christiana, and to radical analyses like Martin Delany's *The Condition, Elevation, Emigration, and Destiny of the Colored People of the United States.*[1]

In the spring of 1852, while temporarily based in New York City, Delany worked feverishly on it and so produced one of the most important documents of black struggle in the nineteenth century. The ideas had begun to take shape back in the 1830s, but the times were not propitious then nor the man fully prepared. By 1852 both had developed in the directions of their earlier promise. Published in May 1852, the work eventually took on a life of its own, becoming a source of some of the most cogent critical analysis of the black condition in America, presenting a program for the rapidly mounting tide of black emigrationism. Indeed, elements of Delany's analysis and program went far beyond emigrationism, and still contain great power and truth more than a century later.

Although there were many differences in their approaches, Delany's radical use of the published word as an act of struggle placed his document in a clear line of succession to David Walker's *Appeal*. Even more than Walker, Delany based his work on the essential ties between the children of Africa in the slave and free states, on the common nature and sources of the oppression and degradation under which they were bound, and on the necessary confluence of the Southern and Northern struggle toward freedom. Moreover, his tones were more measured and his thoughts more fully ordered than Walker's, as he addressed his sober analysis primarily to black people in the North.

The document is often seen primarily as an argument for emigration; however, the key concepts for Delany were "elevation" and "destiny." Thoughts of emigration flowed out of his concern for the elevation of the American black community to its fullest human destiny. As such, his work participated in the best of the fiercely political nationalist thought which had been sweeping Europe and America since the 1840s. Near the beginning, building toward these dual themes, Delany addressed the Northern black population:

"In [the slave states], the bondman is disfranchised, and for the most part so are we. He is denied all civil, religious, and social privileges, except such as he gets by mere suffrance, and so are we. They have no part nor lot in the government of the country, neither have we. They are ruled and governed without representation, existing as mere nonentities among the citizens, and the excrescences on the body politic—a mere dreg in the community, and so are we." Then, after running through his list of grievances, Delany said, "Have we not now sufficient intelligence among us to understand our actual condition, and determine for ourselves what is best to be done? If we have not now, we shall never have."[2]

This approach typified one of the great strengths of Delany's work and life during the crucial prewar decade. He attempted to look with unsparing honesty at the actual situation of black people, to understand its real causes and predict its next stages, and then call for autonomous black action. For Delany, in 1852, the necessary action had to include emigration. He had been pondering the issue for at least fifteen years, but the great ferment produced by the black response to the Fugitive

Slave Law became the natural occasion for his putting the proposals
before black people. In the *Condition* Delany reprinted the text of the
hated law, then wrote a crucial admonition to black people concerning
their white keepers: "A people capable of originating and sustaining
such a law as this, are not the people to whom we are willing to entrust
our liberty at discretion." This was obviously a direct rebuttal to Douglass and others in the protest abolitionist mainstream, attacking their
earlier readiness to turn to whites and cast the black community "on their
hands."[3]

In the light of that basic, justifiable distrust of the white keepers of
black liberty (intrinsic to all radical struggle), Delany, facing the reality
of the Fugitive Slave Law, called out: "What can we do?—What shall we
do? This is the great and important question:—Shall we submit to be
dragged like brutes before heartless men, and sent into degradation and
bondage?—Shall we fly, or shall we resist? Ponder well and reflect."
Answering his own question, he said that black people could count on no
real legal protection in their open resistance to the Fugitive Slave Law:
"We are politically not of them, but aliens to the laws and political privileges of the country. These are truths—fixed facts, that quaint theory and
exhausted moralising, are impregnable to, and fall harmlessly before."
When he considered these things and pondered the history of other distinct peoples, Delany's conclusion was "that there are circumstances
under which emigration is absolutely necessary to [a people's] political
elevation." For Africa's children in America, far more than a minimal,
hounded survival was at stake; Delany envisioned the "elevation" of the
black community to its highest possible destiny, and in view of the American realities, saw no way to achieve that destiny save through emigration.[4]

In 1852 Delany was not yet promoting Africa as the object of black
exodus. Rather, he said, "We must not leave this continent; America is
our destination and our home." To buttress his arguments for a black
stand on the American continent, the thoughtful leader raised certain crucial issues of Afro-American and Native American relationships
which had not been systematically examined before. He also spoke to the
question of black people's historic right to the land. Building on his
extensive research and travel, Delany noted that there had been African
explorers and settlements of African peoples in the New World before
Columbus. This advanced historical and anthropological position was
then used to affirm the right and the reality of pre-European black claims
of possession. Ultimately, Delany was seeking to drive home another of
his critical contributions to nineteenth-century black radical thought: the
common cause between blacks and Native Americans in the struggle to

liberate the land and their lives. Of the Indians, Delany said: "Being descended from the Asiatic, [their] alliance in matrimony with the African is very common—therefore we have even greater claim to this continent on that account, and should unite and make common cause in elevation, with our similarly oppressed brother, the Indian."[5]

Arguing from the right of prior settlement and this special relationship to the Indians, Delany concluded: "Upon the American continent we are determined to stay, in spite of every odds against us." As he recalled his journeys of the late 1830s, he had determined that the new black homeland ought to be located somewhere south of the United States. Canada was a good temporary resting place, but Delany believed it too likely to be annexed by the United States. "Central and South America are evidently the ultimate destination and future home of the colored race on this continent," he maintained. He urged black people to learn Spanish and to prepare themselves to move south. "Go we must, and go we will, as there is no alternative. . . . To remain here in North America, and be crushed to the earth in vassalage and degradation, we never will."[6]

The determined black leader was driving his thoughts, hopes, and plans hard toward the future, toward a radical belief in the renewal of the broken black nation, toward new alliances and new unions. Emigration was a means to these ends. One of the most important hopes expressed by Delany was for the creation of a confederation of nonwhite peoples in the hemisphere, a vision which bore significant similarities to the North American Union that James T. Holly had proposed to the Toronto convention in 1851. In Delany's plans, however, the base would be to the south: "Let us go to whatever parts of Central and South America we may, we shall make common cause with the people, and shall hope . . . to assemble one day . . . in a great representative convention and form a glorious union of South American States . . . inseparably connected one and forever." Consciously using the words of the staunch supporters of the white American union, Delany foresaw a new union, created new visions. Ultimately his focus was on the future, on building, on transforming, on moving forward to a black new world.[7]

Unlike many other emigrationists, Delany stressed that he did not consider this projected exodus an act of desperate escape or angry rejection. Rather, he wrote: "Our common country is the United States. Here were we born, here raised and educated; here are . . . the loved enjoyments of our domestic and fireside relations, and the sacred graves of our departed fathers and mothers, and from here will we not be driven by any policy that may be schemed against us." Instead, insisting on black rights to the land, Delany adamantly defined emigration as an act of self-determination, an autonomous choice of a better land, a better future, a better setting for a new black society. So he doggedly affirmed the rights of black possession in America, but at the same time pointed to the obstacles which stood in the way of their realization, especially if black people sought more than the barest existence at the sufferance of the white world.[8]

Against the background of this tension, in the last sections of the *Condition* Martin Delany attempted to rally the black community to the cause of Central American emigration. "Talk not about consequences. White men seek responsibilities; shall we shun them? They brave dangers and risk consequences; shall we shrink from them? . . . The time has now fully arrived when the colored race is called upon by all the ties of common humanity, and all the claims of consummate justice, to go forward and take their position, and do battle in the struggle now being made for the redemption of the world."[9]

Without an understanding of Delany before the Civil War, it is impossible to appreciate the relationship of such emigration ideas to the black struggle. (Without Delany it is impossible to grasp fully the meaning of Henry McNeill Turner and Marcus Garvey.) At its highest plane, Delany's work suggested that emigration and struggle were not separate, but part of one black movement for self-determination and freedom. "Our race is to be redeemed," he declared, "and it is a great and glorious work, and we are the instrumentalities by which it is to be done. But we must go from among our oppressors; it never can be done by staying among them." Delany apparently knew, too, that any significant black-defined, freedom-oriented emigration would require open struggle against many elements of white American society. That was probably why, near the end of the *Condition*, he said: "They have pressed us to the last retreat—the die is cast—the Rubicon must be crossed—go we will, in defiance of all the slave-power in the Union. . . . That country is the best, in which our manhood can best be developed."[10]

At that moment in history, Martin Delany had no hope in white America or the forces it represented. His only hope—a radical one—was in the capacity of black men and women to move forward and create a new world. For the children of Africa to remake their own history—for an oppressed people consciously to decide to leave the land of their oppressors—*that* would be black radicalism. *That* would constitute a powerful vindication of the fathers and mothers, from the baracoons to the Brazos. It was not the only path of vindication, but its significance for that age was undeniable.

While Martin Delany symbolized the ferment in the Northern black movement, in the South the growing turmoil was no less clear to all who had eyes. A white writer in Virginia remarked that summer: "It is useless to disguise the fact, its truth is undeniable, that a greater degree of in-subordination has been manifested by the negro population, within the last few months, than at any previous period in our history as a state." Many of those responsible for maintaining the system were aware of black resistance. A judge of the North Carolina Supreme Court, in sentencing a black man who had defied a master by acting "impudently and insolently" and by impugning the purity of one of the young white ladies of the household, put forth his own view of the perilous situation: "What acts in a slave towards a white person will amount to insolence, it is manifestly impossible to define—it may consist in a look, the pointing of a finger, a refusal or neglect to step out of the way when a white person is seen to approach. But each of such acts violates the rules of propriety, and if tolerated, would destroy that insubordination, upon which our social system rests."[11]

The concern was justified, for a relentless erosion was at work. Nowhere was it more evident, yet hidden, than in the endless streams of runaways, and in the songs which preceded them into the Southern nights. Black folk gathered in the brush arbors or in the cabins and sang:

> I'm going away, I'm going away,
> I'm going away to live forever,
> I'll never turn back no mo'.

Then, while some singers turned their faces toward heaven and waited for a force outside history to propel them "away," others set out toward the North on their own two feet. Among the fugitives, some committed suicide before allowing their lives to be reclaimed by the white masters, but much more commonly the fugitives used their arms (and they often ran with weapons) not against themselves, but against the masters and slave agents who sought to track them down.[12]

At the same time, even in the midst of their desperate flights, some black men and women maintained a magnificent sense of humor and quickness of wit. (That too was often part of the river's erosive force.) One family's tradition told of a young man named George who, with a friend, ran away from Alabama's slavery.

Him an' annudder fellow had got 'way up in Virginny 'fo' Massa Jim foun' out whar dey was. Soon as Massa Jim foun' de war'bouts of George he went after him. When Massa Jim gits to George an' 'em, George pretended lack he did't know Massa Jim. Massa Jim as' him, "George don't you know me?" George he say, "I never seed you 'fo' in my life." Den dey as' George an' 'em whar did dey come from. George an' [the other] fellow look up in de sky an' say, "I come from above, whar all is love."[13]

In 1852 the testimony came from across the South: blacks were freeing themselves from Randolph County, Missouri; from Bolivar County, Mississippi; from the South Carolina Railroad Company; from a chain gang in New Orleans. From Clinton, Tennessee, from Sparta, Georgia, and the docks of Wilmington, North Carolina, fugitives were eroding the system of slavery. Erosion took many forms, but the system was insistently challenged. Runaways, black men and women wielding scythes and hoes against overseers, others throwing fiery coals into the faces of patrollers— all were part of the welling movement. Always, weaving their way through the river, adding to its relentless power, the songs remained:

> One of dese mornings, five o'clock,
> Dis ole world gonna reel and rock,
> Pharaoh's Army got drownded
> Oh Mary, don't you weep

Any people who really believed in the future drowning of the oppressive Pharaoh and his army—any people who considered themselves chosen by the ruler of the universe—were not a people under firm control.

Of course the keepers of the system saw no alternative but to press down yet more rigidly. Thus in 1852 Alabama enacted an even stricter slave code, repeating the death promise for slave arson, threatening that "every slave who robs . . . or willfully maims . . . or attempts to poison, or to deprive any white person of life . . . must, on conviction, suffer death." And early in 1853 the new President, Franklin Pierce, speaking in the accents of his native New Hampshire's free society, promised fervently in his inaugural address to uphold the spirit and the letter of the Fugitive Slave Law. Yet every such law, on local or national levels, was ultimately another testimony to the active black struggle.[14]

Continued repression from the highest levels of white America, and the persistent and varied black responses from below, increased the pressure on Northern mainstream leaders like Douglass to develop new forms of organized resistance and response. In 1853 the black leader attempted to do this, all this, while fighting the rising power of the movement for emigration, perhaps fearful of his own searing flashes of the visions of Walker and Turner. By the summer of that year Douglass, working with others of his persuasion, had organized another National Black Convention. Meeting in Rochester that July, the convention formed the apogee of the Great Tradition of Black Protest in the antebellum period. When it convened, it was clear that the meeting had attracted more of the men and women who prominently represented that position than ever before. Among those present were James McCune Smith, J. W. C. Pennington, William H. Day, the Langston brothers, Amos Beman, William C. Nell,

Charles L. Remond, and John B. Vashon. Later a commentator claimed that the group represented "one of the grandest arrays of talent and wisdom ever assembled on this continent."[15]

Obviously it was an historic occasion. Many of these gifted black abolitionists were known throughout the Northern states and the British Isles. This meeting was their major co-ordinated attempt to give some clear sense of direction to the beleaguered children of Africa in America —their desperate effort to impose some order on the rising chaos and burgeoning uncertainties of the 1850s.

On one level, the need for such a conference was obvious: The rising dangers and uncertainties demanded a more unified black leadership, a clear sense of direction, some word of protest and appeal. Beyond these general needs, the Rochester convention appears also to have developed out of more specific, concrete, and ambiguous situations. For one, there was Martin Delany. Although he never was mentioned in the call or in the official proceedings of the convention, Rochester was probably meant to be an answer to the mounting forces of nationalism and emigrationism which Delany and the *Condition* represented.

But there was another specific and far more troubling background to the gathering. In 1852 Harriet Beecher Stowe, daughter of one of the major Protestant leaders in white America, published her antislavery novel *Uncle Tom's Cabin*. It was an immediate literary and political sensation, selling more than 300,000 copies in its first year. In February 1853 Mrs. Stowe invited Frederick Douglass to her house in Maine. There she indicated that she would soon travel to England and the European continent, and wanted to help raise money overseas for a major project which would "permanently contribute to the improvement and elevation of the free colored people in the United States." She had not yet decided precisely what sort of project would be appropriate, so after their conversation Mrs. Stowe asked Douglass to send her a letter, proposing what the project ought to be. In March 1853 Douglass wrote to Harriet Stowe, suggesting that a "manual labor college"—in effect, a trade school—be established for black people, preferably in his city of Rochester.[16]

While the details of the proposal were not of great importance, the tone of Douglass's letter was. For it was a letter that Booker T. Washington might have written forty or fifty years later to any similar prospective white benefactor. Denigrating black capacities and praising white power and civilization, at times it came frighteningly close to fawning and groveling—a strange position for a man of Douglass's stature and prestige. For instance, Douglass told Mrs. Stowe that one of the major problems blacks faced was the fact that "colored people are wanting in self-reliance." On the other hand, he said he was sure that whites could work out

the plans for the proposed manual labor school, because "it is the pecu-
liarity of your favored race that they can always do what they think
necessary to be done." This was not meant as sarcasm. Rather, in this
and other ways the contrast was sharply drawn between free blacks as
sadly dependent and unreliable, and whites as all-powerful. In this
context Douglass awaited Mrs. Stowe's beneficence, and organized the
Rochester convention in anticipation of it. Thus the call which announced
the conference emphasized that "there will come before the convention
matters touching the disposition of such funds as our friends abroad,
through Mrs. Harriet Beecher Stowe, may appropriate to the cause of our
progress and improvement."[17]

There were at least 114 persons present at the delegate sessions of the
convention—a comparatively large number for such meetings, and a commentary on the urgency of the time. Douglass was elected one of the vice-
presidents and chairman of the Committee on Declaration of Sentiments.
That declaration came early in the session, and set the tone for much of
the ambivalence which ran like a deep fault through this black abolitionist
gathering. Addressed to "The People of the United States," it was obviously directed to the white population. The major goal of the declaration
was to justify the black claim to common citizenship rights with whites:
"We are Americans, and as Americans, we would speak to Americans. We
address you not as aliens nor as exiles, humbly asking to be permitted to
dwell among you in peace; but we address you as American citizens asserting their rights on their own native soil. Neither do we address you as
enemies (although the recipients for innumerable wrongs); but in the
spirit of patriotic good will." Following a black tradition that went back
at least as far as Toussaint L'Ouverture, the declaration attempted to
appeal to the "best" in America, the writers (primarily Douglass) affirming their belief that "the genuine American, brave and independent himself, will respect bravery and independence in others." But when the
delegates later set forth a long list of grievances and injustices which they
rightly attributed to the majority of Americans, the question could be
asked, which were the "genuine" ones whose ears and hearts they
sought?[18]

Perhaps it was because of this confusing and debilitating search for a
conciliatory relationship with "the genuine American" that these human
trumpets of black agitation were so feeble in their calls for justice, so
impotent before the concrete blows raining down daily on the black community. The leaders at Rochester spoke with far less authority and determination concerning the Fugitive Slave Law than the nationwide black
society was displaying every day. Said Douglass's committee: "We ask
that the Fugitive Slave Law of 1850, that legislative monster of modern

times, by whose atrocious provisions the writ of 'habeas corpus' [and] the 'right of trial by jury' have been virtually abolished, shall be repealed." In the same amazingly passive mode, the convention addressed the need for black suffrage, putting the emphasis not on rights, but on how blacks deserved the suffrage because of their total identification with America's interests. It was an almost obsequious plea which came forth from these fiery orators: "We ask that (inasmuch as we are, in common with other American citizens, supporters of the state, subject to its laws, interested in its welfare, liable to be called to defend it in time of war, contributors to its wealth in time of peace), the complete and unrestricted right of suffrage which is essential to the dignity even of the white man, be extended to the Free Colored man also."[19]

The weakness of their attack was also partly attributable to the inner ideological struggles of the delegates. These were sharply outlined in the "Report of the Committee on Social Relations and Polity," and their reactions to it. The highly respected and assimilationist-oriented William Whipper and Charles Ray were on the committee, and their report turned out to be the most controversial document of the convention. At its heart were the dilemmas and contradictions which then starkly faced the black abolitionist leaders in America. For example, speaking in the vein of American moral reform, they put forward the white family as a model for black people to emulate in the development of their own family life. Yet they knew that white American families had produced all those men and women justly indicted by the convention's address for every sort of attack and cruelty against black people. What sort of model was this?[20]

Further, when it came to the issue of black education, the report sadly admitted that the "whole tendency" of white institutions and teachers, when dealing with black students, was to educate them away from a position of solidarity with their people. Thus the committee reluctantly concluded that it was necessary to develop "the whole process of instruction to meet our particular exigencies"—a task that only blacks could realistically undertake. It was this section that prompted the sharpest and most sustained debate from the delegates, who were concerned about the apparent recommendation of separate and "exclusive" education for black people under the control of other blacks. Many felt they had been fighting too many battles on behalf of black inclusion in white schools and other institutions to accept this proposal readily. Whipper, Ray, and the other committee members denied that they were deserting the traditional struggle, but their report was finally rejected, and the convention went on record as opposing any "complexional exclusiveness" in the development of black education.[21]

At the same time, reflecting the paradoxes and pressures of the day,

the convention called for the development of a set of national black institutions to give direction and help to the desperate black Northern community. An overarching "National Legislature of Colored People" was
initially proposed, but this suggested a far more radical, self-reliant position than most members desired to take, so the idea of a national "Council" was substituted. It was to be a partly appointed, partly elected body,
working in co-operation with similar state councils. Four committees of
the Council would create a number of other national institutions. These
included the manual labor school, a black consumers' co-operative, a
national skills bank and employment agency, and a combined black
archives, bureau of vital statistics, and anti-defamation league.[22]

It was a fascinating, ambitious program, responding simultaneously to
the attacks of the white world and to the forces represented by Delany,
Holly, and others within the black community. On the surface it was a
faint blueprint for black national organizations, a recognition of black
nationality in America. But the delegates at Rochester could not bear
the weight of their own vision. Their final resolution testified to the difficult tension of the abolitionist community in that hard moment of history:
". . . in establishing a National Council for our own special improvement, and a Manual Labor School for the education of our children in
science, literature, and the mechanical arts, this convention do this, not to
build ourselves up as a distinct and separate class in this country, but as
a means to a great end, viz: the equality in political rights, and in civil
rights, and in civil and social privileges with the rest of the American
people." In many ways, this was an understandable position for men who
had persistently fought the virus of Northern segregation, sometimes for
two decades and more. Nevertheless, by their indecisive position, the
black abolitionists tended to enfeeble their own resolve, and to block and
compromise the surge toward black solidarity, self-reliance, and a healthy
sense of African nationality. Instead, they closed the convention eagerly
expressing their "undying affection" to Garrison and his fellow abolitionists, and announcing that *Uncle Tom's Cabin* was "a work plainly
marked by the finger of God" on behalf of black people.[23]

The Great Tradition of Black Protest, with all its magnificent representatives whose lives bore undeniable witness to many hard and valiant
struggles in the past, could speak no word of clear direction for the present. Their faces were turned too fully to the white community and what
it might think and do. Their own minds were unsettled, their wills un-
honed. So they directed the black community neither to open resistance
and rebellion, nor to massive civil disobedience or emigration. If they
heard trumpets, the sound was uncertain. If they were depending upon
Mrs. Stowe's promised financial assistance, like so many other promises

from the white world, it was not kept. By the next year, even the much-discussed plans for black national institutions were swept aside by the indecision of their creators and the fierce movement of history.[24]

It was an instructive experience, even so. Persistent, rampant white nationalist racism, organized and legitimized from the federal level down, had shown black nationalist organizing to be a real and explicit necessity, even though the black people involved were afraid to follow the implications of such a radical thrust. Still, Douglass and his largely assimilationist group had been driven by the sheer necessity of black struggle to explore new possibilities of national black self-reliance, self-definition, and self-determination. In other times and places such organizing could lead to the open drive for national independence. Where it might lead in white-majority America was not clear, but the way surely had to be explored. For blacks determined to remain in America, there was no other logical course.

For in spite of relentless black struggle, in spite of the radicalism being explored across the North, slavery still appeared to be gaining strength, not losing it. On the surface, the South's spokesmen seemed bolder and more confident in their future; the official reopening of the African slave trade was being discussed at Southern business conventions.

Then, in 1854, the tortured issue of the continued expansion of the "peculiar institution" on American soil erupted in Congress again. The subject was bitterly raised anew each time the nation decided to enlarge itself, indicating that Manifest Destiny was impossible without facing the destiny of the nation's black native-aliens, and that the question of the black future was buried deep (as blood?) in the land itself. Now the question was whether or not the future of slavery in the territories of Kansas and Nebraska should be decided on the basis of white popular sovereignty, thus abrogating the $36°30'$ demarcation line between slave and free territory set by the Missouri Compromise of 1820. The fierce, ill-tempered arguments raged in Congress for three months, until a popular sovereignty bill sponsored by Sen. Stephen Douglas of Illinois was passed in May 1854.[25]

In the racial dialectics of America, the struggles and compromises of white leaders in response to the presence and movement of blacks had their profound effects on large numbers of black people, and Douglas's bill was no exception. Indeed, with its passage another tormenting burden was added to the cause of black freedom. The Kansas-Nebraska Territory now offered the advocates of slavery a new possibility to press their exploitation of Afro-Americans further into the West, more brazenly into the North, all the way to Canada's border. At the same time there were renewed and bolder rumblings from the South—and elsewhere—about the possible annexation of that long-envied, African-saturated Caribbean plantation, Cuba. If it happened, as seemed possible in that troubled year, then the bondage of black people would surely be given new life.

It was a bitter time in Canaan, so difficult and frightening that even Frederick Douglass estimated that no less than one quarter of the black population of the North appeared open to the possibilities of emigration. Since the publication of the *Condition* in 1852, Martin Delany had firmly grasped the intellectual leadership of the black emigrationist movement. In the summer of 1853 while the black community of the North was still discussing Douglass's meeting at Rochester, Delany and his friends had felt confident enough in their cause to call for a major convention of their own. Expressly addressing themselves to "all colored men in favor of emigration out of the United States, and opposed to the American Colonization scheme of leaving the Western Hemisphere," the new call maintained the tension between struggle in the United States and movement elsewhere. While it was directed to committed emigrationists, at the same time the call declared, "We . . . ever will stand shoulder to shoulder by our brethren, and all true friends in all good measures adopted by them, for the bettering of our condition in this country, and surrender no rights but with our last breath."[26]

However, not everyone was certain about the meaning and effect of that tension. In the twelve months that elapsed between the issuance of the call in August 1853 and the gathering of the convention in Cleveland, the following summer a spirited, often angry debate stormed through the Northern black community over the question of emigration. Although he published the text of the call to Cleveland in his newspaper, Frederick Douglass declared, "We have no sympathy with the call for this convention," and said he considered it "uncalled for, unwise, unfortunate and premature." He was especially troubled about the open view it would provide to the white public of divisions within the black ranks. His associate editor went further and said that the proposed convention, by admitting that black people could not hope for equality in America, would give "aid and comfort to the enemy." Other opponents were not so restrained: at least one black leader claimed that the emigrationist forces were "no longer . . . friends, but inveterate enemies and haters of the cause [they] once advocated." And some persons suggested that black people in Cleveland ought to use physical force to stop the convention from meeting.[27]

Meanwhile Delany and his friends continued to plan carefully for Cleveland, putting forth a variety of arguments. Some of these ideas were essentially black Zionist in nature, others rose to a level of political messianism not unfamiliar to readers of Delany's writings. For instance, one of the most persistent proemigrationist arguments claimed that "colored men can never be fully and fairly respected as the equals of the whites, in this country, or any other, until they are able to show in some part of the world, men of their own race occupying a primary and independent position, instead of a secondary and inferior one, as is now the case everywhere." Moving beyond this forensic Zionism, the young poet-journalist and barber J. M. Whitfield put forth another version of Delany's hemispheric messianism. Writing from Buffalo in defense of the emigrationist position, he said, "I believe it to be the destiny of the negro, to develop a higher order of civilization and Christianity than the world has yet seen. I also consider it a part of his 'manifest destiny' to possess all the tropical regions of this continent, with the adjacent islands." From such a position of strength, Whitfield claimed, it would be possible for the black race to "exercise its proper influence in moulding the destiny, and shaping the policy of the American continent." It was a bold vision, and not a new one to the thirty-year-old black leader, who claimed to have held it since his adolescence.[28]

Indeed, in contrast to the deep uncertainties which hounded the black abolitionists, audacity and breadth of vision seemed to pervade the emigrationist forces as they prepared for the convention. Delany, H. Ford Douglas, Theodore Holly, Whitfield, and their coworkers appeared to have a clear sense of the direction in which they wished to lead the black community of the North. In spite of the angry attacks on emigrationists, in spite of the differences among them on such details as where blacks should go, the Cleveland organizers sensed momentum sufficient to make possible a relatively disciplined and firmly organized meeting in Cleveland. That discipline and sense of organization had already led them, contrary to the usual black convention style, to declare unequivocally that the meeting would be held "specifically by and for the friends of emigration and NONE OTHERS—and no opposition to them will be entertained." Delany and his core group so controlled the screening of credentials and the admission of delegates that the policy was well upheld. With such sense of purpose and sophistication of organization, it was not surprising that the Cleveland convention became one of the major sources of radical black ideology in the nineteenth century.[29]

From the outset, Delany and his colleagues were developing important new directions. For instance, they accredited twenty-nine black women as voting delegates, nearly one-third of the official representation. Among them were Delany's wife Kate, and Mary E. Bibb, the widow of the recently deceased emigrationist leader, Henry Bibb. (Mrs. Bibb was also elected a second vice-president of the convention.) The mainstream black convention and protest movement had never advanced so fully toward political equality for women. As the sessions began, two carefully wrought documents were the focus of much of the discussion. The first was Delany's report, "The Political Destiny of the Colored Race on the American Continent." Sixteen hundred black people and a few white guests had crowded into the Congregational Church on Prospect Street for the public session of the convention, when Delany presented his report. Much of it was a condensation and elaboration of his 1852 document, including the call for black settlement in the southern part of the American continent. But there were also crucial new elements which had obviously been thrust forward by the experiences of the intervening two years.[30]

In Cleveland in 1854, Delany appeared convinced that the black condition which he had outlined two years before had not improved in the interval, and many members of the audience agreed. Indeed, he said he was convinced that some new compromise would eventually be worked out between the white leadership of the North and South to make it possible for slavery to re-enter the North on a states'-rights basis. Under these circumstances, he insisted, blacks could not sit passively and wait. But as he moved the audience toward his argument for emigration, Delany refused to diminish the hard tension between struggle in America and the struggle to create a new humanity beyond America's shores. Indeed, in the course of this emigrationist statement, the black healer-politician put forward one of the most axiomatic statements of the goals of the black struggle for freedom anywhere: "No people can be free who themselves do not constitute an essential part of the *ruling element* of the country in which they live." In this country Delany saw the goal of the fight for freedom as the right to participate unequivocally, centrally, as governors and determiners of the direction of all American society. The struggle was for the right to rule, and not for a precarious dependence "on the hands" of America, living as its permanent mendicant guests—or later as eternal consumers of "a piece" of its pie.[31]

Nor could Delany foresee or approve of a policy of racial assimilation which would solve the problem of white racism by destroying the black nation. In pressing this point, he produced an insight which the world would later associate with W. E. B. DuBois: "It would be duplicity longer to disguise the fact that the great issue, sooner or later, upon which must be disputed the world's destiny, will be the question of black and white, and every individual will be called upon for his identity with one or the other." Almost a half century before Du Bois's own statement, the issue of the universal color line, and the struggles to be waged around it, had been unmistakably drawn there in Cleveland.[32]

More important, Delany did not stop with the statement of the general principle concerning international color-based conflict. His brilliant, exciting analysis went forward to deal with the specific role of the oppressive American nation in which black people were captive, and here his prophetic insight was stunning. Lifting his full, rich voice with that controlled and slashing anger which so often marked his speeches, Delany said that "the determined aim of the whites has been to crush the colored races wherever found . . . for more than two thousand years." Indeed, he predicted, "the Anglo-Americans" would continue their moves toward control "of every habitable portion of the earth," unless they were stopped.[33]

Continuing where David Walker had left off and moving far beyond, Delany was developing a global analysis of the black-white encounter. As a result, he told the Cleveland audience it was time for black people to move forward with audacious initiative and power; it was time to remember that "the white races are but one-third of the population of the globe —or one of them to two of us—and it cannot much longer continue that two thirds will passively submit to the universal domination of this one third." It was time for black people to move against the bloody white tide, time to resist "by grasping hold of those places [in the world] where chance is in [our] favor, and establishing the rights and power of the colored race."[34]

Emigration, then, was not simply a domestic issue of black struggle for freedom. As Delany posed the matter, it was crucial to the future of the colored races of the world in their international struggles against increasing white incursion and exploitation. In that context, Delany called out to blacks in America: "We must make an issue, create an event, and establish for ourselves a position. This is essentially necessary for our effective elevation as a people, in shaping our national development, directing our destiny, and redeeming ourselves as a race." It was time for the forward movement, the redemptive movement, the movement to create a new history. This was the call of Delany's black radicalism. Beginning with the affirmation of the black right to share *rule* in America, he had expanded his challenge to white power to a worldwide scale. Ideologically, black struggle had never before been pressed so far. In Cleveland, Delany provided a signpost, a watershed.[35]

Hardly had the excitement from Delany's address died away, when it was time for the brash and brilliant H. Ford Douglas to bear down from another direction. He had been chosen to defend the emigrationist position against the unexpected attacks of John Mercer Langston, the popular young graduate of Oberlin who had just become the first black person admitted to the Ohio bar, and who was already a recognized abolitionist leader in his state. Langston had been accepted as a speaker on the record of his earlier emigrationist position, but had surprised the convention by attacking emigration and speaking disparagingly of the "little faith" Delany and his group showed in the ultimate triumph of freedom in America. Langston knew Douglas from the Ohio black conventions and elsewhere, therefore he must have had some sense of what he was provoking. For H. Ford Douglas loved words, loved their very sounds as he crashed them into the arguments of his opponents, loved the feel and shape of them as he hurled them into the struggle. Like Langston, he was in his early twenties, and he was conscious of his youth, aware that he was taking on a popular and highly esteemed black leader, and at the same time challenging not just the immediate antagonist but many of the older leaders of the Great Tradition.[36]

After a harsh personal attack on Langston for his action as "a Judas" to the emigration cause, Douglas assailed the "wisdom" of the elders concerning emigration. Responding to the Rochester convention, he asked, "Because Mr. [Frederick] Douglass, Mr. [J. McCune] Smith or Mr. [John M.] Langston tell me that the principles of emigration are destructive to the best interests of the colored people in this country, am I to act the part of a 'young robin' and swallow it down without ever looking into the merits of the principles involved?" Providing his own emphatic answer, Douglas shouted the central question home to the abolitionist, antiemigrationist group: "No! Gentlemen. You must show me some more plausible reason for the faith which is within you." The quintessential question to the supporters of the Great Tradition had been bluntly posed: if you believe that black people will gain their freedom in this racist land, *why* do you believe it? What is the source of your belief, your faith, your hope?[37]

On that evening of August 27, 1854, H. Ford Douglas, like Delany, was not a believer in the coming of black freedom in America in any foreseeable future.

You must remember that slavery is not a foreign element in this government nor is it really antagonistic to the feelings of the American people. On the contrary, it is an element commencing with our medieval existence, receiving the sanction of the early Fathers of the Republic, sustained by their descendants through a period of nearly three centuries, deep and firmly laid in our [*sic*] organization. Completely interwoven into the passions and prejudices of the American people. It does not constitute a local or sectional institution as the generous prompting of the great and good [Charles] Sumner would have it, but is just as national as the Constitution which gives it an existence.[38]

It was a perfect description of the profound levels of racism ("the passions and prejudices") in America, a warning to all those who looked for an easy end to the institution of slavery. It was this radical analysis and not their "little faith," said Douglas, which "makes us anxious to leave this country." For the emigrationists were convinced that the "life-sustaining resources which slavery is capable of commanding may enable the institution to prolong its existence to an indefinite period of time." According to the young orator, slavery would exist as long as the Union held together: "I firmly believe that the destruction of slavery depends upon the dissolution of these states." However, he was also convinced that such disruption would eventually come, as an act of God's judgment: "It was a guilty copartnership in the first place. It must be and it shall be destroyed." But H. Ford Douglas did not expect to wait in America for that denouement; in 1854, it seemed too far away.[39]

In spite of his overestimation of the Union's power to hold together (which implied a certain underestimation of the power of the black river), Douglas's speech was impressive for its contribution to black radical analysis. Indeed, at one point in his desperately eloquent statement, Douglas anticipated one of the most striking images of the twentieth-century black nationalist movement. He was responding to the vexing, enigmatic issue of the relationship between the black birthright in America and the imperative need to leave America. Should black people really give up their rights to this second native land? John Langston had raised the question in his speech, and Douglas replied: "The gentleman's loud vociferations about remaining here because it happens to be the place of his birth, is a very poor argument indeed. . . . There is just as much force in a black man's standing up and exclaiming after the manner of the 'old Roman'—'I am an American citizen,' as there was in the Irishman who swore he was a loaf of bread, because he happened to be born in a bake oven."[40] (Teaching twentieth-century blacks of their Africanness, Malcolm X would say: "Because a cat has kittens in an oven, it don't make them biscuits.")

Out of a radical analysis came a radical prescription. In addition to affirming emigration, Douglas threw the crowd into tremendous excitement when he declared openly his own willingness to engage in treason against America:

When I remember the many wrongs that have been inflicted upon my unfortunate race, I can scarcely realize the fact that this is my country. I owe it no allegiance because it refused to protect me. . . . I can hate this Government without being disloyal, because it has stricken down my manhood and treated me as a saleable commodity. I can join a foreign enemy and fight against it, without being a traitor, because it treats me as an ALIEN and a STRANGER, and I am free to avow that should such a contingency arise I should not hesitate to take any advantage in order to procure indemnity for the future. I can feel no pride in the glory, growth, greatness or grandeur of this nation.[41]

Although black men and women most often preferred to avoid the thought, Douglas reminded them that in a time like their own the logic of black radicalism might well lead to treason. Indeed, when white racist ideology embedded itself in the very viscera of the state, Douglas saw treason as perfectly justifiable for a black community determined to fight for its freedom. As a result of such fervent and frightening advocacy, black members of the audience may have had to fight hard battles within themselves. Thus the minutes say that Douglas "kept the house in a ferment of emotion." (Emotion, of course, does not lead inevitably to the radicalizing experience, but it gives witness to the inner struggle which must precede all others.)

Before the Cleveland convention was over, there was another product of its work which, combined with Douglas's stunning presentation and Delany's prophetic report, indelibly marked the assembly as a touchstone for the future. It was not possible to predict that the "Declaration of Sentiments and Platform of the Convention" would focus on the root issues of black struggle in America, for such issues did not seem to belong to an emigration convention. But by that time Delany and young Douglas should have made it clear to all that the central issue for the Cleveland forces was not simply emigration or nonemigration in the abstract, but rather the life and renewal of the black nation, the healing of a broken people, the fulfilling of a fiercely sensed destiny, wherever it might take place.

Therefore the Cleveland Declaration spoke to the question of what would have to be done if black people were to surge forward into a self-determining history, courting a destiny no less manifest than that of the Anglo-American world. The declaration also listed the stringent requirements to be met in America, if black people were to work out their destiny in this land. Because of its solid grounding in history, because of the consistency of its concrete analysis of the contemporary situation, because of its faithfulness to the vision of the future that black people needed, much of the Cleveland Declaration moved far beyond the Great Tradition of Protest, and remains alive as a radical prescription today.[42]

The declaration was probably the work of Delany and H. Ford Douglas as much as anyone else. It began with the usual nineteenth-century abolitionist affirmation of natural rights, including the franchise. Then the writers went on to develop certain critical elements of the black struggle which were at once more specific and more universal: "That as men and equals, we demand every political right, privilege and position to which the whites are eligible in the United States, and we will either attain to these, or accept of nothing." Behind that pledge of persistent struggle for total equality in America, there appeared in the convention a constant concern for black unity as well. Thus the document said, "We pledge our integrity to use all honorable means, to unite us, as one people, on this continent."[43]

It was interesting to note the way the Cleveland and Rochester assemblies approached the brutal question of the Fugitive Slave Law. While the Rochester men of the Great Tradition had simply requested the largely racist white rulers to repeal the act, the black men and women at Cleveland said of the law (and implicitly of its creators): "We abhor its existence, dispute its authority, refuse submission to its provisions and hold it in a state of the most contemptuous abrogation." Declaring the hated law null and void, offering the basic challenge to the systems of white authority, the black emigrationist convention refused to legitimize their oppressors with appeals to their power. Indeed, the Cleveland Declaration went beyond this clear challenge to the legitimacy of white power, and restated the demand for effective black power in America as an absolute requirement for any black integrity in this land: "As a people we will never be satisfied nor contented until we occupy a position where we are acknowledged a necessary *constituent* in the *ruling element* of the country in which we live." The Great Tradition had asked only for acceptance by the rulers of the society, for permission to participate as a voting constituency as equals on the minimal level. Ideologically, Cleveland was a profoundly radical challenge because it rammed against the limits of white supremacy—as well as the limits of black aspirations—and dared to propose that the entire society be restructured to move those who had been its captives into the governing councils of its life.[44]

Whether this goal of total black participation was to be realized in America or beyond its boundaries, the creators of the Cleveland Declaration assumed what *The Communist Manifesto* assumed, what the New Testament assumed, what Frederick Douglass sometimes assumed: that where freedom was the issue, struggle was inevitable. For those who sought the liberty to be human, to shape new lives and to create a new society, for those who were trying to move out of the brutal experiences of slavery and mean discrimination, for those who sought those things and were black, in America in 1854, there was no way save the way of the river. Thus the Cleveland convention declared:

That no oppressed people have ever obtained their rights by voluntary acts of generosity on the part of their oppressors.

That it is futile hope on our part to expect such results through the agency of moral goodness on the part of our white American oppressors.

That if we desire liberty, it can only be obtained at the price which others have paid for it.

In the light of those ruthless realities, those great costs, they stated their own commitment: "We are willing to pay that price, *let the cost be what it may*. . . . No people, as such, can ever attain to greatness who lose their identity . . . we shall ever cherish our identity of origin and race, as preferable, in our estimation, to any other people." In Cleveland, black identity and black struggle were inseparable.[45]

Cleveland was perhaps the high point, the deep point, of black radical analysis in the nineteenth century, the best setting forth of black struggle's proper direction in America—or elsewhere. Cleveland carried within itself both the major elements of the river's broad movements, and many of the best aspects of the radical streams. In its call for an authentic black power based on a global vision of struggle and renewal; in its ardent commitment to the coming of the new black nation; in its unflinching identification of the nature and direction of white oppression; in its statement of radical opposition to that oppression, Cleveland was unsurpassed.

The hope which the convention represented flowed out of the history of the river. Later it surfaced again in the ecstatic expectations which grasped black people during the Civil War, in the goals toward which they worked and dreamed in Reconstruction, and in the inarticulate murmurs of thousands of black people who migrated out of the South. Indeed, such hope became a part of what black people relentlessly fought for throughout the twentieth century (and shall no doubt struggle for in the century ahead). But Cleveland was also a link to the past, for Delany's idea of the 1830s finally came to fruition when the convention voted to establish a National Board of Commissioners, with him as its chairman. Out of that board there emerged the mandate to explore three areas for possible black emigration: West Africa, Haiti, and Central America. Meanwhile, seeking temporary alternatives, men like Delany and Douglas soon chose Canada as their base of operations.[46]

That fall, as the search proceeded for a place of black destiny beyond the American furnace, Delany received word from his home community which confirmed all that he knew about the cost of black struggle, even the struggle to leave America. The message came from the white-owned Pittsburgh *Daily Morning Post*, and showed the white world's determination to see no effective black power rise to challenge its domination of this hemisphere. Probably because of Delany's great influence there, the editor felt called upon to discuss those aspects of the Cleveland convention and of Delany's writings which referred specifically to the possibility of a new black nation in Central or Latin America or in the Caribbean. Interestingly enough, the *Post* claimed to believe in emigration to Africa for black people, and said "that anyone will be turned aside from so noble a mission by the delusive dream of conquest and empire in the Western hemisphere is an absurdity too monstrous and mischievous to be believed." The idea of independent black nationhood and confederation in the New World, the *Post* said, "is a vast conception of impossible birth."[47]

Predictably, the white journal proceeded to offer its gratuitous analysis of why such a black plan was "impossible," "monstrous," and "mischievous." In so doing, it actually catalogued the essential realities which faced any black emigration struggle. "The Committee [Delany's commissioners] seems to have entirely overlooked the strength of 'powers on earth' that would oppose Africanization of more than of the Western Hemisphere." In addition to European powers with interests and holdings in the Caribbean area, the paper said,

the United States too, with its routes of commerce across Central America, its friendly relations with the doomed republics of the South, its intention to annex Cuba, *and a little more*, will she not bear a part in this grand tragi-comic emeute [riot, disturbance]? We can assure our colored neighbors that Uncle Sam, Johnny Bull, Johnny Crappeau, Queen Christiana and the Dutch, will all interpose most formidable obstacles to this splendid project. Nothing but a sudden coup de main could give it any chance of success. And for that there is no adequate preparation.[48]

So the accurate if unsolicited white word was given: let black men and women dare to try to break out of the chains forged by this nation, and the experience of the slave ships will be repeated; the warring white nations will unite against them. Let black men and women dare to move toward independent black power which challenges white hegemony, and the response will be what blacks had repeatedly experienced across the North: a riot of white power. There was no ambiguity: whether they stayed or left, if black men and women determined to be free, they faced "most formidable obstacles" of whiteness.

But that was not news, only confirmation of what was already known, even in the mainstream of the struggle. America had made itself very clear, in legal and extralegal ways. That was why even Frederick Douglass's words appeared to become more severe and demanding as the months went by: "Every colored man in the country should keep his revolver under his head, loaded and ready for use. . . . This reproach that blacks are submissive and therefore inferior must be wiped out, and nothing short of resistance on the part of colored men, can wipe it out. Every slave hunter who meets a bloody death in his infernal business, is an argument in favor of the manhood of our race. Resistance is, therefore, wise as well as just." Still, there was something faulty about the honing here. Aside from his simplistic American tendency to equate manhood with armed self-defense, Douglass seemed to focus his call for resistance on the "slave hunter," thereby forgetting the system which supported, maintained, and protected the hunter in his work. Moreover, his solution was a highly individualistic one, contributing little to organized black struggle.[49]

Nevertheless, he was undoubtedly being forced more deeply into radical action, for it was a time when men and women were being annealed even against their will, although imperfectly, incompletely. How else can one explain, in the summer of 1854, the Sunday-morning decision of Elizabeth Jennings, a quiet, respectable schoolteacher and church organist, to defy New York City's Third Avenue Railroad Company in its segregation of black riders in the horse-drawn cars? Probably it was only in such a time of tempering that a woman like this, in search of her rights, would determine to wrestle physically with the conductor and his driver, ending up being "dropped . . . down on the bottom of the platform, so that my feet hung one way and my head the other, nearly on the ground." (Eventually the detour from church led Jennings into the courts for a victory—one which broke the back of segregation on the city's public conveyances a century before Rosa Parks.) How else can one explain the scores of blacks and whites who tried to storm a Boston courthouse filled with fifty armed federal marshals, in order to rescue one black fugitive, Anthony Burns? Though they failed, it was obvious that the great Compromise of 1850 (and all the smaller ones) was not working, could not work, could not dissolve or conceal the overarching evil, the deeper cancer which black slavery revealed in the land, could not break the spirit of human resistance, North or South. Indeed, the very earth itself seemed to resist, to rebel. As the nation pressed its pseudo-legal claims across the expanses of the West, over the memories and mounds of the inhabitants, as it reached out to grab the land, the issue of slavery could not be escaped. The sounds of the river could not be stilled.[50]

On Jordan's Stormy Banks

The Rip Tide of Black Struggle (1855-1860)

Resolved, that if the Dred Scott dictum be the true exposition of the law of the land, then are the founders of the American Republic convicted by their descendants of base hypocrisy, and colored men absolved from all allegiance to a government which withdraws all protection.

Ohio Convention of Colored Men, 1857

By the middle of the decade there were signs everywhere that the white American nation was being driven to the internecine, bloody judgment that David Walker had once announced. Congress's decision to leave the future of slavery in the territories to the will of their white voters had led to guerrilla warfare in Kansas, "bleeding Kansas." In the spring and summer of 1856 a small and brutal civil war was fought there, and it appeared that the American tendency to seek ultimate solutions through the force of arms might prevail. Furthermore, late that spring in Congress, a Southern representative assaulted Sen. Charles Sumner with a heavy cane, striking the abolitionist legislator to the ground unconscious. This flailing attack in the national legislative chamber summed up all the terrible fury and fear then raging throughout the land.[1]

And black people were at the heart of it.

Yet in the minds of the white men and women who were turning on each other so fiercely, the fight still did not include black freedom. For them it was a struggle over the power represented by the slave states: a struggle to delimit their expansion and the degrading influence of slavery, to reserve as much land as possible for the movement of free white labor, for the rise and enrichment of the burgeoning capitalistic forces now clearly identified with the leadership of Northern white

society. And many seemed to struggle for nothing more than the satisfaction of that wild, irrational element in the human spirit which glorifies
warfare, blood, and death.[2]

Still, black people were at the heart of it. Through it all, one unity
remained: none of the major white political forces declared themselves
partisans of black freedom and equality. That was the vocation of black
people, and they did not avoid their calling. Indeed, it was their inexora-
ble movement toward freedom which helped explain why the compromises would not work, why the various white struggles must finally
coalesce in the fiery scourge of war. In that freedom movement, black
folk considered slavery to be the first and most formidable external
obstacle to freedom, and while the white conflicts intensified, individual
acts of black struggle and resistance continued to emerge. Men and
women still risked their lives to use poison against their masters. In the
desperate recourse to scorpions and snakes, others continued faithful to
the African-based arsenal of struggle. Arsonists continued their work in
factories and farms, while in their meeting places black singers cried out:

> Fire, My Saviour, fire
> Satan's camp a-fire;
> Fire, believer, fire,
> Satan's camp a-fire.[3]

Overseers, representing the immediate power of the system, were resisted and often dispatched in strange, mysterious ways. For instance, in
this period we are told that "two slave railroad workers hurriedly jumped
off their hand car, failing to warn their overseer riding with them that
a locomotive was unexpectedly approaching." Elsewhere, a black sugar
miller attempted to dump his overseer "into one of the kettles full of
boiling juice." In Texas it was said that the killing of masters and overseers by their black captive workers had become "painfully frequent,"
and at least one traveler through the Mississippi Valley carefully noted
that "overseers carried arms in constant fear of their lives." Meanwhile,
the swamps—Dismal, Okefenokee, Pasquotank, and others—received
new contingents of outlyers, and the endless stream of fugitives moving
undauntedly north (and sometimes south) continued to exacerbate the
already blood-raw relations between the slave and nonslave states.[4]

By 1856, while white civil conflicts burst forth from the halls of Congress to the sweeping plains of Kansas, reports of black rebelliousness
were rising to the surface everywhere in the South. In North Carolina,
black men were still moving boldly out of the swamps in swift guerrilla
attacks on the slaveowners and other whites. In August 1856 a group
of white citizens complained that in the swamp between Bladen and

Robeson counties "there are several runaways of bad and daring character—destructive to all kinds of stock and dangerous to all persons living
by or near said swamp." The black men had cleared a place for a garden,
and had cows and other livestock in the swamp. When the whites attempted to sweep them out they in fact accomplished nothing, but one
of their own men was killed; and to add insult to this injury, the defiant
black men ran away "cursing and swearing and telling them to come on,
they were ready for them again."[5]

In Tennessee, black iron workers attempted attacks on the mills where
they worked. They were defeated and some were jailed. According to
one testimony, they had planned larger things. It was said

that the negroes all intend rising on the day of the election; and that their plan
was to take advantage of the absence of the white men on that day, and while
they were all from home at the polls voting, to kill all the women and children,
get all the money and arms, and waylay the men on their return home from
the election and murder them; then make for the railroad cars, take them and
go to Memphis, where they could find arms and friends to carry them off to
the Free States if they did not succeed in taking this country.

This attempt by blacks to make their own use of the white elective process was foiled, and at least four persons were sentenced to death in
connection with it. But there was more: a party of some hundred and
fifty black men marched on Dover, Tennessee, in an attempt to rescue
the prisoners. Only a large, well-armed group of whites finally routed
the marchers, and eventually nineteen black participants were hanged.
Thereafter, according to black tradition, many black heads were chopped
off and as a warning to others were placed on poles, creating new signposts in the heart of Tennessee.[6]

In the same year, in Kentucky, caches of arms were found among black
people, as well as materials and plans for blowing up bridges. In Mississippi similar news surfaced, and as usual the state blamed white abolitionists and "black Republicans." It was in Texas, however, that signs
of trouble were most in evidence in that election year. That summer
the whites in Colorado County claimed to have discovered a plot which
would have brought the blacks and Mexicans together in a joint effort
for black freedom. Reportedly, there was a "well-organized and systematic plan for the murder of the entire white population" except for the
young women, who were supposed to be taken as wives when the liberation forces swept down into Mexico. It is difficult to know how reliable
the white information was, on both major and minor points, but at least
five black men were executed, three of them whipped to death, and all
Mexicans were forced to leave the country. At the end of that year, the

Galveston News observed that "never had so many insurrections, or attempts at insurrection, occurred as in the past six months."[7]

In 1856, from the swamps of North Carolina to the hills and rivers of Texas, the movement of black struggle had erupted in quickening ways. Why that year? Was it a desperate hope inspired by the rise of the new Republican Party? Was it the election and its passionately argued issues, its threats of secession and war? Was it Kansas and the fires burning across its plains? Was it the spirit that Nat had heard, the God that Walker knew was just? In black lore some said it was the Knights of Liberty, that mysterious guerrilla force, now fully prepared for its revolution, practicing, launching strategic thrusts across the land.[8]

Whatever the objective causes, the ferment was unmistakably there. As always, radical struggle was expressed through individual black lives like that of one Samuel in Concordia Parish, Louisiana, whose white overseer later testified: "On Tuesday morning the driver Bill came to me and stated that Samuel had become unmanageable, was destroying cotton, that he had ordered Samuel down to be whipped, that Samuel . . . swore that he would not be whipped. Bill then told him he would get the overseer." But the threat did not deter Samuel, who had made his break.

I . . . asked Samuel, if he had refused to get down for punishment when the driver ordered him, he answered at once, "Yes by God, I did and I am not going to be whipped by anybody, either black or white." I told him to stop, as I allowed no negro to talk in that way and he knew that. I then ordered him to throw down his hoe and get down, he swore God damn him if he would. . . . He turned and ran off. I kept my horse standing and called to the rest of the hands to catch that boy, not one of them paid the least attention to me, but kept on at their work. I then started after Samuel myself . . . he wheeled around, with his full force . . . his hoe descending . . . within one or two feet of my head. [I] pulled my horse up, and drew my pistol. Samuel was then standing with his hoe raised. I fired across my bridle arm when he fell.

Even before he fell, Samuel had joined the radical struggle, as had that group of black men and women, bent over, chopping their cotton, refusing to pay "the least attention" to an armed overseer's order to betray one of their own. Bending over their hoes there in Concordia Parish, they were sowing the river.[9]

It caught individual lives in many ways in that year, etching the model of the "bad nigger," the "crazy nigger," into the movement of its flow. However, not all such men met the fate of Samuel. Some resisted and stayed alive to become potential subjects for the honing that would take them beyond the level they had touched. In Mobile, Alabama, it was Battiste. It was said that "various citizens of Mobile frequently complained to the police that they lived in terror . . . of said slave, and

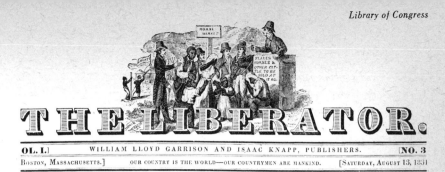

OL. I.]   WILLIAM LLOYD GARRISON AND ISAAC KNAPP, PUBLISHERS.   [NO. 3

BOSTON, MASSACHUSETTS.]   OUR COUNTRY IS THE WORLD—OUR COUNTRYMEN ARE MANKIND.   [SATURDAY, AUGUST 13, 1831

Masthead of the *Liberator*, August 13, 1831, which carried the story of the insurrection in Virginia.

An early portrait of Nat Turner.

Nat Turner and his companions plotting insurrection in Virginia in 1831.

Joseph Cinque,
leader of the July 1839 slave revolt
on board the Spanish ship *Amistad*.

Frederick Douglass,
former slave, abolitionist,
editor of the *North Star*, orator, writer.

Death of Captain Ferrer in the *Amistad* rebellion.

Fugitives defending themselves
against the specially-trained dogs of the slave catchers.

The case gained national prominence in the U.S. courts.

Henry Highland Garnet,
abolitionist and Presbyterian minister,
celebrated for his *Address to the Slaves
of the United States.*

Harriet Tubman during her service
as a Union Army scout.
She led three hundred
of her people to freedom on the
Underground Railroad.

Sojourner Truth,
best known as an abolitionist,
an active protestor against all forms
of injustice.

Martin Delany,
black nationalist theoretician,
first black field officer
to serve in the Civil War.

William Still,
leader of Philadelphia's Vigilance Committee
in the 1850s, abolitionist,
author of *The Underground Railroad*.

Margaret Garner, who killed two of her children rather than have them returned to slavery. When the remaining children were taken away, she committed suicide.

Samuel Ringgold Ward,
Presbyterian minister and
abolitionist lecturer.

Frances Ellen Watkins Harper,
prominent writer and anti-slavery lecturer.

"Twenty-eight Fugitives Escaping from the Eastern Shore of Maryland,"
an illustration from *The Underground Railroad.*.

Black men and women fighting off a group of whites,
including slaveowners, in Christiana, Pennsylvania, in 1851.

Henry Bibb,
a leader of Canada's black population
in the 1850s.

Charles Remond,
an agent of the American Anti-Slavery Society
in the two decades prior to the Civil War.

A poster that appeared in Boston
after slave agents came to the city,
captured Thomas Sims, a black fugitive,
and returned him to Georgia.

New York Public Library

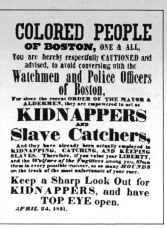

John Mercer Langston,
one of the North's most accomplished
lawyers and political leaders.

Robert Purvis,
an organizer of the first annual
convention of Free Colored People.

were afraid to leave their houses . . . that he . . . stole fowls, and had been in the habit of having unlawful assemblies of slaves at his house." Furthermore, "it was difficult for police officers to find him, and difficult to arrest him when found; that he had gone greased, in order to facilitate his escape, and wore his clothes without buttons, in such a manner that he could and did readily divest himself [of them] when seized."[10]

By nakedness, by grease, by buttonless clothes, the struggle was carried forward. Southern black workers took a different direction from Samuel or Battiste: they organized, stood together, and withheld their labor, demanding more humane conditions for their lives. Usually, a group of enslaved workers simply left the plantation for several days or longer, allowing other blacks to negotiate their grievances with the overseer or owner on their behalf, refusing to return until some settlement had been reached. At times—probably more often than we know now—their early attempts at labor strikes actually prevailed.

At the same time, in the necessary dialectics of struggle, the keepers of the system urged each other, as one said, "to tighten the cords which bind the negro to his condition of servitude—a condition which is to last, if the [Biblical] Apocalypse be inspired, until the end of time." But no cords could stop a river. Black struggle moved sometimes tumultuously, sometimes quietly, marked only by the screeching signal of the outlyers, a sound imitating the cry of the panther to frighten whites, to comfort blacks.[11]

Men like Elijah Anderson and John Mason, both fugitives themselves, continued the dangerous, demanding struggle against slavery by returning South, rescuing more than two thousand black persons in the 1850s. Once, ripped by hounds, Mason was captured and sold back into slavery, but he escaped again to continue his work. Elijah Anderson, less fortunate, died in a Kentucky prison in 1857.[12]

Still, the great power of the moving black fugitives ground against the walls of the system, persistently eroding the links of the political compromises, opening the way to the desperate acts which would finally bring about slavery's end. All the while, the singers sang on. Somewhere in Virginia or Maryland they sang, "Come a-long Moses, don't get lost/ We are the people of God." And Harriet Tubman responded with, "Wade in the water, children," and another group was gone.

In the North, the testing of the black community continued. When the fugitives arrived in that Canaan, whether as successful stowaways, members of Harriet Tubman's latest group, or lonely frightened pilgrims, they would find their highly regarded spokesman, Frederick Douglass, still contending with the spirits of Turner and Walker and Vesey, still wrestling in the deeper, troubling waters. In November 1856, Douglass said he still favored and sought every possible peaceful means to destroy slavery, but was convinced "its peaceful annihilation is almost hopeless . . . and . . . that the slave's right to revolt is perfect, and only wants the occurrence of favorable circumstances to become a duty." Douglass never clearly said what such "favorable circumstances" might be, and perhaps never could, for he admitted that "we cannot but shudder as we call to mind the horrors that have ever marked servile insurrections— we would avert them if we could, but shall the millions forever submit to robbery, to murder, to ignorance . . . because the overthrow of tyranny would be productive of horrors? We say not. The recoil when it comes, will be in exact proportion to the wrongs inflicted; terrible as it will be, we accept and hope for it." Even then he could not bring himself to call actively for the coming of the terrible open conflict. Instead, he spoke ominous though limited words: "The slaveholder has been tried and sentenced, his execution only waits the finish to the training of his executioners. He is training his own executioners."[13]

It was possible to say that Douglass's failure openly to advocate insurrection was further evidence of the limits of his radicalism, but far more important was his continued unwillingness to recognize the fact that the slaveholder was only one element in the system of slavery. He could not— or would not—sharpen and maintain those occasional radical insights which at times had led him to see the involvement of the American people, the American institutions, and the American government in the steel-like web of racism, exploitative economics, and fear which formed the basic undergirding of slavery. For it was not the call to armed insurrection which was the hallmark of antebellum black radicalism, but a careful, sober capacity to see the entire American government, and the institutions and population which it represented, as the basic foe of any serious black struggle, whatever its form might take. It was America, not simply slaveholders, which needed to be transformed, and above all the government and its institutions.

Black men and women did not easily maintain that insight. Its consequences were most often too frightening to face consciously for any sustained period of time. In the expanding campaigns of civil disobedience, men and women recognized the temporary, episodic need for such resistance to the government, but even then the long-range implications were not fully articulated save in moments of extreme rage and under great provocation. True, men like H. Ford Douglas and Martin Delany consistently pressed the message home, but there was a tendency to ascribe their position to their clear emigrationist commitments. Then, in March 1857, the U.S. Supreme Court handed down its long-awaited Dred Scott decision, and the reality of the American government's war against black freedom on behalf of the larger society could no longer be repressed or ignored.[14]

The case of the enslaved black house servant from Missouri had been in the courts for more than a decade. In the 1830s Dred Scott had accompanied his army-officer master to a free state and a free territory, and later, with the aid of some Saint Louis abolitionists, had sued for his freedom on the grounds that he had lived on free Northern soil, including a territory declared free of slavery by the Missouri Compromise of 1820. When Scott's case finally arrived at the Supreme Court in 1856, Roger Taney, who had been Attorney General under Andrew Jackson, was now Chief Justice, and his response was predictable. In March 1857 Taney read the Court's major decision, covering the two central questions: did Scott, as a slave, have a right to sue for his freedom, and had Congress acted constitutionally when it passed the Missouri Compromise legislation back in 1820 and 1821? In approaching the issue of Scott's rights, Taney first proposed another question which was then central to the free black community, especially in the North, but which would eventually touch the entire black population of the nation: "Can a negro, whose ancestors were imported into this country, and sold as slaves, become a member of the political community formed and brought into existence by the Constitution of the United States, and as such become entitled to all the rights, and privileges, and immunities, guaranteed by that instrument to the citizen? One of which rights is the privilege of suing in a court of the United States in the cases specified in the Constitution."[15]

The Court's answer was a resounding *no*. The decision claimed that the founding fathers had never intended African people to be a part of "We the people," the people who formed the nation and were recipients of its citizenship rights, privileges, and responsibilities. Moreover, Taney repeated much of what he had said in 1831 on a similar question: that the treatment of "free" black people since the constitutional period had clearly demonstrated that in practice the federal government, the states, and most of their citizens had never included blacks within the full privileges of the body politic. Therefore, he argued, neither Dred Scott nor any other person of African descent had any citizenship rights which were binding on white American society.[16]

It is interesting to speculate on what might have been the future of the Dred Scott decision, if that first ruling had been the sum of the Court's opinion. For as Taney had said, he was simply basing his statement on the precedents readily found in the treatment of free black people by the Northern states. Would such a judgment by itself have aroused a major furor from any significant portion of the population other than

black people and their closest allies? It is impossible and unnecessary to
say now, for there was a second part to the decision which became the
heart of bitter white controversies that continued right into the Civil War.
The Court ruled that the Missouri Compromise was not constitutional,
because Congress had no authority to deprive white citizens of their
right to enjoy black property north of the Missouri line. Thus the key
compromise in the struggle over slavery's expansion had been thrust
aside by the Supreme Court of the land.

The new American President, James Buchanan, had been inaugurated
just a few days before the Court's decision was announced. Having
obtained advance word of the Court's position, Buchanan declared in his
inaugural address that the decision would end the long decades of bitter
controversy over slavery. Like most official white announcements dealing
with the black presence in America, Buchanan's statement was absolutely
wrong. Antislavery, pro-white labor forces raised a tremendous cry, not
primarily over black rights, but over the nullification of the Missouri
Compromise, since this meant that the nation was now totally exposed
to the untrammeled expansion of "the slave power."[17]

For the black population, the decision carried a supremely offensive
symbolic value more than anything else. As Taney had noted and as they
well knew, it was no novel doctrine. Rather, it confirmed their entire
experience since the establishment of the American nation; but now the
humiliation had been legally focused and justified in the highest court.
Not only had the Court affirmed their lack of citizenship rights, but it
had opened the entire country to slavery. Henceforth there was no hiding
place, neither in the hopes of federal assistance nor in the farthest
reaches of the North. If allowed to stand, the decision would destroy the
already fragile distinction between slavery and freedom for black people.
White America was forcing the Northern and Southern movements of
the struggle still closer. By its own action, the federal government was
guaranteeing the temporary hegemony of black radical thought and
action.

In every part of the country, wherever it was possible for them to do
so, black people flocked angrily to meetings. Frustration and rage filled
their voices as they denounced the Court's decision. But they came together to do more than vent emotions: everywhere they gathered, the
people committed themselves to broader, more defiant acts of civil
disobedience. In many places they made serious plans for emigration.
Never before had they been forced to face so clearly the brutal implications of their beleaguered position. The way was not cloudy, it was dark.
But in the midst of the darkness, all the forces seemed to be converging.
That confluence was evident at a black meeting in Philadelphia in

April 1857, when Robert Purvis and Charles Remond, two of the major voices of the abolitionist tradition, indicated how far they had plunged into the radical flow. Purvis, perhaps the best-known black leader in the state, was now prepared to follow H. Ford Douglas into necessary treason, and accordingly presented several resolutions:

> That to attempt, as some do, to prove that there is no support given to Slavery in the Constitution and essential structure of the American government, is to argue against reason and common sense.
>
> That to persist in supporting a government which holds and exercises the power . . . to trample a class under foot as an inferior and degraded race, is on the part of the colored man at once the height of folly and the depth of pusillanimity.
>
> That the only duty the colored man owes to a constitution under which he is declared to be an inferior and degraded being . . . is to denounce and repudiate it, and to do what he can by all proper means to bring it into contempt.[18]

It was a desperate time, a time when men were being forced to see what they had chosen not to see before, to say what they had said only in the cruelest straits, and to search for actions in keeping with the hour. At the meeting, according to the *Liberator*, Remond "spoke at length and with much fervor." He agreed with Purvis, saying, "We owe no allegiance to a country which grinds us under its iron hoof and treats us like dogs. The time has gone by for colored people to talk of patriotism." Instead, Remond repudiated and denounced the American Union in strong terms. Meanwhile in Pensacola, Florida, many members of the free black population simply left the country.[19]

It was a desperate time, but also one for clearer vision than ever before. The nature of the American government was out into the open. No longer could black people suppose that they were simply dealing with "slaveholders." What H. Ford Douglas had asserted four years before, what David Walker had proclaimed some three decades before, the black community of the North was now forced to see and affirm. At the State Convention of Ohio Colored Men in 1858, the assembly resolved "that if the Dred Scott dictum be the true exposition of the law of the land, then are the founders of the American Republic convicted by their descendants of base hypocrisy, and colored men absolved from all allegiance to a government which withdraws all protection."[20]

In Cincinnati the gifted black writer Frances Ellen Watkins spoke of the recent kidnapping of an enslaved black and with eloquent indignation charged the crime to the United States government, which she said "is the arch traitor to liberty, as shown by the Fugitive Slave Law and the Dred Scott decision." These words were typical of the insights of that desperate decade, which toward its end became even more desperate. But it was also typical that black assessments of the situation were too often swathed in "eloquent" outbursts, in emotional fervor which might guard the people against the continued annealing required. Part of the desperation of the times lay in the search for deeds to accompany the undeniable insights, for action appropriate to the analyses now rushing like a stream. If the federal government was indeed the "arch traitor to liberty"—especially the liberty of black men and women—what should they do?[21]

For some, no response seemed proper other than David Walker's. The struggle of the North must join with, must ultimately encourage, the rising of the masses of the South. In the Massachusetts State Convention of black people in August 1858, the ubiquitous Charles Remond pressed that direction. He moved that a committee be appointed to prepare a Garnet-like address calling on the enslaved brothers and sisters to rise in rebellion. Remond said that "he knew his resolution was in one sense revolutionary, and in another treasonable, but so he meant it. . . . He boldly proclaimed himself a traitor to the government and the Union, so long as his rights were denied him for no fault of his own." Although it was finally voted down, Remond's motion created "the most spirited discussion of the Convention." And when one participant suggested that if such an insurrection occurred, Remond would be conspicuous by his absence, he heatedly denied the charge. But in his denial, he revealed again that "he only regretted that he had not a spear with which he could transfix all the slaveholders at once." Again the focus was on the "slaveholders," and not on the government and the system which made them possible.[22]

Meanwhile Remond's friend Robert Purvis continued in his own path and eventually suggested—somewhat gingerly—that revolution was the only logical answer. Since the American government represented "one of the basest, meanest, most atrocious despotisms that ever saw the face of the sun," he asked, "why not then . . . welcome the overthrow of 'this atrocious government' and construct a better one in its place?" For those black people who desired or needed to remain in America, this was a logical question in 1858. The historical situation had created its own logic, its own forces of tremendous power. As each new attack on black freedom was mounted, the black communities of North and South were driven into deeper confluence, into clearer radicalism. Northern blacks declared themselves traitors, spoke openly of revolution, looked for possible allies among foreign enemies of the United States, repeatedly raised the call for insurrection among the Southern masses, and armed themselves against their own worst times. Those channels, gouged out by the terrible movement of history, seemed the only honorable direction possible if black people were to remain in America, retain their integrity, and struggle to be free.[23]

Still, black freedom could not depend upon attacks from outside forces, and the future of both Northern civil disobedience and Southern insurrection was uncertain. Although the white nation seemed possibly ripe for civil conflict, some persons still saw the only real answer in emigration: if black people were to move toward authentic freedom they would have to move away from America, preferably seeking out their new home under black guidance and control. Thus Martin Delany and his colleagues were being vindicated. Indeed, by that time Delany had already begun what he fully expected to be his own permanent self-exile from America. While searching for a black homeland, while considering Africa more fully than ever before, he had moved his medical practice to Canada, which he viewed as a temporary stopping point in the long search. He was living in the rapidly expanding black community in Chatham, Ontario, when John Brown visited him in the spring of 1858.[24]

Coming as he did out of the bloody precincts of Kansas, accustomed to the guidance of his own harsh visions and voices, John Brown was certain he had discovered a way to move black men and women through the cruel dilemma of the late 1850s. He sought out Delany and the Chatham group partly because it was clear that many of them had taken courageous initiatives which set them apart from the larger black community. But if the various reports of Brown's visit are properly understood, he did not have as clear an answer as he thought he did, nor as accurate a vision of America as did the doubly exiled black men and women. Brown and his comrades asked Delany to organize a meeting of trusted colleagues to confer with them. Then, in May 1858, at a series of semisecret sessions in several Chatham locations, the white-bearded zealot proposed to the group the organization of a biracial armed guerrilla movement to uproot slavery at its core. His language was evidently guarded, but its meaning was this: starting from northern Virginia, moving down through the Appalachian Mountains, Brown's force would extend its way far into the black belt counties of the Deep South. As the movement attracted fugitives from all over the South and comrades from the North, a provisional government of black and white people would be established in the mountains, a kind of guerrilla territory within the United States. Interestingly enough, Brown proposed that this territory be established under the formal aegis of the American government.

It appears that much of the presentation and discussion at Chatham focused not on the daring military action (still being organized in Brown's head), but on the construction and the legal status of the new territory. In the course of one meeting, several of the fugitives from the States asked Brown how he planned to obtain sovereignty for a state with black citizens, especially in the light of the Dred Scott decision. His answer was to propose instead "an independent community [to] be established within and under the United States, but without . . . state sovereignty . . . similar to the Cherokee nation of Indians, or the Mormons." After this was agreed upon—or at least, after the blacks allowed it to rest there—the group considered a constitution which Brown had created for the new community.[25]

The forty-eight articles generally followed the model of the Constitution of the United States (a clear omen to black fugitives from that nation and its laws). However, it was modified for a style of guerrilla life that Brown and his white followers had been living, a style they rightly assumed would also be a necessity for any black and white community of equality in America. But it was not by any means a revolutionary document, at least not in terms of the revolution black people were discussing in that decade. Rather it proclaimed: "The foregoing shall not be construed so as in any way to encourage the overthrow of any State Government, or of the General Government of the United States. and look to no dissolution of the Union, but simply to Amendment and Repeal. And our flag shall be the same that our Fathers fought under in the Revolution." Of course it was possible to attribute such statements to a tactical need for wording which would throw off the federal authorities. But tactics were not what emerged when a black delegate from Ohio staunchly protested that he had no allegiance to the American flag. Brown replied: "The old flag is good enough for me. . . . Under it, freedom was won from the tyrants of the old world, for white men. Now I intend to make it do duty for black men."[26]

Beyond the recruitment of one black man—a young printer named Osborne P. Anderson—it is hard to decipher the larger black response to the Chatham meetings. What seems clear now is that John Brown was still wedded to his America and stood firmly in a major white abolitionist tradition. Evidently he did not grasp that "dissolution of the Union" was precisely what was needed, that black freedom could not be obtained without revolutionary transformation of the entire society. He was ready to take up arms, but the enemy was only vaguely identified. By and large, Brown's approach to the group at Chatham and his subsequent actions marked him more as a courageous white American rebel, with a strong streak of paternalism toward blacks, than as an exemplary white hero of the struggle for black freedom.

Delany's response to Brown's proposal for a black-white liberated territory does not come through sharply in the records. He may have been momentarily tempted to join forces with Brown, but by that time he had his own plans for a new black society and it did not include white men— even militant ones—who were organizing black people under the American flag. Delany's magnificent obsession with the coming of a new African nationhood, and a worldwide destiny for the scattered children of the homeland, had given him no rest. He was determined to go to Africa to carry out the exploration agreed upon at the Cleveland and later emigration conventions, to seek for a Canaan where groups of black people could settle and create a new society. He envisioned even the establishment of a rival kingdom of African cotton which would ultimately challenge the Southern economy in a fight to its death. By 1858 the emigrationist leader was seeking financial resources and associates for the journey, determined that the entire project should be directed and staffed by black persons and funded as fully as possible by the black community.[27]

Many persons discouraged Delany, suggesting that Canada was a sufficiently secure bastion for the time. Besides, a competitive African emigration plan had been developed by the mercurial Henry Highland Garnet and his white-dominated African Civilization Society. As a result, it was even more difficult than usual to obtain funds. But Delany was not deterred. In 1858, in order to raise money, he sold the house that he had bought in Chatham only the year before, and convinced the purchaser to allow Kate Delany and their five children to live there as tenants until he himself returned to take them home to their future.[28]

As part of his search for funds to finance the journey, in 1858 Delany finally finished and published his long-developed project, the novel *Blake*. There is no indication that this work added any significant supply of funds to Delany's meager holdings, but it certainly provided an important insight into the movings of his mind and spirit during the 1850s. Delany had begun the novel most likely around the same time he published his *Condition*. The story's hero, Henry Blake, was a sturdy and brilliant young black man, a native of the West Indies equally at home in the United States and Cuba. The main line of the novel followed him on his extensive travels among the black community in those two countries. For the purposes of black struggle, *Blake*'s primary significance lay in the fact that Delany had created a hero who traveled not as a pilgrim, visitor, or fugitive, but as the originator and organizer of a wide-ranging plan for revolution by the African people of Cuba and the United States.[29]

Probably drawing on Delany's own explorations in 1839–40, and on his intense study of the New World black experience, *Blake*'s theme was the search for pan-African revolution in the Western Hemisphere. As a part of that search, Henry Blake moved among the outlyer communities of the American South, and found determined remnants of Nat Turner's band waiting in the swamps of Virginia and North Carolina, looking for a revolutionary Second Coming. He entered the huts of the humble older black people and discovered that they had established their own role in the struggle as relentless petitioners, offering unending prayers for the coming of the revolution. Throughout the narrative, the songs and traditions of the black South were interwoven with the experiences of Cuba. Included, too, was an important encounter between Blake and the real-life revolutionary Afro-Cuban poet, Placido. In addition, in the novel as in his own life, Delany found ways to tie the African-American struggles for freedom with those of the Indians of the New World.

Taken all together, these elements of the novel constituted a startling and radical piece of work for any black man in antebellum America. But they took on even greater significance when the work came from the pen and soul of Martin Delany, the period's foremost advocate of black emigration. There could be no doubt: Henry Blake *was* Delany, revealing to his readers a striking double consciousness that was at once related to, but different from, the kind that W. E. B. Du Bois would make so well known later. *Blake* showed Delany's inner struggle, his wrestling with the necessity for establishing viable connections between the liberation of African peoples in the Western Hemisphere and those in the homeland.

When the novel is viewed in the light of Delany's own life, it becomes luminously clear that Delany was attempting to maintain a tremendous and painful tension. He was trying to develop and express an African nationality based on the homeland experience, yet at the same time participate responsibly in struggle against the bondage of African people in the Americas. *Blake* was a witness to the fact that Delany was concerned not only with the urgent search for the places of new beginnings for black people, but also—and profoundly—with the need to overturn all the deadly old beginnings which the white exploiters of the New World had made. Placed in the context of the Cleveland documents, *Blake* demonstrates that Delany carried the stream of black radicalism deeper than almost any other man of the post–David Walker generation. During the antebellum period, his double consciousness was not double mindedness but a revolutionary tension, a concern for the redemption and renewal of Africa at home and abroad.

With incessant, mounting pressure, the tensions of that decade continued to wrack and challenge the lives of black men and women across the North, especially when they exposed themselves to the endless flow of black fugitives. In Detroit, that busy crossroads of the runaway movement, it appears that two of the city's black leaders, George De Baptiste and William Lambert, organized a secret society to assist the fugitives—and perhaps to plan a larger freedom role. The group was known by various names: "African-American Mysteries," "Order of the Men of Oppression," and "Order of Emigration." It was probably related to, or identical with, the League of Freedom whose representative was present at the John Brown meeting in Chatham.[30]

Members of this order engaged in secret rituals, utilizing elements from Africa and the slavery experience in America. (Did they know any Knights of Liberty?) To attain the highest degree, one advanced through the successive stages of "rulers, judges and princes, chevaliers of Ethiopia, sterling black Knight, and Knight of St. Domingo." On one level such ritual could have been mere stage effects, escapism, the kind of apparent buffoonery which many persons would later identify with Marcus Garvey. Perhaps. But in those days of heightened conflict and struggle—as in the days of Garvey—it is quite possible that much more was involved. The remembering of Ethiopia and the evoking of Saint Domingo carried potential power. And perhaps there was even more than memories, for at the highest stage of the secret order, when men reached Knight of St. Domingo, they were said to have been introduced to "a ritual of great length dealing with the principles of freedom and the authorities of revolution, revolt, rebellion [and] government." Be that as it may, William Lambert later claimed that on a most concrete level his group had been so active in smuggling fugitives that in one year alone they moved sixteen hundred men, women, and children into Canada. Perhaps some black rituals were meant not as escapism, but as both cover and inspiration to struggle.[31]

In the same way, in spite of much black mobilizing, there were still many uses for interracial action. This, at least, was the experience of Charles H. Langston, the older brother of John M. Langston. In the fall of 1858 he decided to join a biracial group of men near Oberlin, Ohio, in the rescue of a black fugitive named John Price. Price had already been trapped and was about to be placed on a train to Kentucky, but Langston's group snatched him from his captors and sent him on to Canada. Since the Oberlin men had taken Price from an arresting party which included two U.S. marshals, thirty-seven of the rescuers were indicted under the provisions of the Fugitive Slave Law, though only two were brought to trial. Charles Langston was one of them, being tried and convicted in the spring of 1859. Just before his sentencing, Langston spoke to the crowded courtroom, attacking the antiblack animus inherent in the American legal system, citing especially the Fugitive Slave Law, the Dred Scott decision, and the prejudice of the court that had tried him:

"I know that . . . colored men, men of my complexion . . . cannot
expect . . . any mercy from the laws, from the constitution, or from
the courts of the country. . . . I stand here to say that if, for doing
what I did . . . I am to go in jail six months and pay a fine of a
thousand dollars, according to the Fugitive Slave Law . . . I . . . say
that I will do all I can for any man thus seized and held, though the
inevitable penalty . . . hangs over me!" Throughout Langston's speech,
the spectators were so enthusiastic in their cheers and applause that the
judge threatened to clear the court. Still, when the speech was over, the
judge himself admitted much of the just weight it carried, and confined
Langston's sentence to the minimum of twenty days in jail and a hundred-
dollar fine. Langston paid and served; his life had already made its
point.[32]

Among the cheering crowd in the courtroom had been two of Langston's younger black friends and fellow conspirators, Sheridan Leary and
John A. Copeland. By the time of the sentencing, they had already decided
to enter the struggle at even deeper levels. Leary was a saddler and
harness maker who had originally come to Oberlin as a fugitive from
North Carolina; now he had a wife and a young child. Copeland, his
nephew, had left the same Southern state as a free man, and at the time
was a student at Oberlin College. Copeland was the younger, but both
men were in their twenties, with much to live for. Nevertheless, by
1859 both were convinced that only one thing mattered; consequently,
they were preparing to leave trade, college, and family in order to return
to the South and fight slavery on its bloody home grounds. Not long
after the Langston trial was over, Sheridan Leary and his nephew were
on their way to Maryland to meet John Brown.[33]

In the year since he had left the black men of Chatham, Ontario, John
Brown had been working against many obstacles to make final preparations for his rendezvous with destiny, his own final wrestling with the
unbearable tensions of a slave society. By the time he established a base
of operations at the Kennedy Farm in Washington County, Maryland,
it was the late spring of 1859, and Brown was certain of his objectives.
Beginning with a raid on the federal arsenal at Harpers Ferry to secure
arms, he hoped to develop guerrilla operations among the black captives of the South, rally them to a chain of liberated outposts strung along
the Appalachian Mountains deep into the heart of the South, and eventually ignite a widespread uprising of blacks against their masters.
Somewhere in these mountains, the provisional government ratified at
Chatham would be established with Brown as its commander-in-chief, a
group of his white colleagues as officers of the guerrilla army, and Afro-
Americans serving almost exclusively as the line forces. Brown had

studied the accounts of Toussaint and Dessalines in Santo Domingo, had pondered the experience of Nat Turner, and remembered his own days in the West. Out of those bloody memories, in the shadow of the history of black struggle, he shaped his own vision of a new day.[34]

Though not always ready to admit it, Brown was preparing for sedition and treason against the American government—the kind of action which a growing number of black people had been calling for. Pressed on by his own sense of the coming divine judgment, believing that new life could arise out of bloody death, inspired by black martyrs of the struggle, the old soldier-farmer had collected guns, equipment, and money—though not nearly as much money as he had hoped for. Over the summer and into the fall, his forces gathered and waited. During this time, Brown was especially disappointed in the response of well-known black men and women to his invitation to participate in the white-led revolutionary movement. Most of those whom he had approached, including Frederick Douglass, found various ways to refuse. Harriet Tubman promised to participate, but became ill. Finally time ran out, and it was impossible to determine if anyone else from the black community had planned to join. For events pressed John Brown to begin his movement toward Harpers Ferry on the night of October 16, 1859, fully two weeks earlier than originally planned.[35]

By that time five black men had joined his small company of twenty-one insurrectionists. In addition to Leary and Copeland, who arrived from Oberlin the day before the assault, Osborne P. Anderson from Chatham had kept his promise. Shields Green, a fugitive from South Carolina still in his early twenties, had been introduced to Brown by Frederick Douglass and had decided to join the fight. Out of Virginia's Shenandoah Valley came Dangerfield Newby, who in the tradition of those free blacks who had joined Nat Turner, decided to indenture himself in a new way. He was in his forties and thought he had much to live for. His enslaved wife Harriet was about to be sold to a Louisiana buyer, and his seven children to be scattered. So Newby joined the little army in the hope that he, like Delany, would be able to return to the valley and take his wife and family home to a new, unshackled future. In his pocket he carried Harriet's last letter, like an amulet, bearing the words, "Oh dear Dangerfield, com this fall without fail . . . I want to see you so much that is the one bright hope I have before me."[36]

The radical black presence was pressing America to the rivers of fire and blood which men had long seen in their dreams, in their terrified waking hours. Now a white man had chosen revolution, and five black men had come to join with him, urging their own lives into a radicalism which could not be denied. Nor were they alone in this decision. Early

Sunday evening, October 16, hours before the attack, some of Brown's participants went to inform local groups of the enslaved people, and purportedly met with "the greatest enthusiasm." Osborne Anderson later said that "joy and hilarity beamed from every countenance" when black folk were told of the plan. "One old mother, white-haired from age, and borne down with the labors of many years in bonds, when told of the work in hand, replied: 'God bless you! God bless you!' She then kissed the party at her house, and requested all to kneel, which we did, and she offered prayer to God for his blessing on the enterprise, and our success. At the slaves' quarters, there was apparently a general jubilee, and they stepped forward manfully, without impressing or coaxing."[37]

It is not known how many of these black men and women actually stepped out into the threatening night. In their protective, cautionary wisdom, many of them must have recognized how ill prepared was this band of liberators, and there were not nearly as many volunteers as John Brown had hoped for; but it is unlikely that there were as few as the Virginia and Maryland authorities later tried to suggest. Nor can we know how many would have joined Brown if his mission had demonstrated early signs of real success. But almost all of the signs were ominous and they were clear enough for every watchful eye to see. Later that night, after an initial, audacious victory in the capture of the lightly guarded federal armory at Harpers Ferry, Brown allowed himself and his small army of some twenty men—half of whom were posted in areas outside the main battleground—to be trapped in what became a cul de sac. His indecisive maneuverings and attempts at negotiations made it impossible for his men to effect a quick escape into the hills with their hostages and captured weapons. As a result, they became totally vulnerable when the familiar combination of local volunteers, militia companies, and federal forces all mobilized with amazing speed to descend upon them.[38]

By Monday morning, the men in the armory area were trapped in their fortress. Encircled by thousands of antagonists from Harpers Ferry and the surrounding areas who cried out for their death, the group's situation was impossible, and Dangerfield Newby was the first to die, still carrying the letter from Harriet in his pocket. An unending stream of bullets soon cut down others in the armory area, while the attacking forces scattered, captured, mutilated, and killed most of Brown's men who had been stationed at various outposts away from the heart of the action. Finally, after a period of seige and negotiations, on Tuesday morning, October 18, a company of United States Marines led the charge that broke into the stronghold to kill or capture the remnants of the band of visionaries who stood with their confused but courageous general to the end. The attempted insurrection lasted less than thirty-six hours, following a time schedule that bore a fascinating similarity to the long and bloody hours of Nat Turner's rebellion. Like Prophet Nat, John Brown managed to survive the battle.[39]

Of the five black men who had come from outside the area to join the abortive revolutionary action, only Osborne Anderson escaped, to fight again in the Civil War (and to die in 1871, while black men and women were still struggling toward freedom). Leary and Newby were killed in action. Shields Green, after infuriating the representatives of white power with his cool defiance at the trial, was hanged soon after John Brown. Young James Copeland also went to the gallows, but not before writing these words to his family in Oberlin: "I am not terrified by the gallows, which I see staring me in the face, and upon which I am soon to stand and suffer death for doing what George Washington was made a hero for doing. . . . Could I die in a manner and for a cause which would induce true and honest men more to honor me, and the angels more ready to receive me to their happy home of everlasting joy above?" In Nat Turner's Virginia, on the eve of his own death, Copeland himself answered the question he had raised for his family, in the only way it could be: "I imagine that I hear you, and all of you, mother, father, sisters and brothers, say—'No, there is not a cause for which we, with less sorrow, could see you die.' "[40]

A splendid, fierce, and radical urgency was driving black men to die in the river of struggle, proclaiming that their deepest affirmation and justification would come out of the depths of the black community. Shields Green, Sheridan Leary, John Copeland, Dangerfield Newby, Osborne Anderson, and certain others who are nameless now, all enter the company the poet Yeats would later describe when he celebrated the leaders of his own Irish Revolution:—"All changed, changed utterly:/ A terrible beauty is born."[41]

For the black community of the North it was the terrifying beauty of truth. Harpers Ferry and the men who died there under the laws of the Constitution were a symbolic culmination of the radical truth toward which the history of the decade had been forcing black people. The battle there, and the roaring sound of approval it elicited across the black North, represented a final, almost unbearable tightening of the tension of the powerful civil disobedience movement which had been steadily building. Now the implications were clear. The black response could not be confined to the courtrooms and police stations and streets of Ohio and Pennsylvania and Boston. Copeland, Leary, and Anderson had returned to the South to meet Newby and Green and other nameless brothers and sisters. Where the Southern and Northern streams of struggle met, they drew men into radical depths. When would they meet again?

Hope in the federal government was precipitately dying. The North was being faced for what it was, with all of its accommodating racism. The recently formed Republican Party and its spokesmen, like Abraham Lincoln, while generally supporting some qualified civil rights for black people, had made clear their essential commitment to white supremacy and black subordination in the United States. For instance, in the course of one of his 1858 debates with Stephen A. Douglas, Lincoln had said:

I am not, nor ever have been in favor of bringing about in any way the social and political equality of the white and black races . . . I am not nor ever have been in favor of making voters or jurors of negroes, nor of qualifying them to hold office, nor to intermarry with white people; and I will say in addition to this that there is a physical difference between the white and black races which I believe will for ever forbid the two races living together on terms of social and political equality. And insomuch as they cannot so live, while they do remain together there must be the position of superior and inferior, and I as much as any other man am in favor of having the superior position assigned to the white race.[42]

So it was not surprising that black men and women with pride and integrity—and hope for their children—were speaking of emigration as never before; even Frederick Douglass was still looking at the possibilities of Haiti. Black people were moving to armed self-defense, to seditious activities, and now at Harpers Ferry a few had turned to open slave rebellion. Black solidarity was building and deepening; Delany's radical double consciousness was spreading. On an extended speaking tour in New England, H. Ford Douglas was attacking the federal government's continued protection of slavery, declaring "annihilation" of the government as "the highest test of duty." The tension in the black—and white—community was reaching levels which created broad new channels for black radicalism. A new era in the struggle seemed imminent; perhaps this was both the terror and the beauty being born.[43]

Of course there could be no new manifestation of the struggle apart from its great Southern movement. Eighty-nine percent of the children of Africa in America were still in slavery there. And Harpers Ferry had sent tremors through the South unlike any it had known since Nat Turner's avengers scourged the land. Because of John Brown's role, a new wave of physical attacks on white Northerners swept the section, many of those attacked being accused of attempting to foment insurrection. Fear and repression were rising; a tension not unrelated to that of the North hung heavy upon the section. The year 1860 would see a Presidential election. It was generally believed that the Republicans, who were committed to the Free Soil position, had an excellent chance of winning. Therefore talk of secession was constantly heard across the South. Whites were all but at war with one another.[44]

As always, many black people were highly sensitive to these vibrations, seeking to understand how the white conflict might affect their struggles, moving toward freedom wherever the confusion made it possible, biding their time wherever that seemed wise. In 1860—just as in 1856, the previous highly charged Presidential election year—there seemed to be a swelling of the black freedom movement. During the bitter campaign and election, thousands of blacks broke free from slavery. In North Carolina alone some two thousand men, women, and children escaped, including a fugitive from a Martin County plantation named William D. Robeson (later the father of a son named Paul).[45]

To help such persons, black "conductors" continued their often lonely, dangerous work, and the Ohio River was still a major focal point for their activities. From slavery's side Arnold Cragston, a young enslaved black man in Mason County, Kentucky, symbolized their courage: for nearly four years, beginning in 1859, he rowed hundreds of black folk across the river on moonless nights, delivering them to the relative safety of a friendly agent on the other side. Often risking his life, he consistently placed the freedom of his anonymous passengers before his own obvious opportunities to escape. Later, when asked about the Underground Railroad, Cragston said what many others confirmed: "We didn't call it that then. I don't know as we called it anything—we just knew there was a lot of slaves always a-wantin' to get free, and I had to help 'em." On free soil in Ohio other blacks, many of them former slaves, endangered their freedom and their lives to send the fugitives on their way. For instance, from her base at New Lebanon, Ohio, a black woman named Jane Lewis regularly crossed the river in the other direction to bring waiting fugitives across.[46]

All this was occurring in the midst of a highly explosive national situation. In the summer of 1860 the *State Gazette* of Austin, Texas, reported that the northeastern section of the state was almost in "the condition of revolution, which we are forced to regard as a repetition of the horrors enacted at Harpers Ferry." At various points at least nine fires had broken out on a single day, the second Sunday in July. Weapons were said to have been found in the cabins of black people. Representing the fears of many others, one white citizen wrote from Texas: "We sleep upon our arms and the whole country is deeply excited."[47]

Similarly, during that same breathless July, white authorities in Waxahachie, Texas, claimed to have uncovered a plan for a black uprising. According to newspaper accounts, the conspirators had already moved to the point of agreeing on "a tentative division of the land." A letter to the Austin *State Gazette* reported that, in order to handle the situation, "a large mob was assembled, led by the Committee of Vigilance consisting, we are assured, of the most respectable and responsible men of this country." The task of the committee was to execute the three leaders of the insurrection: Sam Smith, Cato, and Patrick. If Patrick was representative then it appears that the threat of death did not shake them, for he was reportedly calm and assured when he told the committee of execution that the attempt at insurrectionary action by his group was "just the beginning of the good work." Indeed, all three men met their fate with what a white correspondent considered "a composure worthy of a better cause."[48]

In the black world, there was no better cause. In Alabama the *Montgomery Advertiser* reported: "We have found out a deep laid plan among the negroes of our neighborhood, and from what we can find out from our negroes, it is generally all over the area. We hear some startling facts. They have gone far enough to divide up our estates, mules, lands and household furniture." At least twenty-five blacks and four whites were executed as a result of these movements. And in December 1860, whites in South Carolina learned that "there exists among the blacks a secret and wide-spread organization of a Masonic character, having its grip, password and oath. It has various grades of leaders, who are competent and earnest men and its ultimate object is FREEDOM." The white writer said that he had warned one of the leading organizers of the group "that such an organization meant mischief." Insisting on his own definitions, the black leader, Scipio, responded, "No, it meant only right and JUSTICE."[49]

And as always, there were solitary acts as well. In that same year of 1860, a black man named Isaac was brought into court in Kentucky, charged with "the offense of administering a deadly poison, called corrosive sublimate, to Isaac Robinson, and his wife and child, with the intention to destroy their lives." The attempt was not successful, but Isaac's break with the system of slavery, with the world of "masters," had already come.[50]

How long would it take for such a transformation to become a universal reality, breaking open the house of bondage? When would justice for black people be established in the land? Another Presidential election was approaching, but it seeemed to offer little hope for the releasing of the tension, the breaking of the dams. In 1860 both major parties had continued to make it clear that the freedom of black men, north or south, had no place in their priorities. Lincoln, the Republican candidate, readily placed the preservation of the white Union above the death of black slavery. The outspoken, New York City–based *Anglo-African* declared: "We have no hope from either [of the] political parties. We must rely on ourselves, the righteousness of our cause, and the advance of just sentiments among the great masses of the . . . people." The writer was correct on the subject of self-reliance, but otherwise terribly misinformed; among the "great masses" of white America, the advance of "just sentiments" regarding justice for black people would be exceedingly slow, if left to develop on its own.[51]

But in 1860 nothing was moving at its normal pace. Now that the Republicans had attained major national status and nominated Lincoln as their standard-bearer, the long-time talk of disunion reached new heights. Immediately after Lincoln's election, the slave states' official move toward secession finally began, starting with South Carolina. It was no longer a threat: Mississippi, Florida, Alabama—one after another, the Southern states left the Union in that winter of 1860–61. This was the way toward the destruction of slavery and the beginning of black freedom which had long been sought in the river. "No union with slavery!" men had cried. "Let the system be cracked, let the government's protection of slavery be ended," they had said. Now the break appeared to be a reality, and H. Ford Douglas boldly declared to the Southern states: "Stand not upon the order of your going, but go at once. . . . There is no union of ideas and interests in this country, and there can be no union between freedom and slavery." And Frederick Douglass proclaimed: "I am for a dissolution of the Union—decidedly for a dissolution of the Union! . . . In case of such a dissolution, I believe that men could be found . . . who would venture into those states and raise the standard of liberty there." Thus one year after Harpers Ferry, Frederick Douglass was foreseeing revolutionary expeditions into the South. (A hope not without basis: already there were reports that several hundred black fugitives had returned from Canada to the South by 1860, risking their lives to bring friends and relatives out with them. Others had the same idea and planned to act, and there were always the legendary Knights of Liberty.)[52]

From the black perspective, then, this Southern move to disunion held crucial possibilities for breaking the ancient dams. But Abraham Lincoln was not looking at matters from the black perspective; his perspective was white, and his supreme goal was to preserve the white-defined Union. So even after the seceding states had formed a new Confederacy in March 1861, Lincoln still spoke of not interfering with slavery in the South, still promised the protection of the United States Constitution for the bondage of black people. In the winter of 1861, there seemed to be no guarantee that the unprecedented state of white disunion would open a clear pathway to black freedom.[53]

It was a perilous and uncertain time. Martin Delany knew it. He had returned from his exploratory journey to Africa in 1860, and was more convinced than ever that since justice for blacks in America would be very long delayed, there was still the need for at least an experimental emigrationist movement. At great cost to his health and with harrowing financial sacrifices, Delany had explored the possibilities of a new Canaan in West Africa. Not all details were in order, but he had signed agreements with West African leaders and was prepared to move forward. Convinced of his sense of direction, in that year he wrote: "I have determined to leave to my children the inheritance of a country, the possession of a territorial domain, the blessings of a national education, and the indisputable right of self-government; that they may not succeed to the servility and degradation bequeathed to us by our fathers."[54]

Delany was still being thrust forward by a radical hope in the New Africa. (In his enthusiasm, he could perhaps be forgiven a certain hyperbolic unfairness to the black "fathers" in America.) By now it was evident that such a move was radical not only in its vision of new black men and women and new black societies, but in a potentially profound challenge to all rising white hopes for the domination of black people and black Africa. This challenge was set forth when he wrote: "Our policy must be . . . *Africa for the African race, and black men to rule them.*" Beginning in 1860, Delany returned to Canada's black communities with that policy in mind, to try to organize a company of pioneering black emigrants to move toward their future in the homeland. (One of his recruits was Osborne P. Anderson, the lone Afro-American survivor of Harpers Ferry.) He was working at this task when the guns erupted in Charleston harbor in the early morning darkness of April 12, 1861.[55]

The Blood-Red Ironies of God

Civil War, Black Freedom, and the Dialectics of Transformation

Although the destruction of the oppressors God may not effect by the oppressed, yet the Lord our God will surely bring other destructions upon them —for not infrequently will he cause them to rise up against one another, to be split and divided, and to oppress each other, and sometimes to open hostilities with sword in hand.

David Walker, 1829

On certain stark and bloody levels, a terrible irony seemed to be at work. For those who interpreted the events of their own times through the wisdom and anguish of the past, the guns of Charleston certainly sounded like the signal for the fulfillment of David Walker's radical prophecies. Here at last was the coming of the righteous God in judgment, preparing to bring "destructions" upon America. Here was the divine culmination of the struggle toward freedom and justice long waged by the oppressed black people. From such a vantage point, the conflict now bursting out was the ultimate justification of the costly freedom movement, a welcome vindication of the trust in Providence. And yet the war was not simply an ally. Like all wars, it brought with it a train of demoralizing, destructive elements, deeply affecting even those persons and causes which seemed to be its chief beneficiaries. In the case of black people, the guns broke in upon their freedom struggle at many levels, diverted and diffused certain of its significant radical elements, and became a source of profound confusion and disarray among its most committed forces. This was especially the case where independent radical black struggle for justice and self-determination was concerned.

Part of the ironic confusion of the Civil War was lodged in the very tradition of David Walker's divine vengeance. In a sense, it was also the tradition of Frederick Douglass's beneficent Providence, of Sojourner Truth's living God, and Henry Garnet's Sovereign of the Universe. In fact, hundreds of thousands of black people, north and south, believed unwaveringly that their God moved in history to deliver his people, and they had been looking eagerly, praying hourly, waiting desperately for the glory of the coming of the Lord. For them, all the raucous, roaring guns of Charleston Harbor and Bull Run, of Antietam and Fort Pillow, of Shiloh and Murfreesboro and Richmond were the certain voice of God, announcing his judgment across the bloody stretches of the South, returning blood for blood to the black river. Then came the critical, human judgment: because the white South was holding millions of black people in bondage while the white North officially held none, the North was designated—with no little fear and trembling—as the force through which God was working his righteous, liberating purpose, the obvious side for black men to join.

But the North was also the federal government, which had repeatedly turned its various faces against black people, denying their citizenship rights and eliciting a mounting storm of black fury, widespread civil disobedience, attempts at insurrection. The North was the state legislatures of the section, with their unjust laws and acts of disfranchisement against their often unwanted black residents. The North was the merchants and the mobs, the school boards and the white farmers. Just yesterday this North, this government, this guarantor of the rights of white slaveholders, had inspired powerful black radical analysis and action. Now, with the firing of a thousand guns—which the North had not initiated—this North was transformed into the instrument of God. With this confused and confusing transformation, the power of black resistance to the real North was subverted. Thus war—so often the supreme honer and harshener of men—in fact blunted and softened much black radicalism. For as the armies reeled their fear-drunken, honor-drunken, pain-drunken ways across the land, and battered their lives against the hills and mountains, against the visions that Prophet Nat and David Walker had seen, they released the revolutionary tension, distorted the terrible beauty, stymied temporarily the movement toward radical, self-reliant, independent black struggle.

To see the meaning of this irony more clearly, one must remember that David Walker had envisioned two distinct possibilities for the final destruction of slavery, racism, and exploitation in America. One was that God would send a black Messiah to lead his people in a righteous crusade against the whole of white, slaveholding, slavery-supporting American society. The second was that the two equally guilty Northern and Southern sections would rise up in civil war, carrying out a sanguinary judgment upon each other with black people on hand, waiting, as the independent, righteous remnant. In those same vision-swept days, Nat Turner had seen only the first shattering possibility: white and black apocalyptic armies, battling each other for victory. Both visions of the end presumed independent black forces, arrayed against the total white-created evil of American society.[1]

Prior to the outbreak of hostilities, the tension in the black community increased as it recognized that the vast majority of white America, represented by its government, was not only prepared to live with slavery, but was opposed to the full development of any black people's rights anywhere. It was this reality which helped to drive the John Copelands to Harpers Ferry, pressed the Martin Delanys to West Africa, sent thousands of others to Canada. But in 1861 the guns of Charleston shattered the tension, broke into the visions, confused the emerging hard radical analysis.

When the war broke out, black men and women were convinced that it had to destroy slavery. Especially in the North, this inner certainty flooded their consciousness, buoyed up their hopes. Now it appeared that God was providing a way out of the darkness of slavery and degradation, a way which would release some of the frightening tension of the previous decade. Because they wanted a way out so desperately, because it was hard to be driven by a fierce urgency, fearsome to experience the personal honing in spite of one's own softer and blunter ways, the children of Africa in America clutched at a solution which would not cause them to be driven into the depths of radicalism. For they must have realized that the chances were good that they might not survive without being seriously, unpredictably transformed. Therefore, when the guns began, black people shunted aside the knowledge of certain fierce realities.[2]

In that mood their men surged forward to volunteer for service in the Union cause, repressing bitter memories. In spite of their misgivings, disregarding the fact that it was not the North which had initiated this righteous war, they offered their bodies for the Northern cause, believing that it was—or would be—the cause of black freedom. If the excited, forgetful young volunteers sought justification, they could find it in the *Anglo-African*: "Talk as we may, we are concerned in this fight and our fate hangs upon its issues. The South must be subjugated, or we shall be enslaved. In aiding the Federal government in whatever way we can, we are aiding to secure our own liberty; for this war can end only in the subjugation of the North or the South." When hard pressed, the journal, like the young men it encouraged, knew very well the nature of the "liberty" they had found so far in the unsubjugated North, and the writer admitted that the North was not consciously fighting for black rights. However, the *Anglo-African* chose to see a power beyond the councils of the North: "Circumstances have been so arranged by the decrees of Providence, that in struggling for their own nationality they are forced to defend our rights."[3]

That was the key to the diverting force of the war as it met the river of struggle. Men and women chose to believe that some mysterious movement of the Divine was among them, forcing a recalcitrant white America, against its will and desire, to fight for the rights of black men. It was a strange theodicy, but it reigned in black America. In January 1862, when the eloquent black physician John Rock announced the doctrine to his black and white abolitionist audience at the Massachusetts Anti-Slavery Society, he drew loud cheers and applause: "I think I see the finger of God in all this. Yes, there is the hand-writing on the wall: *Break every yoke, and let the oppressed go free. I have heard the groans of my people, and am come down to deliver them.*" He too was forced to admit that the government was not intentionally abolitionist, but he was certain that God would break through anyway. "While fighting for its own existence," said Rock, the federal government had been "obliged to take slavery by the throat, and sooner or later *must* choke her to death."[4]

Following such strange turnings of history, and such inspired readings of the writings on the wall, black men ran to volunteer. At the outset of hostilities, in Boston and throughout the North they pledged to "organize themselves immediately into drilling companies, to become better skilled in the use of fire-arms; so that when we shall be called upon by the country, we shall be better prepared to make a ready and fitting response." This was the same Boston and Cincinnati and Chicago where black men had only recently been arming themselves against the courts and the laws and the people. But now God had spoken in the guns.[5]

Early in the war black men were eager not only to participate in the righteous work of the federal government, but to serve their state governments as well. In May 1861 a number of free black men in Pennsylvania offered to go down into the South to try to provoke slave rebellions, but the governor refused to sanction it. (This was, of course, the same Pennsylvania which had readily extradited to Virginia one of John Brown's white followers to be tried and executed.) Following the voices which said that God, in his mysterious ways, had chosen white racist forces to bring about black freedom, black men continued to offer their services to federal and state governments for military duty. These Northern governments, perversely ignorant of any special ordination by

Providence, refused the black volunteers. Afro-Americans could serve as laborers and cooks, doing all the dirty and menial work of the armed forces, but any large-scale arming of these freedom-hungry people seemed out of the question. So in the early period of the war, with very few exceptions (often the light-skinned children of Africa), the black volunteers were refused. In their official language, the government refusals were only a more polite form of the essential message which many white people of the streets shouted and sang in doggerel:

> To the flag we are pledged, all its foes we abhor
> And we ain't for the nigger, but we are for the war.[6]

This sentiment was totally compatible with the history of the North, and the Union leaders were as yet unprepared to try to create any new black-white relations. Abraham Lincoln had not seen the visions which possessed the black people of the North. He had not yet rightly measured "the judgements of the Lord," the movements of Providence. Instead, he was still trapped in his own obsession with saving the white Union at all costs, even the cost of continued black slavery. Sensitively attuned to the feelings of whites, Lincoln believed that the arming of black people would strike deep chords of fear among whites, especially among his tender allies in the "loyal" slave states of Delaware, Maryland, Kentucky, and Missouri. Perhaps of even more importance, he knew that accepting the help of black troops in quelling the Southern rebellion carried with it the moral responsibility of facing their demands for citizenship rights; Lincoln was still convinced that blacks and whites could not live peaceably as equal citizens in the United States. So the black men were refused, and when their eager volunteer companies stubbornly insisted on drilling and marching in the streets and fields of the North, in many cities they were actually attacked by the whites.[7]

Finally such rejection, humiliation, and persecution gave some black people pause for thought, threw their minds back into the recent terrors of the 1850s, suggested again the possibility of other ways in the struggle. One black man put the essential question to all these eager volunteers: "Is this country ready and anxious to initiate a new era for downtrodden humanity, that you now so eagerly propose to make the sacrifice of thousands of our ablest men to encourage and facilitate the great work of regeneration?" Then he answered his own question: "No! No! . . . Our policy must be neutral, ever praying for the success of that party determined to initiate first the policy of justice and equal rights." Obviously, the North had made no such decision.[8]

The same message appeared in a letter from Troy, New York, to the

Anglo-African, signed by one who called himself "Ivanhoe," who urged black men not to volunteer even if invited: "And suppose we were invited, what duty would we then owe to ourselves and our posterity? We are in advance of our fathers. They put confidence in the word of the whites only to feel the dagger of slavery driven still deeper into the heart. . . . We are not going to re-enact that tragedy. Our enslaved brethren must be made freedmen. . . . We of the North must have all the rights which white men enjoy; until then we are in no condition to fight under the flag [which] gives us no protection."[9]

These were echoes of H. Ford Douglas, voices searching toward an independent black position, lives still impelled toward treason. But these were not the dominant voices of the years of war. In spite of rebuffs, the overwhelming call was still to join forces with the North, to proclaim the white Republican leaders as divinely ordained allies in a struggle which only yesterday had carried black people to open defiance of the government, but which now sought desperately to join that same government in its ambiguous forced march toward black freedom. This meant joining the Sewards, the Trumballs, the Greeleys, and the Lincolns, and the white supremacy they unashamedly professed. It meant helping to build the rapidly expanding forces of the industrialists, railroad owners, land speculators, and bankers as they transformed the face of America. God was using most unusual vessels, and it was a most confusing time. Delany cried out: "In God's name, must we ever be subordinate to those of another race? . . . Have we no other destiny in prospect as an inheritance for our children? It is for us to determine whether or not this shall be so." And Delany remained in America to follow the wavering hand of the Divine, to erode his own sense of destiny.[10]

And what of the South? What of those sometimes God-obsessed black believers who had long lifted their cries for deliverance in songs and shouts, in poetry filled with rich and vibrant images? Did they sense the coming of Moses now? Was this finally the day of the delivering God, when he would set his people free? Did they hear Nat Turner's spirit speaking in the guns? Did they believe he was calling them to freedom through all the lines of skirmishers who left their blood upon the leaves? Did they have any difficulty knowing which of the white armies was Pharaoh's?

The answers were as complex as life itself. In many parts of the nation and the world there had been predictions that secession, disunion, and war would lead to a massive black insurrection which would finally vindicate Turner and Walker, and drown the South in blood. Such predictions were made without knowledge of the profound racism and fear which pervaded the white North, and certainly without awareness of the keen perceptions of black people in the South. For most of the enslaved people knew their oppressors, and certainly realized that such a black uprising would expose the presence of Pharaoh's armies everywhere. To choose that path to freedom would surely unite the white North and South more quickly than any other single development, making black men, women, and children the enemy—the isolated, unprepared enemy. For anyone who needed concrete evidence, Gen. George B. McClellan, the commander of the Union's Army of the Ohio, had supplied it in his "Proclamation to the People of Western Virginia" on May 26, 1861: "Not only will we abstain from all interferences with your slaves, but we will, with an iron hand, crush any attempt at insurrection on their part."[11]

So, heeding their own intuitive political wisdom, the black masses confirmed in their actions certain words which had recently appeared in the *Anglo-African*. Thomas Hamilton, the editor, had heard of Lincoln's decision to countermand an emancipation order issued by one of his most fervent Republican generals, John C. Fremont, in Missouri. Hamilton predicted: "The forlorn hope of insurrection among the slaves may as well be abandoned. They are too well informed and too *wise* to court destruction at the hands of the combined Northern and Southern armies—for the man who had reduced back to slavery the slaves of rebels in Missouri would order the army of the United States to put down a slave insurrection in Virginia or Georgia." He was right, of course, and the enslaved population was also right. Therefore, instead of mass insurrection, the Civil War created the context for a vast broadening and intensifying of the self-liberating black movement which had developed prior to the war. Central to this black freedom action, as always, was the continuing series of breaks with the system of slavery, the denials of the system's power, the self-emancipation of steadily increasing thousands of fugitives. Thus, wherever possible, black people avoided the deadly prospects of massive, sustained confrontation, for their ultimate objective was freedom, not martyrdom.[12]

As the guns resounded across the Southern lands, the movement of black folk out of slavery began to build. Quickly it approached and surpassed every level of force previously known. Eventually the flood of fugitives amazed all observers and dismayed not a few, as it sent waves of men, women, and children rushing into the camps of the Northern armies. In this overwhelming human movement, black people of the South offered their own responses to the war, to its conundrums and mysteries.

Their action testified to their belief that deliverance was indeed coming
through the war, but for thousands of them it was not a deliverance to
be bestowed by others. Rather it was to be independently seized and
transformed through all the courage, wisdom, and strength of their waiting black lives.[13]

This rapidly increasing movement of black runaways had been noted
as soon as the reality of Southern secession had been clearly established.
Shortly after the guns of April began to sound in Charleston harbor,
large companies of fugitives broke loose from Virginia and the Carolinas
and moved toward Richmond. Again, one day in Virginia in the spring
of 1861, a black fugitive appeared at the Union-held Fortress Monroe.
Two days later eight more arrived, the next day more than fifty, soon
hundreds. The word spread throughout the area: there was a "freedom
fort," as the fugitives called it, and within a short time thousands were
flooding toward it. Similarly, in Louisiana two families waded six miles
across a swamp, "spending two days and nights in mud and water to
their waists, their children clinging to their backs, and with nothing
to eat." In Georgia, a woman with her twenty-two children and grand-
children floated down the river on "a dilapidated flatboat" until she
made contact with the Union armies. In South Carolina, black folk
floated to freedom on "basket boats made out of reeds," thus reviving
an ancient African craft. A contemporary source said of the black
surge toward freedom in those first two years of the war: "Many thousands of blacks of all ages, ragged, with no possessions, except the
bundles which they carried, had assembled at Norfolk, Hampton, Alexan-
dria and Washington. Others . . . in multitudes . . . flocked north from
Tennessee, Kentucky, Arkansas, and Missouri."

This was black struggle in the South as the guns roared, coming out
of loyal and disloyal states, creating their own liberty. This was the black
movement toward a new history, a new life, a new beginning. W. E. B.
Du Bois later said, "The whole move was not dramatic or hysterical,
rather it was like the great unbroken swell of the ocean before it dashes
on the reefs." Yet there was great drama as that flowing movement of
courageous black men and women and children sensed the movement
of history, heard the voices of God, created and signed their own emancipation proclamations, and seized the time. Their God was moving and
they moved with him.[14]

And wherever this moving army of self-freed men and women and
children went, wherever they stopped to wait and rest and eat and work,
and watch the movements of the armies in the fields and forests—in all
these unlikely sanctuaries, they sent up their poetry of freedom. Some
of them were old songs, taking on new meaning:

> Thus said the Lord, Bold Moses said
> Let my people go
> If not I'll smite your first-born dead
> Let my people go.
> No more shall they in bondage toil
> Let my people go.

But now there was no need to hide behind the stories of thousands of
years gone by, now it was clearly a song of black struggle, of deliverance
for their own time of need. Now the singers themselves understood more
fully what they meant when they sang again:

> One of dese mornings, five o'clock
> Dis ole world gonna reel and rock,
> Pharaoh's Army got drownded
> Oh, Mary, don't you weep.

They were part of the drowning river. Out there, overlooking the battlefields of the South, they were the witnesses to the terrible truth of
their own songs, to the this-worldliness of their prayers and aspirations.
Remembering that morning in Charleston harbor, who could say they
were wrong? "Dis ole world gonna reel and rock . . ."

Every day they came into the Northern lines, in every condition, in
every season of the year, in every state of health. Children came wandering, set in the right direction by falling, dying parents who finally knew
why they had lived until then. Women came, stumbling and screaming,
their wombs bursting with the promise of new and free black life. Old
folks who had lost all track of their age, who knew only that they had
once heard of a war against "the Redcoats," also came, some blind,
some deaf, yet no less eager to taste a bit of that long-anticipated freedom of their dreams. No more auction block, no more driver's lash,
many thousands gone.

This was the river of black struggle in the South, waiting for no one
to declare freedom for them, hearing only the declarations of God in
the sound of the guns, and moving.

By land, by river, creating their own pilgrim armies and their own
modes of travel, they moved south as well as north, heading down to the
captured areas of the coast of South Carolina. *Frederick Douglass's
Monthly* of February 1862 quoted the report of a *New York Times* correspondent in Port Royal: "Everywhere I find the same state of things
existing; everywhere the blacks hurry in droves to our lines; they crowd
in small boats around our ships; they swarm upon our decks; they hurry
to our officers from the cotton houses of their masters, in an hour or

two after our guns are fired. . . . I mean each statement I make to be taken literally; it is not garnished for rhetorical effect." As usual, black people were prepared to take advantage of every disruption in the life of the oppressing white community. When they heard the guns, they were ready, grasping freedom with their own hands, walking to it, swimming to it, sailing to it—determined that it should be theirs. By all these ways, defying masters, patrols, Confederate soldiers, slowly, surely, they pressed themselves into the central reality of the war.[15]

And the songs continued to rend the air, bursting with new meaning, pointing with every word and note toward freedom, filled with a hope and wonder only the captives could know:

> Slavery chain done broke at last!
> Broke at last! Broke at last!
> Slavery chain done broke at last!
> Gonna praise God till I die!

It was a magnificent hope, a commitment purchased with blood; but its ardor could not conceal the fact that the paradoxical war had thrust certain ironies into the Southern struggle for freedom as well. On the one hand, the rapid flow of black fugitives was a critical part of the challenge to the embattled white rulers of the South; by leaving, they denied slavery's power and its profit. But much of their movement out of slavery carried them into the camps of the Union troops, brought them harshly against the incongruous reality of the white North as God's saving agent.

Roaring past and over one set of dams, the black community of escape soon discovered, in the cruelties and racism of the Union camps, yet another set of obstacles to their freedom. For at levels that in those days men dared not explore too fully, the deliverers often seemed to be the enemy. In many places the desperate, weary, uncertain fugitives were mistreated, abused, or chased away by Union soldiers. In some cases the deliverers even returned them to their owners. Still, the black flood did not abate. So while enslaved black people initially took their freedom into their own hands because they had no other apparent options, they were almost immediately forced to entrust that freedom to the hesitant white hands of the armies and leaders of the North. Thus, instead of again connecting with the Northern black movement, they were largely halted in the camps of the federal government, thereby depriving both the Northern and Southern movements of the needed impetus to take them into the next period, when the nature and extent of that hard-won freedom would be viciously questioned and attacked. (Some black fugitives partially avoided the contradiction, but not the problem, by moving far beyond the Union lines, refusing to stop until they reached Canada or Mexico.)[16]

Nevertheless, during the war's first years many variations on the fugitive theme were reported. "A Southern planter wrote a friend in New York that four of his runaway slaves had returned voluntarily after a spell of 'Yankee freedom.' But several months later he complained bitterly that the same four had run away again—this time taking with them two hundred other slaves." Many persons who could not or would not leave their immediate areas joined the struggle in other ways. Shortly after the outbreak of the war, blacks in Georgetown, South Carolina, were jailed for joyously singing:

> We'll soon be free,
> We'll soon be free;
> We'll soon be free,
> When de Lord will call us home.

For the white authorities, the last line could in no way ease the meaning of the song.[17]

Arson continued, too. In May 1861 a dozen ships were burned while at anchor in New Orleans. According to a newspaper correspondent from that area, nobody in the city felt any doubt that the black captives of the area (and probably some of their aggressive free companions) had done the work. That was also the general opinion in Charleston later that same year, when a massive fire swept the city, destroying six hundred buildings and causing seven million dollars in damage. And when, in the fall of 1861, Union gunboats arrived at Beaufort, South Carolina, and many whites fled the city, blacks from the countryside poured into the town to ransack and destroy white property. Meanwhile runaway blacks also served as spies and saboteurs for the Union military forces. One audacious group of families under the leadership of a skilled black harbor pilot, Robert Smalls, actually commandeered and sailed the *Planter*, a Confederate coastal supply ship, past the unwitting Southern keepers of the Charleston harbor batteries and delivered it—and themselves—into Union hands at Beaufort harbor, Smalls' home town.[18]

Although the mass insurrection that men had expected did not take place, in the early years of the war more limited risings were reported in many parts of the South. In Mississippi several plots were supposedly planned to explode on July 4, 1861—that day of black irony; by the end of the summer, some forty black men had been hanged in the Natchez area for their part in the movement. In the same year an attempt at a smaller insurrection led to the hanging of two black men and one woman in northern Arkansas. In South Carolina, whites became suspicious of an increasing number of black funerals and followed a group of mourners to a cemetery, "where it was discovered that the coffin contained arms which were being removed and hidden in a vault." Real mourning followed when "nineteen of the most 'intelligent' conspirators were executed." As for the border states, there too the movement continued unabated, in spite of their special status: In December 1861 some sixty enslaved blacks marched through New Castle, Kentucky, "singing political songs and shouting for Lincoln"; we are told that no one dared stop them.[19]

As the war spread into the South, the black outlyers often found themselves in a crucial and sensitive position. Many of them stepped up their activities against the weakened plantation areas, and successfully resisted patrols sent to capture or destroy them. Some developed strange alliances with white Confederate deserters; together, the two groups created troublesome guerrilla forces in several places behind the Confederate lines. For the blacks, many of whom had always considered themselves at war with Southern society, this was a logical development in their struggle.[20]

Nevertheless, beyond outlyers, arsonists, and insurrectionaries, in the South the major black resistance and struggle was focused in the relentless movement of the self-liberated fugitives into the Union lines. Without speeches, laws, or guns, literally, insistently, with bold force, often organized and led by the trusted black slave drivers, they inserted their bodies into the cauldron of the war. All the denials of Lincoln and his government, all the doggerel of the white Northern population, could not stop them from their own dramatic proclamation, their own announcement that they were at the heart of this conflict. By the end of the spring of 1862, tens of thousands were camped out in whatever areas the Northern armies had occupied, thereby making themselves an unavoidable military and political issue. In Washington, D.C., the commander-in-chief of the Union armies had developed no serious plans for the channeling of the black river. Consequently, in the confusion which all war engenders, his generals in the field made and carried out their own plans. They were badly strapped for manpower, and the black fugitives provided some answers to whatever prayers generals pray. The blacks could relieve white fighting men from garrison duties. They could serve as spies, scouts, and couriers in the countryside they knew so well. They could work the familiar land, growing crops for the food and profit of the Union armies. But as the war dragged on and Northern whites lost some of their early enthusiasm, many Union commanders saw the black men among them primarily as potential soldiers. Many of the black men were eager to fight, but Lincoln was still not prepared to go that far.[21]

Nevertheless, some Union commanders like Gen. David Hunter in South Carolina were again issuing their own emancipation proclamations and beginning to recruit black soldiers. In places like occupied New Orleans it was the unmanageable and threatening movement of the blacks themselves which placed additional pressures on the Union's leader. Reports were pouring into Washington which told not only of the flood of fugitives, but of black unrest everywhere. Black men were literally fighting their way past the local police forces to get themselves and their families into the Union encampments. There was word of agricultural workers killing or otherwise getting rid of their overseers, and taking over entire plantations. Commanders like Gen. Ben Butler warned that only Union bayonets prevented widespread black insurrection. (In August 1862, to preserve order and satisfy his need for manpower, Butler himself had begun to recruit black troups in New Orleans, beginning with the well-known Louisiana Native Guards.) The dark presence at the center of the national conflict could no longer be denied. Lincoln's armies were in the midst of a surging movement of black people who were in effect freeing themselves from slavery. His generals were at once desperate for the military resources represented by the so-called contrabands, and convinced that only through military discipline could this volatile, potentially revolutionary black element be contained. As a result, before 1862 was over, black troops were being enlisted to fight for their own freedom in both South Carolina and Louisiana.[22]

In Washington, Congress was discussing its own plans for emancipation, primarily as a weapon against the South, hoping to deprive the Confederacy of a major source of human power and transfer it into Union hands. Their debates and imminent action represented another critical focus of pressure on the President. While Lincoln continued to hesitate about the legal, constitutional, moral, and military aspects of the matter, he was also being constantly attacked in the North for his conduct of the war. The whites were weary and wanted far better news from the fronts. The blacks were angry about his continued refusal to speak clearly to the issue of their people's freedom and the black right to military service. In the summer of 1862 Frederick Douglass declared in his newspaper: "Abraham Lincoln is no more fit for the place he holds than was James Buchanan. . . . The country is destined to become sick of both [Gen. George B.] McClellan and Lincoln, and the sooner the better. The one plays lawyer for the benefit of the rebels, and the other handles the army for the benefit of the traitors. We should not be surprised if both should be hurled from their places before this rebellion is ended. . . . The signs of the times indicate that the people will have to take this war into their own hands." But Frederick Douglass was not one to dwell on such revolutionary options. (Besides, had he considered what would happen to the black cause, if the white "people" really did take the war into their own hands?) Fortunately, by the time Douglass's words were published, he had seen new and far more hopeful signs of the times.[23]

In September 1862 Abraham Lincoln, in a double-minded attempt both to bargain with and weaken the South while replying to the pressures of the North, finally made public his proposed Emancipation Proclamation. Under its ambiguous terms, the states in rebellion would be given until the close of the year to end their rebellious action. If any did so, their captive black people would not be affected; otherwise, the Emancipation Proclamation would go into effect on January 1, 1863, theoretically freeing all the enslaved population of the Confederate states and promising federal power to maintain that freedom.[24]

What actually was involved was quite another matter. Of great import was the fact that the proclamation excluded from its provisions the "loyal" slave states of Missouri, Kentucky, Delaware, and Maryland, the anti-Confederate West Virginia Territory, and loyal areas in certain other Confederate states. Legally, then, nearly one million black people whose masters were "loyal" to the Union had no part of the emancipation offered. In effect, Lincoln was announcing freedom to the captives over whom he had least control, while allowing those in states clearly under the rule of his government to remain in slavery. However, on another more legalistic level, Lincoln was justifying his armies' use of the Confederates' black "property," and preparing the way for an even more extensive use of black power by the military forces of the Union. Here, the logic of his move was clear, providing an executive confirmation and extension of Congress's Second Confiscation Act of 1862: once the Emancipation Proclamation went into effect, the tens of thousands of black people who were creating their own freedom, and making themselves available as workers in the Union camps, could be used by the North without legal qualms. Technically, they would no longer be private property, no longer cause problems for a President concerned about property rights.[25]

It was indeed a strange vessel that the Lord had chosen, but black folk in the South were not waiting on such legal niceties. Not long after the preliminary proclamation, an insurrectionary plot was uncovered among a group of blacks in Culpepper County, Virginia. Some were slaves and some free, and the message of their action carried a special resonance for South and North alike, and perhaps for the President himself. For a copy of Lincoln's preliminary proclamation was reportedly found among the possessions of one of the conspirators. Though at least seventeen of the group were executed, their death could not expunge the fact that they had attempted to seize the time, to wrest their emancipation out of the hands of an uncertain President. On Nat's old "gaining ground" they had perhaps heard the voice of his God and, forming their own small army, were once again searching for Jerusalem.[26]

Such action symbolized a major difference in the movement of the Southern and Northern branches of the struggle. In the South, though most of the self-liberating black people eventually entered the camps, or came otherwise under the aegis of the Northern armies, they were undoubtedly acting on significant, independent initiatives. During the first years of the war, the mainstream of the struggle in the South continued to bear this independent, self-authenticating character, refusing to wait for an official emancipation.

In such settings black hope blossomed, fed by its own activity. Even in the ambiguous context of the contraband communities the signs were there. In 1862–63, in Corinth, Mississippi, newly free blacks in one of the best of the contraband camps organized themselves under federal oversight, and created the beginnings of an impressive, cohesive community of work, education, family life, and worship. They built their own modest homes, planted and grew their crops (creating thousands of dollars of profit for the Union), supported their own schools, and eventually developed their own military company to fight with the Union armies. It was not surprising, then, that black fugitives flocked there from as far away as Georgia. Nor was it unexpected that, in 1863, federal military plans demanded the dismantling of the model facility. Nevertheless, the self-reliant black thrust toward the future had been initiated, and Corinth was only one among many hopeful contraband communities.[27]

Such movement, and the vision which impelled it, were integral aspects of the freedom struggle in the South. Meanwhile, to aid that struggle, by 1863 Harriet Tubman had entered the South Carolina war zone. Working on behalf of the Union forces, she organized a corps of black contrabands and traveled with them through the countryside to collect information for army raids, and to urge the still-enslaved blacks to leave their masters. Apparently the intrepid leader and her scouts were successful at both tasks, though Tubman complained that her long dresses sometimes impeded her radical activities.[28]

In the North the situation was somewhat different. Word of Lincoln's anticipated proclamation had an electrifying effect on the black community there, but at the same time further removed the focus from the black freedom-seizing movement in the South. The promised proclamation now gave the Northerners more reason than ever to look to others for release, to invest their hope in the Union cause. Now it seemed as if they would not need to be isolated opponents of an antagonistic federal government. Again, because they wanted to believe, needed to hope, yearned to prove themselves worthy, they thought they saw ever more clearly the glory of the coming; before long, in their eyes the proclamation was clothed in what appeared to be almost angelic light. As such, it became an essentially religious rallying point for the development of a new, confusing mainstream struggle: one which, nervous and excited, approached and embraced the central government and the Republican Party as agents of deliverance. Doubts from the past were now cast aside, for their struggle was unquestionably in the hands of Providence and the Grand Army of the Republic. The voice of God was joined to that of Abraham Lincoln.[29]

The way for the full merger was prepared in November 1862, when the putative effects of the Dred Scott decision were essentially annulled. The unexpectedly harsh exigencies of war, the reluctance of whites to fight, the pressure from his generals, the unpredictable freedom activities of blacks in the South, and the constant demands from Northern black leaders—all had combined to convince Lincoln that the North must finally enlist black troops in the federal armies. Of course, it would be somewhat embarrassing to call upon noncitizens and nonaliens to fight and die for the Union and for rights they did not have. So, near the end of November, Attorney General Edward Bates issued an official advisement, saying in part: "Free men of color, if born in the United States, are citizens of the United States." That war-created statement became the first federal admission of black citizenship. A little more than a month later, the Emancipation Proclamation was announced, followed by the first official national recruitment of black troops. Taken together, these three events—rising out of the bitter agonies and unexpected duration of the civil conflict, and inspired in large part by the powerful presence of tens of thousands of Southern blacks who had created their own emancipation—placed the bloody imprimatur of black struggle upon the federal government's pursuit of victory.[30]

Many white persons in the North and in the border states reacted against this obvious change in the war aims of the Union. Some regular army men resigned from the federal service rather than fight for "the niggers." White Northern newspapers warned against an inundation of newly freed blacks, increasing public antipathy. Most whites, like almost every people in the midst of war, simply adjusted themselves to the new situation—so long as it did not touch them too closely—maintaining a continuous, sullen hostility to black people which periodically broke out into violence. Earlier, Sen. Lyman Trumbull of Illinois had spoken accurately for the white Northern majority when he said, "Our people want nothing to do with the negro."[31] Indeed, according to the powerful Republican leader, his own constituents were expressing alarm about the precipitate movement toward black emancipation and were saying, "We do not want them set free to come in among us."

On the other hand, from a certain legal point of view it could be argued that the Emancipation Proclamation set free no enslaved black people at all. Since by December 31, 1862, no Confederate state had accepted Lincoln's invitation to return to the fold with their slaves unthreatened, and since Lincoln acknowledged that he had no real way of enforcing such a proclamation within the rebellious states, the proclamation's power to set anyone free was dubious at best. (Rather, it confirmed and gave ambiguous legal standing to the freedom which black people had already claimed through their own surging, living proclamations.)

Indeed, in his annual address to Congress on December 1, 1862, Lincoln had not seemed primarily concerned with the proclamation. Instead, he had taken that crucial opportunity to propose three constitutional amendments which reaffirmed his long-standing approach to national slavery. The proposed amendments included provisions for gradual emancipation (with a deadline as late as 1900), financial compensation to the owners, and colonization for the freed people. In other words, given the opportunity to place his impending proclamation of limited, immediate emancipation into the firmer context of a constitutional amendment demanding freedom for all enslaved blacks, Lincoln chose another path, one far more in keeping with his own history.[32]

But none of this could dampen the joy of the black North. Within that community, it was the Emancipation Proclamation of January 1, 1863, which especially symbolized all that the people so deeply longed to experience, and its formal announcement sent a storm of long-pent-up emotion surging through the churches and meeting halls. It was almost as if the Northern and Southern struggles had again been joined, this time not through wilderness flights, armed resistance, and civil disobedience, but by a nationwide, centuries-long cord of boundless ecstasy. In spite of its limitations, the proclamation was taken as the greatest sign yet provided by the hand of Providence. The river had burst its boundaries, had shattered slavery's dam. It appeared as if the theodicy of the Northern black experience was finally prevailing. For the freedom struggle, especially in the South, had begun to overwhelm the white man's war, and had forced the President and the nation officially to turn their faces toward the moving black masses. Wherever black people could assemble, by themselves or with whites, they came together to lift joyful voices of thanksgiving, to sing songs of faith, to proclaim, "Jehovah hath triumphed, his people are free." For them, a new year and a new era had been joined in one.[33]

On the evening of December 31, 1862, Frederick Douglass was in Boston attending one of the hundreds of freedom-watch-night services being held across the North in anticipation of the proclamation. That night, a line of messengers had been set up between the telegraph office and the platform of the Tremont Temple, where the Boston meeting was being held. After waiting more than two hours in agonized hope, the crowd was finally rewarded as word of the official proclamation reached them. Douglass said: "The effect of this announcement was startling beyond description, and the scene was wild and grand. Joy and gladness exhausted all forms of expression, from shouts of praise to sobs and tears . . . a Negro preacher, a man of wonderful vocal power, expressed the heartfelt emotion of the hour, when he led all voices in the anthem, 'Sound the loud timbrel o'er Egypt's dark sea, Jehovah hath triumphed, his people are free.' "[34]

Such rapture was understandable, but like all ecstatic experiences, it carried its own enigmatic penalties. Out of it was born the mythology of Abraham Lincoln as Emancipator, a myth less important in its detail than in its larger meaning and consequences for black struggle. The heart of the matter was this: while the concrete historical realities of the time testified to the costly, daring, courageous activities of hundreds of thousands of black people breaking loose from slavery and setting themselves free, the myth gave the credit for this freedom to a white Republican president. In those same times when black men and women saw visions of a new society of equals, and heard voices pressing them against the American Union of white supremacy, Abraham Lincoln was unable to see beyond the limits of his own race, class, and time, and dreamed of a Haitian island and of Central American colonies to rid the country of the constantly accusing, constantly challenging black presence. Yet in the mythology of blacks and whites alike, it was the independent, radical action of the black movement toward freedom which was diminished, and the coerced, ambiguous role of a white deliverer which gained pre-eminence.

In a sense, then, it was these ecstatic Emancipation Proclamation meetings which provided the first real shaping of the unlikely message that the God of the black community had used Abraham Lincoln as his primary agent of freedom—Abraham Lincoln, rather than those many, many thousands of Afro-Americans who had lived and died through blood baptism in the river. In the development of black struggle and black radicalism in America, the consequences of this mythology lasted long and created many difficulties.

Indeed, the consequences began to be evident immediately. Near the end of the Emancipation Proclamation, after Lincoln had counseled the enslaved black population "to abstain from all violence, unless in necessary self-defense," he added this paragraph: "I further declare and make known that such persons, of suitable condition, will be received into the armed service of the United States to garrison forts, positions, stations, and other places, and to man vessels of all sorts in said service." Thus Lincoln had inextricably bound the cause of black emancipation to the military role of black people in preserving his white-defined, white-controlled Union. In a sense, he was indicating which acts of self-defense were "necessary," clarifying why black freedom was being legitimized, preparing to move thousands of black men from the white domination of the Southern plantations to the white domination of the Northern armies.[35]

Now the program of recruitment for the Union forces could move swiftly ahead. Shortly after the proclamation was announced, the state of Massachusetts organized a committee of wealthy and influential white men to supervise the raising of troops for the Union's first Northern-based black regiment. Soon it became clear that the prominent white citizens were not adequate to the job, especially if they confined themselves to the limited number of potential black recruits in Massachusetts. So, under the leadership of George Luther Stearns, a long-time New England abolitionist, the committee secured a national team of black recruiters known as the Black Committee and commissioned them to become fishers of men in all the black communities of the North. The Black Committee never met in one place, but a number of them regularly worked together, and all were paid for their efforts by the original white committee. As a body, the black recruitment force represented much of the heart of the prewar black freedom-movement leadership. Cutting across various elements in that struggle, it included Frederick Douglass, Martin Delany, John M. Langston, Charles L. Remond, Henry Highland Garnet, John S. Rock, William Wells Brown, and several more.[36]

One prominent name missing from the Black Committee was that of H. Ford Douglas, but only because Douglas, then in his early thirties, had already recruited himself. Perhaps with the help of his light skin, during the summer of 1862 he had managed to enlist in the white ranks of the 95th Illinois Infantry, Volunteers. Early in 1863 he was with the Union forces in Tennessee, writing to Frederick Douglass to urge him to raise a regiment and offer his own services to the federal government.

More important, H. Ford Douglas's letter revealed the profound transformation which had taken place in his life in less than a decade—a
transformation symbolic of many others, and surely affected by the confusing, chaotic forces of the war.[37] Understandably, Douglas said he had
enlisted "in order to play my part in the great drama of the Negro's
redemption," but when he spelled out his understanding of that drama,
it was a far cry from the unyielding self-reliance and black messianism
which had been his forte in the early 1850s. For instance, it now appeared
that the younger man, following the lead of some of Frederick Douglass's
earlier statements, was also placing black people "on the hands" of
white America. He seemed to be looking to white America for the redemption of black folk, rather than pressing forward the cause of black
self-elevation and self-determination. Thus Private Douglas claimed that
blacks, especially the newly freed men and women, were now being "cast
morally and mentally helpless (so to speak) into the broad sunlight of
our Republican civilization, there to be educated and lifted to a higher
and nobler life." According to Douglas, the black manhood and woman-
hood which slavery had wasted was "now to be given back to the world
through the patient toil and self-denial of this proud and haughty [white]
race. They must now pay back to the Negro in Spiritual culture, in
opportunities for self-improvement what they had taken from him for
two hundred years."[38]

In a sense it was a stunning turnabout, an expression of a strange,
impossible, and crippling dream, but one obviously not unique to H. Ford
Douglas. All over the war-scarred landscape, profound and tragic ironies
bore their way into scattered black lives and hopes, smashed the firmly
held commitments of strong men and women, and transformed the ethos
of a movement. Less than a decade before, Delany and the younger
Douglas had insisted that black people accept nothing less than a central
role in "the ruling element" of the society they lived in. Now, in the
process of a bloody war, the nation was being shattered and reshaped,
but brilliant black men like those and others were standing outside the
ruling element, organizing other blacks to fight for the purposes of the
white ruling class, while many more, dreaming demoralizing dreams,
marched at the side of white soldiers who denied the rights of blacks
to full citizenship.

Such tragic roles required that men like H. Ford Douglas and the
members of the Black Committee deny certain concrete elements in the
history of black struggle. For instance, the recruiters discovered that in
1863 black men not as eager to volunteer as they had been in
1861. The reluctance came partly because these one-time volunteers were
finding more job opportunities in the expanded war economy of the

North, and partly because they remembered how the North had persistently refused them, how Frederick Douglass himself had once suggested the need for popular revolution against the anti-black Northern leaders. So when Douglass went out to recruit soldiers to serve in the armies of that same government, under the direction of those same leaders, certain acts of self-inflicted amnesia—or magnificent faith—were required of him. Much bitter recent history had to be forgotten, repressed, denied, or transcended. Thus early in July 1863, in the course of one of his recruitment speeches in Philadelphia, Douglass gingerly reviewed the past deeds of the American government, recalling, as one of many examples, the very recent times when "our loyal camps were made slave hunting grounds, and United States officers performed the disgusting duty of slave dogs to hunt down slaves for rebel masters." Then, after exhausting a catalogue of such cruelties, the great abolitionist said to the young men and their parents gathered before him: "These were all dark and terrible days for the Republic. I do not ask you about the dead past. I bring you the living present." Of course, in "the living present" he also brought them enlistment forms for the Union army.[39]

Precisely one week after Douglass's statement, the white past leaped into the present, bearing all the blood and fear and savagery that blacks had experienced before. It came, not on the battlefields of the official Civil War, but on the streets of New York, one of the long-established blood-letting grounds in the unofficial war for white supremacy in America. Admittedly, the situation that summer was exacerbated and complicated by the official war. Some three thousand predominantly white longshoremen had gone on strike for higher wages. Under police protection, black strike-breakers were brought in to take their places. To make things worse, the recently enacted conscription law allowed unemployed workers to be particularly vulnerable to the draft. In the light of the fact that most of the affected white strikers were recent Irish immigrants who likely felt little investment in the nation's long standing conflict over slavery and union, it must have appeared to the longshoremen and their supporters that not only were blacks taking over their jobs, but that they were also being forced to go fight and die for the freedom of these blacks, as well as for the maintenance of a union that was hard for them to claim.

It was too much for them. Goaded on by frustration, they were unable to disguise their hatred and racism with the same sophistication as some of their leaders. And so, beginning on July 13, 1863, these representatives of the white working class engaged for several days in a brutal pogrom, aimed primarily at the city's black community. Hundreds of persons were killed, some in the most savage ways; other thousands were wounded, and many were forced to leave the city. For the black people hiding in barns in New Jersey, for the terrified children in the orphanage set on fire by the mob, for the running, limping Henry Highland Garnet, who narrowly escaped death, *these* were "dark and terrible days." As in every historical situation where no basic transformation has taken place, the past boldly invaded the present, exacting its bitter toll.[40]

Did Frederick Douglass really believe that the past ever died without entering deeply into the present and the future? Was not his own life an eloquent personal testimony to the ever-living quality of the past? Whatever his justification, Douglass symbolized the weaknesses of the Black Committee, forced as it was to apologize for a past which could not be buried, pressed to offer pathetic rationales for blacks dying at white commands.

Nowhere was this pathos and misdirection of struggle seen so clearly as in the life of Martin Delany, another member of the Black Committee. Three years had passed since he had returned from Africa and had offered his solemn pledge to leave to his children "the inheritance of a country . . . and the indisputable right of self-government." Two years had gone by since the guns of April 1861 had halted his voyage to the homeland and the future. Now, in April 1863, Delany was traveling as one of the Western recruiters of the committee, but Africa would give him no rest. While on these recruiting trips, therefore, Delany often dressed in West African garb and lectured about the continent. From Chicago a correspondent described Delany's attire: "The dress which the Doctor wore on the platform was a long dark-colored robe, with curious scrolls upon the neck as a collar. He said it was the wedding dress of a Chief, and that the embroidery was insignia, and had a significance well understood in African high circles. He wore it because he thought it becoming and fitting the occasion."[41]

What *was* the occasion? Did Delany realize it was his marriage to America and its government? Did he guess that he was now on a pathway leading out of the radical channels, taking him inexorably away from his radical goal of "the indisputable right of self-government" for black people? How could he know that the future would primarily view him not in the robes of his West African forebears, but in the military uniform of his white American betrayers?

Perhaps because Martin Delany had carried so much of the essence of prewar black radicalism within him, his movement out of its streams was seared in deeper, more tragic irony. Soon after the Chicago speech, the tragedy closed in. In view of his role on the Black Committee, in the light of all he had said about Africa as an inheritance for his children, it was cruel but inevitable that one day Delany the recruiter would face the searing reality of his seventeen-year-old son, Toussaint L'Ouverture. Toussaint wanted to enlist in the Union army. Here was another deep rending in an already broken life, but Delany felt he had no other choice but to agree. Thus he sent his son off to a war from which Toussaint would never recover, neither spiritually nor physically.[42]

It was a time of ironic occasions, strange marriages, and tragic wounds. It was a time for the Bureau for Colored Troops, for the recruitment of former bondsmen into the armies of the Union, for the battles of Vicksburg and Cabin Creek, for black heroes at Port Hudson and Fort Wagner. Meanwhile the dark heroes in this divinely ordained army were often abused by their white officers, and still paid less than their white counterparts; worse still, in the midst of battle some of them found the guns of their white Union comrades turned against them. It was understandable, then, that signs of black struggle appeared repeatedly within the black sectors of the Union army camps themselves.[43]

All through the period of their service to the Union, there were rumors, fears, reports of organized protest, of mutiny within the black ranks of the army—reports which still deserve further investigation. Although the concrete bases for such fears and intimations were solid, just as they had been in civilian settings, most of the time only fleeting signs were caught on the surface. On occasion, however, the black protest and resistance within the Union armies broke out into tangible incidents like the brief mutiny at Fort Jackson, Louisiana, late in 1863, when Afro-American troops took up arms against a cruel and repressive white officer, but were dissuaded from murder by both words and armed force.[44]

In the same year, Sgt. William Walker of the Third South Carolina Regiment spearheaded a more costly protest, this time against the army's policy of unequal pay. Marching with his company to the captain's tent, Walker led them in stacking their arms there, saying they refused to fight any longer "on the ground that they were released from duty by the refusal of the government to fulfill its share of the contract." His commanders, having no appreciation for fine legal arguments, court-martialed Sergeant Walker and had him shot. Steadily, unmistakably, through events such as these, all the contradictions of the liberating Union army and the Republican deliverers were pressed to the surface of the river.[45]

12

"We Are Coming Up"

The Harsh and Uncertain Path
Toward a New Nation

I travels all dat day and night up de river and follows de north star. Sev'ral times I thunk de blood houn's am trailing me and I gits in de big hurry. I's so tired I couldn't hardly move, but I gits in a trot. I's hopin' and prayin' all de time I meets up wit dat Harriet Tubman woman.

> Thomas Cole
> *Remembering Runaway Days*, 1863

It is not the time to follow in the path of white leaders; it is the time to be leaders ourselves.

> *New Orleans Tribune*, 1865

In spite of contradictions, ironies, and death, black people continued to hope, to focus their eyes and their lives on the possibilities for change created by the war. While the essentially conservative and white-supremacist civilian leaders and most of their generals attempted to contain and suppress the revolutionary potentials of the national conflict, sought to minimize the explosive change in black-white relationships which the war clearly threatened to unleash, the black community, in spite of its reluctant allies, refused to deny its hope for the coming of a new time. Beneath all the often bloody incongruities of the period, that hope persisted. Black men and women had been caught up in a radical expectation of fresh beginnings for America and themselves, believing that the Providence which broke the power of the old slavery would also usher in a new Kingdom. The God who had turned the white Civil War into a death struggle with the Peculiar Institution would surely open the postwar period to the creation of a new society where true freedom would reign.[1]

All through the middle years of the war, Frederick Douglass wrote of his hope, representing a thousand more than himself. But like so many other black—and white—people, Douglass was frantically vague concerning what the mechanisms for the tranformation of America would be. Indeed, one of his greatest weaknesses in this period was the persistence of his earlier tendency to focus on slavery and the South as the major enemies of black freedom. Thus in an article in November 1862 he could say, "Tomorrow we shall have to reconstruct the whole fabric of Southern society, and bring order out of anarchy." Essentially he had no specific contribution of his own to make, and simply agreed with the proposals put forward in the Senate by the abolitionist Charles Sumner. Under this plan the Southern states would be brought back into the Union through the territorial stages and subjected to a form of tutelage in democracy. Douglass concurred: "We shall have to educate the people . . . to make the Southern people see and appreciate Republican government."[2]

But logic had not deserted Douglass. He knew that there is no teaching without teachers, that the question of who would teach the South to "appreciate Republican government" was fully appropriate in the light of the history of black people in the North. For the hard questions were really nationwide: how would the prewar American society be changed, how would its social, political, and economic institutions be purged of white racist commitments? What concrete plans would be made to avoid new forms of political, economic, and psychological enslavement for four million black people? If Providence had finally wrested a formal place for blacks in the military conduct of the war, what part would they have in the creation of the postwar civil society? These were hard questions which ranged far beyond the South and slavery. In his search for the future, Douglass finally did raise some of them, but he had no real answers and fell back on Providence and ineffective rhetoric: "Oh that the heart of this unbelieving nation could be at once brought to a faith in the Eternal laws of justice . . . without reservation or qualifications."[3]

A year later, it was again largely rhetoric that Douglass offered when, near the end of 1863, he spoke at a meeting of the American Anti-Slavery Society, saying that the nation—and certainly the abolitionists—were fighting "for something incomparably better than the Old Union." He said, "We are fighting for unity in which there shall be no North, no South, no East, no West, no black, no white, but a solidarity of the nation, making every slave free, and every free man a voter." The vision was close to ecstasy again, and not untypical of the black community's radical hope at the time; but except for the concern for enfranchisement, there was little that was concrete.[4]

Douglass in fact typified not just the ambiguous radical hope, but the ineffectual situation in which the Northern black protest tradition now found itself. Vagueness and rhetoric were natural to a people who were not a necessary constituent of the ruling element of the nation, and had neither plans for becoming a part of it nor for organizing against it. It was a dangerous and vulnerable position, especially in a society which had already begun to make serious decisions concerning the future of its black people. In this wartime period the Northern black community was even less politicized and internally organized than during the crises of the 1850s. So in spite of the new role of their soldiers on the battlefields, when it came to the political struggles over the future of the society, black people, especially in the North, were left with little more than hope, rhetoric, and appeals to white power—and a Providence which often seemed too white for comfort.

Part of the danger rested in the forced character of the alliance which the war had made necessary. It was one thing for the American government to be driven by military and political exigencies to attack the institution of slavery and enlist black men—primarily as laborers—in its armies. It was another thing for all the black community's hopes to be placed in the hands of those ambiguous allies, the national government and its white constituency. As a result, while the black hope, vision, and goals were radical in their thrust toward a new society, the methods for reaching them were so dependent upon white American leadership that the black struggle in America was powerfully and adversely affected.

During the war, the results of the contradiction were not yet so obvious, but it was not impossible to see manifestations of the dilemma itself. Perhaps this mainstream predicament was put forward most precisely in the speech Robert Purvis made before the annual meeting of the American Anti-Slavery Society in May 1864. The predominantly white audience knew Purvis well. They remembered that he had stood staunchly with them into the 1850s, and that the decade of black harshening had driven him to condemn the government and even to suggest—albeit gingerly—revolution as a logical solution to the oppression of the black community. Now the white abolitionist group held many of the same sanguine hopes for a new day as did their black counterparts, and so were more than pleased to find Purvis in essential agreement.[5]

In his speech Purvis presented crucial examples of two basic problems then plaguing black struggle. One was the expectation that the end of slavery would also mean the end of the oppression which grew out of racism, exploitation, and fear, and bring the dawn of a new freedom. The other problem arose from their belief (or was it desperate hope?) that white political leaders would work on their own initiative to offer true equality to black people. After an introduction by William L. Garrison, Purvis set the enthusiastic tone early in his speech: "Sir, old things are passing away, all things are becoming new. Now a black man has rights, under this government, which every white man, here and everywhere, is bound to respect. [Applause] . . . The black man is a citizen, all honor to Secretary Bates, who has so pronounced him." There, of course, was one of the critical dangers. Anything "pronounced" by whites under the pressure of war could be mispronounced or denied once the situation had changed, especially if unorganized, trusting blacks continued to depend upon white declarations for their citizenship rights.[6]

Such thoughts did not seem to disturb Purvis. Referring specifically to his very recent condemnation of America and its government, he firmly maintained, "I am proud to be an American citizen." Then he said, "You know . . . how bitterly I used to denounce the United States as the basest despotism the sun ever shown upon; and I take nothing back that I ever said." Implicitly, however, much was taken back, for like Douglass, Purvis was in flight from the past. He said he wanted to forget the past, the "old things" which were supposedly "passing away." As a result, Purvis joined in some of the most common and profound mistakes made by those who carried the Northern traditions of black struggle and black radicalism into the Civil War. Forgetting the past, he insisted on blindly charging ahead, declaring, "Joy fills my soul at the prospect of the future."[7]

Still, America's history could not be totally denied, and in the light of that bloody and bitter past, Purvis was forced to acknowledge the fact that some might think him too eager, and consider such joy and assurance premature: "No, sir, I will not wait—I cannot be mistaken," he said. "My instincts, in this matter at least, are unerring. The good time which has so long been coming is at hand. I feel it, I see it in the air, I read it in the signs of the times. . . . The fiat has gone forth which, when this rebellion is crushed . . . in the simple but beautiful language of the President, 'will take all burdens from off all backs, and make everyman a freeman.' " Instincts, messages in the air, signs in the times, mysteriously announced fiats—all led to the white Republican in the White House, to the somber President who was doing very little to put his beautiful words about black freedom into beautiful deeds.[8]

This was shaky ground for a people who needed the most solid possible bases for their assault on the past and their search for a new future. Nevertheless, it was a widely shared and painfully common ground in those confusing days, entirely consistent with many historic black convictions concerning Divine Providence and mysterious forces of deliverance. As a matter of fact, Purvis's semi-mystical expression of faith was a point of confluence for almost all the mainstream protest-abolitionist forces of the time.

Of course, black people did not take that ground without misgivings, and as those latent doubts and questions were articulated, they signaled the direction of the next and far less sanguine stage of the struggle. In October 1864, on the eve of another crucial national election, at a time when men and women saw increasing signs that war might end in a Union victory, black people gathered for another national convention in Syracuse, New York. Some one hundred and fifty delegates—the largest official roster yet—formed the core of the assemblage, and for the first time there was significant representation from Southern states. Prominent men and women like Frederick Douglass, John Mercer Langston, Frances Watkins Harper, Sella Martin, William Wells Brown, and Henry H. Garnet were present, embodying much of the prewar mainstream protest tradition. As the excited delegates and other participants streamed through the streets of the city, white residents asked in hostile tones, "Where are the damned niggers going?"[9]

That, of course, was a key question for everyone everywhere, and it was obvious that the search for answers involved very difficult, tortuous paths. For instance, most if not all the blacks at the Syracuse convention had tied their personal and political destinies to the Republican Party; yet in National Republican circles there was talk now of an armistice with the South, a possible retention of slavery, and a willingness to allow the courts to decide the constitutionality of the Emancipation Proclamation and all other wartime antislavery measures. Apart from the dire threat to black life and hope represented by such thinking, it also revealed the sharp differences within the Republican Party and the Union leadership over the future of American society. But for the delegates at Syracuse, such discussions above all demonstrated the precariousness of a black-Republican alliance. Consequently, there could be no doubt that it was for black people like themselves to provide the answers to the critical question: "Where are the damned niggers going?"

As an attempt to point a way, the Syracuse convention was only a partial and ambiguous success. As usual, its prophetic-rhetorical level of response was moving, and in the long run essentially accurate. Thus the words of one of the New York delegates, Dr. P. B. Randolph: "We are here to ring the bells at the door of the world; proclaiming to the nations, to the white man in his palace, the slave in his hut, kings on their thrones, and to the whole broad universe, that WE ARE COMING UP! [Applause] Yes: we are, at last; and going up to *stay*."[10]

But in the fall of 1864, much more than prophecy was necessary. Throughout the convention the delegates made it clear that they considered the black soldiers fighting and dying on the battlefields to be their people's immediate guarantors of total emancipation. Like blacks across the nation, the men and women at Syracuse deemed the marching men an integral part of a new Jacob's ladder, reaching from slavery to freedom. Understandably, one of the first official demands of the conference was for the removal of all the invidious discriminatory practices in pay, rank, and general treatment which still prevailed against their fighting men.[11]

The delegates went further, calling for the total abolition of slavery and for perpetual federal guarantees against its revival anywhere in the nation or its territories. That was their *sine qua non*. Next among their long-range demands was a call for the political enfranchisement of all black men, and for full citizenship rights for all black people everywhere in the Union. Still treading cautiously, remaining true to their mainstream constituency, the Syracuse delegates stopped short of Delany's Cleveland Declaration of a decade earlier, and avoided talk of the need for blacks to become a "constituent element" of the nation's leadership. On the economic front, the delegates took a similarly limited position: focusing on the needs of Southern blacks, they called for land—a "fair share of the public domain, whether acquired by purchase, treaty, confiscation, or military conquest." Although the call was muted, treated far more discreetly than their discussion of other more conventional political rights, still, the demand was there, recognizable, radical in its potential.[12]

It was, of course, absolutely necessary to direct calls for action on behalf of black freedom to the white leaders of the nation. No less obvious was the fact that almost none of these men in Washington and elsewhere had ever in any way evidenced a deep concern for black rights and liberties in America. As a result of this contradiction, the delegates voted to create a new organization called the National Equal Rights League, whose purposes were twofold: "To encourage [among black people] sound morality, education, temperance, frugality, industry, and promote every thing that pertains to well-ordered and dignified life; to obtain by appeals to the minds and conscience of the American people, or by legal process when possible, a recognition of the rights of the colored people of the nation as American citizens." John Mercer Langston was chosen president of the League, and though it was soon put aside in the high hopes of Reconstruction, the immediate result was to stimulate the formation of many effective local branches in the South and North. Moreover, the League's dual emphasis on internal black self-help and external struggles for citizenship rights caught up much of the Great Tradition and anticipated many future struggles.[13]

If the formation of the League marked the high point of the Syracuse convention, the delegates were not too immersed in the hard history of the time to escape the frightening paradoxes of their relationship to the Republican Party. Though they attacked the Republicans for even considering a truce with slavery, and for excluding blacks from their planning for the nation's future, in convention statements they still relied on the party, some delegates pledging their support to its candidates in the coming Presidential election. More tragically, the staunch black men and women at Syracuse plunged even deeper into the heart of the contradiction, declaring: "That we hereby assert our full confidence in the fundamental principles of this Government, the forces of acknowledged American ideas, the Christian spirit of the age, and the justice of our cause; and we believe that the generosity and sense of honor inherent in the great heart of this nation will ultimately concede us our just claims, accord us our rights, and grant us our full measure of citizenship under the broad shield of the Constitution."[14]

With those words Syracuse delegates voiced the most profound contradictions of the Northern black protest tradition. These Afro-Americans who had lived through slavery and the prewar North, who had survived the white racist riots of the cities, who knew the ways of the white leaders, who had once counseled revolution—these same men and women now spoke of resting their case with the "honor," "generosity," "Christian spirit," and "great heart" of white America and its government. At the same time they condemned that government, demanded rights of it, and formed an Equal Rights League to fight those battles which they knew would continue long after the Civil War had ended.

The contradiction was most likely unavoidable, especially when the group chose to fall back on Douglass's reaffirmation of his earlier anti-emigration views. In the convention's address, written by Douglass, the message went out to the whites: "We are among you, and must remain among you; and it is for you to say whether our presence shall conduce to the general peace and welfare of the country, or be a constant cause of discussion and of irritation,—troubles in the state, troubles in the Church, troubles everywhere." On one level the statement was prophetic, but again it was also much too passive, too removed from the prewar heights of the struggle, and from the self-emancipation movement then raging through the South. Indeed, nowhere was the contradictory agony of the convention more evident than in the document's ultimate acceptance of the idea that the nation belonged to white Americans. Following Douglass's line, in support of this surrender, they said weakly: "To avert these troubles, and to place your great country in safety from them, only one word from you the American people is needed, and that is JUSTICE."[15]

So Syracuse became a witness to the enthrallment of the independent

Northern black movement to a white leadership element which consciously and persistently excluded blacks from its counsels, and planned a national future based on continuing white domination. In time Douglass would repent of such abject dependence on nonexistent white national benignity, would see again (with his intellect, if not his commitments) the tremendous error, the deep flaw in such a position. Then he would declare: "No man can be truly free whose liberty is dependent upon the thought, feeling and actions of others, and who has himself no means in his own hands for guarding, protecting, defending and maintaining that liberty. . . . The law on the side of freedom is of great advantage only where there is power to make the law respected. I know no class of my fellow-men, however just, enlightened, and humane, which can be wisely and safely entrusted absolutely with the liberties of any other class." But even then Douglass found it difficult to speak to the central question implied in his own insight: how were the men and women once in bondage to gain access to the "means," how might they build the black "power" which would offer some security for their rights? The Equal Rights League was an honorable gesture in this direction, but not an adequate force. For the most part, that central issue of black access to power was not joined in the North during the first struggles over the postwar future of the black masses. In the South it was faced in a different way.[16]

As the war pressed its climactic, bloody movements down into the heart of the Confederacy, into the Wilderness, roaring from Tennessee's mountains into Georgia, spreading out along the Mississippi valley into the interior of Louisiana, it continued to be deeply involved and identified with the Southern black struggle. In response to Lincoln's change of policy, thousands of Southern blacks were eagerly enlisting in the blue-clad armies, once more joining their blood and destiny with those of the uniformed black brothers of the North. For many of these once-captive men, the battles began when they decided to enlist. In the "loyal" border states, for instance, white opposition to their recruitment was at times so fierce that black men and boys had to run and fight their way past armed posses and other white gauntlets on their way to the Union enlistment stations. Many blacks did not make it, and were left hanging on trees by the road, while others paid the price of a sheared-off ear or a bloodied head to join the federal forces. (Nor did the friendly uniform worn by black military recruiters spare them from similar experiences.) Still, none of these impediments stanched the black rush to arms. As a result, from the earliest regiments formed in New Orleans and South Carolina, to the massive enlistments in Tennessee and Kentucky—where at least forty to fifty percent of the eligible black male population was under arms—this service of Southern blacks in the "Gospel Army" became a crucial element in the Afro-American freedom struggle—one which no whites, North or South, in the government or out, could ignore.[17]

As for black folk, no one could even dream of ignoring their uniformed heroes, for when the sons of Africa came marching with the Union armies, breaching all the barriers of their long bondage, then black people saw the fullest relevance of the war. For the black soldiers carried within them a desperate determination to defend their own tenuous freedom and the freedom of their people, to seize the only hour that they were given.

In the spring of 1863 one could certainly catch that fierce sense of purpose behind reports like the one from Milliken's Bend, Louisiana, where Southern black men in the Union army fought against those whites who had once maintained their slavery. At the end of the ferocious battle, which included terrible hand-to-hand combat with bayonets and gun butts, there were broken, mangled bodies everywhere. But the black troops held fast and it was said by an officer that "three-fourths of the African troops that were slain were found dead in the ditch where they were ordained to make their stand."[18]

The willingness of men to participate and stand fast in such horrible, costly battles could be attributed to bitterness, vindictiveness, and rage. However, there was always evidence that more creative urgencies were also at work. In Tennessee, toward the end of the war, a black soldier suggested some of those other elements which could drive men like him into the cauldron of battle and at the same time help them find some sanctuary for their humanity in the midst of the carnage. Late in 1864, in Tennessee, following the battle of Nashville, he went on a furlough to visit the plantation where he had been enslaved not long before. According to his later account, the mistress of the place was glad to see him, but not as a Yankee soldier. "She said, 'you remember when you were sick and I had to bring you to the house and nurse you?' and I told her, 'Yes'm, I remember.' And she said, 'and now you are fighting me!' I said 'No'm, I ain't fighting you, I'm fighting to get free.' " It was a simple and profound testimony: He had not chosen her as an enemy, and his fight was not directed against her life, her humanity. But once he had made his choice, it was left to her to decide her own relationship to the freedom struggle of this former slave, to search out for herself what her own humanity demanded. That decision would then determine whether or not the black man must indeed fight her in order to sustain his thrust toward freedom. At Milliken's Bend and Vicksburg and Savannah white men and women were making these decisions, while black men and women fought to get free.[19] ("Ain't gonna let nobody turn me round. . . .")

Everywhere, in spite of their heroic exertions and the apparent simplicity of their yearning for freedom, the fight of the black soldiers continued to be double-sided, filled with contradictions and betrayals, for the enemies to black freedom were still—in the earlier words of Henry H. Garnet—"on both sides of the blood-red waters." Indeed, in several parts of the South the Union army became an agent for controlling thousands of freedom-conscious blacks, including many outlyers. In the period between 1862–65 thousands of such Southern black men who occupied the self-created limbo between slavery and official emancipation were actually forced, impressed into the Union armies. Often the vagrancy laws in the occupied territories were used to round them up, whereupon black resistants either became drafted volunteers or were returned to the plantation owners and overseers. As a result, some of the most determinedly independent black fugitives were caught at last—in the nets of the Union forces. This is not surprising, considering the conservative response of the federal government to the potentially revolutionary situation which the war was creating in the South. Federal leaders recognized such black men as a volatile, self-determining force with tremendous potential for stimulating radical change in black-white relationships. The government judged that it could control them far better as soldiers under military discipline than as quasi-fugitive civilians of undefined status.[20]

Faced with such realities, black struggle continued within the army, not only against white superiors and fellow soldiers, but also against the federal government for having failed to protect the families which these black men had left behind. In Louisiana there were many instances, especially in 1863–64, when black soldiers invaded plantations where their family members—especially women—had been mistreated, and removed them and others to the relative safety of the government's contraband camps and farms. In Plaquemines Parish, where the search for black "bad characters" had never abated, several Afro-American soldiers were arrested for marching on plantations where their families worked, "placing guards over the owners and threatening to shoot any damned white men who interfered." These protective attempts were most often defeated, but their perspective and goals were intrinsically radical. Ever since that time, the role of black American soldiers in the freedom struggle has continued to create lively debates, vast fears, and much paradoxical history.[21]

Of course, like the majority of soldiers in the world's armies, most of the former bondsmen adjusted to the discipline and contradictions of the Union forces, fighting and working in response to white commands, seeking freedom for themselves and their people through service to the government. They continued their fighting and dying, their marching and singing, moving deeper into the Confederate territory where their captive community awaited their coming. Everywhere, in spite of the ironies of the war, Southern blacks were profoundly impressed by the uniformed men and boys who had risen up out of their common enslavement and now marched back among them, guarantors of their freedom. Everywhere, along the roads and by the country squares, they remembered the songs that the black soldiers sang:

> Don't you see the lightning?
> Don't you hear the thunder?
> It isn't the lightning,
> It isn't the thunder,
> It's the buttons on
> The Negro uniforms![22]

And surely some of the newly freed black folk lining the streets and the roads must have remembered their own song of hope before the war:

> Some ob dese days my time will come,
> I'll year dat bugle, I'll year dat drum,
> I'll see dem armies, marchin' along,
> I'll lif my head an' jine der song.[23]

Solitary black fugitives, too, like Thomas Cole, who ran North from Alabama toward the Yankee lines in Tennessee, remembered how it was: "I travels all dat day and night up de river and follows de north star. Sev'ral times I thunk de blood houn's am trailing me and I gits in de big hurry. I's so tired I couldn't hardly move, but I gits in a trot. I's hopin' and prayin' all de time I meets up wit dat Harriet Tubman woman." Young Cole never met Harriet Tubman (who was carrying out her own military operations in South Carolina), but he did find the armies of Gen. William S. Rosecrans, and soon had brass buttons of his own to show on "the Negro uniforms."

Bands of other blacks continued to engage the rebel forces in genuine if uncoordinated guerrilla attacks, harassing their flanks and rear. Toward the end of 1863, reports from North Carolina told of one such black group numbering as many as five hundred who "lead the lives of banditti, roving the country with fire and committing all sorts of horrible crimes upon the inhabitants." Similar reports were rampant in Florida, especially in the western part of the state. Indeed, in that seedbed of disaffection from the Confederate cause, white deserters and black outlyers were again joining forces and "committing depredations against the plantations and troops of loyal citizens of the Confederacy and running off their slaves." These biracial bands were even said to have threatened the cities of Tallahassee, Madison, and Marianna in northern Florida.[24]

Meanwhile, far beneath the surface of these overt acts of struggle, lay a heaving foundation of deeply felt, determined acts of the will. As usual, one of these was prayer. From every corner of the Southern black community, rising like the echoes of some hidden African chorus, the prayers for freedom still went on. Most often they were secret and never detected, but many times they were heard by masters, overseers, or patrols, and those who prayed for freedom were sometimes brutally whipped. In Alabama a hard-praying man named Ned was tied to four pegs in the ground and whipped for his freedom prayers "twell de blood run from him lack he was a hog." But the whipping stopped neither the praying nor the freedom. Not long after, Ned "slipped off an' went . . . to jine de Union Army." ("Not since Cromwell's time," said a contemporary observer of the Southern-based black Union forces, "have we seen so religious an army.")[25]

Near the end of the war, as all the running and fighting, praying and dying took their toll upon the desperate Confederacy, as unparalleled fear and doubt gripped their leaders, the white Southerners reopened earlier discussions about using blacks in their armies. Like the North, they had already used tens of thousands of black men and women as laborers for the military services, but with rare exceptions there was no attempt—or inclination—to arm the enslaved Afro-Americans. By 1864, however, the issue and need were being seriously pressed in Southern leadership circles. Some advocates of the plan to draft bondsmen recognized that it would almost certainly mean the end of their peculiar institution, for as one leader said, "If slaves make good soldiers, our whole theory of slavery is wrong." Nevertheless, as time ran out, some Confederates were willing to trade the death of legal slavery—both in theory and practice—for Southern independence and some other form of domination over their black population.[26]

The proposals obviously held both danger and promise for black struggle in the South. According to at least one source, some black men in the South were prepared for possible recruitment. While the Confederate proposals were under discussion—according to a later report by the *New Orleans Tribune*—"Secret associations were at once organized in Richmond, Va., which rapidly spread throughout Virginia." These associations discussed what the black response should be, and finally agreed "that black men should promptly respond to the call of the Rebel chiefs, whenever it should be made." Then, if they were placed in front of the white Confederate troops on the field of battle, "as soon as the battle began the Negroes were to raise a shout about Abraham Lincoln and the Union, and, satisfied there would be plenty of support from the Federal force, they were to turn like uncaged tigers upon the rebel hordes." If placed to the rear, the black troops were to fire on the white Confederates in front of them. For better or worse, this plan was never given a trial, for the Confederate leaders, even in the utter desperation of the winter of 1864–65, could not bring themselves to arm their bondsmen. And when finally, early in the spring of 1865, they changed their minds, it was too late: Lee surrendered in April.[27]

Nevertheless, it was obvious that the black people of Virginia—and almost everywhere—had decided which of these white forces on the Southern battlefields was actually Pharaoh's army. However, as the war wound down and the issues of the peace began to loom in men's minds, a steadily increasing number of black people would probably have agreed with Henry H. Garnet's earlier observation that "the Pharaohs are on both sides of the blood-red waters." In Kansas, for instance, now that the glory of the battles in the West had passed, letters of complaint from black soldiers testified to the cruel and vicious tortures to which some Union recruiters were resorting to impress black men into the military. Similar stories came from South Carolina and Virginia. There was bad news too from the contraband camps: near the end of the war a federal official admitted that the mortality rate among the former slaves in those places was "frightful," ranging at times above twenty-five percent. And as the military and civilian representatives of the national government and other institutions spread through the conquered South, it became apparent that they were bearing a very mixed set of gifts for blacks. Although some of them came with excellent intentions and initiated crucial services of relief, welfare, and education, they had few answers for the future which could match the newly freed community's radical visions and needs. Besides, too many of these white men and women also bore with them either the racism or the paternalism endemic in their society, and all too often both. Furthermore, the very presence of white helpers, advisers, and guides among the black population tended to inhibit any independent movement among blacks to define their own situation, realize their own hopes, fulfill their own needs.[28]

In a sense, the most perplexing white force was the federal government itself. It is now clear that the reluctant ally of black freedom played an actively conservative role in a situation which, for the best purposes of the freed people, needed to be pushed toward its most profound revolutionary implications. At a time when the trauma of war and the explosive ferment of newly won freedom could have opened the way to entirely redefined black-white relationships in the South, Lincoln and his administration, not being committed to a really new status for black (or white) people anywhere in America, discouraged radical change. With rare exceptions, through its military and civilian agents the national government sought to emphasize continuity, rather than progressive, creative change, in all economic, social, and political relationships between the races. Their actions most often held blacks in subservience to the white-owned land, encouraged continued white political and economic domination, and neutralized and undermined any black attempts at new levels of self-assertion and self-determination. Indeed, one of the most careful students of the federal role in the South during this crucial late wartime period has said: "Whatever changes might have occurred as a result of the war, federal authorities took care to see that they would not be revolutionary."[29]

Of course revolutionary change was precisely what was necessary to advance authentic black freedom, and as always, there were black men and women who saw to the heart of the issue. In those last fading but illuminating days of the war, nowhere in the South did black people speak more clearly to the problems of the ambiguous federal presence, or insist more adamantly on the need for radical postwar change, than in New Orleans. Ever since the earlier days of slavery, this community with its historic free population had had its own special quality of resistance and struggle, its own peculiar internal contradictions. Now black spokesmen there pressed their people, their new white "allies," and themselves toward the fulfillment of the destiny they had seen in the war, and demanded the proper responses to the voices they had heard in the guns.

In Louisiana, as in every other part of the South where black labor had played the central role in transforming the wilderness into sources of wealth, the issue of the land and its future uses for black people provided a focal point for discussion and debate. As in many Southern areas, the federal government had followed its early military conquests in Louisiana with the expropriation of the plantations of rebel military and political leaders. Then, instead of making this land available to the black men and women who had arduously developed it, the government had either eventually returned it to the original owners and their families, or sold or leased it to mostly Northern speculators. In 1864 the newly founded *New Orleans Tribune* called the federally favored owners "avaricious adventurers," and initiated a relentless verbal assault against the federal government for its policy toward the land, the black toilers, and their hope for freedom.[30]

Following the demise of its predecessor, *L'Union*, the *Tribune* had been established in the summer of 1864 by three free black men whose families had originally come from San Domingo. Key financial backing was supplied by a wealthy doctor, J. T. Roudanez, but the major early voice of the *Tribune* was that of Paul Trevigne, the editor, a man of whom it was said, "At great personal peril and with dauntless courage, he battered his way to Negro freedom." Then, before 1864 was over, Roudanez sought out the services of a brilliant Belgian-born scientist and political radical, Jean-Charles Houzeau. By the end of the year, this extraordinary alliance had been secured: a black-owned and controlled newspaper, edited by a gifted white radical ally, a man who had risked his life on two continents in the struggles for human dignity. In the last months of the war, guided by its powerful leadership combination, the *Tribune* kept the land question at the center of that battering force: "It is not too late for the Government to adopt the correct policy in this matter. Sooner or later, this division of property must come about; and the sooner, the better. The land tillers are entitled by a paramount right to the possession of the soil they have so long cultivated. . . . If the Government will not give them the land, let it be rented to them. It is folly now to deny the Rebellion and not accept all its logical results. Revolutions never go backward." There, in the midst of the war, the *Tribune* had spoken the word, identified the real movement, the real struggle, joining itself to the future: "Revolutions never go backward."[31]

In addition to their forthright position concerning the land, both the *Tribune* and *L'Union* raised the equally radical issue of the right of black men—all black men—to the ballot. At the outset of a harsh political struggle for power, they called for black suffrage, and thereby gained for their opinions a peculiar resonance in the battle. By 1864 the ruling whites of Louisiana realized that if their military cause was lost, and if the masses of freed black men were allowed to vote, then a revolution was really upon them, and their political power, once broken, might never be regained. As part of their attempt to block such a revolution, the white Southern leaders who remained in the conquered community tried to exploit the deep-seated differences between the largely quadroon free black community—heavily represented in the black press—and the masses of their darker-skinned, newly freed brothers and sisters. In response to white criticism that it represented an exclusive minority of blacks, the *Tribune* declared that it was "the organ of the oppressed, whether black, yellow, or white," and pressed on toward its goal.[32]

The white opposition also raised the stigmatizing cry of "radicalism" against those who favored the full enfranchisement of the adult black population. The black journalists of New Orleans had indeed been among those who recently formed the Union Radical Association in the black community. In response to the charge of radicalism, *L'Union* had declared: "Radical methods get at the root, at the source of a problem;

they involve the entire achievement of a work, and opposition to half measures." *L'Union* further maintained that "the true friends of liberty should not allow themselves to be intimidated by the denunciations of a false conservatism that wants to conserve nothing except the inalienable rights of traitors and despots." Moreover, it drew a direct line between the American Revolution and the struggles which surged beneath the surface of the Civil War. Claiming strange but illuminating forefathers, it went on to say: "Our revolutionary ancestors were radicals when they undertook to overthrow British despotism . . . and they drafted the most radical political document in the history of mankind—the Declaration of Independence. If we really believe that the grand principles of this Declaration are the only sane base for republican liberty, we cannot be too radical in defending them."[33]

This was more than the usual rhetoric of the mainstream of the Great Tradition of Black Protest, more than the tactical black claim on American heroes. What was at work here was the attempt to redefine the Civil War, to tie it inextricably on the one hand to the struggle for black manhood and full political participation, and on the other hand to the best egalitarian traditions of the unfinished American Revolution. Unasked as always, black people were thrusting themselves into the larger movement of American history, joining that history's paradoxical dialectic. They were demanding the true revolution which would eventually break open the way for all those black man and women who had once been defined as the last to press forward into their rightful places among the first, among "the ruling element" of the nation. Indeed, these most visionary of Africa's children in America boldly proposed that black people themselves be the vanguard of that crucial opening wedge. Shortly before the war ended and the anguished peace began, the editors of the *Tribune* declared, "It is not the time to follow in the path of white leaders; it is the time to be leaders ourselves." In a society uncertain of the way ahead—but certain of white supremacy, whatever the way—the children of the slaveships, the children of Nat Turner, were serving again as a blackhead signpost, believing with exquisite hope that neither revolutions nor rivers go backward, insisting at great cost that their own lives be thrust forward as the ultimate guarantors of that relentless and radical black vision.[34]

Slavery Chain
Done Broke at Last

Claiming "The Land of the Free"

The year 1865 came in, speaking joyful words in our ears. . . . We hail it
with joy, because it finds us surrounded with light. . . . This year, yea, this
present new year, [God] will mount His chariot of power, and will draw his
sword of Vengeance, and will ride from Dan to Beersheba, and will drive out
the Hittites, the Canaanites, and the Jebusites, viz., the rebels, the slaveholders
and the copperheads; and the cry shall be, from the highest mountain to the
lowest valley, that this world is become the Kingdom of our God and of his
Christ, for slavery is abolished forever.

> N. B. Sterett, Sergeant Major,
> 39th U.S. Colored Troops[1]

From the outset they knew. The light was there. The vision did not fail
them, and signs were everywhere. Even before they gathered in churches,
homes, and groves across the North and South on the last night of 1864,
shouting their songs of praise, sending up incantations of hope like
bittersweet trails of African incense, even before those throbbing Watch
Night services had opened the floodgates of racial memories and rituals,
black folk sensed that they had finally come to the crossing point. Wherever they were, they saw, they heard, they felt the signs, bearing witness
to the inescapable truth that 1865 would be the year when the relentless
current of a people's movement joined forces with the mysterious power
of their marching, riding redeemer God. They believed that this was the
moment in history when a suffering, struggling people, in the midst of a
wounded, divided nation, would finally burst out of slavery and move to
the new land of freedom.

Only the blind could miss that light. For although the long dying of
the war had not yet ended, while there were still dark and troubled

nights to be endured, it was clear that the American institution of slavery was finally broken. Black people know that the Senate had already approved the constitutional amendment which would outlaw slavery forever in the United States, and that the House of Representatives was now working toward its own response. They had rejoiced in November 1864, when the legal structures that had held their people in bondage for generations were finally struck down in Frederick Douglass's home state of Maryland. And in the last weeks of the year, from the battlefields of the Civil War, along with all the anguished news of suffering, death, and loss among their men and others, they had heard of how the Union armies had battered their way down to Savannah. Many black people also knew that other seaborne Northern forces were just then preparing to crack the Confederate defenses of Wilmington, North Carolina, the crucial port city that was the home of David Walker and the General of the Swamps. Meanwhile around Richmond, the Confederate capital, Southern white defenders and the ubiquitous black community could both feel the coming fires of the marching Union armies.[2]

The signs were everywhere, even on the calendar. For a people caught up in messianic expectations, looking for the kingdoms of this world to become the liberated kingdoms of their God, it was surely no mere coincidence that the first day of 1865 was also Sunday, the Lord's Day. So after resting briefly from their Watch Night services, they went back again to the Sunday church gatherings, putting off their formal celebration of the Emancipation Proclamation until the next day. Then on that third day of excitement and hope they rose again, this time pouring out of the buildings and the fields, marching, singing, often following the drums and cadences of their black soldiers, carrying their children, helping the old folk, listening to speeches, sermons, and songs, then breaking bread —and much more—together. Since 1863 they had been establishing this new tradition of Emancipation Day celebrations, openly in the North and in the liberated areas of the South, clandestinely elsewhere, uniformly testifying to the fact that freedom was not primarily a legal or political gift from without, but a deeply human quality which had been developing among them within the institution of slavery. Indeed, when the exultant black processions invariably included such fully realized forces as the United Brethren of Mutual Relief, the Morning Star Association, the Ladies of Naomi Court of the Heroines of Jericho, and the Brothers and Sisters of Love and Charity (to say nothing of the many lodges of Masons), who could miss the creative, self-defining genius long at work?

Of course, in the midst of the singing and the eating, through all the love and charity, men and women knew that there was something more

to this new year. The marching black soldiers and their shining guns
reminded them, as did the brothers, husbands, and sons who would
never march again. So reports of the January 2 events often carried
exhortations like that of the Reverend George A. Rue of Boston, who
saw the chariot of God and proclaimed: "Let the battle not cease, nor
the cannons stop their roar, until the chains shall fall from the limbs of
every slave now held in bondage. Then shall songs of praise to the Most
High resound . . . from every hill and valley throughout the land, and
the country will indeed be 'the land of the free.' God speed the day!"[3]

Such signs and messages, often written in blood, were at once chilling
and inspiring to a people poised at the edge of a new moment in their
history. But after the celebrations were over, black men and women—
especially that overwhelming majority in the South—were faced with a
set of very hard questions about this coming land of the free. If 1865
was indeed to be the year of crossing, what was on the other side? The
old institution of slavery was surely dying, but what would be the shape
of the new institution of freedom? How would it be constructed to meet
the needs and dreams of the millions now erupting out of bondage? Who
would combine forces with black people in designing, creating, and maintaining it? After the bloody catharsis of the Civil War, how free would
this America really be—this America so filled with the animus of white
supremacy? Meanwhile, where would black people find work and land
and food and clothing? Who would decide all these things? Moving well
beyond the good feelings of the celebrations, such questions went to the
heart of the postwar black struggle for freedom. For just as slavery had
been an institution with economic, political, religious, and psychological
manifestations and meanings, so it became increasingly clear to many
black persons that freedom must also become a full-blown institution,
affecting the totality of their lives and the lives of others, eventually requiring the entire nation to become "the land of the free."

Neither the Emancipation Proclamation nor the abolition amendment
then making its way through Congress really spoke to these central issues.
Lincoln's wartime document had carried no vision of freedom for all
America's black people. For their part, the framers of the new constitutional amendment seemed intent on simply outlawing slavery, not defining freedom. In a sense this was to be expected: white definitions of
black people's freedom had never been sufficient. As a result, the black
community was not idly waiting for answers and clarifications from
others. Instead, all through the murderous civil conflict which they insisted on calling a "freedom war," black people both in the South and
the North had been working toward their own answers, attempting in
their own wisdom, through their own vision and prayer, to come to

terms with this new stage of the struggle. Especially as the war wound down, they set out in myriad ways and places, individually and in groups, to create, project, and protect their own understanding of the new institution, the new time, the new land. From the editorial offices of the *Tribune* in New Orleans to the convention hall in Syracuse, and in a host of churches and homes, on street corners, and in taverns in between, black people had already begun to ask and answer their own questions about the new land of their freedom. In 1865 that process picked up great force and power.[4]

Just ten days after the Emancipation celebrations, the self-liberating movement of thousands of black people created a paradigmatic moment in the struggle for the new institution. Late in the previous year Gen. William Tecumseh Sherman's Northern army had moved like a fiery juggernaut, smashing its way southeast through Georgia from Atlanta to the sea, capturing the old port city of Savannah just before Christmas. But Sherman's ravaging forces had not come into the Savannah area alone. All the way down—along every road, through every town, crossing each creek and stream—they had encountered and attracted the black community of Georgia. Like hundreds of thousands of black people across the South, especially wherever the Union armies appeared, these black Georgians were already defining their own freedom as they boldly thrust their lives into the wake of the Union lines, into the vortex of that destructive, transforming march.[5]

Here in Georgia, all the way down to Savannah, pressing right to the water's edge, black men, women, and children thronged to the reluctant liberators. In spite of Sherman's low opinion of them, in spite of his refusal to enlist their eager men as soldiers, the people came, working as servants, scouts, teamsters, bridge builders, cooks, working at their freedom. In spite of the hostility of many of the white soldiers and officers, the blacks came on like a river. Though in some places they were left exposed to the fury of the desperate Southern defenders, and in others found that the Northern armies had pulled up the pontoon bridges over rushing country streams and rivers, still the black army followed on, losing many persons in the waters of the Ogeechee and at Ebeneezer Creek. Having known rivers and oceans and drownings before, they kept on. So by the time Sherman reached Savannah, his armies were surrounded, inundated by thousands of black refugees, creators of their own freedom. These blacks had to be dealt with before the white army could slash its bloody way north through the Carolinas, and before the final settling of accounts with Lee's battered forces in Virginia.[6]

All that movement, hope, and dying were part of the setting for a revealing encounter at Sherman's Savannah headquarters on the night of

January 12, 1865. For various political and military reasons the Union's Secretary of War, Edwin M. Stanton, a leading force among the more radical Republicans, had come to the city. He had heard of the cascading black presence, and now he had seen some of it with his own eyes. Responding to the initiative of a black minister, Stanton had requested a meeting with some of the leaders of the newly freed community of that city and its environs. Essentially, Stanton wanted to hear what black people were saying and thinking about the urgent issues of their present and future, about the freedom they envisioned for themselves. For his part, Sherman was now prepared to make use of black troops and wanted to find the speediest way to obtain them, especially since the black community had protested against the forced conscription of their men. That night a delegation of twenty black men, all church leaders, filed into Sherman's quarters to meet with the general and his civilian chief.[7]

The black contingent ranged in age from twenty-six to seventy-two, but most of them were older men well past their forties. The majority had been born into slavery, and almost all of them had lived out their lives in the immediate area. All were pastors, preachers, and lay leaders in the Baptist, Methodist, and Episcopal churches, but like most black men in such positions, they were also barbers and sailors, house servants and field workers. They bore names like Abraham Burke, John Cox, Garrison Frazier, Ulysses Houston, and Arthur Wardell, but their name was legion, for they were the spokesmen of their people. Attired in their best preaching garb, aware of their very special burden and opportunity, they faced Sherman, Stanton, and the other Union representatives. Since in the highest traditions of the black church and the freedom struggle, the congregations behind these men were already providing food, housing, and other material aid to the multitudes of their people who had trooped into the Savannah area, the ministers must have sensed their capacity to speak not only for the blacks of Savannah, but for the newly arrived black armies of freedom as well.[8]

The delegation had chosen Garrison Frazier, an elder with thirty-five years in the Baptist ministry, to speak for them. With one important exception, it was he who responded to the written questions put forward in military/legal style by Stanton and Sherman. Early in the interview the delegation was asked to state its understanding of slavery and to define the freedom provided by the Emancipation Proclamation. Frazier's response was:

Slavery is receiving by irresistible power the work of another man, and not by his consent. The freedom, as I understand it, promised by the proclamation, is taking us from under the yoke of bondage, and placing us where we could reap the fruit of our own labor, take care of ourselves, and assist the government in maintaining our freedom.[9]

As the transcribed response was read again to the group, all the other men concurred. Though each person could have added a set of variations to Frazier's basic themes, he had stated most of the key issues for them.

Stanton and Sherman then raised two crucial questions: "State in what manner you think you can best take care of yourselves, and how can you best assist the government in maintaining your freedom." Again Frazier replied for the others:

The way we can best take care of ourselves is to have land, and turn it and till it by our own labor . . . and to assist the government [in maintaining our freedom], the young men should enlist in the service of the Government, and serve in such manner as they may be wanted.

To make sure that his first point was not overlooked, Frazier repeated, "We want to be placed on land until we are able to buy it and make it our own."[10]

Before they left the general's headquarters, the black men dealt with still another issue, one which had a long history and would resurface throughout the decades of black struggle in the United States. They were asked to "state in what manner you would rather live; whether scattered among the whites or in colonies by yourselves." It is likely that in the minds of the black delegation the term "colonies" did not carry the earlier, antebellum implication of removal of their people to some separate place, away from the land they had nurtured. Rather it was understood as an opportunity for them to have ready access to native land without the hindering, oppressive presence of whites. In that context Frazier responded, using the singular for the first time: "I would prefer to live by ourselves, as there is a prejudice against us in the South that will take years to get over; but I do not know that I can answer for my brethren."[11]

When the other men were polled, it turned out that Frazier spoke for all the brethren save one, twenty-six-year old James Lynch. The youngest member of the group, Lynch was unique in other ways as well. Born free in Baltimore, he had attended school in the North and was a presiding elder in the African Methodist Episcopal Church. In 1863 he had been assigned by his denomination to work with the black communities of South Carolina and Georgia as they emerged from slavery. Generally, this impressive young leader advised his people to cultivate friendship with the whites of the South, and it was through one of Lynch's white friends that the initial contact with Stanton had been made. Eventually the young clergyman found his way to Mississippi, where his significant gifts as preacher, politician, and conciliator made him an important leader in the Republican Party of that state. Here in Savannah, however, he was the sole dissenter on the question of "in what manner you would rather live"; according to the record, "Mr. Lynch says he thinks they should not be separated, but live together."[12]

Considering the different experiences of Lynch and the other black ministers, the difference in views on this matter was at once understandable and illuminating. However, at that moment it was not of signal importance. (When one considers the clear implication of self-government which went along with the ministers' view of black colonies, it is obvious that in the development of the postwar South, neither black view really prevailed.) Far more significant at the time was the meeting itself, and the subterranean process it revealed.

The people had been moving, thinking, working their way through to new understandings of their needs. Moreover, they had gone beyond words to deeds. In Savannah, as elsewhere, they had continued to create the institutions of freedom, institutions which had seen their first tender life in the midst of slavery. So even while the guns of war were roaring around them, James Lynch and others had organized the black community to create the Savannah Educational Association, and by the time the ministers met with Sherman and Stanton, Savannah's black people were ready to open and support two schools for their children and themselves. The site they chose for one of the schools carried an eloquent message of its own, for they decided to take Bryan's Slave Market, the city's slave-trading center, and transform it into Bryan's Free School.[13]

Savannah was both symbol and microcosm. Here, before their freedom from slavery had been officially recognized by the nation—while many white Americans were fiercely holding back, convinced that this nation could never contain both free black and free white men and women—the black community was moving forward. Still searching for the trail of the chariots of God, seeking out their own way, defining their own freedom, taking the initiative to build their own institutions and speak their own convictions, black people necessarily addressed the future of the larger society as well. Whether from Frazier or Lynch, Houston or Cox, or the thousands who sat in their churches, or those who worked the land in the refugee villages, a central message was being worked out: freedom for black people meant taking care of themselves—a profound sense of independence. Indeed, the word from Garrison Frazier and the evidence from the contraband camps suggested that, for him and others, freedom at best required significant levels of political autonomy. It meant too the right to protect themselves, and the guarantee of federal aid—especially through the use of black troops—to assist in maintaining their liberty against the still lively spirit of slavery and white domination. Freedom meant education. Freedom meant land: "We want . . . land . . . to . . . make it our own." Soon the deeper message began to emerge: such a vision of black freedom demanded a new vision of America itself.[14]

Even in that first month of the frighteningly new year, anyone who looked closely at the emerging freed community of the South, anyone who listened to their messages, must have sensed something more: this community had its own authentic leaders, its legitimate spokespersons who had been nurtured among the people and their indigenous institutions for decades and longer. In no way could such men and the women who stood with them be essentially described as products of white paternalism, of an internalized white work ethic or a concentration-camp system. Rather, such persons were products of their own struggles against all of these and other aspects of slavery, the continuing harvest of their own will to be free. Thus many of the black ministers who met Sherman and Stanton in Savannah were direct and living products of the struggles for independent black churches that the Reverend Andrew Bryant and his courageous band of Baptists had waged in and around the port city at the end of the eighteenth century. These products of the river—men like Frazier, Houston, and others—testified to its continuing creative force. They helped to explain why in 1865 Savannah's black community, and many others like it, felt ready to walk directly out of slavery into the dangerous and necessary freedom of self-government; why they seemed prepared to challenge all America to a new vision of itself; why they were their own best signs of the new times.[15]

The challenge that such men and women represented was dramatically heightened by the fact that black people were not the only ones organizing in the South during that winter of transformation. As the war subsided, the defeated and occupied states of the Confederacy began to organize in order to work their way back into the Union. So white men too were meeting, holding official conventions, negotiating with Lincoln over the terms of their readmission to the Union, over the requirements for their new "loyal" governments. As a result, the rising power and demands for freedom of the unofficial black conventions, and the white gatherings determined to hold back the coming of the new time, were often juxtaposed.[16]

Such a gathering of opposing forces was evident in Nashville that January, when Tennessee's official all-white constitutional convention met to develop a body of laws meeting Lincoln's mild requirements for readmission to the Union. Those requirements called for a minimum of ten percent of the state's 1860 voting population to pledge loyalty to the Union and to approve a new constitution abolishing slavery and repudiating secession—a plan whereby blacks were consciously excluded from the Reconstruction process. The obvious intention of the Nashville convention was to establish a government which denied black participation on every level of citizenship, leaving the former slaves in a limbo similar to that of the free black people of the antebellum South.

However, this was not the antebellum South, and the new, free black people of Tennessee had other ideas about their future. They had been busy holding their own meetings, organizing petition campaigns, sending lobbyists to Washington, preparing their own definitions of their role in the reconstructed state. The day after the white convention began, a strong black petition was set before it, calling for full citizenship and unrestricted suffrage, based largely on the Afro-American sacrifices for the Union cause. The Tennessee blacks could not forget the large proportion of their men still in the Union armies. Said the black petition in part: "The government has asked the colored man to fight for its preservation and gladly has he done it. It can afford to trust him with a vote as safely as it trusted him with a bayonet."[17]

About the same time, black people were meeting in convention in New Orleans, urged on by the determined voice of the *Tribune*: "The age of guardianship is past forever. We now think for ourselves, and we shall act for ourselves." Acting for themselves, they gathered in January to form the Louisiana branch of the National Equal Rights League. In doing so, the black community of the Crescent City seemed to find a new basis for unity within its own often-fractured life. Conscious of the social, complexional, economic, and linguistic divisions which had so often plagued black New Orleans, the *Tribune* declared:

The meeting of this convention has inaugurated a new era. It was the first political move ever made by the colored people of the State acting in a body. . . . There were seated side by side the rich and the poor, the literate and educated man, and the country laborer, hardly released from bondage, distinguished only by the natural gifts of the mind. There, the rich landowner, the opulent tradesman, seconded motions offered by humble mechanics and freedmen. Ministers of the Gospel, officers and privates of the U.S. Army, men who handle the sword or the pen, merchants and clerks, all classes of society were represented, and united in a common thought: the actual liberation from social and political bondage.[18]

Such a convention was an act of struggle in itself, bringing together the black community, challenging the white leaders of the state and the nation to respond to black visions and to their claims to the rights of citizens. But there were other implications for the movement toward freedom, especially in the persons of the "officers and privates of the U.S. Army" who were present, and who indeed always seemed present wherever such gatherings were held. In New Orleans as elsewhere, these black military men were a force of great transformative potential. Already they had challenged the city's segregation laws on the streetcars and had won the special right to ride without restriction. Now in January 1865, in keeping with the spirit and direction of the Equal Rights League meeting, the men in blue pressed the issue beyond special treatment. At a mass meeting one of the black officers urged all of his people to rally behind the example of the soldiers, telling both soldiers and civilians, "We must claim the right of riding for every one of us, and claim it unconditionally." In a campaign that extended over two years, the New Orleans black community finally won the right.[19]

Some results of the early black struggles to define and establish their freedom were far more immediate and significant. Indeed, before January 1865 had ended, it appeared as if the self-liberating movement of contrabands and fugitives, which had originally helped to bring on the nighttime meeting in Savannah between the ministers and Sherman and Stanton, would actually mark the dawning of a new era. For one of the major reasons for the conference had been the Union's desire to find a way to deal with the flood of black people, some of whom were impeding the movements of Sherman's armies, while others were already claiming and working the land that the Confederate owners had deserted. Then, on January 16, only a few days after the black ministers had called for land, self-government, and protection, Sherman responded by issuing his famous Field Order Number 15, embodying and legitimizing the action that black men and women had already taken toward those goals. In turn, the order emboldened the freedom-seeking community to continue and expand its forward movement.

Under the terms of the military edict, the demand for land was immediately, though imperfectly, addressed. More than four hundred thousand acres of land abandoned by Confederate owners on the Georgia and South Carolina Sea Islands and along the coast were set aside for black settlement and temporary possession, confirming what thousands of black folk were already doing, appearing to answer the prayers of generations. Plots of forty acres per family were proposed, and following the wisdom of the black ministers and the logic of the situation, Sherman's order also directed that no whites, except necessary military personnel or others in helping roles, were to reside in the new black settlements. Indeed, the order affirmed what black men had declared as their people's need and capacity for self-government, stating that "the sole and exclusive management of affairs will be left to the freed people themselves, subject only to the United States military authority and the acts of Congress."[20]

Of course this decision—like all military actions, including the Emancipation Proclamation—was no mark of sheer altruism. Not only did it provide at least a temporary solution to the problem of the heaving, uncontrolled army of black refugees which threatened to impede Sherman's planned assault into the heart of the Carolinas, but it also made provision for a black army which he could control. Crucial in the field order, as in the Emancipation Proclamation before it, was the insistence that "the young and able-bodied Negroes must be encouraged to enlist as soldiers in the service of the United States."[21]

Coming as it did in January 1865, when so many persons could see and hear the last, anguished dying of the Confederate dream, Field Order 15 and its land provisions created an explosion of hope within the black communities of the South and the North. Word of its existence and its possible wider applications spread quickly. Obviously, black movement toward freedom had been crucial in forcing the action, and now it appeared as if access to the land, self-government, and protection—was that not the essential meaning of black soldiers for black people?—had been accepted by the government as legitimate elements in the definition of their freedom.

Immediately the hope which had grown out of action and vision now became the source of greater action and renewed vision. Nowhere was this more evident than in the struggle for land, and once more the Savannah meeting provided a symbolic focus. The Reverend Ulysses Houston, pastor of the Third African Baptist Church of the port city, had been one of the delegates to the meeting with Stanton and Sherman, and if his experience is an accurate indicator of the situation, it strongly suggests that the black men had come to the encounter not only with an agenda, but with a carefully worked-out plan of action.

Houston was forty years old at the time. He had been born into slavery, and in his youth had served as a nurse in the federal naval hospital in Savannah. Later, in addition to his service as a pastor, he had established himself as a butcher in the city. It was said that he always used his spare time well, learning how to read, studying the Bible and theology— apparently also studying the uses of freedom. Almost immediately after Field Order 15 was issued, Houston led a group of blacks to set up a self-governing community on Skidaway Island, off the Georgia coast. This was obviously a carefully planned venture, awaiting only the formal approval of the military government. A contemporary account of the experiment said that "[Houston] and his fellow colonists selected their lots, laid out a village, numbered the lots, put the numbers in a hat, and drew them out. It was Plymouth colony repeating itself." More important, it was black men and women indicating that they were fully in earnest and fully confident when they told Sherman and Stanton that they were prepared to govern themselves. Thus Houston declared of his Skidaway community, "We shall build our cabins, and organize our town government for the maintenance of order and the settlement of all difficulties."[22]

At the same time, in the midst of this exhilarating hope, these black people refused to deceive themselves about the precariousness of their situation. They knew that they had not been given any permanent title to the land. Already they had spied the old owners returning to the scene, investigating the situation, petitioning the military forces, predicting that the plantations would be taken back once the war was officially over and the military occupation ended. Besides, apart from the black occupants of the land, all the official decision makers were white. So it was not possible to rest easy. As a result, there were many occasions like the one in early February when representatives of the Skidaway group pressed their questions to government agents. A white observer noted: "They wanted to know what title they would have to their land—what assurance they could have that it would be theirs after they had improved it. Their questions were plain, straightforward, and showed a shrewdness which I had not looked for."[23]

Regardless of what a Northern white observer had looked for, the Skidaway experience was not uncommon in those days when so many things seemed at once possible and very precarious. Not only in the area covered by Sherman's order, but wherever blacks were able to gain a tenuous hold on land across the South, they had organized in groups of families and set up communities which had many self-governing aspects. They stretched from Slabtown in Virginia and Roanoke Island off the coast of North Carolina, across to Carrolton, below New Orleans. Thousands of black families were organized in communities in New Bern, North Carolina, and at Shiloh near Memphis. They established Zion Town near Richmond, and Contraband up the Tennessee River from Chattanooga. Communities with significant levels of autonomy were based as far north as Cairo, Illinois, and at White River, Holly Springs, and Grand Junction in Mississippi. The two best-known settlements in the latter state were at Corinth in the northeast and Davis Bend in the west. In almost every instance, there were local black governing councils and executives giving guidance from within, and black troops providing protection from a variety of external enemies.[24]

A sense of tenuousness marked all these hopeful experiments in black freedom, for they were on borrowed land and time. By 1865 some of them had been eliminated by the exigencies of the war and the lack of sympathy of the Union military commanders. Thus the focus of the black community and much of the nation at large was on the area covered by Field Order 15. This was the most extensive arena of experimentation, representing the pinnacle of both hope and of danger. Throughout that area blacks were moving, especially on the offshore islands. Often the vanguard was their soldiers, securing the land for Union control. The actions of the troops then provided an opportunity for those blacks already on the islands, and the new pilgrims who joined them (not without internal conflicts at times), to carry out the plans which they had been making all along. So settlements took place on islands like Wadmalaw, John's, Edisto, James. Eventually, some forty thousand men, women, and children established themselves on the lands covered by Sherman's order. In the winter of 1865 they were tilling, planting, building, organizing, governing themselves, all the while palpably experiencing the immediate protection of the sons and lovers, brothers and fathers they had sent into the Union armies. And everywhere there were men like Ulysses Houston, born in slavery to lead his people in establishing their freedom.[25]

So when Congress finally passed the Thirteenth Amendment to the Constitution on January 31, 1865, its members were well behind the movement of the Southern black community, pressing forward beyond slavery to a new life. Even so, it was only natural that black people celebrated the Congressional action, expressing great thankfulness to God and their white friends; for if the amendment were ratified, it would finally outlaw slavery in the United States. A people still feeling the pain of the lash and the injustice of bondage knew that this was a great development, the answer to many prayers, the result of much suffering, struggle, and hope.

Still, nothing in the forty-three words of the legal document reflected the lofty vision and commitment of black people at work in Slabtown, Contraband, or Savannah. No amendment could bear the ecstasy—or the political implications—of the Union chaplain who preached to sixteen hundred of his people in a church in Wilmington, North Carolina, that winter of their legal liberation. After they poured out their hearts in the hymn, "Sing unto the Lord a New Song," the members of the Front Street Methodist Church carried on this kind of exchange with the Reverend Hunter:

One week ago you were all slaves; now you are all free. [Uproarious screamings] Thank God the armies of the Lord and of Gideon has [sic] triumphed and the Rebels have been driven back in confusion and scattered like chaff before the wind. [Amen! Hallelujah!][26]

By their very nature, acts of Congress could contain neither the vital power of the encounter between that former slave and his rapturous new congregation, nor the political vision of a man like Tunis Campbell, one of the many leaders whose role in the postwar struggle is yet to be fully understood. Campbell had been born in New Jersey in 1812, and was one of those many thousands of black men who were refused when they first volunteered to serve in the Union army at the outset of the war. Nevertheless, like many others, Campbell persisted. Indeed, this ordained Methodist minister went directly to Washington (a popular path for black leaders after the Emancipation Proclamation), to offer his services to Lincoln and Stanton. As a result, the New Jerseyan was commissioned to go into South Carolina to help black people establish their new life.[27]

Eventually appointed an agent of the Freedmen's Bureau and assigned to work with the black communities on Saint Catherine's, Sapelo, and Ossabaw Islands off the coast of Georgia, Tunis Campbell soon revealed his special version of new black life. Closely assisted by his son, Tunis, Jr., and using Saint Catherine's as a base, the aggressive black leader set up a formal government for the islands, including a bicameral legislature and a court whose chief justice was said to be "a Negro from the African Congo." All this was based on a written constitution. How much of the idea Campbell and his family brought with them, and how much developed out of their participation in the heady new society arising in the coastal zones, is not yet clear, but according to some reports one of the first acts of Campbell's legislature "was to pass a law forbidding any white person to set foot on the islands." In addition, a defense force of more than two hundred men was soon established. Before long, it was obvious that such a vision was not quite what Stanton and Sherman had foreseen when Savannah's respectable black churchmen spoke of needing land, taking care of themselves, and assisting the government in maintaining their freedom. In time, white Northern newspapers learned of the Campbells' intriguing experiment in democracy, and at least one journal labeled it a "Nigger Empire."

Labels could not extinguish hope. For a while—for a brief and perilous period, as Sherman pressed his augmented armies up through the Carolinas from Ridgeland to Columbia, from Fayetteville to Durham Station, trailing fire and blood—it appeared that the black vision of land, self-government, and protection might prevail, in spite of the myopia of white journalists and presidents. So when some Confederate plantation owners began to drift back toward the coastal areas, exploring the new situation, it was not unusual to hear a former slave, speaking for others, say to the former owners, "We own this land now, put it out of your head that it will ever be yours again." And when some white men tried to go out in boats to survey their island plantations, they were stopped at the docks by armed black men and sent back to the mainland.[28]

For a time, for a brief and dangerously exciting time, as the remaining Southern armies in Virginia and North Carolina felt the terrors of defeat all around them, and as Robert E. Lee faced the harsh realities of his demoralized forces, decimated by desertion, casualties, and disease, it appeared possible that the revived black struggle for new life and new beginning might emerge triumphant from such anguished crucibles of death. In some places, at least, black people had possessed the land, had taken control of their own lives, were fulfilling hopes which had lain buried ever since those first days of captivity in the African forests. Indeed, sometimes it seemed as if they were a resurrected people. Consider the testimony of the white man who wrote from Ladies Island off South Carolina:

I never knew during forty years of plantation life so little sickness. Formerly every man had a fever of some kind, and now the veriest old cripple, who did nothing under secesh rule, will row a boat three nights in succession to Edisto, or will pick up corn about the corn house. There are twenty people whom I know were considered worn out and too old to work under the slave system, who are now working cotton, as well as their two acres of provisions; and their crops look very well.[29]

In those days, as winter succumbed to spring, all things seemed possible, even resurrection. Perhaps the black men in the room in Savannah and the editors of the *New Orleans Tribune* had been prophets. Perhaps the prayer meetings and town meetings and miniature legislatures now rising on the islands were harbingers of a new freedom, a new life coming into being right there, practically in the same harbors where the old African life had been wrenched into a new captivity. Was it spring or freedom or Jesus that people felt in the air? Or did all of these together fuel the hope that seemed now to drive black folk by the hundreds and then thousands out of the upcountry areas down to the coasts, drawn by the magnet of land, self-government, and protection? Did they see the old man rowing his boat, no longer a cripple, and dream of their own possibilities? Did they sing a new song, beyond the antiphonies of the slave ships and the ocean waves: "Michael row the boat ashore, Hallelujah"?

Whatever the songs, whatever the hopes, black people all across the South were moving, surging toward the promise of land, daring to believe that Field Order 15 was only the beginning of the new time. Then, early in March 1865, when Congress passed the Freedmen's Bureau Act, specifically ordering that the abandoned lands of the unpardoned white Confederate supporters be set aside—at least temporarily—to provide forty-acre allocations to free black families, there seemed every reason to give unbridled rein to hope and expectation. But there were other forces, other dreams, other people moving during those last days of the war, and other plans for the land which brooked no vision of black ownership. There were other plans for black people which meant to minimize their new freedom. And where there were no concrete plans, there were ancient, visceral white supremacist reactions, telling white American men and women that black people simply could not, must not govern themselves, must not become independent, must not be allowed to determine what they would plant, whom they would work for, what their own future would be, and thus what the future of the land, of the South, of the nation would be.[30]

These forces which pressed against the best black revolutionary hopes for freedom, land, and self-determination were not confined to the minds, hearts, and institutions of Southern whites. Often they were present in the Republican Party, in the board rooms of the Northern industrialists who supported that party, in the conference rooms of its Congressional leaders. And in spite of the Great Emancipator myth which had already begun to surround him in the eyes of Afro-Americans, there was no assurance of succor from the complex and brooding man in the White House, when it came to the hard, central issues of black political equality and the promise of land.

Nevertheless, spring seemed irresistible, and the movement toward black freedom, the flooding of black hope went on. In Savannah, on the Sea Islands, at New Bern, Vicksburg, and Contraband, everywhere the experiments in black self-government persisted. The words and deeds and songs of black leaders like Houston and Lynch and Campbell, and of nameless rowers of boats, continued to resound across the countryside. All these, of course, were only the heart of an intense, microcosmic experience which spanned the entire South and spilled over into the North. For wherever black people ventured forth from slavery, they were groping for the appropriate deeds which would give new life and sharper reality to the institution of their freedom.

Most often, the black actions which defined and demanded freedom were a combination of symbolic and political movement. For instance, early in the spring of 1865, when no one could doubt the outcome of the war any longer, Charleston's black community held a massive parade. Some four thousand took part, including artisans, schoolchildren, church and fraternal groups, firemen, and armed black soldiers. The procession stretched out for three miles, and one float in the parade told the essential story as it moved along, bearing a coffin with a large sign, "Slavery is Dead." Of course the parade said more. It was also another black announcement of the birth of freedom, stated not only in the signs, displays, and songs, but in the major action itself: the gathered, marching, self-affirming movement of the former slaves. This was a sure indication

that new times were coming. Black folk were moving literally and figura-
tively out of the side streets and the gutters, claiming the thoroughfares,
claiming the right to parade, to beat their drums, to celebrate the reality
of their freedom and resurrection, ultimately claiming the right to one
another. As 1865 passed from the time of war to the strange and hopeful
illusions of peace, such parades and processions—announcing, claiming,
and rejoicing in freedom—became an integral part of black life across
the South. Almost always, several essential elements were present: the
children who embodied the best hopes of the community; the religious
and political ecstasy of dancing, shouting, clapping men and women,
acting out their joy and expectation; the singing, marching black soldiers
who were their protection; and the drums.[31]

Of course at no time was the spontaneous, ecstatic quality of the war-
born freedom celebrations captured so fully as in those days surrounding
the historic moment which black people would always remember as "the
Surrender." At the end of March 1865, as the Northern armies came
surging down Virginia's roads toward Richmond and Petersburg, the
final, crumbling strongholds of Southern resistance, black Union troops
were prominent in the moving lines of men, and their people's excited
responses to these dark messengers of light often seemed intensified into
religious transport, into a reshaping of history. Then, at the beginning of
April, as the blacks and blues marched smartly into Richmond, capital of
the Confederacy, the joy of their ancestral community was unbounded.
While the white population generally hid itself behind locked doors, black
people streamed out into the roads, flooded the avenues. As the singing,
shouting soldiers paraded by on foot and sat tall on prancing horses, they
exchanged shouts and screams and songs of glory with black civilians
thronging the streets.[32]

For a time, as the black and conquering army sang its victorious
songs, some of the aged men and women who watched and sang with
them might have justifiably wondered if General Nat had finally come,
if Jerusalem had at last been taken, if their hearts were deceiving them
when they heard another song pounding in their bosoms:

> You might be Carroll from Carrollton
> Arrive here night afo' Lawd make creation
> But you can't keep the World from movering round
> And not turn her back from the gaining ground.[33]

For a time, under the transforming sun of early April, as the songs and
shouts leaped back and forth from marching soldiers to flowing crowd,
as memories sprang up like flowers in a field, the scene could have suggested a magnificent metamorphosis of history, recalling those days of

terrible heroism on the Atlantic, when the songs of the Africans on the ship decks were joined with those of their companions overboard whose heads and hearts for one last time defied the power of the churning waters. Nowhere did this restaging and reshaping of history seem more apt than in the center of the city, where the black troops and their tumultuous supporters gathered at Richmond's infamous slave market to proclaim "freedom to all mankind." At the request of the crowd, an army chaplain who had once escaped from Virginia's slavery lifted his voice to the heavens. Filled with passion and breaking with sorrow and joy, his words were suddenly interrupted by a sound which came from behind the heavily barred windows of nearby Lumpkins' Jail and began to fill the air like the distant roaring of an ocean. Finally it pressed aside all other reverberations of freedom and joy, and became the triumphant singing of the black men and women still occupying one of the nation's last slave prisons, who knew that the long journey was over, who shouted more than they sang:

> Slavery chain done broke at last!
> Broke at last! Broke at last!
> Slavery chain done broke at last!
> Gonna praise God till I die![34]

As it was in the time of slavery, so even now at the dawning of freedom, neither the massed voices in the prison nor the surging crowds on Richmond's liberated streets could tell the full story of the struggle. As ever, the deepest human responses could be known only in the solitary lives whose entire beings were now electrified with hope. How else could one understand the reactions of the black woman far away from the exulting city, out on a plantation near Yorktown, Virginia, who heard the great news and went off from the house to a sequestered place, looked around to see if anyone was watching her, and then;

I jump up an' scream, "Glory, glory, hallelujah to Jesus! I's free! I's free! Glory to God, you come down an' free us; no big man could do it." An' I got sort o' scared, afeared somebody hear me, an' I takes another good look, an' fall on de groun', an' roll over, an' kiss de groun' for de Lord's sake, I's so full o' praise to Masser Jesus. He do all dis great work. De soul buyers can nebber take my two chillen lef' me; no, nebber can take 'em from me no mo'.[35]

Still, it is possible that the deepest, richest level of all the cascading joy was revealed in the account of another black woman in Virginia who saw the flag of surrender being raised on April 9 and then was caught up on the whirlwind of her people's ecstasy, running with them everywhere, to everyone, to everything, shouting freedom:

Run to de kitchen an' shout in de winder:
   Mammy, don't you cook no mo'
   You's free! You's free!
Run to de henhouse an' shout:
   Rooster, don't you crow no mo'
   You's free! You's free!
  Ol' hen, don't you lay no mo' eggs,
   You's free! You's free!
Go to de pigpen an' tell de pig:
   Ol' pig, don't you grunt no mo'
   You's free! You's free!
Tell de cows:
   Ol' cow, don't you give no mo' milk,
   You's free! You's free![36]

By the time they were finished with their running and shouting, it may be that Fanny Berry and her celebrating community had caught up in their lives all the great genius of that moment, of that people, had somehow expressed its ineffable fullness for all their brothers and sisters across the land. Shouting and singing, feeling and knowing, running in the currents of the river's most African depths, Fanny Berry and her companions had identified this coming freedom as a condition which extended beyond the small realm of human life, sweeping up the entire created order of nature and of history in its transcendent, numinous power.

No mo!
You's free!
Praising Father God,
Kissing Mother Earth,
Running and loving with all their creatures,
You's free!
You's free!

14

The Challenge of the Children

Creating a New Vision of America

> Now rally, Black Republicans,
>   Wherever you may be,
> Brave soldiers on the battle-field,
>   And sailors on the sea.
> Now rally, Black Republicans—
>   Aye, rally! we are free!
>   We've waited long
>   To sing the song—
>   The song of liberty.
>
> Song from the *Black Republican*
> New Orleans, 1865

> . . . traitors shall not dictate or prescribe to us the terms or conditions of our citizenship, so help us God.
>
> Black Convention
> Norfolk, Va., 1865

Passing through Norfolk, Virginia, on his way south during that spring of 1865, a Northern newspaper man noted that every black dwelling in the city "exhibited the tender tokens of mourning for the good, dead President." Everywhere in the nation, the story was the same. In the midst of the ecstasy of this year of freedom, just days after word of "the Surrender" had sent paroxysms of thanksgiving and joy flooding through their lives, the black communities of America were stunned and sobered by the assassination of Abraham Lincoln. In the terrible darkness of mid-April some ways of Providence seemed hard to fathom; the chariot of vengeance had stopped at strange doors. So in their memorial meetings they spoke of "a national calamity . . . an irrepressible loss beyond the power of words to express." In the Capitol, soon after Lincoln's death was announced a black woman cried out, "My good President! I would rather have died myself! . . . Oh, Jesus! Oh, Jesus!" Down on one of the South Carolina Sea Islands, a man who had risked his life to escape from slavery now wondered if there was any purpose to it all, any hope, saying, "The rebs won't let us alone. If they can't kill us, they'll kill all our frien's sure."[1]

In spite of the difficulties they had had with him during the war, the children of Africa in America considered Lincoln a friend, an ally, a leader in their developing struggle to create the institution of freedom, to chart the new land. Now his death in a heroic, sacrificial mode made it possible for the emerging black community to avoid the harsh and certain clashes between their soaring visionary projections and the President's attempts to keep the future of black freedom in narrow bounds, to hold the rushing river within limits that he and other well-meaning whites could manage. So, after April 15, Abraham Lincoln could serve as a mythic symbol of Emancipation, a companion to John Brown, while black people tried to size up the flesh-and-blood realities and prospects of Andrew Johnson, Lincoln's Vice-President and successor. They had heard that Johnson, a Tennessee loyalist, hated the Southern aristocrats who had been the leaders of the Confederacy. At one point, while military governor of Tennessee, he had told its newly freed people that he was willing to be their Moses. Time alone would reveal what that meant. Meanwhile black people refused either to be mesmerized by their mourning for "the good, dead President," or to live on false hope concerning the self-proclaimed Moses. Rather, in that spring of grief and exaltation, where the paths of God were not always clear and their friends not easily identifiable, they continued to move forward, making their own way.[2]

In thousands of individual and collective actions black men and women persistently experimented with freedom, tentatively creating its forms and content. Working at the communal bedrock of their religion, blacks made it clear that freedom meant independence from white control of their churches, of their organized religious lives. So in Wilmington, North Carolina, those black church people who had responded to Chaplain Hunter in such spirited, ecstatic ways, quickly demonstrated their sense of the connection between rapture and political decision-making. Their nervous white Methodist pastor, L. S. Burkhead, had already sensed what was coming when he complained that the Reverend Hunter's liberation preaching had unsettled all the congregation's "former principles and ideas of subordination." Under the influence of the black preacher, said Burkhead, the people "seemed already in imagination to be walking the streets of the capital of the nation and listening to their own silver-toned voices dispensing the 'glad tidings' of the Greeley and Sumner gospel to the Congress of the United States." To lift the imaginative powers of recently enslaved people to the point of seeing themselves as leaders of the entire nation was, of course, a great feat. However, the congregation at Front Street Church soon moved beyond imagination to create their own new reality, demanding that the Southern Methodist leadership dismiss their complaining white pastor and let them ally themselves with the burgeoning forces of the African Methodist Episcopal Church. This was what freedom required.[3]

In Raleigh, North Carolina, another Methodist congregation left no doubts in the minds of their former masters about their reasons for wanting to move toward a new, free, black way. Indeed, they taught their own lesson in religion and politics as they challenged the white Christians. The Wesley Chapel members said they were determined to separate from the white Southern Methodist connection because that church believed in "perpetuating slavery," and had seceded from the Northern Methodists over the issue. Moreover, they accused their erstwhile religious leaders of having "taught rebellion" against the national government in order to maintain human bondage, *their* bondage. In the old time, they said, they had been compelled to put up with such corruption of the Gospel, such attacks on their integrity, but this was a new time. Now, as these black pilgrims forged their way toward freedom, struggling successfully with unfaithful white Christians, with their own tender consciences, and with the structures of the written word, they finally declared: "we Desiar to despence with the Services of men whos fidelity to the government by us is doubted in order therefore that we may be able to worship God according to the dictates of our consciences."[4]

In other situations the struggle to define freedom was much more individual, eccentric, unique. For instance, in many places black folk simply assumed new forms of dress, the women wearing brighter colors than ever before, donning white gloves, carrying parasols, writing their own speeches of freedom in each formerly forbidden item of apparel, in each proud movement of their bodies. For their part, the men kept dogs and guns, hunted whenever they chose, traveled around the countryside without passes. Both men and women often refused to yield the sidewalks to white folks when they met. They omitted the long-standing and deeply understood obeisances and signs of inferior status. They rode horses or mules or drove carriages, taking the right of way from white pedestrians. They argued with white people, refusing any longer to say yes when they meant no. They met in public with any blacks they chose and with as many as they chose, at any hour and for as long as they chose. They changed their names. They made new demands on white people, based on their own sense of dignity and their new freedom to express it. Thus one army officer wrote that black people had obviously resolved "that in their present condition as free men their former masters and present employers should address them in a more respectful manner than formerly."[5]

Nor could any whites predict where this kind of localized black independence would find its next expression. Not even the most trusted of the old servants could be counted on any longer. In Washington, Georgia, one young white woman complained to her diary that with the coming of freedom and the military occupation forces, several of the most dependable and apparently subservient black folk, among them house servants, had radically changed (or revealed) their character. Eliza Andrews cited one man who had been known to them all as kindly Uncle Lewis. Now, she reported, "Uncle Lewis, the pious, the honored, the venerated, gets his poor old head turned with false notions of freedom and independence, runs off to the Yankees with a pack of lies against his mistress, and sets up a claim to part of her land!"[6]

There were many resurrections, many former cripples now rowing toward freedom, many "uncles" seeing visions of justice in the lands of their "nieces." But the price could be high, for almost every black act of assertion was seen by whites—in a sense, accurately—as "insubordination" and "insolence." White people knew that such spirit and action were dangerous to the world they were seeking to maintain, and wherever possible they attempted to contain the force, to break its assertive movement. In Savannah a delegation of black people from the surrounding rural areas called on Chief Justice Salmon Chase, who was making a Southern tour that spring, and complained that "their old masters were abusing them, were whipping those who said they thought they were free." In Alabama, Chase's party heard of black people in the rural sections who had come into Montgomery "with their ears cut off by their former masters, in punishment for their assertion of their freedom." Such practices were common in many parts of the South, especially the rural districts, and often the news came from persons who spoke for friends and relatives who could not come, men and women who had lost their lives in those early movements toward hope.[7]

The costs were familiar, but neither whippings nor torture nor death had ever stopped the black movement toward freedom, and they did not stop it now. Indeed, there was a spirit at work in this special year which could not be broken. One native white political leader in Alabama caught some of its character when he described the black reaction to the official announcement of freedom: "They were disposed . . . to get into a drunken disposition—I use that expression in its literal sense—to assert

their rights, thinking that such assertion was necessary to their maintenance." Inspired by what might well be called an intoxication with freedom, the black people would "rush right into a church, without any
change having taken place, where the white people were sitting; not that
they had no place to sit [i.e., the Negro pew], but simply to show their
equality."[8]

Of course a change *had* taken place, and because it had begun within
them black people knew it, and knew that it was indeed necessary to
assert—to demonstrate—their rights, if they were determined to maintain
them. A quintessential example of this consciousness arose in the Laurens
area of South Carolina where, once emancipation was official, a black
woman named Patience Johnson was asked by her former mistress if she
would remain with her and work for wages. As mistresses went, she was
not bad, so there was reason for Patience to consider the request. But the
young woman's response was simple: "No, Miss, I must go; if I stay here
I'll never know I am free."[9]

And yet it was not simple. Compressed in that one woman's words was
the great power of the sweeping, explosive black movement of 1865,
announcing that, beyond the laws and proclamations of others, black
people themselves, through their own action of freedom, must not only
shape their emancipation but also develop some fundamental self-knowl-
edge, some palpable assurance of their freedom, upon which all else
would have to be built. So Patience left, as so many had left and would
leave, risking the dangers of freedom—dangers which were more than
psychological, as the white community organized itself to hold its black
work force, its black mudsill, its black mirror, in place.

Who knew all this and appreciated it more than Sojourner Truth? That
sturdy, seasoned walker into freedom, creator of liberty, was still on the
road in the year of change, asserting the transformation which had begun
in her own life decades before. During the latter part of the war she had
come to Arlington, Virginia, just outside Washington, D.C., to work
among the newly freed black community, inspiring them with her indomitable spirit, ministering to their material needs. In the late winter of 1865,
when Congress finally passed a bill prohibiting segregation on all the District's horsecar lines, Sojourner knew that rights must be tested, fought
for, seized, and defined through struggle. Out on the street, one spring
day, she tried to flag down one of the horsecars. One passed and refused
to stop. Another went by, with the driver ignoring her long, waving arms.
At that point, according to her biographer, Sojourner "gave three tremendous yelps," shouting, "I want to ride! I want to ride! *I want to
ride!!*" Her shouts and vivid gestures drew a crowd that made it impos-

sible for the next car to go by without stopping. Then, when Sojourner Truth got on and took her seat with the other passengers, the conductor told her that either she would ride outside on the front platform directly behind the horses, or he would throw her off. Probably the man did not know to whom he was talking, and the powerful Truth remained firmly in her seat. Indeed, to make her point, she stayed on beyond her stop. Finally, she left the car and said joyfully, "Bless God! I have had a ride." In addition, later she had the conductor arrested, caused him to lose his job, and did much to establish the right of blacks to ride all the horsecars in the nation's capital. It was, to be sure, quite a ride.[10]

All through that year when the contours of freedom were being searched out and created through words and deeds of assertion and hope, black women were deeply involved in the process. It was not always as direct an engagement as Sojourner's, but it was real. For instance, one of the most significant movements toward the definition of freedom came as black families all over the South made a momentous decision to withdraw their women from the full-time agricultural labor force. In many cases children moved out of the role of full-time field hands as well. Everywhere in slavery's former domain, black families were openly declaring the autonomy they had fought so hard to develop and maintain under the old regime; they were establishing their right to decide who should work and how. Now mothers and wives were often free to give more attention to their own families and work; children could attend the schools now being created at great cost by blacks and their white allies.[11]

Indeed, it was a group of the school children on Saint Helena's Island off the South Carolina coast who offered one of the most powerful testimonies to the meaning of black freedom. On a warm day in May, a prestigious group of white visitors from the North had stopped to visit this place which had produced so many men for the first black Union regiment and so much hope for the possibilities of black self-reliance on the land. Hundreds of newly freed residents gathered for the occasion in the open field between their old church and their new school. Then, after speeches and songs, a group of young children from the school was called up to the outdoor platform. "Mothers passed up their little four-year olds, decked in all the cheap finery they could command; fathers pressed forward and made room for sons and daughters, whom they followed with eyes of paternal pride; and there was a general smiling, and bustling, and eagerness to show off the shiny-faced, large-eyed little creatures." Then the black children sang:

"My country, 'tis of thee,/Sweet land of liberty,/Of thee I sing./Land where my fathers died,/Land of the pilgrim's pride,/From every mountainside,/ Let freedom ring."[12]

Whatever the quality of the singing or the consciousness of the young chorus, the symbolism of that afternoon in May was overwhelming. Members of the last generation of Africa's children to be born into American bondage were adding their own small voices, their eager, trusting spirits as counterpoints to the grinding sounds of the chariot of divine vengeance. Pressed forward by their parents, their lives were being offered as a promise, as another deeply moving element of the great black hope that America would soon become their land, "the land of the free."

Who heard the children of Saint Helena as they staked their claims to these United States? Who heard the voices of H. Ford Douglas and Martin Delany, of Harriet Tubman and David Walker beneath the singing of the children? In May 1865 it was easy to miss the young singers, to try to avoid the hard and painful implications of their song and its vital connections to the past and future black struggle for America. The war had finally ended. The ratification process for the Thirteenth Amendment was working its way through the states. Even long-standing abolitionist allies like William Lloyd Garrison were so eager to move on with the things that made for peace among white people that he proposed disbanding the American Anti-Slavery Society. Garrison and many like him were still trapped in one of the most fundamental abolitionist flaws: convinced that all the evils of racial discrimination, subordination, and oppression flowed out of the institution of slavery, he was certain that once the legal institution was destroyed, the other evils would very quickly disappear. Filled with this strangely optimistic (or deluded) view of human development, Garrison, as he watched the approaching ratification of the Thirteenth Amendment, expressed his absolute certainty that black men and women would now, without any special help, "win their way to wealth, distinction, eminence and official station."[13]

Indeed, Garrison seemed so sanguine about the result of legal abolition, and so unclear about the rights due to black people as citizens, that he expressed severe doubts about whether or not the newly freed community should have the vote. Perhaps he was tired, and having decided that his days of active struggle for black freedom were over, he needed some way to rationalize his withdrawal, some way to forget that at the founding convention in 1833 it was he who had demanded that abolitionists of the new American Anti-Slavery Society "secure to the colored population . . . all the rights and privileges that belong to them as men and as Americans." At any rate it was also he, the Society's founder and president, who in the spring of 1865 proposed that, since its work was now ended, the organization should be dissolved.[14]

Of course most black people who watched these developments were in full accord with Frederick Douglass as the black leader staunchly opposed the self-destruction of the best-known abolitionist organization. For a time such wisdom prevailed. Nevertheless, it was hard for most white persons to hear the voices of the children. They represented the claims of a black community moving toward freedom, a community whose right to make such assertions, to engage in such movement was hardly recognized by the larger society. For just as they had done in the war, so now in the chaos of transition these freedom-possessed people were forcing themselves and the issue of their role in America's future onto the center of the national stage. Although many white political leaders were willing to transmute the issues at stake into such simple matters as the creation and domination of new black voters, in order to assure continuing Republican control over the South and the party's preeminence in the nation, there was obviously far more involved, and black people knew it.

Since the crisis of secession, a series of crucial transformations had taken place in the life of the young nation, and the fundamental questions at hand for the entire society turned out to be national versions of the questions black people were raising concerning the institution of freedom and the nature of the new land. As such they carried profound political, economic, social, and constitutional implications for the government and for all the people of the United States, whether they recognized it or not. At stake were such constitutional questions as: what would be the new relationships between the central government and the seceded states, and through what processes would these relationships be developed? Since for all practical purposes black people were now free, how would representation be allocated in each of the former slaveholding states? Who would be their citizens, their voters, their elected officials? What would be the role and rights of black people in the future of these former slave states? How would their protection be guaranteed? A central corollary concern was the matter of who would make such judgments—the President, Congress, the military commanders in the defeated states, the provisional governments, or some other body? How would blacks be related to any decision-making bodies? Would Congress's being in recess for most of this critical transitional year make a difference? Would Andrew Johnson call it back into session to deal with the momentous issues at hand? Or would he, like Lincoln, attempt to hold most of these decisions under the aegis of an executive office whose power had greatly expanded during the war?[15]

Just as the constitutional issues constantly intersected questions of human justice and destiny, so too did the economic problems. The economic life and resources of entire sections of the South had been disrupted, destroyed, or badly damaged. Atlanta, Columbia, Fredericksburg, and scores of other cities were filled with the rubble and shells of burned-out, battered buildings. Thousands of miles of railroad were in disrepair. Hundreds of thousands of acres lay uncultivated or with their crops destroyed, and millions of acres had been deserted by supporters of the Confederacy as they fled the Union armies. What was the future of that land? Who would work it, own it, and under what conditions? The slaves who had worked the fields in bondage were now free, often claiming the land as their just due. Many had left the places where they had labored for decades, and others were eager to follow the path of Patience Johnson. Meanwhile, hundreds of thousands of Confederate veterans were returning, looking for work that did not exist, unable to envision themselves in jobs once held by slaves, carrying currency which usually could buy nothing but pity. In the light of these developments, few could imagine how the basic agricultural life of the region would be reorganized without slavery.

At the same time, in the course of the war the factories and mills of the North had greatly expanded, moving that section toward a rate of industrialization which would not slow down for a century. Equally important, the Northern-based banking institutions and railroad corporations which provided the economic undergirding for this rapid growth were also gaining more power, and were setting their eyes on the resources of the South. How would all these forces relate to the insistent black demands for land, for autonomy, for independence and full citizenship?

Obviously these were no abstract issues. They affected millions of black and white men, women, and children. Thus the question of the legal status of the white Southerners who had been active leaders of the Confederacy was not simply an argument over whether or not they had committed treason. By and large, such persons constituted the leadership class of the South. Would they resume leadership? If not, who would? What were the constitutional rights of this old leadership group? Did they retain any rights to the land that they had owned and abandoned during the war—land which, under some circumstances, could have justifiably been confiscated for the use of the landless black people?

By way of the harrowing chariots of war, a situation of tremendous revolutionary potential had been created. At its heart lay the fragile, explosive relationships between a people actively freeing themselves and those who only yesterday had held them in bondage or had acquiesced in and profited from their exploitation. A new community was creating itself and being created: African-Americans, Afro-Americans, were now at hand. What would be the shape of their life with their former masters, the white Southerners, and with all the white supremacist Euro-Americans? This common thread ran through many of the other issues, providing an integument of flesh and blood to the national economic, constitutional, and political questions. Was there really to be a new society in America, based on a new set of national and local political, economic, and social relationships? Would white men and women hear the children singing, the conventions petitioning, see the old folks rowing, the Brothers and Sisters of Love and Charity marching, and enter into that spirit? Or was there to be instead a "restoration," as Andrew Johnson had begun to call it, a brutal replacing of as much of the old order as possible, proving that revolutions indeed can go backward? Or would some flattened compromise between the two visions emerge? And if it did, what would another white-imposed national compromise cost black folk? Here was the ground on which all the other questions converged to meet the black surge toward freedom.

Of course neither the questions nor the conditions were new in the spring of 1865. Whether in embryo or in full form, they had been present ever since that moment four years earlier when the first Confederate guns launched their shells into the early morning darkness of Charleston harbor, and the first wartime black fugitives surged toward freedom. Throughout the war the questions had been nagging and the conditions expanding, and whenever the exigencies of the armed conflict would allow it, Lincoln and his cabinet as well as the Republican-dominated Congress had been searching for their own sometimes discordant approaches. And while the Confederate government had been stubbornly fighting to maintain its costly views, black people had been building their own persistent, often subterranean positions. Now, even though neither the questions nor the conditions were new, the spring of 1865 represented a new moment, a new opportunity. The end of the war, the defeat of the Confederacy, and the active, articulate, ubiquitous presence of four million newly freed black people sharpened all the issues and added a profound sense of urgency to the search for solutions.

Well into the spring of the year, it was still not clear where Andrew Johnson stood as he addressed the critical questions of the nation's future, especially the issues which defined black freedom. Within his own party there were increasingly conflicting views over the future of these new "Americans of African descent," as they were sometimes derisively labeled. But black people were generally satisfied with the label and had determined not to wait for white Republicans to make up their minds about its meaning. For just as they were laying immediate claim to the country, so too they boldly assumed their right to participate in the life of the Republican Party itself. Even without the paradoxical black theodicies that had arisen out of the flames of war and identified this party as the Almighty's tool of redemption, even without the dramatic force of

Lincoln's martyrdom, there was a certain cool and simple logic in the need for a black approach to the Republicans. This was the ruling party of the nation, the leaders of the government which controlled the occupying forces in the South. This was the party whose decisions would go far to determine which aspects of the evolving black freedom platform would be nationally legitimized and which would not, which black initiatives would be affirmed and which would be fought, smashed, or betrayed. It was the Republicans who would play a central role in determining the basis on which unity would come to the ruptured body of the United States, moving the society either toward the new human solidarity envisioned by the best black hopes, or toward the restoration of the forces of exploitation, reaction, and fear.

Of course no Afro-American, no matter how uninformed politically, could miss the fact that this was a party of white men which therefore—now that the sanctified war had come to an end—could never be trusted to nurture the same dreams, hopes, and convictions concerning freedom that were the substance of black life. But a people who knew paradox and contradiction intimately could not allow such problems to destroy their determination. A people desperate for freedom had to come to terms with the limitations of their options as they negotiated the cruel shoals of the newest stage of their struggle. Some of these contradictions might favor the cause, others might shatter it; the chances would have to be taken.[16]

Still, there was something more than chance at work. As the former slaves explored the possibilities of their Republican allies, new realities began to appear. For instance, it was immediately apparent (as any careful reader of a journal like the *New Orleans Tribune* could have predicted) that these black men and women were not approaching the Republican Party as abject, imploring dependents, seeking help from their powerful potential helpers, or simply hoping to take advantage of white disagreements. Rather, some came to the new moment with their own definitions of what it might mean to join certain elements of the Republican forces. Indeed, the hopeful, audacious mood in which many first entered this political arena, the assumptions they brought, cannot be overemphasized; for black people were preparing themselves to join, to participate, and not simply to serve as wards, passive recipients, or voting pawns in the new relationship.

Early in the struggle to define their role in the Republican Party, some of the black leadership seemed no less intent on transforming Lincoln's party than the nation. Nor did one have to look only at the pages of the *New Orleans Tribune* to see this. In that same city, near the end of the war, Dr. S. W. Rogers, a former slave who had become a highly respected and educated clergyman, now began to publish a newspaper called the

Black Republican. Here the familiar term took on new meaning, not as an accusation or epithet bandied among white men, but as a statement of black determination and pride. In the first issue of the paper, published in April 1865, Rogers wrote:

Black Republican is a proper name for the newspaper organ of American colored men.

We mean to maintain our race—not deny it. The name of our paper asserts at once our race and our principles.

White men may be monarchists, aristocrats or oligarchs, but American colored men should be nothing but Republicans. In the prevalence of Republican ideas and the establishment of Republican institutions, are the hope and the safety of our people.

As we have fought for these ideas on the field, and have suffered for them through revolution, so shall we proclaim and defend them on the forum and through the press in the face of all foes whatever.[17]

Refusing to quibble over small or capital Rs, black men and women were not simply seeking help from the Republican Party. Moving onto the political stage with a spirit far more radical than the mainstream of the Northern business-based party, the newcomers were, as usual, challenging white men and women to live by their announced principles. They were determined to force the Republican Party to deal with the vibrant presence of a new democratic-republican constituency within its gates. Meanwhile they continued to urge their people to move from a position of strength, saying, "Let us be the allies of the Republicans, not their tools; let us retain our individuality, our banner, and our name."[18]

Nor was the *Black Republican* content that the struggle to maintain the spirit, opinions, and identity of black Republicans should be confined to "the forum and . . . the press," or to the kinds of persons usually associated with those settings. With his eye on the larger, less literate black community, with his sense of the potential they held for bringing this new spirit into the Republican Party, Rogers soon printed "The Song of the Black Republicans." In its own fascinating way, it carried certain echoes from the river, especially reminiscent of the freedom song attributed to Sea Island black men and women during the War of 1812. Now in the spring of 1865 it was proposed that the people sing a new song, and it was surely not accidental which element of "the people" should be called upon first:

> Now rally, Black Republicans,
>   Wherever you may be,
> Brave soldiers on the battle-field,
>   And sailors on the sea.

Now rally, Black Republicans—
   Aye, rally! we are free!
      We've waited long
      To sing the song—
   The song of liberty.

Free workmen in the cotton-field,
   And in the sugar cane;
Free children in the common school,
   With nevermore a chain.
Then rally, Black Republicans—
   Aye, rally! we are free!
      We've waited long
      To sing the song—
   The song of liberty.[19]

A people whose songs of liberty had been disguised and muted in a minor key so long was a people to be reckoned with when the new time for singing began. For the waiting had not been passive; a flooding force had built up, and new black Republicans surging out of slavery and challenging the semifreedom of the nation's white supremacy might well turn out to be more than dark copies of white Republicans.

Some white persons recognized this reality. In May 1865, as he traveled through the South, Chief Justice Chase witnessed something of the rising tide. He reported that "everywhere throughout the country colored citizens are organizing Union Leagues." While there is still some debate about the precise line of descent and role of the Union Leagues in the early postwar South, there can be no question about the significance of these politico-religious clubs. Appearing at least as soon as Congress passed the Thirteenth Amendment in January 1865, and taking their name and perhaps more from the war-created Northern Republican organization, the Leagues became one of the most important mechanisms for creating and organizing black Republicans in the tumultuous three-and-a-half-year period from the end of the war to Grant's election in 1868. Nor is there any question that black people took this white institution, as they had taken so much else, and shaped it to their own needs.[20]

Though that transformation became most apparent after 1865, it could not be ignored that spring. The League was already so active and organized in Wilmington, North Carolina, that when Chase visited the city the leaders of the group arranged for an interview with him. One of the Justice's companions noted: "They have a Union League formed among themselves, the object of which is to stimulate industry and education, and to secure combined effort for suffrage, without which they insist that they will soon be practically enslaved again." A few months after the Chief Justice's visit they indicated their clear intention to continue forward, petitioning the city government to appoint black policemen and inspectors of fuel. Wherever the League was encountered, observers like Chase and his party noted that there were primarily black organizers at work. Some money and direction had begun to come from white Republicans with motives of their own, but a people ready to transform their songs into the living of their lives did not need much prodding; they were ready. Thus Chase advised Andrew Johnson that the black-dominated Leagues rising in the South constituted "a power which no wise statesman will despise."[21]

Well beyond the confines of the Union Leagues, often at levels not accessible to Chief Justices or Presidents, serious black organizing had been going on all year. The former slaves had determined that this activity was essential to the creation of their freedom. So, ever since those initial conventions in Nashville and New Orleans in January, they had been coming together all winter and spring, gathering in churches, homes, and fields, sometimes in newly accessible public buildings. They met and argued and prayed over the wording of petitions and addresses. Calling themselves by many names—"Colored Peoples Convention," "Convention of Loyal Citizens," "Convention of Colored Men"—they organized hundreds of preparatory meetings and scores of conventions. Everywhere one turned—especially in the towns and cities of the South, but not there alone—thousands of black people were convening. In Norfolk, New Orleans, and Knoxville, in Petersburg and Vicksburg, in Wilmington and Chapel Hill, in Baltimore and Little Rock, black men and women insisted that the nation and its leaders face the determination of the former slaves to help define and create the free, new time.[22]

Such vision, determination, and passion were costly, especially when they welled up in men and women who only yesterday were supposed to have been servants of all white people. So the delegates often had to leave their homes in the middle of the night and walk for miles to a rendezvous, eluding white patrols while perhaps nursing memories of other night journeys toward freedom. Sometimes the meetings were held under threat of armed attack or arson from a white community deeply troubled by such thoughts and actions from their former slaves. Many times black patrols had to be set out on the road and guards had to be placed around the buildings where they met. In places like Chapel Hill, North Carolina, and elsewhere, attacks against the black conventions were actually carried out. Still, the meetings went on, the speeches were made, the committees were organized, the petitions were written and proclaimed.[23]

Although the records are scanty, there is also evidence of a good deal of formal and informal Republican organizing at the major statewide black conventions. Almost invariably, one of the important features of each gathering was a speech, or a series of them, from a visiting black political exhorter. Apparently a network of contacts already existed which made it possible to bring these itinerant organizers to conventions and mass meetings in many places. Sometimes it was James Lynch, the brilliant young Methodist churchman, who combined his ecclesiastical and political organizing with consummate skill, and who became one of the great orators of his time. On other occasions it was James Rapier, the articulate leader who, born free in Alabama and educated in Canada, had returned to exhort and organize his people toward defining their freedom and shaping the Republican Party in the South. Elsewhere the excited crowds would hear John Mercer Langston, hero of the antebellum struggles in the North and now a Freedmen's Bureau official. No less ubiquitous was Frances Ellen Watkins Harper, the essayist and poet who had given so much of her life to the antislavery circuit. Here at the beginning of the new time, dealing with the men and women she had worked so hard to help free, Harper was just as selfless in her commitment and as effective in her organizing. Only Langston, in his role as a Freedmen's Bureau educational supervisor, was an official representative of the Republican-dominated federal government; still, the functions of most men and women like these were essentially the same: to encourage their people to define and demand freedom, and to help them organize for such action, including participation in creating the new Republican Party of the South.[24]

At the springtime and summer conventions, many of the basic themes and demands rising from the people remained the same. Black delegates constantly pressed the relationship between the military service of their men and the demand for the vote. The connection was obvious in a petition circulated that spring throughout the black community of North Carolina, and then broadcast in newspapers across the nation. Originating in the dynamic and self-sufficient leadership of New Bern, North Carolina, the petition was on its way to Andrew Johnson, saying:

Some of us are soldiers and have had the privilege of fighting for our country in this war. . . . We want the privilege of voting. It seems to us that men who are willing on the field of danger to carry the musket of Republics in the days of Peace ought to be permitted to carry its ballots; and certainly we cannot understand the justice of denying the elective franchise to men who have been fighting for the country, while it is freely given to men who have just returned from four years of fighting against it.[25]

Everywhere that idea was insistently raised: blacks had won their citizenship rights through the sacrifices of their husbands, brothers, sons, and fathers on the battlefields in the armies of the Union. Simple justice required the right, the reward, of nothing less than full suffrage. Indeed, that spring the *Black Republican* of New Orleans based a critical prediction on the justly earned black right: "If the loyal black men, if the scarred veterans who have freely shed their blood to save the nation from destruction, are denied equality before the law we shall have no permanent peace, for the reason that it will not be a peace founded on the eternal principles of right and justice."[26] In New Orleans and across the land, black men and women continued their stewardship of the wounded nation's conscience, demanded that the issue of social justice be taken seriously, insisted that principles were important in the human community, that some things were right and some not. To reward white "traitors" with full citizenship privileges, allowing them to control the land and the new governments, while denying essential rights to black "patriots," did not seem right at all. As they continued to press such issues in their speeches, sermons, and petitions, it became increasingly evident that black people were again being forced not only to define the nature of their own freedom, but also to play a crucial role in the creation of a new political and moral philosophy for the entire nation, a nation patently unprepared for freedom, equality, or justice.

Late that spring in Vicksburg, Mississippi, black men again put forward profound ideological and ethical challenges to the nature of the state and national governments. In a mass meeting chaired by Jacob Richardson, a member of the 49th U.S. Colored Infantry Regiment, the newly freed community boldly petitioned Congress not to seat Mississippi's delegates while black people were disfranchised there. They demanded that "the State of Mississippi be not restored to federal relations unless by her constitution she shall enfranchise her loyal colored citizens." In Tennessee the same voice was raised. There, following the all-white constitutional convention, the state's black communities petitioned the first session of the postwar legislature for full citizenship rights and were again rebuffed. So they too turned to Congress and said, "We protest against the Congressional delegation from Tennessee being received into the Congress of the United States, if the Legislature of Tennessee does not grant [our] petition . . . prior to December 1, 1865." From Norfolk, Virginia, the word of challenge and confrontation was put forward in even sharper, bolder terms, as a black convention looked at the returning Confederates and resolved "that traitors shall not dictate or prescribe to us the terms or conditions of our citizenship, so help us God."[27]

Throughout the South, in almost every state of the former Confederacy, the same potentially revolutionary situation was developing. The men and women who had been legally enslaved just months earlier were now meeting in public not only to discuss the political affairs of the state and the nation which they immediately claimed as their own, but to challenge the political legitimacy of their former owners, overseers, and oppressors. They were demanding that national political recognition of their erstwhile masters be denied until full enfranchisement was granted them. They were nominating, debating, and voting, reclaiming all the democratic mechanisms for truly democratic purposes. They were sending delegations to the state and national capitols to plead their cause. In some places they were transmitting revolutionary messages in words as well as deeds, evoking images which seemed to combine elements of David Walker, the spirit of San Domingo and the Bastille, and the Old Testament prophets. At least that seemed to be the meaning of the message which came out of David Walker's native town of Wilmington, North Carolina, that summer. As his spiritual descendents urged their people to organize for a black convention, they called out:

Freedmen of North Carolina, Arouse!!! Men and Brethern, these are the times foretold by the Prophets, "when a Nation shall be born in a day," the good time coming. Four millions of chattels, branded mercantile commodity, shake off the bands, drop the chains, and rise up in the dignity of men. The time has arrived when we can strike one blow to secure those rights of Freemen that have been so long withheld from us.[28]

Of course the challenging black voices were not all raised at the same pitch of defiance. Indeed, when the North Carolina convention did meet in Raleigh in the fall, it was controlled by men with more moderate public voices, men whom a Northern white observer considered "wise and judicious." The tone of the gathering was set by the banner hung across the front of the crowded sanctuary in the African Methodist Episcopal church where they met: "With malice toward none, with charity for all, with firmness in the right." The resolutions were all respectful in tone, mindful of the white men who were even then gathering for the meeting of the new state legislature. Still, when all the humble pleas for rights were over, the black delegates voted to form a North Carolina branch of the Equal Rights League, knowing that no matter how polite and moderate their requests, there would be no effective rights for them without the continuation of their own hard, dangerous organizing work.[29]

In Georgia the issues were also put forward in a quiet voice, but one threatening to the essential assumptions of American society. Here the black word was again directed to Andrew Johnson, who was considering a petition from Georgia's white population for the appointment of a provisional military governor for the state. Aware of events around them, quietly insisting on their new role, the black petitioners said:

Should your excellency grant the Petition now in circulation among the White People . . . we humbly and most earnestly pray that our interests, as well as theirs, may be regarded in your selection of the proper person for the important office. We ask not for a Black Man's Governor, nor a White Man's Governor, but for a People's Governor, who shall impartially protect the rights of all, and faithfully sustain the Union.[30]

So simple and yet so grand a vision was beyond the comprehension of most of white America, yet the struggle to define their new freedom required that black men and women dream such radical, quietly eloquent dreams, complementing the fiery visions which were rising out of Wilmington. For here, as in decades past and in the time to come, prophecy was intrinsic to the river. Blacks across the South were declaring an ultimately undeniable truth to the entire nation: if black people's freedom were to be real, America and its ideas and structures of racial supremacy would have to be fundamentally transformed; the old white America would have to die with slavery, and the children of Africa would need to become co-creators of the new United States.

In Virginia, Norfolk was a major center of such visionary activity and leadership. There, ever since winter the black community had begun to develop a new set of organizations and to hold mass meetings, at times involving two thousand or more persons. In April, at one of their fervent, overflowing sessions, the Norfolk blacks had organized the Colored Monitor Union Club, whose main function was to keep the issue of equal rights for blacks before Congress, to publicize their views concerning the rights of free people across the state, and "to assist the present [national] administration in putting down the enemies of the government, and to protect, strengthen and defend all friends of the Union." The club quickly became a leading force in the organizing of Virginia's black people as they proclaimed and acted out their freedom.[31]

Within the Union Club the central, driving leadership appeared to come from Dr. Thomas Bayne, who had started life in the state as a slave, seized his own freedom by fleeing North well before the Civil War, and then returned to his native ground during the conflict to continue the deeper struggle. Now, he was a dentist and also, like so many other leaders of the time, an itinerant preacher. With the tools of his profession, the conviction of his ministry, and the sharply honed will to be free, he moved through the communities of eastern Virginia like an envoy of the new times, insisting that the good news he carried must include the gospel of freedom.[32]

In the course of that spring of hope and danger, Bayne chaired a meeting in Norfolk which produced a series of militant resolutions, including demands from the black community for the right to be heard, as well as proclamations of their responsibility "to speak and act as freemen . . . to claim and insist on equality before the law, and equal rights of suffrage at the ballot-box." Referring to the last-ditch attempts of the Virginia legislature to enact Black Codes which sharply proscribed their freedom, the Norfolk black community vowed civil disobedience. In a spirit reminiscent of the late 1850s in the North, Norfolk's black people said that obedience to such laws was absolutely wrong. In their view it would be "inconsistent with our own self-respect, or . . . the respect of others" to submit voluntarily to "invidious political or legal distinctions, on account of color merely." As the city's Afro-American community developed its positions, it offered insight into the varied emphases coming from different black centers in the South. Thus land and self-government were central to the agricultural areas of Georgia, South Carolina, and Mississippi, whereas in this port city a major emphasis was placed on the vote, on the right to participate in the political process, with somewhat less attention to land.

Here, recognizing the significance of their numbers as a powerful minority of more than forty percent in the state, the black Virginians said they would prove themselves worthy of the franchise by "insisting on it as a right." They vowed that "traitors shall not dictate or prescribe to us the terms or conditions of our citizenship, so help us God." Believing that God helped those who were self-reliant, the Norfolk group went further, declaring that they were ready to back up their demand for equal rights by organizing a boycott, resolving "that as far as in us lies, we will not patronize or hold business relations with those who deny to us our equal rights."[33]

Whether or not the boycott attempt was successful is not presently clear, but the Norfolk group did not stop at that. They were afforded another opportunity for action that spring when the presidentially appointed provisional governor called for the election of a new state assembly. The call to vote was unmistakably issued to white male Virginians only, but blacks had vowed to insist on their rights, to refuse to obey "traitors" in high places. So they issued their own call and offered a direct challenge to the all-white balloting. On May 25, the election day, approximately one thousand black men and women gathered at the Bute Street African Methodist Church in the city. Most had once been enslaved, others had been fugitives, some had been born free. Now on this momentous morning they gathered as free men and women, proclaiming their status through their deeds.

At first they planned to move from the church as one body and march to the various polling places in the four wards of the city, so as to establish their right to share the franchise; but some argued persuasively that their numbers and their determination might well provide a convenient excuse for white violence. So instead, the group decided to send a reconnoitering committee to each ward, where they would attempt to vote and thereby test the policies of the white officials. It was a dangerous situation in which to assay the range and meaning of black freedom, but the committees went out on their mission, and the masses who remained behind filled Bute Street Church with songs and prayers, continuing a long tradition that combined religion and revolutionary action. When the scouting/voting parties returned, they reported that black people were being turned back in three of the wards, but in the fourth they were allowed to place their names on a special contested-vote list. Immediately men who lived in that ward began to move out in groups of ten, leaving the church to enter the fight, to be without external sanctuary.

Meanwhile the rest of the males in the freedom congregation cast their votes right in the church, legitimizing themselves, refusing to submit to the mandates of disloyal white men. Here was the birth of the freedom ballot among blacks, which in Norfolk went beyond the symbolic in its revolutionary significance. For not only did it give men (and women?) an opportunity to act out their commitment to freedom, to define their own liberation, but eventually the highly organized community used the contested ballots to challenge the legality of the white election. Their example led to similar action elsewhere in the state, and the entire determined movement not only forced Andrew Johnson to meet with a black delegation, but eventually brought about the repeal of the Virginia codes which denied political rights to the black community.[34]

By word, by deed, by the singing of children, the people who had been the slaves of American society were now engaged not only in creating the definitions of their own freedom but in suggesting the outlines of the new nation which would be necessary to contain them. As the tumultuous spring of 1865 ended, the initial word was there for all who had eyes and ears—and hearts. Black people were saying that freedom meant above all the right to participate in the process of creating it. In a democratic society, freedom meant not only the right to vote, but the right to participate in all the political decision-making processes. From their petitions pouring into state and national legislatures, indeed, it was obvious that the black community was even proposing that yesterday's slaves must have the right to help define the means by which the former slaveholding states would be brought back into the Union. Thereby, they were claiming the right to participate in the re-creation of the United States.

In an agrarian society, they said, freedom meant the right to land—the land they had nurtured. Freedom meant the right to work, both off and on the land. In a country now shedding the coils of racially defined slavery, freedom meant independence from white domination of every kind; it meant the right to protection—self-protection and governmental protection—from the worst white intentions and actions. Moreover, in all the conventions and messages, in all the newly organized educational associations, it was clear that black people considered the right to education crucial to their future as a free people. As a matter of fact, a people who knew the nurturing power of a loving community naturally defined freedom as the right and opportunity to develop themselves and all the institutions of their common experience, whether families, churches, or schools, or "The Ladies of Naomi Court of the Heroines of Jericho" and "The Brothers and Sisters of Love and Charity." This was the message. The confluence of the river of struggle and the terrible chariots of war had broken open the way, and the children of bondage were crossing over, bearing visions of a new land, challenging white America to a new life.

> *My country. My country.*
> *Tis of thee I sing.*
> *Country still unborn.*
> *Sweet land yet to be.*

15

Black Hope, Black Soldiers, and Black Codes

The Clashing Versions of Justice

My children, my little children, are singing to the sunshine.

W. E. B. Du Bois[1]

When the first summer of freedom began, the children were still singing, children of promise, children of hope, singing to the sunshine: My country, my country, sweet land of liberty. Saint Helena children, Memphis children, Vicksburg children, Slabtown children, Boston children, Wilmington children, Southhampton County children, Harpers Ferry children, Dismal Swamp children, Plaquemine children, Christiana children, everywhere children, all God's children, singing to the sunshine. My country.

In the first summer of freedom, the children sang, standing on bloody ground, land where their fathers died, challenging history, transcending history, flowing with the river to overcome history, calling on the sunshine to remake history. Slavery's children, freedom's children, Nat Turner's children, Harriet Tubman's children, Frederick Douglass's children, children first seen in visions while mothers hung from the mast of a ship named *Jesus*, children of parents last heard singing above the ocean's roar, children born in swamps and caves, children of promise, children of hope, Sojourner's lost/found children, claiming a country by the power of their hope, by the strength of their innocence, by the warmth of their embrace, by the history of the river, drawing America to their breasts, singing to the healing sun, singing warmth and wholeness to a cold and broken land. "My children, my little children, are singing to the sunshine."

In that year of parades and conventions, in those days of celebration and anxiety, through all the anguish and joy of the crossing over, there were many times when black and white America's history was transcended and transformed, if only for a blazing moment in the sun. It may be that none of those brief periods of epiphany were more dramatic and widespread than the scores of occasions, especially in the South, when black people, led by their marching, singing soldiers, lay special claim to the Fourth of July. By the time of the Civil War, the white nation had already forgotten much of the revolutionary significance of this central but ambiguous national symbol. The mocking existence of slavery, the bitter debates caused by it, the harsh reality of other sectional conflicts, and the emergence of various antilibertarian forces had all sucked the essence out of the symbol. Thus it was not easy for white people to hold the Fourth as a celebration of revolution and a memory of a struggle for freedom and independence. Up to that time, of course, the black people of the South had never had any reason to make such connections. Then came the war and the Emancipation Proclamation, accompanied by their own flooding toward freedom, as well as the promise of the Thirteenth Amendment, all of which marked the vital change. So in 1865, even while the nature and extent of their freedom were being argued and fought through a bloody transitional year, black communities across the South seized on this symbol of American freedom and made it their own, challenging history itself. Invariably, white citizens retreated even farther from the public celebrations, leaving the streets and the squares to the new "Americans of African descent."[2]

Like their brothers and sisters elsewhere, the African-American community of Augusta, Georgia, called on the black troops stationed there to lead a procession of some four thousand marchers through the streets of the city on the Fourth. Among the participants was a contingent of black women who carried banners high in the summer's breeze, proclaiming "Freedom and equality is our motto" to a crowd of more than ten thousand who watched and listened to the speeches that filled out the meaning of the slogan, including a stirring oration by the ubiquitous James Lynch. But nowhere was the multiple meaning of the act of possession more clearly demonstrated than in the "loyal" state of Kentucky. Because this slave state had not joined the Confederacy, because the provisions of the Emancipation Proclamation therefore did not apply to it, as the war ended there was great confusion about the official status of its enslaved population. Among black people, however, there was far less confusion than among others. With their marvelous feeling for the internal logic of the situation and for the deepest meanings of American history, they began to look forward to July Fourth as the date on which their freedom would publicly be announced and acknowledged by the

military and civilian authorities. Reporting to his superiors with an understandable edge of nervousness, the commanding general of the region,
John M. Palmer, claimed that Kentucky's Afro-American population was
"inflamed by this belief" in the Fourth as their official jubilee day. Thus
fired by hope, as spring flowed into summer, "thousands of [black
people] left their masters' houses, and came into our posts at different
points in the State," Palmer said. "Every nook and hiding-place . . .
was filled with them."[3]

But there was much more than hiding and waiting going on. Late that
spring a delegation of black men from Louisville met with Palmer to
ask him when he was going to announce the official emancipation of
those persons still enslaved in the state. Though Palmer told them that
he had no such authority, this did not discourage the delegation or their
community. Acting on their own authority, aware of the actions of their
brothers and sisters across the South, black people in the Louisville area
planned a mammoth freedom celebration for the Fourth. When the day
came, it was immediately apparent that a new time had begun, for the
procession that made its way to the meeting place in Johnson's Woods,
just outside the city, was surely one of the largest anywhere that year.
Estimates ranged from twelve thousand to twenty thousand marchers,
including the ever present children, workmen's organizations, church
groups, mutual aid societies, and others. At the head of the parade on
that very warm day was a contingent of some eight hundred black soldiers and a military band, marching, strutting, and singing as only black
soldiers could do. Another six hundred uniformed black men and their
band brought up the rear. The hiding was over. Emerging from the nooks
and crannies, the fugitives had joined the public march to freedom, creating their own emancipation proclamation, with the words rolling forth in
every drumbeat, every children's song, each ecstatic shout, syncopated to
the rhythms of their spirits and hopes.

When the singing, swaying mass arrived at Johnson's Woods, they
found a regiment of black artillery encircling the area to protect them.
They were greeted too by a throng of nearly one hundred thousand persons—including some whites—who immediately surrounded and absorbed them. Every black person from Kentucky and lower Ohio seemed
to be there, for no one intended to miss freedom. Soon the soldiers were
served a magnificent meal and everyone else managed to feed themselves
in one way or another. The gigantic freedom assembly was then addressed by John M. Langston, carrying within himself many memories
of earlier Northern struggles. Naturally, at the proper time the Declaration of Independence was read aloud. Finally, before it was all over, the
black action evoked a most interesting response, for General Palmer

was on hand; recognizing the force of the black movement toward Johnson's Woods, he had managed to find the authority he needed and so
announced:

By the Declaration of Independence, by the Constitution of the United States,
by the law of our country which makes all of its inhabitants free, since our
government is a democracy; as commanding officer of this Commonwealth,
by the power and authority invested in me and upon the instruction and approval of the President of the United States, I do declare slavery forever
abolished in this State.[4]

Though they gave him thunderous applause, the black people at Johnson's Woods surely knew that this general and his President, along with
their Constitution and Declaration of Independence, had all followed
the black vanguard into this assembly of freedom. Annealing them
through the fire of their hope, molding the best white revolutionary traditions to their people's needs, those former slaves were teaching the
generals and the presidents the way toward truth, while at the same time
declaring, creating, and acting out their own freedom.

In any assessment of that freedom march through the streets of Louisville and many cities like it, the presence of the black infantry at the
beginning and end of the line, and the encircling force of the black
artillery men at the grove, must be understood as neither ornamental nor
accidental. The black soldiers were present both as reminders of the cost
their community paid in the Civil War, and as immediate guardians and
leaders of this community as it set forth toward new life and freedom
in the heart of a hostile, bitter, frightened white society. All through the
chaotic year of transition the black soldiers were present, often playing
the protective role the Savannah ministers originally envisioned or, as in
New Orleans, setting examples of protest and direct action. Frequently
they were forced to move beyond marches, guard duty, and protest to
engage in harsh, armed struggles on behalf of their people, for the sake
of their own dignity. Indeed, those black men in blue are central to any
proper understanding of the self-liberating movement of their emerging
community in the year of jubilee. Only when we comprehend the meaning of their presence do we see the powerful potential for revolutionary
transformation in the South which they represented. Only then can we
sense the logic of the white Southerners who stood rigidly against that
rushing black tide, and understand what was lost to the struggle when
the black military vanguard was eventually removed.

By the time of Louisville's Fourth of July celebration, black troops
comprised some thirteen percent of the Union army, and the very
presence of the Blacks and Blues, as they were often called, had become

both a part of the overall irony of the war and a critical element in the
struggle for freedom. For in spite of their desire to enlist from the outset,
black soldiers had not been accepted in any significant numbers until
after the Emancipation Proclamation, in the winter and spring of 1863.
At that time, when they began to stream into the Union armies, the
majority came out of slavery, and their term of enlistment was for three
years or the duration of the war, whichever was longer. This meant that
when the war ended in the spring of 1865 and the white volunteers, many
of whom had been in for a longer time, began demanding to be mustered
out, the Union army was forced to use its black soldiers as a major
force in occupying the defeated Confederate states. In the summer of
1865 there were more than 120,000 black troops in the army, most of
them in the South, serving now as the official agents of the military governments which continued to oversee and share political power with the
emerging provisional white civilian governments in the region.[5]

An explosive and potentially revolutionary situation had again developed out of the accidents of war. By now these black soldiers, many of
whom had been through the searing, transforming experiences of combat,
considered themselves at once representatives of the conquering Union
government, protectors of their ancestral community, and guarantors of
their people's best dreams. In the uniform of the Northern armies they
had fought to destroy slavery and its power over their lives. They had
risked themselves to create their own freedom and the freedom of their
people, to resurrect themselves and develop new lives. As loyalists and
armed enforcers, they were prepared to play a powerful, radical role:
former slaves turned soldiers of freedom. From all that anyone could
tell, large numbers of these men were serious when they sang the powerful words of the most popular marching song of all: "As he died to make
men holy, let us die to make men free." In their own minds, they were
still the primary bearers of the terrible swift sword.

Of course, their people felt and understood all this. So a correspondent
to the *Christian Recorder* wrote from Wilmington, North Carolina, late
that spring about how good it was to have black troops replace the white
Union occupation forces there. "We have so long been annoyed by 'rebs'
in the garb of Union soldiers," he said, "that it was almost like the
transition from slavery to liberty, to feel that we had those around us
who would be our protectors indeed. . . ." Unfortunately, a deep and
widespread resistance to that transition had welled up in other quarters,
and the soldiers in the army of black guardians were not the ultimate
arbiters of their role, not even the owners of their own swords. All
around them raged clashing, antagonistic visions. Everywhere white
supremacy, fear, and greed were at work. At the head of the conquering

government, as commander-in-chief of these black soldiers, was Andrew Johnson, and it was ever more obvious that this was a man who did not believe in black people's right even to be full and equal citizens, much less liberators and cocreators of a new age in America.

On an even more immediately explosive level, the black vision had to encounter the angry, bitter, frightened wills of all those white Confederate soldiers who now straggled back to their homes, many bearing the scars of their defeats, some without limbs, others dreaming all the terror-filled dreams of cannon shot and piercing screams and unstanched fountains of blood. These men in tattered gray uniforms returned to their communities to find devastation on the earth, to see black Union soldiers representing the conquering armies. They knew that some of these armed black men had probably met them or their relatives on the fields of death. How were they to deal with former slaves whose first acts of freedom had apparently included the killing of Southern white men, legally, officially, with the approval of other white men? For some of the angry Confederate veterans it was like a fever on the brain, and the burning did not diminish when they saw the black soldiers marching in freedom parades, singing their songs of religious fervor, or encountered them on the streets and roads and sometimes had their military buttons cut off by these bold, assertive black men.[6]

Finally, ranged against the black armies of hope were the Southern white men and women who never went to war, who sent their sons and fathers, their husbands and sweethearts off to die. Sometimes their bitterness and rage seemed the deepest of all, their blindness the most antagonistic to the dreams of liberation in the hearts of the Blacks and Blues. It was this group whose reaction to the black soldiers of freedom was caught vividly by one of their representatives, writing in a New Orleans newspaper in 1865:

Our citizens who had been accustomed to meet and treat the negroes only as respectful servants, were mortified, pained and shocked to encounter them in towns and villages, and on the public road, by scores and hundreds and thousands, wearing Federal uniforms, and bearing bright muskets and gleaming bayonets. They often recognized among them those who had once been their own servants. . . . All felt the quartering of negro guards among them to be a deliberate, wanton, cruel act of insult and oppression.

In Georgia one editor looked at the black troops and came to a far more direct and summary conclusion: "We shall never be loyal until they are taken away."[7]

One of the major responsibilities the black soldiers took upon themselves was to protect their people's struggle for land. Though whites found this role insufferable, the soldiers were constantly encouraging the others to hold out for land of their own, rather than go back to working for whites. This recognition of black soldiers as supporters of black rights to the land and to their own labor was widespread in the South. In Florida, as in many other places, white military and civilian authorities identified black troops as those spreading the belief that the forty acres would be distributed around Christmas of 1865 or New Year's Day of 1866. Since many of the black troops in Florida had come out of the area in South Carolina and Georgia where Field Order 15 applied, this was probably an accurate statement. Nevertheless, in the context of America's moral, political, and economic climate, such action was considered seditious by many. That was the meaning of a report by Gen. Quincy Adams Gillmore, Union commander in South Carolina, where in the first half of 1865 more than eighty percent of the fourteen thousand occupation troops were black. Gillmore complained that "I have found . . . many bad men among the non-commissioned officers and privates of some of my colored regiments—men, who by their false representations and seditious advice, have exercised a most baleful influence upon the plantation laborers." In Alabama a white resident of Sumpter County was more direct when he said that "negroes will *not work* surrounded and encouraged with black troops encouraging them to insubordination."[8]

What whites called "insubordination" and "sedition" were, of course, black freedom and independence, and the Alabamian was right at least about the role of the black troops. For not only did they march in parades, participate in and lead conventions, secure land, and generally protect their community, but they also led that community toward new levels of freedom, sometimes in the most unexpected places. One Sunday morning early in the summer of 1865, in Aiken, South Carolina—one of the most difficult and threatening areas for blacks—a group of some twenty Blacks and Blues, with bayonets on their belts, entered the Baptist church. According to the story told later by the white minister, the soldiers were directed to the galleries by the ushers. Some started up to that section traditionally assigned to black worshipers, but others called them back. Together the group then sought out seats in the main section of the church. When some white men tried to block this black invasion of their holy sanctuary, the minister claimed that "the soldiers flourished their bayonets and began to curse." After those actions of freedom they were allowed to seat themselves, but the congregation decided not to hold its evening service. How long the whites closed themselves against the spirit and body of black freedom is not clear, but many sources confirm that black soldiers continued to lead the way in a variety of bold ventures beyond the old boundaries of servitude and white supremacy.[9]

As the provisional white civilian governments began to move back into power under Johnson's "restoration" of the South, and set out to block the black movement toward freedom, such action led to inevitable and widespread conflicts between black soldiers and white civilian and military authorities. In Vicksburg and Memphis they fought the Irish police. In Wilmington, North Carolina, the soldiers were accused of "defying and insulting" the police; indeed, on at least one occasion the black soldiers arrested the white chief of police and paraded him through the streets before an appreciative crowd of black people. Clashes between black and white soldiers—often over the treatment of the local black communities—were reported in Charleston, Atlanta, Danville, Chattanooga, and Jacksonville. Almost everywhere that black military men were stationed, it was said that "the Negro soldiers clashed with all forms of white authority." In some places black soldiers managed to break their people loose from jail, claiming that there was no real justice available to them. Considering the example set by these soldiers, it was not surprising to hear from various quarters the complaint raised by a white editor in Montgomery, Alabama: "We have heard freedmen declare that they will not submit to overhauling or arrest by any damned rebel police."[10]

Indeed, as it became increasingly clear that a major goal of "white authority"—from the White House down to the smallest county jurisdictions—was to contain and limit black freedom, and hold the line for white supremacy, neither the clashes nor the attitudes behind them were surprising. As long as armed black soldiers were around, as long as a self-liberating black community kept insisting on defining, creating, and expanding the precincts of its freedom, and as long as white men and women sought to maintain maximum control over black lives and black labor, the explosive possibilities were clear to all. In the summer of 1865 Martin Delany, now an agent of the Freedmen's Bureau, explained a key aspect of the situation to a group of newly freed men and women on Saint Helena's Island. Under discussion was the burning question of the black right to freedom and the land. Delany held forth on how those rights had been won and how they must be maintained. He told the excited audience: "I want you to understand that we would not have become free, had we not armed ourselves and fought out our independence." Later, picking up that theme and suggesting its explosive potential, he added, "I tell you slavery is over, and shall never return again. We have now two hundred thousand of our men well drilled in arms and used to warfare, and I tell you it is with you and them that slavery shall not come back again, and if you are determined it will not return again."[11]

Martin Delany saw part of the picture, but missed the rest. Having clearly explained the powerful potential of the black troops, he called upon the black people of Saint Helena to depend not upon the soldiers but upon the government to keep its word in making land available to them and in protecting them. Almost at the same time, in New Orleans the *Tribune* also saw the tremendous revolutionary possibilities of the black soldiers. According to the editors, "a system of terror" had been let loose upon the black people of the state as they sought to exercise their freedom: "Several have already been murdered and many more will be if we do not resist. The right of self defense is a sacred right." But the editors felt there was a better way than for individual black citizens to take up arms: "It would probably be sufficient to send a few companies of colored troops into the worst parishes. The presence of our armed brethren, wearing the United States uniform, would do a great deal toward bringing the slaveholders to their senses. The black regiments carry with them the vivid and forcible image of the revolution, i.e. of the elevation of the downtrodden race to the level of citizens."[12]

Because, as usual, the *Tribune* was absolutely right about the significance of the black troops, and because the white government which controlled them had no interest in allowing that kind of revolution to move any further than it had, black people could not count on any consistent, official dispatching of their soldiers to help them in time of need. Rather, just the opposite was happening. Petitions and protests from white people across the South were pouring into the White House, calling for the removal of the black troops. Typical was the action in Georgia, where the state legislature sent a special commission to the nation's capital to protest vigorously against the presence of the occupying black soldiers. The commission said it objected to the placing of "our former slaves with arms in their hands, to arrest, fine or imprison . . . to maltreat our citizens and insult their wives and daughters." This was the context in which the Georgia editor had declared, "We shall never be loyal until they are taken away." Because this view was shared by the President and his highest military leaders, the black troops began to be taken away, and quickly. But as long as they were present, black soldiers continued to do what they thought necessary in their confrontations with white police and military forces which were often made up of Confederate veterans, most of them determined to crush the fragile new institution of freedom.[13]

In Mississippi, where one of the bastions of black troops was located, there continued to be clashes. On several occasions it was reported that groups of these ambiguous soldiers of the Union "met and engaged in minor skirmishes" with white militiamen. In addition, "individual clashes resulting in violence between whites and Negro soldiers were not uncommon." The similarity between the black soldiers and the free blacks and outlyers of an earlier time was striking, and it was highlighted when Mississippi's provisional governor reported to President Johnson that local blacks "congregate around the negro garrisons in great numbers, and are idle and guilty of many petty crimes."[14]

Even as they recognized that soon they would not be able to serve officially as protectors of their people's freedom, the soldiers continued to set an example of resistance and struggle. A contemporary account from the fall of 1865 in South Carolina perhaps tells the story best:

In Newberry District . . . it appears that in a [railway] car which was standing on the track were three or four women and two Rebel soldiers,—one of them a Texan. A negro sergeant had occasion to enter the car, and was roughly ordered out by the Texan. He responded to the effect that he knew his business and should mind it. The two Rebel soldiers thereupon seized him and undertook to thrust him out. He resisted, and the Texan stabbed him, inflicting what was supposed to be a mortal wound. In an hour the two Rebels were caught by the negro soldiers of the regiment to which the sergeant belonged; and in three hours more, the Texan had been tried by a drum-head court-martial, shot, and buried. The other Confederate escaped while they were taking him up for trial, and will not be retaken.[15]

Obviously, there was no room in the South—or anywhere else in the United States—for black soldiers like these. Indeed, there seemed to be no place in the minds or hearts, or the social and political structures, of most white Americans for a community of four million former slaves whose words and deeds demanded for them a role of parity within the society, who claimed the traditional American right of self-defense, whose children were taught to sing of a "sweet land of liberty," while their fathers and mothers literally fought to possess their share of it.

How should people who only yesterday had been part of an exploitative master class now deal with the news that summer from Georgia that "the negroes are frequently out very late at night, attending the meetings of a society they have formed . . . for the protection of female virtue"? Or what should white women say about the black washerwomen of Jackson who seemed to believe that their freedom and virtue required the organization of their own protective association? The new images and realities were hard to deal with. For instance, what could one make of yesterday's "ignorant slaves" who now seemed fiercely determined to educate themselves and their people? At least one white man was deeply moved when he saw the epitome of this quest in Macon, Georgia: "a young negro woman with her spelling book fastened to the fence, that she might study while at work over the wash tub." Such testimony of black determination to master the printed word came from every corner of the South, and no one summed up its ubiquitous fascination more adequately than Sidney Andrews, a young white Northern journalist:

Many of the negroes . . . common plantation negroes, and day laborers in the towns and villages, were supporting little schools themselves. Everywhere, I found among them a disposition to get their children into schools, if possible. I had occasion very frequently to notice that porters in stores and laboring men about cotton warehouses, and cart drivers on the streets, had spelling books with them, and were studying them during the time they were not occupied with their work. Go into the outskirts of any large town and walk among the negro inhabitants, and you will see the children, and in many instances grown negroes, sitting in the sun alongside their cabins studying.[16]

Such black people, who not only sang but studied in the sun, were a threat to many white Southerners, and the smouldering ashes of their "little schools" often provided mute testimony to that fact. But if reading, writing, sunlit former slaves were threats, what were a frightened people to make of the ever dangerous black preachers, many of whom now seemed to be exploding with sun, like a group in Mobile, Alabama, accused of "inculcating the freedmen with doctrines of murder, arson, violence and hatred of white people"? It was said that these men preached sermons in which whites were described as "white devils," "demons," or "proslavery devils." Following the traditions of David Walker and Nat Turner and anticipating much to come, Mobile's black prophets spoke of an impending race war in which all whites would be exterminated. According to the local newspaper, one of the preachers who was arrested "frequently cried out 'In this hour of blood who will stand by me?' and his question ever met with most enthusiastic replies of 'I will, bless God!' from the assembled auditory." Obviously, such men were clear and present dangers to all white definitions of good news.[17]

So it was not strange that so many white Americans found these developments hard to grasp. For even if the terrible blindness of race and fear had not been at work, the nation was actually being called upon to respond to a remarkable event in human transformation—one not easily absorbed. A people just emerging from the supposedly dehumanizing experience of slavery, a people for the most part desperately poor and materially deprived, a people assumed to be ignorant of "civilization," was announcing in words and deeds an agenda for the continuing movement toward freedom and new humanity in the United States. Supposedly subdued by paternalist domination, these former slaves were prophesying a new nation for all, including the paternalists. Instead of adopting the masters' values, a significant body of men and women had sensed the necessity of reshaping themselves and the entire society to address their definitions of freedom. At great cost, and with a vision exceeding that of their allies or enemies, black people were declaring that freedom meant the death of white supremacy and the creation of a new philosophy and a new politics for the United States. In 1865, this was something that almost no one in America could see. Instead, the generally approved white dreams involved new steel mills and railroad tracks, miles of grain and loaded ships, and the conquest of nonwhite savages and unbounded markets across the globe. Still, the fundamental tragedy was not that there were such clashing visions, or that whites could not immediately grasp the black revelation. Rather it inhered in the fact that men and women consciously chose not only to set themselves against the coming of the light, but to try to break the spirit and hold captive the lives of the human channels of hope.

Resistance to the black vision and the bold actions which often accompanied it came from everywhere, beginning with Andrew Johnson in the White House. His earlier promises to be a Moses to black people and his highly publicized disdain for the Confederate aristocracy had originally suggested some ground for hope. However, by the summer of 1865 clear-minded observers of either race could see that this erstwhile slaveowner was no Moses that any freedom-oriented black person would want to follow. It was obvious, too, that his supposed dislike for the Southern aristocracy seemed to fade quickly as their representatives—including a significant number of women—came to pay court to him and seek pardons allowing them to reclaim the land they had abandoned and the political leadership they had renounced. By summer's end Johnson's direction was frighteningly clear, and in turn newspapers were quoting his announcement that "This is a country for white men, and by God, so long as I am President, it shall be a government for white men." Thus, he was not only permitting an unrepentant Southern white ruling class to move back into power, but he was making every effort, and giving the Southern leadership every license, to curb the rising black movement toward authentic freedom, beginning with the search for basic political rights and land.[18]

Andrew Johnson was a Southern white supremacist, as well as a stubborn, insecure, and volatile man. Thus he was one of the most unfortunate leaders possible for a moment in history when the best future of the nation required great vision, courage, humanity, and strength—a moment in which a society might have moved to overcome its own past, respond creatively to its former slaves, and begun the struggle to create an authentically new future, starting in the South. Instead, as they considered the postwar Southern situation, neither Lincoln nor Johnson had envisioned any radically new departures. Indeed, as penalties for treason and armed rebellion go, the arrangement that Johnson and his supporters, and Lincoln before them, offered these white Southerners was rather gentle. No demands were made for fundamental change in the antebellum Southern order of things, except that the death of slavery had to be acknowledged through the ratification of the Thirteenth Amendment, and that the Confederate war debts had to be repudiated. When he was called upon to determine what portion of the white population had to be loyal for a state to rejoin the Union, Johnson set no percentage or proportion at all, simply declaring that whenever "that portion of the people . . . who are loyal" had rewritten the constitution and established the new government, the state could rejoin the Union. In Johnson's mind there was no question but that "the people" who would do all these things were the white people. Black men and women were not slaves any longer, but they were surely not to be participating, decision-making citizens.[19]

On the other hand, by the time the hot-tempered Tennessean had begun to settle into his new role, black men and women all over the South and across the nation had spoken their own minds, were continually projecting their own vision of citizenship, of collective rebirth. Not only were they meeting, voting, and marching, but they were creating churches, claiming land, establishing newspapers, developing protective associations, and taking special pride in the creation of schools everywhere. So when the first white teachers from the American Missionary Association arrived that summer in Raleigh, North Carolina, they found a school already established in the local African Methodist Episcopalian church. In Atlanta others discovered a school organized by two former slaves in the basement of a church, and another developing in the confines of an old railroad car. Blacks were moving with their vision, refusing to wait: in one place the school was simply an awning stretched over a framework of pine poles; in another, the front yard of the teacher's bare shack, or a mule stable, or an abandoned white school, or the overhang of a rocky ledge where fugitives once hid but hid no more, standing now in the sun.

It was a powerful dynamic. Indeed, this refusal to hide, to wait, this black insistence on defining their freedom and re-creating themselves, carried with it a fundamental challenge to the old order. Thus it was not surprising that the new white state governments felt they had to respond quickly and directly. The former slaves had imaginatively seized the initiative in defining the possibilities of a transformed South. In response to the black demands for freedom and justice, in reaction to the black insistence on new lives and new institutions, the old white supremacist reaction came thundering back from every one of the "restored" governors' mansions, constitutional conventions, and legislatures. Fearful, reactive, selfish, and arrogant, they sought to force back the tide. Understandably, they felt that the President of the United States was on their side.

In Georgia Benjamin F. Perry, the provisional governor appointed by Johnson, was a far cry from the "people's governor" that the black community of that state had asked for. He opened the constitutional convention with a speech announcing that "this is a white man's government, and intended for white men only." In neighboring Alabama another Johnson appointee echoed Perry's statements, saying, "It must be remembered that politically and socially ours is a white man's government." In North Carolina the Speaker of the House added truthful sarcasm: "This is a white man's government, and intended for white men only, as even Connecticut, in New England itself, has just decided."[20]

The appointed and elected white officials were reflecting and leading the opinions of their people, who sometimes put the case more directly and ominously. One Alabama planter said, "If we cannot whip the Negro, they and I cannot live in the same country." In Virginia, as befitted the people's genteel ways, the *Richmond Whig* was much more delicate: "There must be a mudsill to society. In the South that mudsill is, or was, the negro. . . . These people are negroes, they are free, and let them continue free—but let them be *free negroes*. . . . The negroes' happiness and safety are best promoted by . . . conformity to his manifest destiny and that is social and political inferiority to whites."[21]

But it was in Mississippi, dark heart of the frontier of the South, that the most fundamental statement of the white supremacist vision was expressed—appropriately enough, in reaction to the demands of the black men and women of Vicksburg for full political participation in the reconstruction of their state. Recognizing the power of the black argument, and the danger it represented to white supremacy, the *Natchez Courier* set forth the essential philosophy which guided the majority of whites in the South—and the North—as they responded to all black demands for equality and national transformation. The editor claimed that no two dissimilar races could live together on a basis of equality anywhere: "One *must* be superior—one *must* be dominant. If the negro should be the master, the whites must either abandon the territory, or there would be another civil war in the South—a war of the races—the whites against the blacks—and that war would be a war of extermination."[22]

In the context of this narrow, beleaguered, but very common American view, any move by black men and women to define their freedom as the act of sharing power was perceived as a total threat to the power of the whites. Of course what the black movement really represented was a threat to *total* white power, which was not the same. However, white men were not making such distinctions, and where confusion reigned or doubts arose, members of the planter-entrepreneur classes were always ready to force the issue of black power *or* white power as the only real question at hand. They were aided in this action by the fact that most white people, north and south, agreed with Joseph E. Brown, the outgoing governor of Georgia, who said he believed in the essential, God-created inferiority of blacks and then told the new legislature: "Unless madness rules the hour, they will never be placed upon a basis of political equality with us . . . they are not competent to the task of self-government, much less to aid in governing a great nation of white people."[23]

Given the fact that the emerging black thrust toward freedom had to deal with such vehement definitions of sanity and madness, it was understandable that many of their conventions, petitions, and individual actions tried to move with caution to allay these white fears, especially in those counties where blacks outnumbered whites in overwhelming proportions. Nevertheless these same white fears, so antithetical to the coming of a new time, made it absolutely necessary that the newly freed black community continue to work out—and live out—a theory of society which could counter this deeply held racial supremacist point of view.

It is in such a setting of black initiative and white reaction, of creativity and vision from the former slaves and narrow, frightened rigidity from the former master class, that the Black Codes of 1865 are best understood. When that newly restored sector of the "great nation of white people" who lived in the South began to create the laws for their state and local governments, those laws had to reflect their world view, their fears of black (and white) freedom, their delusions, their definitions of themselves and the black people who lived all around them, who lived within them, who filled the surreal world of their dreams. Only when these realities are added to the obvious issues of economic and political privilege and unenlightened self-interest, can one fully appreciate the reactive nature of the Codes. They were a direct response to the rising power and revolutionary potential of the black surge toward freedom. The Codes were a reply to the creative and thoughtful proposals, pleas, and demands for an interdependent black and white society of equals coming from the conventions, petitions, sermons, and life of the newly freed community. At their deepest level the Black Codes were a declaration of white people's incapacity—or unwillingness—to envision such unprecedented freedom and equality in the South, or to face its necessary accompaniments: the death of their own distorted self-vision, their own narrow definitions of self-interest, and their own least authentic selves.[24]

Though the laws dealing with black people varied from state to state, from city to city, essential patterns were constant across the South. Everywhere the Black Codes attempted to set up hard barriers against the forward movement of black men and women toward freedom, attempted to press them as far back into slavery as possible. Reacting against the basic black demand to possess the land, several states imposed restrictions against land ownership or rental by black people. For instance Mississippi, whose laws set much of the pattern, prohibited its black population from renting or leasing any land outside the towns and cities. On the other hand the city of Opelousas, Louisiana, denied the rights of blacks to own or rent a house in the town, if they did not already do so on January 1, 1866. Laws like these were not simply aimed against the ownership of property; they were part of a network of legal and extralegal attempts to guard against untrammeled physical movement by black people. They were meant to keep blacks bound to jobs and land controlled by white people. If freedom meant the right to move about in search of new jobs and new lives, then these laws were set against freedom, and new versions of the slave patrols were established to enforce them.[25]

Vagrancy laws were another crucial element of control. In Alabama a vagrant could be any "laborer or servant who loiters away his time, or refuses to comply with any contract for a term of service without just cause." Mississippi's laws demanded that, by the second Monday of January 1866, every black person must have a "lawful home or employment and . . . written evidence thereof." South Carolina was vaguer in its definitions, but a vagrant there could be sentenced to as much as a year of hard labor and be hired out to an individual. Whatever the details, one obvious intent was to make it as difficult as possible for black people to refuse to sign work contracts while holding out for the long-expected forty acres.

In reaction to the rising black movement toward self-reliance, every state created harsh penalties against any black workers who broke their contracts with landowners or other employers. In the same vein, the laws placed severe limits on the kinds of independent work and trades that black men could enter. Some states like Mississippi included sections in their codes which could only be called fugitive worker clauses, because of their similarity to the earlier fugitive slave laws. So-called apprenticeship laws were another thrust back toward slavery, denying the black community's attempts to shore up its family life; providing easy ways for children to be taken away from any black parents or guardians deemed unable to support or guide them, these laws placed such children as unpaid laborers in the hands of white families.

Throughout the structures of this postwar legal assault, black people were subjected to many special punishments which did not apply to whites. They were also barred from service in the state militia, and from ownership of a military weapon. The patterns were clear: in almost every situation having to do with black-white relationships, freedom of movement, freedom of choice in jobs, a personal sense of independence, and control over their own families, the Black Codes were the slave codes revived, with the sole exception of certain limited, specially defined rights to hold property, to have marriages legally recognized, to enter into contracts, and to sue and be sued. But under no circumstances whatsoever did any of these newly loyal states make provision for black men to govern themselves, vote, or hold office, or for black children to receive publicly funded education.[26]

In the final analysis, though they were cruel reactions against black hope, the Codes were not surprising. For a people with the world view of white Americans, such laws were a predictable response to the black thrust toward self-defined freedom, especially in the absence of white national leadership or any other contrary pressure. Moreover, these Southerners were the only white Americans who shared the land and daily life with large numbers of black people; they were the ones who most depended on controlled mass black labor; they had seen and felt at first hand the revolutionary potential of the black movement surging toward the future. For such people, the Black Codes were an almost foreseeable response to the breakdown of slavery as well as to the unmistakable black will to be free. In other parts of the nation, to be sure, many white Americans had already demonstrated the deadly uses of the law against the best aspirations of those nonwhite natives of the land who sought to live free and independent among them; so Southerners were really doing nothing new.[27]

Important though they were, the Black Codes were only the official white Southern reaction. As soon as it was clear that black men and women meant to create new realities, as soon as their hunger for freedom was perceived as a threat to the white vision of the world, then other forms of reaction developed. Whether there were laws or not, white men and women in local communities across the South conspired to keep land out of black hands, refusing to sell, lease, or rent. In addition, in the summer of 1865 white men, led by veterans of the Confederate armies, began forming paramilitary organizations to supply the extralegal force which they knew would be needed if they were to contain the rising black river. In some states they organized as official militia units. Eventually, in the post-1865 period, many of these local organizations expanded and took names like the Ku Klux Klan and the Knights of the White Camelia, but even before they had names they had chosen their purpose, their methods, and their weapons. Before 1865 was over the stories of shootings, burnings, drownings, hangings, and decapitations abounded; word of black bodies putrefying on the ground began to come out of the South. The two visions were in conflict, and wherever black men could keep their weapons, could find ground to stand on, the armed struggle to defend their vision went on.[28]

Of course the search for land, the need to hold on to land, was still central to the black hope for a new life in America. Near the end of September Sidney Andrews, a young journalist wandering in the South, provided eloquent testimony to that reality. As he traveled in the South Carolina upcountry, passing through Orangeburg and the rubble of Columbia, he was constantly approached by blacks who had come in from the rural areas seeking news, asserting their freedom of movement, asking the central question: "When is de land goin' fur to be devided?" Unable to hear, unable to see the central issues as blacks saw them, Andrews was often incredulous: "Some of them believe the land which they are to have is on the coast; others believe the plantations on which they have lived are to be divided among themselves."[29]

From the angle of vision of the rising black people, from the standpoint of any intrinsic justice, these were not wild ideas, but Andrews found them so. Not understanding the significance of Field Order 15 and the Freedmen's Bureau legislation for the black communities, he was surprised to encounter constantly "a widespread idea that the whites are to be driven out of the lower section of the state, and that the negroes are there to live by themselves." Did this not appear to have happened on Edisto and Wardmelaw and Saint John's and Saint Catherine's? Was there not some real ground for such vision and hope? Not for Andrews: he could only comment that "other absurd notions well known to prevail are, that freedom can only be found 'down-country,' i.e. in the neighborhood of Charleston; that it is inseparable from the presence of the army, etc."[30]

So the wisdom of the black men and women thrusting toward freedom was only foolishness to the young white who would soon become an instant expert on the South and its two races. For as long as they could, of course, the moving black community followed their own wisdom, surging toward the coasts, toward the experiments with independence and black self-government which they had heard about. Moving like a tattered, hopeful, visionary army, they went down to the waters, toward Charleston, toward the islands, toward the precincts of freedom. As Andrews headed in the same direction (but followed a different compass), he said, "[I] met scores of them trudging along with their whole earthly possessions in a bundle on the head . . . I spoke with many. They had but few words; 'Goin' to Char'ston,' was often their only reply."[31]

In other states like Alabama and Mississippi, where the experiments in freedom were not so concentrated or on such a grand scale, blacks simply left the plantations where they had been enslaved and moved away toward relatives, toward that sense of concrete assurance that Patience Johnson described. Everywhere too they moved because they had heard that land would be available by New Year's Day of 1866, and in spite of the Black Codes they did not want to be tied to the old places when the new time began.[32]

They were convinced the land was coming. It was rightfully theirs, not only by the threefold claim of cultivation, loyalty, and warfare, but as part of the all-consuming justice of God. In spite of every discouraging sign, they were determined to believe that the land was coming and wanted to be ready to receive it. While many felt that they could do no more than position themselves strategically for the coming of the new age, others believed that they could be instruments in the process of creation. Perhaps some of these heard voices echoing the sounds which had filled Nat Turner's mind. Whatever they heard, they decided to fight for the land. Reports of such struggles surfaced all over the South. That fall in Georgia, black people near Augusta were said to have "taken forcible possession of several plantations and will not allow any white persons thereon." Near Georgetown, South Carolina, scenes reminiscent of antebellum resistance were enacted as blacks armed themselves with hoes, sticks, and bricks, determined to hold on to their land. From Duplin, North Carolina, the cry was raised, the vow was made that black people would have lands "even if they had to shed blood to obtain them."[33]

Such words and actions flowed in from many places that autumn, but the focus was again on the Sea Islands. There black residents pulled up the bridges from the mainland, established dockside barricades, and organized bands of armed men who repeatedly repelled white owners. Reports of such resistance were common from Fenwick, Edisto, Wardmelaw, and other islands. Understandably, these men and women at first had expected the Union army to be their ally in this struggle for the land and all that it meant. Apparently, hundreds and perhaps thousands of persons had memorized whole sections of Sherman's Field Order 15, as if it were a reading from the Bible. But field orders were not gospels, and in almost every instance of black resistance from Louisiana to Norfolk, Virginia, the white soldiers of the Union army (occasionally assisted by their reluctant black comrades-in-arms) became the ultimate recourse of the former owners. Since Johnson's policy of pardons for the Confederate supporters who held title to the land had effectively countermanded Sherman's field order, and since Johnson was Commander-in-Chief of the armed forces, the black resistants could expect little else. Nevertheless the quest for land went on. How else could adults keep faith with the singing children, with the voices of the river?[34]

16

The Struggle Ends, the Struggle Begins

There Is a River

. . . it inspires us with hope when we reflect, that our cause is not alone the cause of four millions of black men in this country, but we are intensely alive to the fact that it is also the cause of millions of oppressed men in other "parts of God's beautiful earth," who are now struggling to be free in the fullest sense of the word, and God and nature are pledged to their triumph.

Black Convention
Charleston, S.C., 1865

When the showdown came between the black quest for land and justice on the one hand, and Andrew Johnson's policy of easy pardons for the Confederate landowners on the other, it did not take place all at once. The hope was not exploded in any one moment—in fact, the dream of "forty acres and a mule" never died within the black communities of America. But one place, one time was so powerful a symbol that it cannot be ignored. On Thursday, October 19, 1865, on Edisto Island, some twenty-five miles southwest of Charleston, the time and the place were joined.

As the drama unfolded, the Freedmen's Bureau and its leader, Gen. Oliver O. Howard, played crucial, tragic roles. By that time Johnson's actions had already effectively undermined one of the Bureau's most important original functions as a protector of black people in their independent use of the land. Instead, as the fall wore on, as the pardoned owners came back to their black-occupied plantations on the Sea Islands and the coast, the Bureau assisted the owners' attempts to regain control over both the land and the resisting Afro-American labor force. Howard, known as "the Christian General," was caught in the midst of this disastrous transformation. After having made clear promises of land to the freedmen all through the late spring and early summer, he had been subsequently ordered by Johnson to reverse himself. Going against his own conscience, Howard betrayed the hopes of the black people who considered him one of their best friends, and capitulated to Johnson. As he made his choice, it is likely that the young, disabled general thought long thoughts about the promise of a bright future in the military that was still before him.[1]

In October Howard was on a tour, trying to explain to black men and women why it was impossible for them to have the land he had originally promised them. He requested that Edisto's overwhelmingly black community be brought together so that he might address them. Word of trouble and betrayal had already flashed through the islands, and when the one-armed general arrived, his choices were signaled in the makeup of his party, which included one of the biggest white landowners in the area. Meanwhile, more than two thousand black men, women, and children had gathered in the large Episcopal church at the center of the island, filled with apprehension and desperate hope. According to a white woman who attended the meeting, Howard told the people "that he, being their friend, had been sent by the President to tell them that the owners of the land, their old masters, had been pardoned, and their plantations were to be given back to them; that they wanted to come back to cultivate the land, and would hire the blacks to work for them."[2]

This was the message borne by their friend. Naturally, it outraged the black people who had been cultivating the land for generations, and had now begun to work for and govern themselves. They had trusted Howard and his more courageous assistant, Gen. Rufus Saxton, and the other white and black friends who had assured them that the government would be fair, that the land would be theirs. Now angry shouts of "No! No!" erupted immediately. Chilling cries, anguished moans broke out everywhere in the building. Some persons sprang up to leave, refusing to hear such an insult to their intelligence, their trust, and their hope. One black man shouted from the balcony: "Why, General Howard, why do you take away our lands? You take them from us who are true, always true to the Government! You give them to our all-time enemies. That is not right!"[3]

The Christian General had no answer for such a question, no response to such an accusation. He knew that generals, whatever their religious persuasions, do not often deal in issues of right and wrong, at least not for long—not when they disagree with their superiors, not if they want to continue to be generals, which Howard wanted very much. He also knew that the anger of the black community was justified and that it was steadily becoming more and more difficult to control. So instead of answering, he sought a temporary way out. Claiming that it was impossible to carry on a reasonable discussion in the large, excited meeting, Howard asked that a small committee be formed to meet apart from the general session, to try to come up with a solution. A committee of three was formed, consisting of one black man, one landowner, and one representative of the Freedmen's Bureau. While the committee met, Howard proposed that the people occupy their time not with debate, clarifying discussion, and the continued airing of their grievances, but with singing. One man cried out, "How shall we sing the Lord's songs in a strange land?" Already they knew: the land that they had cared for and nurtured, the land which had nurtured them, was now being estranged from them. So they sang "Nobody Knows the Trouble I Seen," and they cried out, in all its long-metered mourning, "Wandering in the Wilderness of Sorrow and Gloom," filling the church with echoes and memories deep as a river. Yet these were not songs of total resignation and hopelessness, but a statement of truth—truth greater than the Christian General dared admit.[4]

While the songs were being sung in the church, the black representative on the committee continued to struggle for the truth. He insisted on his people's need for the land, offering to buy it from the white owners, if necessary, pressing the connection between the land and the sense of selfhood and independence which were so much a part of the new institution of freedom. The representative of the owners refused everything short of abject dependence. He knew that Howard had already surrendered to Johnson's vision of the "restored" South, a vision which essentially excluded large numbers of independent black landowners. So the black demand was denied, and as the Christian General left the island, he warned the angry, betrayed men and women of the dangers of resistance.[5]

Such a warning was necessary. The struggle for land had already aroused black resistance throughout the South, including the Sea Islands, and Howard knew that there would likely be more. Even young Sidney Andrews realized that "the negroes . . . almost universally believe that the islands have been given to them, and they are not likely to readily relinquish that belief. . . . An attempt to force them from the islands at present, or to compel them to the acceptance of the terms proposed by the planters, will overthrow their faith in the Government, and there will be—bloodshed." A few weeks later, when a white man who owned one of the islands near Edisto tried to return, he was turned back by its black defenders; later he told a friend that "the Negroes on that Island were armed and have announced their purpose to allow no white man on it."[6]

Over on the mainland in Savannah, the resistance was led by a charis-matic lawyer, teacher, and organizer named Aaron A. Bradley. A native of Augusta, Bradley was one of the many black leaders who had escaped to the North during the antebellum period. When, toward the end of the war, Bradley returned to Georgia as a teacher, he was almost fifty years old, an advanced age for the time. But the short, slightly built, light-skinned man was also a highly concentrated dynamo of energy who had no intention of slowing down. Although he was operating a school in Savannah, Bradley made skillful use as well of the black churches of that community as a base for some highly effective organizing of his people against the loss of the land they had possessed under Field Or-der 15. Articulate, flamboyant, and aggressive, Bradley not only urged black people not to make contracts with the white owners that fall, but said that if they wanted to take the crops from the lands they had cultivated, they should do so. "It was not stealing," he reasoned, "for whom would they be stealing from but themselves." Outside of the Field Order 15 area, the same spirit was evident. In Greensboro, Alabama, black men and women gathered early in December to elect delegates to a statewide convention of their people. In their meeting, the demand for land was central, with speaker after speaker declaring that they would have "lands or blood."[7]

Here, of course, was the time for Maj. Martin Delany to appear, trail-ing all the glory and hope of his antebellum years, leading some part of those "two hundred thousand men well drilled in arms" to support the revolutionary claims of his people to the land on Edisto and elsewhere. But neither current rhetoric nor earlier glory would suffice in this situa-tion. Like the white Christian General, this visionary black major was now bound down by his own choices, by his decision to remain an agent of the federal government, of Andrew Johnson. Therefore when the Union troops eventually came to evict the desperate black people from the disputed land, Major Delany was not available to stand by their side. Delany's calls for black power and solidarity were largely behind him. Instead, as a functionary of the United States government, he was now permitting himself to be pitted against the potential revolu-tion, against the legitimate demands of his people. So on island after island and along the coastal areas, the black families who refused to sign contracts which locked them into a kind of serfdom were put off the land, often with military force.[8]

Nor was there any recourse in the North. For even respectable sympa-thizers there, like the editor of the influential *Nation*, vehemently de-nounced "the assumption that the distribution of other people's land to the Negroes is necessary to complete the work of emancipation." Rather,

the *Nation* declared that "division of rich men's lands among the landless . . . would give a shock to our whole social and political system
from which it could hardly recover without the loss of liberty"—meaning especially, one must assume, the liberty of wealthy white men to
grow wealthier. Here again, white visions of black freedom were inadequate at best, and at worst dangerous to the lives and self-respect of
black people.[9]

As fall ended, the tension mounted. The Freedmen's Bureau and the
rest of the army were by now clearly allied against the black determination to possess the land. Instead of receiving titles to forty acres of their
own, blacks were being coerced by federal and local government agen-
cies into signing unfavorable farm-labor contracts, pressed to give up
their dream of independence. Meanwhile a people based on the land
could not avoid the facts of the changing season, their material needs,
and the rising, powerful white opposition. For according to traditions—
according to the rhythms of agricultural work, the texts of the Black
Codes, and the military rulings of what once had been a glorious "Freedom Army"—early January was the time by which the working members
of the newly freed black community had to sign labor contracts with
the rightful owners of the land or be considered vagrants, rebels, outlaws, and according to the *Nation*, attackers of white liberty.

In this unjust and volatile situation, a flood of rumors poured over the
South, rumors of black insurrection, rumors that if there were no redis-
tribution of the land by Christmas, then "New Year's would bring a
black uprising." Though the rumors were on one level understandable,
it was just as hard in 1865 as it had been in 1855 and 1835—and in
all the years and nights of white nightmares before and ever since—to
be certain about what they were really based on. Still, some things were
clear: black people were deeply troubled about the denial of their right
to the land. Not only were they passing resolutions and in some places
physically guarding their new settlements against former white owners,
but apparently tens of thousands of them across the South were simply
refusing to sign any work contracts for the new year, refusing to recognize the old owners, refusing to be caught under legal contract, should
the distribution of land somehow still take place. And they were ready
to defend themselves: one report to President Johnson near the end of
the year stated that "in one way or another they have procured great
numbers of army muskets and revolvers." Of course the source of these
weapons was not really obscure: wherever they were based, black soldiers
were still backing up their people, often secretly holding on to their
weapons after being mustered out. By every possible means black men

and women continued to try to impose their own definitions on this year of perilous crossing.[10]

From a certain perspective, such determination and actions were in themselves rebellious. It took only a short leap of the imagination to what Sidney Andrews heard that fall in South Carolina: that "the negroes have an organized military force in all sections of the State, and are almost certain to rise and massacre the whites about Christmas time." Indeed, in the minds of some whites this had already happened. There was word—albeit false—in the late fall that "there had been a rising of the Negroes in Maryland; that a great many whites had been killed; and that some considerable portion of Baltimore and many of the plantations had been seized by the Negroes." No part of the South was free of such white dreams of terror, reminiscent of other times of turmoil and deep shakings. From Florida one white resident wrote to his President: "There is really danger of an insurrection . . . raised principally from the secret admonitions of colored troops."[11]

The rumors, of course, were based on certain solid realities. But the flames of white fear were also fanned by persons who sought to create an environment of anxiety and panic, so as to carry out and justify acts of terrorism for their own purposes. In many places across the South, rumors of black insurrection were accompanied by white violence and coercion. Many blacks were beaten and tortured in efforts to break up alleged plots, confiscate weapons, crush all local leadership, and deny black definitions of freedom. Communities from Virginia to Texas were invaded by white men who moved as enforcers of the new Black Codes and disarmed black people under force of arms and the power of an unjust legal system. Newly formed white militia units, looking very much like the old slave patrols, took up arms against the resisting black community, often with the active or passive cooperation of the U.S. Army and the Freedmen's Bureau. All this was usually geared toward forcing black people away from any independent relationship to the land, pressing them into the hands of the men and women determined to possess not only their labor, but as much of their souls as possible.[12]

Yet there is still reason to wonder about some of the deepest fountains which fed these rumors of black insurrection. After identifying and affirming all the logical, concrete bases for white dread, when all the manipulations and engineering of the terror are understood, there is still something about the pressurized depths of the fears themselves which bears consideration, especially when they appear so similar to the rumors of armed black insurrection and rebellion which inundated the South periodically during the height of slavery's power. Is it possible that after all the logical grounds are covered, something more was at work, something less amenable to precise and systematic explanation? Could it be that there raged through the hearts of the white community a terrible, logic-defying demand for punishment and death? Hidden among the fantasies and dreams, was there some fierce yearning for scourging, for unmediated justice to be raked across their lives and burned into the marrow of their beings by the black men and women whom they had so often, so carelessly, at times so harshly abused and destroyed? Would bloody insurrection against themselves have satisfied some necessity deeper than words and consciousness, something in them that searched frantically for the pathway back toward humanity and community? Were these rampant rumors actually the gathering up of all the speechless groans of a lost and tortured white people in search of help, health, and freedom? Did they sometimes suspect that their white God was also a consuming fire? Did they possibly hold, perhaps share with black people the searing conviction that without the shedding of blood there is no remission of sins?

It may be that all the rumors, fears, and antiblack violence were nothing more than shields against the piercing songs of the children, who boldly claimed the country. They may have been desperate attempts to drown out the clear and sober black voices all around them, inviting them to a common destiny more hopeful, though more difficult, than mutual extermination. The persistent invitations were everywhere. That fall, in the midst of the reports of insurrection, such voices clearly arose out of Charleston, South Carolina, when the black people of that state convened one of the last major African-American conventions of the year. Held near the end of November, the gathering commanded the attention of many of both races in the North as well as the South. To a large degree, such attention was mandated by demography. It was a matter of numbers, essentially the same black numbers which had provoked white nightmares and hunting parties over the decades of slavery, and now raised new fears of freedom. Not only were black people still a majority in the state, but in many of the lowland plantation counties and on the Sea Islands, they outnumbered whites by as much as seven and eight to one.[13]

Of course there was also a special history at work which filled the South Carolina situation with rich irony. Here was the state which had provided some of the most resolute and fiery defenders of slavery. Its representatives and spokesmen had blazed the way through all the harsh antebellum debates which tortured the nation's white community and finally helped rend their Union. So when it came time for the black people of that state to hold their first major convention, many eyes from all over the nation were upon them. In their turn, the black South Carolinians were fully aware of the situation and played their role to its fullest. Indeed, their Colored People's Convention provided a culmination and quintessence of the convention movement of black people across the South in that critical year of transition. Their resolutions, presence, and spirit spoke directly to the Black Codes, to the subject of black freedom, and to the necessary requirements for establishing a true community of black and white people in America.

The convention met in Zion Presbyterian Church, the largest gathering place for Charleston's black community. With a seating capacity of two thousand, it was overflowing with life and evangelical excitement when the convention opened on the last Saturday of November. Black people of many kinds and circumstances made their way from the city and the countryside, from the mainland and the islands, bringing various understandings of the significance of this momentous occasion. But all seemed to sense the absolute necessity of forcefully demanding their rights as new citizens, rejecting all of the less-than-equal Black Code categories into which the white people and the state legislature of South Carolina were trying to place them. In that spirit, to the fervent accompaniment of hymns and spirituals and many prayers, they formulated an "Address to the White Inhabitants of the State of South Carolina":

The laws which have made white men powerful have degraded us, because we were black and because we were reduced to the condition of chattels. But now that we are freemen—now that we are elevated, by the Providence of God, to manhood, we have resolved to stand up, and like men, speak and act for ourselves. We fully recognize the truth of the maxim, "The gods help those who help themselves."

Speaking and acting for itself with the Black Codes obviously in mind, the convention approved a statement summarizing its definition of the rights necessary to black freedom:

We simply ask that we shall be recognized as *men*; that there be *no obstructions* placed in our way; that the same laws which govern *white men* shall govern *black men*; that we have the right of trial by jury of our peers; that schools be established for the education of *colored children* as well as white; and that the advantages of both colors shall, in this respect, be *equal*; that no impediments be put in the way of our acquiring homesteads for ourselves and our people; that, in short, we be dealt with as others are—in equity and justice.

In their memorial to Congress they asked for the same equality of treatment, but went on to claim the right "to assemble in peaceful convention to discuss the political questions of the day," and the right "to enter all avenues of trade, commerce, agriculture, to amass wealth by thrift and industry." To all this they added a summary human right not normally found in the public documents of the nation: "the right to develop our whole *being*, by all the appliances that belong to civilized society."

Benefiting from the experiences and documents of the earlier conventions in this Southern movement toward freedom, building on their own powerful indigenous leadership, the South Carolina convention pressed some of its ideas more deeply, more fully than most of the other black assemblies. Indeed, it grappled with one of the most difficult and most important traditions of black struggle in a way unmatched by any other black assembly that year. For the convention's address to the white people of the state placed the black struggle for freedom in its full international context, remembering David Walker and the antebellum Delany, anticipating the coming DuBois and the marching Garvey:

It is some consolation to know, and it inspires us with hope when we reflect, that our cause is not alone the cause of four millions of black men in this country, but we are intensely alive to the fact that it is also the cause of millions of oppressed men in other "parts of God's beautiful earth," who are now struggling to be free in the fullest sense of the word, and God and nature are pledged to their triumph.

At the same time, while placing the struggle for black freedom in the United States in its larger setting, they demanded that the signal importance of their new native land be recognized, that the voices of the children be heard. So their statement of international vision was immediately followed by the declaration, "We are American by birth, and we assure you that we are Americans in feeling; and in spite of all the wrongs which we have so long and *silently* endured in this country, we can yet exclaim, with a full heart, 'O, America, with all thy faults we love thee still.' " By then, of course, the aroused black populace had made it clear in South Carolina and elsewhere that they did not love the faults, and would no longer endure silently. Rather, they were simply clearing the grounds for the ongoing movement toward justice.

So the black Carolinians again directly addressed their fellow citizens: Facing all the former masters and current employers, all their future oppressors and persecutors, all the fearful masses who raged against real or fancied insurrection, all the men and women whose hands too often bore the blood of black innocents—facing all of them, these black lovers of a new America, these citizens of a country yet unborn, spoke to the white people of South Carolina and of every other state in the Union: "We would address you—not as Rebels and enemies, but as friends and fellow-countrymen, who desire to dwell among you in peace, and whose

Black fugitives from Virginia
defending themselves against
slave catchers in Maryland
in 1853.
All were captured,
but Wesley Harris
(center foreground)
again escaped.

Armed fugitives
from Virginia
resisting recapture
at the Maryland state line
in December 1855.

Runaway slaves approaching federal sentinels near Fortress Monroe,
seeking freedom and protection.

Osborne P. Anderson,
who came from Canada to join John Brown's
band of revolutionaries.
He was the only black survivor of
their Harpers Ferry raid.

Library of Congress

John A. Copeland,
a student at Oberlin College
who was executed for his participation
in the Harpers Ferry action.

Library of Congress

Shields Green,
a fugitive from South Carolina
who was hanged
soon after John Brown was.

From "Purge This Land" by Stephen Oates,
attributed by Boyd Stutler, Harper & Row, 1970

Lewis S. Leary,
a native of North Carolina
who was only in his twenties
when he lost his life
on John Brown's mission.

Dangerfield Newby,
a free man from Virginia
who joined John Brown's revolutionaries
and died in action.

Library of Congress

Library of Congress

ohn Brown and his surviving black and white companions as they were arraigned.
From "The Old Man" by Nelson Truman, courtesy Holt, Rinehart & Winston, 1973

Robert Smalls (top) and three of his companions who captured the Confederate gunboat *Planter* and delivered it to Union forces off the shore of South Carolina in 1862.

Library of Congress

A humorous rendering of the black initiative during the Civil War which changed the status of thousands of enslaved people into official "contraband" of war. As such, they were no longer under their masters' control.

Can't come back nohow massa
Dis chile's contraban

Come back you black n

A recruiting poster in the Union's campaign
in North Carolina in 1865.

Black troops defending Union positions
at Milliken's Bend, Louisiana, in June 1863.

BATTLE OF
MILLIKEN'S BEND

Black Union troops liberating enslaved plantation workers
in North Carolina in 1865.

A black corporal
in the Union Army.

Black people who joined Gen. William T. Sherman's army
as it cut its way through Georgia.

Black troops among the liberating forces marching into Richmond, Virginia, in April 1865.

Black people gathering to discuss their futur
in the post-slavery perioc

A girl
who attends a freedmen's school
sharing her new reading skills
with her grandfather.

Black cavalrymer
bringing in Confederate prisoners

destinies are interwoven and linked with those of the whole American people, and hence must be fulfilled in this country."

Once again a black community gathered in struggle had raised a prophetic voice. Recognizing their own place among the oppressed and rising peoples of the world, they nevertheless affirmed their full right to the land they had made native through the fire of their trials and the labor of their hands. The prophets of Wilmington were correct: a new people was straining to be born, and somehow they knew that they could not be born in isolation from the destiny of the nation. More than anyone else in America, these black men and women in Charleston and Savannah, Knoxville and Norfolk, Vicksburg and New Orleans understood that there could be no redemption of America's best hopes unless they played a central role in the re-creation of the nation, that there could be no true borning for them unless the nation were made new, beginning in their own state, with the creation of a new, humane community of "friends and fellow-countrymen." Only then could the promise of the children, the longing of the parents, and the movement of the river be fulfilled. My country. My country.

It was a fearful dialectic, especially as the emerging Afro-Americans realized that if their vision prevailed, they must ultimately do the work of rebuilding in concert with the people who had been their legal owners, who had been despoilers of their women, breakers of their men, exploiters of their labor, murderers of their children, or a host of guilty bystanders. Still, at great inner cost they were calling for a new beginning —not forgetting the past, never forgetting it, but seeking to overcome it, to transform its meaning through the creation of a new future.

One can easily imagine the inner struggles which the black delegates had to wage in order to approve a document calling their former masters "friends and fellow-countrymen." Still, they persisted. After what the published reports referred to as "an animated debate" (the only such reference in the records of the meeting), the black people, driven by a strangely beautiful but desperate hope, passed a special resolution calling for the process of reconciliation to begin:

As American chattel Slavery has now passed forever away, we would cherish in our hearts no malice nor hatred toward those who were implicated in the crime of slaveholding; but would extend the right hand of fellowship to all; and would make it our special aim to establish unity, peace and brotherhood among all men.

What manner of men and women were these? Refusing to flinch in the face of the past, attacking the criminal system which had bound them, they extended "the right hand of fellowship"—a distinctly Christian phrasing—to the former criminals, offering to build together a new society. Who were these prophets and potential lovers who came to the convention in work clothes and uniforms, wrapped their hair in bright turbans and bandannas, and made Zion Church a precinct of sanctified hope? Whoever they were, however they managed to control the memories, fears, and anguish of the past, they were not fools, for among the rights they demanded was the right "to keep and bear arms." Dreamers, prophets, and lovers though they were, they were also rooted in the brutal realities of their own experiences and those of their forebears. So they knew that in a land where slavery, fear, and greed, beginning in the deep recesses of human hearts, had created a world of their own, the pathway to "unity, peace and brotherhood among all men" would be very long and very hard; would be at best cruelly difficult to negotiate, and at worst drenched in blood.

Just as it was hard to know who heard the singing children of Saint Helena, so now it was difficult to probe the hearts and minds of white America, to assess the effects of such a call to unity from South Carolina's black majority. To be sure, as the winter solstice approached, there were signs and intimations of various kinds. In Washington, when the Thirty-ninth Congress convened at the beginning of December, its members refused to seat the representatives from the Southern states, among whom were many former political and military leaders of the Confederacy. Congress took this action partly because of its determination to wrest the Reconstruction process from the hands of the President, but also because many Northern leaders were deeply troubled by the ruthless and regressive Black Codes. In a sense, then, black people's continuous struggle toward freedom helped create a serious rupture in the process of white reconciliation, a development which eventually led to new openings for the thrust toward justice. Of course almost no one in Congress was really responding to the black invitation to make this a community of "friends and fellow-countrymen." Nevertheless, the action against the Confederate states was important, in line with the requests of the black conventions, offering a source of hope for a more humane approach to the Reconstruction of the South and a recognition of the black demands for true freedom and community.[14]

On the other hand, no less a national leader than Gen. Ulysses S. Grant, the hero of Appomattox, offered another kind of response to the black struggle for a new America. In the last month of the year, Grant made a perfunctory tour of the South for Andrew Johnson. One of the issues on his agenda was the future of black soldiers in the volatile South. In Grant's opinion, there was no doubt about what and where their future should be, especially in regard to the life of their people:

The good of the country, and economy, require that the force kept in the interior, where there are many freedmen . . . should all be white troops. The reasons for this are obvious without mentioning many of them. The presence of black troops, lately slaves, demoralizes labor, both by their advice and by furnishing in their camps a resort for the freedmen for long distances around. White troops generally excite no opposition, and therefore a small number of them can maintain order in a given district. Colored troops must be kept in bodies sufficient to defend themselves.[15]

Inadvertently, Grant's conclusions provided a vivid summary of the contribution of race, politics, and economics to the white American refusal of "the right hand of fellowship." To accept that offer would mean letting go of too much that was precious. Meanwhile his recommendation to remove the black troops from the South was both an acknowledgment of their actual and potential power and a serious blow to the freedom movement.

By then, the mustering out process had already begun, exposing hundreds of thousands of people to their enemies. But the struggle did not stop: the river continued, because black people could not be mustered out of its flow. Men and women like Tunis Campbell, Patience Johnson, Ulysses Houston, and Dr. Thomas Bayne could not be discharged, for they were permanent soldiers. Aaron A. Bradley, looking like a professor with his wire-framed glasses, orating like an actor and packing a derringer, was a soldier. As the Blacks and Blues were forced to march away, he kept organizing in Savannah and the surrounding "Gechee" areas, telling the people to take up arms, if necessary, to save their land. Trying to stop such dangerous, seditious, and economically radical talk, the army closed down his school. But Bradley could not be mustered out that way, for he carried his case right to the top, wiring President Johnson: "My private school . . . was ordered discontinued . . . because I spoke against your reconstruction. Sir, will you please open my school." Then, ultimately with the involvement of General Howard himself, Bradley was arrested and another telegram went to Johnson, this time from the Christian General: "A man named Bradley has been making speeches at S[avannah] to the colored people criticising President's policy, advising Negroes not to make contracts except at point of bayonet, and to disobey your orders; have arrested him, he does not deny charges, proof conclusive." Bradley was convicted and jailed for a short time, but he was soon back in the heart of the struggle, bold and flamboyant as ever.[16]

There were soldiers of freedom like Bradley embedded everywhere in the life and flow of the newly freed black community. In those hard and beautiful times of crossing over, they continually supported, sustained, and challenged their people. Though their external appearance might vary, though they were obviously endowed with the usual supply of weaknesses and eccentricities, internally they were marked by an essential courage, an unflagging commitment to the cause of their people and a powerful sense of vision of the new land. Along with thousands of others, known and unknown, they bore the heritage of the long struggle, the traditions of the ever-moving river. They helped a pilgrim people to remember the grand procession of men and women who had nurtured the hope of the coming time in every generation.

Such men and women were present, scattered from Virginia to Texas, from California to Massachusetts, when the historic word finally came. On December 18, 1865, the Thirteenth Amendment to the Constitution of the United States ended its difficult journey through Congress and the state legislatures and was finally proclaimed for all the people to hear. After so long a time of waiting and praying, of hoping and dying, the central announcement now seemed passive, compressed, and strangely flat: "Neither slavery nor involuntary servitude . . . shall exist within the United States, or any place subject to their jurisdiction."

> *My Lord!*
> *No more!*
> *No more auction block for me.*
> *No more.*
> *No more driver's lash for me.*
> *Many thousands gone.*

In spite of all the troubles, in spite of all the trials, in spite of all the betrayals of the year of jubilee, it was still a time to shout, to sing and pray and dance. No more! So the black celebrations went on into the night of liberation, but as usual the free people who rejoiced were doing much more than extolling the actions of a Congress or a group of individual states. Far more deeply ran the river. In the midst of a harsh new struggle, they were celebrating their God, seeing again his divine chariots of vengeance, feeling the power of his terrible swift sword. Near the end of this cruel and beautiful year of transition, they were celebrating themselves, remembering all the meetings and petitions, all the conventions and boycotts, all the women in their new bonnets carrying parasols and freedom signs, all the men marching out to vote when the world said they had no vote, all the ears cut off for the love of freedom, all the lives lost on this pilgrim way.

Even as the forces of oppression began to be marshaled again, the black community was celebrating all its former crippled members who now rowed boats and raised corn, and testified to new birth. In the midst of fear and violence and orders for mustering out, they were celebrating the black soldiers who tried in war and peace to guarantee their freedom; they were holding on to the black children who embodied this hope in their lives and in their songs. Even as presidents, generals, and editors turned deaf ears, black folk were celebrating the ways they had stood together to support one another in the harsh struggles for land, to hear each other in the town meetings and prayer meetings, in the legislatures on the Sea Islands and in the mass meetings in the big churches of Norfolk, Charleston, and Nashville. While white men and women rose up again to deny them their freedom, while representatives in Congress discussed their freedom, black families rejoiced in the night, recognizing the life-long mixture of bitter and sweet, of birth and death, determined not to be turned back, refusing to lose hope. For they were celebrating themselves.

This new amendment was their creation. These were the words that the waiting, struggling, dying, living community had heard in the first guns of dawn in Charleston harbor. These were the words they had written in all the marching and singing, in all the fighting and praying, through all the running and falling, with all the poisons and fire. These were the words they had brought up from the terror-filled depths. No more. This was the amendment they had shaped with their hopes, written in the flow of their blood.

Always the blood, blood of life, blood of death. Knowing that more would be shed, they were remembering the blood streaking the waves of the Atlantic, remembering the blood on Nat Turner's dying ground, remembering the blood in the tracks of the Underground Railroad, remembering the blood on a thousand thousand white hands, remembering the blood crying out from the battlegrounds of the Freedom War, blood so freely shed in that year of jubilee, blood for the remission of sins. Many thousands gone.

Near the close of that chaotic, brooding year, black people were remembering the past and moving forward, committing their lives to all the unfinished struggles of the river. With the crossing over just begun, with the requisites of true freedom still beyond their grasp, still beyond the vision of white America, with fierce but needful battles just ahead, black people were celebrating their God and themselves, for a great victory had surely been won. It had been a brutal, magnificent struggle, reaching over more than three centuries, over thousands of miles, from the sunburned coasts of the homeland to the cold and dreary trenches near Petersburg, Fort Wagner, and Milliken's Bend. And they were the soldiers, their people were the soldiers, the singers, the petitioners, the creators of the new time.

So as they sang and prayed and cried into the night, the night when slavery was officially ended in the United States, black people were celebrating themselves, honoring their forebears, holding up their children to the midnight sun, praising the mysterious, delivering God who had made it possible for them, and all who lived before them, to come so far and stand so firm in the deep red flooding of Jordan.

Acknowledgments

Coming to the end of a work like this, I recognize more clearly than ever before the fundamental inadequacy of the traditional word "acknowledgments." Somehow the term does not quite embrace all the profound sense of gratitude, grace, and simple awe that fills me as I think of all the people and forces that have marvelously conspired to make this book a reality at last.

In the Introduction, I identify some of the individuals whose life and work, whose influence and example have been of particular help to me. However, there is more that needs to be said. First, even at the risk of redundancy, I am moved to reaffirm the obvious fact that this entire undertaking would have been inconceivable without the African-American people whose persistent struggle for freedom is its central subject matter and raison d'être. Their lives, their hope, their failures and triumphs are the deepest sources of inspiration and authentication for all that I have done here. I shall be forever grateful for the privilege of participating in and interpreting the experiences of this evolving, transformative community.

At the same time, the level and quality of my personal engagement in movement, research, reflection, and writing would have been impossible without the loving and sacrificial commitment of my own immediate family: Rosemarie, my wife and precious companion for more than two decades; Rachel Sojourner, our daughter and inspiration, and Jonathan DuBois, our beloved son. Sharing, forgiving, holding on through all the hard times, ministering, enduring absences, healing, hoping, encouraging, persisting, searching through libraries, reading hundreds of pages of manuscript, offering critical insights, loving, always loving, they have given more to the completion of this work than any words can convey. My thankfulness to them and for them is boundless.

Also, even though they were not so aware of or actively engaged in my work, I am deeply grateful for the faith in me that I have continued to feel from my mother, Mabel Harding, and—even beyond the bounds of death—from my uncle, Gordon McDonald Broome. (And yes, I am grateful, too, to Graham Harding, wherever he may be, for helping to bring me into this world.)

Constantly surrounding and interwoven with our immediate household has always been a nurturing, extended family of blood relatives and others who have supported me, our family, and this demanding work in many ways: Charles Freeney, nephew and comrade, offering great assistance as professional archivist and builder of fallen spirits; Lee, Harvey, Walter, and Mildred Dozier, graciously sharing the substance of their lives and the complete openness of their home; Gloria Jackson James, generously, faithfully serving as secretary and research assistant; Alma and Louis Campbell, Sue Verrett, Alberta Freeney, Norma Jackson, Dock ("Son") Freeney, Jr., Ella and Dock Freeney, sharing our burdens on many essential levels.

These are the core of a helping, supporting community of men and women whose totality can never be fully encompassed here, but who must still be recognized and thanked, even in the most imperfect and inadequate of ways. Foremost among them is Howard Thurman, that magnificent American mystic, whose belief in me, my family, and my vocation, whose deep grounding in the river and in the spirit were a source of profound strength and inspiration through the long years of this work. It was this surrogate father and spiritual guide who sought out his close friend, Dr. Daniel Collins, a vice-president at Harcourt Brace Jovanovich, and urged him to read an earlier version of *There Is a River,* thereby setting in motion the immediate train of events that led to this publication. Since his death this spring, Thurman's supporting presence has continued with me as a powerful reality.

Among the living members of the far-flung, encircling, nurturing community, I count with special gratitude George and Farrell Thomas, constantly sharing themselves, their home, and their marvelous extended family. From the outset of this work, C. L. R. James and St. Clair Drake have offered special encouragement and important criticism. Ella Baker also provided early inspiration, advice, and support. Herman Blake has been generous in every sense of the word. Howard Dodson and Pat Daly, through their creative leadership of the Institute of the Black World, helped set me free to work on this book in the knowledge that the organization was in excellent hands. Also, although they are officially counted as my publishers, I cannot help but identify Dan Collins and William Jovanovich as part of the community of support behind this endeavor. For each of them has taken a personal interest in me, my family, and the work, that goes far beyond the requirements of any professional relationship. This has been a most important source of strength.

Others who have been part of the community of concern have been Tandy and Thulani Gcabashe and their children, James and Grace Boggs, James and Leola McFarland, and other members of the National Organization for an American Revolution; Bob and Janet Moses, Bill Davis, Katherine Dunham, Lerone and Gloria Bennett, C. T. and Octavia Vivian, Earl Thorpe, Carl Holman, Hoyt Fuller, Lamont Yeakey, Tom and Gloria Gordon, Tran Van Dinh, Walter and Yvonne Hutchins, Spencer Weston, Robert Harris, James Turner, Sonia Sanchez, John Oliver Killens, Mack Jones, Haki Mhadibuti and the Institute for Positive Education, George Lamming, Kalamu and Tiara Ya Salaam, Dewitt Dykes, Lucius Outlaw, Allan Ballard, Wilfred Cartey, Len Jeffries, and Charles Long.

As I consider such a sustaining network, two groups must be mentioned, in spite of the fact that my association with them began before the manuscript was conceived. One is the Peace Section of the Mennonite Central Committee, under the leadership of Elmer Neufeld, who originally provided the support that made it possible for Rosemarie and me to be present in the South at the height of the Freedom Movement. The other group goes back further, goes in deeper; it is that gathering of men, women, and children, living and dead, who were my initial nurturing community at Victory Tabernacle Seventh Day Christian Church in Harlem. I am grateful to them for my earliest conscious immersion in the collective hope and religion of the black community, grateful for first learning among them that "There is a river . . ."

In addition to this larger, sustaining circle of friends, relatives, and coworkers, there were many persons who carried out a number of specific tasks that were central to the development of the work. For instance, in addition to the family members who helped with the research, there were a number of assistants who performed crucial functions. They include Willie Paul Berrien, Michael Fisher, Bryce Smith, Christine Coleman, Kenneth Dossar, Vincent Jubilee, James Early, Patricia Paden, Raymond Trent, Keith Lashley, Iris Eaton, Judith Harkison, Lee Owens, and Jonathan Hibbs.

I am also indebted to the many librarians who have been such a valuable source of aid. Among these were Miles Jackson and Casper Jordan at the Trevor Arnett Library of the Atlanta University Center; Wilson Flemister, librarian of the Interdenominational Theological Center in Atlanta; Jean Hutson, Ernest Kaiser, and Stanton Biddle at the

Schomburg Center in Harlem; Jessie Carney Smith, Ann Shockley and
Vallie Pursley, at the Fisk University Library; Dorothy Porter and Michael
Winston, directors of the Moorland Spingarn Research Collection at
Howard University; and Sylvia Render of the Library of Congress;
Joy Allsop with the Richard B. Moore Collection at the Center for
Multi-Racial Studies at the Barbados campus of the University of the West
Indies; Louise Coursey, especially during her tenure as librarian of the
Moton Center for Independent Study in Philadelphia; and Yuki Brinton,
librarian at Pendle Hill. In addition, I received significant assistance
from the staffs of the libraries at Union Seminary, Duke University, the
University of North Carolina, Yale University, the University of the
West Indies at Cave Hill, Barbados and at Mona, Jamaica, as well as at
Temple University, the University of Pennsylvania, Swarthmore College,
the University of Denver, the University of New Mexico at Albuquerque,
and the Henry Regenstein Library at the University of Chicago.

A group of committed and concerned people who participated in this
collective project as typists made a major contribution to the effort. They
include Sharon Bourke (of whom more will be said), Barbara Harkins,
Sandra Randolph Norris, Farrel Thomas, Olivia Richardson, Gloria
Jackson James, and Senona Shields. I was consistently gratified by their
skillful attention to detail and substance, which made my own work so
much easier.

At various points in the evolution of the work I have needed (or
thought I needed) a place to be apart from the demands of my all-too-
active life, or a base of operations while doing research in institutions
away from home. Unfailingly, through the kindness of others, I have
found such settings. I am therefore especially grateful to the friends and
loved ones who helped in this way, including: John and Eugenia Clarke,
who consistently opened their home in Harlem to me and my family;
Andrew and Amy Billingsley at Morgan State University, who gave so
much of their life and their home; Bill and Francis Pauley, Andy and
Jean Young, and George and Farrel Thomas, my Atlanta friends who
freely shared their living space with me. I bear a special debt of gratitude
to the beloved community at the Monastery of the Holy Spirit, near
Conyers, Georgia, who put aside their normal rules and offered me sustenance of many kinds (including great Sunday morning basketball
games).

When he was president of Fisk University, James Lawson graciously
made it possible for me to live and work there for a summer. Will and
Brenda Campbell welcomed me to their land and their hearts in Mt. Juliet,
Tennessee. Emory and Dorothy Guy of West Mount Airy in Philadelphia
also shared their home with me. I am grateful, too, for the time our

family was able to spend in the homes of Robert Lynn and Staughton and Alice Lynd while I was doing research. Nor can I forget the special kindness of Ella Baker and her niece, Jacqueline Brockington, in making their family home in North Carolina available to me. Over the past two years, the Swarthmore Friends Meeting has generously provided me with a spacious working area.

During the closing phases of the work it has also been very good to experience the life of the unique educational and religious community called Pendle Hill. Those who are responsible for its leadership have consistently made many helpful efforts to accommodate the special needs of space and time connected with this task. I am especially grateful to Parker Palmer, Ed Sanders, Janet Shepherd, Barbara Parsons, Robin Harper, as well as all the rest of the Pendle Hill community for their cooperation and support, and I treasure the special beauty that Sudarshan and Sita Kapur and their family have brought into my life at Pendle Hill.

In every place that I have worked, whether at home or in one of the outposts, I have been accompanied and sustained by the creations of a group of black artists whose music and graphic art have provided great nourishment for my spirit. Foremost among these have been musicians John Coltrane, Aretha Franklin, Otis Redding, and Nina Simone, as well as Herman Kofi Bailey the artist. There were times when I simply could not have made it through without them.

Over the years, as this work has developed, I have been blessed also with three magnificent editors, each of them contributing a special gift at the time it was most needed. Sharon Bourke, who worked with me at the Institute of the Black World, voluntarily took on the double responsibility of typing one of the earlier drafts of the book and then editing it with a sympathetic, informed, and creatively critical spirit. Phil Petrie, who was at William Morrow when we first met, encouraged me to write from the depths of my own sensibility and commitment; and even after he was no longer officially responsible for the manuscript, Phil continued to offer support and advice. Finally, when William Jovanovich took a personal interest in the manuscript and assigned Drenka Willen to work with me, none of us could know how long and complex the journey toward publication would be, nor how this Serbian-born editor and her Afro-American author would work together. But this turned out to be a magnificent choice—at least for me—and at every moment along the way I have been profoundly grateful for Drenka's rare gifts of critical intelligence and gentle persistence, and for her humanistic vision that encouraged the expression of my own. The work is unquestionably stronger because of such persons and their gifts. I consider their presence at critical moments of the book's development as an evolving act of grace.

I am, of course, especially appreciative of all those persons, organizations, and institutions, whose belief in the work I was doing helped to provide the funds that I needed to carry it forward. I feel a particular sense of thanks for Charles Williams of the Lily Endowment who was an early and generous supporter of the Institute of the Black World and of my own work. So, too, Carol Bernstein and Robert Browne of the DJB Foundation, and James Joseph, Stanley Wise, and Ivanhoe Donnelson of the Cummins Engine Foundation were very helpful at an early stage. Eldridge Macmillan of the Southern Education Foundation and Charles Cobb of the United Church of Christ more than once came to the aid of the Institute and helped me as well. Leslie Dunbar of the Field Foundation, Benjamin Payton of the Ford Foundation, Jeffrey Fields of the National Endowment for the Humanities, Victor Rabinowitz of the Rabinowitz Foundation, and Joel Colton of the Rockefeller Foundation all provided valuable assistance. I also appreciated the cooperative spirit with which William Chafe, Lawrence Goodwyn, and Thelma Kithcart supported my work as a Visiting Fellow of the Oral History Program at Duke University. It is important to note, too, that Barbara Moffatt and her colleagues in the Community Service Division of the American Friends Service Committee, as well as Aaron and Rosalyn Wallace, Walter and Yvonne Hutchins, Walter Dozier, and Andrew and Amy Billingsley, were especially helpful to me in times of serious financial emergency along the way.

Finally, I marvel at and appreciate the many persons who were willing to read this manuscript at various stages of its development. Their responses have been important sources of insight, correction, re-visioning and encouragement. Among these were C. L. R. James, St. Clair Drake, Ella Baker, Benjamin Quarles, Robert Hill, William Strickland, Howard Dodson, Eugene Genovese, Herbert Gutman, Michael Winston, Mary F. Berry, Earl Thorpe, Staughton Lynd, Harvey Cox, Howard Thurman, and Andrew Billingsley.

But I marvel most of all at the fact that this first volume is finally complete. When I consider the "many trials, snares and toils" through which it has come, I am amazed and convinced that the same renewing, transforming spirit that has moved in the river of our struggle has been graciously available to me, flowing through the lives of the sustaining community that has done so much to help bring this work into being. So I marvel, rejoice, and give thanks, looking forward to the continuing movement of creation, believing that the best is yet to come for us all.

Notes

CHAPTER 1: FROM THE SHORES OF AFRICA

1. Such names of ships are found throughout Elizabeth Donnan's invaluable *Documents Illustrative of the Slave Trade to America*, 4 vols. (1935; rpt. New York: Octagon Books, 1965).

2. Among a number of helpful sources for an understanding of the slave trade and particularly the process of collecting captives are Roger Anstey, *The Atlantic Slave Trade and British Abolition, 1760–1810* (Atlantic Highlands, N.J.: Humanities Press, 1975), especially pp. 20–66; K. G. Davies, *The Royal African Company* (London: Longmans, 1957), pp. 240ff; C. Duncan Rice, *The Rise and Fall of Black Slavery* (New York: Harper and Row, 1975), pp. 111–16; Basil Davidson, *The African Slave Trade* (Boston: Atlantic Little-Brown, 1961), especially Ch. 3; Daniel P. Mannix and Malcolm Cowley, *Black Cargoes: A History of the Atlantic Slave Trade* (New York: Penguin, 1962), Ch. 1, 4. An older and still important work is George E. Dow, *Slave Ships and Slaving* (1927; rpt. New York: Marine Research Society, 1970). In a more personal and often moving vein, Nathan Huggins, *Black Odyssey* (New York: Pantheon, 1977), pp. 1–56, has provided an important humanized version of the story.

3. Several illuminating general introductions to African life and history have become available during the last decade. Included among these are two works by Basil Davidson, *Africa: History of a Continent* (New York: Macmillan, 1972), and *The African Genius: An Introduction to Social and Cultural History* (Boston: Atlantic Monthly Press, 1970); also [Alvin M. Josephy, Jr., ed.], *The Horizon History of Africa* (New York: American Heritage, 1971). Though not a general history, Walter Rodney's incisive Marxist analysis in *How Europe Underdeveloped Africa* (Washington, D.C.: Howard University Press, 1974) is invaluable, especially Ch. 2.

4. The quotation is from Claude McKay's poem, "Outcast," in Wayne Cooper, ed., *The Passion of Claude McKay: Selected Prose and Poetry, 1912–1948* (New York: Schocken Books, 1973), p. 121.

5. There are several informative discussions of these early contacts and connections. Among the most valuable are A. Ade Boahen, "The Coming of the Europeans," in Josephy, *Horizon History*, pp. 305–27; Carlo M. Cipolla, *Guns, Sails and Empires* (New York: Funk & Wagnalls, 1965), pp. 21–89, 132–48; William H. McNeill, *The Rise of the West* (Chicago: University of Chicago Press, 1963), pp. 569–78 (McNeill's focus on European "pugnacity" is intriguing); Rodney, *How Europe*, Ch. 3, 4; Eric Williams, *Capitalism and Slavery* (New York: Russell and Russell, 1961), pp. 30–50.

6. Some of the most incisive discussions of this overworked issue are found in Davidson, *African Genius*, Part 4; Davidson, "Slaves or Captives? Some Notes on Fantasy and Fact," in *Key Issues in the Afro-American Experience*, Nathan J. Huggins, Martin Kilson, and Daniel M. Fox, eds., 2 vols. (New York: Harcourt Brace Jovanovich, 1971), I, 54–73; Rodney, "African Slavery

and Other Forms of Social Oppression on the Upper Guinea Coast," *Journal of African History*, 7 (1966), 431–43.

7. One of the most recent discussions of the ways in which Native Americans, Europeans, and Africans were approached as a labor force is in Peter H. Wood, *Black Majority* (New York: Knopf, 1974), pp. 37–62. Wood focuses on South Carolina. The Virginia experience has been explored by Edmund S. Morgan, *American Slavery, American Freedom* (New York: W. W. Norton, 1975).

8. The standard monograph on white servitude in the colonies is Abbot E. Smith, *Colonists in Bondage* (1947; rpt. Gloucester, Mass.: Peter Smith, 1965). For important treatments since then, see Lerone Bennett, *The Shaping of Black America* (Chicago: Johnson Publishing, 1975), pp. 18–57; Morgan, *American Slavery*, pp. 108–79, 216–18; and Winthrop D. Jordan, *White Over Black* (Chapel Hill: University of North Carolina Press, 1968), pp. 52–95. Much insight on this subject was presented even earlier by E. Williams in the first chapter of *Capitalism*.

9. On the development of the slave trade, see Davies, *Royal African*, pp. 213–90; Davidson, *African Slave Trade*, pp. 53–68; Mannix and Cowley, Ch. 2, 3; E. Williams, *Capitalism*, pp. 30–50. Malachi Postlewayt, the eighteenth-century economist, is quoted in Harold Baron, "The Demand for Black Labor," *Radical America*, 2 (Mar./Apr., 1971), 2–6. The profitability of slavery and its relationship to European economic, political, and social development is still under debate. For a sample of some positions see C. L. R. James, *The Black Jacobins* (1938; rpt. New York: Vintage Books, 1963), pp. 45–61; Rodney, *How Europe*, Ch. 3; E. Williams, *Capitalism*, passim; Robert P. Thomas and Richard N. Bean, "The Fishers of Men: Profits of the Slave Trade," *Journal of Economic History*, 34 (Dec. 1974), 885–914.

10. The destructive effect of the slave trade on African life and culture is noted in Davies, *Royal African*, pp. 278–84; Josephy, *Horizon History*, pp. 305–27; Anstey, *Atlantic*, pp. 69–88, 404; Rice, *Rise and Fall*, pp. 17–21. See also Rodney, "African Slavery," pp. 431–33, and his "Upper Guinea and the Significance of the Origins of Africans Enslaved in the New World," *Journal of Negro History* (hereafter cited as *JNH*), 54 (Oct. 1969), 327–45; also Davidson, "Slaves or Captives?"

11. Quoted in Mannix and Cowley, p. 108. No extensive work has yet been done on the struggles for black freedom during the middle passage. Two helpful essays are Lorenzo Greene, "Mutiny on the Slave Ships," *Phylon*, 5 (Jan. 1944), 346–54, and Darold D. Wax, "Negro Resistance to the Early American Slave Trade," *JNH*, 51 (Jan. 1966), 1–15. The starting point for any new major study would still be Elizabeth Donnan's monumental *Documents*.

12. Mannix and Cowley, p. 108.

13. Readily accessible works which focus on the middle passage include Davidson, *African Slave Trade*; James Pope-Hennessy, *Sins of the Fathers* (New York: Knopf, 1968); Thomas Howard, ed., *Black Voyage: Eyewitness Accounts of the Atlantic Slave Trade* (Boston: Little, Brown, 1971); Mannix and Cowley. For suggestions on the deadly costs of the trade to the largely white crew members, see Philip D. Curtin, *The Atlantic Slave Trade: A Census* (Madison: University of Wisconsin Press, 1969), pp. 282–86; contemporary testimonies on the same point are in Howard, Ch. 3.

14. Quoted in Donnan, II, 359.

15. *Ibid.*, I, 438, 443.

16. See Mannix and Cowley, p. 104.

17. Donnan, III, 45.

18. *Ibid.*, 226. (One can only speculate about this Captain Tomba's possible relation to a leader with the same name among the Baga people of West Africa about the same period. He is briefly mentioned in Rodney, *How Europe*, p. 80.)

19. Donnan, III, 226. This cannibalism did not die out among white oppressors. In many American lynchings, blacks experienced it well into the twentieth century in various tormented forms. For one example, see Ralph Ginzburg, ed., *100 Years of Lynchings* (New York: Lancer Books, 1962), p. 223.

20. Donnan, III, 226.

21. Greene, "Mutiny," p. 349; Donnan, II, 486; Wood, *Black Majority*, pp. 221–22.

22. Benjamin Brawley, *A Social History of the American Negro* (1921; rpt. New York: Macmillan, 1970), p. 43; Donnan, IV, 374.

23. Donnan, II, 354–55.

24. For instance, see Harvey Wish, "American Slave Insurrections Before 1861," *JNH*, 22 (July 1937), pp. 299–320.

25. Davidson, *African Slave Trade*. Mannix and Cowley and Pope-Hennessy offer summary accounts of the voyages. Note also McNeill's brief statement on the role of diseases in the European conquests: *Rise of the West*, pp. 571–73. See as well Curtin's cautious statement, *Atlantic Slave Trade*, p. 270.

26. Mannix and Cowley, p. 114.

27. The *Young Hero* event is reported in Mannix and Cowley, pp. 114–16. A similar story of the mournful nighttime songs appears in Robert Dale Owen, *The Wrong of Slavery* (Philadelphia, 1864), p. 52. The hymn in question was composed by one of the most famous of the Christian slaving captains, John Newton: Mannix and Cowley, pp. 133–37.

28. Donnan, II, 281–82.

29. *Ibid.*, I, 456–57.

30. *Ibid.*; my emphasis.

31. For example, Mannix and Cowley, pp. 117–22. In addition to other suicides cited below, pp. 18–20, note also the account of the African, Olaudah Equiano (Gustavas Vassa), in Philip D. Curtin, ed., *Africa Remembered: Narratives by West Africans from the Era of the Slave Trade* (Madison: University of Wisconsin Press, 1967), p. 96.

32. Howard, *Black Voyage*, p. 94.

33. Mannix and Cowley, p. 118.

34. Donnan, II, 361 n. Also Mannix and Cowley, p. 110.

35. Donnan, II, 360–61.

36. *Ibid.*

37. *Ibid.*, III, 213. The same incident is recorded in a slightly different form by Greene, "Mutiny," p. 352.

38. Donnan, II, 323–24.

39. *Ibid.*

40. *Ibid.*, III, 374–75.

41. Mannix and Cowley, pp. 110–11.

CHAPTER 2: AMERICAN BONDAGE, AMERICAN FREEDOM

1. Quoted in Roi Ottley and William Weatherby, eds., *The Negro in New York* (New York Public Library, Oceana Publications, 1967), p. 12.

2. Paul Jacobs and Saul Landau, eds., *To Serve the Devil*, 2 vols. (New York: Vintage Books, 1971), I, 44–45. An important account of this disputed event, including contemporary Dutch documents, appears in Allen Trelease, *Indian Affairs in Colonial New York* (Ithaca, N.Y.: Cornell University Press, 1960), pp. 71–74. On the overall history of the encounter between the Native Americans and the newcomers, one of the most helpful recent studies is Gary B. Nash, *Red, White and Black: The Peoples of Early America* (Englewood Cliffs, N.J.: Prentice Hall, 1974). Francis Jennings, *The Invasion of America* (New York: W. W. Norton, 1976), provides a stern and incisive examination of the New England phase of those early, bloody meetings.

3. Such last-minute struggles are cited in Donnan, II, 460–85. Mannix and Cowley, p. 127, mention some of the suicides at the end of the journey. Two helpful sources for West Indian enslavement are Richard S. Dunn, *Sugar and Slaves* (Institute of Early American History and Culture, Williamsburg, Va.: University of North Carolina Press, 1972), and Carl Bridenbaugh, *No Peace Beyond the Line* (New York: Oxford University Press, 1972).

4. There is still an important ongoing debate over the nature of the black (and laboring white) status in seventeenth-century America. For a time, Jordan's *White Over Black*, especially pp. 44–98, had been considered a standard treatment. During the 1970s that work came under renewed scrutiny; for instance, it was the main subject of a special session on "Sex, Racism and Democracy: Alternatives to the Jordan Hypothesis," during the Nov. 1974 Southern Historical Society meeting. See *Journal of Southern History*, 41 (Feb. 1975), 67–68. A significant new wrestling with the subject then appeared in Morgan's *American Slavery*. The major statement from a black historian is found in Bennett, *The Shaping of Black America*, pp. 5–80 —a provocative and important treatment.

5. One of the best collections of the slavery-related laws is John C. Hurd, *The Law of Freedom and Bondage in the United States*, 2 vols. (Boston, 1858), especially I, 228–311. Another significant source is Helen G. Catterall, ed., *Judicial Cases Concerning American Slavery and the Negro*, 5 vols. (1926–37; rpt. New York: Octagon Books, 1968), I, 53–61; IV, 1–3, 445–58. See also Samuel Shepherd, ed, *The Statutes at Large of Virginia*, 3 vols. (1835; rpt. New York: Arno Press, 1970). A helpful survey of the legal developments is found in Paul C. Palmer, "Servant Into Slave: The Evolution of the Legal Status of the Negro Laborer in Colonial Virginia," *South Atlantic Quarterly*, 65 (Summer 1966), 355–70. Also M. E. Sirmans, "The Legal Status of the Slave in South Carolina, 1670–1740," *Journal of Southern History*, 28 (Nov. 1962), 426–73; Jordan, *White Over Black*, pp. 71–98. Unfortunately, the best-focused collection of these laws deals primarily with eighteenth- and nineteenth-century examples: William Goddell, *The American Slave Code* (New York, 1853).

6. John Blassingame, *The Slave Community: Plantation Life in the Antebellum South* (New York: Oxford University Press, 1973), p. 29; Hurd, I, 234, 250, 253, 306; Miles Mark Fisher, *Negro Slave Songs in the United States* (1953; rpt. New York: Citadel Press, 1968), p. 29.

7. See for example the Virginia law on Christian baptism and continued slavery in Catterall, *Judicial*, I, 57; also P. Palmer, "Servant," pp. 360–61.

8. In the "Fundamental Constitutions," Locke said, "every freeman of Carolina shall have absolute power and authority over his negro slaves, of what opinion or religion soever." Quoted in John Hope Franklin, *From Slavery to Freedom*, 3rd ed. (New York: Knopf, 1967), p. 77. Morgan, *American Slavery*, p. 381, provides an interesting commentary on the inadequacies of Locke's lauded liberalism where poor English whites were concerned. For an important discussion of the class tensions among whites, see not only Morgan and Wood but also T. H. Breen, "A Changing Labor Force and Race Relations in Virginia, 1660–1710," *Journal of Social History*, 7 (Fall 1973), 3–18.

9. The class conflict between the white landowners and the laboring classes, especially in colonial Virginia, is a major theme of Morgan's *American Slavery*. At times he seems hard-pressed to follow the logic of his own arguments, and his rather tortured and ambiguous treatment of the issue is challenged and clarified by the more direct approach of Theodore Allen, " 'They Would Have Destroyed Me': Slavery and the Origins of Racism," *Radical America*, 9 (May/June 1975), 41–63.

10. On runaways and outlyers, Herbert Aptheker's seminal essay, "Maroons Within the Present Limits of the United States," *JNH*, 24 (Apr. 1939), 167–84, is crucial. For the runaways in colonial South Carolina, see Wood, *Black Majority*, pp. 239–68. A hemispheric perspective on the runaway/outlyer/maroon experience is provided through the essays in Richard Price, ed., *Maroon Societies: Rebel Slave Communities in the Americas* (New York: Anchor Books, 1973), beginning with Price's excellent introductory essay, pp. 1–30. (Aptheker's *JNH* article cited above is also included in Price's volume, pp. 151–67.) Also see Hurd, I, 228–311.

11. Herbert Aptheker, *American Negro Slave Revolts* (1943; rpt. New York: International Publishers, 1963), pp. 165–66. Breen, "Changing Labor Force," pp. 9–12; Wilcomb E. Washburn, *The Governor and the Rebel* (Chapel Hill: University of North Carolina Press, 1957), pp. 80, 88, 209; Morgan, *American Slavery*, pp. 250–70; T. Allen, "They Would Have," pp. 44–45.

12. Aptheker, *Slave Revolts*, pp. 166–67. On Mingoe, see Aptheker, "Maroons," p. 168. It appears that the enslaved people often used their funerals for certain African cultic renewals, as well as other activities which were best carried on beyond the sweep of white surveillance. See Howell M. Henry, *The Police Control of the Slave in South Carolina* (Emory, Va.: The author, 1914), pp. 143–44. See below, p. 55, for another creative nineteenth-century use of the black funeral.

13. Andros is quoted in Aptheker, *Slave Revolts*, p. 167. The estimates of Virginia's black population at the end of the seventeenth century vary from 10 to 30 percent of the whites. See Adele Hast, "The Legal Status of the Negro in Virginia, 1705–1765," *JNH*, 54 (July 1969), 218; Breen, "Changing Labor Force," p. 16. See also Morgan's tentative extrapolations from the experience of two Virginia counties, *American Slavery*, pp. 420–23. I incline toward the higher figure.

14. The developing black presence in Saint Augustine is discussed in Russell Garvin, "The Free Negro in Florida Before the Civil War," *Florida Historical Quarterly*, 46 (July 1967), 1; Wood, *Black Majority*, pp. 50–51, 239; Philip S.

Foner, *History of Black Americans* (Westport, Conn.: Greenwood Press, 1975), I, 261.

15. In this early period even more than in later times, we depend heavily on reports and observations by white governing authorities for our picture of the movements of the African peoples. This carries the danger of much distortion, of course. But it also reveals much about the significance of the black struggle and its effects on those who would suppress it. Lord Cornbury is quoted in Ottley and Weatherby, *The Negro in New York*, p. xvii.

16. For other examples of black resistance and rebellion, see Catterall, *Judicial*, I, 77–79; IV, 11, 12, 31, 355; Aptheker, *Slave Revolts*, pp. 162–71. The New York rebellion is reported in Kenneth Scott, "The Slave Insurrection in New York in 1712," *New York Historical Society Quarterly*, 45 (Jan. 1961), 43–74.

17. Scott, "Slave Insurrection," pp. 46–47. This use of African rituals in the struggle for freedom in America continued into the twentieth century, marked for instance by the name of a post–World War I black revolutionary organization, the African Blood Brotherhood. On the ABB, see Theodore G. Vincent, *Black Power and the Garvey Movement* (Berkeley, Calif.: Ramparts Press, 1971), pp. 74–85.

18. The Boston incident is cited in P. Foner, *History*, p. 266.

19. Wood, *Black Majority*, pp. 298–301.

20. *Ibid.*, p. 274; T. Allen, "They Would Have," p. 57.

21. Accounts of Samba's conspiracy appear in Willie Lee Rose, ed., *A Documentary History of Slavery in North America* (New York: Oxford University Press, 1976), pp. 104–05, as well as in St. Clair Drake, "Black Nationalism and White Power," Ch. 15 of an unpublished manuscript in my possession. For the South Carolina incidents, see Wood, *Black Majority*, pp. 243, 298–301.

22. Donnan, IV, 132. It is interesting to note the assumption by Byrd—following his Cataline reference—that it would take a free white leader to give direction to black revolt in America. That belief did not die easily, living into the 1940s in the writing of an outstanding black Marxist, Oliver Cromwell Cox. See his discussion of the need of white leadership in *Caste, Class and Race* (1948; rpt. New York: Monthly Review Press, 1959), pp. 571–73.

23. The best and most recent account of the Stono uprising appears in Wood, *Black Majority*, pp. 308–26. There the rebellion is well placed within the larger context of black struggle and white repression in Carolina. (Wood, by the way, finds the name Jemmy most consistent with the documents.) Also Aptheker, *Slave Revolts*, pp. 187–88; William F. Cheek, *Black Resistance Before the Civil War* (Beverly Hills, Calif.: Glencoe Press, 1970), pp. 105–06.

24. This tradition of boldly marching black men continued in the history of black struggle; see below, pp. 113–14. On the larger, international scene, one also finds striking examples, especially in peasant uprisings. Eric J. Hobsbawn, *Primitive Rebels* (New York: W. W. Norton, 1965), pp. 66, 78, 104, 152, 160, is especially helpful here.

25. Wood, pp. 317–19; Aptheker, *Slave Revolts*, pp. 187–88.

26. Wood, pp. 285–307, 318–26; John Oliver Killens, ed., *The Trial Record of Denmark Vesey* (Boston: Beacon Press, 1970), p. 157; Catterall, IV, 35. Regarding white vigilance, see Sirmans, "Legal Status," pp. 426–73; Morgan, *American Slavery*, pp. 14–29; and Wood, pp. 271–84.

27. Daniel Horsmanden, *The New York Conspiracy* (1744; rpt. Boston: Beacon

Press, 1971), pp. i–xxv. The modern introduction to this work by Thomas J. Davis is enlightening.

28. On the plans for a black governor, see *ibid.*, pp. 41–42. The list of names appears on pp. 467–73 of that volume. A number of writers have claimed that there was no conspiracy, merely a series of unconnected events. This view, with some modification, is put forward by Ferenc M. Szasz, "The New York Slave Revolt of 1741: A Re-Examination," *New York History*, 48 (July 1967), 215–30. Szasz says that the criminal activities were more likely class-motivated acts directed by blacks and whites against the wealthy settlers. Even if such an interpretation proved correct, it would still not remove the black actions from the struggle for freedom and new definitions. Rather, it would simply remind us of the alliances between black and white servants and slaves in those days. Information on the New Jersey situation is in the *Boston Evening Post* of July 6, 1741, quoted in P. Foner, *History*, I, 266.

29. Among the sources for eighteenth-century fugitives are: "Eighteenth Century Slaves as Advertised by Their Masters," *JNH*, 1 (Apr. 1916), 163–216; Lorenzo Greene, "The New England Negro as Seen in Advertisements for Runaway Slaves," *JNH*, 29 (Apr. 1944), 125–146; Daniel E. Meaders, "South Carolina Fugitives as Viewed Through Local Colonial Newspapers," *JNH*, 60 (Apr. 1975), 288–319; Edgar J. McManus, *Black Bondage in the North* (Syracuse: Syracuse University Press, 1973), pp. 108–24; Richard K. Murdoch, "The Seagrove-White Stolen Property Agreement of 1797," *Georgia Historical Quarterly*, 42 (Sept. 1958), 258–76.

30. "Eighteenth Century Slaves," pp. 173–216; Wood, *Black Majority*, p. 250.

31. "Eighteenth Century Slaves," p. 177.

32. *Ibid.*, p. 210.

33. *Ibid.*, pp. 211–16.

34. On the uses of poisons, see Wood, *Black Majority*, pp. 289–292. Michael [Gerald W.] Mullin, ed., *American Negro Slavery* (New York: Harper and Row, 1976), p. 9, calls attention to the significant amount of "passive resistance," especially among the newly arrived Africans in the colonies. My own views on the essentially *active* nature of such resistance appear above, p. 19.

35. *Virginia Gazette*, January 25, 1770, cited in Mullin, *American Negro*, pp. 94–95.

36. Catterall, *Judicial*, III, 424. On Captain Tomba, see above, pp. 12–13.

37. Lorenzo Greene, *The Negro in Colonial New England* (1942; rpt. New York: Atheneum, 1968), pp. 154–55; P. Foner, *History*, I, 277.

38. Catterall, *Judicial*, III, 6.

39. See Richard Price's stimulating essay in *Maroon Societies*, pp. 1–30.

40. Greene, "New England," p. 136; Wax, "Negro Resistance," pp. 14–15.

41. Wax, pp. 14–15.

42. See any of the several competent histories of the Revolutionary period, such as Lawrence H. Gipson, *The Coming of the Revolution, 1763–1775* (New York: Harper and Row, 1954), or John C. Miller, *Origins of the American Revolution* (Stanford, Calif.: Stanford University Press, 1959). For examples of the black activity, see Catterall, *Judicial*, I, 101–19. Also note Franklin, *From Slavery*, pp. 133–34, on the runaways and the estimate by Jefferson. In addition, see George W. Williams, *History of the Negro Race in America, 1619–*

1880, 2 vols. (1883; rpt. New York: Arno Press, 1968), I, 355–59; McManus, *Black Bondage*, pp. 152–59.

43. Williams, *History of Negro Race*, I, 339–62; Franklin, *From Slavery*, p. 132; Benjamin Quarles, *The Negro in the American Revolution* (Chapel Hill: University of North Carolina Press, 1961), pp. 13–32, 51–60.

44. An important discussion of the serious shortcomings of this action by the Continental Congress appears in Donald L. Robinson, *Slavery in the Structure of American Politics, 1765–1820* (New York: W. W. Norton, 1971), pp. 78–80, 470.

45. For examples of certain black uses of Revolutionary ideology and fervor, see Herbert Aptheker, ed., *Documentary History of the Negro People in the United States*, 3 vols. (New York: Citadel Press, 1951–74), I, 5–16; Quarles, *American Revolution*, pp. 43–50; Jordan, *White Over Black*, pp. 291–92; McManus, *Black Bondage*, p. 153. Important information and insights are also available in Arthur Zilversmit, "Quok Walker, Mumbet, and the Abolition of Slavery in Massachusetts," *William and Mary Quarterly*, 25 (Oct. 1968), 614–24; and Elaine MacEacheren, "Emancipation of Slavery in Massachusetts: A Reexamination, 1770–1790," *JNH*, 55 (Oct. 1970), 289–306.

46. Aptheker, *Documentary*, I, 9–10.

47. *Ibid.*, pp. 10–12.

48. Gayraud S. Wilmore, *Black Religion and Black Radicalism* (New York: Anchor Press, 1973), pp. 103–16; Franklin, *From Slavery*, p. 161; Carter G. Woodson, *The History of the Negro Church* (Washington, D.C.: Associated Publishers, 1945), pp. 40–45. Albert J. Raboteau, *Slave Religion* (New York: Oxford University Press, 1978), is also helpful here, especially pp. 96–150.

49. Richard Allen, *The Life Experience and Gospel Labors of the Rt. Rev. Richard Allen* (1793; rpt. New York: Abingdon Press, 1960), pp. 23–28. The best available modern treatment of Allen and his work will be found in Carol V. R. George, *Segregated Sabbaths: Richard Allen and the Emergence of Independent Black Churches, 1760–1840* (New York: Oxford University Press, 1973), especially pp. 49–59, on Allen's break with St. George's. See also John H. Bracey, August Meier, and Elliot Rudwick, eds., *Black Nationalism in America* (Indianapolis and New York: Bobbs-Merrill, 1970), pp. 9–10. For an interesting observation on Allen's larger conservatism, see St. Clair Drake, *The Redemption of Africa and Black Religion* (Chicago: Third World Press and Institute of the Black World, 1970), pp. 32–33.

50. Richard Allen, pp. 1–30; George, *Segregated*, pp. 22–59.

51. On Vesey and his connection to the African Methodist Church movement, see below, pp. 67–69.

52. Quoted in John H. Clarke and Vincent Harding, eds., *Slave Trade and Slavery* (New York: Holt-Rinehart, 1970), p. 58. See also my discussion above, p. 42.

53. Robinson, *Slavery*, pp. 81–83. It is revealing to compare the statements on slavery in the first draft of the Declaration with Jefferson's even more cautious earlier position in "A Summary View of the Rights of British America" (1774). The full text of both documents appears, among other places, in Richard N. Current and John A. Garraty, eds., *Words That Made American History*, 2 vols. (Boston: Little, Brown, 1965), 1, 165–82. For the comparison between Jefferson's draft of the Declaration and the final document, as well as his own comments on the struggle in the Continental Congress, see Adrienne Koch and

William Peden, eds., *The Life and Selected Writings of Thomas Jefferson* (New York: Modern Library, 1944), pp. 12–36. William Cohen, "Thomas Jefferson and the Problem of Slavery," *Journal of American History*, 55 (Dec. 1968), 503–26, is revealing on Jefferson's role as a slaveowner. Staughton Lynd's treatment of the larger issue is helpful in *Class Conflict, Slavery and the United States Constitution* (Indianapolis: Bobbs-Merrill, 1968), especially pp. 135–213.

54. Donnan, III, 358; Curtin, *Atlantic Slave Trade*, pp. 71–73, 210–14, 265–67. See also Mannix and Cowley, pp. 186–90; Robert W. Fogel and Stanley L. Engerman, *Time on the Cross* (Boston: Little, Brown, 1974), I, 86–89.

55. The story of the late-eighteenth-century movement toward emancipation is well summarized in Arthur Zilversmit, *The First Emancipation* (Chicago: University of Chicago Press, 1967), pp. 169–229. The philosophical and political roots of the post-1770 white American struggle against slavery are discussed in fascinating detail throughout David B. Davis, *The Problem of Slavery in the Age of Revolution, 1770–1823* (Ithaca, N.Y.: Cornell University Press, 1975). Unfortunately, Davis gives no serious attention to antislavery activities carried out by blacks.

56. The most important single study of the Haitian revolution is still James, *Black Jacobins*. Other suggestions on the significance of that revolution to the black struggle in America are offered below, pp. 46–47, 58–59. Also Aptheker, *Slave Revolts*, pp. 41–45; Jordan, *White Over Black*, pp. 377–91; and John E. Baur, "International Repercussions of the Haitian Revolution," *Americas*, 26 (Apr. 1970), 394–418, especially 403, 416–17. The quotations from Boukman and Toussaint appear in James, pp. 87, 90. The sense of radical break with the past, of religiously experienced new beginnings and new life, has continued to characterize many revolutionary settings and expressions. See for instance Frantz Fanon's inspirational peroration in his classic *The Wretched of the Earth* (New York: Grove Press), pp. 252–55.

57. Aptheker, *Slave Revolts*, p. 210; Cheek, *Black Resistance*, p. 101.

58. Marion G. McDougall, *Fugitive Slaves* (1891; rpt. New York: Bergman Publications, 1967), pp. 14–18, traces the movement from a constitutional article to the law of 1793. See also Robinson, *Slavery*, pp. 285–86, and Lynd, *Class Conflict*, pp. 135–213.

59. Aptheker, "Maroons," pp. 168–69; Franklin, *From Slavery*, pp. 133–34. There were also numerous occasions on which Indians were hired to capture black fugitives. The story of the "General" is in Aptheker, *Slave Revolts*, p. 217. On the larger issue of outlyers and their activities, see also Aptheker, "Additional Data on American Maroons," *JNH*, 23 (Oct. 1947), 452–60.

60. Aptheker, *Slave Revolts*, p. 218; Jordan, *White Over Black*, p. 392. In addition, Catterall's documents, in *Judicial*, reveal a constant refrain of arson and poison against white property and white lives. For the Haitian comparison, see James, *Black Jacobins*, p. 88.

61. A most stimulating treatment of the interpenetration of economic, political, and ethical issues involved in the crucial choices of the young nation may be found in William A. Williams, *The Contours of American History* (Chicago: Quadrangle Books, 1966), pp. 75–223. These are the same concerns raised throughout Robinson's *Slavery*.

62. For example, Sheldon H. Harris and Paul Cuffee, *Black America and the African Return* (New York: Simon and Schuster, 1972), pp. 13–72.

348

CHAPTER 3: REBELS, RESISTANTS, AND OUTLYERS

1. On the Louisiana Territory and its connection to San Domingo's revolution, see Franklin, *From Slavery*, p. 151, and W. E. B. DuBois, *The Suppression of the African Slave Trade* (1898; rpt. New York: Russell and Russell, 1965), pp. 70–93.

2. The most helpful compendium of demographic information on the black situation at the beginning of the new century may be found in [U.S. Department of Commerce, Bureau of the Census], *Negro Population, 1790–1915* (1918; rpt. New York: Arno Press, 1968), especially pp. 21–57.

3. E. Williams, *Capitalism*, pp. 72, 126–28; Fogel and Engerman, *Time*, I, 60, 86–89.

4. Curtin, *Atlantic Slave Trade*, pp. 210–13; DuBois, *Suppression*, pp. 48–50, 85–90. Regarding the status of blacks in the antebellum North, the best available study is still Leon Litwack, *North of Slavery* (Chicago: University of Chicago Press, 1965). Slave/free figures are available in *Negro Population*, p. 57. On the larger black Northern experience in the early decades of the century, see also Franklin, *From Slavery*, pp. 151–64; and Aptheker, *Documentary*, I, 29–44.

5. Litwack, *North*, pp. 33–34.

6. Among the more helpful sources on the insurrection by Gabriel and others are: Aptheker, *Slave Revolts*, pp. 219–26; Gerald W. Mullin, *Flight and Rebellion: Slave Resistance in Eighteenth-Century Virginia* (New York: Oxford University Press, 1972), pp. 140–61; Joseph C. Carroll, *Slave Insurrections in the United States, 1800–1865* (1938; rpt. New York: Negro Universities Press, 1968), pp. 47–57; Orville Victor, *History of American Conspiracies* (New York, 1863), pp. 27–28. Anyone interested in the event should read Arna Bontemps' evocative and important novel, *Black Thunder* (1936; rpt. Boston: Beacon Press, 1968).

7. Aptheker, *Slave Revolts*, p. 219.

8. Mullin, *Flight*, p. 149. It is interesting to compare Martin's statement with a similar development in the life of Toussaint L'Ouverture; see above, p. 47.

9. Mullin, *Flight*, p. 159.

10. Aptheker, *Slave Revolts*, p. 220.

11. Quoted in Cheek, *Black Resistance*, p. 111.

12. The Mississippi governor is quoted in Davidson B. McKibben, "Negro Slave Insurrections in Mississippi, 1800–1865," *JNH*, 34 (Jan. 1949), 74.

13. Jordan, *White Over Black*, pp. 391–402, provides an important statement on the pervasiveness of black resistance and rebellion during those early years of the nineteenth century. See also Aptheker, *Slave Revolts*, pp. 224–43; and Carrol, *Slave Insurrections*, pp. 57–82.

14. Aptheker, *Slave Revolts*, p. 239.

15. Originally, the newly independent country's name was spelled "Hayti." We have used the modern spelling for consistency and clarity. Dessalines is quoted in Drake, "Black Nationalism," p. 19. See also James, *Black Jacobins*, pp. 369–74.

16. James, pp. 369–74.

17. Examples of the continuing black responses appear below, pp. 56, 68. Discussions of this white reaction are found, among other places, in Jordan,

White Over Black, pp. 375–402; DuBois, *Suppression*, pp. 70–93; and Baur, "International Repercussions," pp. 394–418.

18. The Louisiana action is documented in Donnan, IV, 663. Often the black revolutionary statement has been mistakenly attributed to Gabriel or one of his coworkers, as for instance in Franklin, *From Slavery*, p. 211, and Aptheker, *Slave Revolts*, pp. 223–24. However, the original source for the quotation, an English traveler in the South, was very likely referring to another black, unnamed Virginia insurrectionist who was on trial in 1804, during the Englishman's visit to the state. Robert Sutcliff, *Travels in Some Parts of North America in the Years 1804, 1805 and 1806* (York, England, 1811), p. 50.

19. Franklin, *From Slavery*, p. 206.

20. Excerpts from the address appear in Aptheker, *Documentary*, I, 52.

21. Byrd is quoted in Aptheker, *Slave Revolts*, p. 246. The North Carolina message appears in Aptheker, *Documentary*, I, 53–54.

22. Jack D. L. Holmes, "The Abortive Slave Revolt at Pointe Coupée, Louisiana, 1795," *Louisiana History*, 11 (Fall 1970), 341–62; Aptheker, *Slave Revolts*, pp. 249–250. See the account in Wish, "American Slave Insurrections," 319; also the contemporary Louisiana newspaper report reproduced in Richard Hofstadter and Michael Wallace, eds., *American Violence* (New York: Knopf, 1970), pp. 190–92.

23. The words of the song and an account of its transmission are in John H. Moore, "A Hymn of Freedom—South Carolina, 1813," *JNH*, 50 (Jan. 1965), 50–53. There is a significant similarity in words and meter between the South Carolina "Hymn" and songs which emerged from struggles more than a century later in places like Elaine, Arkansas. See Arthur I. Waskow, *From Race Riot to Sit-In, 1919 and the 1960s* (New York: Anchor Books, 1967), pp. 121ff.

24. Gary Nash presents a stimulating account of certain aspects of that ambiguous black-Indian relationship in *Red, White*, pp. 290–97. See also Kenneth W. Porter's important essays on the earlier period, collected in *The Negro on the American Frontier* (New York: Arno Press, 1971), pp. 15–62, 139–81.

25. Garvin, "The Free Negro," pp. 1–17. One of the most instructive accounts of the larger diplomatic and international setting of the First Seminole War (really Black and Seminole War) is provided by Leitch J. Wright, Jr., "A Note on the First Seminole War as Seen by the Indians, Negroes and Their British Advisors," *Journal of Southern History*, 34 (Nov. 1968), 565–75.

26. John D. Milligan, "Slave Rebelliousness and the Florida Maroon," *Prologue*, 6 (Spring 1974), 5–18; also Aptheker, *Slave Revolts*, p. 259.

27. The Savannah statement is quoted in Aptheker, *Slave Revolts*, p. 31. The story of the 1816 military action is in Milligan, "Slave Rebelliousness," p. 12.

28. Milligan, "Slave Rebelliousness," pp. 16–17.

29. *Ibid.*; Aptheker, *Slave Revolts*, p. 259. The role of the federal government as a persistent antagonist of black freedom is delineated by Mary Frances Berry in *Black Resistance, White Law* (New York: Meredith Corporation, 1971), especially pp. 40–49 for her treatment of the First Seminole War.

30. Africa was not the only alternative outside the North American continent. In 1819 King Henri Christophe of Haiti informally offered to provide transportation and funds for all black persons in the United States of America who wanted to emigrate to his sector of the divided Haitian nation. His illness and death in the midst of a revolution against his rule prevented the emigration

plan from being carried out. See the documents quoted in Drake, "Black
Nationalism," pp. 48–64. The letter from Africa is quoted in August Meier,
"The Emergence of Negro Nationalism: A Study in Ideologies," unpublished
Master's thesis, Department of History, Columbia University, 1949, pp. 26–27.
Also see Harris and Cuffee, *passim*.

31. Vesey and the insurrection he organized have not yet received the precise and
full-blown treatment they deserve. However, several works are helpful: Killens,
Trial; Killens, *Great Gittin' Up Morning* (New York: Doubleday, 1972);
John Lofton, *Insurrection in South Carolina* (Yellow Springs, Ohio: Antioch
Press, 1964); Robert Starobin, "Denmark Vesey's Slave Conspiracy of 1822:
A Study in Rebellion and Repression," in John Bracey, August Meier, and
Elliot Rudwick, eds., *American Slavery: The Question of Resistance* (Belmont,
Calif.: Wadsworth Publishing, 1970), pp. 142–57. Also Marion L. Starkey,
Striving to Make It My Home (New York: W. W. Norton, 1964), pp. 167–207.
One scholar has argued that there really was no attempted insurrection: Rich-
ard Wade, "The Vesey Plot: A Reconsideration," *Journal of Southern History*,
30 (May 1964), 143–61. A direct and effective reply to Wade is offered by
Sterling Stuckey, "Remembering Denmark Vesey," *Negro Digest* (*Black
World*), 15 (Feb. 1966), 28–41. The Philadelphia statement is quoted in
Aptheker, *Documentary*, I, 71.

32. Killens, *Trial*, p. 12.

33. For details on the African church struggles, see Lofton, *Insurrection*, pp.
92–94, 132–33; and Ulrich B. Phillips, *American Negro Slavery* (1918; rpt.
Baton Rouge: Louisiana State University Press, 1966), pp. 420–421. The
general religious foundations of the Vesey conspiracy are discussed in Vincent
Harding, "Religion and Resistance among Antebellum Negroes, 1800–1860,"
in August Meier and Elliot Rudwick, eds., *The Making of Black America*,
2 vols. (New York: Atheneum, 1969), I, 184–87.

34. Killens, *Trial*, pp. 14, 58.

35. There are many references in Killens, *Trial*, to Vesey's uses of the black
revolution in San Domingo/Haiti, as for instance pp. 42, 43, 46, 59, 62, 111.
The role of Gullah Jack is discussed on pp. 13–16.

36. *Ibid.*, p. 45. The connection of Vesey to the song is picked up by Starkey in
Striving, p. 209. However, Miles Mark Fisher's significant but enigmatic study,
Negro Slave Songs, p. 40, attributes the first uses of the spiritual to an earlier
period.

37. One trial witness claimed that the book of *Tobit* in the Old Testament
Apocrypha (the non-canonical books) was among the sources used by Vesey's
men; see Killens, *Trial*, p. 85.

38. *Ibid.*, pp. 24–28; Starkey, *Striving*, pp. 167–80; Lofton, *Insurrection*, pp.
131–40. There was testimony at the trials that Vesey and his comrades had
established some real contact with Haiti: Killens, *Trial*, pp. 28, 70–71, 111.
That tradition of pan-African assistance in the black American struggle persisted well into the mid-twentieth century. (In Africa, its obverse expectation of help from the New World was also present.)

39. Killens, *Trial*, pp. 12, 42, 62.

40. *Ibid.*, pp. 15–16.

41. *Ibid.*, pp. 17, 27–28. Starobin, "Denmark Vesey's Slave Conspiracy," is especially sensitive to the diversity of the movement.

42. Killens, *Trial*, p. 2; Starobin, pp. 147–48.

43. Killens, *Trial*, p. 136.

44. *Ibid.*, pp. 135, 30–31.

45. *Ibid.*, p. 60.

46. Aptheker, *Slave Revolts*, pp. 272–73; Killens, *Trial*, p. 4.

47. Starobin, p. 148.

48. Aptheker, "Maroons," p. 176. Accounts of similar contemporary outlyer activities in North Carolina appear in R. H. Taylor, "Slave Conspiracies in North Carolina," *North Carolina Historical Review*, 5 (Jan. 1928), 20–34.

49. Aptheker, "Maroons," p. 176.

50. Aptheker, *Slave Revolts*, pp. 276–77.

51. The runaway experience is briefly recorded in Turner's *Confessions*. Of the many available editions of the latter, we are using Henry Irving Tragle, ed., *The Southampton Slave Revolt of 1831* (Amherst: University of Massachusetts Press, 1971), pp. 300–21; note p. 308 regarding Turner's running away. In addition, Tragle reprints a fascinating contemporary description of the Dismal Swamp, pp. 297–99. The fugitive experience is also recorded in Stephen B. Oates's biography of Turner, *The Fires of Jubilee* (New York: Harper and Row, 1975), p. 28.

CHAPTER 4: SYMPTOMS OF LIBERTY AND BLACKHEAD SIGNPOSTS

1. The following overview of America in the late 1820s is based on many sources, including: Robert Baird, *Religion in America* (New York, 1844); Charles I. Foster, *An Errand of Mercy: The Evangelical United Front, 1790–1837* (Chapel Hill: University of North Carolina Press, 1960); Sidney E. Ahlstrom, *A Religious History of the American People* (New Haven: Yale University Press, 1972); John B. McMaster, *A History of the People of the United States*, 8 vols. (New York: D. Appleton and Company, 1918–24), IV, V; Perry Miller, *The Life of the Mind in America* (New York: Harcourt, Brace & World, 1965); Alice Felt Tyler, *Freedom's Ferment: Phases of American Social History to 1860* (Minneapolis: University of Minnesota Press, 1944); George Dangerfield, *The Era of Good Feelings* (New York: Harcourt, Brace & World, 1963). Of course the interpretation is largely my own.

2. See for instance Helen Hunt Jackson, *A Century of Dishonor* (1885; rpt. Minneapolis: Scholarly Press, 1964), *passim*; Grant Foreman, *Indian Removal* (Norman: University of Oklahoma Press, 1953), *passim*. See also the excellent collection of documents on the dispossession in Virgil J. Vogel, ed., *This Country Was Ours: A Documentary History of the American Indian* (New York: Harper and Row, 1972).

3. On the Missouri Compromise debates, see Dangerfield, *The Era*, pp. 95–245; and Glover Moore, *The Missouri Controversy, 1819–1821* (Lexington: University of Kentucky Press, 1953), *passim*.

4. *Negro Population*, pp. 24–57. The internal slave trade is discussed fully in Frederic Bancroft, *Slave Trading in the Old South* (1931; rpt. New York: Frederic Ungar, 1959), pp. 19–66; also Robinson, *Slavery*, pp. 427–66.

5. *Negro Population*, pp. 24–57. Examples of the references are to be found, for instance, in Aptheker, *Slave Revolts*, pp. 18–45, and Tragle, *Southampton*, p. 17.

6. In dealing with the local attorney, Thomas Gray, and his version of Turner's

Confession (Tragle, pp. 300–21), we are faced with many problems. Tragle offers a helpful analysis of the document and its authenticity in the course of his sharp and telling criticism of the novelist William Styron, pp. 401–09. I suspect that there is much truth in the *Confession,* that Gray inserts himself more than is helpful, and that Nat Turner conceals a good deal. Oates's biography, *The Fires of Jubilee,* is competent but flat, missing the mystery inherent in a man like Turner.

7. Tragle, *Southampton,* pp. 306–07.

8. *Ibid.,* p. 308.

9. *Ibid.*

10. Indeed, there soon developed a belief among many blacks that Nat was endowed with the gift of healing; others said he had power to control the clouds. Such stories, clearly drawing on the lively traditions of Africa, only added to the young man's renown. See Tragle, *Southampton,* pp. 222, 420–21, 100, 309–10; Oates, *Fires,* pp. 35–41; Aptheker, *Slave Revolts,* pp. 294–95.

11. On Nat Turner's marital status, the documents and suggestions provided by Tragle (*Southampton,* pp. 90, 281, 327) are valuable; also Oates, *Fires,* pp. 29, 162–63, 308–09.

12. The millenarian setting of early nineteenth-century Christianity is discussed in H. Shelton Smith, Robert T. Handy, Lefferts A. Loetscher, eds., *American Christianity,* 2 vols. (New York: Charles Scribner's Sons, 1960), II, 12, 16, 18; Nelson Burr, *A Critical Bibliography of Religion in America,* Vol. IV of James W. Smith and A. Leland Jamison, eds., *Religion in American Life,* 4 vols. (Princeton: Princeton University Press, 1961), I, 326–27; Ahlstrom, *Religious History,* pp. 474–78.

13. Tragle, *Southampton,* p. 310; Herbert Aptheker, *Nat Turner's Slave Rebellion* (New York: Humanities Press, 1966), pp. 137–38; Oates, *Fires,* p. 41.

14. Robert Hayden, "Ballad of Nat Turner," *Selected Poems* (New York: October House, 1966), pp. 72–74.

15. Tragle, *Southampton,* p. 92; Oates, *Fires;* p. 42.

16. Aptheker, *Slave Revolts,* p. 265. On the subject of these other uprisings, there is a helpful bibliography in Eugene D. Genovese, *Roll, Jordan, Roll: The World the Slaves Made* (New York: Pantheon, 1974), pp. 709–11; an important, expanded version of his treatment and of his bibliography on the subject is available in *From Rebellion to Revolution: Afro-American Slave Revolts in the Making of the Modern World* (Baton Rouge: Louisiana State University Press, 1979). See also Aptheker, *Slave Revolts,* p. 278.

17. The story of the shipboard suicides is found in Austin Bearse, *Reminiscences of Fugitive-Slave Law Days in Boston* (1880; rpt. New York: Arno Press, 1969), p. 9.

18. Aptheker, *Slave Revolts,* pp. 279–80; a continued movement of rebellion and resistance by Alabama outlyers in this period is confirmed by James B. Sellers, *Slavery in Alabama* (University: University of Alabama Press, 1950), pp. 282–83. Also see Franklin, *From Slavery,* pp. 210–11.

19. Unfortunately, we still have nothing more comprehensive on David Walker's life than Henry Highland Garnet's "A Brief Sketch on the Life and Character of David Walker," first published in 1848 and reprinted in Herbert Aptheker, ed., *One Continual Cry: David Walker's Appeal to the Colored Citizens of the World* (New York: Humanities Press, 1965), pp. 40–44. A modern essay focusing especially on Walker's Boston years indicates a number of the perti-

nent questions about him: Donald M. Jacobs, "David Walker: Boston Race Leader, 1825–1830," *Essex Institute Historical Collections*, 107 (Jan. 1971), 94–107.

20. Garnet, "Brief Sketch," p. 41; *Freedom's Journal*, Mar. 16, 1827; Jacobs, "David Walker," pp. 95–97.

21. For examples of such words and their costliness, see Ira Berlin, *Slaves Without Masters* (New York: Pantheon, 1975), pp. 89–97, 336–38; Samuel Ringgold Ward, *Autobiography of a Fugitive Negro* (1855; rpt. Chicago: Johnson Publishing, 1970), p. 12; Robert S. Starobin, ed., *Blacks in Bondage: Letters of American Slaves* (New York: Franklin Watts, 1974), pp. 107–10. Moreover, persons like Nat Turner (above, p. 80) and Frederick Douglass (below, p. 103) could also testify to these realities.

22. For the dangers faced by black abolitionists in the North, see Aptheker, *Documentary*, I, 220; Dorothy Sterling, ed., *Speak Out in Thunder Tones* (New York: Doubleday, 1973), pp. 132–36; Ward, *Autobiography*, pp. 35–37.

23. Quoted in Bracey et al., *Black Nationalism*, p. 25.

24. The text of the speech appeared in *Freedom's Journal*, Dec. 19, 1828.

25. [Robert Alexander Young], *The Ethiopian Manifesto* (New York, 1829). The most readily available source of the full text is Sterling Stuckey, ed., *The Ideological Origins of Black Nationalism* (Boston: Beacon Press, 1972), pp. 30–38.

26. Stuckey, *Ideological Origins*, p. 30. In the light of Young's reference to Grenada as the source of the mulatto Messiah, a few alert twentieth-century black nationalists have noted that the mother of Malcolm X came to the United States from Grenada. However, internal evidence in the *Manifesto* suggests that Young was really pointing to himself as the promised deliverer. It is also important to note that, like so many similar manifestoes in the later black struggle, this one was addressed at least as fully to whites as to "Ethiopians."

27. There are several modern editions of the complete text of the *Appeal*. Among the most accessible are Charles M. Wiltse, *David Walker's Appeal* (New York: Hill and Wang, 1965), and Aptheker's *One Continual Cry*. Aptheker's introduction and footnotes are by far the most helpful; his text is used in this study.

28. Walker/Aptheker, pp. 64–65. Certainly the line of spiritual heirs reaches at least from Henry Highland Garnet (below, pp. 133–35, 140–43) to Malcolm X.

29. Walker/Aptheker, pp. 73–74.

30. *Ibid.*, p. 89.

31. *Ibid.*, p. 75. It is fascinating to note how directly Walker is related to the traditions of religious/political revolution. For instance, very similar sentiments were expressed by the Anabaptist revolutionary Thomas Muntzer during the German Peasants' War of the sixteenth century; see Guenther Lewy, *Religion and Revolution* (New York: Oxford University Press, 1974), p. vii. Also, many concepts and even certain stylistic aspects of the *Appeal* suggest that Walker had had access to the April 1804 proclamation by Jacques Dessalines, the Haitian liberator. See the Dessalines document in Drake, "Black Nationalism," pp. 28–35.

32. Drake, "Black Nationalism," p. 30; above, pp. 58–59.

33. Walker/Aptheker, pp. 83–85, 65–66.

34. Confidence in God's retributive justice is a constant in the literature of black struggle. Many of its modern manifestations were most deeply lodged in the

teachings of the Nation of Islam and their foremost heretic, Malcolm X. Compare Malcolm X, *The Autobiography of Malcolm X* (New York: Grove Press, 1964), pp. 246, 370; Elijah Muhammad, *The Fall of America* (Chicago: Muhammad's Temple of Islam No. 2, 1973), pp. 52–55, 108–11; and Louis E. Lomax, *When the Word Is Given* (New York: New American Library, 1964), pp. 175–76.

35. Walker/Aptheker, pp. 76, 126–28. Again, Walker seems very close to Dessalines. Indeed, his description of whites as the "natural enemies" of black people is precisely the same as Dessalines's in the 1804 proclamation: Drake, "Black Nationalism," p. 29.

36. Walker/Aptheker, pp. 139, 140, n.

37. *Ibid.*, pp. 77–78.

38. *Ibid.*, pp. 93–94. Consciously or not, Walker, the church member, introduced here a pan-African parallel to the New Testament concept of the Christian Church as the indivisible "body of Christ."

39. *Ibid.*, p. 104.

40. *Ibid.*, pp. 137–38.

41. *Ibid.* In our own post–Montgomery Boycott generation, we have seen leaders and institutions as varied as Martin Luther King, Jr., Malcolm X, James Forman, the Nation of Islam, and the Urban League, struggle mightily with the issue of what *would* be the appropriate restitution and reparations due to the black community.

42. Walker/Aptheker, pp. 45–50; William H. Pease and Jane H. Pease, "Document: Walker's *Appeal* Comes to Charleston: A Note and Documents," *JNH*, 59 (July 1974), 287–92; H. E. Sterkx, *The Free Negro in Ante-Bellum Louisiana* (Rutherford, N.J.: Fairleigh Dickinson University Press, 1972), p. 98.

43. Quoted in Litwack, *North*, p. 234.

44. Walker/Aptheker, p. 43. Eventually the bounty on Walker was raised to $3,000.

45. *Ibid.*, pp. 45–50.

46. Aptheker, *Slave Revolts*, p. 290.

47. Walker/Aptheker, pp. 43–44. Jacobs, "David Walker," pp. 106–07, does not accept the poisoning theory, and raises an interesting question about Walker's age when he died.

48. Tragle, *Southampton*, p. xv. Oates, *Fires*, p. 51, identifies the marriage year as late 1829.

49. According to his *Confessions* (Tragle, p. 310), the four men named comprised the first group to whom Nat revealed his plans. By the time of the actual event, two more persons, Jack Reese and Will Francis, were included. See also Oates, *Fires*, pp. 52–53.

50. Tragle, *Southampton*, p. 310. The final words are quoted in G. Williams, *History of Negro Race*, II, 88. Williams knew and appreciated the oral traditions of the black community. This quotation may well have been reconstructed from such a source.

51. Tragle, *Southampton*, pp. 310–13. In addition, for all their lack of precision and accuracy, several contemporary newspaper reports suggest the impact of the event on the surrounding population. They are quoted in Tragle, pp. 31–72. See Oates, *Fires*, pp. 66–91.

52. On the poor supply of arms, see a contemporary statement quoted in Aptheker, *Nat Turner's Slave Rebellion*, p. 55.

53. On the involvement of the U.S. military, two different emphases appear in

Aptheker, *Slave Revolts*, p. 300, and Tragle, *Southampton*, pp. 16–17. Also note Oates, *Fires*, p. 97.

54. Tragle, pp. 34, 69, 74–75, 92; Aptheker, *Nat Turner's Slave Rebellion*, pp. 60–62.

55. Aptheker, *Nat Turner's Slave Rebellion*, pp. 37–38.

56. [Samuel Warner], *Authentic and Impartial Narrative of the Tragical Scene . . . in Southampton County* (New York, 1831), p. 23. The Warner document is also reproduced in Tragle, *Southampton*, pp. 279–300.

57. Ira Berlin, "Documents: After Nat Turner, A Letter from the North," *JNH*, 55 (Apr. 1970), 144–51.

58. The wording of the formal charge against Nat Turner is found in the Minute Book of the Court of Southampton County. The more familiar formulation: ". . . making insurrection, and plotting to take away the lives of divers free white persons," is evidently Gray's own version: Tragle, *Southampton*, pp. 221, 318.

59. Tragle, pp. 221, 132, 317; Oates, *Fires*, p. 119.

60. G. Williams, *History of Negro Race*, II, 90.

61. Tragle, p. 7.

CHAPTER 5: MANY THOUSANDS CROSSING OVER

1. The statement from Richmond is quoted in G. Williams, *History of Negro Race*, II, 90. The other appears in [Warner], *Authentic Narrative*, p. 20.

2. W. E. B. DuBois, ed., *The Negro Church* (Atlanta: Atlanta University Press, 1903), pp. 24–25; Eric Foner, ed., *Nat Turner* (Englewood Cliffs, N.J.: Prentice-Hall, 1971), pp. 94–118; Catterall, *Judicial*, III, 277.

3. Quoted in Russell Ames, "Protest and Irony in Negro Folksong," *Science and Society*, 14 (Summer 1950), 194.

4. Aptheker, *Slave Revolts*, pp. 28–52. Frank A. [Frances] Rollin, *Life and Public Services of Martin R. Delany* (Boston, 1868; rpt. New York: Kraus Reprint, 1969), pp. 39–40; Dorothy Sterling, *Freedom Train: The Story of Harriet Tubman* (New York: Doubleday, 1954), pp. 31–34; Frederick Douglass, *My Bondage and My Freedom* (1855; rpt. New York: Arno Press, 1968), pp. 198ff.

5. Douglass, *My Bondage*, p. 200. Of course Douglass and his antagonists were wrong about the details of Nat's ending, but the essential point was still the same.

6. *Ibid.*, p. 220; Frederick Douglass, *Narrative of the Life of Frederick Douglass* (Boston: American Anti-Slavery Society, 1845), pp. 64–65.

7. Douglass, *Narrative*, pp. 69–72; Douglass, *My Bondage*, pp. 236–46. See Shirley Graham's imaginative rendering of the experience with Sandy the Conjurer and with Covey in her biography of Douglass, *There Once Was a Slave* (New York: Julian Messner, 1947), pp. 8–15, 24–28. It is interesting to compare Douglass's account of the Covey struggle with the story that a lesser known black leader, William Parker, tells of his battle with his master. [William Parker], "The Freedman's Story," *Atlantic Monthly* 17 (Feb./Mar. 1866), 157–60. For Parker's role in black struggle, see below, pp. 169–71.

8. Quoted in Benjamin Drew, ed., *The Refugee: Or the Narratives of Fugitive*

Slaves in Canada (Boston: John P. Jewett and Company, 1856), p. 345. The Drew volume has been reprinted with a helpful introduction in Tilden Edelstein, ed., *The Refugee: A Northside View of Slavery, by Benjamin Drew* (Reading, Mass.: Addison-Wesley, 1969); the Brant quote appears on pp. 242–43.

9. Kenneth M. Stampp, *The Peculiar Institution* (New York: Vintage Books, 1956), pp. 144–48. In his own work Stampp lists five elements; I saw two distinct factors in his fourth item, and so divided it into my numbers 4 and 5.

10. [William Parker], pp. 152–66.

11. Douglass, *Narrative*, pp. 84–86; Douglass, *My Bondage*, pp. 280–83.

12. Douglass, *My Bondage*, pp. 280–83.

13. The persistence of black resistance, on varying levels of life and activity, is documented in such sources as Raymond A. Bauer and Alice H. Bauer, "Day to Day Resistance to Slavery," *JNH*, 27 (Oct. 1942), 388–419; Genovese, *Roll, Jordan*, pp. 613–21; Blassingame, *Slave Community*, pp. 104–31, 209–16. Moreover, the tradition of resistance is endemic to the narratives of black men and women who survived slavery, published, with an introductory volume, in George P. Rawick, ed., *The American Slave: A Composite Autobiography*, 31 vols. (Westport, Conn.: Greenwood Press, 1972, 1978).

14. Joseph G. Tregle, "Early New Orleans Society: A Reappraisal," *Journal of Southern History*, 18 (Feb. 1952), 33.

15. Aptheker, *Slave Revolts*, p. 93; W. G. Addington, "Slave Insurrections in Texas," *JNH*, 35 (Oct. 1950), 412.

16. Jackson's own participation in slavery and Indian removal is discussed in Melvin Steinfield, ed., *Our Racist Presidents: From Washington to Nixon* (San Ramon, Calif.: Consensus Publishers, Jan. 1972), pp. 79–93; there is also a more extensive essay in Frederick Binder, *The Color Problem in Early National America* (The Hague: Mouton, 1968), pp. 120–56. For a much kinder view of Jackson's policies, see F. P. Prucha, "Andrew Jackson's Indian Policy: A Reassessment," *Journal of American History*, 56 (Dec. 1969), 527–39. On the larger national policies involved, see Foreman, *Indian Removal, passim*. Of course at the time some of the most perceptive observations concerning the white American uses of law for immoral purposes were made by Alexis de Tocqueville in his *Democracy in America*; in the edition edited by J. P. Mayer and Max Lerner (New York: Doubleday, 1966), note especially pp. 207–08, 243–48, 308–12.

17. The categories of black persons and the descriptive quotation are part of Kenneth W. Porter's pioneering discussion of the black-red alliance, "Florida Slaves and Free Negroes in the Seminole War, 1835–1842," *JNH*, 28 (Oct. 1943), 390–421, also 262–94. Note too the more recent summary approach of Mary Berry, *Black Resistance*, pp. 53–67. The following account is taken essentially from these two sources.

18. Quoted in Porter, "Florida," p. 392.

19. *Ibid.*, pp. 398–400.

20. See Berry, *Black Resistance*, pp. 63–65, for the completion of these events.

21. Douglass, *My Bondage*, p. 278. Douglass clearly stated in the same place that "the north was our Canaan." Moreover, he also offered another version of the familiar second song: "I thought I heard them say / There were lions in the way, / I don't expect to stay / Much longer here" (*ibid.*). The "Valiant Soldier" song is quoted in Lawrence Levine, "Slave Songs and Slave Con-

sciousness," in Tamara Hareven, ed., *Anonymous Americans* (Englewood Cliffs, N.J.: Prentice-Hall, 1971), p. 116.

22. Richard C. Wade, *Slavery in the Cities* (New York: Oxford University Press, 1964), pp. 83–84.

23. Catterall, *Judicial*, II, 516–17.

24. *Ibid.*

25. Rawick, *American Slave*, XVIII, 49. By a fascinating coincidence, the song was also recorded in Tennessee.

26. Aptheker, *Slave Revolts*, p. 333.

27. Brawley, *A Social History*, pp. 152–53; Howard Jones, "The Peculiar Institution and National Honor: The Case of the *Creole* Slave Revolt," *Civil War History*, 21 (Mar. 1975), 28–50. Sometime in the late 1840s or early 1850s Frederick Douglass wrote a fictional account of the Creole incident, "The Heroic Slave." An important and revealing document, it appears in Ronald T. Takaki, *Violence in the Black Imagination* (New York: G. P. Putnam's Sons, 1972), pp. 37–77.

28. Aptheker, *Slave Revolts*, pp. 335–36.

29. *Ibid.*, p. 336. See also Nicholas Halasz, *The Rattling Chains* (New York: David McKay, 1966), p. 209.

30. The discussion of black fugitives is based on a variety of sources, including Blassingame, *Slave Community*; Harriet Buckmaster, *Let My People Go* (1941; rpt. Boston: Beacon Press, 1966); Larry Gara, *The Liberty Line* (Lexington: University of Kentucky Press, 1961); Genovese, *Roll, Jordan*; Rawick, *American Slave*; Wilbur H. Siebert, *The Underground Railroad from Slavery to Freedom* (1898; rpt. New York: Arno Press, 1968); William Still, *The Underground Railroad* (1871; rpt. Chicago: Johnson Publishing, 1970). Gara differs with most other sources (and, to some degree, with me) in suggesting that there were far fewer fugitives than generally estimated in 1830–60. Basing his position largely on the 1850 and 1860 census reports and other contemporary documents, he estimates that there were no more than 1,000 fugitives per year. However, some of his own figures (pp. 96–99) suggest that the census figures were unrealistically low. Also, Gara does not deal adequately with Siebert's section (pp. 340–58) on Southern losses. My own estimate falls somewhere between Siebert and Gara; but I tend in Siebert's direction, which would triple or quadruple Gara's estimates. The story of Fanny appears in Harriet Beecher Stowe, *The Key to Uncle Tom's Cabin* (1853; rpt. New York: Arno Press, 1969), p. 363.

31. Hayden, *Selected Poems*, p. 75.

CHAPTER 6: STRANGE RIVER IN CANAAN

1. My generalizations on the problems of blacks in the antebellum North are based on many sources, but they may be most readily summarized in the following works: Leonard L. Richards, *"Gentlemen of Property and Standing": Anti-Abolitionist Mobs in Jacksonian America* (New York: Oxford University Press, 1970); Eugene Berwanger, *The Frontier Against Slavery* (Urbana: University of Illinois Press, 1967); Lorman Ratner, *Powder Keg: Northern Opposition to the Anti-Slavery Movement, 1831–1840* (New York: Basic Books, 1968); Jane H. Pease and William H. Pease, *They Who Would Be Free: Blacks Search for Freedom, 1830–1861* (New York: Atheneum,

1974). See also Aptheker, *Documentary*, I; Franklin, *From Slavery*, pp. 213–38; Litwack, *North*, *passim*; and *Negro Population*, pp. 21–57. The "Jim Crow" reference here is to the thesis originally put forward by C. Vann Woodward in his important work, *The Strange Career of Jim Crow* (New York: Oxford University Press, 1957). As originally stated, it tended largely to ignore the presence of a *de jure* and *de facto* segregation in Northern cities that clearly predated the racial patterns he noted in the post-Reconstruction South. Later, especially in "The Strange Career of a Historical Controversy" in his *American Counterpoint* (Boston: Little, Brown, 1971), Woodward acknowledged that problem.

2. The July Fourth practice in Philadelphia is recorded in Franklin, *From Slavery*, p. 231.

3. There are examples of such mob action in Ratner, *Powder Keg*, pp. 71–72, 78–79, 40–41; Richards, *"Gentlemen,"* pp. 33–35, 116–20, 125–29. The basic survey work on the Colonization Society is still P. J. Staudenraus, *The African Colonization Movement, 1816–1865* (New York: Columbia University Press, 1961).

4. Howard H. Bell, *A Survey of the Negro Convention Movement, 1830–1861* (New York: Arno Press, 1969), pp. 12–13.

5. Katherine DuPre Lumpkin, "The General Plan was Freedom: A Negro Secret Order on the Underground Railroad," *Phylon*, 28 (Spring 1967), 65.

6. Quoted in Aptheker, *Documentary*, I, 159.

7. Benjamin Quarles, *Black Abolitionists* (New York: Oxford University Press, 1969), pp. 143–56; Gara, *Liberty Line*, pp. 93–100; Pease and Pease, *They Who*, pp. 207–12.

8. Quarles, *Black Abolitionists*, pp. 204–05.

9. Cheek, *Black Resistance*, p. 28; Siebert, *Underground Railroad*, pp. 251–53.

10. The best source on Ruggles is Dorothy B. Porter, "David M. Ruggles, Apostle of Human Rights," *JNH*, 28 (Jan. 1943), 23–50. See also Charles H. Wesley, "The Negroes of New York in the Emancipation Movement," *JNH*, 24 (Jan. 1939), 86–88; Ottley and Weatherby, *The Negro in New York*, p. 85.

11. Douglass, *My Bondage*, p. 341.

12. Some of Douglass's own sense of his career may be traced through his initial *Narrative* (1845), and its two later expanded versions, *My Bondage* (1855) and the *Life and Times of Frederick Douglass* (1892). Each of these is available in several modern editions. The best available biography is still Benjamin Quarles, *Frederick Douglass* (Washington, D.C.: Association Press, 1948; rpt. New York: Atheneum, 1968); the most accessible collection of his writings is Philip S. Foner, ed., *The Life and Writings of Frederick Douglass*, 4 vols. (New York: International Publishers, 1950). The publication of a major new edition of Douglass's papers has begun recently: John W. Blassingame, ed., *The Frederick Douglass Papers: Series One: Speeches, Debates and Interviews* (New Haven, Conn.: Yale University Press, 1979), I. A modern biography is still sorely needed; Nathan Huggins, *Slave and Citizen: The Life of Frederick Douglass* (Boston: Little, Brown, 1980) is a significant, popularized step in that direction.

13. See for instance Franklin, *From Slavery*, p. 32; Litwack, *North*, pp. 214–46; Quarles, *Black Abolitionists*, pp. 3–36, 83; George P. Rawick, *From Sundown to Sun Up: The Making of the Black Community*, Vol. I of *The American Slave*, p. 10.

14. Among the most helpful works on the organized, white-controlled abolitionist movement are Martin Duberman, ed., *The Anti-Slavery Vanguard* (Princeton: Princeton University Press, 1965); Dwight Dumond, *Anti-Slavery* (Ann Arbor: University of Michigan Press, 1961); Louis Filler, *The Crusade Against Slavery, 1830–1860* (New York: Harper and Row, 1963); Aileen S. Kraditor, *Means and Ends in American Abolitionism* (New York: Pantheon, 1969); William H. Pease and Jane H. Pease, eds., *The Anti-Slavery Argument* (Indianapolis: Bobbs-Merrill, 1965); Lewis Perry, *Radical Abolitionism: Anarchy and the Government of God in Anti-Slavery Thought* (Ithaca, N.Y.: Cornell University Press, 1973); Gerald Sorin, *Abolitionism: A New Perspective* (New York: Praeger, 1972). Also valuable is Woodward's "The Northern Crusade against Slavery" in *American Counterpoint*, pp. 140–62.

15. Henry Steele Commager, ed., *Documents of American History*, 2 vols. (New York: Prentice-Hall, 1963), I, 279; Quarles, *Black Abolitionists*, pp. 49–50.

16. Concerning the larger, Protestant religious context of the mainstream abolitionist movement, in addition to the titles mentioned in note 14, see Whitney R. Cross, *The Burned-Over District* (Ithaca, N.Y.: Cornell University Press, 1950); David B. Davis, ed., *Ante-Bellum Reform* (New York: Harper and Row, 1967); Clifford S. Griffin, *Their Brothers' Keepers* (New Brunswick, N.J.: Rutgers University Press, 1960); and Timothy L. Smith, *Revivalism and Social Reform in Mid-nineteenth Century America* (New York: Peter Smith, 1957).

17. The initial "Declaration of Sentiments" of the American Anti-Slavery Society is instructive on this point: Pease and Pease, *Anti-Slavery*, pp. 65–71.

18. The black-white struggles within the abolitionist movement are discussed in Robert Allen, *Reluctant Reformers* (Washington, D.C.: Howard University Press, 1974), pp. 31–42; Quarles, *Black Abolitionists*, pp. 49–50; Pease and Pease, *They Who*, pp. 68–93; Filler, *Crusade*, pp. 142–45; Litwack, *North*, pp. 214–46. See also Litwack's "The Emancipation of the Negro Abolitionist" in Duberman, *Vanguard*, pp. 137–55. For a somewhat different emphasis, see James M. McPherson, "A Brief for Equality: The Abolitionist Reply to the Racist Myth, 1860–1865," in Duberman, *Vanguard*, pp. 156–77.

19. Martin R. Delany, *The Condition, Elevation, Emigration and Destiny of the Colored People of the United States Politically Considered* (Philadelphia, 1852), p. 27. Delany, of course, was not alone in his observations of the black-white dynamics; for another black contemporary expression, see Aptheker, *Documentary*, I, 169–74.

20. For introductions to the life and work of these men, see notes 14 and 16.

21. Quarles, *Black Abolitionists*, tells the basic black abolitionist story, including some discussion of the persons mentioned here. However, a more extended analysis would have been helpful.

22. There are two modern biographies of Delany: Dorothy Sterling, *The Making of an Afro-American: Martin Robison Delany, 1812–1885* (New York: Doubleday, 1971); and Victor Ullman, *Martin R. Delany: The Beginnings of Black Nationalism* (Boston: Beacon Press, 1971). Rollin's *Life* was done at least partly under Delany's direction, and has all the strengths and weaknesses of such an "authorized" work. Woodson is treated in Floyd J. Miller, "The Father of Black Nationalism: Another Contender," *Civil War History*, 17 (Dec. 1971), 310–19.

23. Rollin, *Life*, pp. 39–40.

24. In his preface to *Condition*, Delany claims to have originally "laid out" his plan "at twenty-four years of age" (pp. 9–10). According to Miller, Delany's teacher Woodson used the pseudonym "Augustine," which was also the signature for a series of articles dealing with much of the same material in the *Colored American* in 1837–41. If Delany's chronology is correct, his work antedated "Augustine"'s by at least one year. However, rather than debate who was "the Father of Black Nationalism," I would suggest that the ideas in question developed out of experiences and reflections that were the common property of these two brilliant and closely associated black men.

25. Delany, *Condition*, pp. 209–12.

26. For other examples of contemporary black emigrationist thought, see Bracey et al., *Black Nationalism*, pp. 38–48; Joan R. Sherman, "James Monroe Whitfield, Poet and Emigrationist," *JNH*, 57 (Apr. 1972), 169–76.

27. Litwack, *North*, pp. 25–28, 235–36; Sterling, *The Making*, pp. 58–59; Bell, *Survey*, pp. 31–34; Staudenraus, *African Colonization*, pp. 188–93.

28. Sterling, *The Making*, pp. 55–74; Ullman, *Delany*, pp. 38–39; Rollin, *Life*, pp. 46–47.

29. Note, for example, the contemporary discussion of emigration to the Caribbean as reflected in the *Colored American* of Apr. 4, 11, and 18, 1840.

30. *Ibid.*, May 9, 1840.

31. Stampp, *Peculiar Institution*, pp. 144–48, and above.

32. The only book-length biography of Garnet is Earl Ofari, *Let Your Motto Be Resistance* (Boston: Beacon Press, 1972), a work that is not comprehensive in scope. A briefer, more recent biographical treatment that makes more use of contemporary documents is Jane H. Pease and William H. Pease, "The Black Militant: Henry Highland Garnet," in their collection, *Bound With Them in Chains* (Westport, Conn.: Greenwood Press, 1972), pp. 162–90. For an earlier estimate of Garnet written by his former classmate, Alexander Crummell, see that author's *Africa and America: Addresses and Discourses* (Springfield, Mass., 1891; rpt. New York: Arno Press, 1969), pp. 271–305.

33. Ofari, *Motto*, pp. 2–14; Pease and Pease, *Bound With Them*, pp. 162–65, 169–70; Quarles, *Black Abolitionists*, p. 90.

34. Documents on the division among the abolitionists are available below, note 35. All quotations from Garnet's speech are taken from the *Colored American*, May 30, 1840.

35. The split in the white antislavery movement, the rise of the Liberty Party, and the black responses to these developments are treated in Dumond, *Anti-Slavery*, pp. 282–304; Filler, *Crusade*, pp. 120–36, 145–59; Kraditor, *Means*, pp. 118–77; and Quarles, *Black Abolitionists*, pp. 54–56, 183–88.

36. *Colored American*, Oct. 10, 1840.

37. *Ibid.*, Jan. 23, 1941.

38. *Ibid.*, Feb. 13, 1841.

39. On Remond, see Quarles, *Black Abolitionists*, pp. 131–33; Pease and Pease, *They Who*, pp. 44–46, 55–80. His statement is quoted in Arthur L. Smith, *Rhetoric of Black Revolution* (Boston: Allyn and Bacon, 1969), p. 118.

40. Informative discussions of the disunionist position are found in Carlton Mabee, *Black Freedom* (New York: Macmillan, 1970), pp. 244–66, 363–75; Kraditor, *Means*, pp. 196–208, 211–17; and Perry, *Radical*, pp. 161–66. See below, p. 217.

41. Hugh D. Graham and Ted R. Gurr, eds., *The History of Violence in America* (New York: Frederick A. Praeger, 1969), p. 409.
42. *Colored American*, June 27, 1840.
43. Quoted in Pease and Pease, "Black Power—the Debate in 1840," *Phylon*, 29 (Spring 1968), 24.

CHAPTER 7: BEYOND THE NORTH STAR

1. Bell, *Survey*, pp. 63–110; Bell, ed., *Minutes of the Proceedings of the National Negro Conventions, 1830–1864* (New York: Arno Press, 1969), 1843, 1847, 1848 (no consecutive pagination); Pease and Pease, "The Negro Convention Movement," in Huggins et al., *Key Issues*, I, 196–99. Garnet is quoted in Quarles, *Black Abolitionists*, pp. 225–26.
2. Bell, *Minutes*, 1843, [pp. 5–7]. Also helpful in setting the context for the Buffalo meeting are Quarles, *Black Abolitionists*, pp. 226–27; Pease and Pease, *Bound with Them*, pp. 179–80; Ofari, *Motto*, pp. 34–50. The most accessible sources for Garnet's speech are Bracey et al., *Black Nationalism*, pp. 67–76; and Ofari, pp. 144–53. The speech was actually the report of the convention's official committee on "Business," but Garnet had prepared it and he presented it.
3. Bracey et al., *Black Nationalism*, p. 71.
4. *Ibid.*, p. 73.
5. *Ibid.* In one form or another, paraphrased or directly quoted, that statement from Hebrews 9:22 ("without shedding of blood is no remission [of sins]," KJV) became a continuing, relentless theme in black commentary on the struggle for freedom in America. See above, p. 97; Bracey et al., *Black Nationalism*, pp. 75–76.
6. My own judgment of Garnet should be balanced by the more admiring opinion of one of his classmates, the distinguished black intellectual Alexander Crummell, who later said of Garnet, "If he had remained a slave, he would have become a leader and fomenter of insurrection." See Crummell's *Africa and America*, p. 300. In this eulogy on Garnet, Crummell had much more to say along the same line (pp. 271–305). The audience reaction was noted by a contemporary quoted in Bell, *Minutes*, p. 251.
7. Bell, *Minutes*, 1843, [pp. 6–26, *passim*]. The second vote was 19–18. However, most secondary accounts of the convention have missed the fact of the third and final 19–9 vote against issuing the *Address*.
8. The German immigrants were responding specifically to a plan to settle in their area some five hundred black persons who had been slaves of John Randolph, the Virginia political leader, and had been freed when he died. So the white farmers were not only resisting any new black presence, but were seeking as well to separate themselves from the old. Their statement appeared in the *African Repository*, Mar. 1847, quoted in Sterling, *Speak Out*, p. 207.
9. Tocqueville, in Mayer and Lerner edition, p. 315.
10. The only solid written evidence for the existence of such a group comes from the work of Moses Dickson, a black native of Cincinnati who later became a leader in the post-Reconstruction benevolent society movement among black people. In 1846, when twenty-two years old, he claimed to have been the key

organizer of the Knights. See his *Manual of the International Order of Twelve* (St. Louis, 1891), pp. 7-15. (Interestingly enough, an 1879 edition of the *Manual* does not present the same story.) Apparently, one of the most conscientious of the earlier black scholars of this century, Monroe Work, took Dickson's story seriously. The existence of the Knights of Liberty is reported as fact in Work's "Secret Societies as Factors in the Social and Economic Life of the Negro," in James E. McCulloch, ed., *Democracy in Earnest* (Washington, D.C.: Southern Sociological Congress, 1918). However, another scholar has disparaged Dickson's story, claiming that the black leader "invented" it: Edward Nelson Palmer, "Negro Secret Societies," *Social Forces*, 23 (Oct. 1944–May 1945), 207–12. Another possible clue to the Knights of Liberty is discussed in chapter 10, note 26.

11. Douglass's earliest career in the organized abolitionist movement receives very brief treatment in his *Narrative*, p. 153, but there is a larger description in *My Bondage*, pp. 268–83. See also P. Foner, *Life*, I, pp. 45–62, 103–12; and Quarles, *Douglass*, pp. 9–37.

12. Betty Fladeland's *Men and Brothers Anglo-American Anti-Slavery Cooperation* (Urbana: University of Illinois Press, 1972) is a good survey of the British-American linkages. Douglass's experiences overseas are reported in *My Bondage*, pp. 283–303; P. Foner, *Life*, I, 62–75, 115–234; and Quarles, *Douglass*, pp. 38–54. His struggle with the legal purchase issue can be noted in P. Foner, *Life*, I, 200–06.

13. Bell, *Minutes*, 1847, [p. 32].

14. P. Foner, *Life*, I, 282–84.

15. For instance, Quarles, *Douglass*, pp. 32, 61, 168; also P. Foner, *Life*, I, 52–53, 57, 79, 256–59, 384–87.

16. Douglass, *Narrative*, p. 31.

17. Sterling, *The Making*, pp. 80–92, 97.

18. Douglass's statement about Delaney's black consciousness is quoted in Rollin, *Life*, p. 19. That work is also the best source for the children's names (p. 29).

19. Ullman, *Delany*, pp. 78–79.

20. Sterling, *The Making*, p. 102; Ullman, pp. 78, 79. The "military tactics" motion is quoted in Sterling, pp. 111–12; however, it does not appear in the minutes of the convention. The Northern perception of the growing strength of "the slave power" during this period is explored in Larry Gara, "Slavery and the Slave Power: A Crucial Distinction," *Civil War History*, 15 (Mar. 1969), 5–18.

21. See above, pp. 140–43; also Bracey et al., *Black Nationalism*, p. 73. The movement of Garnet's thinking is recorded in Quarles, *Black Abolitionists*, p. 216, and in Pease and Pease, *Bound With Them*, pp. 182–84.

22. Quoted in Bell, "The Negro Emigration Movement, 1849–1854: A Phase of Negro Nationalism," *Phylon*, 9 (Summer 1959), p. 138.

23. Stephen B. Oates, *To Purge This Land with Blood* (New York: Harper and Row, 1970), p. 61.

24. Quoted in Aptheker, *Documents*, I, 290–91. See also Pease and Pease, *They Who*, p. 86, on Van Rensselaer.

25. Aptheker, *Documents*, I, 290–91.

26. Both the Michigan and Cincinnati incidents were reported in the *North Star*

of July 28 and Aug. 11, 1848, respectively, as cited in Sterling, *Speak Out*, pp. 154–55.

27. Regarding the actions by Northern states, see Litwack, *North*, pp. 69–72; Berwanger, *The Frontier*, pp. 43–51, 66–73. The situation of free blacks in the South is treated in Berlin, *Slaves Without Masters*, especially pp. 203–12, 360–63. On the Maryland action see Penelope Campbell, *Maryland in Africa* (Urbana: University of Illinois Press, 1971), pp. 190–91. Douglass is quoted in Ullman, *Delany*, p. 100.

28. P. Foner, *Life*, I, 398–99.

29. Earl Conrad, *Harriet Tubman, Negro Soldier and Abolitionist* (New York: International Publishers, 1942), pp. 30–43; Buckmaster, *Let My People Go*, pp. 213–16; Edgar Toppin, *A Biographical History of Blacks in America Since 1528* (New York: David McKay, 1971), pp. 427–31.

30. Elizabeth M. Geffen, "Violence in Philadelphia in the 1840's and 1850's," *Pennsylvania History*, 36 (Oct. 1969), 388.

CHAPTER 8: A FERMENT OF FUGITIVES

1. P. Foner, *Life*, I, 417.

2. There are several helpful studies of the national debates over the extension of slavery during this period, as for instance Allan Nevins, *Ordeal of the Union: A House Dividing, 1852–1857*, II (New York: Charles Scribner's Sons, 1950); Roy F. Nichols, *The Disruption of American Democracy* (New York: Macmillan, 1948); and Elbert B. Smith, *The Death of Slavery: The United States, 1837–65* (Chicago: University of Chicago Press, 1967). It also provides the major background for Eric Foner, *Free Soil, Free Labor, Free Men: The Ideology of the Republican Party before the Civil War* (New York: Oxford University Press, 1971). Of course it is forever present in all the works on abolitionism cited in chapter 6, note 16.

3. See the sources in note 2. One readily available source of the Compromise acts is Commager, *Documents*, I, 319–23.

4. *Ibid.*, pp. 321–23. An important earlier monograph on the legal and political problems presented by the fugitives is McDougall, *Fugitive Slaves*, especially pp. 27–33, 44, 112–15.

5. The black response to the act is discussed in Pease and Pease, *They Who*, pp. 217–32; Quarles, *Black Abolitionists*, pp. 197–222; and Litwack, *North*, pp. 247–79. Also note Aptheker, *Documents*, I, 299–316. Ward is quoted in Carter G. Woodson, ed., *Negro Orators and Their Orations* (Washington, D.C.: Associated Publishers, 1925), p. 196.

6. Quarles, *Black Abolitionists*, p. 199.

7. *Ibid.*, p. 201.

8. Quoted in Ullman, *Delany*, p. 112. See also Sterling, *The Making*, pp. 119–20.

9. P. Foner, *Life*, II, 47–48, 57–58; Quarles, *Douglass*, pp. 91–95, 105–07.

10. Quoted in Quarles, *Black Abolitionists*, p. 203.

11. The League of Freedom is mentioned in the *Liberator* of Oct. 11, 1850, cited in Sterling, *Speak Out*, p. 257. Leadership in the formation of what is probably the same group—though called a Committee of Vigilance—is attributed to William C. Nell by Robert P. Smith, "William Cooper Nell: Crusading Black Abolitionist," *JNH*, 55 (July 1970), 182–99.

12. Quoted in Cheek, *Black Resistance*, pp. 148–49.

13. Quoted in St. Clair Drake and Horace R. Cayton, *Black Metropolis* (New York: Harcourt, Brace and Company, 1945), p. 34.

14. Also Cheek, *Black Resistance*, pp. 34–45. Jonathan Katz, ed., *Resistance at Christiana* (New York: Thomas Crowell, 1974), is the best source on the Pennsylvania group.

15. Quarles, *Black Abolitionists*, p. 200; Sterling, *The Making*, p. 120. The source for the estimated black migration—a work used by Quarles, *Black Abolitionists*, p. 217, and Litwack, *North*, p. 249, for instance—is an earlier study: Fred Landon, "The Negro Migration to Canada after . . . 1850," *JNH*, 5 (Jan. 1920), 22–23. Robin Winks, who has done the most authoritative modern study of the black experience in Canada, thinks Landon's figures too high, but cannot substitute any of his own for the period in question. See Winks's *The Blacks in Canada* (New Haven: Yale University Press, 1971), pp. 233–40, 484–96.

16. Aptheker, *Slave Revolts*, p. 342; K. Porter, *The Negro*, pp. 424–29.

17. Aptheker, *Slave Revolts*, p. 343; Addington, "Slave Insurrections," p. 433.

18. In a frightened, secular, "post-Christian" age, such forms of resistance may seem foolish, naive, and self-deceptive. However, in a time and a community when "prayer warriors" were taken very seriously, and spiritual struggles were amazingly concrete, black men and women considered this a real contribution to the struggle against slavery. Certain fascinating, semifictional statements of this kind appear in Martin R. Delany, *Blake: Or the Huts of America* (1859; rpt. Boston: Beacon Press, 1970), pp. 38, 39, 112.

19. Rawick, *American Slave*, XVII, 142, 215; XVIII, 259.

20. *Ibid.*, XIII, 97. Meanwhile, in a border-state city like St. Louis, the black population was no less ingenious in the struggle for education. There a Baptist minister circumvented the laws against his people's instruction by buying a steamboat and setting up his school on the Mississippi River, which was federal property. Judy Day and M. James Kedro, "Free Blacks in St. Louis: Antebellum Conditions, Emancipation, and the Post-War Era," *Bulletin of the Missouri Historical Society*, 30 (Jan. 1974), 123–24.

21. Rawick, XVIII, 116. Similar stories, often told by men and women about their parents, are found throughout Rawick's narratives, as for example IV, 48; II, 27; II, Part 2, 36.

22. James McKaye, *The Emancipated Slave* (New York: 1864), p. 12.

23. See Rawick, XIII, 6; IV, Part 2, 191.

24. *Ibid.*, XVIII, 144–45.

25. Quoted in Conrad, *Harriet Tubman*, p. 49. Henry Gross's account is in Drew, *The Refugee*, p. 85.

26. Quarles, *Black Abolitionists*, pp. 205–06. Pease and Pease, *They Who*, pp. 219–21, includes an important account of the rescue. Evidently, Shadrach's real name was Frederick Wilkins, though one source—Stanley W. Campbell, *The Slave Catchers* (New York: W. W. Norton, 1972), pp. 148–51—uses the surname Jenkins. Quarles, *Black Abolitionists*, pp. 209–11, and Pease and Pease, *They Who*, pp. 223–25, are helpful on the "Jerry" McHenry case. Larry Gara demonstrates in two significant articles that the Fugitive Slave Law of 1850 was ineffective in both its main purposes: recapturing fugitives (only some 200 were returned) and healing the growing division between the sections; instead, the law exacerbated the political situation and helped split

the nation. See Gara, "The Fugitive Slave Law in the Eastern Ohio Valley," *Ohio History*, 73 (Apr. 1963), 116–28, 170–71; and "The Fugitive Slave Law: A Double Paradox," *Civil War History*, 10 (Jan. 1964), 229–40.

27. P. Foner, *Life*, II, 155–56.

28. An important initial essay as a biographical study of Douglas is Robert L. Harris, Jr., "H. Ford Douglas: Afro-American Anti-Slavery Emigrationist," an unpublished paper in the author's possession. Some sketchy but valuable information on Douglas is available in *Records of the Adjutant General's Office, 1780–1917*, Record Group 94, National Archives.

29. Aptheker, *Documentary*, I, 316–17.

30. Bibb's own autobiographical narrative is most readily found in Gilbert Osofsky, ed., *Puttin' On Ole Massa: The Slave Narratives of Henry Bibb, William Wells Brown and Solomon Northup* (New York: Harper and Row, 1969), pp. 53–171. Other helpful sources are Ullman, *Delany*, pp. 130–46; and Winks, *Blacks*, pp. 396–97.

31. In addition to the works in the preceding note, see Bell, *Survey*, pp. 149–50. Holly's message is quoted in Ullman, p. 136.

32. The most extended treatment of the Christiana incident is Katz's *Resistance*. An older work is H. U. Hensel, *The Christiana Riot* (Lancaster, Pa.: New Era, 1911). See also Richard Grau, "The Christiana Riot of 1851: A Reappraisal," *Journal of the Lancaster County Historical Society*, 68 (Michaelmas 1964), 147–63; and Roderick W. Nash, "The Christiana Riot: An Evaluation of Its National Significance," *ibid.*, 65 (Spring 1961), 65–91. The one published eyewitness account, attributed to William Parker but probably the product of several persons' efforts, appeared as "The Freedman's Story" in the *Atlantic Monthly*.

33. [William Parker], pp. 162–66.

34. Katz, *Resistance*, pp. 86, 89.

35. Hensel, *Christiana*, p. 33.

36. The federal government, operating in ways which would become familiar to many later resistants, was at least as interested in harassment, intimidation, and disruption as it was in conviction. See Katz, *Resistance*, pp. 162–64, 247–61, as well as S. Campbell, *Slave Catchers*, pp. 152–54, and [William Parker], pp. 288–90.

37. Katz, pp. 137–46, 147–55; Quarles, *Black Abolitionists*, pp. 211–12; R. W. Nash, "Christiana Riot," pp. 74–86.

CHAPTER 9: CALLED TO GO FORWARD

1. Philadelphia, 1852.

2. Delany, *Condition*, pp. 14–15. The tremendous rise of nationalism in Europe was vividly symbolized in the revolution of 1848, while in the United States the spirit of "Young America" and other nationalist movements was most fully expressed in the slogan and ideology of "Manifest Destiny." See McMaster, *History*, pp. 95ff.

3. Delany, *Condition*, pp. 147–56; see above, p. 154.

4. Delany, *Condition*, pp. 156–59.

5. *Ibid.*, pp. 171–73. The theme of black and native American solidarity was later given prominence again in Delany's novel, *Blake*.

6. Delany, *Condition*, pp. 173, 178–81.

7. *Ibid.*, p. 182. Delany's last words concerning a new Union were obviously meant to evoke (and transform) the famous passage from Daniel Webster's speech in the 1830 Senate debate against the proponents of states' rights: "Liberty *and* Union, now and forever, one and inseparable!" Current and Garraty, *Words*, I, 367.

8. Delany, *Condition*, p. 48. It is interesting to compare Delany's statement here with the affirmation of a right to this country which was made a century later by Paul Robeson, the politically conscious black artist and spokesman: Paul Robeson, *Here I Stand* (New York: Othello Associates, 1958), p. 56 (1971 ed., p. 48).

9. Delany, *Condition*, pp. 182–83.

10. *Ibid.*, p. 183.

11. Aptheker, *Slave Revolts*, p. 340. The North Carolina judge is quoted in Catterall, *Judicial*, II, 168.

12. Rawick, *American Slave*, VI, 160–161. For an example of a runaway with a weapon, see testimony in *ibid.*, p. 390.

13. *Ibid.*, 161.

14. One accessible source for the prophetic spiritual "Oh Mary" is Sterling A. Brown et al., eds., *The Negro Caravan* (New York: Dryden Press, 1941), p. 439. On the fugitive slave laws, see S. Campbell, *Slave Catchers*, pp. 102–03; Filler, *Crusade*, p. 213.

15. The best single source for the 1853 convention is its "Proceedings," available in Bell, *Minutes*, 1853. The comment on the assemblage was by J. Theodore Holly in his introduction to Frederick Douglass, W. J. Watkins, and J. M. Whitfield, *Arguments Pro and Con . . . on . . . a National Emigration Convention* (Detroit, 1854), p. 3.

16. The letter, which sketches some of the context, was reproduced in the "Proceedings" of the convention, pp. 33–38. It is also reprinted in P. Foner, *Life*, II, 229–36.

17. "Proceedings," pp. 36–37.

18. *Ibid.*, pp. 8–10.

19. *Ibid.*

20. The Social Relations Committee documents appear on pp. 20–25 of the "Proceedings."

21. *Ibid.*, pp. 23–26, 46.

22. *Ibid.*, pp. 18, 19, 44. These black institutions are somewhat inaccurately described in Howard Bell's otherwise informative essay, "Negro Emigration," pp. 132–42.

23. "Proceedings," p. 40.

24. P. Foner, *Life*, II, 36.

25. Brief, usually bland summaries of the crucial Kansas-Nebraska struggles are presented in any survey of American history, as for instance John Blum et al., *The National Experience* (New York: Harcourt, Brace & World, 1963), pp. 306, 310. For more detailed discussions, see Nevins, *Ordeal*, II, 78–159, 301–46; Roy F. Nichols, "The Kansas-Nebraska Act: A Century of Historiography," *Mississippi Valley Historical Review*, 43 (Sept. 1956), 187–212; Nichols, *The Stakes of Power* (New York: Hill and Wang, 1961), pp. 47–62.

26. The *Call* appears in Douglass et al., *Arguments*, pp. 5–7. This document in

cludes attacks against the emigrationist movement and its coming conference by Frederick Douglass and his assistant editor, W. J. Watkins (primarily the latter), along with very capable rejoinders by Whitfield. On him see J. Sherman, "James Monroe Whitfield," *JNH*, pp. 169–76; also Brown et al., *Negro Caravan*, p. 290. On the national developments, see Franklin, *From Slavery*, p. 182.

27. Douglas et al., *Arguments*, pp. 7, 8, 16.
28. *Ibid.*, pp. 9, 16–17, 24.
29. *Ibid.*, p. 6.
30. The convention report is reproduced in Rollin, *Life*, pp. 327–67. It is also available in Bracey et al., *Black Nationalism*, pp. 87–110. Dorothy Sterling, *The Making*, pp. 155–57, provides information on the setting of the convention. Ullman, *Delany*, pp. 163–64, is helpful on women at the Cleveland convention. At Rochester, in spite of Frederick Douglass's own advanced public position on women's rights, there had been only one female delegate, and that was considered an accomplishment. See P. Foner, *Life*, II, 19.
31. Rollin, *Life*, p. 329.
32. *Ibid.*, p. 335. DuBois's best-known statement, "the problem of the Twentieth Century is the problem of the color line," appeared in the introduction to *The Souls of Black Folk* (1903; rpt. Greenwich, Conn.: Fawcett, 1961). However, DuBois, in his usual style, was quoting from himself, for he had used that very phrase in his "Address to the Nations of the World," written for the first Pan-African Conference in London in July 1900. The conference document appears in Alexander Walters, *My Life and Work* (New York: Fleming H. Revell, 1917), pp. 257–60.
33. Rollin, *Life*, pp. 336–37.
34. *Ibid.*, p. 337.
35. *Ibid.*, p. 338. As with so many visionaries before and after him, Delany's best hopes and dreams went well beyond his own capacities and were counter to the urgent movement of history. Nevertheless, the grandeur of the vision remains, and there can be no gainsaying the writer who claimed that this 1854 report and the convention platform together "constitute the philosophical bedrock [of] black nationalism" in America. See Ullman, *Delany*, p. 170.
36. William F. Cheek presents a useful sketch of Langston's life in "John Mercer Langston: Black Protest Leader and Abolitionist," *Civil War History*, 16 (June 1970), 101–20. Cheek's essay also appears in Bracey, Meier, Rudwick, eds., *Blacks in the Abolitionist Movement* (Belmont, Calif.: Wadsworth Publishing, 1971), pp. 25–43.
37. H. Ford Douglas, *Speech . . . Before the Emigration Convention . . . August, 1854* (Chicago, 1854), pp. 3–6. Portions of the speech are reproduced in Aptheker, *Documentary*, I, 366–68.
38. Douglas, *Speech*, p. 9.
39. *Ibid.*, p. 13.
40. *Ibid.*, p. 15.
41. *Ibid.*, pp. 11–12.
42. The text of the Declaration is available in Aptheker, *Documentary*, I, 363–66.
43. *Ibid.*, p. 365.
44. *Ibid.* Ullman's work on Delany initially called my attention to the contrasts in the approach of the two conventions. Ullman, pp. 154–56; Aptheker, *Documentary*, I, 363–66.

45. Aptheker, *Documentary*, I, 365–66.
46. Ullman, *Delany*, pp. 165–72; Sterling, *The Making*, pp. 157–58.
47. R. Harris, "H. Ford Douglas," pp. 9–12; the *Post* editorial is quoted in Ullman, *Delany*, pp. 175–76.
48. Ullman, *Delany*, pp. 175–76.
49. Quoted in Cheek, *Black Resistance*, p. 33; P. Foner, *Life*, II, 287.
50. Elizabeth Jennings told her own story in *Frederick Douglass' Paper*, July 28, 1854, cited in Sterling, *Speak Out*, pp. 140–43. One of the more recent accounts of the famous Anthony Burns rescue is David R. Maginnes, "The Case of the Court House Rioters," *JNH*, 56 (Jan. 1971), 31–42.

CHAPTER 10: ON JORDAN'S STORMY BANKS

1. The sampling of references to Kansas-Nebraska literature which are cited in chapter 9, note 25, would be helpful here as well. One fascinating view of the Kansas-Nebraska developments comes through the activities of John Brown: Oates, *Purge*, pp. 97–177. A full account of the Sumner affair is found in David Donald, *Charles Sumner and the Coming of the Civil War* (New York: Knopf, 1960), pp. 288–97.
2. The best summary of the white Free Soil position, in relation to its competing ideologies, is E. Foner, *Free Soil.*
3. On the uses of scorpions and snakes, see R. H. Taylor, "Slave Conspiracies," p. 33.
4. Robert S. Starobin, *Industrial Slavery in the Old South* (New York: Oxford University Press, 1970), p. 87; Genovese, *Roll Jordan*, pp. 615–17.
5. Aptheker, *Slave Revolts*, pp. 345–46.
6. Starobin, *Industrial Slavery*, pp. 89–91; Harvey Wish, "The Slave Insurrection Panic of 1856," *Journal of Southern History*, 5 (May 1939), 210–13; Aptheker, *Slave Revolts*, p. 347; Rawick, *American Slave*, XVIII, 84.
7. Aptheker, *Slave Revolts*, p. 347; McKibben, "Negro Slave Insurrections," p. 81; Addington, "Slave Insurrections," pp. 414–18.
8. Dickson, *Manual*, p. 16; Aptheker, *Documentary*, I, 380.
9. Melvin Drimmer, ed., *Black History: A Reappraisal* (New York: Doubleday, 1968), p. 132.
10. Catterall, *Judicial*, III, 242.
11. *Ibid.*, p. 45. Delany's *Blake*, p. 79, tells of the panther call.
12. Franklin, *From Slavery*, p. 255.
13. P. Foner, *Life*, II, 406.
14. A popular history of the decision is Vincent C. Hopkins, *Dred Scott's Case* (New York: Fordham University Press, 1951). Two more recent scholarly examinations are Walter Ehrlich, *They Have No Rights: Dred Scott's Struggle for Freedom* (Westport, Conn.: Greenwood Press, 1979); and Don E. Fehrenbacher, *The Dred Scott Case* (New York: Oxford University Press, 1978). For the black responses to the decision see also Quarles, *Black Abolitionists*, pp. 230–34; Aptheker, *Documentary*, I, 392–94, 411–12; Pease and Pease, *They Who*, pp. 240–44.
15. Anyone who had read Taney's earlier opinion on black legal inferiority when he was Attorney General could not have been surprised; see Carl B. Swisher, *Roger B. Taney* (New York: Macmillan, 1935), pp. 151–54. In 1831 Attorney General Taney said: "The African race in the United States even

when free, are every where a degraded class, and exercise no political influence. The privileges they are allowed to enjoy, are accorded to them as a matter of kindness and benevolence rather than right" (Swisher, p. 154). Taney's personal experience with slavery is outlined in Charles W. Smith, Jr., *Roger B. Taney: Jacksonian Jurist* (Chapel Hill: University of North Carolina Press, 1936), pp. 141–54; Litwack, *North*, pp. 52–53. The text of the decision is readily available in Commager, *Documents*, I, 340.

16. Commager, I, 340; Litwack, *North*, pp. 52–53.

17. Edwin C. Rozwenc, *The Making of American Society*, 2 vols. (Boston: Allyn and Bacon, 1972), I, 510–11. Larry Gara in "Slavery and the Slave Power," pp. 5–6, 10–18, offers a concise statement of the moral, emotional, and political force which had built up behind that term by the 1850s.

18. Quoted in Aptheker, *Documentary*, I, 392–93.

19. *Ibid.*, p. 394; Garvin, "The Free Negro," p. 11.

20. Aptheker, *Documentary*, I, 412.

21. Brown et al., *Negro Caravan*, p. 641.

22. Aptheker, *Documentary*, I, 407; Quarles, *Black Abolitionists*, p. 232.

23. Quoted in Litwack, *North*, pp. 265–66.

24. Among the more helpful sources for Brown's visit to Chatham are W. E. B. DuBois, *John Brown* (1909; rpt. New York: International Publishers, 1962), pp. 251–66; Richard J. Hinton, *John Brown and His Men* (1894; rpt. New York: Arno Press, 1968), pp. 170–85, 619–37; Oates, *Purge*, pp. 243–47; Rollin, *Life*, pp. 85–90; Sterling, *The Making*, pp. 167–75; Victor, *American Conspiracies*, pp. 527–29, 573–77; and Winks, *Blacks*, pp. 267–71.

25. Rollin, *Life*, pp. 88–89.

26. The black delegate who opposed the pledge of allegiance at Chatham was George J. Reynolds, a coppersmith of Sandusky, Ohio. Reynolds was reputedly a member of a secret armed black organization, the Liberty League, whose major function was to assure fugitives a safe passage across the Canadian border, but which was also rumored to have other, more insurrectionary plans. Whether the Liberty League was related to the Knights of Liberty is not now known. For references to Reynolds and his League, see Hinton, *John Brown*, pp. 180, 185, 635. Brown's response to Reynolds is quoted in Sterling, *The Making*, p. 172.

27. The most important readily available sources on the emigration project are found in Martin R. Delany and Robert Campbell, *Search for a Place: Black Separatism and Africa* (1860; rpt. Ann Arbor: University of Michigan Press, 1969); and A. H. M. Kirk-Greene, "America in the Niger Valley: A Colonization Centenary," *Phylon*, 22 (Fall 1962), 225–39. See also Sterling, *The Making*, pp. 178–79; and Rollin, *Life*, pp. 83–85. It is important to note that Rollin's work, which was clearly guided by Delany, gives very short shrift—less than five pages in the main body—to the nationalist-emigrationist period of the man's life. That fact is probably a commentary on what Delany had become and, by 1868, what he wanted history to record.

28. Richard K. MacMaster, "Henry Highland Garnet and the African Civilization Society," *Journal of Presbyterian History*, 48 (Jan. 1970), 95–112. MacMaster reminds us that the idea of African-produced cotton as a rival to the Southern kingdom had been raised sometime earlier by proponents of Liberian settlement. Eventually there was some co-operation established between Delany's venture and Garnet's Society—a move which seemed only to

confuse most of their colleagues and supporters. See MacMaster, pp. 103–12.

29. Floyd J. Miller, who rediscovered many formerly neglected sections of the novel, provides a useful introduction and notes for the work. See Delany, *Blake*, pp. xi–xxix, 315–21.

30. Lumpkin, "General Plan," pp. 63–72.

31. *Ibid.*

32. Summary accounts of the Oberlin-Wellington incidents are available in S. Campbell, *Slave Catchers*, pp. 164–67; Gara, *Liberty Line*, pp. 138–40; and Quarles, *Black Abolitionists*, pp. 213–14. Langston's speech is quoted in Cheek, *Black Resistance*, pp. 155–61.

33. DuBois, *John Brown*, pp. 280–82; Hinton, *John Brown*, pp. 246–47, 263, 504–05; Oates, *Purge*, pp. 268, 291.

34. DuBois, *John Brown*, pp. 273–76; Hinton, *John Brown*, pp. 182–84; Oates, *Purge*, pp. 243–47, 276–79.

35. Oates, *Purge*, pp. 274–89.

36. Concerning the black men in Brown's company, see DuBois, *John Brown*, pp. 280–83; Hinton, *John Brown*, pp. 504–08; Oates, *Purge*, pp. 224, 268, 276, 282–83, 286. The quotation from Harriet Newby's letter appears in Oates, *Purge*, p. 294.

37. Osborne P. Anderson, *A Voice from Harper's Ferry* (1861; rpt. New York: World View Publishers, 1974), p. 96.

38. There remains some dispute about the response of local enslaved (and free) blacks. Anderson (pp. 96–99) insists that many blacks were responsive and prepared to act with Brown, and that some were actual participants in the engagement. Oates, citing Oswald G. Villard's study—*John Brown, 1800–1859: A Biography Fifty Years After* (Boston: Houghton Mifflin, 1910)—as his sole source of information on this matter, is equally adamant in claiming a total absence of voluntary participation from the surrounding black population (pp. 301–02). DuBois, following Anderson's firsthand account, speaks of from twenty-five to fifty blacks armed by the Brown forces. The figure of seven black deaths comes from Anderson, pp. 97–98. My own tendency is to accept Anderson's account.

39. Oates, *Purge*, pp. 290–302, provides a helpful summary of the main action.

40. Quoted in Hinton, *John Brown*, p. 509. Copeland was executed on Dec. 16, 1859.

41. William Butler Yeats, "Easter, 1916," in *The Collected Poems of William Butler Yeats* (New York: Macmillan, 1956), pp. 177–78. /

42. Roy P. Basler, ed., *The Collected Works of Abraham Lincoln*, 9 vols. (New Brunswick, N.J.: Rutgers University Press, 1953), III, 145–46.

43. "Speech of H. Ford Douglas," *National Anti-Slavery Standard*, 21 (Aug. 25, 1860).

44. Much of the bitter, divisive mood of the time was focused and reflected in the American Anti-Slavery Society's pamphlet, *Southern Outrages Upon Northern Citizens* (New York, 1860). A standard and informative overview of the period is provided by Allan Nevins in *The Emergence of Lincoln: Prologue to the Civil War, 1859–1861* (New York: Charles Scribner's Sons, 1950), II, 98–202.

45. William Robeson eventually had a son named Paul. Paul Robeson, *Here I Stand*, p. 14 (new ed., p. 6). The annual report of the American Anti-

Slavery Society for 1861 provides information from contemporary newspapers on the ferment in the South.

46. Rawick, *American Slave*, XVII, 146–53.
47. William W. White, "The Texas Slave Insurrection of 1860," *Southwestern Historical Quarterly*, 52 (Jan. 1949), 270, 259–62; Addington, "Slave Insurrections," pp. 423–24.
48. Addington, p. 421.
49. Quoted in Aptheker, *Slave Revolts*, p. 357.
50. Catterall, *Judicial*, I, 440.
51. *Anglo-African*, Mar. 17, 1860, quoted in James M. McPherson, *The Negro's Civil War* (New York: Pantheon, 1965), p. 4.
52. *Ibid.*, pp. 11–13; Siebert, *Underground Railroad*, p. 28.
53. Lincoln's First Inaugural Address (Mar. 4, 1861) contains a summary of his noninterference position. Basler, *Collected Works*, IV, 249–71.
54. Delany's own account of the African voyage is presented in his *Official Report of the Niger Valley Exploring Party* (New York, 1861). The document is reprinted in Delany and Campbell, *Search*, pp. 23–148. See also Ullman's review and analysis, *Delany*, pp. 216–37.
55. Delany and Campbell, *Search*, p. 121.

CHAPTER 11: THE BLOOD-RED IRONIES OF GOD

1. See above, pp. 88–89.
2. Among the most available and useful sources for documenting the black response to the coming of the war are McPherson, *Negro's Civil War*, pp. 19–36; Aptheker, *Documentary*, I, 459–480; and the pages of the *Christian Recorder* for 1861.
3. Aug. 24, 1861. Quoted in McPherson, p. 31.
4. Aptheker, *Documentary*, I, 469. It must be recognized, of course, that black abolitionists were not alone in this position. Across the North the vast majority of their white antislavery colleagues moved quickly to an unwavering, patriotic, pro-Union position and maintained it throughout the war. A helpful discussion of the white abolitionist mood appears in John S. Rosenberg, "Toward a New Civil War Revisionism," *American Scholar*, 38 (Spring 1969), 262–63. Also James M. McPherson, *The Struggle for Equality* (Princeton: Princeton University Press, 1964), pp. 47–74ff.
5. Aptheker, *Documentary*, I, 465.
6. On the Pennsylvania offer, see Herbert Aptheker, *To Be Free: Studies in American Negro History* (1948; rpt. New York: International Publishers, 1969), pp. 71–72. The doggerel is quoted in W. E. B. DuBois, *Black Reconstruction in America* (1935; rpt. New York: World Publishing, 1962), p. 56. For other examples of similar white responses, see McPherson, *Struggle*, pp. 21–33; Dudley Cornish, *The Sable Arm* (New York: W. W. Norton, 1965), pp. 1–28; Benjamin Quarles, *The Negro in the Civil War* (New York: Russell and Russell, 1953), pp. 24–31. However, by the time the war had opened up deep fountains of blood in white families across the land, a new song was being sung:

> Some tell us 'tis a burning shame
> To make the naygers fight;

An' that the thrade of bein' kilt
   Belongs but to the white;
But as for me, upon my soul!
   So liberal are we here,
I'll let Sambo be murthered instead of myself
   On every day of the year.

Quoted in Leon Litwick, *Been in the Storm So Long* (New York: Knopf, 1979), p. 71.

7. During most of his time in the Presidency, Lincoln's preferred alternative to equal black citizenship was colonization. The most complete single statement of his position may be found in Basler, *Collected Works*, V, 370–75. Discussions of this and other aspects of Lincoln's racial policies and views are available in Benjamin Quarles, *Lincoln and the Negro* (New York: Oxford University Press, 1962), pp. 106–23; George Sinkler, *The Racial Attitudes of American Presidents* (New York: Doubleday, 1972), pp. 34–93; Warren A. Beck, "Lincoln and Negro Colonization in Central America," *Abraham Lincoln Quarterly*, 4 (Sept. 1950), 162–83; Paul J. Scheips, "Lincoln and the Chiriqui Colonization Project," *JNH*, 37 (Oct. 1952), 418–53; Ludwell H. Johnson, "Lincoln and Equal Rights: A Reply," *Civil War History*, 13 (Mar. 1967), 66–73, especially p. 69. Also George M. Frederickson, "A Man but Not a Brother," *Journal of Southern History*, 41 (Feb. 1975), 39–58.

8. *Anglo-African*, Sept. 28, 1861, quoted in McPherson, *Struggle*, pp. 31–32.

9. *Anglo-African*, Oct. 19, 1861, quoted in McPherson, *Struggle*, p. 34.

10. One of the best surveys of the Republican Party's ideology as it entered the Civil War is found in E. Foner's *Free Soil*. His assessment of the party's economic position and its relationship to black people is more sympathetic than my own, but nonetheless invaluable. For a good summary, see Litwack, *North*, pp. 269–74. Delany is quoted in Sterling, *The Making*, p. 219.

11. George B. McClellan, *Report on the Organization and Campaigns of the Army of the Potomac* (New York, 1864), pp. 15–16.

12. *Anglo-African*, Sept. 21, 1861, quoted in McPherson, *Struggle*, p. 42. The general whose order was countermanded was John C. Fremont. There is some evidence that a few Union officers attempted to encourage insurrection among the enslaved blacks: DuBois, *Black Reconstruction*, p. 65.

13. See especially DuBois, *Black Reconstruction*, pp. 57–82, for a fascinating statement of this black activity, which DuBois called "the General Strike," thereby somewhat overstating the nature of the movement. It is dealt with in many other sources as well, ranging from Carter G. Woodson's early study, *A Century of Negro Migration* (Washington, D.C.: Association for the Study of Negro Life and History, 1918), to the important, provocative work by Louis L. Gerteis, *From Contraband to Freedman: Federal Policy Toward Southern Blacks, 1861–1865* (Westport, Conn.: Greenwood Press, 1973), pp. 11–14. One of the fullest modern treatments of that wartime black movement to freedom is Leon Litwack, "Free At Last," in Hareven, *Anonymous Americans*, pp. 131–71, creatively expanded in Litwack's *Been in the Storm*.

14. Accounts of the early black flooding toward freedom are found in many places. Among them are DuBois, *Black Reconstruction*, pp. 54–65; Elizabeth Botume, *First Days Amongst the Contrabands* (1892; rpt. New York: Arno Press, 1969), pp. 10–15; Robert F. Engs, "Freedom's First Generation," unpublished

manuscript in the author's possession; Litwack, *Been in the Storm*, pp. 135–37. See also Gerteis, *From Contraband*, pp. 11–16.

15. Undated *New York Times* clipping reprinted in *Douglass' Monthly* (Feb. 1862), p. 599.

16. Gerteis, *From Contraband*, is the best available source on this subject; see also DuBois, *Black Reconstruction*, pp. 67ff. A most helpful more recent treatment of one concrete example is William F. Messner, "Black Violence and White Response: Louisiana, 1862," *Journal of Southern History*, 41 (Feb. 1975), 19–38.

17. The mass escape is reported in Ottley and Weatherby, *The Negro in New York*, p. iii. The South Carolina incident appears in Thomas W. Higginson, "Negro Spirituals," *Atlantic Monthly*, 19 (June 1867), pp. 685–94.

18. Aptheker, *Slave Revolts*, p. 365. The experience of Robert Smalls and the *Planter* is treated in many places, but his biography is most fully covered in Okon E. Uya, *From Slavery to Public Service: Robert Smalls, 1839–1915* (New York: Oxford University Press, 1971). See McPherson, *Negro's Civil War*, pp. 154–58, for a contemporary account of the *Planter* incident.

19. McKibben, *Negro Slave Insurrections*, pp. 73–90; Georgia Lee Tatum, *Disloyalty in the Confederacy* (Chapel Hill: University of North Carolina Press, 1934), p. 3; Ottley and Weatherby, *The Negro in New York*, pp. 111–12; Aptheker, *Slave Revolts*, p. 94.

20. Aptheker, *Slave Revolts*, pp. 360ff.

21. Gerteis, *From Contraband*, pp. 11–98, *passim*; Messner, "Black Violence," pp. 19–38; Franklin, *From Slavery*, pp. 273–74; DuBois, *Black Reconstruction*, p. 92; Cornish, *Sable Arm*, pp. 69–111.

22. Messner, "Black Violence," pp. 19–31.

23. The best summary of the various emancipation discussions and proposals appears in John Hope Franklin, *The Emancipation Proclamation* (New York: Anchor Books, 1965); for the Congressional pressures on Lincoln, see especially pp. 16–28. The rise of a strong antislavery, anti–slave power sentiment is described—but not analyzed—in P. J. Staudenraus, "The Popular Origins of the Thirteenth Amendment," *Mid-America*, 50 (Apr. 1968), 108–15. Douglass's statement appears in *Douglass' Monthly*, August 1862, p. 694.

24. Franklin, *Emancipation*, pp. 29–54.

25. *Ibid.*, p. 76; Gerteis, *From Contraband*, pp. 65–82.

26. Aptheker, *Slave Revolts*, pp. 94–95.

27. Cam Walker, "Corinth: The Story of a Contraband Camp," *Civil War History*, 20 (Mar. 1974), 5–22.

28. Sterling, *Speak Out*, pp. 353–54.

29. Quarles, *Negro in Civil War*, pp. 161–66.

30. Litwack, *North*, p. 63.

31. Franklin, *Emancipation*, pp. 114–17. For an example of a resolution passed by a Northern state (Illinois) against the Proclamation, see Commager, *Documents*, I, 421–22. The speech by Trumbull, an Illinois Senator and a leader in the Republican Party, appeared in the *Congressional Globe*, 37th Cong., 2nd session (Feb. 25, 1862), p. 994. Similar Northern white responses are provided in James McPherson's introduction to *Anti-Negro Riots in the North* (1863; rpt. New York: Arno Press, 1969), pp. iii, iv.

32. Basler, *Collected Works*, V, 527–37.

33. Franklin, *Emancipation*, pp. 101–04; McPherson, *Negro's Civil War*, pp. 49–53; Charles, *Lincoln*, pp. 139–50. There is some evidence in the oral tradition of the slave narratives that most enslaved blacks did not consider Jan. 1, 1863, to be as important to their freedom as the ending of the Civil War or the passage of the 13th Amendment. See Rawick, *American Slave*, VI, 362; XIII, 204; IX, 156.

34. Quoted in Aptheker, *Documentary*, I, 476–77.

35. Basler, *Collected Works*, VI, 30.

36. Helpful information on the black (and white) recruiters is in Peter Burchard, *One Gallant Rush* (New York: St. Martin's, 1965), pp. 77–78, 84; Henry G. Pearson, *The Life of John A. Andrew, Governor of Massachusetts*, 2 vols. (Boston: Houghton Mifflin, 1904), II, 81–86, 91; Cornish, *Sable Arm*, pp. 108, 110; Quarles, *Negro in Civil War*, pp. 8–9, 184–85.

37. On H. Ford Douglas's wartime experiences, the National Archives materials and the Harris essay cited in chapter 8, note 28, are most helpful. His letter to Frederick Douglass, dated Jan. 8, 1863, appeared in *Douglass' Monthly*, Feb. 1863, p. 786. ·

38. *Douglass' Monthly*, Feb. 1863, p. 786. Yet less than a month later H. Ford Douglas wrote another, rather different letter, complaining to Owen Lovejoy about the racial prejudice he was encountering in the military. Quoted in Sterling, *Speak Out*, pp. 322–24.

39. The reluctance of some potential black recruits, as well as other related problems, are treated in McPherson, *Negro's Civil War*, pp. 173–75, and Cornish, *Sable Arm*, pp. 105–11. The Douglass incident is reported in P. Foner, *Life*, III, 363–64.

40. There is a full-scale, somewhat flamboyant treatment of the draft riots in James McCague, *The Second Rebellion: The Story of the New York City Draft Riots of 1863* (New York: Dial Press, 1968); see also McPherson, *Negro's Civil War*, pp. 69–76.

41. Quoted in Ullman, *Delany*, p. 257.

42. *Ibid.*, p. 283; Sterling, *The Making*, pp. 231–32, 275–76. Rollin, *Life*, pp. 145–54, relates Delany's recruitment experiences as interpreted by him from his post–Civil War perspective.

43. Cornish, *Sable Arm*, pp. 181–96; DuBois, *Black Reconstruction*, p. 107.

44. Gerteis, *From Contraband*, pp. 108–09.

45. Franklin, *From Slavery*, pp. 287–88; McPherson, *Negro's Civil War*, p. 201.

CHAPTER 12: "WE ARE COMING UP"

1. The role of the federal government in suppressing the revolutionary potential of the black movement out of slavery is treated with great care in Gerteis, *From Contraband*, passim.

2. "The Work of the Future," *Douglass' Monthly*, Nov. 1862, quoted in P. Foner, *Life*, III, 290–93.

3. *Ibid.*

4. "Our Work Is Not Done," *Proceedings of the American Anti-Slavery Society*, Dec. 3–4, 1863; quoted in P. Foner, *Life*, III, 386.

5. The address is reproduced in Robert Purvis, *Speeches and Correspondence* (Philadelphia, 1898[?]), pp. 6–11.

6. *Ibid.*, p. 7. The reference to "Secretary Bates" is to Attorney General Edward Bates's advisement of Nov. 1862, concerning the citizenship of free blacks. See above, p. 234. On the larger issue of the interrelationships among the war, black self-liberating activity, and Republican policies, one of the most perceptive treatments is provided by Mary F. Berry, *Military Necessity and Civil Rights Policy* (Port Washington, N.Y.: Kennicat Press, 1977).

7. Purvis, *Speeches*, pp. 7–8.

8. *Ibid.*

9. The best source for the Syracuse convention is "Proceedings of the National Convention of Colored Men" in Bell, *Minutes*, 1864, [pp. 1–62]. It provides the basic documentation for the following treatment of the convention. The question from the white residents of Syracuse is quoted there, [pp. 13–14].

10. *Ibid.*, [p. 22].

11. *Ibid.*, [pp. 4, 23, 33, 53, 56–58].

12. *Ibid.*, [pp. 33–36, 41–43].

13. *Ibid.*, [pp. 17–19, 36–39]. In 1869, the high tide of Reconstruction's hope, another black convention voted not to revive the already weakened League. August Meier, *Negro Thought in America 1880–1915* (Ann Arbor: University of Michigan Press, 1966), pp. 4–8. However, it is also interesting to note that the name and function were revived again in a difficult period by William Monroe Trotter, a true heir of the black abolitionist tradition. See Stephen R. Fox, *The Guardian of Boston: William Monroe Trotter* (New York: Atheneum, 1970), pp. 140, 179. The work of an active branch of the first League is briefly reported in James M. McPherson, *Struggle*, pp. 234–35.

14. "Proceedings," in Bell, *Minutes*, 1864, [pp. 15, 33–34, 46–61].

15. *Ibid.*, [p. 62].

16. Douglass, *Life and Times*, p. 377.

17. The price paid by some blacks for their recruitment is explored in John W. Blassingame, "The Recruitment of Colored Troops in Kentucky, Maryland and Missouri, 1860–1863," *The Historian*, 24 (Aug. 1967), 533–45.

18. Harvey Wish, "Slave Disloyalty Under the Confederacy," *JNH*, 23 (Oct. 1938), 445; Cornish, *Sable Arm*, pp. 144–45; DuBois, *Black Reconstruction*, p. 108.

19. Rawick, *American Slave*, XVIII, 253.

20. Gerteis, *From Contraband*, pp. 106–11, and Cornish, *Sable Arm*, pp. 236–37, deal with the use of impressment and vagrancy laws to bring blacks into the military. (A poignant document by black troops who had been impressed appears in the H. Ford Douglas papers; see note 28.) On the role of military recruitment as a means of controlling volatile black power, see Messner, "Black Violence," pp. 27–31, as well as Gerteis.

21. Gerteis, *From Contraband*, pp. 110ff, and Messner, "Black Violence," pp. 19–38, provide an overview as well as concrete examples of such developments in the relationship between self-liberated blacks in the South and the federal government. See also Wish, "Slave Disloyalty," pp. 441–42, 444.

22. Rawick, *American Slave*, XVIII, 232.

23. Quoted in Vernon L. Wharton, *The Negro in Mississippi, 1865–1890* (1947; rpt. New York: Harper and Row, 1965), p. 20.

24. Rawick, *American Slave*, IV, 229. The interviewer for this narrative set the date of Cole's flight in 1861; but since Cole tells of running toward Gen.

William Rosencrans's army in Tennessee, the year has to be 1863. See also
Litwack, "Free At Last," pp. 131–71; Aptheker, "Maroons," p. 165; John F.
Reiger, "Deprivation, Disaffection and Desertion in Confederate Florida,"
Florida Historical Quarterly, 48 (Jan. 1970), 293; Wish, "Slave Disloyalty,"
p. 445.

25. Rawick, *American Slave*, VI, 416–17. See above, pp. 163, 208, for other references to the determined use of prayer as an element of the black struggle. The
comment about the religious element of the black Union forces was made by
Thomas W. Higginson, *Army Life in a Black Regiment* (1869; rpt. Boston:
Beacon Press, 1962), p. 255.

26. T. R. Hay, "The South and the Arming of Slaves," *Mississippi Historical Review*, 6 (June 1919), 34–73; N. W. Stephenson, "The Question of Arming the
Slaves," *American Historical Review*, 18 (Jan. 1913), 295–308; see also Du-
Bois's well-documented discussion of the subject in *Black Reconstruction*,
pp. 115–20.

27. DuBois, *Black Reconstruction*, pp. 119–20.

28. For an example of the brutal tactics of impressment, note the "Letter from 53
Enlisted Men of the Light Colored Battery, Ft. Leavenworth, Kansas, to Capt.
H. Ford Douglas, June 14, 1865," in *Records*. Gerteis, *From Contraband*,
p. 102, and Blassingame, "Recruitment," pp. 538–39, present other examples.
The contraband camp mortality figure is quoted in Franklin, *From Slavery*,
p. 21.

29. Gerteis, *From Contraband*, p. 5.

30. The best-known set of problems regarding black land rights developed in the
coastal areas of South Carolina. See Willie Lee Rose, *Rehearsal for Reconstruction: The Port Royal Experiment* (New York: Vintage Books, 1967),
especially pp. 272–96. Concerning the larger Southern scene, see Gerteis,
From Contraband, pp. 40–44, 55–58, 169–81; LaWanda Cox, "The Promise
of Land for the Freedman," *Mississippi Valley Historical Review*, 45 (Dec.
1958), 413–39; William S. McFeeley, *Yankee Stepfather: General O. O.
Howard and the Freedman* (New Haven: Yale University Press, 1968),
pp. 92–148; McPherson, *Struggle*, pp. 249–55. Also DuBois, *Black Reconstruction*, pp. 456ff; McPherson, *Negro's Civil War*, p. 295.

31. The most helpful study of the two newspapers and of the men who gave them
life is Finnian Patrick Leavens, *"L'Union* and the *New Orleans Tribune* and
Louisiana Reconstruction," unpublished Master's thesis, Louisiana State University, 1966. There is also significant information in Donald E. Everett, "Demands of the New Orleans Free Colored Population for Political Equality,
1862–1865," *Louisiana Historical Quarterly*, 38 (Apr. 1955), 43–64. Although
they provide important information, both Leavens and Everett leave much to be
desired in the realm of analysis. See also DuBois, *Black Reconstruction*, p.
456. The quotation on revolutions appears in McPherson, *Negro's Civil War*,
p. 295. Its earliest American source appears to be Sen. William H. Seward's
"Irrepressible Conflict" speech of October 1858; Frederic Bancroft, *The Life
of William H. Seward* (New York: Harper and Brothers, 1900), I, 406.

32. Everett, "Demands," pp. 48–55.

33. McPherson, *Negro's Civil War*, pp. 281–82.

34. The *Tribune* statement is quoted in David C. Rankin, "The Origins of Black
Leadership in New Orleans During Reconstruction," *Journal of Southern His-*

tory, 40 (Aug. 1974), 417–40. Rankin's excellent study makes the point that many of the persons who shared such a vision in New Orleans had been free before the war and had often gained access to literacy as well as property.

CHAPTER 13: SLAVERY CHAIN DONE BROKE AT LAST

1. *Christian Recorder*, Feb. 4, 1865.
2. The black community's awareness of the wartime events and their implications is readily apparent in the pages of the *Recorder*. See especially Jan. 7–28 and Feb. 4, 1865.
3. *Ibid.*, Jan. 14, 1865.
4. See above, pp. 246–49 for references to the *Tribune* and to the Syracuse convention.
5. W. T. Sherman, *Memoirs* (New York, 1892), II, 201–52, and Edmund L. Drago, "How Sherman's March Through Georgia Affected the Slaves," *Georgia Historical Quarterly*, 57 (Fall 1973), 361–75.
6. Drago, "How Sherman's March," p. 361ff.
7. This account of the Savannah meeting is based on "The Freedmen in Georgia," *The National Freedman*, 1 (Apr. 1865), 98–101; a letter from James Lynch, *Christian Recorder*, Feb. 4, 1865; *New York Tribune*, Feb. 13, 1865; Rose, *Rehearsal*, pp. 326–27.
8. The list of black participants appears in "Freedmen," pp. 98–99. Twenty persons are named there, while Lynch's letter to the *Recorder* mentions a group of nineteen, including himself.
9. "Freedmen," pp. 99–100.
10. *Ibid.*, p. 99.
11. *Ibid.*
12. Lynch, a major black Reconstruction leader, has not yet been given the attention he deserves. The only sketch of his life available is William C. Harris, "James Lynch: Black Leader in Southern Reconstruction," *The Historian*, 34 (Nov. 1971), 40–61, a significant but not entirely accurate account. For other important information on Lynch, see two articles by William B. Gravely: "A Black Methodist on Reconstruction in Mississippi: Three Letters by James Lynch in 1868–1869," *Methodist History*, 11 (July 1973), 3–18; and "The Decision of A.M.E. Leader, James Lynch, to Join the Methodist Episcopal Church," *Methodist History*, 15 (July 1977), 263–69.
13. John Blassingame, "Before the Ghetto: The Making of the Black Community in Savannah, Georgia, 1865–1880," *Journal of Social History*, 6 (Summer 1973), 471–73.
14. The quotation is from Frazier's statement above, p. 263.
15. On Bryan and his followers, see above, p. 44.
16. Two works provide useful summaries of the black conventions in this transitional period: Herbert Aptheker, "Organizational Activities of Southern Negroes, 1865," in his *To Be Free*, pp. 136–62; and Martin Abbot, "Freedom's Cry: Negroes and Their Meetings in South Carolina, 1865–1869," *JNH*, 20 (Spring 1959), 263–72. A sampling of the documents produced by the conventions appears in Aptheker, *Documentary*, II, 533–47.
17. Alrutheus A. Taylor, *The Negro in Tennessee, 1865–1880* (Washington, D.C.: Associated Publishers, 1941), p. 2.
18. *New Orleans Tribune*, Jan. 20, 1865; Litwack, *Been in the Storm*, pp. 508–09.

19. Roger A. Fischer, "A Pioneer Protest: The New Orleans Street-Car Controversy of 1867," *JNH*, 53 (Jan. 1968), 220-21.

20. Rose, *Rehearsal*, pp. 320-21, provides a good description of the context of the field order's land policies. James S. Allen, *Reconstruction, The Battle for Democracy* (New York: International Publishers, 1937), pp. 225-27, is also informative and stimulating. One of the most accessible sources for the text of the field order itself is W. T. Sherman, *Memoirs*, II, 250-52.

21. W. T. Sherman, *Memoirs*, II, 250-52.

22. An account of Houston's life and activities appears in "The Bone and Sinew of the South," *The National Freedman*, 1 (Apr. 1865), 82-83.

23. *Ibid.*

24. One of the best and most concise sources of information on the new communities of black freed persons is Edward Magdol, *A Right to the Land* (Westport, Conn.: Greenwood Press, 1977), pp. 90-108.

25. Joel Williamson, *After Slavery* (Chapel Hill: University of North Carolina Press, 1965), p. 61; Dorothy Sterling, ed., *The Trouble They Seen* (New York: Doubleday, 1976), pp. 30-46; Rose, *Rehearsal*, pp. 320-31.

26. Litwack, *Been in the Storm*, pp. 465-66; Roberta Sue Alexander, "North Carolina Churches Face Emancipation and the Freedmen," *University of Dayton Review*, 9 (Winter 1972), 52-55.

27. Unfortunately, the only available account of Campbell's life and work is a study which is at best unsympathetic and at times scurrilous: E. Merton Coulter, "Tunis G. Campbell, Negro Reconstructionist in Georgia," *Georgia Historical Quarterly*, 51 (Dec. 1967), 401-24; 52 (Mar. 1968), 16-52. This account is based on Coulter's work as well as on Campbell's testimony in U.S. Congress, *Report of the Joint Select Committee to Inquire into the Condition of Affairs in the Late Insurrectionary States*, 42nd Congress, 2nd Session (Washington, D.C.: Government Printing Office, 1872), VI, VII: 845-64. (The Select Committee's work was also known as the Ku Klux Klan investigation.)

28. Sterling, *The Trouble*, pp. 30-46; Williamson, *After Slavery*, p. 63.

29. Edwin D. Hoffman, "From Slavery to Self-Reliance," *JNH*, 41 (Jan. 1956), 16.

30. For important studies of the Freedmen's Bureau and its relationship to the black struggle for land, as well as the white counterforces, see L. Cox, "The Promise," pp. 413-40; Rose, *Rehearsal*, pp. 337-40, 350-52; McFeeley, *Yankee Stepfather*, pp. 92-148; Robert Cruden, *The Negro in Reconstruction* (Englewood Cliffs, N.J.: Prentice-Hall, 1969), pp. 13-26.

31. Williamson, *After Slavery*, pp. 47-48.

32. For the Richmond story, see *Christian Recorder*, Apr. 22, 1865; [Writers Program, Works Projects Administration, Virginia], *The Negro in Virginia* (1940; rpt. New York: Arno Press, 1969), pp. 164-65, 212; Litwack, *Been in the Storm*, pp. 167-71.

33. Above, pp. 102-03.

34. *Christian Recorder*, Apr. 22, 1865; Litwack, *Been in the Storm*, pp. 167-69.

35. The experience is reported secondhand in Laura Haviland, *A Woman's Life* (Grand Rapids, Mich., 1881), pp. 414-15. See also Litwack, *Been in the Storm*, p. 171.

36. Rawick, *American Slave*, XVI, 6; Litwack, *Been in the Storm*, p. 171.

CHAPTER 14: THE CHALLENGE OF THE CHILDREN

1. The journalist was Whitelaw Reid; see his account in *After the War* (New York, 1866), p. 19. The black sentiments of mourning and apprehension are cited in Botume, *First Days*, p. 178; McPherson, *Negro's Civil War*, pp. 307–08; and Quarles, *Lincoln*, p. 240.

2. Johnson's statement to the free black people of Tennessee is reported, among other places, in Lately Thomas, *The First President Johnson* (New York: William Morrow, 1968), p. 279.

3. Litwack, *Been in the Storm*, pp. 465–66; Alexander, "North Carolina Churches," pp. 52–55.

4. Alexander, "North Carolina Churches," pp. 54–55.

5. The contemporary testimony concerning the transformation in black public attitudes and actions is widespread. See reports of it in Williamson, *After Slavery*, p. 47; Nell Irvin Painter, *Exodusters* (New York: Knopf, 1976), pp. 5–6; U.S. Congress, *Report of the Select Committee to Inquire into the Mississippi Election of 1875*, 44th Congress, 2nd Session (Washington, D.C.: Government Printing Office, 1876), I, 1315. The quotation is from Painter, pp. 5–6.

6. Quoted in Grady McWhiney, ed., *Reconstruction and the Freedmen* (Chicago: Rand McNally, 1963), p. 27.

7. Reid, *After the War*, pp. 145, 222, 352; John B. Myers, "Reaction and Adjustment: The Struggle of Alabama Freedmen in Post-Bellum Alabama, 1865–1867," *Alabama Historical Quarterly*, 32 (Spring/Summer 1970), 5–22. Important contemporary information on the persecution of blacks who sought freedom is also provided in Carl Schurz, *Report on the Condition of the South* (1865; rpt. New York: Arno Press, 1969), pp. 18–20, 58, 70–79.

8. Quoted in Horace Mann Bond, *Negro Education in Alabama* (New York: Atheneum, 1969), p. 27.

9. Williamson, *After Slavery*, p. 33.

10. [Olive Gilbert], *Narrative of Sojourner Truth* (Battle Creek, Mich.: The author, 1878), pp. 140–41.

11. For examples of this withdrawal in Mississippi and Alabama, see Wharton, *The Negro*, p. 118, and Peter Kolchin, *First Freedom* (Westport, Conn.: Greenwood Press, 1972), p. 9.

12. Reid, *After the War*, p. 108.

13. Garrison is quoted in Cruden, *The Negro*, p. 36.

14. James B. Stewart, *Holy Warriors* (New York: Hill and Wang, 1976), pp. 51–53. On the struggle among Garrison and others over his proposal to dissolve the AAAS, see Walter Merrill, ed., *Let The Oppressed Go Free, 1861–1867*, Vol. V of *The Letters of William Lloyd Garrison* (Cambridge: Harvard University Press, 1979), pp. 247–48, 269–70. Garrison continued to grow in his postwar understanding of the need for broad-ranging black rights. See Merrill, *Letters*, V, 365–66, and McPherson, *Struggle*, pp. 297–307.

15. Many of the issues summarized below are treated in far greater detail—though not always from my perspective—in general accounts of Reconstruction and the postwar issues already cited: Cruden, *The Negro*; John Hope Franklin, *Reconstruction: After the Civil War* (Chicago: University of Chicago Press,

1961); Kolchin, *First Freedom*; Litwack, *Been in the Storm*; Magdol, *Right to the Land*; Williamson, *After Slavery*. See also Rembert W. Patrick, *The Reconstruction of the Nation* (New York: Oxford University Press, 1967).

16. One of the more illuminating recent works on the relationship of the Republican Party to the newly freed black community is Herman Belz, *A New Birth of Freedom* (Westport, Conn.: Greenwood Press, 1976). See also Michael Les Benedict, *A Compromise of Principle* (New York: W. W. Norton, 1974).

17. Quoted in Martin E. Dann, ed., *The Black Press, 1827–1890* (New York: Capricorn Books, 1971), pp. 58–59. Rogers and *The Black Republican* are briefly discussed in John W. Blassingame, *Black New Orleans, 1860–1880* (Chicago: University of Chicago Press, 1973), pp. 122, 155–57. Blassingame described Rogers as "the most learned Negro minister in the state" (p. 122).

18. *Black Republican*, Sept. 1865, quoted in Litwack, *Been in the Storm*, p. 536.

19. *Black Republican*, April 29, 1865, quoted in Dann, *Black Press*, pp. 138–40.

20. Chase is quoted in Franklin, *Reconstruction*, pp. 123–25, as a part of that author's perceptive assessment of the League phenomenon.

21. The Wilmington encounter is recorded in Reid, *After the War*, p. 51. See also W. McKee Evans, *Ballots and Fence Rails* (Chapel Hill: University of North Carolina Press, 1967), p. 87, and Magdol, *Right to the Land*, pp. 50–51. The advice from Chase to Johnson is quoted in J. Allen, *Reconstruction*, p. 93.

22. Aptheker, *To Be Free*, pp. 136–62; Abbott, "Freedom's Cry," pp. 263–72.

23. Aptheker, *To Be Free*, pp. 150–62.

24. For more on the itinerant exhorters and organizers, see A. Taylor, *Negro in Tennessee*, p. 8; McPherson, *Struggle*, p. 338; Loren Schweninger, "Black Citizenship and the Republican Party in Reconstruction Alabama," *Alabama Review*, 29 (Apr. 1976), 83–102; Still, *Underground Railroad*, pp. 795–98. On the Equal Rights League in this period, see Evans, *Ballots*, p. 93, and Sidney Andrews, *The South Since the War* (1866; rpt. New York: Arno Press, 1969), pp. 128–30.

25. Quoted in Aptheker, *Documentary*, II, 534–35.

26. *Black Republican*, April 29, 1865, quoted in Dann, *Black Press*, p. 141.

27. The petitions from Mississippi, Tennessee, and Virginia appear in Aptheker, *Documentary*, II, 535–39. The meetings are discussed in his *To Be Free*, pp. 138–42, and in Wharton, *The Negro*, p. 140.

28. Quoted in Evans, *Ballots*, p. 87.

29. S. Andrews, *The South*, pp. 119–31; Litwack, *Been in the Storm*, pp. 502–06.

30. *The Liberator*, June 30, 1865, quoted in Sterling, *The Trouble*, p. 61.

31. Aptheker, *To Be Free*, pp. 138–48; *Documentary*, II, 535–36.

32. Thomas Bayne is another member of that large and impressive company of black fugitives who returned to the South during and after the war to join the struggle for a new society, and who deserve to be far more fully known. Aptheker, *To Be Free*, pp. 138–40.

33. *Ibid.*, pp. 140–48.

34. *Ibid.*

CHAPTER 15: BLACK HOPE, BLACK SOLDIERS, AND BLACK CODES

1. DuBois, *Souls of Black Folk*, p. 190.

2. Carl Schurz, in an account from Mobile, Alabama, provides a typical example

of the white flight from July Fourth celebrations and the enthusiastic black participation; see *Report*, p. 58.

3. The Augusta march is reported in Alan Conway, *The Reconstruction of Georgia* (Minneapolis: University of Minnesota Press, 1966), p. 72. On the Kentucky celebration, see *Christian Recorder*, July 29, 1865; John Mercer Langston, *From the Virginia Plantation to the National Capitol* (Hartford, 1894), pp. 237–40; Herbert G. Gutman, *The Black Family in Slavery and Freedom, 1750–1925* (New York: Pantheon, 1976), pp. 379–81.

4. Langston, *Virginia Plantation*, p. 239.

5. Statistics on the black military presence are provided in Marvin E. Fletcher, "The Negro Volunteer in Reconstruction, 1865–1866," *Military Affairs*, 32 (Dec. 1968), 124–31.

6. For examples of the psychological effects on white Southerners, see Jerrell H. Shofner, *Nor Is It Over Yet* (Gainesville: University of Florida Press, 1974), p. 21.

7. The New Orleans statement is quoted in Walter L. Fleming, ed., *Documentary History of Reconstruction* (Cleveland: Arthur H. Clarke, 1906), I, 48–49. The Georgia editor's words are cited in Fletcher, "Negro Volunteer," p. 127. Such sentiments and experiences recur in the documents of the period.

8. On the Florida situation, see Shofner, *Nor Is It*, p. 38. Gillmore's statement is quoted in James E. Sefton, *The United States Army and Reconstruction, 1865–1877* (Baton Rouge: Louisiana State University Press, 1967), p. 52. The Alabamian's comment appears in Kolchin, *First Freedom*, p. 33. Magdol, *Right to the Land*, pp. 144–46, and Litwack, *Been in the Storm*, p. 269, are also helpful. It should be noted, too, that black soldiers were sometimes used to evict their people from the land; see Sterling, *The Trouble*, p. 43.

9. Williamson, *After Slavery*, p. 53.

10. For confrontations between black soldiers and white civilians, see Sefton, *United States Army*, pp. 50–53; Fletcher, "Negro Volunteer," p. 127; Litwack, *Been in the Storm*, pp. 83–84; Francis Simkins and Robert H. Woody, *South Carolina During Reconstruction* (Chapel Hill: University of North Carolina Press, 1932), p. 30; Robert E. Purdue, "The Negro in Savannah, 1865–1900," Ph.D. Dissertation, University of Georgia, 1971, pp. 67–68; Jerry Thornberry, "Northerners and the Atlanta Freedmen, 1865–1869," *Prologue*, 6 (Winter 1974), 236–51. The Alabama editor is quoted in Howard N. Rabinowitz, "The Conflict Between Blacks and the Police in the Urban South, 1865–1900," *The Historian*, 36 (Nov. 1976), 62–76.

11. Edward Magdol, "Martin Delany Counsels Freedmen, July 23, 1865," *JNH*, 56 (Oct. 1971), 303–09.

12. Quoted in Dann, *Black Press*, pp. 88–89.

13. The Georgia statements are cited in Conway, *Reconstruction*, pp. 27, 65. For similar views from Mississippi, see James W. Garner, *Reconstruction in Mississippi* (New York: Macmillan, 1901), pp. 104–07.

14. William C. Harris, *Presidential Reconstruction in Mississippi* (Baton Rouge: Louisiana State University Press, 1967), pp. 70–71.

15. Quoted in S. Andrews, *The South*, p. 221. Similar stories of black resistance led by soldiers came from many parts of the South. See Alrutheus A. Taylor, *The Negro in the Reconstruction of Virginia* (Washington, D.C.: Association for the Study of Negro Life and History, 1926), p. 70; Williamson, *After Slavery*, pp. 28–29; Fischer, "Pioneer Protest," pp. 219–21.

16. The meetings of the Georgia society are reported in Eliza Andrews, *The War-Time Journal of a Georgia Girl, 1864–1865* (New York: D. Appleton, 1908), pp. 349–50. The young woman with the spelling book was noted by S. Andrews, *The South*, p. 338. Andrews's testimony concerning the ubiquitous black self-educating activity appears in W. P. Fessenden et al., *Report of the Joint Committee on Reconstruction*, U.S. 39th Congress, 1st Session (1866; rpt. Freeport, N.Y.: Books for Libraries Press, 1971), III, 174. See also Kolchin, *First Freedom*, pp. 83–86, and Simkins and Woody, *South Carolina*, p. 426.

17. On the Mobile preachers, see Litwack, *Been in the Storm*, p. 469. The same kind of report from North Carolina appeared in the *Christian Recorder*, Aug. 19 and Sept. 9, 1865.

18. The standard modern biographical study of Johnson is Eric L. McKitrick, *Andrew Johnson and Reconstruction* (Chicago: University of Chicago Press, 1960). McKitrick has also edited a collection of essays on Johnson and his situation by several authors, *Andrew Johnson: A Profile* (New York: Hill and Wang, 1969). The quotation from the Northern newspapers is cited in Cruden, *The Negro*, p. 5.

19. McKitrick, *Johnson and Reconstruction*, pp. 134–213; Franklin, *Reconstruction*, pp. 40–41. McKitrick's and Franklin's views of Johnson parallel my own. For somewhat more sympathetic accounts see James E. Sefton, *Andrew Johnson and the Uses of Constitutional Power* (Boston: Little, Brown, 1980); Albert Castel, *The Presidency of Andrew Johnson* (Lawrence, Kans.: Regents Press, 1979); and L. Thomas, *First President Johnson*.

20. The Georgia and Alabama gubernatorial statements are quoted in Aptheker, *To Be Free*, pp. 137, 232. The statement from North Carolina is cited in Andrews, *The South*, p. 154. The reference to Connecticut's white voters and their decision to continue barring black people from the state franchise is discussed in Benedict, *Compromise*, pp. 100–16.

21. The Alabama planter, typical of thousands of others, is quoted in Bond, *Negro Education*, p. 25. The *Whig* quotation is in Engs, "Freedom's First Generation," p. 87.

22. Quoted in Wharton, *The Negro*, pp. 140–41. Carl Schurz was one of the many travelers in the South who noted the intense and widespread white resistance to conceding any rights to black people; see *Report*, p. 81.

23. Conway, *Reconstruction*, p. 55.

24. The most complete study of the Black Codes available is Theodore B. Wilson, *The Black Codes of the South* (University: University of Alabama Press, 1965). Wilson's work is very sympathetic to the Southern governments, and neither he nor anyone else calls attention to the Codes as a white reaction to the black determination to be free. Since Mississippi's laws received most attention, it is helpful to see them in the context of Wharton's *The Negro*, pp. 82–92. Wilson and Wharton are the primary sources of the summary of the Codes presented here.

25. For a full examination and citation of the Opelousas document, see Schurz, *Report*, pp. 23–24, 92–96.

26. In his subdued but persistent defense of the Southern white governments under Presidential Reconstruction, Wilson calls attention to the important fact that the occupying U.S. Army and the Freedmen's Bureau had already developed their own equivalent of the Black Codes. The essential purpose of these regulations, he rightly says, was to "protect the Negroes from violence and actual

enslavement, but keep as many as possible on the plantations and *compel* them to work." See *Black Codes*, p. 57.

27. The white American uses of the law against Indian rights and aspirations is documented in many places. One of the most helpful works is Vogel, *This Country Was Ours*. Vine Deloria, the Sioux scholar, is currently completing a massive volume on the subject under the aegis of the Smithsonian Institution.

28. Concerning early white terrorist violence, harrowing contemporary accounts appear in Schurz, *Report*, pp. 19, 36, 59, 62–63, 68, and Fleming, *Documentary*, I, 68–71. See also John Hope Franklin, *The Militant South* (Cambridge: Harvard University Press, 1956), pp. 24–25, and his *Reconstruction*, p. 154.

29. S. Andrews, *The South*, p. 97.

30. *Ibid.*, p. 98.

31. *Ibid.*

32. Schurz's *Report*, pp. 15–16, provides an important contemporary summary of this movement. See also Kolchin, *First Freedom*, pp. 4–23, and Williamson, *After Slavery*, p. 34.

33. The best summary of these struggles for the land appears in Magdol, *Right to the Land*, pp. 162–70, 257. See also S. Andrews, *The South*, pp. 232–33; Litwack, *Been in the Storm*, p. 406; and Williamson, *After Slavery*, p. 82.

34. Magdol, *Right to the Land*, pp. 162–70.

CHAPTER 16: THE STRUGGLE ENDS, THE STRUGGLE BEGINS

1. The most complete modern version of the story of Howard and the Bureau is found in McFeeley, *Yankee Stepfather*, and in his essay, "Unfinished Business: The Freedmen's Bureau and Federal Action in Race Relations," in Huggins et al., *Key Issues*, II, 5–25. Of course all twentieth-century treatments of Howard and the Bureau probably owe some debt to W. E. B. DuBois's seminal essay, "Of the Dawn of Freedom," in *Souls of Black Folk*, pp. 23–41. Important contributions are found in L. Cox, "The Promise," pp. 413–37; Gerteis, *From Contraband*, pp. 185–88; Cruden, *The Negro*, pp. 14–26. See also Belz, *A New Birth*, p. 105, for a somewhat different emphasis.

2. This account of the Edisto confrontation is based on several sources: Mary Ames, *From a New England Woman's Diary in Dixie in 1865* (Springfield, Mass.: Plimpton Press, 1906), pp. 95–103; S. Andrews, *The South*, pp. 212, 213; Hoffman, "From Slavery," pp. 23–26; Oliver Otis Howard, *Autobiography*, 2 vols. (New York: Baker and Taylor, 1907), II, 237–40; Magdol, *Right to the Land*, pp. 157–61; and McFeeley, *Yankee Stepfather*, pp. 140–43. The paraphrase of Howard's statement appears in M. Ames, *New England*, p. 96.

3. O. Howard, *Autobiography*, II, 238–39.

4. *Ibid.*; M. Ames, *New England*, pp. 96–97; S. Andrews, *The South*, p. 212; Hoffman, "From Slavery," pp. 23–24.

5. McFeeley, *Yankee Stepfather*, pp. 140–44; Magdol, *Right to the Land*, pp. 161–64; Hoffman, "From Slavery," pp. 23–26.

6. S. Andrews, *The South*, p. 213; Williamson, *After Slavery*, p. 82.

7. On the many sources of black leadership, see Williamson, *After Slavery*, pp. 369–70, and Sterling, *The Trouble*, pp. 146–53. The rich, complex, and im-

portant story of Aaron A. Bradley has yet to be fully told by a sympathetic historian. The most complete account is E. Merton Coulter, "Aaron Alpeoria Bradley, Georgia Negro Politician During Reconstruction Times," Parts I, II, and III, *Georgia Historical Quarterly*, 51 (Mar., June, Sept. 1967), 15–41, 154–74, 264–306. The Alabama speakers are quoted in Magdol, *Right to the Land*, pp. 167–68.

8. Magdol, *Right to the Land*, pp. 162–70.
9. The *Nation*'s opinion is quoted in Cruden, *The Negro*, p. 36.
10. Concerning the postwar white fear of black rebellion, see S. Andrews, *The South*, p. 36; Wharton, *The Negro*, pp. 59, 218–19; Kolchin, *First Freedom*, pp. 37–38; Litwack, *Been in the Storm*, pp. 425–30. The report on black arms supplies appears in Fleming, *Documentary*, I, 83; see also Allen, *Reconstruction*, pp. 54–55.
11. S. Andrews, *The South*, p. 36; J. Allen, *Reconstruction*, p. 55.
12. W. P. Fessenden et al., *Report*, III, 140; Myers, "Reaction and Adjustment," pp. 5–22; Litwack, *Been in the Storm*, pp. 428–29; Reid, *After the War*, pp. 145, 222; Gutman, *Black Family*, p. 321.
13. There is a full and valuable collection of the South Carolina black convention reports in the *New York Tribune* of Nov. 29, 1865; all quotations are from that issue. In addition, see Williamson, *After Slavery*, pp. 47–52.
14. The Congressional activity may be followed in papers like the *New York Tribune* and the *New York Times* of Dec. 1865. It is also summarized in works like Patrick, *The Reconstruction*, pp. 62–65.
15. Quoted in Fleming, *Documentary*, I, 51–52.
16. Coulter, "Aaron Alpeoria Bradley," pp. 15–41. The telegrams to Johnson are quoted in McFeeley, *Yankee Stepfather*, pp. 202–03.

A Select Bibliography of Books, Articles, and Congressional Reports

Abbott, Martin. "Freedom's Cry: Negroes and Their Meetings in South Carolina, 1865–1869." *Journal of Negro History*, 20 (Spring 1959): 263–72.

Addington, W. G. "Slave Insurrections in Texas." *Journal of Negro History*, 35 (Oct. 1950): 408–34.

Ahlstrom, Sidney E. *A Religious History of the American People.* New Haven: Yale University Press, 1972.

Alexander, Roberta Sue. "North Carolina Churches Face Emancipation and the Freedman." *University of Dayton Review*, 9 (Winter 1972): 47–65.

Allen, James S. *Reconstruction, The Battle for Democracy.* New York: International Publishers, 1937.

Allen, Richard. *The Life Experience and Gospel Labors of the Rt. Rev. Richard Allen.* New York: Abingdon Press, 1960 (originally published 1793).

Allen, Robert. *Reluctant Reformers.* Washington, D.C.: Howard University Press, 1974.

Allen, Theodore. " 'They Would Have Destroyed Me': Slavery and the Origins of Racism." *Radical America*, 9 (May-June 1975): 41–63.

American Anti-Slavery Society. *Southern Outrages Upon Northern Citizens.* New York: 1860.

Ames, Mary. *From a New England Woman's Diary in Dixie in 1865.* Springfield, Mass.: Plimpton Press, 1906.

Ames, Russell. "Protest and Irony in Negro Folksong." *Science and Society*, 14 (Summer 1950): 193–213.

Anderson, Osborne P. *A Voice from Harper's Ferry.* New York: World View Publishers, 1974 (originally published 1861).

Andrews, Eliza. *The War-Time Journal of a Georgia Girl, 1864–1865.* New York: D. Appleton, 1908.

Andrews, Sidney. *The South Since the War.* New York: Arno Press, 1969 (originally published 1866).

Anstey, Roger. *The Atlantic Slave Trade and British Abolition, 1760–1810.* Atlantic Highlands, N.J.: Humanities Press, 1975.

Anti-Negro Riots in the North. New York: Arno Press, 1969 (originally published 1863).

Aptheker, Herbert. "Additional Data on American Maroons." *Journal of Negro History*, 23 (Oct. 1947): 452–60.

——. *American Negro Slave Revolts.* New York: International Publishers, 1963 (originally published 1943).

——, ed. *Documentary History of the Negro People in the United States.* 3 vols. New York: Citadel Press, 1951–74.

——. "Maroons Within the Present Limits of the United States." *Journal of Negro History*, 24 (Apr. 1939): 167–84.

——. *Nat Turner's Slave Rebellion.* New York: Humanities Press, 1966.

——, ed. *One Continual Cry: David Walker's Appeal to the Colored Citizens of the World.* New York: Humanities Press, 1965.

————. *To Be Free: Studies in American Negro History.* New York: International Publishers, 1969 (originally published 1948).

Baird, Robert. *Religion in America.* New York, 1844.

Bancroft, Frederic. *The Life of William H. Seward.* New York: Harper and Brothers, 1900.

————. *Slave Trading in the Old South.* New York: Frederick Ungar, 1959 (originally published 1931).

Baron, Harold. "The Demand for Black Labor." *Radical America,* 2 (Mar./Apr. 1971): 2–6.

Basler, Roy P., ed. *The Collected Works of Abraham Lincoln.* 9 vols. New Brunswick, N.J.: Rutgers University Press, 1953.

Bauer, Raymond A., and Bauer, Alice H. "Day to Day Resistance to Slavery." *Journal of Negro History,* 27 (Oct. 1942): 388–419.

Baur, John E. "International Repercussions of the Haitian Revolution." *Americas,* 26 (Apr. 1970): 394–418.

Bearse, Austin. *Reminiscences of Fugitive-Slave Law Days in Boston.* New York: Arno Press, 1969 (originally published 1880).

Beck, Warren A. "Lincoln and Negro Colonization in Central America." *Abraham Lincoln Quarterly,* 4 (Sept. 1950): 162–83.

Bell, Howard H., ed. *Minutes of the Proceedings of the National Negro Conventions, 1830–1864.* New York: Arno Press, 1969.

————. "The Negro Emigration Movement, 1849–1854: A Phase of Negro Nationalism." *Phylon,* 9 (Summer 1959): 132–42.

————. *A Survey of the Negro Convention Movement, 1830–1861.* New York: Arno Press, 1969.

Belz, Herman. *A New Birth of Freedom.* Westport, Conn.: Greenwood Press, 1976.

Benedict, Michael Les. *A Compromise of Principle.* New York: W. W. Norton, 1974.

Bennett, Lerone. *The Shaping of Black America.* Chicago: Johnson Publishing, 1975.

Berlin, Ira. "Documents: After Nat Turner, A Letter from the North." *Journal of Negro History,* 55 (Apr. 1970): 144–51.

————. *Slaves Without Masters.* New York: Pantheon, 1975.

Berry, Mary Frances. *Black Resistance, White Law.* New York: Meredith Corporation, 1971.

————. *Military Necessity and Civil Rights Policy.* Port Washington, N.Y.: Kennikat Press, 1977.

Berwanger, Eugene. *The Frontier Against Slavery.* Urbana: University of Illinois Press, 1967.

Binder, Frederick. *The Color Problem in Early National America.* The Hague: Mouton, 1968.

Blassingame, John W. *Black New Orleans, 1860–1880.* Chicago: University of Chicago Press, 1973.

————, ed. *The Frederick Douglass Papers: Series One: Speeches, Debates and Interviews.* New Haven: Yale University Press, 1979.

————. "The Recruitment of Colored Troops in Kentucky, Maryland and Missouri, 1860–1863." *The Historian,* 24 (Aug. 1967): 533–45.

————. "Before the Ghetto: The Making of the Black Community in Savannah, Georgia, 1865–1880." *Journal of Social History,* 6 (Summer 1973): 463–88.

————. *The Slave Community: Plantation Life in the Antebellum South.* New York: Oxford University Press, 1973.

Blum, John, et al. *The National Experience.* New York: Harcourt, Brace & World, 1963.

Bond, Horace Mann. *Negro Education in Alabama.* New York: Atheneum, 1969.

"The Bone and Sinew of the South." *The National Freedman,* 1 (Apr. 1865): 82–83.

Bontemps, Arna. *Black Thunder.* Boston: Beacon Press, 1968 (originally published 1936).

Botume, Elizabeth H. *First Days Amongst the Contrabands.* New York: Arno Press, 1968 (originally published 1892).

Bracey, John; Meier, August; and Rudwick, Elliot, eds. *American Slavery: The Question of Resistance.* Belmont, Calif.: Wadsworth Publishing, 1970.

————, eds. *Black Nationalism in America.* Indianapolis and New York: Bobbs-Merrill, 1970.

————. *Blacks in the Abolitionist Movement.* Belmont, Calif.: Wadsworth Publishing, 1971.

Brawley, Benjamin. *A Social History of the American Negro.* New York: Macmillan, 1970 (originally published 1921).

Breen, T. H. "A Changing Labor Force and Race Relations in Virginia, 1660–1710." *Journal of Social History,* 7 (Fall 1973), 3–18.

Bridenbaugh, Carl. *No Peace Beyond the Line.* New York: Oxford University Press, 1972.

Brown, Sterling A., et al., eds. *The Negro Caravan.* New York: Dryden Press, 1941.

Buckmaster, Harriet. *Let My People Go.* Boston: Beacon Press, 1966 (originally published 1941).

Burchard, Peter. *One Gallant Rush.* New York: St. Martin's, 1965.

Burr, Nelson. *A Critical Bibliography of Religion in America.* Vol. IV of *Religion in American Life.* Edited by James W. Smith and A. Leland Jamison. 4 vols. Princeton: Princeton University Press, 1961.

Campbell, Penelope. *Maryland in Africa.* Urbana: University of Illinois Press, 1971.

Campbell, Stanley W. *The Slave Catchers.* New York: W. W. Norton, 1972.

Carroll, Joseph C. *Slave Insurrections in the United States, 1800–1865.* New York: Negro Universities Press, 1968 (originally published 1938).

Castel, Albert. *The Presidency of Andrew Johnson.* Lawrence, Kans.: Regents Press, 1979.

Catterall, Helen T., ed. *Judicial Cases Concerning American Slavery and the Negro.* 5 vols. New York: Octagon Books, 1968 (originally published 1926–37).

Cheek, William F. *Black Resistance Before the Civil War.* Beverly Hills, Calif.: Glencoe Press, 1970.

————. "John Mercer Langston: Black Protest Leader and Abolitionist." *Civil War History,* 16 (June 1970): 101–20.

Cipolla, Carlo M. *Guns, Sails and Empires.* New York: Funk & Wagnalls, 1965.

Clarke, John H., and Harding, Vincent, eds. *Slave Trade and Slavery.* New York: Holt-Rinehart, 1970.

Cohen, William. "Thomas Jefferson and the Problem of Slavery." *Journal of American History,* 55 (Dec. 1968): 503–26.

Commager, Henry Steele, ed. *Documents of American History.* 2 vols. New York: Prentice-Hall, 1963.

Conrad, Earl. *Harriet Tubman, Negro Soldier and Abolitionist.* New York: International Publishers, 1942.

Conway, Alan. *The Reconstruction of Georgia.* Minneapolis: University of Minnesota Press, 1966.

Cooper, Wayne, ed. *The Passion of Claude McKay: Selected Prose and Poetry 1912–1948.* New York: Schocken Books, 1973.

Cornish, Dudley. *The Sable Arm.* New York: W. W. Norton, 1965.

Coulter, E. Merton. "Aaron Alpeoria Bradley, Georgia Negro Politician During Reconstruction Times." Parts I, II, and III. *Georgia Historical Quarterly,* 51 (Mar. 1967): 15–41; 51 (June 1967): 154–74; 51 (Sept. 1967): 264–306.

———. "Tunis G. Campbell, Negro Reconstructionist in Georgia." Parts I and II. *Georgia Historical Quarterly,* 51 (Dec. 1967): 401–24; 52 (Mar. 1968): 16–52.

Cox, LaWanda. "The Promise of Land for the Freedman." *Mississippi Valley Historical Review,* 45 (Dec. 1958): 413–39.

Cox, Oliver Cromwell. *Caste, Class, and Race.* New York: Monthly Review Press, 1959 (originally published 1948).

Cross, Whitney R. *The Burned-Over District.* Ithaca: Cornell University Press, 1950.

Cruden, Robert. *The Negro in Reconstruction.* Englewood Cliffs, N.J.: Prentice-Hall, 1969.

Crummell, Alexander. *Africa and America: Addresses and Discourses.* New York: Arno Press, 1969 (originally published Springfield, Mass., 1891).

Current, Richard N., and Garraty, John A., eds. *Words That Made American History.* 2 vols. Boston: Little, Brown, 1965.

Curtin, Philip J., ed. *Africa Remembered: Narratives by West Africans from the Era of the Slave Trade.* Madison: University of Wisconsin Press, 1967.

———. *The Atlantic Slave Trade: A Census.* Madison: University of Wisconsin Press, 1969.

Dangerfield, George. *The Era of Good Feelings.* New York: Harcourt, Brace & World, 1963.

Dann, Martin E., ed. *The Black Press, 1827–1890.* New York: Capricorn Books, 1971.

Davidson, Basil. *Africa: History of a Continent.* New York: Macmillan, 1972.

———. *The African Genius: An Introduction to African Social and Cultural History.* Boston: Atlantic Monthly Press, 1970.

———. *The African Slave Trade.* Boston: Atlantic, Little-Brown, 1961.

Davies, K. G. *The Royal African Company.* London: Longmans, 1957.

Davis, David B., ed. *Ante-Bellum Reform.* New York: Harper and Row, 1967.

———. *The Problem of Slavery in the Age of Revolution, 1770–1823.* Ithaca, N.Y.: Cornell University Press, 1975.

Day, Judy, and Kedro, M. James. "Free Blacks in St. Louis: Antebellum Conditions, Emancipation, and the Post-War Era." *Bulletin of the Missouri Historical Society,* 30 (Jan. 1974): 117–35.

Delany, Martin R. *Blake: Or the Huts of America.* Boston: Beacon Press, 1970 (originally published 1859).

———. *The Condition, Elevation, Emigration and Destiny of the Colored People of the United States Politically Considered.* Philadelphia, 1852.

————. *Official Report of the Niger Valley Exploring Party.* New York, 1861.

Delaney, Martin R., and Campbell, Robert. *Search for a Place: Black Separatism and Africa.* Ann Arbor: University of Michigan Press, 1969 (originally published 1860).

Dickson, Moses. *Manual of the International Order of Twelve.* St. Louis, 1891.

Donald, David. *Charles Sumner and the Coming of the Civil War.* New York: Knopf, 1960.

Donnan, Elizabeth. *Documents Illustrative of the History of the Slave Trade to America.* 4 vols. New York: Octagon Books, 1965 (originally published 1935).

Douglas, H. Ford. File, *Records of the Adjutant General's Office, 1780–1917.* Record Group 94, National Archives.

————. *Speech . . . Before the Emigration Convention . . . August, 1854.* Chicago, 1854.

————. "Speech of." *National Anti-Slavery Standard,* 21 (Aug. 25, 1860).

Douglass, Frederick. *The Life and Times of Frederick Douglass.* New York: Collier Books, 1962 (originally published 1892).

————. *My Bondage and My Freedom.* New York: Arno Press, 1968 (originally published 1855).

————. *Narrative of the Life of Frederick Douglass.* Boston: American Anti-Slavery Society, 1845.

Douglass, Frederick; Watkins, W. J.; and Whitfield, J. M. *Arguments Pro and Con . . . on . . . a National Emigration Convention.* Detroit, 1854.

Dow, George F. *Slave Ships and Slaving.* Salem, Mass.: Marine Research Society, 1927.

Drago, Edmund L. "How Sherman's March Through Georgia Affected the Slaves." *Georgia Historical Quarterly,* 57 (Fall 1973) : 361–75.

Drake, St. Clair. "Black Nationalism and White Power." Chapter 15 of an unpublished manuscript.

————. *The Redemption of Africa and Black Religion.* Chicago and Atlanta: Third World Press and Institute of the Black World, 1970.

Drake, St. Clair, and Cayton, Horace R. *Black Metropolis.* New York: Harcourt, Brace and Company, 1945.

Drew, Benjamin, ed. *The Refugee: Or the Narratives of Fugitive Slaves in Canada.* Boston: John P. Jewett and Company, 1856. (This was republished as Edelstein, Tilden [ed.], *The Refugee: A North-side View of Slavery, by Benjamin Drew.* Reading, Mass.: Addison-Wesley, 1969.)

Drimmer, Melvin, ed. *Black History: A Reappraisal.* New York: Doubleday, 1968.

Duberman, Martin, ed. *The Anti-Slavery Vanguard.* Princeton: Princeton University Press, 1965.

DuBois, W. E. B. *Black Reconstruction in America.* New York: World Publishing, 1962 (originally published 1935).

————. *John Brown.* New York: International Publishers, 1962 (originally published 1909).

————. *The Negro Church.* Atlanta: Atlanta University Press, 1903.

————. *The Souls of Black Folk.* Greenwich, Conn.: Fawcett, 1961 (originally published 1903).

————. *The Suppression of the African Slave Trade.* New York: Russell and Russell, 1965 (originally published 1898).

Dumond, Dwight. *Anti-Slavery.* Ann Arbor: University of Michigan Press, 1961.

Dunn, Richard S. *Sugar and Slaves.* Institute of Early American History and Culture, Williamsburg, Va.: University of North Carolina Press, 1972.

Ehrlich, Walter. *They Have No Rights: Dred Scott's Struggle for Freedom.* Westport, Conn.: Greenwood Press, 1979.

"Eighteenth Century Slaves as Advertised by Their Masters." *Journal of Negro History,* 1 (Apr. 1916): 163–216.

Engs, Robert F. "Freedom's First Generation." Unpublished manuscript in author's possession.

Evans, W. McKee. *Ballots and Fence Rails.* Chapel Hill: University of North Carolina Press, 1967.

Everett, Donald E. "Demands of the New Orleans Free Colored Population for Political Equality, 1862–1865." *Louisiana Historical Quarterly,* 38 (Apr. 1955): 43–64.

Fanon, Frantz. *The Wretched of the Earth.* New York: Grove Press, 1963.

Fehrenbacher, Don E. *The Dred Scott Case.* New York: Oxford University Press, 1978.

Fessenden, W. P., et al. *Report of the Joint Committee on Reconstruction.* 4 parts. U.S. 39th Congress, 1st Session. Freeport, N.Y.: Books for Libraries Press, 1971 (originally published 1866).

Filler, Louis. *The Crusade Against Slavery, 1830–1860.* New York: Harper and Row, 1963.

Fischer, Roger A. "A Pioneer Protest: The New Orleans Street-Car Controversy of 1867." *Journal of Negro History,* 53 (Jan. 1968): 219–33.

Fisher, Miles Mark. *Negro Slave Songs in the United States.* New York: Citadel Press, 1968 (originally published 1953).

Fladeland, Betty. *Men and Brothers: Anglo-American Anti-Slavery Cooperation.* Urbana, Ill.: University of Illinois Press, 1972.

Fleming, Walter L., ed. *Documentary History of Reconstruction.* 2 vols. Cleveland: Arthur H. Clarke, 1906.

Fletcher, Marvin E. "The Negro Volunteer in Reconstruction, 1865–1866." *Military Affairs,* 32 (Dec. 1968): 124–31.

Fogel, Robert W., and Engerman, Stanley L. *Time on the Cross.* 2 vols. Boston: Little, Brown, 1974.

Foner, Eric. *Free Soil, Free Labor, Free Men: The Ideology of the Republican Party before the Civil War.* New York: Oxford University Press, 1971.

———, ed. *Nat Turner.* Englewood Cliffs, N.J.: Prentice-Hall, 1971.

Foner, Philip S. *History of Black Americans.* Westport, Conn.: Greenwood Press, 1975.

———, ed. *The Life and Writings of Frederick Douglass.* 4 vols. New York: International Publishers, 1950.

Foreman, Grant. *Indian Removal.* Norman: University of Oklahoma Press, 1953.

Foster, Charles I. *An Errand of Mercy: The Evangelical United Front, 1790–1837.* Chapel Hill: University of North Carolina Press, 1960.

Fox, Stephen R. *The Guardian of Boston: William Monroe Trotter.* New York: Atheneum, 1970.

Franklin, John Hope. *The Emancipation Proclamation.* New York: Anchor Books, 1965.

———. *From Slavery to Freedom.* 3rd edition. New York: Knopf, 1967.

———. *The Militant South.* Cambridge: Harvard University Press, 1956.

———. *Reconstruction: After the Civil War*. Chicago: University of Chicago Press, 1961.

Frederickson, George M. "A Man but Not a Brother." *Journal of Southern History*, 41 (Feb. 1975): 39–58.

"The Freedmen in Georgia." *The National Freedman*, 1 (Apr. 1865): 98–101.

Gara, Larry. "The Fugitive Slave Law: A Double Paradox," *Civil War History*, 10 (Jan. 1964): 229–40.

———. "The Fugitive Slave Law in the Eastern Ohio Valley." *Ohio History*, 73 (Apr. 1963): 116–28, 170–71.

———. *The Liberty Line*. Lexington: University of Kentucky Press, 1961.

———. "Slavery and the Slave Power: A Crucial Distinction." *Civil War History*, 15 (Mar. 1969): 5–18.

Garner, James W. *Reconstruction in Mississippi*. New York: Macmillan, 1901.

Garvin, Russell. "The Free Negro in Florida Before the Civil War." *Florida Historical Quarterly*, 46 (July 1967): 1–12.

Geffen, Elizabeth M. "Violence in Philadelphia in the 1840's and 1850's." *Pennsylvania History*, 36 (Oct. 1969): 381–410.

Genovese, Eugene D. *From Rebellion to Revolution: Afro-American Slave Revolts in the Making of the Modern World*. Baton Rouge: Louisiana University Press, 1979.

———. *Roll, Jordan, Roll: The World the Slaves Made*. New York: Pantheon, 1974.

George, Carol V. R. *Segregated Sabbaths: Richard Allen and the Emergence of Independent Black Churches, 1760–1840*. New York: Oxford University Press, 1973.

Gerteis, Louis S. *From Contraband to Freedman: Federal Policy Toward Southern Blacks, 1861–1865*. Westport, Conn.: Greenwood Press, 1973.

[Gilbert, Olive.] *Narrative of Sojourner Truth*. Battle Creek, Mich.: The author, 1878.

Ginzburg, Ralph, ed. *100 Years of Lynchings*. New York: Lancer Books, 1962.

Gipson, Lawrence H. *The Coming of the Revolution: 1763–1775*. New York: Harper and Row, 1954.

Goddell, William. *The American Slave Code*. New York, 1853.

Graham, Hugh D., and Gurr, Ted R., eds. *The History of Violence in America*. New York: Frederick A. Praeger, 1969.

Graham, Shirley. *There Once Was a Slave*. New York: Julian Messner, 1947.

Grau, Richard. "The Christiana Riot of 1851: A Reappraisal." *Journal of the Lancaster County Historical Society*, 68 (Michaelmas 1964): 147–75.

Gravely, William B. "A Black Methodist on Reconstruction in Mississippi: Three Letters by James Lynch in 1868–1869." *Methodist History*, 11 (July 1973): 3–18.

———. "The Decision of A.M.E. Leader, James Lynch, to Join the Methodist Episcopal Church." *Methodist History*, 15 (July 1977): 263–69.

Greene, Lorenzo. "Mutiny on the Slave Ships." *Phylon*, 5 (Jan. 1944): 346–54.

———. *The Negro in Colonial New England*. New York: Atheneum, 1968 (originally published 1942).

———. "The New England Negro as Seen in Advertisements for Runaway Slaves." *Journal of Negro History*, 29 (Apr. 1944): 125–46.

Griffin, Clifford S. *Their Brothers' Keepers.* New Brunswick, N.J.: Rutgers University Press, 1960.

Gutman, Herbert G. *The Black Family in Slavery and Freedom, 1750–1925.* New York: Pantheon, 1976.

Halasz, Nicholas. *The Rattling Chains.* New York: David McKay, 1966.

Hareven, Tamara K., ed. *Anonymous Americans.* Englewood Cliffs, N.J.: Prentice-Hall, 1971.

Harris, Robert L., Jr. "H. Ford Douglas: Afro-American Anti-Slavery Emigrationist." Unpublished paper.

Harris, Sheldon H., and Cuffee, Paul. *Black America and the African Return.* New York: Simon and Schuster, 1972.

Harris, William C. "James Lynch: Black Leader in Southern Reconstruction." *The Historian,* 34 (Nov. 1971): 40–61.

———. *Presidential Reconstruction in Mississippi.* Baton Rouge: Louisiana State University Press, 1967.

Hast, Adele. "The Legal Status of the Negro in Virginia, 1705–1765." *Journal of Negro History,* 54 (July 1969): 217–39.

Haviland, Laura. *A Woman's Life.* Grand Rapids, Mich., 1881.

Hay, T. R. "The South and the Arming of Slaves." *Mississippi Historical Review,* 6 (June 1919): 34–73.

Hayden, Robert. *Selected Poems.* New York: October House, 1966.

Henry, Howell M. *The Police Control of the Slave in South Carolina.* Emory, Va.: The author, 1914.

Hensel, H. U. *The Christiana Riot.* Lancaster, Pa.: New Era, 1911.

Higginson, Thomas W. *Army Life in a Black Regiment.* Boston: Beacon Press, 1962 (originally published 1869).

———. "Negro Spirituals." *Atlantic Monthly,* 19 (June 1867): 685–94.

Hinton, Richard J. *John Brown and His Men.* New York: Arno Press, 1968 (originally published 1894).

Hobsbawn, Eric J. *Primitive Rebels.* New York: W. W. Norton, 1965.

Hoffman, Edwin D. "From Slavery to Self-Reliance." *Journal of Negro History,* 41 (Jan. 1956): 8–42.

Hofstadter, Richard, and Wallace, Michael, eds. *American Violence.* New York: Knopf, 1970.

Holmes, Jack D. L. "The Abortive Slave Revolt at Pointe Coupée, Louisiana, 1795." *Louisiana History,* 11 (Fall 1970): 341–62.

Hopkins, Vincent C. *Dred Scott's Case.* New York: Fordham University Press, 1951.

Horsmanden, Daniel. *The New York Conspiracy.* Boston: Beacon Press, 1971 (originally published 1744).

Howard, Oliver Otis. *Autobiography.* 2 vols. New York: Baker and Taylor, 1907.

Howard, Thomas, ed. *Black Voyage: Eyewitness Accounts of the Atlantic Slave Trade.* Boston: Little, Brown, 1971.

Huggins, Nathan. *Black Odyssey.* New York: Pantheon, 1977.

———. *Slave and Citizen: The Life of Frederick Douglass.* Boston: Little, Brown, 1980.

Huggins, Nathan; Kilson, Martin; and Fox, Daniel M., eds. *Key Issues in the Afro-American Experience.* New York: Harcourt Brace Jovanovich, 1971.

Hurd, John C. *The Law of Freedom and Bondage in the United States.* 2 vols. Boston, 1858.

Jackson, Helen Hunt. *A Century of Dishonor*. Minneapolis: Scholarly Press, 1964 (originally published 1885).

Jacobs, Donald M. "David Walker: Boston Race Leader, 1825–1830." *Essex Institute Historical Collections*, 107 (Jan. 1971) : 94–107.

Jacobs, Paul, and Landau, Saul, eds. *To Serve the Devil*. 2 vols. New York: Vintage Books, 1971.

James, C. L. R. *The Black Jacobins*. 2nd edition. New York: Vintage Books, 1963 (originally published 1938).

Jennings, Francis. *The Invasion of America*. New York: W. W. Norton, 1976.

Johnson, Ludwell H. "Lincoln and Equal Rights: A Reply." *Civil War History*, 13 (Mar. 1967) : 66–73.

Jones, Howard. "The Peculiar Institution and National Honor: The Case of the *Creole* Slave Revolt." *Civil War History*, 21 (Mar. 1975) : 28–50.

Jordan, Winthrop D. *White Over Black*. Chapel Hill: University of North Carolina Press, 1968.

[Josephy, Alvin M., Jr.] *The Horizon History of Africa*. New York: American Heritage, 1971.

Katz, Jonathan, ed. *Resistance at Christiana*. New York: Thomas Crowell, 1974.

Killens, John Oliver. *Great Gittin' Up Morning*. New York: Doubleday, 1972.

———. *The Trial Record of Denmark Vesey*. Boston: Beacon Press, 1970.

Kirk-Greene, A. H. M. "America in the Niger Valley: A Colonization Centenary." *Phylon*, 22 (Fall 1962) : 225–39.

Koch, Adrienne, and Peden, William, eds. *The Life and Selected Writings of Thomas Jefferson*. New York: Modern Library, 1944.

Kolchin, Peter. *First Freedom*. Westport, Conn.: Greenwood Press, 1972.

Kraditor, Aileen S. *Means and Ends in American Abolitionism*. New York: Pantheon, 1969.

Landon, Fred. "The Negro Migration to Canada After . . . 1850." *Journal of Negro History*, 5 (Jan. 1920) : 22–23.

Langston, John Mercer. *From the Virginia Plantation to the National Capitol*. Hartford, 1894.

Leavens, Finnian Patrick. "*L'Union* and the *New Orleans Tribune* and Louisiana Reconstruction." Unpublished Master's thesis, Louisiana State University, 1966.

Lewy, Guenther. *Religion and Revolution*. New York: Oxford University Press, 1974.

Litwack, Leon F. *Been in the Storm So Long*. New York: Knopf, 1979.

———. *North of Slavery*. Chicago: University of Chicago Press, 1965.

Lofton, John. *Insurrection in South Carolina*. Yellow Springs, Ohio: Antioch Press, 1964.

Lomax, Louis E. *When the Word is Given*. New York: New American Library, 1964.

Lumpkin, Katherine DuPre. "The General Plan was Freedom: A Negro Secret Order on the Underground Railroad." *Phylon*, 28 (Spring 1967) : 63–77.

Lynd, Staughton. *Class Conflict, Slavery and the United States Constitution*. Indianapolis: Bobbs-Merrill, 1968.

Mabee, Carlton. *Black Freedom*. New York: Macmillan, 1970.

MacEacheren, Elaine. "Emancipation of Slavery in Massachusetts: A Reexamination, 1770–1790." *Journal of Negro History*, 55 (Oct. 1970) : 289–306.

McCague, James. *The Second Rebellion: The Story of the New York City Draft Riots of 1863.* New York: Dial Press, 1968.

McClellan, George B. *Report on the Organization and Campaigns of the Army of the Potomac. . . .* New York, 1864.

McDougall, Marion G. *Fugitive Slaves.* New York: Bergman Publishers, 1967 (originally published 1891).

McFeeley, William S. *Yankee Stepfather: General O. O. Howard and the Freedmen.* New Haven: Yale University Press, 1968.

McKaye, James. *The Emancipated Slave.* New York, 1864.

McKibben, Davidson B. "Negro Slave Insurrections in Mississippi, 1800–1865." *Journal of Negro History,* 34 (Jan. 1949) : 73–90.

McKitrick, Eric L., ed. *Andrew Johnson, A Profile.* New York: Hill and Wang, 1969.

———. *Andrew Johnson and Reconstruction.* Chicago: University of Chicago Press, 1960.

McManus, Edgar J. *Black Bondage in the North.* Syracuse: University of Syracuse Press, 1973.

McMaster, John B. *A History of the People of the United States.* 8 vols. New York: D. Appleton and Company, 1918–24.

MacMaster, Richard K. "Henry Highland Garnet and the African Civilization Society." *Journal of Presbyterian History,* 48 (Jan. 1970) : 95–112.

McNeill, William H. *The Rise of the West.* Chicago: University of Chicago Press, 1963.

McPherson, James M. *The Negro's Civil War.* New York: Pantheon Books, 1965.

———. *The Struggle for Equality.* Princeton: Princeton University Press, 1964.

McWhiney, Grady, ed. *Reconstruction and the Freedmen.* Chicago: Rand McNally, 1963.

Magdol, Edward. "Martin Delany Counsels Freedmen, July 23, 1865." *Journal of Negro History,* 56 (Oct. 1971) : 303–09.

———. *A Right to the Land.* Westport, Conn.: Greenwood Press, 1977.

Maginnes, David R. "The Case of the Court House Rioters." *Journal of Negro History,* 56 (Jan. 1971) : 31–42.

Mannix, Daniel P., and Cowley, Malcolm. *Black Cargoes: A History of the Atlantic Slave Trade.* New York: Penguin Books, 1962.

Meaders, Daniel E. "South Carolina Fugitives as Viewed Through Local Colonial Newspapers." *Journal of Negro History,* 60 (Apr. 1975) : 288–319.

Meier, August. "The Emergence of Negro Nationalism: A Study in Ideologies." Unpublished Master's thesis, Department of History, Columbia University, 1949.

———. *Negro Thought in America 1880–1915.* Ann Arbor: University of Michigan Press, 1966.

Meier, August, and Rudwick, Elliot, eds. *The Making of Black America.* 2 vols. New York: Atheneum, 1969.

Merrill, Walter, ed. *The Letters of William Lloyd Garrison,* V, *Let the Oppressed Go Free, 1861–1867.* Cambridge: Harvard University Press, 1979.

Messner, William F. "Black Violence and White Response: Louisiana, 1862." *Journal of Southern History,* 41 (Feb. 1975) : 19–38.

Miller, Floyd J. "The Father of Black Nationalism: Another Contender." *Civil War History,* 17 (Dec. 1971) : 310–19.

Miller, John C. *Origins of the American Revolution*. Stanford, Calif.: Stanford University Press, 1959.

Miller, Perry. *The Life of the Mind in America*. New York: Harcourt, Brace & World, 1965.

Milligan, John D. "Slave Rebelliousness and the Florida Maroon." *Prologue*, 6 (Spring 1974): 5–18.

Moore, Glover. *The Missouri Controversy, 1819–1821*. Lexington: University of Kentucky Press, 1953.

Moore, John H. "A Hymn of Freedom—South Carolina, 1813." *Journal of Negro History*, 50 (Jan. 1965): 50–53.

Morgan, Edmund S. *American Slavery, American Freedom*. New York: W. W. Norton, 1975.

Muhammad, Elijah. *The Fall of America*. Chicago: Muhammad's Temple of Islam No. 2, 1973.

Mullin, Gerald W. *Flight and Rebellion: Slave Resistance in Eighteenth-Century Virginia*. New York: Oxford University Press, 1972.

Mullin, Michael [Gerald W.], ed. *American Negro Slavery*. New York: Harper and Row, 1976.

Murdoch, Richard K. "The Seagrove-White Stolen Property Agreement of 1797." *Georgia Historical Quarterly*, 42 (Sept. 1958): 258–76.

Myers, John B. "Reaction and Adjustment: The Struggle of Alabama Freedmen in Post-Bellum Alabama, 1865–1867." *Alabama Historical Quarterly*, 32 (Spring/Summer 1970): 5–22.

Nash, Gary B. *Red, White and Black: The Peoples of Early America*. Englewood Cliffs, N.J.: Prentice-Hall, 1974.

Nash, Roderick W. "The Christiana Riot: An Evaluation of Its National Significance." *Journal of the Lancaster County Historical Society*, 65 (Spring 1961): 65–91.

Nevins, Allan. *The Emergence of Lincoln: Prologue to the Civil War, 1859–1861*. Vol. II. New York: Charles Scribner's Sons, 1950.

———. *Ordeal of the Union: A House Dividing, 1852–1857*. Vol. II. New York: Charles Scribner's Sons, 1950.

Nichols, Roy F. *The Disruption of American Democracy*. New York: Macmillan, 1948.

———. "The Kansas-Nebraska Act: A Century of Historiography." *Mississippi Valley Historical Review*, 43 (Sept. 1956): 187–212.

Oates, Stephen B. *The Fires of Jubilee*. New York: Harper and Row, 1975.

———. *To Purge This Land with Blood*. New York: Harper and Row, 1970.

Ofari, Earl. *Let Your Motto Be Resistance*. Boston: Beacon Press, 1972.

Osofsky, Gilbert, ed. *Puttin' On Ole Massa: The Slave Narratives of Henry Bibb, William Wells Brown and Soloman Northup*. New York: Harper and Row, 1969.

Ottley, Roi, and Weatherby, William, eds. *The Negro in New York*. New York Public Library, Oceana Publications, 1967.

Owen, Robert Dale. *The Wrong of Slavery*. Philadelphia, 1864.

Painter, Nell Irvin. *Exodusters*. New York: Knopf, 1976.

Palmer, Edward Nelson. "Negro Secret Societies." *Social Forces*, 23 (Oct. 1944– May 1945): 207–12.

Palmer, Paul C. "Servant Into Slave: The Evolution of the Legal Status of the

Negro Laborer in Colonial Virginia." *South Atlantic Quarterly*, 65 (Summer 1966) : 355–70.

[William Parker.] "The Freedman's Story." *Atlantic Monthly*, 17 (Feb./Mar. 1866) : 152–66, 276–95.

Patrick, Rembert W. *The Reconstruction of the Nation.* New York: Oxford University Press, 1967.

Pearson, Henry G. *The Life of John A. Andrew, Governor of Massachusetts.* 2 vols. Boston: Houghton Mifflin, 1904.

Pease, William H., and Pease, Jane H., eds. *The Anti-Slavery Argument.* Indianapolis: Bobbs-Merrill, 1965.

———. "Black Power—The Debate in 1840." *Phylon*, 29 (Spring 1968) : 19–26.

———. *Bound With Them in Chains.* Westport, Conn.: Greenwood Press, 1972.

———. "Document: Walker's *Appeal* Comes to Charleston: A Note and Documents." *Journal of Negro History*, 59 (July 1974) : 287–92.

———. "The Negro Convention Movement" in *Key Issues in the Afro-American Experience.* Edited by Nathan Huggins, Martin Kilson, and Daniel M. Fox. New York: Harcourt Brace Jovanovich, 1971, I, 191–205.

———. *They Who Would Be Free: Blacks Search for Freedom, 1830–1861.* New York: Atheneum, 1974.

Perry, Lewis. *Radical Abolitionism: Anarchy and the Government of God in Anti-Slavery Thought.* Ithaca: Cornell University Press, 1973.

Phillips, Ulrich B. *American Negro Slavery.* Baton Rouge: Louisiana State University Press, 1966 (originally published 1918).

Pope-Hennessy, James. *Sins of the Fathers.* New York: Knopf, 1968.

Porter, Dorothy B. "David M. Ruggles, Apostle of Human Rights." *Journal of Negro History*, 28 (Jan. 1943) : 23–50.

Porter, Kenneth W. "Florida Slaves and Free Negroes in the Seminole War, 1835–1842." *Journal of Negro History*, 28 (Oct. 1943) : 390–421.

———. *The Negro on the American Frontier.* New York: Arno, 1971.

Price, Richard, ed. *Maroon Societies: Rebel Slave Communities in the Americas.* New York: Anchor Books, 1973.

Prucha, F. P. "Andrew Jackson's Indian Policy: A Reassessment." *Journal of American History*, 56 (Dec. 1969) : 527–39.

Purdue, Robert E. "The Negro in Savannah, 1865–1900." Ph.D. dissertation, University of Georgia, 1971.

Purvis, Robert. *Speeches and Correspondence.* Philadelphia, 1898 [?].

Quarles, Benjamin. *Black Abolitionists.* New York: Oxford University Press, 1969.

———. *Frederick Douglass.* New York: Atheneum, 1968 (originally published Washington, D.C.: Association Press, 1948.)

———. *Lincoln and the Negro.* New York: Oxford University Press, 1962.

———. *The Negro in the American Revolution.* Chapel Hill: University of North Carolina Press, 1961.

———. *The Negro in the Civil War.* New York: Russell and Russell, 1953.

Rabinowitz, Howard N. "The Conflict Between Blacks and the Police in the Urban South, 1865–1900." *The Historian*, 36 (Nov. 1976) : 62–76.

Raboteau, Albert J. *Slave Religion.* New York: Oxford University Press, 1978.

Rankin, David C. "The Origins of Black Leadership in New Orleans During Reconstruction." *Journal of Southern History*, 40 (Aug. 1974) : 417–40.

Ratner, Lorman. *Powder Keg: Northern Opposition to the Anti-Slavery Movement, 1831–1840.* New York: Basic Books, 1968.

Rawick, George P., ed. *The American Slave: A Composite Autobiography*. 31 vols. Westport, Conn.: Greenwood Press, 1972, 1978.

————. *From Sundown to Sun Up: The Making of the Black Community*. (Vol. 1 in *The American Slave: A Composite Autobiography*, 31 vols.) Westport, Conn.: Greenwood Publishing Co., 1972.

Reid, Whitelaw. *After the War*. New York, 1866.

Reiger, John F. "Deprivation, Disaffection and Desertion in Confederate Florida." *Florida Historical Quarterly*, 48 (Jan. 1970) : 279–98.

Rice, C. Duncan. *The Rise and Fall of Black Slavery*. New York: Harper and Row, 1975.

Richards, Leonard L. *"Gentlemen of Property and Standing": Anti-Abolition Mobs in Jacksonian America*. New York: Oxford University Press, 1970.

Robeson, Paul. *Here I Stand*. New York: Othello Associates, 1958 (republished 1971).

Robinson, Donald L. *Slavery in the Structure of American Politics, 1765–1820*. New York: W. W. Norton, 1971.

Rodney, Walter. "African Slavery and Other Forms of Social Oppression on the Upper Guinea Coast." *Journal of African History*, 7 (1966) : 431–43.

————. *How Europe Underdeveloped Africa*. Washington, D.C.: Howard University Press, 1974.

————. "Upper Guinea and the Significance of the Origins of Africans Enslaved in the New World." *Journal of Negro History*, 54 (Oct. 1969) : 327–45.

Rollin, Frank A. [Frances]. *Life and Public Services of Martin R. Delany*. New York: Kraus Reprint, 1969 (originally published Boston, 1868).

Rose, Willie Lee, ed. *A Documentary History of Slavery in North America*. New York: Oxford University Press, 1976.

————. *Rehearsal for Reconstruction: The Port Royal Experiment*. New York: Vintage Books, 1967.

Rosenberg, John S. "Toward a New Civil War Revisionism." *American Scholar*, 38 (Spring 1969) : 250–72.

Rozwenc, Edwin C. *The Making of American Society*. 2 vols. Boston: Allyn and Bacon, 1972.

Scheips, Paul J. "Lincoln and the Chiriqui Colonization Project." *Journal of Negro History*, 37 (Oct. 1952) : 418–53.

Schurz, Carl. *Report on the Condition of the South*. New York: Arno Press, 1969 (originally published 1865).

Schweninger, Loren. "Black Citizenship and the Republican Party in Reconstruction Alabama." *Alabama Review*, 29 (Apr. 1976) : 83–102.

Scott, Kenneth. "The Slave Insurrection in New York in 1712." *New-York Historical Society Quarterly*, 45 (Jan. 1961) : 43–74.

Sefton, James E. *Andrew Johnson and the Uses of Constitutional Power*. Boston: Little, Brown, 1980.

————. *The United States Army and Reconstruction, 1865–1877*. Baton Rouge: Louisiana State University Press, 1967.

Sellers, James B. *Slavery in Alabama*. University: University of Alabama Press, 1950.

Shepherd, Samuel, ed. *The Statutes at Large of Virginia*. 3 vols. New York: Arno Press, 1970 (originally published 1835).

Sherman, Joan R. "James Monroe Whitfield, Poet and Emigrationist." *Journal of Negro History*, 57 (Apr. 1972) : 169–76.

Sherman, W. T. *Memoirs*. II. New York, 1892.

Shofner, Jerrell H. *Nor Is It Over Yet*. Gainesville: University of Florida Press, 1974.

Siebert, Wilbur H. *The Underground Railroad from Slavery to Freedom*. New York: Arno Press, 1968 (originally published 1898).

Simkins, Francis B., and Woody, Robert H., eds. *South Carolina During Reconstruction*. Chapel Hill: University of North Carolina Press, 1932.

Sinkler, George. *The Racial Attitudes of American Presidents*. New York: Doubleday, 1972.

Sirmans, M. E. "The Legal Status of the Slave in South Carolina, 1670–1740." *Journal of Southern History*, 28 (Nov. 1962) : 426–73.

Smith, Abbot E. *Colonists in Bondage*. Gloucester, Mass.: Peter Smith, 1965 (originally published 1947).

Smith, Arthur L. *Rhetoric of Black Revolution*. Boston: Allyn and Bacon, 1969.

Smith, Charles W., Jr. *Roger B. Taney: Jacksonian Jurist*. Chapel Hill: University of North Carolina Press, 1936.

Smith, Elbert B. *The Death of Slavery: The United States, 1837–1865*. Chicago: University of Chicago Press, 1967.

Smith, H. Shelton; Handy, Robert; and Loetscher, Lefforts, A., eds. *American Christianity*. 2 vols. New York: Charles Scribner's Sons, 1960.

Smith, Robert P. "William Cooper Nell: Crusading Black Abolitionist." *Journal of Negro History*, 55 (July 1970) : 182–99.

Smith, Timothy L. *Revivalism and Social Reform in Mid-nineteenth Century America*. New York: Peter Smith, 1957.

Sorin, Gerald. *Abolitionism: A New Perspective*. New York: Praeger, 1972.

Stampp, Kenneth M. *The Peculiar Institution*. New York: Vintage Books, 1956.

Starkey, Marion L. *Striving to Make It My Home*. New York: W. W. Norton, 1964.

Starobin, Robert S., ed. *Blacks in Bondage: Letters of American Slaves*. New York: Franklin Watts, 1974.

———. *Industrial Slavery in the Old South*. New York: Oxford University Press, 1970.

Staudenraus, P. J. *The African Colonization Movement, 1816–1865*. New York: Columbia University Press, 1961.

———. "The Popular Origins of the Thirteenth Amendment." *Mid-America*, 50 (Apr. 1968) : 108–25.

Steinfield, Melvin, ed. *Our Racist Presidents: From Washington to Nixon*. Ramon, Calif.: Consensus Publishers, Jan. 1972.

Stephenson, N. W. "The Question of Arming the Slaves." *American Historical Review*, 18 (Jan. 1913) : 295–308.

Sterkx, H. E. *The Free Negro in Ante-Bellum Louisiana*. Rutherford, N.J.: Fairleigh Dickinson University Press, 1972.

Sterling, Dorothy. *Freedom Train: The Story of Harriet Tubman*. New York: Doubleday, 1954.

———. *The Making of an Afro-American: Martin Robison Delany, 1812–1885*. New York: Doubleday, 1971.

———, ed. *Speak Out in Thunder Tones*. New York: Doubleday, 1973.

———, ed. *The Trouble They Seen*. New York: Doubleday, 1976.

Stewart, James B. *Holy Warriors*. New York: Hill and Wang, 1976.

Still, William. *The Underground Railroad*. Chicago: Johnson Publishing, 1970 (originally published 1871).

Stowe, Harriet Beecher. *The Key to Uncle Tom's Cabin.* New York: Arno Press, 1969 (originally published 1853).

Stuckey, Sterling, ed. *The Ideological Origins of Black Nationalism.* Boston: Beacon Press, 1972.

———. "Remembering Denmark Vesey." *Negro Digest (Black World),* 15 (Feb. 1966): 28–41.

Sutcliff, Robert. *Travels in Some Parts of North America in the Years 1804, 1805 and 1806.* York, England, 1811.

Swisher, Carl B. *Roger B. Taney.* New York: Macmillan, 1935.

Szasz, Ferenc M. "The New York Slave Revolt of 1741: A Re-Examination." *New York History,* 48 (July 1967): 215–30.

Takaki, Ronald T. *Violence in the Black Imagination.* New York: G. P. Putnam's Sons, 1972.

Tatum, Georgia Lee. *Disloyalty in the Confederacy.* Chapel Hill: University of North Carolina Press, 1934.

Taylor, Alrutheus A. *The Negro in Tennessee, 1865–1880.* Washington, D.C.: Associated Publishers, 1941.

———. *The Negro in the Reconstruction of Virginia.* Washington, D.C.: Association for the Study of Negro Life and History, 1926.

Taylor, R. H. "Slave Conspiracies in North Carolina." *North Carolina Historical Review,* 5 (Jan. 1928): 20–34.

Thomas, Lately. *The First President Johnson.* New York: William Morrow, 1968.

Thomas, Robert P. and Bean, Richard N. "The Fishers of Men: Profits of the Slave Trade." *Journal of Economic History,* 34 (Dec. 1974): 885–914.

Thornberry, Jerry. "Northerners and the Atlanta Freedmen, 1865–1869." *Prologue,* 6 (Winter 1974): 236–51.

Tocqueville, Alexis de. *Democracy in America.* Edited by J. P. Mayer and Max Lerner. New York: Doubleday, 1966.

Toppin, Edgar. *A Biographical History of Blacks in America Since 1528.* New York: David McKay, 1971.

Tragle, Henry Irving, ed. *The Southampton Slave Revolt of 1831.* Amherst: University of Massachusetts Press, 1971.

Tregle, Joseph G., Jr. "Early New Orleans Society: A Reappraisal." *Journal of Southern History,* 18 (Feb. 1952): 20–36.

Trelease, Allen. *Indian Affairs in Colonial New York.* Ithaca, N.Y.: Cornell University Press, 1960.

Tyler, Alice Felt. *Freedom's Ferment: Phases of American Social History to 1860.* Minneapolis: University of Minnesota Press, 1944.

Ullman, Victor. *Martin R. Delany: The Beginnings of Black Nationalism.* Boston: Beacon Press, 1971.

U.S. Congress. *Report of the Joint Committee on Reconstruction.* 39th Congress, 1st Session. Washington, D.C.: Government Printing Office, 1866.

U.S. Congress. *Report of the Joint Select Committee to Inquire into the Condition of Affairs in the Late Insurrectionary States.* 42nd Congress, 2nd Session. Washington, D.C.: Government Printing Office, 1872.

U.S. Congress. *[Mississippi in 1875] Report of the Select Committee to Inquire into the Mississippi Election of 1875.* 2 vols. 44th Congress, 2nd Session. Washington, D.C.: Government Printing Office, 1876.

[U.S. Department of Commerce, Bureau of the Census.] *Negro Population, 1790–1915.* New York: Arno Press, 1968 (originally published 1918).

Uya, Okon E. *From Slavery to Public Service: Robert Smalls, 1839–1915.* New York: Oxford University Press, 1971.

Victor, Orville J. *History of American Conspiracies.* New York, 1863.

Villard, Oswald G. *John Brown, 1800–1859: A Biography Fifty Years After.* Boston: Houghton Mifflin, 1910.

Vincent, Theodore G. *Black Power and the Garvey Movement.* Berkeley, Calif.: Ramparts Press, 1971.

Vogel, Virgil J., ed. *This Country Was Ours: A Documentary History of the American Indian.* New York: Harper and Row, 1972.

Wade, Richard C. *Slavery in the Cities.* New York: Oxford University Press, 1964.

————. "The Vesey Plot: A Reconsideration." *Journal of Southern History,* 30 (May 1964) : 143–61.

Walker, Cam. "Corinth: The Story of a Contraband Camp." *Civil War History,* 20 (Mar. 1974) : 5–22.

Walters, Alexander. *My Life and Work.* New York: Fleming H. Revell, 1917.

Ward, Samuel Ringgold. *Autobiography of a Fugitive Negro.* Chicago: Johnson Publishing, 1970 (originally published 1855).

[Warner, Samuel.] *Authentic and Impartial Narrative of the Tragical Scene . . . In Southampton County.* New York, 1831.

Washburn, Wilcomb E. *The Governor and the Rebel.* Chapel Hill: University of North Carolina Press, 1957.

Waskow, Arthur I. *From Race Riot to Sit-In, 1919 and the 1960's.* New York: Anchor Books, 1967.

Wax, Darold D. "Negro Resistance to the Early American Slave Trade." *Journal of Negro History,* 51 (Jan. 1966) : 1–15.

Wesley, Charles H. "The Negroes of New York in the Emancipation Movement." *Journal of Negro History,* 24 (Jan. 1939) : 65–103.

Wharton, Vernon L. *The Negro in Mississippi, 1865–1890.* New York: Harper and Row, 1965 (originally published 1947).

White, William W. "The Texas Slave Insurrection of 1860." *Southwestern Historical Quarterly,* 52 (Jan. 1949) : 259–85.

Williams, Eric. *Capitalism and Slavery.* New York: Russell and Russell, 1961.

Williams, George W. *History of the Negro Race in America, 1619–1880.* 2 vols. New York: Arno Press, 1968 (originally published 1883).

Williams, William A. *The Contours of American History.* Chicago: Quadrangle Books, 1966.

Williamson, Joel. *After Slavery.* Chapel Hill: University of North Carolina Press, 1965.

Wilmore, Gayraud S. *Black Religion and Black Radicalism.* New York: Anchor Press, 1973.

Wilson, Theodore B. *The Black Codes of the South.* University: University of Alabama Press, 1965.

Wiltse, Charles M. *David Walker's Appeal.* New York: Hill and Wang, 1965.

Winks, Robin. *The Blacks in Canada.* New Haven: Yale University Press, 1971.

Wish, Harvey. "American Slave Insurrections Before 1861." *Journal of Negro History,* 22 (July 1937) : 299–320.

————. "Slave Disloyalty Under the Confederacy." *Journal of Negro History,* 23 (Oct. 1938) 435–50.

————. "The Slave Insurrection Panic of 1856." *Journal of Southern History,* 5 (May 1939) : 210–13.

Wood, Peter H. *Black Majority.* New York: Knopf, 1974.

Woodson, Carter G. *A Century of Negro Migration.* Washington, D.C.: Association for the Study of Negro Life and History, 1918.

———. *The History of the Negro Church.* Washington, D.C.: Associated Publishers, 1945.

———. *Negro Orators and Their Orations.* Washington, D.C.: Associated Publishers, 1925.

Woodward, C. Vann. *American Counterpoint.* Boston: Little, Brown, 1971.

———. *The Strange Career of Jim Crow.* New York: Oxford University Press, 1957.

Work, Monroe. "Secret Societies as Factors in the Social and Economic Life of the Negro" in *Democracy in Earnest.* Edited by James E. McCulloch. Washington, D.C.: Southern Sociological Congress, 1918.

Wright, Leitch J., Jr. "A Note on the First Seminole War as Seen by the Indians, Negroes and Their British Advisors." *Journal of Southern History,* 34 (Nov. 1968) : 565–75.

[Writers Program, Works Project Administration, Virginia.] *The Negro in Virginia.* New York: Arno Press, 1969 (originally published 1940).

X, Malcolm. *The Autobiography of Malcolm X.* New York: Grove Press, 1965.

Yeats, William Butler. *The Collected Poems of William Butler Yeats.* New York: Macmillan, 1956.

[Young, Robert Alexander.] *The Ethiopian Manifesto.* New York, 1829.

Zilversmit, Arthur. *The First Emancipation.* Chicago: University of Chicago Press, 1967.

———. "Quok Walker, Mumbet, and the Abolition of Slavery in Massachusetts." *William and Mary Quarterly,* 25 (Oct. 1968) : 614–24.

Index

VINCENT HARDING is a native of New York City and is a graduate of the City University of New York and Columbia University School of Journalism. He also holds an M.A. and a Ph.D. in history from the University of Chicago. With his wife, Rosemarie, he worked full-time in the Southern-based black freedom movement in the early 1960s, before becoming chairman of the Department of History and Sociology at Spelman College in Atlanta, Georgia. In 1968 he became director of the Martin Luther King, Jr., Memorial Center and the coordinator of the nationally televised CBS "Black Heritage" series. Harding was one of the organizers of the Institute of the Black World, and in 1969 became its first director; he is now chairman of the Institute's board. His previously published books include *Must Walls Divide?* and *The Other American Revolution.* Harding is now on the faculty of the Iliff School of Theology at the University of Denver in Denver, Colorado.

V-791	**REICH, WILHELM AND LEE BAXANDALL (ed.)** / Sex-Pol.: Essays 1929-1934
V-159	**REISCHAUER, EDWIN O.** / Toward the 21st Century: Education for a Changing World
V-622	**ROAZEN, PAUL** / Freud: Political and Social Thought
V-204	**ROTHSCHILD, EMMA** / Paradise Lost: The Decline of the Auto-Industrial Age
V-954	**ROWBOTHAM, SHEILA** / Women, Resistance and Revolution
V-288	**RUDOLPH, FREDERICK** / The American College and University
V-226	**RYAN, WILLIAM** / Blaming the Victim, (Revised edition)
V-130	**SALE, KIRKPATRICK** / Power Shift
V-965	**SALE, KIRKPATRICK** / SDS
V-902	**SALOMA, JOHN S. III AND FREDERICK H. SONTAG** / Parties: The Real Opportunity for Effective Citizen Politics
V-375	**SCHELL, ORVILLE AND FRANZ SCHURMANN (eds.)** / The China Reader, Vol. I: Imperial China
V-376	**SCHELL, ORVILLE AND FRANZ SCHURMANN (eds.)** / The China Reader, Vol. II: Republican China
V-377	**SCHELL, ORVILLE AND FRANZ SCHURMANN (eds.)** / The China Reader, Vol. III: Communist China
V-738	**SCHNEIR, MIRIAM (ed.)** / Feminism
V-375	**SCHURMANN, FRANZ AND ORVILLE SCHELL (eds.)** / The China Reader, Vol. I: Imperial China
V-376	**SCHURMANN, FRANZ AND ORVILLE SCHELL (eds.)** / The China Reader, Vol. II: Republican China
V-377	**SCHURMANN, FRANZ AND ORVILLE SCHELL (eds.)** / The China Reader, Vol. III: Communist China
V-971	**SCHURMANN, FRANZ AND NANCY AND DAVID MILTON (eds.)** / The China Reader, Vol. IV: People's China
V-89	**SENNETT, RICHARD** / Families Against the City: Middle Class Homes of Industrial Chicago 1872-1890
V-940	**SENNETT, RICHARD AND JONATHAN COBB** / The Hidden Injuries of Class
V-308	**SENNETT, RICHARD** / The Uses of Disorder
V-974	**SERRIN, WILLIAM** / The Company and the Union
V-405	**SERVICE, JOHN S. AND JOSEPH W. ESHERICK (ed.)** / Lost Chance in China: The World War II Despatches of John S. Service
V-798	**SEXTON, BRENDAN AND PATRICIA** / Blue Collars and Hard Hats
V-279	**SILBERMAN, CHARLES E.** / Crisis in Black and White
V-353	**SILBERMAN, CHARLES E.** / Crisis in the Classroom
V-850	**SILBERMAN, CHARLES E.** / The Open Classroom Reader
V-681	**SNOW, EDGAR** / Red China Today: The Other Side of the River
V-930	**SNOW, EDGAR** / The Long Revolution
V-902	**SONTAG, FREDERICK H. AND JOHN S. SALOMA III** / Parties: The Real Opportunity for Effective Citizen Politics
V-388	**STAMPP, KENNETH** / The Era of Reconstruction 1865-1877
V-253	**STAMPP, KENNETH** / The Peculiar Institution
V-959	**STERN, PHILIP M.** / The Rape of the Taxpayer
V-547	**STONE, I. F.** / The Haunted Fifties
V-307	**STONE, I. F. AND NEIL MIDDLETON (ed.)** / The I. F. Stone's Weekly Reader
V-231	**TANNENBAUM, FRANK** / Slave and Citizen: The Negro in the Americas
V-312	**TANNENBAUM, FRANK** / Ten Keys to Latin America
V-984	**THOMAS, PIRI** / Down These Mean Streets
V-322	**THOMPSON, E. P.** / The Making of the English Working Class
V-810	**TITMUSS, RICHARD** / The Gift Relationship: From Human Blood to Social Policy
V-848	**TOFFLER, ALVIN** / The Culture Consumers
V-980	**TOFFLER, ALVIN (ed.)** / Learning for Tomorrow: The Role of the Future in Education